BROADWAY NATION

ADVANCE PRAISE FOR BROADWAY NATION

"David Armstrong's Broadway Nation is a lively, engaging, and fascinating journey through the vibrant history of the Broadway musical. With thoughtful, insightful readings of numerous productions, Armstrong uncovers the ground-breaking contributions of immigrant, Jewish, queer, and Black artists—many of whom were marginalized yet shaped one of America's most enduring art forms. Through rich anecdotes and keen insights, this compelling book reclaims their legacies, offering a fresh perspective on theater history. Whether you're a historian, a theatermaker, or a passionate fan, Broadway Nation is an important and impossible-to-put-down tribute to the diverse voices behind the Great White Way."

Stacy Wolf, Princeton University, author of *Beyond Broadway* and *Changed for Good*

"A fascinating, comprehensive, and timely gem of a book that more than lives up to its promise of delivering no less than five books in one. Kudos to David Armstrong for his masterful exploration of the origins, continuities, and connections among five indispensable groups of artists that made the American musical and the musical American: Immigrants, Jews, Queers, Blacks, and Women (I, J, Q, B, and W)."

Geoffrey Block, author of *Enchanted Evenings: The Broadway Musical from "Show Boat" to Sondheim and Lloyd Webber*

"Through his passion and intellect, David sheds a light on the communities that collectively crafted the Broadway musical. His experience as a writer, director, producer, and educator comes together in a refreshing examination of the histories that make up the art form."

Ian Eisendrath, Olivier Award-winning and Grammy-nominated Music Producer, Music Supervisor, Conductor, and Arranger of theater and film, including *Come From Away, A Christmas Story*, Disney's live-action *Snow White*, and Hulu's *Only Murders In The Building*

"David Armstrong's insightful history of the evolution of the Broadway Musical and its creators is captivating and comprehensive as well as indispensable."

Tony Award-winning lyricist David Zippel

"Everyone interested in musical theatre—students, working professionals, and passionate fans — will be entirely captivated by this comprehensive history of the Broadway musical and its story of the Black, Gay, Jewish, and Immigrant men and women who invented it. I said it when I first worked with him in 1982, and I say it again now in 2025, 'David Armstrong is a genius!'"

Jenifer Lewis, actress and author of *The Mother of Black Hollywood*

BROADWAY NATION

HOW IMMIGRANT, JEWISH, QUEER, AND BLACK ARTISTS INVENTED THE BROADWAY MUSICAL

David Armstrong

LONDON • NEW YORK • OXFORD • NEW DELHI • SYDNEY

METHUEN DRAMA
Bloomsbury Publishing Plc
50 Bedford Square, London, WC1B 3DP, UK
1385 Broadway, New York, NY 10018, USA
29 Earlsfort Terrace, Dublin 2, Ireland

BLOOMSBURY, METHUEN DRAMA and the Methuen Drama logo are trademarks of Bloomsbury Publishing Plc

First published in Great Britain 2025

Copyright © David Armstrong, 2025

David Armstrong has asserted his right under the Copyright, Designs and Patents Act, 1988, to be identified as author of this work.

For legal purposes the Acknowledgments on p. xxi constitute an extension of this copyright page.

Cover design by Namkwan Cho
Cover Images @ George M. Cohan (George M. Cohan, c. 1918, Public Domain)
Dorothy Fields (Dorothy Fields & Arthur Schwartz work on score of "A Tree Grows in Brooklyn" / World Telegram & Sun photo by Walter Albertin, Public Domain)
Bob Cole and J. Rosamond Johnson (https://commons.wikimedia.org/wiki/File:Coleandjohnson.jpg)
Oscar Hammerstein II. (https://commons.wikimedia.org/wiki/File:Oscar_Hammerstein_-_portrait.jpg)
Lorenz Hart, (Composers Richard Rodgers and Lorenz Hart Posing Together (Original Caption) American composer Richard Rodgers (1902–1979) and lyricist Lorenz Hart (1895–1943, Getty Images)
Katherine Dunham, https://commons.wikimedia.org/wiki/File:Katherine_Dunham_by_Annemarie_Heinrich,_1954.jpg
Albertina Rasch, Austrian prima ballerina, Albertina Rasch, seen from the back, looking over her shoulder, with a shawl draped low on her back. (Photo by Maurice Goldberg/Condé Nast via Getty Images)
Lin-Manuel Miranda, IN THE HEIGHTS by Miranda ; Lin-Manuel Miranda (as Usnavi) ; Directed by Kail ;
at Richard Rodgers
Theatre, New York City, US ; 9 March 2008 ; Credit : Joan Marcus / ArenaPAL ; www.arenapal.com
Stephen Sondheim (28th August 1962: American songwriter Stephen Sondheim, whose works include the musicals 'A Funny Thing Happened on the Way to the Forum', 'Into the Woods' and 'Passion'.
(Photo by Michael Hardy/Express/Getty Images))
Irving Berlin (Photo still of Irving Berlin, with signature, 1920, Public Domain)

All rights reserved. No part of this publication may be: i) reproduced or transmitted in any form, electronic or mechanical, including photocopying, recording or by means of any information storage or retrieval system without prior permission in writing from the publishers; or ii) used or reproduced in any way for the training, development or operation of artificial intelligence (AI) technologies, including generative AI technologies. The rights holders expressly reserve this publication from the text and data mining exception as per Article 4(3) of the Digital Single Market Directive (EU) 2019/790.

Bloomsbury Publishing Plc does not have any control over, or responsibility for, any third-party websites referred to or in this book. All internet addresses given in this book were correct at the time of going to press. The author and publisher regret any inconvenience caused if addresses have changed or sites have ceased to exist, but can accept no responsibility for any such changes.

A catalogue record for this book is available from the British Library.

A catalog record for this book is available from the Library of Congress.

ISBN: HB: 978-1-3504-2832-4
PB: 978-1-3504-2831-7
ePDF: 978-1-3504-2834-8
eBook: 978-1-3504-2833-1

Typeset by RefineCatch Limited, Bungay, Suffolk
Printed and bound in Great Britain

For product safety related questions contact productsafety@bloomsbury.com.

To find out more about our authors and books visit www.bloomsbury.com and sign up for our newsletters.

*For the many inspiring educators and theater artists who mentored and believed in me
well before they had any actual reason to do so, especially:
Bobby Ziegler, Kay King, Dale C. Banks, Ruth Cormier, Lillie Gravely,
F. Paul Ruttledge, Elinore Dial, Worth Gardner, Charles Kondek, Tommy Brent,
Michael Murray, Robert Tolan, John Going, Gene Frankel, and Helen Gallagher.*

CONTENTS

List of Illustrations	xii
List of Boxes	xix
Acknowledgments	xxi

Introduction	1
How to Use This Book	2
A Few Words About Words	3
Overture: What is a Broadway Musical?	4
The Elements of a Musical	7
The Writing	8
The Staging, Direction, and Choreography	8
The Music Department	9
The Design	9
The Producing Team	10
The Performance	10
Prologue: Before Broadway	12
The Ballad Opera	12
European Operetta	13
Burlesque	13
The Spectacular Extravaganza	14
Vaudeville	16
Tin Pan Alley	17
The Yiddish Theater	18
Edwardian Musical Comedy	18

Act I: The Genesis Period

1	**Yearning to Breathe Free—The Immigrants Who Invented the Broadway Musical (♪, ♩)**	23
	The Irish Immigrants	24
	The German, Eastern European, and Jewish Immigrants	24
	"There's No Business Like Show Business"	25
	Not Quite Yet Musicals—The Shows of Harrigan & Hart, Weber & Fields, and Williams & Walker (♪, ♩, 🅑)	25
	The Father of the Musical Comedy: George M. Cohan	28
	Father of the American Operetta: Victor Herbert	30

Contents

	Defining American Music: Irving Berlin	32
	"The Song is You"—Jerome Kern	34
	The Princess Theatre Musicals	36
	"A Dainty Bit of Salt and Sweetness"—Best Practices Create a Blockbuster—*Irene!* (Q)	37
	"Hey, Mr. Producer!"—Hammerstein, Ziegfeld, and the Shuberts (I, J)	39
	The Greatest Stars: The Performers	40
2	**Forgotten Forefathers (and Foremothers)—The Black Artists Who Invented the Broadway Musical (B)**	41
	The African Grove Theater	41
	A Shameful Legacy: The Minstrel Show	42
	"Ring, Ring, Da Banjo"—The Music of the Minstrelsy	43
	Legacies of the Minstrel Show	44
	Black Variety and Burlesque	45
	The First Black Broadway Musicals	47
	"There's a Boat That's Leavin' Soon for New York"—Black Migration Transforms the Musical	48
	Williams & Walker on Broadway	48
	Bob Cole and the Johnson Brothers	50
	Women of Color, Women of Note (B, J)	52
	"Mr. Cellophane"—Bert Williams	53
	The End of an Era	54
3	**"Out on That Gay White Way"—The Queer Artists Who Invented Broadway (I, J, Q)**	57
	A Queer Broadway Power Couple: Frohman and Dillingham	58
	"Oh, You Don't Know the Half of it, Dearie!"—Broadway's Drag Superstars, Part 1	59
4	**"Anything You Can Do, I Can Do Better"—The Founding Mothers of Broadway (I, J, W)**	62
	"Ah, Sweet Mystery of Life!"—The Writers	62

Act II: The Silver Age

5	**"All That Jazz"—The Silver Age of Broadway, Part 1: The 1920s (I, J, Q, B, W)**	71
	Fascinating Rhythms: Jazz and the Showtune	72
	The Jews and the Blues (I, J, B)	73
	"Side by Side by Side"—Musical Comedy, Operetta, and Revue	75
	"I'm Just Simply Full of Jazz"—The Harlem Renaissance and *Shuffle Along* (B)	77
	"Full of Pep and Syncopation"—Black Broadway in the 1920s (B, W)	79
	"Sweet and Hot!"—Time Travel Destination #1: September 1925 (I, J, Q)	84
	"I Want To Be Happy"—Vincent Youmans and *No, No, Nannette* (I, J, Q)	88

Contents

Flagrant Disguise—Queer Artists of the 1920s (I, J, Q)	90
"Masculine Women, Feminine Men"—Broadway's Drag Superstars, Part 2	101
"Just *Keep Shufflin'*"—More Black Musicals (I, J, B, W)	102
Another Setback for Black Artists (B)	106
"Life is Just a Bowl of Cherries"—De Sylva, Brown, and Henderson (I, J)	106
Life on the Mississippi—The Arrival of *Show Boat* (I, J, B, W)	108

6   **"Old Man Trouble, I Don't Mind Him"—The Silver Age of the Broadway Musical, Part 2: The 1930s** (I, J, Q, B, W)   109
    "Brother Can You Spare A Dime?" (I, J)   110
    Girl Crazy—"Who Could Ask For Anything More?"   111
    "The Sunny Side of the Street": Women of the Silver Age (I, J, W)   111
    Cole Porter and "The Set That's Smart" (Q)   113
    Anything Goes: "A Rowdy, Naughty, Subversive Masterpiece"   115
    "Wintergreen for President!"—Political Satire on Broadway (I, J, Q, B, W)   119
    "Dancing in the Dark"—Dietz and Schwartz and the Intimate Revue   120
    Going Hollywood—Broadway Heads West (I, J, Q, B, W)   123
    "Our Little Den of Iniquity"—*Pal Joey* and the Beginning of the End (I, J, Q)   129

Intermission

7   **"By Your Pupils You'll Be Taught": A Broadway Legacy Chain from Harbach, to Hammerstein, to Sondheim, to Miranda** (I, J, Q)   151
    Away We Go!—The Revolution of *Oklahoma!*   157
    "You've Got to be Taught"—The Ethos of *South Pacific*   160
    "Lights up on Washington Heights"   164

Act III: The Golden Age

8   **"Something's Coming, Something Good"—The Golden Age of Broadway, Part 1: The Transition Between *Oklahoma!* and *Carousel*** (I, J, Q, B, W)   171
    "Out of Your Dreams"—The Innovations of *Lady in the Dark*   171
    Carmen Jones (I, J, Q, B)   183
    Follow the Girls to the *Mexican Hayride* (I, J, Q, B, W)   184
    "The Indivisibility of Human Freedom"—Yip Harburg and *Bloomer Girl* (I, J, B)   185
    "A Helluva Town!" (I, J, Q, W)   188
    "Round in Circles"—Rodgers and Hammerstein's *Carousel* (I, J, W)   191

9   **"Another Op'nin', Another Show!" The Golden Age of Broadway, Part 2: The 1940s and 1950s** (I, J, Q, W)   194
    The Street Where They Lived—Lerner and Loewe   194
    Musical Comedy 2.0   197

Contents

"Doin' What Comes Naturally"—Irving Berlin, Herbert and
    Dorothy Fields, and *Annie Get Your Gun* (J, J, W, Q)   198
"Brush Up Your Shakespeare"—Cole Porter and *Kiss Me, Kate* (J, J, W, Q)   201
New Kids on the Block: Styne, Loesser, and Adler and Ross (J, J)   203
"Colorful"—Black Broadway in the Golden Age (B)   212
1958: *West Side Story* vs *The Music Man* (J, J, Q)   217
1960: *Gypsy* vs *The Sound of Music* (and Mary vs Ethel) (J, J, Q, W)   227

10   "Open A New Window"—The Golden Age of Broadway,
    Part 3: The 1960s (J, J, Q)   238
    "I Can See It!"—*The Fantasticks* and the Rise of the Off-Broadway
        Musical (Q)   238
    "The Other Generation": The Boomers and *Bye Bye Birdie* (J, Q)   239
    "A World Outside of Yonkers"— Jerry Herman and *Hello, Dolly!* (J, J, Q, B, W)   244
    "She's The One!"—The Big Transgressive Lady Shows (J, J, Q, W)   247
    Broadway Goes Avant-Garde (J, Q, W)   248
    "Miracle of Miracles": *Fiddler on the Roof* (J, J)   249

Act IV: The Modern Era

11   "Let the Sunshine In"—The Modern Era of Broadway,
    Part 1: The Multiple Revolutions of the 1970s (J, Q, B, W)   253
    Time Travel Destination #2: April 1968   253
    Hair and the Rise of the (pop)Rock Musical (J, Q)   254
    "The Beat Goes On"—More (pop)Rock Musicals   258
    "Everybody Rejoice!"—The Return of the Black Musical (J, Q, B, W)   261
    "Everything Old is New Again"—The (so-called) Nostalgia Craze   264
    "Next!"—Hal Prince and the Concept Musical (J, Q)   270
    5, 6, 7, 8!—The Dance Explosion   278
    "I Am What I Am"—Gay Liberation on Broadway (J, Q)   279

12   "Do You Hear the People Sing?"—The Modern Era of Broadway,
    Part 2: Cameron Mackintosh and the British Invasion (J, Q)   285
    "Music of the Night"—The Unexpected Return of the Operetta   286
    "Look, I Made a Hat"—Sondheim Just Keeps Moving on   291
    "Famous Feet"—Tommy Tune (Q)   293

13   "Defying Gravity"—The Modern Era of Broadway,
    Part 3: Broadway in the Twenty-first Century (J, Q, B, W)   295
    "You Can't Stop the Beat"—The Musical Comedy Strikes Back! (J, Q, W)   295
    "Let it Go!"—*The Full Monty* (J, Q, B)   301
    "It's Good to be the King" (of Broadway)—Mel Brooks and
        The Producers (J, J, Q, W)   303
    "Mamma, I'm a Big Girl Now"—Post-Modern Musical Comedy
        and *Hairspray*   306

Contents

"A Whole New World"—Disney on Broadway (J, Q, B, W)   311
"I've Heard That Song Before"—The Jukebox Musical(W)   313
"Good News!"—The Return of the Musical Play   315
"One Song Glory"—Jonathan Larson and the Enduring Legacy of *Rent*   316
The Wizard and Stephen (J, W)   317
Second Wave—Twenty-First Century Concept Musicals   318

Act V: The Principal Themes

14 "Goodbye to Blueberry Pie!"—The Trials and Triumphs of Transgressive Women (I, J, Q, B, W)   339
"Don't Rain on my Parade"—Rebellious Ingenues and Feisty Leading Ladies   341
"I Wanna be Bad"—The Sexual Mavericks   342
"Don't be Afraid of the Dark"—Wise Women and Caretakers   343
"There'll Be Some Changes Made"—The Disruptors   343
"Life is a Banquet!"—The Forces of Life   346

15 "Make Them Hear You"—Equity, Social Justice, and Inclusion (I, J, Q, B, W)   349
"While the White Folks Play"   350
Tales of the South Pacific   352
"A Puzzlement"—Anna and the King of Siam   353
"A Place for Us"   354
"And They Called It, Ragtime"   355
"A Struggle We Have Yet to Win"   355

16 "We Know We Belong To The Land"—The Vital Importance of Community (I, J, Q, B, W)   358
"Territory Folks Should Stick Together"   360
"Sit Down, You're Rocking the Boat"   361
The Outsiders   362
"There's a Hole in the World Like a Great Black Pit"   365
"Welcome to the Rock"   366

Notes   368
Bibliography   404
Index   408

ILLUSTRATIONS

1 The Broadway Theater District and Times Square at night in 1955. Because of its spectacular display of illuminated theater marquees and billboards, it was early on dubbed "The Great White Way." 4
2 Map of Broadway Theater District. 6
3 Irish American composer, lyricist, playwright, director, choreographer, and song and dance man superstar George M. Cohan (center with cane) leads the cast in "Anyplace The Old Flag Flies," the rousing act one finale of his 1911 musical *The Little Millionaire*. 21
4 Ethel Merman and chorus perform "Blow, Gabriel, Blow" in the 1934 hit musical comedy *Anything Goes*—music and lyrics by Cole Porter, book by Howard Lindsay and Russell Crouse, (revised from an earlier version by Guy Bolton and P. G. Wodehouse), directed by Lindsay, and with choreography by Robert Alton. 69
5 The vaudeville team of Harrigan and Hart were among the first theatrical artists to create what were at least embryonic versions of the Broadway musical. Between 1873 and 1893, Edward Harrigan (right), in partnership with Tony Hart (left, in drag), produced, directed, and co-starred in forty-one not-quite-yet-musicals featuring a revolving cast of ethnic character types from the streets of New York—Irish, Germans, Italians, Jews, and African Americans. 132
6 Classically trained Irish immigrant composer Victor Herbert pioneered a new, distinctly American form of operetta. Among his principal collaborators was Rida Johnson Young, who between 1910 and 1924 wrote the book and lyrics for eleven musicals and operettas, including Herbert's greatest success, *Naughty Marietta* (1910), which introduced the hit song, "Ah, Sweet Mystery of Life." 133
7 Left to right, star Eddie Cantor, producer Florenz Ziegfeld, Jr., songwriter Irving Berlin (at piano), director-choreographer Sammy Lee, and the Ziegfeld Girls rehearse for *The Ziegfeld Follies of 1927*. 133
8 Composer Will Marion Cook contributed songs to thirteen Broadway musicals, including *Clorindy, or The Origin of the Cakewalk* (1898), *The Casino Girl* (1900), *In Dahomey* (1903), *Abyssinia* (1906), *Bandana Land* (1908), and *The Ziegfeld Follies of 1910*. 134
9 Lyricist, bookwriter, director, producer, and performer Bob Cole (seated) and composer, lyricist, and performer J. Rosamond Johnson created songs for at least twenty Broadway musicals (often in collaboration with

	Rosamond's brother James Weldon Johnson), including Weber and Fields' *Whoop-De-Doo* (1903), *Humpty-Dumpty* (1904), *The Shoo-Fly Regiment* (1907), and *The Red Moon* (1909).	134
10	Top vaudeville and Broadway stars Bert Williams and George Walker flank the "Queen of the Cakewalk," choreographer and performer Aida Overton Walker, in their 1904 musical *In Dahomey* (music by Will Marion Cook, lyrics by Paul Dunbar, book by Jesse Shipp). Williams would later become the first Black star of *The Ziegfeld Follies*.	135
11	In 1921, the songwriting and vaudeville team of Noble Sissle and Eubie Blake kicked Broadway into the Jazz Age with their smash hit musical comedy *Shuffle Along*. This dynamic, long-running show helped to spark the Harlem Renaissance and initiated a vibrant second decade of Black musicals on Broadway that included their follow-up musical, *The Chocolate Dandies* (1924).	135
12	Broadway, vaudeville, and film star, Bill "Bojangles" Robinson, perhaps the most influential tap dancer of all time, celebrated his sixty-first birthday by dancing down sixty-one blocks of Broadway, cheered on the entire way by adoring crowds.	136
13	Irving Berlin and Moss Hart's 1933 "sophisticated" revue, *As Thousands Cheer*, staged by Hassard Short, employed a newspaper format as its unifying theme. In Act One, Broadway star Ethel Waters electrified the audience with the weather report, "Heat Wave" (pictured here), choreographed by Charles Weidman, and then, in the second act, devastated the audience with the dramatic song "Supper Time."	137
14	Producers Charles Frohman (left) and Charles Dillingham (right) were a Queer Broadway power couple who, during the earliest decades of the Broadway musical, were remarkably visible, even in the press, as unusually close friends and business partners. Together and separately, they helped launch the careers of many of the Queer theater artists who played significant roles in inventing the musical.	137
15	One of the most popular and highest-paid stars of the Genesis Period was Julian Eltinge. Between 1905 and 1915, he starred in five Broadway musicals created especially for him by top talents such as Cohan, Berlin, Harbach, and Kern to showcase his extraordinary talents for "female impersonation." In this trick photo, Eltinge appears as both the groom and the bride.	138
16	Queer director, choreographer, and lighting designer Hassard Short, whose thirty-year career included fifty Broadway shows, was constantly in demand as one of the most innovative and acclaimed "stagers" of musical comedies and revues.	139
17	Between 1925 and 1943, Richard Rodgers (music) and Lorenz Hart (lyrics) created the scores for thirty-one witty, tuneful, and often quite innovative and experimental Broadway musicals. However, the loose, ramshackle,	

yet wildly entertaining Rodgers and Hart-style musical comedies of the Silver Age would eventually be replaced by the story-driven, character-rich, impeccably crafted, and cohesive musical plays of Rodgers and Hammerstein. 140

18 Actor, playwright, composer, lyricist, and director Noel Coward with Broadway director and producer John (Jack) Wilson on the deck of a ship. The pair frequently traveled the world together as creative, business, and romantic partners. 141

19 Director Josh Logan (center, in chair) and choreographer Robert Alton (right), on the stage of a Broadway theatre, in rehearsal for the 1942 Rodgers and Hart musical *By Jupiter*, with stars Constance Moore and Ray Bolger. 142

20 From left, director Agnes De Mille, producer Saint-Subber, songwriter Cole Porter, and choreographer Hanya Holm in rehearsal for the 1950 musical *Out of this World*. 142

21 Prolific bookwriter Herbert Fields and his equally prolific sister, lyricist, and bookwriter Dorothy Fields, photographed by *Vogue* magazine in 1943, presumably backstage at *Something for the Boys*, the hit Cole Porter musical for which they collaborated on the book. Together and separately, they were central to the creation of dozens of hit Broadway musicals. 143

22 Actress, playwright, librettist, producer, and director Dorothy Donnelly was a leading Broadway actress before she turned her attention to playwriting. Between 1916 and 1927, she created the book and lyrics for eight Broadway musicals and operettas, including the blockbusters *Blossom Time* and *The Student Prince*. 144

23 Choreographer and star dancer Gertrude Hoffmann was the first woman to be credited with the "dance direction" of a Broadway show (although other uncredited women, including Aida Overton Walker, likely preceded her). Between 1903 and 1927, Hoffmann designed the dances for fifteen Broadway musical comedies and revues. 145

24 Polish-Russian-Jewish immigrant Albertina Rasch choreographed thirty-three Broadway shows, including many of the biggest hits of the 1920s and 1930s, such as *The Ziegfeld Follies of 1927*, *Rio Rita*, and *Mlle. Modiste*; the legendary Dietz and Schwartz musical revues: *Three's A Crowd*, *Flying Colors*, and *The Band Wagon*; and the landmark 1941 Moss Hart/Kurt Weill/Ira Gershwin musical *Lady in the Dark*. 146

25 In her choreography for nine Broadway productions, including *Cabin in the Sky*, in which she starred as the temptress "Georgia Brown," the extraordinary dancer, choreographer, and anthropologist Katherine Dunham created highly theatrical evocations of indigenous dances from around the world, all derived from her anthropological research. She also mined the rich history of African American dance, from the cakewalk to the hot swing dances of the 1940s. 147

Illustrations

26 Actor Bobby Watson (flanked by co-stars Gladys Miller and Eva Puck) was acclaimed for his performance as the flamboyant "male modiste Madam Lucy" in the 1919 smash hit musical *Irene*. Twenty-two years would go by before audiences would see another overtly Queer principal character in a Broadway musical. 148

27, 28, 29, 30 The Broadway musical as a craft and artform has been passed down directly from one artist to the next, generation to generation. One of the most direct and significant examples of this kind of "legacy chain" is the connection between (clockwise from top left) Otto Harbach, Oscar Hammerstein II, Stephen Sondheim, and Lin-Manuel Miranda. 149

31 In Rodgers and Hammerstein's Pulitzer Prize-winning musical *South Pacific* (1949), both of the show's parallel love stories hinge on issues of internalized racism and social justice. In the emotional final scene, American nurse, "Ensign Nellie Forbush" (originally played by Mary Martin), joins hands with French planter, "Emile De Becque" (Ezio Pinza), as his mixed-race children (Barbara Luna, Michael or Noel De Leon) welcome him home. 169

32 The original London cast of *Hair* (1968), book and lyrics by Gerome Ragni and James Rado, musical by Galt MacDermit, directed by Tom O'Horgan, choreographed by Julie Arenal. 251

33 Set just before and during the American Civil War, the central character of *Bloomer Girl* (1944) is Evelina Applegate (Celeste Holm), a hoop-skirt manufacturer's daughter who has fallen under the sway of her feminist aunt, Dolly Bloomer (Margaret Douglass, left), who is also active in the Underground Railroad. Here, Pompey (Dooley Wilson, center), a runaway slave, is delivered to Bloomer's office, where she is assisted by Daisy (Joan McCracken, right). Although *Bloomer Girl* never entered the canon of classic, enduring Broadway musicals, it was a highly influential show in its day. 321

34 In the original production of *Annie Get Your Gun* (music and lyrics by Irving Berlin, book by Herbert Fields and Dorothy Fields, direction by Joshua Logan, choreography by Helen Tamiris), sharpshooter Annie Oakley (Ethel Merman) shows off her chest full of championship medals to her rival and fiancé Frank Butler (Ray Middleton). 322

35, 36 Three pioneering women have dominated the history of Broadway lighting design: Jean Rosenthal (left), Peggy Clark, and Tharon Musser (right). 323

37 The *West Side Story* creative team: (left to right) Stephen Sondheim (lyrics), Arthur Laurents (with his hand on his shoulder—book), Hal Prince (producer), Robert Griffith (producer—seated), Leonard Bernstein (music), and Jerome Robbins (director and choreographer). 323

38 Lena Horne, star of the 1957 Broadway musical *Jamaica*, sits for a portrait painted by Geoffrey Holder, who, eighteen years later, would win two Tony Awards for his direction and costume design of *The Wiz*. 324

Illustrations

39. *No Strings* (1962) was Richard Rodgers' first Broadway musical after the death of Hammerstein and the only show for which Rodgers wrote both music and lyrics. Featuring stylish, inventive direction, and choreography by Joe Layton, the musical was set in Paris and focused on a romance between a glamorous Black fashion model (Diahann Carroll) and a white expat writer (Richard Kiley). It became a major box office hit, running for 580 performances and winning Tony Awards for Carroll, Layton, and Rodgers. 325
40. Crowds flood into the Majestic Theatre to see Sammy Davis Jr. in the 1964 Broadway musical *Golden Boy*. With a book by Clifford Odets and William Gibson (based on Odets' 1937 play), and an often-thrilling contemporary score by Charles Strouse and Lee Adams, the musical climaxed in an exciting and visceral fight sequence choreographed by Donald McKayle. 326
41. The blockbuster 1964 "musical comedy dream," *Hello, Dolly!*— produced by David Merrick, with book by Michael Stewart, music and lyrics by Jerry Herman, and direction and choreography by Gower Champion—applied the unusual tactic of following its original Tony-winning star, Carol Channing, with a series of even bigger stars: Ginger Rodgers, Martha Raye, Betty Grable, Phylis Diller, Pear Bailey, and Ethel Merman. Herman (center) appeared at the 1969 Tony Awards with two of his Dollys: Pearl Bailey (left) and Carol Channing (right). 326
42. In 1960, choreographer Joe Layton had three shows running on Broadway simultaneously: *Once Upon a Mattress*, *Greenwillow*, and *The Sound of Music*. He would go on to choreograph and/or direct more than twenty Broadway shows, including *No Strings* and *George M*, both of which earned him Tony Awards for "Best Choreography," and the long-running hit musical *Barnum*. 327
43. The West End stars of the musical *Hair* with the show's creative team. From left, actor Oliver Tobias, co-authors James Rado and Gerome Ragni, actor Paul Nicholas, and director Tom O'Horgan. 328
44. The 1970 Tony-winning "Best Musical" *Applause* (book by Betty Comden and Adolph Green, score by Charles Strouse and Lee Adams, direction and choreography by Ron Field) featured Lee Roy Reams (center) as "Duane," one of the first openly gay characters seen in a Broadway musical since 1941's *Lady in the Dark*. Here, he escorts the show's central character, "Margo Channing," played by Lauren Bacall (left), out for a night on the town at a Greenwich Village gay bar, where they encounter dancer Sammy Williams (right), who, five years later, received a Tony for his performance as the groundbreaking gay character, "Paul," in *A Chorus Line*. 328
45. With her staging of the 1972 hit gospel revue *Don't Bother Me I Can't Cope* (book, music, and lyrics by Micki Grant), Vinnette Carroll became the first Black woman to direct a Broadway musical, as well as the first to be

Illustrations

	nominated for a Tony Award for "Best Director." In 1978, she directed and wrote the book for another long-running hit, *Your Arms Too Short To Box With God* (music and lyrics by Alex Bradford, and additional songs by Micki Grant).	329
46	Left to right, Tony nominee Vivian Reed, Newton Winters, and Lonnie McNeil stopped the show cold with their performance of "Sweet Georgia Brown" (choreographed by Billy Wilson) in *Bubbling Brown Sugar* (1976), the first of a series of Black songwriter revues that captivated Broadway during the "nostalgia craze" of the 1970s and early '80s that included *Ain't Misbehavin'*, *Eubie*, and *Sophisticated Ladies*.	330
47	Director-choreographer and star performer Tommy Tune won the third of his ten Tony Awards for his direction of the 1982 musical *Nine*, which was also awarded "Best Musical." Here, Tune clowns with classic Broadway and Hollywood stars Ann Miller and Milton Berle at the awards ceremony.	331
48	Gillian Lynne, seen here working in her West London home in 1971, choreographed seven Broadway musicals, including two of the longest-running hits of all time: *Cats* and *The Phantom of the Opera*.	332
49	Another Broadway songwriting "legacy chain": (left to right) Stephen Schwartz (*Godspell*, *Pippin*, *Wicked*) poses with Kristen Anderson-Lopez (*In Transit*, *Frozen*) and Robert Lopez (*Avenue Q*, *Book of Mormon*, *Frozen*) at the Dramatists Guild Foundation's Celebration Concert honoring Schwartz's 70th birthday in 2018.	332
50	The dynamic trio of women behind the international mega-hit jukebox musical *Mamma Mia!*: (left to right) director Phyllida Lloyd, producer Judy Craymer, and bookwriter Catherine Johnson on the red carpet at the 2014 Laurence Olivier Awards.	333
51	Director-choreographer Jerry Mitchell (right) with bookwriter Harvey Fierstein (left) and composer-lyricist Cyndi Lauper (center), in rehearsal for a touring production of their 2013 Tony Award-winning "Best Musical" *Kinky Boots*.	333
52	Since 1992, five-time Tony Award winner Susan Stroman has directed and/or choreographed eighteen Broadway musicals and plays, including *Crazy For You*, the 1994 revival of *Show Boat*, *Contact*, and *The Producers*.	334
53	Director-choreographer Casey Nicholaw (center) joins the creative team and cast of *Disney's Aladdin* on stage during the show's opening night curtain call. Front row, left to right, music supervisor Michael Kosarin, dance arranger Glen Kelly, bookwriter/lyricist Chad Beguelin, (Nicholaw), composer Alan Menken, scenic designer Bob Crowley, and lighting designer Natasha Katz. Second row, left to right, Jonathan Schwartz, Brandon O'Neil, Brian Gonzales, James Monroe Iglehart, Adam Jacobs (hidden behind Mencken), Courtney Reed, and Jonathan Freeman. Walter McBride / Contributor.	335

Illustrations

54 The original cast of the 2017 musical *Come From Away* (book, music, and lyrics by Irene Sankoff and David Hein, direction by Christopher Ashley, musical staging by Kelly Devine, musical supervision by Ian Eisendrath). This musical demonstrated very effectively that, even within the financial limits and reduced cast sizes of twenty-first-century Broadway, inspired creative teams can still find effective ways to continue the Broadway musical's long tradition of bringing entire communities to life on stage.　　　　337

BOXES

Acknowledged and Unacknowledged Songs	27
"Ev'ry Touch of Fingers Tells Me What I Know": *The Merry Widow* on Broadway	31
Broadway Dance #1: A Brief History of The Cakewalk	44
Broadway Dance #2: Tap Dance—An African American / Irish American Co-Creation (I, B)	54
Broadway Dance #3: Dancing Ladies—The Stagers and Choreographers (I, J, B, W)	64
Broadway Dance #4: "The Charleston" (B, W)	81
Golden Days—Dorothy Donnelly (I, W)	86
Rodgers and Hart take Manhattan (the Bronx and Staten Island, too) (I, J, Q)	87
"A Perfect Blendship"—Monty Wooley	98
Broadway Dance #5: Mr. Bojangles (B)	103
"Ladies Don't Write Lyrics"—Dorothy Fields (I, J, W)	105
"Broadway Baby": Moss Hart (J, Q)	117
The Great Collaborator: George S. Kaufman	120
"Heat Wave": Ethel Waters (B, Q, W)	122
Broadway Dance #6: Queer Choreographers of the Silver Age (Q, I)	125
"This is New": Kurt Weill in America (I, J)	172
Broadway Dance #7: Agnes DeMille and the Dancing Ladies of the Golden Age (I, J, B, W)	174
The Music That Made Them Dance—Trude Rittmann and the Unsung Art of the Broadway Dance Arranger	178
Broadway Dance #8: Americana and the Musical	189
"A Perfect Relationship": Betty Comden and Adolph Green (I, J, W)	190
The Bench Scene: "The Singular Most Important Moment in the Evolution of Contemporary Musicals"	191
Powerhouse: Joshua Logan (Q)	199
Broadway Dance #9: Jerry Robbins and Company (Q, I, J, W)	205
Designing Women—Jean Rosenthal, Peggy Clark, and Tharon Musser Invent Broadway Lighting Design (I, J, Q, W)	209
A Dancer's Life: Chita Rivera	220
"Here's To Us!"—Women Writers of The Golden Age (I, J, W)	225
Greatest of All Time: The Merm (W)	229
"A Cockeyed Optimist": Mary Martin (Q, W)	234
Broadway Dance #10: The Rise of the Director-Choreographer (J, Q)	241
"Tune The Grand Up"—Jerry Herman (J, Q)	246
Broadway Dance #11: Black Choreographers Take Centerstage (B, Q)	269

Boxes

"I Can Do That"—Michael Bennett	274
Broadway Dance #12: Daughters of DeMille—Dancing Ladies of the Modern Era (W)	296
Something Different—The Songs of David Yazbek	301
Yazbek's Favorite Musicals	302
Twenty-first Century Musical Comedy	307
Broadway Dance #13: Queer Choreographers of the New Millennium (Q)	308
"Money Makes the World Go Around"—The Perilous Economics of Modern Broadway	312
Dancing Queens—The Women Behind *Mamma Mia!*	314
Twenty-first Century Musical Plays	318
"Who Tells Your Story?"—Record-Breaking Broadway Herstory	319
Other Hit Musicals that Center on Transgressive Women Include:	347
Thirty-five Musicals Dealing with Equity, Social Justice, and Inclusion	349

ACKNOWLEDGMENTS

In many ways, *Broadway Nation* is the culmination of my (to date) forty-seven-year career in the American theater as a director, choreographer, artistic director, bookwriter, producer, and, more recently, educator and podcaster—which has included involvement in at least two hundred productions of musicals both classic and new. I am certain that every one of those shows provided me with some insight or tidbit of knowledge that, in one form or another, has now found its way into this book. So, first and foremost, I must thank the thousands of actors, singers, dancers, designers, directors, choreographers, bookwriters, composers, lyricists, orchestrators, music directors, stage managers, producers, administrative staff members, musicians, technicians, and craftspeople I have had the privilege of collaborating with over the years—most especially my former colleagues at The 5th Avenue Theatre.

When I stepped down from my position there in 2018, I was unsure what my "third act" would entail. I will be forever grateful to Geoff Korf, Executive Director, and Lynn M. Thomas, former Interim Executive Director of the University of Washington School of Drama, for inviting me to create a lecture course on the history of the Broadway musical and to Scott Magelesson, Sue Bruns, Megan Gurdine Thornberry, Eloise Boyle, Stefka Milaylova, L. Zane Jones, Tina Swenson, Guillaume C. Tourniare, Jonathan Rizzardi, and Mackenzie L. Bounds for their invaluable guidance and assistance in devising and teaching *Drama 171a: The Broadway Musical*, which has inspired both my podcast and this book.

I am equally indebted to the co-founders of the Broadway Podcast Network, Dori Berinstein, and Alan Seales, for welcoming the podcast, *Broadway Nation,* onto their outstanding roster of shows and to Susan McCabe, Jeff Hoyt, and Chris Austin at KVSH, "the Voice of Vashon;" and particularly Nick Tarabini, Nik Hagan, and Pauls Macs, for helping me to create it. I also want to thank the stellar lineup of guest authors and practitioners who have been so generous with their time, memories, and musical theater knowledge; the nearly 3000 members of the *Broadway Nation* Facebook Group; the generous patrons of the podcast; and the more than 300,000 people worldwide who have listened.

This book would certainly not exist if my wonderfully supportive and extremely patient editor, Dom O'Hanlon, had not reached out to me about writing it. Dom's vision, along with his insightful feedback and guidance, has been crucial throughout the process, especially in regard to the book's structure. His entire team at Methuen Drama/Bloomsbury—Sam Nicholls, Rebecca Heselton, Eleanor Rose, and Ronnie Hanna—could not have been more helpful and reassuring to a first-time author. Special thanks to my attorney and dear friend, Mark Sendroff; Jonathan Stevens for his help tracking

Acknowledgments

down permissions; and Gail Leander Wright for her encouragement and wise counsel regarding my book proposal.

Thanks must also go to Annemarie van Roessel, Doug Reside, and the staff of the New York Library for the Performing Arts Billy Rose Theatre Division and Theater On Film and Tape Archive, as well as to Sylvia Wang and the staff of the Shubert Archive. I am also indebted to the many brilliant authors who have been guests on the podcast and have provided me with much support and advice as I embarked on my own book. Their outstanding scholarship also greatly inspired me. They include Adam Abraham, Grace Barnes, Misha Berson, Geoffrey Block, Ken Bloom, Trevor Boffone, Maya Cantu, Richard Carlin, Ted Chapin, Stephen Cole, Elizabeth T. Craft, Sheldon Epps, Andrew L. Erdman, Peter Filichia, Ben Francis, Laura Frankos, Caseen Gaines, Elysa Gardner, Liza Gennaro, Jesse Green, Margaret Hall, Tomas Hischak, Mark Eden Horowitz, Barry Kester, Dustin Martinich, Dominick McHugh, Sunny Stalter Pace, Rick Pender, Deborah Phillips, Doug Reside, Phoebe Rumsey, Adam Rush, Paul Salsini, Rob W. Schneider, Oliver Soden, Millie Taylor, Jack Viertel, Rebecca Applin Warner, Ben West, Laurie Winer, Kevin Winkler, and Stacy Wolf.

I not only need to sincerely thank but also beg much forgiveness from my valued circle of close friends and family—Doug Tompos, James Rocco, Margaret Inouye, Tracy Wellens, Marie and Robert Berry, Lisa Fleischman, and my sister, Gail Enterline—who had to put up with nearly two years of me researching, writing, revising, and editing this manuscript in the midst of weekend and holiday meals, gatherings, vacations, and events. In addition, they always graciously indulged me as I no doubt annoyingly read countless sections aloud for their approval or critique. Most of all, in this regard and every other, my eternal love and gratitude goes to my husband, Bill Berry, who by now has been at my side for more than twenty years and who I cannot imagine navigating life's journey without.

Finally, perhaps the largest measure of thanks must go to my longtime colleague, collaborator, and bosom buddy, Albert Evans. Over thirty years, we have enjoyed countless explorations, discussions, and debates regarding the art and craft of the Broadway musical, and *Broadway Nation* is deeply infused with his astute insights, perceptions, and observations at every turn of the page. It simply would not be what it is without him.

INTRODUCTION

From time immemorial, humans have told stories through some combination of speech, music, song, and dance. This kind of storytelling is embedded in our humanity, and possibly our DNA. In fact, in 2022, researchers discovered human neurons that respond only to singing—not speech or instrumental music.[1] As a result of this inherent "primal urge," every region and culture worldwide has created its own distinct forms of music-dance-theater. The earliest incarnations were closely tied to religious, cultural, and community rituals which eventually, over the centuries, evolved into Greek tragedy, Roman comedy, Indian dance-drama (Kathakali and others), medieval mystery and miracle plays, Javanese shadow puppets (Wayang Kulit), Japanese noh and kabuki theater, commedia dell'arte, Elizabethan drama, Renaissance masques, Thai dance-drama (Khon), Baroque opera, Peking opera, grand opera, classical ballet, modern dance, and many, many others. Each of those unique forms of music-dance-theater was a product of the specific cultural forces and unique historical circumstances that combined to create it. *Broadway Nation* will focus on the most recent manifestation of this timeless human instinct—**the Broadway Musical**—and will examine the diverse cultural and historical forces that gave birth to it and have made this uniquely American art form the dominant theatrical form of the twentieth and twenty-first centuries.

Central to this will be a demonstration of how the Broadway musical was created almost entirely by people who were marginalized from mainstream society—Immigrant, Jewish, Queer, and Black artists—including a much larger percentage of women than is generally acknowledged. Simultaneously, *Broadway Nation* will trace the evolution of the art form they invented from its embryonic origins at the end of the nineteenth century, through its mid-twentieth-century "Golden Age," and right up to its current twenty-first-century resurgence that continues despite the disruptions and set-backs caused by the global pandemic. *Broadway Nation* will also demonstrate how, throughout its history, the Broadway musical has always both reflected and shaped American culture.

Following an "Overture" that explores what exactly a Broadway musical is and details its major components, this book will relate its history largely chronologically, beginning with a "Prologue" briefly detailing the musical's immediate precursors. This is followed by four main "Acts" relating to the four major epochs in its history, which I have named "The Genesis Period," "The Silver Age," "The Golden Age," and "The Modern Era."

Surprisingly, in the field of musical theater history, there are remarkably few agreed-upon names or dates to define the various time periods in Broadway history. Almost everyone will refer in some way or other to the "Golden Age of Broadway," but opinions vary widely regarding exactly when, or even if, that occurred. Some writers apply the Golden Age label to the entire period from the 1910s through the 1950s—and if we were only considering it in terms of the brilliant, classic, timeless songs that Broadway produced during that period, that might make sense.

In my view, however, the overall form, structure, nature, and intent of the Broadway musical changed significantly about halfway through those four decades, so I find it much more useful and instructive to divide that period in half and create a definite distinction between the first half, which I have dubbed the *Silver Age*, and the *Golden Age* that follows it. The musical then significantly changed again, if less definitively, at the end of the 1960s, which is how I arrived at these four distinct periods of development.

Broadway Nation's first major section, Act I, includes four chapters covering the formative period of the Broadway musical, The Genesis Period, which I have determined begins around 1890 and continues through to the end of World War I. Then, the two chapters that make up Act II relate the history of The Silver Age, which includes the 1920s and 1930s and continues up to the opening of Rodgers and Hammerstein's *Oklahoma!* in 1943. That groundbreaking show firmly launches the Golden Age, which Act III relates in three chapters that span the period from *Oklahoma!* to the opening night of *Hair* in 1968, which kicks off Act IV and The Modern Era of the Broadway musical with three chapters bringing us up to the present day.

At the top of Act III, however, *Broadway Nation* will take a sort of intermission break from the chronological format to illustrate another central emphasis of this book: the great degree to which the art and craft of the Broadway musical has been handed down directly from one artist to the next, throughout its history. To that end, Chapter 7 will explore the extraordinary "legacy chain" that extends from Otto Harbach to Oscar Hammerstein II to Stephen Sondheim to Lin-Manuel Miranda and, in the process, encompasses nearly the entire history of the Broadway musical.

Finally, *Broadway Nation* concludes with three chapters that explore the social and cultural impact of Broadway musicals by analyzing its three most prevalent, ubiquitous, and pervasive themes: transgressive women; equity, social justice, and inclusion; and community.

How to Use This Book

Broadway Nation can be used in several ways. As noted above, if read straight through from beginning to end, this book will relate the history of the Broadway musical in a primarily chronological manner. Alternatively, readers could choose to follow the individual story threads of the groups of artists who invented it by locating the icons placed at the beginning of each chapter and subsection. For example, if you wish to focus primarily on Black theater artists and the musicals they have been involved in, you go through the book reading the sections headed by the symbol: B. Or, if you wish to focus on the women who invented the Broadway musical, you would look for this symbol: W. Here is a chart of the symbols that can be followed:

Introduction

Chart of Individual Story Thread Symbols

Immigrant artists: I

Jewish artists: J

Queer artists: Q

Black artists: B

Women artists: W

The symbols are also included in the Chapter and Section listings in the Table of Contents.

A Few Words About Words

Throughout this book, I use the terms "Black" and "African American" interchangeably. Although Black is often preferred today because it is more inclusive, virtually all of the individuals profiled in this book were or are descendants of Africans who were kidnapped and then enslaved in the Americas. On a very few occasions, I have included the historical terms, "negro," "colored," and other more offensive terms if they are part of a direct quote or the title of a song, book, or show.

Similarly, I use the terms "Queer," "Gay," and "LGBTQ" interchangeably and in their most inclusive connotations to identify homosexual, bisexual, non-normative, non-heterosexual, and/or sexually fluid individuals while acknowledging that many of these individuals would likely not have identified themselves as such during their lifetimes and may not have been comfortable with these designations. In particular, I have used the term "Queer" in the book's subtitle and elsewhere with the understanding that even though in recent decades, this term has been reclaimed, repurposed, widely adopted by young people, academia, and the media, and championed as being more inclusive than "Gay"—for many people this word can sometimes still bear the sting of the ugly slur it once was.

OVERTURE: WHAT IS A BROADWAY MUSICAL?

Fig. 1: The Broadway Theater District and Times Square at night in 1955. Because of its spectacular display of illuminated theater marquees and billboards, it was early on dubbed "The Great White Way." R. Krubner / ClassicStock / Getty Images.

The most significant Broadway musical of the twenty-first century (so far) is, without a doubt, *Hamilton*. Following its 2016 opening on Broadway, *Hamilton* received a record-setting sixteen Tony Award nominations and won eleven—including "Best Musical," "Best Book," and "Best Score." It also received seven Olivier Awards, the 2016 Grammy Award for "Best Musical Theater Album," two Emmy Awards for the show's video capture, and the 2016 Pulitzer Prize for Drama. It is one of those very rare shows that receive both unanimous critical praise and unprecedented ticket sales. To date, more than 8 million people worldwide have seen a live production of *Hamilton*, with an even greater amount estimated to have seen the video capture. Its creator and original star, Lin-Manuel Miranda, is one of very few people in recent decades to go from Broadway to superstardom in nearly every medium. He is everywhere: writing music, starring in and directing movies, producing albums and television shows, and speaking out regarding political and humanitarian issues. However, as he has stated many times, his first love remains musical theater, for which he has great respect. As he told the *New York Times* in 2018:

> One of the hardest things to do is to make a successful musical. I don't mean financially successful, I mean artistically. Where all of the art forms—the choreography, the music, the dancing, the sets, the songs, all build toward these moments. When they're all working in tandem, I do not think there is a more thrilling art form.[1]

I certainly agree with him, and I would rank the scale of difficulty of creating a successful Broadway musical right up there with designing, building, and launching whatever new manned flight space shuttle NASA has in the works. It takes a similar team of experts to plan, assemble, test, and launch one; there are just as many interconnected moving parts that all must work together perfectly; there are just as many things that can go wrong, and the final result can be a fizzle, an explosion, or a glorious flight. But before we explore that issue further, we need to ask—what exactly is a Broadway musical?

A Broadway musical is a musical that's performed on Broadway, of course—and at least the first half of the term is fairly easy to define. In a strictly physical sense, Broadway is a street in New York City—the longest street in the world, in fact—which begins at the southern tip of Manhattan and continues 150 miles north, all the way to the state capitol in Albany. However, in relationship to the subject of this book, the only section of "the big street" we need to be concerned with is the section that cuts a northwest diagonal path across Times Square in the midtown Broadway Theater District, which is bordered on the south by West 41st Street, on the north by West 54th Street, and spans from Eighth Avenue in the West to Sixth Avenue in the East. With one exception, only theaters located within this district can be considered Broadway theaters—but not every theater there qualifies. Movie theaters and concert halls are not eligible. Only live theater performance venues (so-called "legitimate" theaters) count, and then only if they have more than 500 seats. Currently, there are forty-one theaters that meet these criteria, only four of which, however, are actually located on Broadway itself—the majority are situated on the numbered streets that cross it (see map on page 6.).[2]

So, to answer our question:

A Broadway Musical is a musical presented live in one of the official Broadway theaters. But of course, Broadway is more than just a physical location—it is also a style, an essence, a concept, a mark of quality, a state of mind, and a worldwide brand.

Now comes the more difficult question: What is a musical? Dictionaries, textbooks, and scholars offer dozens of definitions, some varying only slightly, others much more divergent. After looking them over, and for the purpose of this discussion, here is the one that I think comes closest to the mark:

Broadway Nation

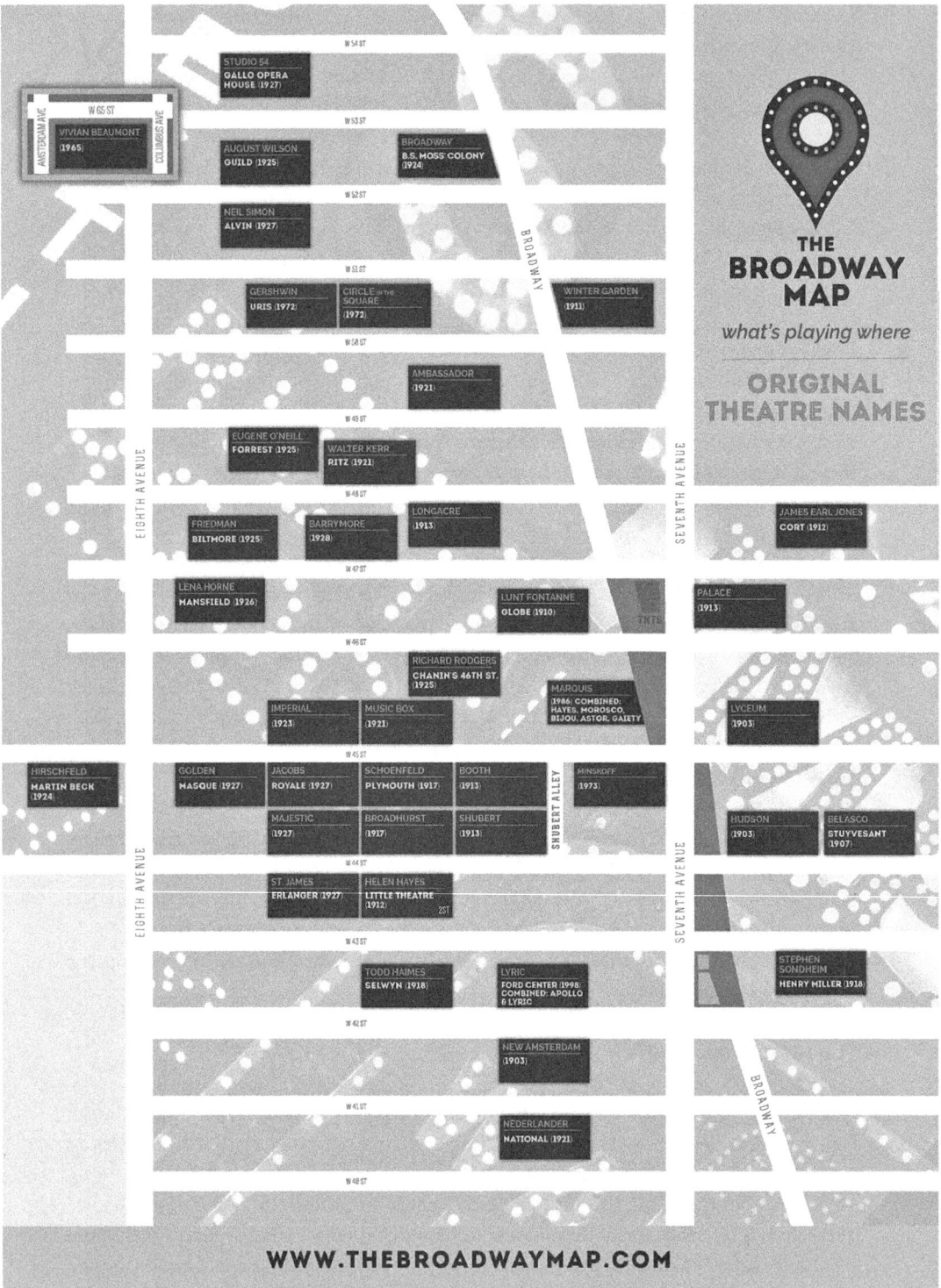

Fig. 2: Map of Broadway Theater District. ©2404 The Broadway Map. All rights reserved.

A musical is a theatrical performance in which music, lyrics, and dance are employed as the primary and most important elements in the telling of the story.

Combine those, and you get:

A Broadway musical is a theatrical performance presented live in one of the official Broadway theaters in which music, lyrics, and dance are employed as the primary and most important elements in the telling of the story.

A key aspect here is that Broadway musicals are live performances. Many books, documentaries, podcasts, and scholars will discuss and analyze stage and film musicals together. And of course, many Broadway stage musicals have been adapted into film musicals (and a few have gone the other way). This book, however, will focus almost exclusively on musicals created to be performed live on stage in front of a live audience, mostly because of what I see as a fundamental difference between the two forms.

From the very first movie musicals of the late 1920s and right up to today, the stories of original made-for-film musicals have almost always centered on "boy meets girl" romance plotlines—which, as we will see, Broadway musicals almost never do. Even more importantly, made-for-film musicals have only rarely even attempted to do what I argue is the essence of the Broadway musical—to use song and dance to tell stories and define characters in ways that make those musical sequences indispensable to the storytelling. In most made-for-film musicals, you could edit out any or all of the musical numbers, and the story would be unaffected.

Now, let's go back to what makes musicals so challenging to pull off. A Broadway musical is by far the most intensely collaborative of art forms. Even a relatively small show requires a large team of creators to effectively bring it to the stage. In addition, to be successful, a musical needs to feel as if it came from a unified vision and unique point of view.

The Elements of a Musical

- The Writing—book, music, and lyrics (created by the Bookwriter,[3] Composer, and Lyricist).[4]
- The Staging—direction and choreography (created by the Director and Choreographer).[5]
- The Music Department—consisting of the Music Supervisor, Music Director, Conductor, Orchestrator, Vocal Arranger, and Dance Arranger.[6]
- The Design—sets, costumes, lighting, sound, and video (created by the Set Designer,[7] Costume Designer, Lighting Designer, Sound Designer, and Video Designer).[8]
- The Producing Team—consisting of the Lead Producer, Co-Producers, General Manager, Company Manager, and Investors.
- The Performance—Actors,[9] Musicians, Stage Managers, and Technical Crews.[10]

The Writing

The most tangible and enduring aspect of a Broadway musical is the product of the show's writers—**the book, the music,** and **the lyrics.** As might be expected, this is because if the show is a hit, those elements are written down, published, recorded, and licensed for performance beyond Broadway. Above all, the show's songs, which often attain significant popularity outside of the context of the musical itself, may continue to have currency long after other aspects of the show have faded from fashion and memory. Dozens, if not hundreds, of songs from musicals that debuted on Broadway more than a century ago are still widely known, performed, and beloved.

What exactly constitutes the "book" of a show is much harder to pin down. As a result, bookwriters usually receive the least amount of credit for the success of a show and the maximum amount of blame if it fails. This is because their role is so ill-defined and misunderstood. Some observers think of "book" as analogous to "libretto," a term used primarily in opera, where it refers to all of the words in a work, sung and spoken (if any). In that way of thinking, the "book" of a musical would be made up of all of the spoken dialogue combined with the lyrics. But more often than not, on Broadway, the dialogue and lyrics are the creation of two separate theater artists—only one of whom is credited as the bookwriter. In another view, the "book" refers only to the spoken dialogue sections of a musical, but that leaves out the most important aspect of this job: the shaping of how the story is told. In my view, the "book" of a musical is best defined as the *story structure* of the show, and the bookwriter's primary job is to construct the "architectural skeleton" of a musical that will hold it up and support the show's more visible elements: the dramatic scenes, comic interludes, jokes, musical sequences, dances, and songs. Another significant thread of this book is how, over the history of the Broadway musical, the book and the bookwriter have become increasingly more crucial to the success of a musical, even as they remain undervalued and discounted. Exactly why the script or text of a musical is called "the book" in the first place seems to be lost to history.

The Staging, Direction, and Choreography

In a similar way, the artists responsible for the "staging" of a musical also have confusing roles. The role of the choreographer is the easiest to understand. The word "choreography" literally means "dance writing," and they are often thought of as the "fourth author" of a show, alongside the bookwriter, lyricist, and composer. And because their work can be written down, video recorded, copyrighted, and reproduced in a clear and ongoing manner, the choreography of a hit Broadway show often lives on as part of the show in a similar manner to the text and music. Sometimes, the choreography establishes itself so strongly that it becomes a standard and expected part of that musical for decades as it moves into regional and amateur productions and major revivals. On a few occasions, Broadway dances have even established a presence outside of their show's original context.[11]

The work of a director, however, is much harder to describe and grasp. In most cases, the director is the proverbial "captain of the ship," involved in supervising and overseeing every aspect of the production, from working with the writers in finalizing the script, score, and concept to casting the actors, organizing the rehearsals, and guiding and shaping the performances. The director also usually plays a significant role in figuring out how to physicalize the work of the writers and take it from the page to the stage. They do this by working with the designers on the look, atmosphere, and style of the physical production—sets, lights, costumes, and sound—and, most importantly, by collaborating with the choreographer (and set designer) on how the show will move. How the responsibility of staging a show gets divided between a director and choreographer varies wildly from team to team and show to show. With some musicals, the choreographer will stage every second of the show during which there is music playing, but with others, the director may do all of the musical staging except for the most overt dancing. Most shows end up somewhere between those extremes, and with the most effective collaborations, it's a moot point because the staging is so seamless that it's impossible to tell where the director's work left off and the choreographer's began. Another key thread of this book is the evolution of how Broadway musicals move and flow and how their staging has become increasingly more continuous, epic, and cinematic.

The Music Department

Throughout most of Broadway history, the musical aspects of a show were the responsibility of the Music Director/Conductor. However, in recent decades, most Broadway musicals have installed a "Music Supervisor" to head the team. Whatever title you apply, the primary job remains the same: to oversee the teaching and mastering of the show's musical score by the cast and orchestra and to organize and oversee the creation and implementation of the show's orchestrations and vocal and dance arrangements.[12] Traditionally, they would also conduct the orchestra. The fast-paced production process of most Broadway musicals makes it almost impossible for the composer to create the show's orchestrations and musical arrangements themself, even if they possess those skills and want to do that work. Instead, those jobs are, in essence, sub-contracted to the Orchestrator, Vocal Arranger, and Dance Arranger. The Music Director/Supervisor will also collaborate closely with the Sound Designer regarding all the musical aspects of a show.

The Design

The Set, Costume, and Lighting Designers of a musical work closely with the Director and Choreographer (as stated above) to determine how to best support and augment the work of the writers and bring a dynamic, three-dimensional life to the show. Their designs not only create a physical reality for the show—they also convey mood, emotion, and metaphor, as with the set design for *Hamilton*, which its designer, David Korins, describes as an "unfinished foundation with scaffolding around it [that is] meant to represent our brand-new, unfinished country."[13] The design of a musical is often one of its most potent and memorable aspects, and its original design choices, such as *Hello, Dolly!*'s famous red dress for its title number, *Bye Bye Birdie*'s Mondrian-inspired pop art multi-level set for "The Telephone Hour," or *Les Miz*'s enormous jackknifing barricade. Potent images like these can become bonded to a show forever. In contrast, fresh new designs can seemingly reinvent a classic musical and make it feel much more modern. The most recent additions to the Broadway design team are the Sound Designer—who in the modern era has become crucial to the success of a show—and the Video/Projection Designer.

The Producing Team

Despite the fairly recent incursion into the Broadway sphere of big corporate entities such as the Walt Disney Co. and Universal Pictures, the majority of Broadway shows are, in essence, small businesses headed by a "Lead Producer" and funded by a small team of "Associate Producers" and investors. The Lead Producer is the "top decision maker on a show," and their impact "is both financial and creative."[14] Broadway producer Kevin McCollum, whose productions have included *Rent*, *Avenue Q*, *In the Heights*, and *Six*, believes that "'Producer' is one of the most maligned and misunderstood words in our culture," in part because the job is so mysterious and "hard to define—because we have to know enough about every department." The Lead Producer's job, he says, "is to help shepherd a show artistically, logistically, and promotionally to capture the public's imagination." As we will see, from Ziegfeld to McCollum, the role of the Lead Producer has not changed all that much over the past 100 years, but the specifics of their involvement in the artistic aspects of a musical can vary widely from show to show, and producer to producer.

The Performance

The most visible and tangible aspect of any Broadway musical is, of course, its performance. Eight times a week, a team of expert actors, singers, dancers, musicians, stage managers, and backstage crews—in most cases, adding up to well over 100 highly trained professionals—present the work of the musical's creative and producing teams to a live audience. Even though the casts, orchestras, and crews of Broadway musicals have been drastically reduced in size over the last fifty or so years, live musical theater, by its very nature, remains an extremely labor-intensive undertaking, and this ties directly to the significant expense of mounting a Broadway musical and the cost of tickets. Unfortunately, a detailed analysis of Broadway's complex economics is beyond this book's scope, except in the most general way.

Every Broadway musical is the creation of a team of artists and creators, much as outlined above, who must somehow arrive at a shared vision of how and why to tell the story they have joined together to bring to the stage. Usually, one member, or faction, of the team holds the most power and influence and functions as the de facto leader of the group. As we will see, that center of power has shifted over time, from producers and performers during the Genesis Era, to songwriters during the Silver Age, to bookwriters/lyricists in the Golden Age, and to directors and director-choreographers in the Modern Era.

PROLOGUE: BEFORE BROADWAY

The nineteenth century gave birth to a number of theatrical and musical forms that would have a strong influence on the men and women who invented the Broadway musical. Entire books could, and should, be written detailing the full influence and impact of these precursors. In this chapter, however, I will touch on them in just enough detail to provide context for what will follow.

The Ballad Opera

This first of these precursors, the ballad opera, originated back in the eighteenth century, more than one hundred years before any of the others. But remarkably, in many ways, it is the most similar to the Broadway musicals of the twenty-first century, especially the *jukebox musicals* (see Chapter 12). The most outstanding example of a ballad opera was the first and most popular of the genre: *The Beggar's Opera*. It was created by the playwright, poet, and ballad writer[1] **John Gay** as a reaction to the British vogue for Italian opera that began in the early 1700s and intensified with the arrival of composer George Frideric Handel in London in 1710.[2] Even though Gay was well-versed in Italian opera, having even written the libretto for Handel's *Acis and Galatea* (1719), he now set out to create a theater piece that was its polar opposite. Instead of a pastoral, tragic love story set in mythical Arcadia about a nymph and a shepherd, *The Beggar's Opera* is a cynically comic tale set in the gritty underworld of (then) present-day London populated by thieves, murderers, sex workers, and seemingly respectable, but actually corrupt, businessmen. Rather than collaborating with a composer on a new operatic score, Gay selected sixty-nine well-known tunes that included traditional folk songs, popular dance tunes, the latest love ballads, and even some of Handel's operatic arias—the "Top 40" of the day—and then fitted them with new lyrics that tied them into the story. The result was seen as both a hilarious satire of Italian opera and a pointed social and political satire of the aristocracy and the government—the music of the people in service of a story taken from the streets. This created a sensation.

Following the debut of *The Beggar's Opera* in London in 1728, it ran for sixty-two consecutive performances, breaking all previous records. It was first produced in New York in 1750 and soon became part of the standard repertory of every theatrical company in Britain and America, as well as the most produced stagework of the eighteenth century.[3] Many other ballad operas would follow it, but none equaled the popularity of the original. In addition to its general influence on musical theater in Europe and America, *The Beggar's Opera* specifically served as the basis for two other musical works: *The Threepenny Opera* (1928), with book and lyrics by Bertolt Brecht and music by Kurt

Weill; and *The Beggars Holiday* (1946), with book and lyrics by John Latouche and music by Duke Ellington.

European Operetta

Beginning in the 1850s, operettas (sometimes called light operas, comic operas, or opera bouffe) began to emerge in nearly every part of Europe, and each region had its own local form and flavor: sexy and satiric in Paris (where composer Jacques Offenbach essentially invented the form); lush and romantic in Vienna, Berlin, and Budapest (led by "waltz king" Johan Strauss II and later Franz Lehár), and patriotic and heroic in Madrid (where they are called "Zarzuelas").[4] Most significant with regard to their impact on the Broadway musical are the fourteen tuneful and hilariously topsy-turvy operettas created by the British team of **Gilbert and Sullivan** between 1871 and 1896. These captivating works swept the English-speaking world, including America, where they remained wildly popular throughout much of the twentieth century. Every major U.S. city and university had its own Gilbert and Sullivan Society (some still do), and the most popular of their shows, such as *H.M.S Pinafore*, *The Mikado*, and *The Pirates of Penzance*, are still produced today. As a result, nearly every Broadway songwriter, past and present, has been inspired and influenced by Gilbert and Sullivan's extended musical sequences, show-stopping "patter songs," and especially Gilbert's perfect rhyming technique which set a standard that nearly every Broadway lyricist has emulated. Unlike *grand opera*, in which usually all of the words are set to music, operettas include spoken dialogue scenes that alternate with songs and musical sequences. Given the focus of this book, it is interesting to note how many of the creators of European operetta were Jewish, including Offenbach and most of the librettists and lyricists of the German and Viennese iterations.

Burlesque

Another wildly popular theatrical form of the nineteenth century was burlesque. This was not, however, what we think of in regard to that term today. Originally, a burlesque show was a production that employed a mostly female cast to perform outrageous parodies—or burlesques—of famous plays, novels, operas, or literary works that were popular at the time. These could be anything from classic Greek myths to *Robin Hood*, *Robinson Caruso*, or *Faust*. These shows used song and dance to augment (if not actually tell) the story, and by all accounts, they were hilariously funny. This tradition has remained with us in parody films such as Mel Brooks' *Young Frankenstein*, the Austin Powers series, and the *Scary Movie* franchise, to name only a few. They employ exactly the same formula as the early burlesque shows: start with something inherently serious and then send it up by making irreverent, unrelenting fun of it. And yes, part of what made these early burlesque shows a sensation was that the leading male hero roles were played by women dressed in short tunics and tights that showed off their legs. That kind of provocative display would eventually evolve into the "girly show" and "striptease" aspects of later burlesque shows. Both styles of burlesque have had a major impact on the Broadway musical. (Early burlesque is explored further in the section on Lydia Thompson on page 64.)

The Spectacular Extravaganza

In 1866, a curious hodgepodge called *The Black Crook* opened in downtown New York and became "an instant sensation"[5] and an unprecedented success. Although this show is frequently cited as "the first musical," it is difficult to justify this claim since the story and score of *The Black Crook* had almost no discernible influence on the form or content of what would become the Broadway musical. *The Black Crook* was, however, a landmark event in the history of show business, and its legendary backstory has understandably captivated theater historians. In brief, a young producer named Henry Jarrett "brought a European ballet troupe to America and outfitted it with beautiful sets and the latest sexy French costumes."[6] European ballet dancers had been big attractions in the U.S. since the late 1840s, not so much for their dancing but because the young female dancers wore short (for the period) skirts and daringly displayed their legs sheathed in flesh-colored tights. But before the ballet could open, the theater it was booked into[7] burned down, and the entire company was left stranded with nowhere to perform. Meanwhile, a new fantastical melodrama—a rip-off of *Faust* titled *The Black Crook*—was scheduled to open at Niblo's Garden, but the manager of that theater, William Wheatley, was growing "uncertain about his shaky new production" and jumped at the idea of combining the ballet with the melodrama and melding it into one enormous production.[8] Although the story was incomprehensible (just try reading it), the spectacular production featured more than 100 performers and a dazzling series of special-effects-filled transformation scenes featuring elaborate scenery "magically rising out of the floor, fairies soaring through the air, shimmering stalagmites and stalactites glistening in [the fairy queen] Stalacata's crystal grotto."[9] And on it went for five and a half hours—"American audiences had never seen anything like it."[10]

The Black Crook was loaded with orchestral music to accompany its many ballets and scenic transformations, but there were only a few songs, and, as historian Larry Stempel notes, those vocal numbers were selected not by the show's writers but by the singers themselves. For example, the show's biggest hit song, "You Naughty, Naughty Men," a "saucy music hall ditty that had virtually no bearing on the story," was written specifically for its singer, Millie Cavendish, and when she "left the show early in the run, the song left with her."[11] The show itself, however, went on to an unprecedented sixteen-month run of 474 consecutive performances and earned more than a million dollars in ticket sales. Over the following twenty-five years, *The Black Crook* would be revived on Broadway ten times. Meanwhile, multiple "franchised" touring productions brought the show to nearly every city and town in America. In this way, *The Black Crook* revolutionized American show business by setting new standards for success that before it had seemed impossible to achieve.

Inevitably, a series of lavish musical extravaganzas quickly emerged to try to capitalize on that success, led by **Humpty Dumpty**, starring pantomime comedian George L. Fox, which opened in 1868 and would go on to run even longer than *The Black Crook*. Its plot "bore scant resemblance to the Mother Goose stories from which it drew its title,"[12] since the original fairytale characters appeared only briefly before a Fairy Queen transformed them into commedia dell'arte characters. It did, however, feature "the first American roller-skating troupe, circus acts, bieyclists [sic], subterranean grottos, a lavish panorama of Naples, and . . . a steamboat explosion and fire."[13] In 1874, *Evangeline*, "nominally a parody of Longfellow's poem,"[14] became the first show to be billed as a "musical comedy." It featured such gimmicks as a balloon trip to Arizona, a dancing cow (played by two men in one costume), a shapely woman in tights playing the leading male hero role, and a 300-pound male comedian in the leading female role.[15] Meanwhile, a trio of Hungarian immigrant brothers—Imre, Bollossy, and Arnold Kiralfy—who had arrived in America in 1868, and worked as dancers in both *The Black Crook* and *Humpty Dumpty*, began creating their own lavish shows, beginning with a new and improved 1873 revival of *The Black Crook*, followed by a mammoth production of Jules Verne's **Around The World In 80 Days**, featuring a live elephant and what was billed as the "Greatest Terpsichorean Ensemble ever united on any stage," including "a corps de Ballet of 250 Dansueses and a Supurb Cast."[16] The show focused on the most exotic and sensational aspects of the story, including "Fettish Dances, and Oriental Groupings by Lovely Maidens in Sumptuous Attire."[17]

The best remembered of these shows is the 1903 stage adaptation of L. Frank Baum's children's book, **The Wizard of Oz**, which had been published just three years earlier. Director Julian Mitchell was the driving force behind this production, and he persuaded a reluctant Baum to turn the show into a "send-up of the previous twenty-five years of musical extravaganzas,"[18] as well as a vehicle for the comedy team of David Montgomery and Fred Stone, who starred as the Scarecrow and Tin Woodsman. With its tornado scene, all-girl dancing poppy field, glittering Emerald City, and in place of Toto, another dancing cow named Imogene, *The Wizard of Oz* played nine months on Broadway and then toured America for the next six years. In the process, it became "the favorite of a generation." It would eventually inspire MGM to make a very different movie musical version, which in turn would inspire both the 1971 Broadway hit *The Wiz* and the current Broadway extravaganza *Wicked*.

Even if *The Black Crook* was not "the first musical," it did pass on three essential and lasting elements to the form. First, the idea that a musical show could, and should, become a money-making blockbuster hit. Secondly, it established an expectation in the audience that lavish and spectacular scenery, costumes, lighting, and special effects would be a vital part of the staging of a musical show. Finally, despite strong condemnation from conservative newspaper editors and clergymen, it "firmly established women in tights as a major feature of American show business, the first big step in making the chorus girl a fixture on the American musical stage."[19]

In a series of outraged editorials, the *New York Herald* denounced the show and called on "the respectable portion of the community [to] proclaim an unflinching war against

The Black Crook,"[20] and even urged them to burn Niblo's Garden to the ground.[21] One article stated that the writer had believed that the "dramatizations from the French with which we have been favored from time to time were obscene enough to suit the most depraved taste. But it seems not so. New York required something more loose and obscene yet, and . . . has now got it in the shape of a play called *The Black Crook*," a show which "depended for its popularity upon the lascivious pictures formed upon the stage." And in provocative language that must have thrilled the show's press agents, the writer singled out the "demon dance" during which "fifty-three girls, selected for the beauty of their features and perfection of their form, take part in an entirely nude state, except a narrow clout of thin gauze that conceals nothing . . . How long will this devil's work be allowed?" In reality, the dancers were completely covered from neck to toe, but repressed Victorian-era audiences were not accustomed to seeing even the shape of the human form, and so were excited and thrilled by this display—even as it inspired comparisons with "scenes in Sodom and Gomorrah just before fire and brimstone rained down on them."[22] In the end, the objections were all to no avail because, as one disgruntled reformer lamented, "multitudes are turned away nightly." In its assault on conservative morality, *The Black Crook* had become:

> . . . the magnet whose power of attraction nobody can resist. Editors write against it, ministers preach against it, and lecturers hurl their thunderbolts against it, and the more they write and preach and thunder, the more the people go to see it. Everybody condemns it, and nearly everybody patronizes it. The young are swept as by the tide, and the old go to see what draws the young—the saints go to see what dread monster is threatening to swallow up the small remnant of morality left to the country, and the sinners to see what ungodly phenomenon is stirring the wrath of the saints. Laymen go to see the target of their minister's weekly lampoons, and the clergy to see how many of their flocks are under the influence of the charmer. Thus one and another turn the heads and feet of all classes towards *The Black Crook*, and still the enthusiasm is without abatement, after a year of almost continuous repetition.[23]

This heady and complex mix of objectification and liberation will become a potent and ongoing feature of the Broadway musical and, thus, a recurring topic of discussion throughout this book.

Vaudeville

From the early 1880s through the late 1920s the preeminent form of entertainment in America was vaudeville.[24] At its peak, thousands of Vaudeville theaters were spread across every city and town in America, and more than five million Americans attended a Vaudeville show every week. A vaudeville performance was essentially a traveling variety show made up of a dozen or so individual, self-contained acts of all kinds—singers, dancers, comedians, musicians, magicians, escape artists, acrobats, jugglers, family acts, animal acts, kid acts, dramatic scenes: anything that might captivate an audience—and every show would be programmed to create contrast and variety. Each of these individual acts was between eleven and twenty minutes long, with the longest segments reserved for the most popular stars "at the top of the bill." Live Vaudeville was eventually dealt a death blow by sound movies, but many of its most popular performers became Broadway, film, and early television superstars. Echoes of vaudeville are still very much with us in television talent contests such as *America's Got Talent*.

Tin Pan Alley

Before the invention of sound recording, the phonograph, and the radio, anyone who wanted to hear music had only two choices: attend a live performance (if one was available) or sing and/or play the music themselves. After the conclusion of the Civil War, as cities in the North began to prosper, the number of homes in America with pianos skyrocketed. It was estimated that in 1887, more than 500,000 young people were studying piano.[25] As a result, sheet music became a very big industry run mostly by German immigrants, because many of them had been involved in music publishing back in Europe. At first, these music publishing companies were spread throughout the midwestern cities where early German immigrants had settled in large numbers—Cincinnati, Milwaukee, St. Louis, and so on. However, as New York established itself as the center of American show business, the music publishing industry consolidated there as well.

For more than forty years—from approximately 1885 through the 1920s—a one-block-long section of 28th Street between 5th Avenue and Broadway in NYC was the music publishing center of the world. Dozens of music publishing companies were crammed into that one street where songs were written, arranged, and auditioned and where professional musical artists came to find new songs to perform. On a typical day, there were so many pianos in so many offices and song demonstration rooms, all pounding out tunes simultaneously, that one journalist described the resulting cacophony as sounding like hundreds of people banging on tin pans. This image caught on, and before long, both that street and the music publishing industry itself became ironically and proudly known as "Tin Pan Alley."

During its first two decades, Tin Pan Alley produced an unprecedented succession of hit songs, including the 1892 ballad "After The Ball." With words and music by German Jewish songwriter Charles K. Harris, it was the first song to sell more than a million copies of sheet music. That got people's attention. Then it went on to sell more than five million. Songwriting was a brand new, disruptive industry that now became a new and exciting, if not entirely respectable, profession. For the first time in history, composers wrote songs that were aimed at a mass audience rather than for aristocratic patrons. This established patterns and standards for American pop music that are still largely followed today.

Broadway Nation

In those days, the only way to make a song known to the public was to have it performed live, as frequently and in front of as many people as possible. It soon became clear that the most impactful and lucrative exposure that any new song could receive was for it to be featured in a Broadway revue or musical comedy. Soon, Tin Pan Alley's top songwriters began creating full scores for Broadway shows, and Broadway "showtunes" were considered to be the highest levels of craft and artistry in songwriting. Every Tin Pan Alley songwriter now aspired to write for Broadway because it meant that they had reached the pinnacle of their profession, and music publishing companies became actively involved in the world of Broadway musicals.

The Yiddish Theater

The first professional Yiddish[26] theater company was founded in Romania in 1876, and this new art form quickly spread throughout the Yiddish-speaking world, which at that time included Poland, Ukraine (and other parts of the Russian Empire), Germany, England, France, Argentina, Canada, and by the 1880s, Yiddish Theater had arrived in America. At its height, twenty-two Yiddish playhouses lined the "Jewish Rialto"—the Yiddish theater district centered on Second Avenue on New York's Lower East Side. Thousands of Jewish immigrants flocked to its vibrant mix of plays, operettas, vaudeville, and other kinds of musical performances, all written in or translated into Yiddish. As we will see, many of the Jewish inventors of the Broadway musical grew up attending the Yiddish Theatre and were strongly influenced by its music and drama.

Edwardian Musical Comedy

When Gilbert and Sullivan acrimoniously split up in the 1890s, a newer, even lighter form of entertainment emerged to fill the void—Edwardian Musical Comedy. Its originator was an impresario named George Edwards (1855–1915), although the name of this theatrical form refers to the historical period and not to him. Edwards had worked for producer Richard D'Oyly Carte and had assisted him in mounting the Gilbert and Sullivan operettas. In 1885, Edwards was put in charge of the Gaiety Theater in London, where he initially produced the kind of burlesque shows discussed above, but he wanted to create classier kinds of productions that would attract a more upscale audience. The first was *In Town*, in 1893, which the *Sunday Times* described as "a curious medley of song, dance, and nonsense."[27] Then came *The Gaiety Girl*, the first of these shows to be billed as "a musical comedy." It also was the first to establish what quickly became one of the key attractions of these shows—a singing and dancing chorus of six "Gaiety Girls." Somewhat more refined than similar groups in burlesque, these beautiful and fashionable young women became the media celebrities of their day, as epitomized by the "Florodora Girls" who stopped their show (*Florodora*) nightly with their still famous double sextette ("Tell Me Pretty Maiden"), and who according to legend all married millionaires.

Edwards' shows combined elements of burlesque, Gilbert and Sullivan, and music hall. Their plots and stories were very slight, but unlike the burlesques, they were set in the modern day and featured characters dressed in the absolute height of fashion. The songs were a mix of styles and could be switched out and replaced as needed during the run to encourage audiences to return again and again. *The Gaiety Girl* was the first in a long string of "girl titles" that would follow it, including *The Shop Girl* (1894), *The Circus Girl* (1895), *A Runaway Girl* (1898), *The Quaker Girl* (1910), and a late entry that will come up again when its American version plays a key role in the evolution of the Broadway showtune, *The Girl From Utah* (1915).

The influence and impact of these precursors is often very clear and specific—and sometimes very unexpected. Black composer Eubie Blake, who, as we will see in Chapter 2, was the initial force in bringing jazz to Broadway, told an interviewer that as a teenager, he had seen *Florodora* at Ford's Theater in his hometown of Baltimore and effusively went on to credit that show's composer/lyricist, Leslie Stewart, with being the "direct cause" of him becoming a composer. "I liked his style," Blake said, "I loved that tune, and I said I can write tunes like that!"[28]

Edwardian musical comedies, Yiddish Theater, spectacle, Tin Pan Alley, vaudeville, operetta, burlesque, and the minstrel show provided lifeblood, bones, and sinew to the Broadway musical as it was being born. That birth, however, might never have happened if not for the remarkable confluence of the giant waves of immigration that swept into NYC during the nineteenth and early twentieth centuries.

ACT I
THE GENESIS PERIOD

Fig. 3: Irish American composer, lyricist, playwright, director, choreographer, and song and dance man superstar George M. Cohan (center with cane) leads the cast in "Anyplace The Old Flag Flies," the rousing act one finale of his 1911 musical *The Little Millionaire*. Bettmann / Contributor.

CHAPTER 1
YEARNING TO BREATHE FREE—
THE IMMIGRANTS WHO INVENTED
THE BROADWAY MUSICAL (I, J)

The Broadway musical was born around the turn of the twentieth century and emerged out of what used to be called "the melting pot"—that simmering confluence of cultures and races that were packed into the teeming tenement neighborhoods of New York City. To an enormous extent, the Broadway musical can be seen as an "immigrant art form" as well as an "outcast art form." It certainly was almost entirely invented by men and women from outside the mainstream of society. What they created was something new: an immensely popular, democratic kind of music-theater that—like most great American inventions—was inspired by both a strong desire for self-expression and a strong necessity to make money and put food on the table. The concept of "the melting pot" has lost favor with many historians, but it remains a very apt description of how various multicultural artistic traditions and art forms blended together to create the American musical.

Between 1820 and 1920, over 30 million immigrants came to the United States. Almost all of them were escaping famine, oppression, or both in their home countries, and when they arrived on America's shores, most of them were desperately poor. Prior to this, the entire population of the United States amounted to only 9.7 million, and they were overwhelmingly homogeneous: almost all of them were what are sometimes called WASPS (White Anglo-Saxon Protestants.) At that time, most Americans were descended from those early waves of pilgrim Puritans, whom Cole Porter would later characterize in the title song of his musical *Anything Goes* as having "got a shock when they landed on Plymouth Rock." Despite their own immigrant roots, many in the WASP establishment majority regarded this onslaught of newcomers as a threat to their "American way of life." In language that sounds remarkably like anti-immigrant speech used today, they accused these newcomers of being dirty, dangerous, disease-ridden foreigners who practiced alien religions and warned they would bring drugs and violent crime and take jobs away from "real Americans." One journalist described "streams of undersized, peculiar, alien people ... on their way from the slums of Europe to the slums of America ... the defeated, incompetent and the unsuccessful ... the very lowest layer of European society."[1] Astoundingly, at least from our contemporary point of view, the immigrants of this period that the WASP establishment objected to so fiercely came from Ireland, Germany, Italy, and Eastern Europe and would all be considered "white" by today's standards. That is not, however, how they were perceived at the time.[2]

The Irish Immigrants

Nearly four and a half million of these immigrants came from Ireland, most of them fleeing the starvation and disease that resulted from the Irish Potato Famine, which stretched from 1845 to 1849. By 1910, more people of Irish ancestry were living in New York City than in Dublin. They were largely unskilled and illiterate. Even worse—at least in the eyes of the WASP establishment—the vast majority of them were Roman Catholic. Anti-Catholic propaganda insinuated that they would be more faithful to the Vatican than they would be to the American government, and Catholics were even accused of being sent by the Pope to subvert American democracy. Political cartoons of the day viciously caricatured Irish immigrants as shiftless drunkards and "wild beasts" with simian features, and even as late as 1899, a pseudoscientific illustration in *Harper's Weekly* presented "Irish Iberians" as a different race that was "believed to have been originally an African race" and "descendants of savages of the stone age."[3] The daily prejudice and discrimination Irish immigrants faced was far from subtle and "Help Wanted" advertisements and "Rooms For Rent'" signs stated outright and plainly that "No Irish Need Apply."

The German, Eastern European, and Jewish Immigrants

Nearly six million Germans emigrated to the United States between 1820 and World War I. They, too, were escaping economic hardship, political revolution, and unrest. However, unlike the Irish, many in this first wave of German immigration had just enough money to travel past New York to the Midwest in search of farmland and employment. As a result, significant German populations soon grew up in Cincinnati, St. Louis, Chicago, and Milwaukee, but millions stayed right where they had landed in New York City. They, too, faced severe religious and cultural prejudice. Just like the Irish, a large percentage of these German immigrants were Catholic, and since Catholics tended to have deeply cultural and relatively liberal attitudes towards the consumption of alcohol, this placed them in direct conflict with conservative Protestant values. (The enactment of Prohibition was, to a large extent, an attempt to tame the "immoral" habits of Catholic immigrants.)

Even more disturbing from the establishment's point of view was that another large percentage of German immigrants were Jewish. Soon, they were followed to America by another two million Jews who were being driven out of their homes in the Russian Empire and Eastern Europe. They came to America in search of what they called "Di Goldene Medine"—"The Golden Land." (Their stories are dramatized with great emotional power and historical accuracy in the Broadway musicals *Fiddler on the Roof*, *Rags*, and *Ragtime*.) These immigrants—Irish, German, Jewish—took the most menial, dangerous, and low-paying jobs—work that established Americans would not do. They dug canals, built railroads, swept streets, cleaned houses, and toiled long hours in textile mills and "sweatshop" garment factories. Most significant to this discussion, a large number of them found opportunity and employment in a very different, if no less rigorous, field of endeavor that was just beginning to emerge at this time. It was called "The Show Business."

"There's No Business Like Show Business"

In this new simmering pot of cultures that made up New York City just before the turn of the century, "the show business" was gathering steam. As urban life and modern culture were being invented, theaters began springing up throughout New York City, especially on that street called "Broadway." Meanwhile, nationwide vaudeville circuits were being formed, sheet music publishing was becoming a major industry, and soon phonograph records and "moving pictures" would be added to the mix. However, as has been the case throughout most of world history, "show people"—actors, singers, dancers, comedians, playwrights, songwriters, and so on—were still largely regarded by the establishment culture as being low class and disreputable, no matter how much their talent might be valued and rewarded. To display oneself on a stage was viewed as being morally suspect. In the eyes of so-called "polite society," show people were only a small step away from being vagabonds and prostitutes. This attitude made "the show business," even as it was growing in popularity, a line of work that respectable Americans would not do. This void would largely be filled by immigrants, who could scarcely afford to harbor that kind of prejudice or pass up any kind of opportunity to get ahead, as they were already relegated to the fringes of society. Luckily, their Irish, German, Eastern European, and Jewish cultures all included rich musical, dance, and theatrical traditions that they could draw on and tap into. So, for those ambitious young immigrants who possessed the necessary talent and determination, show business became one of the fastest possible ways to escape the slums and sweatshops. It was this unusual combination of circumstances that set the stage for the birth of what we have come to call "the Broadway musical."

Not Quite Yet Musicals—The Shows of Harrigan & Hart, Weber & Fields, and Williams & Walker (I, J, B)

The first theatrical artists to create what were at least embryonic versions of the musical as we know it were three Vaudeville song and dance comedy teams—the Irish American duo of Harrigan and Hart, the Polish Jewish American duo of Weber and Fields, and the African American duo of Williams and Walker.

Edward (Ned) Harrigan and Tony Hart began their fourteen-year partnership in 1871. They became headline Variety stars by performing short comic skits in which Harrigan served as the straight man to Hart's outrageous clowning and exceptional talent for female impersonation. Eventually, the duo got booked into New York's *Theatre*

Comique, where they became such a hit that they eventually took over management of the theater and began to expand their signature routines into full-length plays with songs—but they weren't quite musicals. Between 1873 and 1893, Harrigan, the "self-educated son of a seaman" who had "grown up in Manhattan's Irish slums and run away to sea in his teens,"[4] produced, directed, and co-starred in forty-one of these plays, all set in a fictional tenement block he named "Mulligan Alley," and featuring a revolving cast of ethnic character-types from the neighborhood—Irish, Germans, Italians, Jews, and, significantly, African Americans. In 1889, Harrigan wrote, "If I have given undue prominence to the Irish and the negro, it is because they form about the most salient features of Gotham humanity, and they are the two races who care the most for song and dance."[5] Regrettably, the Black characters in these shows were played by white actors in blackface. Still, it seems that Harrigan, who had performed with Manning's Minstrels, was endeavoring in his plays to break away from Minstrel show stereotypes.[6] His goal was to put the "melting pot" onstage in front of an audience made up of those same diverse groups, as demonstrated by Harrigan's lyric (which echoes some of the everyday casual racism of the period) for the song, "McNally's Row of Flats" from his 1882 play, *The McSorleys*:

It's Ireland and Italy,
Jerusalem and Germany,
Oh, Chinaman and naggars [sic],
And a paradise for rats,
All jumbled up togayther [sic]
In the snow or rainy weather,
They represent the tenants
In McSorley's row of flats.[7]

As critic William Dean Howells wrote in 1886, "Mr. Harrigan shows us the street-cleaners and contractors, the grocery men, the shysters, the politicians, the washerwomen, the servant girls, the truckmen, the policemen, the risen Irishman and Irishwoman of contemporary New York."[8] Harrigan and Hart's shows always "carried the cheapest ticket in town and their most devoted spectators were the orphaned newsboys whom New York had by the thousands."[9]

Harrigan and Hart mounted a new show every few months, placing these now beloved characters into new variations. With titles such as *The Mulligan Guard Ball* (1879), *The Mulligan Guard Picnic* (1880), and *The Mulligan Guard Christmas* (1880), these shows were much like episodes of a television sitcom. Ned Harrigan wrote the lyrics to the songs featured in their shows, set to music composed by David Braham (originally Abraham). Braham had been born into a Jewish family in London in 1834 and had emigrated to New York City when he was fifteen. He would later become Harrigan's father-in-law when Ned married his daughter, Annie. Although virtually forgotten today, these Harrigan/Braham songs were international sensations at the time, especially "The Mulligan Guard Marching Song," which became the best-selling hit song of the

1870s.[10] Like virtually all of the songs in Harrigan and Hart's shows, "Mulligan Guard" was an *acknowledged song* (see Box below). These songs augmented the story and added excitement and color to the staging but were not used to tell the story or reveal the inner world of the story's characters in any direct way. This is the principal reason that Harrigan and Hart's shows were not quite yet musicals.

> ### Acknowledged and Unacknowledged Songs
>
> > "Our fifes and drums, so sweetly they did play
> > as we marched, marched, marched with the Mulligan Guard."
>
> The songs in the Harrigan and Hart shows were what many academics label as "diegetic." However, because that term has been somewhat awkwardly borrowed from Film Studies, where it refers to something quite different, I believe it is much less confusing to call them ***acknowledged songs***. These are songs that the characters in the story (along with the writers of the show and the audience watching it) acknowledge to be songs. For example, in the musical *Guys and Dolls*, when Adelaide sings "A Bushel and A Peck," she and all of the other characters in the scene understand and acknowledge that this is (for the purposes of the story) a "pre-written song" being performed by her and the Hot Box girls as part of the floor show at that nightclub. In contrast, just a few moments later, she is alone in the club after it has closed for the night, and sings "Adelaide's Lament." This song, however, is *not* a song—at least not as far as Adelaide or the story is concerned. Rather, it is an inner monologue that the show's composer/lyricist, Frank Loesser, has set to music; therefore, it is an ***unacknowledged song***. Near the end of that show, Adelaide and Sarah Brown sing "Marry The Man Today." This duet is a conversation—a dialogue scene set to music—and, as such, it is also an unacknowledged song. The critical aspect is that the characters in the story who are involved in these songs do not think (acknowledge) that they are singing. Any musical sequence that takes the place of what instead could have been written as non-musical dialogue or monologue is an *unacknowledged song*. A *play* can include *acknowledged songs*, but *unacknowledged songs* can only exist in a *musical*—and to a great degree, *unacknowledged songs* are what make a musical a musical. It should be noted, however, that many songwriters very effectively blur the line between these two kinds of songs for theatrical effect.

Joe Weber and Lew Fields were both born in 1867, and both were the children of Polish Jewish immigrants. They met while growing up in extreme poverty on New York's Lower East Side. By the age of nine, **Weber and Fields** were already performing a knockabout comedy act in the beer gardens and smoky dives of New York's rough and tumble, working-class entertainment district called "The Bowery." Sporting derby hats, checkered suits, and fake beards, they portrayed a pair of German immigrants—a wise guy and a greenhorn just off the boat. Their act became so popular that, like Harrigan and Hart, they eventually gained control of their own Broadway theater and expanded their vaudeville skits into full-length shows. With titles such as *Whirl-i-Gig, Fiddle De Dee, Hoity-Toity,* and *Twirly-Whirly,* their shows featured a company of fifty performers headed by Weber and Fields and half a dozen other stars, including Lillian Russell, the biggest female star of the day. All of the Weber and Fields shows were "burlesques"—in the original meaning of that word (see page xxx): broadly comic entertainments that made fun of popular plays and novels of the day. In many ways, Weber and Fields' shows were remarkably similar to Monty Python's *Spamalot,* and the way it spoofs the legend of "King Arthur and the Knights of the Round Table." Their show *Hokey Pokey* (1912) even included a song titled "If it Wasn't for the Irish and the Jews," which includes the lyric: "I once heard Dave Belasco say[11] / you couldn't stage a play today / if it wasn't for the Irish and the Jews." This is remarkably similar to *Spamalot*'s "You Won't Succeed on Broadway (If You Don't Have Any Jews)," written a century later. This brand of parody and satire has continued as one of the distinctive flavors of the Broadway musical throughout its history.

Weber and Fields productions also established the kind of elaborate visual displays that have remained a major aspect of most Broadway musicals right up to today—spectacular sets, colorful costumes, special effects, dynamic choreography, and elaborate production numbers showcasing full chorus lines of dancers. Since then, musicals have almost always included a feast for both the eyes and the ears. However, their greatest contribution to the development of the Broadway musical was the theatrical dynasty Lew Fields established. He was the father of not only Herbert and Joseph Fields—two of the most important and prolific bookwriters—but also their sister Dorothy Fields, who would be one of Broadway's top lyricists for over forty years.

The team of Williams and Walker will be profiled in the next chapter, which focuses on the contributions of Black creators to the development of the Broadway musical. What I find fascinating is that simultaneously, all three of these teams—Williams and Walker, Weber and Fields, and Harrigan and Hart—were doing very nearly the exact same thing at roughly the same time: expanding their successful vaudeville song and dance acts into full-length entertainments. While none of these added up to an actual musical as we would define it today, they did inspire and point the way for two other Irish songwriters who would bring the musical into a form we would most certainly recognize.

The Father of the Musical Comedy: George M. Cohan

George M. Cohan was Broadway's first superstar, adored by audiences for his distinctive and dynamic stage presence as well as for his phenomenal range of first-class talents that included song and dance man, actor, lyricist, composer, playwright, director, choreographer, and producer—and often he undertook many of those roles simultaneously. He was born in 1879 in Providence, Rhode Island, on the 3rd, rather than "on the 4th of July" as he would famously proclaim in his song, "Yankee Doodle Boy."[12]

His mother, Helen "Nellie" (Costigan) Cohan, had emigrated from Ireland with her parents, while his father, Jerry, was the son of Irish Catholic immigrants from County Cork. Over the years, the family name had been modified from "O'Caomhan" to "Keohane" and finally, to "Cohan," when Jerry decided to capitalize on his early success as an amateur Irish clog dance champion and embark on a career in the emerging field of show business. Eventually, he incorporated Nellie and daughter, Josie, into the act, and by the time little Georgie was seven, the entire family was barnstorming the country as a headlining Vaudeville team—"The Four Cohans."

Although he received almost no formal education, George began writing tunes and song lyrics by the age of ten and began creating comedy sketches and routines for The Four Cohans while still in his teens. His earliest songs were primarily written in waltz-time or occasionally in a bouncy 4/4 "Schottische" tempo.[13] However, sometime in the 1890s, while touring in vaudeville with his family, "Cohan became more and more aware of and fascinated by the emerging style of 'rag-time'—the underground urban folk music of Midwestern African Americans" and began to incorporate "the rhythmic palate" of ragtime music into his songs.[14]

"I Am That Yankee Doodle Boy!"

Success in vaudeville, however, wasn't enough for young George. Inspired by the shows of Harrigan and Hart,[15] he set his sights on Broadway and quickly burst onto the scene by writing the book, music, and lyrics for a show called *Little Johnny Jones*, in which he also played the title role. Cohan stated that his goal (just like his idol Harrigan) was to "bring actual living characters from the street to the stage." However, his real achievement was to place those characters in dramatically plausible and coherent stories. Compared to everything that had come before, Cohan significantly upped the stakes of musical theater bookwriting by combining melodrama with farce and folding in vaudeville-style comedy, rapid-fire action, and snappy dialogue. Cohan's shows were both funny and dramatic, and his catchy, rhythmic, Tin Pan Alley-type songs were (at least loosely) tied into the storylines. *Little Johnny Jones* introduced two unforgettable tunes, "Yankee Doodle Boy" and a song that, more than a century later, is still Broadway's anthem, "Give My Regards to Broadway." Both songs were performed by Cohan himself, in his own indelible, trademark style: he would strut across the front of the stage with his hat cocked down over his eyes in an iconic manner that would be copied, honored, and echoed by everyone from Jimmy Durante to Gene Kelly to Bob Fosse, and still lives on as the embodiment of Broadway style.[16]

Audiences adored Cohan, but early critics were nearly unanimous in their disdain. In a 1906 *Life* magazine review of Cohan's musical comedy *George Washington Jr.* (which introduced the song, "You're A Grand Old Flag"),[17] critic James Metcalf described Cohan as "a vulgar, cheap, blatant, ill-mannered, flashily dressed, insolent smart Aleck, who for some reason unexplainable appeals to the imagination and apparent approval of large American audience." He also recommended that *Life*'s readers "go see Mr. Cohan's performance. There could be no stronger appeal for the betterment of the American stage—no fiercer commentary on the debased condition of the intelligence of a large part of the theater-going public."

What was it about Cohan, his shows, and his songs that inspired such derision? In music historian Mick Moloney's view, it's because Cohan was "kind of a one-man revolt against the inherited tastes of high art from Europe, especially from England ... He's brash, he's loud, he's arrogant, he's pushy, he's obnoxious—but by God he's successful!" And, of course, any kind of art that is extremely popular is often looked down upon by the critics. However, it may be that a deeper prejudice inspired these negative reactions. We have to consider what it meant for an Irish American to stand on a stage in 1904 and sing, "I'm A Yankee Doodle Dandy" or cast himself as the title character in *George Washington, Jr.* The days of "No Irish Need Apply" signs were not so long in the past, and anti-Catholic sentiment was still going strong and would continue through the 1920s. So, waving a flag and declaring himself to be "a real live nephew of my Uncle Sam" can very much be seen as a social and political statement. The not-so-subtle message of Cohan's flag waving was, "I'm just as American as anyone else," and furthermore, that "we Irish are America"—"we immigrants are America." This seems remarkably similar to the statement that Lin-Manual Miranda is making more than 100 years later by having BIPOC actors portray America's founding fathers and mothers in his musical *Hamilton*.

During his long career, George M. Cohan created twenty Broadway musicals and more than 500 songs—a surprising number of which still have currency today. Perhaps most significantly, as Rick Benjamin, the founder and conductor of the Paragon Ragtime Orchestra, tells us, Cohan was the first "major white theater composer to inject the rhythms of ragtime music into musical comedy scores," and the resulting popularity of his songs and shows would expose "vast numbers of white theatergoers to ragtime, helping it to gain acceptance as the 'language' of modern theater."[18] However, as Benjamin points out, it is important to note that in the early 1900s the term "ragtime" referred to any and all kinds of syncopated pop songs and instrumental pieces. It was not until the 1940s that music historians narrowed the definition of "ragtime" to include only a very specific form of piano pieces by Scott Joplin and other ragtime composers.

I don't believe it is an overstatement to assert that Cohan invented the "Musical Comedy" as we know it. Virtually every musical that came after him was built on the patterns he established. So, it seems entirely appropriate that Cohan is the only figure in the history of Broadway to be honored with a statue in the center of Times Square.

Father of the American Operetta: Victor Herbert

Victor Herbert was born in Dublin, Ireland, but he studied in Germany to be a classical cellist. He must have been very good because in 1886, at the age of twenty-seven, he emigrated to New York to play in the orchestra of the Metropolitan Opera. Early on, he achieved success as a cellist, composer, and conductor of classical music—but he was interested in a larger audience. Like Cohan, Herbert had also been captivated by the works of Harrigan and Hart, and his original intention was to create a similar kind of "folk theater." However, his classical training and technique led him first to create a series of European-style operettas featuring lyrical music and stories that took place in glamorous foreign settings—Venice, India, Persia, Egypt, and, most exotic of all, "the land of Mother Goose" in his wildly popular fantasy extravaganza, *Babes in Toyland*. Building on that success and influenced by the arrival of Franz Lehár's blockbuster, *The Merry Widow* (see Box below), Herbert then began to pioneer a new version of the operetta—and one that was distinctly American.

In three smash hit shows—*Mlle. Modiste* (1905), *The Red Mill* (1906), and *Naughty Marietta* (1910)—he combined upscale old-world-style classical melodies with syncopated ragtime rhythms, boisterous Bowery-type waltzes, and other Tin Pan Alley pop-music styles of the day. The stories of these shows still took place in faraway Europe, but they were set in the modern day, and the plots hinged on contemporary Americans, usually brash but charming New Yorkers, who, while traveling abroad, helped the locals sort out their problems. Most importantly, the music and lyrics for the most part related to the plot, revealed the inner life of the characters, and often were woven into extended musical sequences that moved the story forward. In the process, Herbert and his main collaborators, Rida Johnson Young[19] and Henry Blossom, created a string of hit songs, including "Ah! Sweet Mystery of Life," "The Italian Street Song," "Streets of New York," and "Kiss Me Again." Even though Herbert died in 1924, many of his shows, and especially his songs, remained immensely popular throughout the entire twentieth century.

With Victor Herbert and George M. Cohan, the two main genres of the Broadway musical had now been firmly established: the *musical comedy* and the *operetta*. Eventually, these two forms will be fused together by Rodgers and Hammerstein into what they called the *musical play*—and today, we just call a *musical*.

"Ev'ry Touch of Fingers Tells Me What I Know": *The Merry Widow* on Broadway

> It was nearly 10:30 o'clock [sic] last night when the strains of the celebrated "Merry Widow Waltz" floated over the footlights of the New Amsterdam Theatre. But it was not necessary to wait until then to know that this operetta was to become as popular in America as it has been in Europe since it was produced in Vienna in January 1905. The theater was packed, and all the available standing room was taken . . . for the fame of this "widow" had preceded her . . . the applause was almost terrifying in its intensity at times, and there were many shouts of "Bravo!" as at a performance of "Pagliacci" when Caruso sings.
>
> *New York Times*, October 27, 1907.[20]

In 1907, when the Viennese operetta *The Merry Widow* opened in New York, it became an instant sensation and inspired what historian Larry Stempel has called a new "Silver Age" of American operetta.[21] With sparkling music by Franz Léhar and a witty, racy libretto by the Jewish-Austrian-Hungarian writing team of Viktor Léon and Leo Stein,[22] the show had premiered in Vienna just two years earlier as *Die Lustige Witwe*. Its enormous success there was quickly replicated in other European cities in multiple languages, including an English adaptation by Basil Hood, with lyrics by Adrian Ross, presented in a dazzling production by George Edwardes that took London by storm. Just months later, that version opened on Broadway, "with perhaps a few suggestive lines and situations accepted in Munich or Vienna eliminated."[23] The story is about a glamorous and immensely wealthy young widow from a fictional Balkan country living the highlife in Paris. Amid the usual stock operetta characters, including a secondary couple involved in an adulterous love triangle, *The Merry Widow*'s book, score, and staging[24] brought unusual life to its two central figures: the widow, Sonia, and Prince Danilo, her fellow countryman and ex-lover who has been sent to Paris to woo and wed Sonia and ensure that her vast fortune stays in their homeland. As might be expected of a work of art born in Sigmund Freud's Vienna, underneath the surface of their rocky relationship, their true feelings for one another are revealed by a haunting and sensuous waltz. As Larry Stempel observes, "What most people think of as 'The Merry Widow Waltz' went to the heart of the new (American) operetta genre in its psychological use of music and movement to reveal emotional truths where words failed."[25] From this point on, this kind of use of ballroom dancing as a potent erotic metaphor for lovemaking will be replicated in countless stage and film musicals, including every Fred Astaire and Ginger Rodgers movie and *The King And I*'s climactic "Shall We Dance."

Defining American Music: Irving Berlin

Meanwhile, among the masses of desperately poor Jewish immigrants who packed the rag boats coming to America was a desperately poor, illiterate six-year-old boy named Israel Baline. He was born in 1888 in a small village in Siberia and spent his earliest years in a shtetl in today's Belarus[26]—much like the fictional town of Anatevka in *Fiddler on the Roof*. Israel would, in fact, have been roughly the same age as Tevye's youngest daughter, Bielke, in the musical. Later in life, Irving Berlin (as he would eventually rename himself) would remember almost nothing of his childhood in Russia except for the images and emotions of being held in his weeping mother's arms as they watched his family's home being burned to the ground during a pogrom. When he was five, the Balines, fearing for their lives, joined the mass Jewish exodus to the United States.

Anyone familiar with the musical *Ragtime* (1998) will have a pretty good idea of the world that Berlin grew up in—the bustling streets of New York's Lower East Side filled with pushcart peddlers hawking their wares, exhausted young women toiling in garment industry sweatshops, children dancing on the street for pennies, large families crowded into small airless tenement apartments. This was not a promising beginning. However, like so many Jews of his generation, Berlin would go on to have a tremendous impact on American culture and, in many ways, define what it means to be an American.

Young Izzy Baline (as he was still known at the time) got a job selling newspapers. Much like it is depicted in the musical *Newsies*, Izzy was one of those newsboys (although probably with a bit less dancing). However, the few coins he was able to earn and bring home to his struggling family were barely enough to pay for his own room and board, and when his father unexpectedly died, thirteen-year-old Izzy, not wishing to be a burden on his mother, left home and set out on his own. Perhaps because his father had been a cantor—the chief vocalist and clergy member who leads the music in a Jewish religious service—Izzy decided that singing might be a way to earn a living, and although he didn't have much of a voice, he had plenty of energy and loads of chutzpah. He started by making the rounds, from one Bowery saloon to another, singing for loose change. Then, after getting fired from a short-lived stint as a chorus boy in a musical called *The Show Girl*, he got a job as a Tin Pan Alley "song plugger."[27]

As we will see, many of the inventors of the musical started out as song-pluggers, but this job title can refer to several different kinds of activity. In this case, sheet music publishers paid Izzy to sit in the audience of a Vaudeville theater and applaud vigorously for the songs they published. Sometimes, he would even jump up on his seat and "spontaneously" lead the crowd in a sing-along of the tune he was being paid to "plug." At the same time, the performers onstage would act surprised by this "unexpected" audience participation. If his ruse was effective, audience members would be inspired to purchase the sheet music of this new song that had caused such a commotion. It's important to remember that sound recording was only in its infancy at this time, and sheet music publishing was big business. So, the only way for a songwriter to make money was through the sale of sheet music. Almost every home in this period had a piano and a family member who could play it at least moderately well, and in the evenings, the family would gather around the piano and sing the latest hits.

By 1907, Izzy had found a new job as a singing waiter in a Chinatown dance hall where he was able to earn a weekly salary plus tips. Soon, a rival saloon down the block began pulling in big crowds with a new Italian novelty song written by their house pianist and bouncer. So, Izzy's boss commanded him and their pianist to write their own song. They came up with a ditty that they titled "Marie From Sunny Italy." It wasn't much of a song, but somehow it got published, and on the sheet music cover, Izzy received the credit: "Lyrics by I. Berlin." This new name was carefully chosen—close to his birth name, but with a "formal, Teutonic ring."[28] This was quite smart because German immigrants ran the music publishing industry. The song was enough of a success that Berlin soon decided to pursue songwriting full-time—both words and music. This leap of faith required a great deal more chutzpah, considering he couldn't read music and could only play the piano in one key.

Despite these limitations, Irving Berlin wrote dozens of songs during this period, with enough success that it brought him to the attention of George M. Cohan, who "took a great shine to the young Russian immigrant and opened many doors for him."[29] Cohan introduced Berlin to Tin Pan Alley publishers, as well as Broadway producers and performers, and eventually surprised him with a crucial gift: a Weser transposing piano. This ingenious instrument allowed self-taught pianists like Cohan and Berlin, who could only play in one key, to mechanically shift the keyboard so that the music would come out in any key they wanted. According to biographer Laurence Bergreen, this freed Berlin to:

> develop the harmonies, nuances, rhythms, and fill notes he needed to embellish his tunes. At the touch of a lever, he could test a chord or a phrase in a different key; he could experiment with interactions between chords and melodies without having to seek out a collaborator whose patience and endurance was as great as his.[30]

Then in 1911, Berlin composed a snappy march, fitted it out with catchy lyrics, and sold the song to a producer who immediately plugged it into his new Broadway show. Unfortunately, that show quickly flopped, but somehow, the song found its way to the singer Al Jolson, the biggest star of the era, who made it an instant hit. It sold half a million copies, then a million more, then two million. With that one song, the still captivating and infectious "Alexander's Ragtime Band," Irving Berlin became a songwriting superstar and a very wealthy young man.

In 1914, he made the leap from writing individual songs for Tin Pan Alley to creating full scores for Broadway musicals with the hit show *Watch Your Step*, which starred the ballroom dance sensations Vernon and Irene Castle. As we will see, over the next fifty-two years, Irving Berlin would go on to write twenty-five Broadway musicals in a remarkable one-of-a-kind Broadway career that spanned all the way from the Genesis Period to the final decade of the Golden Age. Meanwhile, he also became a major force in Hollywood, contributing songs to dozens of films, beginning with the very first talking/singing picture, *The Jazz Singer* (1927), in which Al Jolson introduced Berlin's "Blue Skies," and continuing through *White Christmas* and *There's No Business Like Show Business*, both in 1954. Over that time, Berlin created over 1,000 songs, at least 100 of which have become beloved and enduring standards that have stayed alive in our culture—including quite a few written more than a century ago; songs that are still recorded and performed by contemporary stars such as Lady Gaga. Even in the twenty-first century, two "new" Irving Berlin musicals opened on Broadway, *White Christmas* in 2009 and *Holiday Inn* in 2016, both inspired by his classic film musicals.

"The Song is You"—Jerome Kern

Meanwhile, another pioneering Jewish songwriter was coming of age further uptown. Jerome Kern was born in 1885 in New York on Sutton Place, which at that time was a famous beer district. In sharp contrast to Irving Berlin, Kern's parents were fairly prosperous German Jewish immigrants. Kern received a substantial musical education—first at the New York College of Music and later with private tutors in Germany and England, and first began composing music. Kern returned to New York in 1904, and over the next decade, he contributed songs to more than two dozen Broadway musicals and revues.

"They Didn't Believe Me"—A One Song Revolution

In the Genesis Period, musicals were usually put together so quickly and loosely that they would often include tunes by several different songwriting teams. In 1914, Kern was engaged to write a few songs to spruce up an Edwardian musical comedy that was being imported from London called *The Girl From Utah*. The title character was a young Mormon woman who, to avoid being trapped in a polygamous marriage, escapes to London, where she falls in love with a handsome actor.[31] One of the songs that Kern wrote for that show (in collaboration with lyricist Herbert Reynolds) would prove to be a groundbreaking step forward in the development of the Broadway musical. In fact, singer and composer Mel Tormé would later contend that "when Jerome Kern composed 'They Didn't Believe Me' he invented the popular song."

What was it that made this song so revolutionary? To begin with, most songs of that era were composed either as waltzes in three-quarter time (such as "After the Ball" or "The Band Played On") or as marches in 2/4 time (like Cohan's "Yankee Doodle Boy" and Berlin's "Alexander's Ragtime Band"). However, those time signatures do not allow a singer much leeway to interpret the lyric. Kern's big innovation was composing "They Didn't Believe Me" in 4/4 time—which made every measure of music twice the length. This provided the vocalist with more time and space to bring out the meaning and intention of the lyric—holding some notes longer, releasing other notes early, and expanding and contracting the lyric for dramatic effect. It also allowed the singer to phrase the words more naturally and conversationally—much like an actor might do with a spoken monologue or dialogue. And the innovations did not stop there! Songs in this period usually included lengthy "verses" that conveyed most of the story content of the song, which then alternated with short 16-bar "choruses" (much like "hooks" in contemporary pop/rock songwriting). Kern and Reynolds, however, took a decidedly different approach. They expanded the chorus to thirty-two bars (and the bars themselves were longer because they now had four beats instead of two). From this point on, it was the chorus (aka the refrain) that became the central feature of most Broadway songs, and the verses were reduced to relatively brief setups before or between the choruses. "They Didn't Believe Me" was not the first musical theater song composed in 4/4 time, and it may not have even been the first musical theater love ballad created in 4/4 time. It is, however, the first one we can identify—and certainly the first to become a popular hit.

Reportedly, the song created such a tremendous impact as originally performed by Julia Sanderson (the girl from Utah) and Donald Brian (her British suitor) that by the end, the entire audience was singing along. Most significantly, it was a revelation to the next generation of musical dramatists, including sixteen-year-old George Gershwin, who first heard this song at his aunt's wedding reception at a New York hotel and was instantly captivated by it. "Who wrote that?" he asked. The answer intensified his desire to become a composer for the Broadway stage. He wanted to tell stories through song—

just like Kern. Only a few years later, Gershwin would have the opportunity to work directly with his idol when he took a job as a rehearsal pianist on Jerome Kern's musical *Miss 1917*. Music historian Mark Steyn considers "They Didn't Believe Me" to be a game-changing innovation and contends that Gershwin and Rodgers were able to "write their own 4/4 conversational love songs because 'They Didn't Believe Me' had made such songs possible. A single song became the template for the Broadway ballad."[32]

The Princess Theatre Musicals

Just before this, Kern, in collaboration with bookwriters and lyricists **Guy Bolton** and **P. G. Wodehouse**, began creating a series of musicals at the intimate 299-seat Princess Theatre. Because of this theater's diminutive size, Kern and his collaborators had to design shows that could be produced on a smaller scale and employ a more intimate and informal style of performance than was typical. This lack of spectacle placed a much more intense focus on the stories and characters of these musicals, and as a result, critics of the day often compared their plots and dialogue quite favorably to those of well-made non-musical plays. This was because most of the Princess musicals were actually based on recent hit plays that provided strong frameworks for these musical versions to expand upon. This established a pattern that would become standard practice right up to today: from that point on, the overwhelming majority of all musicals have been adapted from preexisting source material—principally plays, novels, and films. In addition, because there were not enough seats at the Princess to support paying star salaries, the writers did not have to customize these musicals to suit star performers who often demanded that their well-known personalities and unique talents be showcased. Instead, the writers of the Princess shows were able to focus on creating smart, cohesive, and more coherent stories. In an interview from the period, Bolton explained what he and his collaborators were trying to accomplish:

> Our musical comedies depend as much upon plot and the development of their characters for success as upon their music, and they deal with subjects and peoples near to the audiences. We endeavor to make everything count. Every line, funny or serious, is supposed to help the plot continue to hold. Every song and lyric contributes to the action. The humor is based on situations, not interjected by comedians.[33]

The Princess Theatre musicals—*Very Good Eddie*, *Have A Heart*, *Oh, Boy!*, *Leave It To Jane*, and *Oh, Lady! Lady!*—were all popular hits in their time but are virtually never performed today, but they are still enormously important because of the significant influence they had on the next generation of musical theater creators. In addition to inspiring George Gershwin, fourteen-year-old Richard Rodgers became so captivated by *Very Good Eddie* that he saw it at least a dozen times, later stating that, "If you were at all sensitive to music, Kern had to be your idol."[34]

To a great extent, the Princess Theatre musicals initiated the transition from the Genesis Period—during which shows were dominated by producers and performers—to the Silver Age in which songwriters became the controlling force in the creation of Broadway musicals.

"A Dainty Bit of Salt and Sweetness"—Best Practices Create a Blockbuster: *Irene*! (♩)

In many ways, the first two decades of the musical can be seen as a lively conversation, and often a fierce competition, between the Irish, Jewish, and, as we will see in the next chapter, the Black inventors of the musical—each of them responding to and building upon the inventions and innovations of their colleagues. The Genesis Period climaxed in 1919 when a songwriting team of first-generation Irish Americans, **Joe McCarthy and Harry Tierney**, created the "outstanding musical comedy success of recent times"[35]—*Irene*.

According to the *Daily News*, *Irene* was "the sort of music comedy [sic] one recommends to one's friends with the proud light of discovery in one's eye,"[36] and this "delightful entertainment"[37] quickly became Broadway's biggest hit musical so far. It would go on to an unprecedented run of 675 performances, which was not only significantly longer than any other previous Genesis Period show, but eighteen years would have to go by before any subsequent musical could break that record![38] By 1921, there were four companies of *Irene* touring America, along with "four in the United Kingdom . . . and one each in India, Australia, New Zealand, Sweden, Hungary, South Africa and South America."[39]

What made *Irene* so captivating and so incredibly successful? In short, it incorporated all the best practices of the most successful musicals that had come before it. Just like the Princess Theatre shows, *Irene* was adapted from a preexisting play by James Montgomery (who also wrote the musical's book), and as one critic noted, "Harry Tierney, who wrote the music, and Joseph McCarthy, responsible for the lyrics, have co-operated with Mr. Montgomery to a remarkable extent and as a result, *Irene* can rightfully take its place among the leading productions of the kind in this or any other period of the stage."[40] The show's book was unanimously considered to be "far better than the average run of them because it has a plot that is worthwhile" and even "amid a hurricane of laughs [it] occasionally halts to give you a flash at real life and brings a grip in your throat, and now and then a hint of moisture to your eye."[41] That surprisingly affecting plot was a modern rags-to-riches Cinderella story about a plucky Irish immigrant girl who falls in love with a wealthy Long Island society boy. As historian Ethen Mordden has pointed out, "Her name is Irene O'Dare, which implies right from the start that she will dare to take a chance on life—she will dare to go out into the world and seize the day—like a female version of Cohan himself." And *Irene*'s songs were built on the templates that Kern, Berlin, Herbert, and Cohan had established and were closely tied to the events of the story. The result is a delightful and captivating score that produced several hit songs, including the blockbuster "Alice Blue Gown."

Irene's second act opened with a song titled "We're Getting Away With It," led by a character named Madam Lucy, and one of the things the show got away with was introducing what seems to be the first major Queer character ever to appear in a Broadway musical. A central aspect of the show's story is that Irene O'Dare gets a job as a model for an aspiring society fashion designer, who for professional reasons goes by the name of "Madame Lucille" and who, as one critic noted, "is, of course, a man, and Bobbie Watson who played] the part, with his ridiculously effeminate manner, carries much of the comedy."[42] It is clear from the reviews that this role was one of the show's highlights, and every actor who played it, either on Broadway or on those multiple national tours, received widespread acclaim for their portrayal. Its originator, Bobby Watson (who would go on to play leading roles in eight other Broadway musicals), was said to have been "perfect as the male modiste,"[43] which he "played . . . with ecstasy and a lisp,"[44] and while he "burlesqued entertainingly the traditional peculiarities of the class,"[45] he "never even approached the thin line that would have ruined the impression upon the audience. He was refreshingly comic."[46] That thin line seems to have been of great concern to several critics, but only Haywood Broun of the *New York Tribune* found the role itself to be "occasionally objectionable." Still, he credited Watson for "in the main" keeping "within the reasonable bounds, and at such times he was highly amusing."[47] Out on tour, "laurels for the real comedy" went to Raymond Crane, who as the "lady-like modiste,[48] takes the difficult role of acting the part of a very effeminate male,"[49] but "does not overdo his part and produces many laughs."[50] In another company, actor Jere Delaney was said to have given "a regular powder puff performance in the role of Mme. Lucy"[51] and was praised for "injecting comedy of the sidesplitting type into the plot."[52] However, in a feature article titled "Pugilistic Star Plays Role of Male Modiste," the *Boston Globe* made sure to point out that it had been only "a few years ago that Jere was aspiring to be the lightweight ring [boxing] champion of New Jersey."[53] Robert H. Burns, who also toured in the role, was said to have escaped "wholly the odium of male impersonators of women," and his "humor and his frisky dancing make his part a veritable contribution."[54] Finally, a young actor named Busby Berkley (who would go on to a legendary career as a Broadway and Hollywood choreographer) was acclaimed for being "all that could be desired in an effeminate role,"[55] and "as near perfection as possible" in playing "a comedy part in a manner that might easily be overdone." Like all the actors who played this role, Berkley was highly praised for his dancing: "It is many moons since theatergoers here have seen a man with legs and feet so thoroughly educated in the art of Terpsichore."[56] Twenty-two years would go by before Broadway audiences would see another Queer principal character in a musical.

In 1921, the *Los Angeles Times* called *Irene* "the outstanding musical comedy success of recent times . . . It has been the rage all over the world for the past two years, and there is no slackening noticeable in its drawing qualities . . . the plot is bright and clever in dialogue and rich in musical numbers, the costumes are visions of loveliness and the whole is admirably staged."[57] And *Irene* was well-crafted enough that even half of a century later, during the "Nostalgia Craze" of the 1970s, it was able to be retooled and resurrected in a hit Broadway "revisal" starring Debbie Reynolds.

Irene was McCarthy and Tierney's biggest Broadway hit, but certainly not their only one. During the teens and '20s they worked together, and in collaboration with other songwriters such as Italian immigrant James Monaco, to create a string of long-running shows and enduring hit songs.

Of course, not all of the immigrants who went into "the show business" became composers, bookwriters, or lyricists, and writers were not the only early inventors of the Broadway musical. During this period, both producers and star performers often had an equal, if not even greater, impact on the content and style of Broadway musicals.

"Hey, Mr. Producer!"—Hammerstein, Ziegfeld, and the Shuberts (♩, ♪)

In the Genesis Period, Broadway producers were entrepreneurs who wielded total control over their shows and often oversaw every aspect of them. Although, as holds true today, most producers stayed in the background and were unknown to the general public, the names of three of the most powerful and successful early producers still have significant cultural currency more than a century later—Hammerstein, Shubert, and Ziegfeld.

Oscar Hammerstein I was born to German Jewish parents in an area of Prussia that is now part of Poland, and he came to America in 1864. By the turn of the century, Oscar and his two sons, Willie and Arthur, had created a theatrical empire that included twelve New York theaters and had become significant producers of opera, vaudeville, musical comedy, and operetta. However, their most significant contribution to the musical theater is, without a doubt, Willie's son, Oscar Hammerstein II, whose historic partnership with Richard Rodgers forty years later led the musical into its Golden Age.

The Shubert Brothers—Sam, Jacob (J. J.), and Lee—were Russian Jews who emigrated to America as children in 1882. By 1900, they had leased their first New York theater, the Herald Square, and within a few years, they controlled thirty-one Broadway theaters and sixty-three more in other cities across the country. To keep their theaters filled, the Shubert Brothers produced more than 500 plays and musicals. Even today, the Shubert Organization remains the largest theater owner on Broadway.

More than eighty years after his death, **Florenz Ziegfeld** is still arguably the most famous producer in the history of Broadway. He was born in Chicago in 1867, the child of German and Belgian immigrants. Today, his illustrious name and his legendary creation—*The Ziegfeld Follies*—still epitomize Broadway at its most spectacular and glamorous. He mounted his first *Follies* in 1907 and went on to produce a new edition every year through 1927. These dazzlingly extravagant musical revues showcased the most brilliant performers, the most beautiful showgirls, and the most captivating new hit songs of the day. With his impeccable taste and incredible gift for publicity, Ziegfeld has often been called "the greatest showman the theater will ever know." All the top songwriters of the era—Victor Herbert, Jerome Kern, McCarthy and Tierney—contributed numerous songs to multiple incarnations of the *Follies*, and Irving Berlin wrote music and lyrics for nine editions, including the hit tune that became the *Follies*' virtual theme song. "A Pretty Girl is Like a Melody."

The Greatest Stars: The Performers

Perhaps even more than the producers, the most popular performers of the era were just as important to the creation and success of these musicals as were the writers. Almost all musicals in the Genesis Period were "star vehicles," designed and built to showcase the specific talents and dynamic personas of one or more of the biggest stars of the day. At the top of the pack, without a doubt, was **Al Jolson** (c. 1886–1950). He was born Asa Yoelson in a part of the Russian Empire that is now in Lithuania sometime between 1883 and 1886. At the age of six, he emigrated to New York City with his father, who was a rabbi and cantor. Jolson made his Broadway debut in a show called *La Belle Paree* in 1911 at the Winter Garden Theatre and instantly became a major sensation. The Shubert Brothers quickly signed him to a seven-year contract, and in almost every season from 1912 to 1921, they produced a new Broadway musical comedy created specifically to showcase Jolson's dynamic talents.

The greatest female star of this period was **Fanny Brice** (1891–1950). Born on New York's Lower East Side, her parents were Hungarian German Jewish immigrants. On Broadway, she starred in nineteen musicals, including ten editions of *The Ziegfeld Follies*. Brice is best remembered today as the title character in the biographical Broadway musical *Funny Girl* (1964) and its 1968 film adaptation.

Comic **Ed Wynn** (1886–1966) was born into a Jewish family in Philadelphia. His father was from Bohemia, and his Romanian Turkish mother had emigrated from Istanbul. Wynn debuted in the *Ziegfeld Follies of 1914* and went on to work for both Ziegfeld and the Shubert brothers in a series of star vehicles over several decades. His unique and distinct comic persona, which all of those shows were designed to showcase, would be perfectly captured many years later in the 1964 Disney film *Mary Poppins*, in which Wynn played the role of "Uncle Albert," who "loves to laugh."

Jolson's greatest rival was **Eddie Cantor** (1892–1964). Cantor was born in New York, the son of Russian Jewish immigrants. He made his Broadway debut in the *Ziegfeld Follies of 1917* and went on to star in fifteen Broadway musicals and revues, becoming a major motion picture and radio star as well.

This unlikely collection of immigrants and children of immigrants—Irish and German Catholics, along with Jews from all over Eastern Europe, almost all of whom started out impoverished, uneducated, and with English as their second language—were somehow able to draw on the rich musical, dance, and theatrical traditions that they had brought with them from the "old country" and combine those with new African American music and dance forms they were drawn to in America, to become the writers, composers, lyricists, producers, and performers who originated what was about to become America's signature art form: the Broadway musical.

CHAPTER 2
FORGOTTEN FOREFATHERS (AND FOREMOTHERS)—THE BLACK ARTISTS WHO INVENTED THE BROADWAY MUSICAL (B)

Black theater artists played a much larger role in the creation of the Broadway musical than has generally been reported or acknowledged. Most notably, this includes an entire decade of hit shows and songs that have been egregiously underreported and, consequently, are almost entirely forgotten today. This chapter aims to rediscover those musicals and shine a much-deserved spotlight on the amazingly multi-talented men and women who created them and whose legacy still inspires Broadway today—even if most people are entirely unaware of their contributions. The precursors of Black musical theater in America have also been underreported and go back much further in history than is generally discussed.

The African Grove Theater

From the colonial period through the early nineteenth century, Black performers and Black audiences were excluded from virtually all formal American theaters, but that doesn't mean there were no Black theater makers, performers, or productions. It simply means that shows made by and for Black audiences had to be staged in whatever makeshift spaces could be found. Unfortunately, there are very few surviving records or details about such performances. What we do know is that in 1821, a free Black man named William Alexander Brown purchased a house in a section of lower New York called "Little Africa" and, not long after, opened a theater in his garden. He then built a 300-seat theater on the second floor. He named it the **African Grove Theater** and opened it with a production of Shakespeare's *Richard III* presented for "Ladies and Gentlemen of Colour . . . by persons of Colour [sic]." As with most Shakespearean productions in that era, the text was heavily revised, a program of lighthearted songs was presented prior to the play, and a "Ballet" pantomime titled *Asama* was presented after.[1] Two years later, The African Grove presented *The Drama of King Shottaway*, the first known play written by an African American. Unfortunately, because of financial difficulties and ongoing harassment by rowdy white patrons who would attend the shows just to heckle the Black performers, the African Grove Theater closed after only a few seasons.

During that same decade, a white performer named **Thomas Dartmouth "Daddy" Rice** darkened his face with burnt cork and portrayed a character he named "Jim Crow." Dressed in tattered clothes, dancing in a herky-jerky style, and speaking and singing in an exaggerated southern Black dialect, he performed a song called "Jump Jim Crow." He claimed his routine was based on a Black street performer whose singing and dancing had intrigued and captivated him. Rice and his caricature became so popular and so famous that "Jim Crow" became a widely used insult for Black men and eventually became the ubiquitous nickname for the oppressive and unjust laws that enforced strict and inequitable racial segregation for nearly 100 years following the abolition of slavery. Inspired by Rice's success, other individuals and eventually entire companies of white men in blackface began performing what came to be called "minstrel shows."

A Shameful Legacy: The Minstrel Show

As uncomfortable and repugnant as it most certainly is, it is impossible to relate the history of the Broadway musical (or indeed the history of any aspect of American popular entertainment) without at least some focus on the ***minstrel show***. Of all the many precursors of the Broadway musical, this is arguably the most influential. In the beginning, all of the performers in these shows were white men, and a typical minstrel show performance featured highly accomplished solo and group singing, expert dancing, accomplished musicianship, skillfully performed comedy routines, and (at least in part) extremely derogatory and demeaning characterizations of both rural and urban African Americans, including racist stereotypes of Black culture that included patronizing, sentimental, idealized images of carefree, dimwitted enslaved people who seemed to want nothing more than to happily sing and dance. By the 1850s, minstrel shows had become major attractions in cities and towns across America. In New York alone, there were ten theaters devoted to minstrel shows.

Why were these shows so popular? In writer and critic Margo Jefferson's assessment, "Some of this came out of a genuine fascination with the music, the songs, the dances, the performance styles of Black people," and scholar Eric Lott suggests that blackface performance represented "a strange mix of envy, fascination, desire, and fear."[2] It's important to keep in mind that the majority of white theatergoers in the North had experienced very little contact with actual African Americans. Even as late as 1860, when NYC had a population of more than 800,000—less than 2 percent of them were Black.[3] As a result, white Northerners were largely ignorant of the actual harsh realities of slavery, and they often, therefore, assumed that minstrel shows represented accurate portrayals of enslaved people. Or perhaps they just wanted to believe that. Perhaps the minstrel show's nostalgic, sugar-coated depiction of "life on the old Plantation" helped them to turn a blind eye to the pleas of the Abolitionists and allowed them to ignore the inequitable treatment of free Blacks in their own communities.

Surprisingly, the free Black people who did live in the North also began attending minstrel shows in significant numbers, and theater owners who had not previously allowed Blacks into their venues now swept aside the policies that had excluded them. It is not clear why free Blacks showed up in such relatively large numbers to see these shows—shows that made fun of the way Black people walked, talked, sang, and danced. Some historians surmise that they went to laugh at the ludicrous, over-the-top caricatures these crazy white people had dreamed up, while others believe that Black audience members were genuinely attracted to the authentic elements of Black music and culture that had survived the ridicule and gross exaggeration.

However, it is much easier to understand why, after the end of the Civil War, Black performers themselves started appearing in minstrel shows. In that period, minstrel shows were virtually the only form of show business that existed and, therefore, the only opportunity for anyone—Black or white—to earn a living as a performer or musician. Soon, all-Black minstrel troupes performing in blackface began touring the U.S., Canada, England, and even Australia. In 1890, the U.S. Census reported that almost all of America's 1,490 Black actors were employed in touring minstrel shows, and many of the greatest early Black star performers got their start in these all-Black minstrel troupes. Why would Black artists demean themselves by performing in blackface? "Look, this is the 19th Century," Margo Jefferson tells us. "They had limited options. They were expected to."[4] Broadway and film star Ben Vereen, who has portrayed both fictional and historical nineteenth-century performers, surmised that it happened like this:

> African Americans are sitting out there looking at white (Minstrel) entertainers and they go, "Wait a minute, we can do us better than they're doing us. Why don't we go into show business?" . . . But the white audiences in this country told them, "If you want to be on our stage, in this country, you better black up." And that's where the Black minstrel show came from. And from out of that—from behind the mask, genius was born.[5]

Promoters advertised these Black minstrel companies as being "real and original" and more "authentic"—and perhaps they were. It may be true that larger portions of the music, dance, and comedy that was presented by Black minstrel troupes was more genuinely representative of actual African American culture—even as the performers still had to perpetuate racist stereotypes. This dichotomy is part of what makes this subject so complicated and confusing.

"Ring, Ring, Da Banjo"—The Music of Minstrelsy

Both white and Black minstrel shows included authentic elements of Black culture. Minstrel show bands featured banjos, tambourines, and bones (wooden spoons), all of which were derived from African musical instruments brought to the U.S. by enslaved people. In addition, many of the songs and instrumental pieces performed in these shows were adaptations of actual African American folk music. A surprising number of minstrel show songs created by both white and Black songwriters are still heard and performed today. These include "Oh! Susanna," "Camptown Races," "Old Folks At Home" (aka Swanee River), and many others with words and music by **Stephen Foster,** who is considered to be the first American to make a career as a professional songwriter.[6] America's first prominent Black songwriter was **James Bland,** who wrote music and lyrics for more than 700 songs, including "In The Evening By The Moonlight," "Oh, Dem

Golden Slippers," and "Carry Me Back to Old Virginny," which in 1940 became the official state song of Virginia. Minstrel show songs by Bland, Foster, and others were the first American popular songs, and they have had a profound influence on both American pop music and the Broadway showtune.

Broadway Dance #1: A Brief History of The Cakewalk

Dance was also a central element of minstrel shows, and here, too, they often drew on authentic African American folk dance forms—most notably, **the cakewalk**. This dance originated in the antebellum period when enslaved Blacks "began making fun of the stiff, pretentious, highfalutin ballroom dancing of their white owners. They caricatured and mocked their oppressors by employing ostentatious bows, exaggerated curtsies, and showy, high-stepping struts. And in this way, the cakewalk became a covert but powerful expression of both Black joy and Black resistance in the face of white supremacy."[7] Ironically, the white owners, who were oblivious to being mocked, loved the dance and took it up themselves, copying and imitating the dancing of their slaves. Soon, cakewalk dance competitions became a part of both white and Black plantation life, with the winner receiving a cake as a prize. This is the origin of the expression "take the cake." Eventually, the dance migrated from the plantations to towns and cities in the North where it was danced at parties and balls and became one of the first social dance crazes to spread around the world. Most importantly for this discussion, a theatricalized version of the dance became an exuberant, kinetic high point of every minstrel show performance when the entire company—Black or white—would join in the "grand cakewalk" or "walkaround." The layers of irony here are mind-blowing! Think of it: Black performers in blackface were imitating white performers in blackface who were mocking Black people by performing a dance created by Black people to make fun of white people. And the crowd went wild!

Eventually, the cakewalk evolved into the ballroom dance crazes of the Ragtime Era, including the one step, two-step, bunny hug, grizzly bear, and foxtrot—and served as the foundation of Jazz Age and Swing Era dances such as the Charleston, Black Bottom, Big Apple, Lindy hop, and jitterbug. The cakewalk's signature steps and style are still very much alive in the vocabulary of Broadway dance. In fact, echoes of it can be seen in the choreography of such twenty-first-century musicals as *Hadestown*, *Chicago*, *Disney's Aladdin*, *The Book of Mormon*, and *Hamilton*.

Legacies of the Minstrel Show

The standard minstrel show format included three sections. The first part, called the *minstrel line*, was the blackface section of the show and is often misremembered today as being the entire minstrel show. The second part was called the Olio (which means mixture) and consisted of a variety program of songs, dances, and specialty acts, often not performed in blackface. The final section was a half-hour musical comedy sketch—often a burlesque of a current hit play—and also not always incorporating blackface. (These would be similar to the parodies of films or television shows we might see today on *Saturday Night Live*.) Following the Civil War, the three sections of the minstrel show began to go their separate ways: the Olio expanded into variety and eventually vaudeville, and the sketch evolved into burlesque and eventually musical comedy. And appallingly, the first section, including its degrading, racist stereotypes, would linger on as an insidious part of American entertainment and culture for more than half a century, if not longer.

In addition to this shameful racist legacy, minstrel shows contributed many other enduring elements to pop culture:

- The concept and format of an MC or "Master of Ceremonies" began with the minstrel show's "Interlocutor" who would host the evening by introducing each of the acts and supplying jokes and wry comments in between—as can still be seen on awards shows, comedy roasts, and in the classic "Tonight Show," late-night talk show format.
- The minstrel show's practice of rewriting the lyrics of popular songs for comic effect—especially to comment on current topical events and personalities—was transferred to early burlesque and has continued unabated into contemporary times through the song parodies of Alan Sherman, Weird Al Yankovic, Randy Rainbow, and Gerard Alessandrini's long-running off-Broadway revue *Forbidden Broadway*.
- Because of their all-male casts, minstrel shows prominently featured drag performances, and quite a few of the male performers became renowned for their portrayals of female characters. This performance style would cross over into all areas of American entertainment.
- Another important legacy is the comedy duo—a comedy act in which two comedians feed each other "setups," trade punchlines, and generally serve as foils for each other's comic material. Both including and divested of its negative racial overtones, this dynamic has remained a mainstay of American show business ever since.

Most importantly, minstrel shows opened the door for Black performers and songwriters, who were then able to establish themselves as professional performers on the American stage. As we will see, this positioned them to be ready to move into other emerging forms of early American show business and to play a major role in the invention of the Broadway musical.

Black Variety and Burlesque

Burlesque (again in the original sense of the word) was in many respects similar in form to the minstrel show. But instead of making fun of African Americans, burlesque shows made fun of the social habits and pretensions of middle-class and upper-class white people, and both forms featured parodies of "high" art and culture. The growing popularity of burlesque eventually led to **Sam T. Jack's Creole Burlesque Company**, billed as "the only show of its kind on earth." This production was designed for white audiences but was performed by an all-Black cast of both men and women—and none of them in blackface. From 1890 to 1897, an edition of Jack's show might feature "20 very funny male comedians," "soulful songstresses," a cake-walk dance team, a "male impersonator," and a line of sixteen "lively, lovely ladies," with every performance concluding with "a one-act burlesque," one of which was titled "The Beauty of the Nile, or, Doomed by Fire."[8] Then, in 1896, a show called *The Black Patti Troubadours*, billed as "The Greatest Colored Show On Earth," made its debut. This troupe of more than fifty African American singers, dancers, comedians, jugglers, acrobats, and other entertainers was the brainchild of the internationally renowned Black soprano **Matilda Sissoretta Joyner Jones**. Born in 1869 in Virginia, she was an immensely talented classically trained opera singer who was invited twice to sing at the White House for presidents Benjamin Harrison and Grover Cleveland. When she performed at Madison Square Garden in 1892, she was favorably compared to the most famous opera singer of the day, Adelina Patti, and hailed as "the Black Patti." Even though it seems that Jones was not fond of this nickname, she recognized its publicity value and formed her own show. *The Black Patti Troubadours* show was described as half "musical farce" and half "operatic kaleidoscope," and from 1895 to 1916, her troupe toured extensively throughout the U.S. and Europe. In the process, it became a crucial training ground for hundreds of black theater artists, including a multi-talented young man named Bob Cole.

Bob Cole was born in 1888 in Athens, Georgia, where his parents had been enslaved. Cole became a star performer in *Sam T. Jack's Creole Show* and also began writing music and comedy material for the show. After publishing his first songs in 1884, he formed the Worth's Museum All-Star Stock Company in New York—the first Black repertory theater. There, he became adept in all aspects of theater-making—he directed, choreographed, and wrote the songs and comic and dramatic sketches that made the company immensely popular. Its two dozen performers would go on to become the stars of nearly every Black show of the following decade. Cole then joined the Black Patti show, and it was there that he began creating what were, in essence, one-act mini-musicals—one of which he would expand into the first all-Black musical comedy to be performed on Broadway.

Meanwhile, another multi-talented Black artist was forging a parallel path. **Will Marion Cook** was born in 1869 in Washington, D.C., to middle-class parents—his father was the first Dean of Howard University. Will began studying classical music as a teenager and became so accomplished that he was sent to Germany to study composition and violin with a disciple of Johannes Brahms. He returned to the U.S. in the 1890s but found it was nearly impossible for a Black man to find work as a violinist or composer in the white world of classical music. Instead, he turned his focus to composing ragtime music, possibly inspired by the success of another classically trained Black composer, Scott Joplin.

Both Will Cook and Bob Cole began to dream of presenting an all-Black musical show on Broadway. However, they had radically different ideas about what kind of show that should be. Cole believed that Black artists should directly compete with white authors and strive to achieve the same high artistic standards and goals as they did. Cook, however, felt that Black artists should create work that reflected the soul of Black people and not try to mimic the works of white artists. Anytime the two songwriters were in the same room, they would violently argue and disagree, and their mutual friends tried to keep them away from each other as much as possible. However, in 1896, within months of each other, they debuted the first two Black Broadway musicals.

The First Black Broadway Musicals

Bob Cole's show was called **A Trip to Coontown**, and it has the distinction of being the first full-length musical show written, directed, performed, and produced by Black artists to open on Broadway—and this was twenty-five years prior to *Shuffle Along*, which is often credited with that distinction. The show's unfortunate title was clearly intended to echo the 1891 hit show *A Trip to Chinatown*. Like that show, it offered audiences a visit to one of New York's ethnic neighborhoods and included a loosely structured story about a con artist named Jim Flimflammer who attempts to swindle an old man out of his $5,000 pension until the hero, Willie Wayside (played by Bob Cole), foils his plans and eventually saves the day. The story, however, was frequently interrupted by specialty acts and musical performers, including a contortionist, singer Juvia Roan ("the Cuban Nightingale"), the Freeman Sisters, and Lloyd G. Gibbs, who was billed as "The Greatest Living Black Tenor." Overall, the show was very similar to the Sam T. Jack and Black Patti variety shows, except for including its very thin storyline to tie it all together.

Four months later, Will Marion Cook's show, **Clorindy, or The Origin of the Cakewalk**—billed as a "negro operetta"—opened at the roof-top Casino Theatre featuring a cast of twenty-six, including leading Black comedian Ernest Hogan. Although the show originally had a storyline, it seems the book was eliminated during rehearsals because the uncovered roof garden setting made it impossible to hear extended sections of dialogue.[9] So the actual performance consisted of only the songs—with music by Will Marion Cook and lyrics by poet, novelist, and playwright **Paul Laurence Dunbar**. Dunbar was born in 1872 in Dayton, Ohio, but his parents had been enslaved in Kentucky before the Civil War. He wrote his first poem at the age of six and gave his first public recital at nine. He was the only Black student at Dayton's Central High, where Orville Wright, of the Wright Brothers, was a classmate and friend. Dunbar was elected president of the school's literary society, served as editor of the school newspaper, and was a member of its debate club.

Years later, Cook recalled the thrilling first night of *Clorindy*: "I was so delirious that I drank a glass of water thinking it was wine and got glorious drunk. Negroes were at last on Broadway and here to stay . . . We were artists and we were going a long way." Will Cook went on to compose the scores of several other Broadway musicals, including *In Dahomey*, and he was equally successful as a concert artist. In 1912, he led a 150-voice chorus in a concert at Carnegie Hall in a performance of his choral piece *Swing Along!*, which was written for *In Dahomey*. Cook toured Europe with his all-Black Southern Syncopated Orchestra, with his wife Abbie Mitchel as the lead singer, and also served as a teacher and mentor to many young Black musicians, most significantly, the great jazz composer "Duke" Ellington.

"There's a Boat That's Leavin' Soon for New York" — Black Migration Transforms the Musical

Although what historians call the "Great Migration" didn't officially begin until 1910,[10] a significant stream of Black Southerners poured into NYC from as early as 1890. They came in search of greater social and economic opportunity and were met with similar, and often worse, discrimination to what Irish, Jewish, Italian, and other immigrants faced. But just like those other groups, they discovered that show business offered them opportunities for advancement not available to them in most other professions.

Many talented African Americans found work even in mainstream (white) vaudeville, and major acts like Williams and Walker, Ma Rainey, and Bessie Smith became headliners. In fact, vaudeville bills often featured white, Black, Asian, Latin American, and Jewish performers all in the same show. It was surprisingly multicultural. Offstage, however, racism was still rampant. Performers of color were not allowed to stay in the same hotels or boarding houses as the white performers, and many vaudeville theaters refused to admit Black audience members or segregated them in the balcony. To serve that African American audience, a nationwide network of all-Black vaudeville theaters emerged, which Black performers nicknamed "the Chitlin' Circuit." Among the biggest stars of both Black and white vaudeville was the team of **Williams and Walker.**

Williams & Walker on Broadway

George Walker was born in Kansas in 1873 and began his career in a Black minstrel troupe. **Bert Williams** was born in the Bahamas around 1874 and migrated to California, where, as a teenager, he also began working in various minstrel shows. The two men met in San Francisco in 1893 and decided to team up. They formed an act in which Walker played the role of a fast-talking con man, and Williams the dimwitted oaf who becomes the victim of Walker's schemes.

Much like Harrigan and Hart and Weber and Fields, Williams and Walker's productions started out as little more than variety acts, but eventually they incorporated characters, situations, and plot threads combined with songs that at least in some ways related to those story elements. In 1903, Williams and Walker joined with other talented Black artists to produce *In Dahomey*, a show that was a step toward the duo's ambitious dream to explore their African heritage onstage.[11] It told the story of a group of African Americans who, after finding a pot of gold, move to Africa and become the rulers of Dahomey. (During the eighteenth and nineteenth centuries, Dahomey was an actual

African kingdom located where the country of Benin is today.) The show's score was very eclectic, with music by **Will Marion Cook** that ran the gamut from Viennese-style waltzes to syncopated ragtime tunes, and lyrics by **Paul Laurence Dunbar** that in some songs employed very proper, high-toned English, and in others used contemporary Black dialect and slang, as in the show's captivating choral number, "Swing Along," with its encouragement of Black pride:

> Come along, Mandy, come along Sue,
> White folks watchin' and seein' what you do
> White folks jelous when you'se walkin' two by two,
> So swing along Chillun, swing along!
> Well-a, swing along, yes-swing along,
> An-a lif'-a yo' heads up high
> Wif pride and gladness beamin' from yo' eye . . .

But *In Dahomey's* New York premiere was not without controversy. The *New York Times* reported that:

> A thundercloud has been gathering of late in the faces of the established Broadway managers. Since it was announced that Williams and Walker, with their all-Negro musical comedy, *In Dahomey*, were booked to appear at the New York Theatre, there have been times when trouble breeders foreboded a race war.[12]

Apparently the "trouble breeders" were mistaken since "all went merrily"[13] on the show's opening night, and this "three hours of solid amusement"[14] became a significant hit that critics declared was "filled with bright sayings and amusing situations and the audience, which filled every seat in the house, was kept in a continuous roar of laughter."[15] And on its subsequent tour of England, the entire production was summoned to give a command performance at Buckingham Palace for the Prince of Wales. Financially, the show was also a tremendous success, with its backers receiving a 400 percent return on their investment. This made it abundantly clear that an all-Black show could compete on Broadway.

Three years later, Williams and Walker "sang and danced themselves into to exhaustion"[16] in ***Abyssinia***, another hit show set in Africa that related "the adventures of colored tourists from Kansas who reach then present-day Abyssinia [Ethiopia] en route to Jerusalem [sic],"[17] and featured the country's actual ruler King Menelik II as a character. This "handsomely costumed show"[18] featured a score by the team of Will Marion Cook, Bert Williams, **Jesse A. Shipp** and **Alex Rogers** that was acclaimed as "the best ever attempted by any colored company."[19] It was reported that the production was "beautifully staged" with "the whole company trained to perfection"[20] by Jesse Shipp who, with this show, became the first credited Black director of a Broadway musical.

In contrast, Williams and Walker's 1908 show was set in the U.S. and called ***Bandana Land***. The *New York Mail* called it "An emphatic hit" And declared that "half the shows on Broadway are deadly compared to this latest offering of Williams and Walker."[21] And the *Brooklyn Daily Eagle* described it as:

> a play dealing with the humors [sic] of the Southern negroes of the present day as they are seen by humorists of their own race. For the most part, white managers have kept their hands off this time and allowed the authors J.A. Shipp, Alex Rodgers, the composer of the music, Will Marion Cook, and the three chief actors to work out and build up a play which should be to the life of their race what "The Old Homestead"[22] is to the life of New England . . . it is genuine and honest and—what matters most is that it is so funny that you laugh yourself tired over it . . . The piece is naturally full of songs and dances, and those are the things which arouse the white spectators to something like a fury of applause. The touches which portray the life and character of the ordinary negro arouse quick and hilarious laughter among the colored auditors, pretty good evidence that the authors have told the truth.[23]

The highlights of the show reportedly included Aida Overton and George Walker performing "The Merry Widow Waltz"; Abbie Mitchell Cook, who with "her phenomenal soprano voice" sang the song "Red, Red Rose," by Alex Rodgers "well enough for any opera house";[24] and Bert Williams singing "his new song 'I'd Rather Have Nothin' All of the Time Than Something for a Little While.'"[25]

As the *New York Age* reported in March of 1908, during the run of *Bandana Land*, Williams and Walker "aroused a race controversy among the New York theatrical folk" when George M. Cohan and Sam Harris invited them to perform with Weber and Fields and other top stars in a special Sunday night performance to raise money for the Newsboys' Home Club. Williams and Walker agreed to appear, and "in billing the benefit in the newspapers they were put ahead of every [white] star act on the bill." However, when some of the other "less important and insignificant performers" booked for the show saw the billing, they attempted to rally the other white performers to boycott the event. The newsboys themselves "were indignant," and at a meeting they "resolved to send letters to every leading show house in the country" informing them of the racist attitudes of those performers.[26] In the end, only two acts withdrew and "were not in any manner missed," and the show turned out to be "the greatest success ever given for the benefit of the 'newsies' and over $5000[27] was raised for the fund."[28]

Unfortunately, *Bandana Land* was the final Williams and Walker production because a year later, during the show's post-Broadway tour, Walker became seriously ill and had to drop out. He died in 1911, most likely of syphilis.

Bob Cole and the Johnson Brothers

As important as Williams and Walker were, they were not the only Black pioneers of the musical during this time. Another important songwriting team was **James Weldon**

Johnson and J. Rosamond Johnson. These college-educated brothers from Jacksonville, Florida, came to New York in 1899 with a dream of presenting their original operetta, *Talosa*, on Broadway. They had presented their musical tale of life on a South Sea island before Jacksonville's leading white patrons the previous year and been encouraged to take it to Broadway. James later acknowledged that going to New York was an "absurd and improbable venture" made possible only by their "invincible faith in themselves." That faith certainly paid off because shortly after arriving in NYC, they were taken under the wing of Oscar Hammerstein I, who was very impressed with their songs, and his subsequent recommendations opened many doors for the songwriting team. Soon, they were interacting with the leaders of both white and Black theater in New York, especially Bob Cole, with whom they became partners. The Johnsons' raw, youthful talent and Cole's copious experience proved to be a vibrant combination. Cole and the Johnson Brothers wanted to do away with minstrel show stereotypes. Cole even wrote a manifesto that he called the "Colored Actors Declaration of Independence," which read in part:

> We are going to have our own shows. We are going to write them ourselves. We are going to have our own stage manager and our own orchestra leader and our own manager out front to count up. And no divided houses—our race must be seated from the front row back.[29]

Their first collaboration, *The Shoo-Fly Regiment*, demonstrated what they had in mind. It told the story of a graduate of a Black college, much like the Tuskegee Institute, which was founded in Alabama in 1881. Against his girlfriend's wishes, he gives up his dream of becoming a teacher to enlist in the army to fight in the Spanish–American War. Eventually, after a successful combat mission and other plot complications, he returns and marries his sweetheart. The characters in the story were smart, educated, brave, and patriotic, and significantly, the central love story was treated seriously. Before this, it was assumed that white audiences would not accept a sincere depiction of Black romance. *The Shoo-Fly Regiment* had a total run of almost two years, including a long tour and several months on Broadway, where it received mostly favorable reviews. However, at least one critic was of the opinion that Blacks should "continue to write shows of a minstrel nature and leave modern musicals to white authors."

Needless to say, Cole and the Johnsons ignored that critic's advice. Their next hit was ***The Red Moon*** (1909), written in collaboration with Black composer **Joe Jordan**. The show's leading character was a young college-educated woman (originally played by Abbe Mitchel) who is the daughter of a Black woman and an Indigenous man, and the story revolved around the conflict and eventual reconciliation between these two cultures, as represented by her family. In his book, *Black Musical Theatre*, author Allen Woll describes *The Red Moon* as follows:

> The folklore of two of America's minorities—Blacks and Native Americans—was the basis of this musical comedy. Bob Cole claimed that they had decided to do the

show while traveling through the western United States with their Vaudeville act. Cole and Johnson performed on an Apache reservation, and they discussed Indian music and folklore with their hosts. Rosamond eventually integrated Indian-style melodies into his score for *The Red Moon*.[30]

The press hailed the show as "brilliant," "ambitious," and "well worth seeing," and following its success in New York, it toured America for almost a year. Tragically, this was this team's last musical because, in 1911, following a period of illness and depression, Bob Cole committed suicide. Over the course of their brief career, Cole and the Johnson Brothers wrote more than 200 songs, the most famous of which was their 1902 hit "Under the Bamboo Tree," which was interpolated by Broadway star Marie Cahill into her musical *Sally In Our Alley*, and went on to sell more than 400,000 copies of sheet music. This song was so emblematic of its turn-of-the-century period that it was revived and memorably performed by Judy Garland and Margaret O'Brien in the classic 1944 MGM film musical *Meet Me in St. Louis*.

Women of Color, Women of Note (B, J)

In addition to these talented men, several Black women also became significant Broadway stars during the Genesis Period. Most prominent were Abbie Mitchel and Aida Overton Walker. **Abrea "Abbie" Mitchell** was born on the Lower East Side of New York and was the daughter of a German Jewish father and a Black mother. She began studying voice as a child and by all accounts had a glorious, pure soprano voice. Her first major role was in *Clorindy, The Origin of the Cakewalk* in 1898, and later that year she married the show's composer, Will Marion Cook. Abbie went on to enjoy a very long career that included leading roles in *In Dahomey* and *The Red Moon*, while, thirty years later, she originated the role of Clara in the premiere of *Porgy and Bess*, in which she introduced the song "Summertime."

Aida Overton Walker was an acclaimed dancer, singer, and actor—who was often billed as "The Queen of The Cakewalk." She was born in Virginia in 1880 but grew up in NYC, where, during her childhood, she received an unusual amount of education and musical training. While still a teenager, she joined *Black Patti's Troubadours*, where she met her soon-to-be-husband George Walker. Aida became a centerpiece of Williams and Walker's vaudeville act and then "the leading star lady" of their musicals *In Dahomey*, *Abyssinia*, and *Bandana Land*, in which critics hailed her as "one of the best dancers we have ever seen," "the life of the whole company," and "a born actress who could shine in serious parts, and even in Shakespearean drama." When George Walker became seriously ill and had to drop out of the tour of *Bandana Land*, Aida literally stepped into her husband's shoes and played his (male) role throughout the rest of the show's run, and to great acclaim. In addition to her performing talents, Aida was also a gifted choreographer (see Chapter 4, page 66). Tragically, she died of kidney failure in 1914 when she was only thirty-four.

During this period, talented Black artists also began to be employed in predominantly white productions, including one of the most famous entertainment brands of all time: *The Ziegfeld Follies*. To be clear, overall, the *Follies* were extremely white. There were no Black "Ziegfeld Girls" (although there were likely women of color who "passed" as white), and African American theatergoers were not allowed to sit in the audience of these shows. Ziegfeld, however, was always on the lookout for outstanding talent and often employed Black musical arrangers, orchestrators, and choreographers, and at least ten editions of the *Follies* featured songs by Black songwriters, including Joe Jordan, Will Vodery, Alex Rodgers, J. Turner Layton, and Henry Creamer.[31] Most famously, Ziegfeld created a central role in the *Follies* for one legendary Black star.

"Mr. Cellophane" — Bert Williams

The year after George Walker died, Ziegfeld engaged Bert Williams to co-star in the 1910 edition of his *Follies*. Legend has it that several of the show's white stars and other performers objected to sharing a stage with a Black man and threatened to quit unless Williams was fired. Reportedly, Ziegfeld's response was, "Go if you want to. I can replace every one of you except Bert Williams." Ziegfeld's bold stand paid off—no one quit, and Williams' performance became a highlight of the show, with *Theatre Magazine* declaring, "Bert Williams is a vastly funnier man than any white comedian now on the American stage."

Sixty-five years later, songwriters Kander and Ebb and director/choreographer Bob Fosse paid homage to Bert Williams in their musical *Chicago* with the song "Mr. Cellophane." They modeled the music, lyrics, and staging of that musical number on Williams' legendary performance of his signature song, "Nobody":

> When life seems full of clouds an' rain
> And I am filled with naught but pain
> Who soothes my thumpin', bumpin' brain?
> . . . Nobody

Originally written for *Abyssinia* (with music by Williams and lyrics by Alex Rodgers), "Nobody" personifies a wistful, sad sack, "Jonah man" character who just can't get a break from life.[32]

Williams would go on to star in nearly every annual edition of the *Ziegfeld Follies* from 1910 through 1919. Although he became one of the most famous and acclaimed performers of the era and played to packed houses on Broadway and in theaters across the nation, he still faced soul-crushing racial prejudice and discrimination almost every day, and everywhere he traveled. In most cities, he was not allowed to ride in elevators with white passengers, or stay at the same hotels or eat in the same restaurants as his white co-stars. He told his friend Eddie Cantor, "It wouldn't be so bad, Eddie, if I didn't hear the applause still ringing in my ears."[33] His *Follies* co-star, comic W. C. Fields, called

Williams "the funniest man I ever saw and the saddest man I ever knew." When Williams died in 1922, more than 5,000 people filed by his casket. Pioneering Black educator and leader Booker T. Washington noted that "Bert Williams has done more for the race than I have. He smiled his way into people's hearts. I have been obliged to fight my way."[34]

The End of an Era

Unfortunately, the untimely deaths of George Walker, Aida Overton Walker, and Bob Cole, combined with a sharp increase in racial discrimination during the years just before World War I, would lead to a nearly ten-year period in which musicals created by Black artists, and to a great extent Black performers, would be entirely absent from Broadway.

Broadway Dance #2: Tap Dance—An African American / Irish American Co-Creation (🎵, 🎵)

In the popular imagination, **tap dancing** has come to be nearly synonymous with the Broadway musical itself. A solo dancer, male or female, rhythmically strutting across the stage dressed in top hat and tails or an entire chorus exuberantly pounding out infectiously syncopated beats is, for many, the very essence of Broadway. But where did this uniquely American and remarkably enduring form of dance come from? This section will explore the complex, fascinating, and difficult-to-pin-down history of this African American and Irish American co-creation.

Between 1619 and 1866, an estimated 388,000 enslaved Africans were kidnapped and brought to the United States. They came from a wide variety of regions and cultures and carried with them many diverse music and dance traditions, and during the centuries of slavery, these traditions blended and intermingled. And, like all people throughout history, no matter how oppressed or persecuted, these enslaved people sang and danced—as part of religious rituals, as expressions of joy and sorrow, to reinforce a sense of community, or simply for enjoyment or entertainment. Meanwhile, white Southerners were exposed to this singing and dancing on a regular basis. Generations of white children often spent more time with the enslaved people who nursed and cared for them than they did with their own parents, and the children of both the whites and enslaved Blacks played together and grew up in close contact. In this way, music and dance were exchanged back and forth between them continuously over hundreds of years.

The music of enslaved Africans centered on various kinds of drums and rhythmic beats. However, after an unsuccessful (but for the white owners very alarming) slave rebellion in 1739, during which it was believed that enslaved Blacks had used drums to send messages to each other to coordinate the uprising, laws were passed forbidding "the beating of drums, blowing of horns or the like which might . . . be used to arouse slaves to insurrectionary activity."³⁵ So, as a way around this problem, enslaved Blacks transferred the drum rhythms to their feet and hands, rattled tambourines, clacked bones together like castanets, and transformed the bonja (an African string instrument made out of a gourd) into the banjo—a musical instrument found nowhere else in the world.³⁶ As the legendary Broadway choreographer, writer, and dance historian, Agnes De Mille relates the story, "By 1840, they had developed a highly complicated and brilliant form of dancing, brand-new and all their own."³⁷

Meanwhile, the Irish Famine was forcing millions of immigrants to flee to America. Among them were thousands of the members of an outcast itinerant group known as the Irish Travelers. Prior to the American Civil War, they traveled throughout the Southern states, performing their jigs, reels, and clog dances wherever they went. The footwork of the Irish Travelers intrigued the enslaved Blacks, who quickly picked it up, eventually transforming the Irish downbeat into a syncopated off-rhythm. But instead of adopting the stiff upper body and rigid arms that the Irish were locked into, the Black dancers moved their arms and entire upper body freely and in exuberant ways. In DeMille's view, "The Blacks threw away all the restraints until the decorous hornpipe and the Irish clog became the exuberant American buck-and-wing, tap and jazz."³⁸

That's one version of the story. Another thread centers on immensely popular dance competitions that were held in and around New York's "Five Points" district in the 1840s, involving the champion Black dancer **William Henry Lane,** also known as "Master Juba," and his Irish American rival, **John Diamond**.

The Five Points was New York's poorest, most dangerous, and most infamous neighborhood, where thousands of the most impoverished Irish, Jewish, German, Chinese, and Black Americans lived, all packed together in tenement buildings. Martin Scorsese's 2002 film *Gangs Of New York* is set in the Five Points district, and the reality of life there was probably even gritter than depicted in that film. When writer Charles Dickens visited the area, including one of its dance halls, in 1841, he was appalled by the poverty he found there but was thrilled by the dancing of sixteen-year-old William Henry Luce, "the greatest dancer known," which he described in detail:

> Single shuffle, double shuffle, cut and cross-cut, snapping fingers, rolling his eyes, turning in his knees, presenting the backs of his legs in front, spinning about on his toes and heels . . . dancing with two left legs, two right legs, two wooden legs, two wire legs, two spring legs—all sorts of legs and no legs—what's it to him? And in the walk of life, or dance of life, does man ever get such stimulating applause as thunders about him when . . . he finishes by leaping on the bar counter and calling for something to drink.³⁹

In the same way that boxing promoters would later pit Black prizefighters against champion white boxers with the intent of stirring up interest in the fight, beginning in 1844 theatrical agents organized dance contests between William Henry Luce, known as "Master Juba," and twenty-one-year-old Jim Diamond, who was billed as Juba's "greatest white contemporary," and whom the press hailed as "one of, if not the, greatest jig dancers the world has ever known."[40] The contestants were each paid $500,[41] an enormous sum equivalent to more than $20,000 today. This can only mean that these competitions drew large and lucrative crowds. Although the "winners" of these contests have been lost to history, as historian Tyler Anbinder tells us in his book *Five Points*:

> We do know that such contests, as well as the friendly rivalries between native-born whites, Irish immigrants, and African Americans within the Five Points' dance halls, had a profound influence on the direction of American dance. Each group incorporated favorite steps from their competitors' dance idioms into their own. In Juba's case, he adopted some of the high-stepping, foot-stomping style of the jig into his own footwork. It was from this interaction between African Americans dancing the shuffle and the Irish dancing the jig that "tap dancing" developed.[42]

Juba and Diamond competed in a series of these competitions in New York and across the U.S., during which they continued to influence each other's dancing. Diamond later became a star performer in minstrel shows, and Juba became one of the first Black performers to "guest star" with white minstrel troupes. Juba's fame even took him to London, where he performed before royalty and where he died in 1852 at the age of twenty-seven. Dance historian Marion Hannah Winter called Juba "the most influential single performer of nineteenth-century American dance."[43] Nearly 175 years after his death, Juba's influence has not been forgotten. In his 1995 Tony Award-winning dance musical *Bring In Da Noise, Bring In Da Funk*, dancer/choreographer Savion Glover included a segment in homage to Master Juba.

Which of these versions of the origin of tap dancing is true? Probably both, along with many other similar cultural exchanges and intersections that were never recorded.

CHAPTER 3
"OUT ON THAT GAY WHITE WAY"— THE QUEER ARTISTS WHO INVENTED BROADWAY (I, J, Q)

To a considerable degree, the Broadway musical is a Queer creation. From the very beginning and continuing throughout its history, American musical theater has included LGBTQ people throughout its ranks, including the most important and powerful positions and at the highest levels of leadership. And to a remarkable extent, these Queer creators have always been out, accepted, and acknowledged—at least within the world of Broadway.

Several key factors have contributed to this high level of Queer representation within the art form. As discussed in Chapter 1, until quite recently show business as a profession has always existed on the outermost fringes of social respectability. So, it makes sense that an industry already made up of outcasts would naturally be more accepting of other kinds of diversity and unconventional lifestyles. Author Patrick McGilligan points to a long tradition of "show business as an open door for all types of humanity."[1] And there is evidence that theater, dance, music, and the arts in general have been a haven for Queer people throughout history and around the world.

While one can certainly make a case that the so-called "legitimate" (non-musical) Broadway theater world has experienced a similar level of Queer dominance and influence—and, of course, many of the same creative artists, performers, and producers have worked in both spheres—for the purposes of this book, I will keep the focus on the musical.

I have compiled a list of the 350 most significant leaders and creators of the Broadway musical, and well over 100 of them can be identified as Queer—a designation that may be especially appropriate for those artists who worked during the first half of the twentieth century, because many of them were, to at least some degree, sexually fluid and involved in both same-sex and traditional heterosexual relationships and marriages, either by necessity or inclination.

It is often quite difficult for historians and researchers to determine the sexuality of individuals who lived fifty to one hundred years ago and left behind very little documentation as to their sexual preferences or identities. And it would be fair to ask if it is any of our business. From a cultural and historical perspective, however, I believe that it is absolutely worth discovering and occasionally even speculating about the sexuality of theater practitioners from the past because it can help to reveal the actual and immense contribution that Queer artists have made to our world and culture. In a positive way, this challenges, disrupts, and expands the conventional, received version of history. And since everyone concerned died long ago, I do not see how any harm can come from it. Even if, during their lifetimes, they wanted to keep their sexuality a secret, we now should view it with no shame attached.

In his groundbreaking study of gay life in New York from 1890 to 1940, author George Chauncey states that while gay men working on Broadway in the early twentieth century "did not enjoy unalloyed acceptance in this work environment, to be sure," it did offer them significantly greater tolerance than most workplaces, and in fact, "some men could be openly gay among their coworkers, and many others were at least unlikely to suffer serious retribution if their homosexuality were discovered."[2] In an unpublished memoir written in the 1980s, the Academy Award-winning set designer George James Hopkins (1896–1985)—who arrived in NYC in 1911—recalls the Broadway theater scene of that era as being "saturated with gay culture" but noted that "homosexuality wasn't the casual topic of conversation it is today." Hopkins (whose earliest work involved designing racy costumes for the *Ziegfeld Follies*) was mentored by one of the most powerful showmen of the era, Charles Frohman.[3]

A Queer Broadway Power Couple: Frohman and Dillingham

Charles Frohman was born into a Jewish family in Sandusky, Ohio in 1860. By the turn of the century, he had established a theatrical empire and had become one of Broadway's most important producers. During his career, he produced 700 plays and musicals in New York and London, including the American premieres of *The Importance of Being Earnest*, *Sherlock Holmes*, *Peter Pan*, and *The Girl From Utah*. Frohman was at the center of a vibrant Queer circle of leading theater artists that included playwrights Oscar Wilde, Clyde Fitch, and Somerset Maugham; theatrical agent and Broadway producer Elizabeth Marbury; megastar Maude Adams; and, most significantly, Frohman's producing and life partner, **Charles Dillingham**.[4]

Frohman and Dillingham were partners in every way. They shared offices and lived quite openly together in town and country homes. They also frequently vacationed and traveled the world together, and by all reports, their theatrical colleagues treated them as the equivalent of a heterosexual married couple. Their close relationship continued even after Dillingham married in 1913. His wife may also have been Gay, and their marriage was very likely a "lavender marriage" that allowed both of them (and Frohman) to mask their queerness from the outside world.[5]

This kind of subterfuge was not unusual at the time, and it was certainly understandable, considering the significant risks of being outed publicly, which would have been quite evident to Frohman and Dillingham. Both men were close friends of Oscar Wilde, and Frohman was his American producer. In 1895, Frohman went forward with the New York premiere of Wilde's play *The Importance of Being Earnest*, even as Wilde was being put on trial in London for "gross indecency." So, the idea that you could be sent to prison for being Queer was in no way theoretical for Frohman and Dillingham. Even so, the couple remained remarkably visible, even in the press, as being unusually close friends and business partners.

In 1915, Frohman embarked for England on the *Lusitania*, and Dillingham accompanied him to the dock and promised to be there to meet him when he returned. A few days later, in an event that helped spark America's entry into World War I, the ocean liner was sunk by German torpedoes, and more than a thousand of its crew and passengers, including Frohman, went down with the ship. Numerous letters of heartfelt condolence were sent to Dillingham by Lee Shubert and other theatrical luminaries of the day, who addressed him as they would any other widowed spouse.[6] Dillingham continued his long and spectacular career into the Silver Age, producing dozens of hit shows, including musicals by Victor Herbert, Irving Berlin, and Jerome Kern, and co-producing with Florenz Ziegfeld. Perhaps most significantly, Frohman and Dillingham helped launch the careers of many of the Queer theater artists who played major roles in inventing the Broadway musical.

"Oh, You Don't Know the Half of it, Dearie!"—Broadway's Drag Superstars, Part 1

Remarkably, one of the most popular and highest-paid stars of the Genesis Period—on a par with Al Jolson, Eddie Cantor, and Fanny Brice—was the "female impersonator" **Julian Eltinge**. Although almost entirely forgotten today, Eltinge (rhymes with "belting") was so beloved and famous in his day that he even had a theater named after him—an honor awarded to only a handful of other stars.

Eltinge was born William J. Dalton in 1881 near Boston, MA, where his Irish Catholic paternal grandfather had emigrated from County Tipperary.[7] He soon moved with his family to Butte, Montana, where his father ran a barbershop. Because the population of the American West in this era was predominantly male, saloons in mining towns like Butte were often desperate for female entertainers, and proprietors sometimes hired young teenage boys to fill out their chorus lines of dancing girls.[8] At some point in the late 1890s, Eltinge became one of those performers, at least until his father discovered what he was doing and whipped the boy so severely that his mother sent him to live with his aunt in Boston, where he found work in a milliner's shop where he learned tricks of the trade that would serve him well in his future career.[9] Still determined to go into show business, the seventeen-year-old began studying dance and performing in amateur theatricals sponsored by various civic organizations. In these all-male productions, Eltinge was always cast in the leading female role and performed them to great acclaim. Finally, he was seen in one of those productions by a New York producer who cast him in his first Broadway show, *Mr. Wix of Wickham*, in 1904.

By all reports, Eltinge's "gender illusions" were extraordinary, and there was very little camp or comment involved in his performances. Instead, he had the ability to "completely deceive"[10] an audience into believing that he was actually a woman and then make them gasp in surprise when he ripped off his wig and revealed that he was not. Between 1905 and 1915, Eltinge starred in five Broadway musicals, all created specifically for him by top talents such as George M. Cohan, Irving Berlin, Otto Harbach, P. G. Wodehouse, and Jerome Kern. And often they included lyrics written by Eltinge himself. The plots of his shows were modeled on the famous play *Charley's Aunt*, with farcical situations that required the leading male hero character (Eltinge) to disguise himself as a woman in order to solve a crisis, foil the villain, and marry the girl of his dreams. And they always required Eltinge to execute a series of lightning-fast costume changes that would astound the audience as he switched back and forth between genders with remarkable speed.

His most fervent fans were women who worshiped him as an icon of fashion and femininity. At the height of his fame, he published *Julian Eltinge's Magazine of Beauty Hints and Tips* and promoted his own line of women's cosmetics, corsets, and shoes. Offstage, however, Eltinge made every effort to counter any possible suggestion of his (apparently) true Queer identity. He released publicity photos of himself engaging in stereotypically "manly" pursuits such as chopping wood, smoking cigars, riding horses, and sparring with world champion boxer "Gentleman" Jim Corbet. Sometimes, he hired actors to pose as audience members who would make disparaging comments about his masculinity during his performances. In response, Eltinge would gather up his skirts, jump off the stage, punch the heckler in the face, and then leap back on the stage and pick up the show right where he left off, to cheers and applause from the crowd. Eventually, his immense fame and popularity took him to Hollywood, where between 1914 and 1931, he starred in twelve silent movies, including film versions of his stage hits *The Fascinating Widow* and *The Crinoline Girl*. Late in his career, the social politics of the 1930s grew more conservative, and laws and restrictions were implemented, making drag performances illegal (remarkably similar to laws passed in Tennessee and Florida in 2023). This, in tandem with his advancing age, sent Eltinge's career into a steep decline, and following his death in 1941, he faded into undeserved obscurity. The Eltinge Theater, however, is still there. In 1998, as part of the redevelopment of Times Square, the entire building was moved on rails and relocated to the opposite end of 42nd Street, where today it's the AMC Empire 25 movie theater. The ceiling of its lobby still features a large, elaborate mural depicting a trio of dancing Muses from Greek mythology frolicking in flowing gowns—and all three are images of Julian Eltinge.

Many other performers tried to emulate Eltinge's fame and success, but his only serious rival was **Bothwell Browne**. Born in Denmark in 1877, Browne emigrated to San Francisco with his family as a child. He became one of the most popular acts in vaudeville; however, unlike Eltinge, whose female persona was always very demure and proper, Browne offended some critics and audiences with his sexy and suggestive dance routines, especially his portrayal of Cleopatra in which he supposedly performed with a live poisonous snake! In 1911, he also starred in his own Broadway musical, *Miss Jack*, playing a college student who is forced to disguise himself as a sorority girl.

Following in the dainty footsteps of Eltinge and Browne was **Bert Savoy**. He was born Everett McKenzie in 1888[11] in Boston and reportedly began his drag career performing a "hoochie-coochie" dance in a carnival sideshow there. Then, in a remarkable parallel with Julian Eltinge's story, he perfected that routine in the rough saloons and dance halls of Alaska during the gold rush. Savoy's career really took off in 1915 when he teamed up with Jay Brennan, who became both his performing and life partner. Their racy dialogue and campy songs soon turned Brennan and Savoy into a vaudeville sensation. They made their Broadway debut in a lavish musical revue, co-produced by Charles Dillingham and Florenz Ziegfeld, titled **Miss 1917**, which included songs by Victor Herbert, Jerome Kern, McCarthy and Tierney, and Bob Cole and J. Rosamund Johnson. The following season, Brennan and Savoy became "the two most talked about actors the length and breadth of 'Flash Alley' [Broadway],"[12] when they starred in the **Ziegfeld Follies of 1918** alongside Eddie Cantor and Will Rogers, where their routine was acclaimed as "a scream from start to finish!"[13] Their careers crossed over into the Silver Age with **The Greenwich Village Follies of 1920** and **The Greenwich Village Follies of 1922**.

Savoy was one of the first drag performers to develop an overtly Gay persona, presenting himself not as a woman but as a drag queen. He was flamboyant, loud, and irreverently bawdy in a style that has been passed down to the *RuPaul's Drag Race* stars of today. With Savoy decked out from ankles to wig in gaudy, exaggerated versions of the latest fashions, and with Brennan as his dapper "straight man," the jokes and banter flew fast and furiously and were "coupled with a leer and a swish." Savoy always ended their routines by walking off waving a chiffon handkerchief and practically screaming at Brennan, "Oh, you don't know the half of it, Dearie!" This much-repeated catchphrase became so famous that it inspired the Ira and George Gershwin song, "The Half of Dearie, Blues," introduced by Fred Astaire in the musical *Lady, Be Good!* (1924).

Bert Savoy was the epitome of camp both on and off the stage, and the story of his dramatic death is legendary and, by all accounts, absolutely true. On June 26, 1923, accompanied by his half-brother and two friends, Savoy was walking along the shore at Long Beach, NY, watching an incoming storm when a stunningly loud thunderclap prompted him to remark, "Well, ain't Miss God cuttin' up somethin' fierce?!" After which, he was immediately struck by a bolt of lightning and died.[14] Brennan went on to appear in four more Broadway revues[15] with a new partner, Stanley Rogers, who successfully replicated all of Savoy's mannerisms and catchphrases, and the act still managed to "set the audience roaring."[16]

Brennan then went to Hollywood, where he became a screenwriter. He died in 1961 at the age of seventy-eight. Mae West, the fabled Broadway and film superstar, would later confess that she had based much of her distinctive persona on the affectations, physicality, and comedy stylings of Bert Savoy.

CHAPTER 4
"ANYTHING YOU CAN DO, I CAN DO BETTER"—THE FOUNDING MOTHERS OF BROADWAY (I, J, W)

We often read or hear the assertion that Broadway is, and has always been, a male-dominated industry. As with nearly every other twentieth- and even twenty-first-century field of endeavor, this is undoubtedly true. Still, we would have to acknowledge that the overwhelming majority of those males who have dominated Broadway have themselves been members of marginalized groups: LGBTQ, African Americans, Jews, and other immigrants. A deeper investigation soon reveals that women have played a much more significant role and have had a substantially more consistent and profound impact on the musical than has generally been reported or acknowledged. Despite being outnumbered by their male counterparts, from the very beginning, female bookwriters, composers, lyricists, choreographers, producers, and designers have nevertheless played indispensable roles in the creation and development of the American musical theater—even if they are seldom appropriately acknowledged and remembered today. While they have never been officially designated as the "Founding Mothers of Broadway," that seems to me an appropriate title for the extraordinary women explored in this chapter, whose remarkable contribution to the genesis of the Broadway musical is certainly as significant as many of their better-known male counterparts.

"Ah! Sweet Mystery of Life!"—The Writers

One of the earliest notable women is playwright, bookwriter, lyricist, and composer **Anne Caldwell**, who was born in Boston, MA, in 1867. Between 1905 and 1920, she worked on thirty Broadway musicals—contributing both book and lyrics to sixteen of them—many of which were substantial hits in their day. Caldwell entered show business as a performer at the age of fourteen and later began writing songs with her husband, James O'Dea, composing music to his words. In 1912, they collaborated with Victor Herbert on the Cinderella musical *The Lady and the Slipper*. After the death of her husband in 1915, Caldwell turned her focus to lyrics, collaborating with such leading composers as Vincent Youmans, Harry Tierney, and especially Jerome Kern. She appears to have been a particular favorite of Charles Dillingham, who produced sixteen of the musicals she was involved with, including *The Night Boat*, the first show on which she was paired with Kern. Caldwell and Kern would go on to create songs for eight Broadway musicals, including their biggest hits, **Good Morning Dearie**, **Chris Cross**, and **Stepping**

Stones, a musical comedy version of Little Red Riding Hood. Although none of Caldwell's shows—and only a handful of her songs—are ever performed or heard today, at the time, she was one of Broadway's top writers. Her songs were interpolated into musical comedies alongside those of George M. Cohan, Irving Berlin, Otto Harbach, P. G. Wodehouse, George and Ira Gershwin, Bob Cole and J. Rosamond Johnson, and she was a founding charter member of the American Society of Composers, Authors, and Publishers (ASCAP).[1] Most recently, four Caldwell/Kern songs were interpolated into the hit 1975 Broadway revival of ***Very Good Eddie*** and can be heard on that show's original cast album.

Somewhat better known is **Rida Johnson Young**, who was born in 1869 in Baltimore, Maryland. Between 1910 and 1924, she wrote the book and lyrics for eleven musicals and operettas, including Victor Herbert's greatest success, ***Naughty Marietta*** (1910). She had another huge hit when she collaborated with the Hungarian Jewish immigrant composer Sigmund Romberg on the smash hit ***Maytime*** (1917), which became the second longest-running show of the 1910s. Overall, Young penned the lyrics to more than 500 songs, at least two of which twenty-first-century audiences may be familiar with since they were incorporated into the 2002 Broadway musical *Thoroughly Modern Millie*: "I'm Falling In Love With Someone" and "Ah, Sweet Mystery Of Life!." That second song was also a comic highlight of the 1974 film *Young Frankenstein*.

Other songwriting women of the Genesis Period were singers who wrote material for themselves, and sometimes others, to perform. Most significant in this regard was singer, comedian, actress, and producer **Nora Bayes**, one of the biggest vaudeville and Broadway stars of the era, in a similar stratosphere to that of Al Jolson, Eddie Cantor, and Fanny Brice. In fact, Bayes grew so famous that in 1919 she became the first woman to have a theater named after her. Born Rachel Elenora Goldberg into an orthodox Jewish family,[2] she adopted the stage name "Nora Bayes" to better complement the Irish-themed songs that made up much of her repertoire. As a songwriter, she contributed lyrics to eleven Broadway shows, including ***The Ziegfeld Follies of 1908***, in which Bayes and her co-writer, performing partner, and second husband, Jack Norworth, introduced one of the most popular songs of the twentieth century, "Shine On, Harvest Moon." Bayes' flamboyant, bohemian, and unconventional lifestyle, along with her shrewd business sense, often challenged traditional roles and values for women of the era, and her very public defiance of the authority and control of male managers and producers, such as Florenz Ziegfeld, along with her five marriages and divorces, made front-page news. One newspaper quoted her shocking advice to wives: "As soon as one becomes bored, one should secure a divorce,"[3] a statement that was outrageously scandalous for the time.

The songs of Nora Bayes, Rida Johnson Young, and Anne Caldwell demonstrated that female writers "could create works for the stage that were equally as satirical, witty, timely, and simply as comical as the work of any man" and helped to establish "that writing American musical comedy was not solely a male domain."[4]

Broadway Dance #3: Dancing Ladies—The Stagers and Choreographers (I, J, B, W)

Before Harrigan and Hart, Weber and Fields, and Williams and Walker, a dynamic woman named **Lydia Thompson** was equally influential in inspiring this new soon-to-be art form through her creation of early embryonic, not-quite-yet musicals. Thompson was an acclaimed English dancer, singer, actress, director, and producer who formed her own company of performers which she called "Lydia Thompson and Her British Blondes." When she first brought them to New York in 1868, Lydia and her troupe quickly became a sensation. The shows they presented were burlesques of well-known stories drawn from novels, plays, poems, operas, classical myths, fairy tales, and legends, such as *Orpheus and Euridice*, *Faust*, *Aladdin*, *Sinbad*, *Robinson Caruso*, and *Robin Hood*. As described by Kurt Gänzl in his book *Lydia Thompson—Queen of Burlesque*, Thompson presented these stories in "zanily grotesque"[5] and ridiculous versions that were loaded with puns, witty wordplay, rhyming couplets, slapstick comedy, "and parodies on the present times,"[6] combined with "songs made up from popular tunes set with topical, satirical, and suitable-to-the-subject (more or less)[7] new lyrics, and a goodly dose of dance, both graceful and comical—not to mention some dashing examples of the scene painters' and mechanists' arts."[8]

In addition, Lydia smartly added a heavy dollop of sex into the mix. Her shows were quite racy for the time, featuring both sexual innuendo and dozens of women wearing what were considered at the time to be very revealing costumes. Lydia, herself often played the male hero or "principal boy" roles that provided her with the opportunity to dress in short tunics and display her much-admired legs in form-fitting tights. We must remember that this was still the puritanical Victorian age, when respectable women went to great lengths to obscure their bodies under hoop skirts, bustles, and multiple layers of fabric, and when even the legs of tables and pianos were sometimes draped to make them less provocative! So, the idea of young ladies choosing to exhibit themselves on a stage in form-fitting costumes was truly shocking. As one critic wrote, "Such a display of legs was never before seen in this city, even *The Black Crook* and *The White Fawn* could not equal this production. It *outstrips* them all . . ."[9] The eventual evolution of satirical burlesque into sexy "girly shows" began here with Lydia and her many imitators, but it would be decades later before the striptease acts that became synonymous with the term would be introduced.

In Gänzl's estimation, Lydia was "one of the most technically skilled and effective dancers of her generation, a dazzling comedienne . . . and possessor of both a pretty, if unambitious soprano, and of a deliciously winning way with popular song . . ."[10] As one critic declared, "Miss Thompson breathes life into everything she does. She is charming to look at, a good singer, a really clever dancer, and the life and soul of every scene." Lydia specialized in lampooning the swaggering, swashbuckling, romantic male heroes of legendary tales, and in recent years she has been hailed as "the first drag king."[11] Often, her entire troupe of British Blondes would follow her into battle dressed as sexy soldiers and marching in military drills and formations. This seems to have given birth, at least in part, to the now classic showbiz concept of chorus lines of dancing girls dressed in tights and executing high-kicking precision choreography. Indeed, there might have been no Radio City Music Hall Rockettes and no finale to *A Chorus Line* without Lydia blazing the trail.

The music in Lydia's shows was a pre-copyright era hodgepodge of well-known tunes borrowed from classical music, operas, operettas, folk songs, popular songs, and marches—the "Top 40" of the Victorian age. As one contemporary critic observed:

> The music is taken from all quarters. Offenbach's lively airs are liberally used, and the latest popular songs are introduced freely. The dances—especially one that resembles very much the walkaround [cakewalk] of the negro minstrels—are all comical, and the ensembles are delightfully absurd.

Another of Lydia's enduring contributions to the vocabulary of Broadway dance was her popularization of the can-can, which she and her troupe performed in her Ali Baba burlesque, *The Forty Thieves*, "with the abandon of the genuine French article."[12] Although French opera-bouffe star Lucile Tostee had introduced the can-can to America the previous year, it was Thompson, "the best and most magnetic theatrical dancer"[13] of the era, who turned that daring dance into a sensation.

Thompson's unique combination of "comedy, parody, satire, improvisation, song and dance, cross-dressing, extravagant stage effects, risqué jokes, and saucy costumes took New York by storm." It also provoked fierce criticism from conservative factions who questioned Lydia's morality and condemned her and her troupe for going far beyond what they considered the bounds of decency. Others seemed more disturbed by "the impertinence of a woman who had the audacity to swagger boldly about the stage acting like a man."[14] Theater historian John Kenrick has described the overall effect of Lydia's shows:

> Underdressed women playing sexual aggressors, combining good looks with impertinent comedy—and in a production written and managed by a woman? Unthinkable! No wonder men and adventurous wives turned out in droves, making Thompson and her "British blondes" the hottest thing in American show business.[15]

Thompson's first New York season played to standing-room-only business and grossed over $370,000 (more than $11 million today)! Over the following five years, from 1868 to 1873, as a result of her astute management and genius for publicity, Thompson brought seventeen productions to Broadway—produced and directed by, and starring, Lydia herself. In between, she took her troupe of players on coast-to-coast, cross-country tours of America. Lydia Thompson represented a new kind of independent woman that had seldom been seen before, and everywhere she traveled, she was met with the same wildly enthusiastic acclaim accompanied by fierce disapproval. Lydia's shows were only precursors to the musical, but they had a tremendous influence on the emerging form and especially on three powerful women who followed her—Aida Overton Walker, Gertrude Hoffmann, and Albertina Rauch.

Aida Overton Walker, the "Queen of The Cakewalk," has been profiled in Chapter 2, but it's important to note that in addition to being one of the most famous Black performers of the Genesis Period, she was also a gifted and influential choreographer. She first began creating dances for Williams and Walker's vaudeville act, which she joined in 1897, and the innovative ragtime versions of the cakewalk she staged for the duo and herself to perform became such "a genuine sensation" that the team was catapulted to the "front rank of the topliners."[16] Overton Walker's choreography played a major role in propelling the cakewalk into an international dance craze, and she commanded high fees for instructing white high society in the finer points of the dance. She then became the first Black woman to choreograph a Broadway musical (and possibly the first woman to do so) when she created the dances for *In Dahomey* in 1903, *Abyssinia* in 1906, and *Bandanna Land* in 1909 (the first show for which she was credited for "musical staging by"). Whatever remnants and reverberations of the cakewalk still linger in Broadway choreography today (and there are many!) have likely been handed down to us from Aida Overton Walker.

Gertrude Hoffmann was another star performer and choreographer. She was born around 1883 and grew up in the vibrant theatrical world of late nineteenth-century San Francisco, where her Irish immigrant mother was a dressmaker who catered to singers, dancers, and actresses. At that time, the San Francisco theater scene was dominated by extravaganzas, burlesques, and pantomimes, a style of performance that had, in part, been introduced to the city by Lydia Thompson during her appearances there in 1871. That visit had culminated in what the newspapers called "the Battle of the Blondes," during which Lydia's troupe played across the street from a rival troupe of copycat imitators.[17] Interestingly, Gertrude would later recall that the first moment she knew she wanted to work in theater was as a little girl when she saw a production of *Ali Baba and the Forty Thieves* and "from the moment that curtain went up . . . [I] began producing in the theater."[18] Although Lydia Thompson had gone home to England years before Gertrude was born, *The Forty Thieves* had been one of Lydia's most acclaimed productions and her style and sensibilities still held strong in San Francisco. By the age of fourteen,

Gertrude was performing as one of hundreds of "Ballet girls" in spectacular productions in the city's numerous theaters and opera houses, and early on she began to be assigned featured bits and specialty dance solos that, no matter how brief, would often be remarked upon by the press. By the age of seventeen, Gertrude was headed to New York as a dancer in a show slated to play Hammerstein's Victoria Theatre, and along the way, she met and married the show's music director and composer, Max Hoffmann.[19] That show flopped in New York, but Gertrude and Max discovered that they were a dynamic team and soon formed their own touring company, Max Hoffmann Troubadours, and from 1901 to 1903, Gertrude was dance director, stage manager, and costume designer for all of the troupe's productions. This was an invaluable training ground, and as biographer Sunny Stalter-Pace tells us, "By the summer of 1903, she was sufficiently skilled and prepared to do her work in the high-stakes world of New York theater." There, working for Oscar Hammerstein I, she became "the first woman to be credited for her dance direction in a Broadway show."[20] At least a few other uncredited female choreographers (including Aida Overton Walker) had worked on shows before her—but Gertrude Hoffmann is officially the first. Between 1903 and 1927, she would go on to design the dances for fifteen Broadway shows.

Hoffmann career had many other phases as well. She became a top vaudeville star, headlining her own elaborate mini-revue in which she sang, danced, and performed celebrity impersonations and parodies of the biggest stars of the day, both female and male. In 1908, she created a scandalous controversy when she produced, choreographed, and performed a sexy, dramatic dance act titled "A Vision of Salome," in which she portrayed the biblical temptress. Her performance was so racy that following one of her New York performances, she was arrested for indecency. However, the judge threw out the case based on Hoffman's very reasonable defense that she had already performed that dance more than 400 times without being arrested. In fact, it may all have been a publicity stunt, but whatever the case, it jump-started a "Salomania" craze in which everyone from Fanny Brice to Aida Overton Walker and Julian Eltinge performed their own "Dance of The Seven Veils" in imitation of Hoffmann. Gertrude Hoffmann never stopped reinventing herself, and her career thrived well into the Silver Age (see page 112).

ACT II
THE SILVER AGE

Fig. 4: Ethel Merman and chorus perform "Blow, Gabriel, Blow" in the 1934 hit musical comedy *Anything Goes*—music and lyrics by Cole Porter, book by Howard Lindsay and Russell Crouse, (revised from an earlier version by Guy Bolton and P. G. Wodehouse), directed by Lindsay, and with choreography by Robert Alton. Photo by Vandamm Studio© Billy Rose Theatre Division, The New York Public Library for the Performing Arts.

CHAPTER 5
"ALL THAT JAZZ"—THE SILVER AGE OF BROADWAY, PART 1: THE 1920S (I, J, Q, B, W)

Between the end of World War I in 1918 and the opening of Rodgers and Hammerstein's *Oklahoma!* in 1943—the period which I have designated the Silver Age of Broadway—more than 300 musical shows opened on Broadway, and overwhelmingly they were the creation of a vibrant second wave of Jewish, Irish, Black, and Queer artists—including an increasing number of women. By this point, a majority of the white artists in this wave were "second generation" children of immigrants who, in a major shift from the harsh poverty and limited education of their predecessors, now mostly came from families who had navigated their way, at least, into the lower middle class, and many of these young people had even graduated from college. The new generation of Black creators was also quite different from the previous generation.

Beginning around 1910—in an event historians call "The Great Migration"—thousands of African Americans endeavored to escape from the overt violence and oppression of the rural Jim Crow South by moving to the urban North—especially New York City—in search of greater economic and educational opportunities. This sudden influx of enterprising young Black people, combined with the series of dynamic social changes that emerged in American society after the war, transformed the uptown neighborhood of Harlem into a vibrant breeding ground for modern Black culture. After a nearly ten-year absence of Black musicals on Broadway, a new and even more significant decade of African-American-generated musical theater was preparing to burst onto the scene.

The status of women was also undergoing a significant shift. World War I had already greatly expanded women's employment, but by 1920, for the first time in history, more than half of all Americans lived in cities rather than in rural areas, and this increase in urbanization, along with increased economic growth, prompted young, unmarried women to enter the workforce in even greater numbers. By the end of the decade, 25 percent of all women and more than 50 percent of single women would be employed.[1] Meanwhile, in January of 1920, the Eighteenth Amendment[2] to the U.S. Constitution went into effect, banning the sale and distribution of alcohol, and the era of Prohibition began. In author Jerome Charyn's view, this happened because "White Protestant America had declared war on Catholics, immigrants, and big cities like Chicago and New York. It was rural America's last stand."[3] Just seven months later, the Nineteenth Amendment was ratified, granting women the right to vote in all national and local elections. Although this did not immediately affect politics in significant ways (it was not a very political era), the cultural and presumably psychological effect of this newfound sense of power and importance was immense, resulting in a decade-long burst of women's liberation.

The most visible representative of this new paradigm was "the Flapper," a cultural icon who emerged in full force right as the decade got underway. In fact, by May of 1920, Hollywood had already released *The Flapper*, a hit movie starring Ziegfeld showgirl Olive Thomas in the title role, and this, along with the release of F. Scott Fitzgerald's short story collection *Flappers and Philosophers* that same year, spread the (somewhat sensationalized) image and ideology of the flapper across the nation. Flappers were modern, independent, free-spirited, highly social young women who publicly rebelled against the traditional nineteenth-century rules of society, especially the Victorian dictate that "a woman's place is in the home." Instead, flappers boldly ventured out into what had been a man's world: working in offices, driving cars, riding bicycles, smoking cigarettes, and (illegally) drinking cocktails in nightclubs and speakeasies. They also rejected the traditional conservative values of modesty and chastity and transformed the traditional image of women by wearing makeup, chopping their hair into a boyish bob, and rejecting the multiple body-obscuring layers of Edwardian fashion in favor of unstructured sheath dresses with scandalously short hemlines and low necklines that provocatively revealed their bare arms, shoulders, and knees. This new fashion, along with their rejection of stiff corsets and girdles, is what allowed them the freedom of movement necessary to execute wild new dances such as the shimmy and the Charleston (see page 81). Flappers were also at the center of a sexual revolution. World War I had drastically increased access to sex education and contraception, and while it is impossible to estimate whatever increase in premarital sex may have resulted from this, the sexually charged atmosphere of the 1920s, as exemplified by the widespread popularity of "petting parties" and other playful forms of erotic experimentation, undoubtedly led to an increase in sexual activity for both men and women.[4] Perhaps most outrageously, the flapper represented the spirit of jazz, which itself was originally a slang term for sex.

Fascinating Rhythms: Jazz and the Showtune

While all of these events and developments had a major impact on this new generation of theater artists, of equal importance, at least for them, was an event that took place back in 1917—although they likely did not understand the magnitude of its significance at the time. On January 27 of that year, jazz arrived in New York City with the debut of the Original Dixieland Jass [sic] Band. This contingent of five white musicians (founded in New Orleans the previous year by Nick LaRocca, the son of poor Sicilian immigrants) debuted at Reisenweber's 400 Club, a swanky, popular gathering spot for Broadway producers, performers, and stars located at West 58th Street and Eighth Avenue. In fact, it was Al Jolson who had heard the band play in Chicago and recommended that they be booked into this early restaurant/nightclub for what turned out to be an extended engagement. The *New York Clipper* covered the band's debut with a one-line review: "Its weird music must be heard to be appreciated."[5] And, indeed, their "weird music" would begin to be much more widely appreciated a month later when the Original Dixieland

Jass Band released the very first jazz recordings, "Livery Stable Blues" and "Dixie Jass Band One Step," which became instant hits and introduced millions of people around the world to this new genre of music.

There is, of course, no doubt that Black musicians had performed this new style of music in NYC prior to this date. After all, jazz had been brewing in New Orleans and other cities in the South and Midwest for more than a decade. It had evolved "from the work songs of slaves, from spirituals and blues, from funeral marches, from ragtime, from Creole songs, from the 'jass' bands inside a honky-tonk car that was 'sometimes hooked onto the train that carried (Black) itinerant workers from job to job.'"[6] This, however, is the first NYC jazz performance that can be documented. It marked the end of the "Ragtime Era" and brought the "Jazz Age" to Broadway. For the next fourteen years, The Original Dixieland Jazz Band, as it was soon renamed, remained a top attraction at Reisenweber's, the Folies Bergère on the roof of the Wintergarden Theater,[7] and other hot New York nightspots through to the end of the 1920s.

At the same time that jazz music was emerging, the distinctive sound, form, and structure of the "Broadway Showtune" was also taking shape. Over the following two decades, Silver Age Broadway musicals produced an incredibly rich trove of perfectly crafted, wonderfully expressive, endlessly captivating, and enduring works of art that today are at the center of what is known as the Great American Songbook. While it is true that jazz and the showtune are closely related and interconnected—they are not exactly the same thing. Yes, the showtune was strongly influenced by jazz, and many elements of jazz were incorporated into it. And indeed, the standard repertoire of nearly every jazz musician and vocalist has primarily been made up of Broadway showtunes. However, the purpose and intention behind the creation and composition of these forms of music are very different. The primary goal of a jazz composer (much like a classical composer) is to create *musical impact*, and the lyrics of a jazz composition (if there even are any) are of secondary importance to the music. And both the music and lyrics are intended, at least in part, to provide a groundwork for improvisation and are expected to be interpreted freely and differently every time the work is performed. In contrast, the principal intention of a Broadway songwriter is *dramatic impact*. Their main goal is to tell a story and to bring to life the characters within that story. The lyrics of a showtune are always of equal, if not even greater, importance as the music, and Broadway composers and lyricists usually expect their work to be performed in a close replication of the way it appears in the printed score. The two forms, however, do share a fascinating origin story.

The Jews and the Blues (I, J, B)

In his audio documentary tracing the roots of jazz, titled *Jews and Blues: Inside Out*, radio commentator Michael Goldfarb asserts that:

> The story of how Jewish and African American music came to be mingled is the story of how the soundtrack of the American Century came to be written. Beyond

the music, the tale is social history—a chronicle of migration and immigration defining, culturally at least, how newcomers become Americans. It's also a tale of race and progressive politics.[8]

That also perfectly describes the origin story of the Broadway showtune. Both stories center on the remarkably close affinity and relationship between two *musical scales* that came from different parts of the world and evolved from very diverse cultural roots. The first is the **Phrygian scale,** which serves as the basis of most forms of Jewish music, including Hebrew prayers and Klezmer. It is also at the root of many forms of Indian, Arabic, Egyptian, Middle Eastern, Central Asian, Eastern European, and Spanish music.

How did the Phrygian scale come to be embraced by so many disparate cultures and regions across the world? It appears to have originated with the Roma people, a long-persecuted group historically referred to as "Gypsies."[9] This is a very complicated and controversial term. Many people who identify as Roma (also called Romani or Romany) consider it to be a slur, while others embrace the term, and several Roma organizations use "Gypsy" in their official names. To further complicate this issue, the word has several long-standing connections to show business and Broadway musicals. For centuries, the Roma have often made their living as accomplished entertainers, and as such, they have spread their vibrant traditional music and dance across the world. This began way back in the Middle Ages when, for unknown reasons, the Roma left their homeland in Northern India and began a centuries-long migration that would take them through Persia, the Middle East, Turkey, and North Africa and eventually spread their people throughout Eastern and Western Europe. Everywhere the Roma went, their traditional music and dance forms (including the Phrygian scale) went with them and were absorbed into the local culture. Simultaneously, elements of the music and dance they encountered in each of the local cultures were absorbed and assimilated into Roma music and dance, and they then took those additions with them on their subsequent journeys, and so on.[10] The exact time and place of the cultural exchange between the Jewish and Roma peoples is not clear and may have occurred multiple times over the centuries.[11] But certainly, by the end of the nineteenth century, when Jews began to be driven out of the Pale of Settlement and other areas of Eastern Europe, the religious and secular (Klezmer) music they brought with them to America was built on the Phrygian scale.

The other musical scale, commonly called the **Blues scale**, is also a complex hybrid form with a long history. It descended from the African folk music of the forty-five distinct ethnic groups from Western and Central Africa whose people were kidnapped and enslaved in the Americas. Over the 400 years of slavery, the cultures, religions, and music of those various groups were blended into a new and unique African American culture, which had also absorbed many influences from white European American culture, religion, and music.

These two musical scales—Blues and Phrygian—sound amazingly similar, and the Black and Jewish music that arose from them often have striking similarities. As can be heard on Goldfarb's broadcast, the "hazanuth" (chanting/singing) of a Jewish cantor at times sounds nearly identical to the *work song* of an early twentieth-century Black laborer working in the fields. This did not go unnoticed. And since art tends to dissolve cultural barriers, during the first decades of the twentieth century, Black musicians and composers such as Eubie Blake and J. Rosamond Johnson perceived familiar sounds in the music of Jewish Tin Pan Alley songwriters and were inspired to emulate them. Simultaneously, as ragtime, blues, Negro spirituals, jubilee songs, and eventually jazz began to emerge into mainstream (white) culture, Jewish songwriters, including Irving Berlin, George Gershwin, and Harold Arlen, found themselves deeply drawn to Black music and began to incorporate aspects of it into their work. So it appears that this remarkable affinity between the sounds of the Phrygian scale and the Blues scale led to the creation of both jazz and the Broadway showtune. In Michael Goldfarb's view:

> The music of Blacks from the south and Jews from Europe shares these things: both are deeply emotional; both sprang from the effort to transcend harsh environments; both seek to reach a higher ground through musical expression. The convergence of old worlds in the new created something that changed the sound of music forever.[12]

"Side by Side by Side"—Musical Comedy, Operetta, and Revue

Showtunes became the central building blocks and main events of three distinct but interrelated genres of musical theater that vied for dominance on Broadway during the Silver Age: the *musical comedy*, the *operetta*, and the *revue*. None of these were new, of course, but they came into their own in the Silver Age, reaching new levels of quality, confidence, and panache. However, only a handful of the hundreds of wildly popular musical shows that premiered during this era are ever revived today.

Why? One reason is that the tastes and expectations of Broadway audiences were quite different back in the day. As one contemporary critic wryly noted, what Broadway theatergoers most wanted from a Silver Age **musical comedy** was "fun, melody, grace, pretty girls and costumes, lively dances, and a story slight enough to make no demands on the audience but sufficiently ridiculous to allow the characters to disport themselves with abandon impossible in any other form of dramatic fare." Much like a modern television sitcom, the stories of these shows were divertingly disposable— enjoyable in the moment but largely forgotten by the next day. The plots were not expected to be cohesive, and the characters were not required to have significant depth as long as the shows were funny, racy, topical, tuneful, and overall entertaining. The primary purpose of these shows was to showcase the distinctive talents of their star performers and provide a framework for introducing new (hopefully soon-to-be hit) songs.

Side by side with the musical comedies were the **operettas**. Their principal purpose was to provide a vehicle for highly romantic, lushly melodic, light-classical music performed by beautifully trained, near-operatic voices. Operetta songs were usually more specifically tied into their books' plotlines, which were more carefully crafted than the average musical comedy. Modern audiences, however, would likely find the books of most Silver Age operettas to be creaky and leaden with overly melodramatic stories, cardboard heroes and heroines, and overly broad comic sidekicks whose jokes were not very fresh even back in the day.

Finally, these were the glory days of the Broadway *musical revue*, and two young men who had previously worked for Ziegfeld now had the temerity to challenge their former employer by launching their own eponymous series of lavish revues: **The George White Scandals** and **Earl Carrol's Vanities**. Another close competitor was **John Murray Anderson** and his string of **Greenwich Village Follies**. Like the musical comedies, these revues introduced hundreds of hit songs, many of which remain popular today, and like their Genesis Period predecessors, Silver Age revues were built around the great performers who starred in them and featured comedy sketches and musical numbers that were often extremely topical. To revive any of these revues today would be much like restaging an episode of *Saturday Night Live* decades after it first aired and with a different cast. Most of the jokes would be incomprehensible to that later audience because the topical subject matter would be long forgotten. And because the writing had been expertly tailored to specific stars, it would likely not sit well on other performers. By the Golden Age of Broadway, the revue format had largely migrated to television and morphed into the TV variety shows of the late 1940s and 1950s that showcased performers such as Jimmy Durante, Milton Berle, Jack Benny, and Bob Hope—the exact same stars who had headlined some of the great revues of the Silver Age. As a result, revues largely died out on Broadway around the same time. However, as we will see, the structure and format of the revue will heavily influence many of the Modern Era musicals in the 1970s.

So, even though the titles of many Silver Age shows are still widely known, as a result of the limitations listed above, almost none of the hit musicals of this era—revues, operettas, or musical comedies—are ever performed today. It should not really be surprising that these shows mostly lie dormant. The overwhelming majority of all theatrical works from the past have faded away entirely. That's why we consider the relatively small number that have managed to stick around to be "classics." They have endured and retained much of their freshness, impact, and meaning over many years and through changing times, culture, and values—even if some of their specific content has become dated or out of sync with the contemporary moment. I wonder what Broadway shows, songs, books, movies, or TV shows from our current era will still be in the mix a hundred years from now?

In their day, these Silver Age shows were wildly entertaining, hilariously funny, and often moving—and they left a tremendous legacy. In addition to the hundreds of enduring songs that came from them, many of the theatrical innovations and techniques that originated in these shows have been passed down to the musicals of today.

"I'm Just Simply Full of Jazz"—The Harlem Renaissance and *Shuffle Along* (🔊)

As lyricist Alan Jay Lerner wrote in *The Street Where I Lived*:

> The American Theater had never known and, sadly enough, probably never will know another decade like it [the 1920s]. Radio was in its infancy. No T.V. Motion pictures were still silent. And sixty-three theaters on Broadway. One season there were over thirty musicals running simultaneously, and in December of 1927, eleven shows opened on the same night.[13]

The decade had actually kicked off with *Irene*, the unprecedented musical comedy hit that had opened in 1919 and (as outlined in Chapter 3) brought together all of the most vital elements and best practices of the Genesis Period. McCarthy and Tierneys's score for *Irene* was still very much rooted in traditional European musical forms, with perhaps just a hint of ragtime. But then, in the spring of 1921, the sounds and rhythms of the Jazz Age roared onto Broadway with the sensational ***Shuffle Along***.

As writer, poet, lyricist, and social activist Langston Hughes remembered it, "The 1920s were the years of Manhattan's Black Renaissance. It began with *Shuffle Along*, *Running Wild*, and the Charleston." Indeed, when *Shuffle Along* opened on Broadway, it created such a sensation and brought so much attention to emerging Black artists that it not only jump-started a vibrant new wave of Black musicals on Broadway, but also helped to inspire that sudden blossoming of Black literary, visual, and performing arts known as the Harlem Renaissance. In his book *Harlem: The Crucible of Modern African American Culture*, author Lionel Bascom describes it as a seismic cultural change that "created an unprecedented opportunity to use art to recast the Negro as a deserving, worthwhile American, no longer to be seen as just the downtrodden descendants of slaves." Meanwhile, when Langston Hughes was deciding where he wanted to go to college, he chose Columbia University specifically because he wanted to see this smash hit Black Broadway musical whose fame had spread all the way to Ohio. After arriving in NYC, Hughes "sat up in the gallery, night after night at *Shuffle Along*," which he later recalled as "a honey of a show. Swift, bright, funny, and gay, with a dozen danceable, singable tunes . . . Everybody was in the audience—including me. It was always packed." He specifically credited the show with providing "a scintillating send-off and pre-Charleston kick to the Negro vogue in Manhattan that soon spread to books, African sculpture, music, and dancing."[14]

The four Black creators of *Shuffle Along* were all talented and accomplished mainstream vaudeville headliners. The show's book was written by the comedy team of **Flournoy Miller** and **Aubry Lyles**, who were both born in Tennessee in the mid-1880s and met while attending Fisk University. Their act consisted of songs, jokes, and physical humor and included a sketch called "The Mayor of Dixie'" that they believed could be expanded into a full-length musical comedy. The show's score was the creation of **Sissle and Blake**.

Noble Sissle was born in Indianapolis in 1889 and began singing in his high school glee club. He dropped out of college to join James Reese Europe's Society Orchestra, and during World War I, he played under Europe's leadership in the regimental band of the all-Black 369th Infantry Regiment, famously known as the "Harlem Hellfighters." **James Hubert (Eubie) Blake** was born in Baltimore in 1887. Before Emancipation, both of his parents had been enslaved. Eubie began exhibiting extraordinary piano skills at the age of six, and by the age of twelve, he had already composed the "Charleston Rag'" and other ragtime tunes, all to the great disapproval of his mother, who did not want "the devil's music" in her house. Eubie's professional career began as a piano player in the summer resort of Atlantic City, New Jersey, where he interacted with both George M. Cohan and Irving Berlin. It was around this time that Blake met Noble Sissle, and together they wrote their first songs. Blake then moved to New York, where, after the tragic death of James Reece Europe, he briefly took over leadership of the Society Orchestra. Eventually, Sissle and Blake teamed up to form their own very classy vaudeville act called "The Dixie Duo," although neither of them was from the South. Instead of appearing in blackface and wearing comically garish or tattered costumes as was still common practice for Black vaudeville performers at the time, Sissle and Blake glided onto the stage sporting elegant tuxedos and their natural skin tones, then Blake took his seat at a sleek grand piano as the duo launched into a selection of popular hit tunes of the day, nostalgic ballads, and new original songs with music by Eubie Blake and lyrics by Noble Sissle.

In 1921, Miller and Lyles shared a bill with Sissle and Blake at a fundraising performance for the NAACP.[15] The comedy team was greatly impressed by the songwriters' creations and proposed that they join forces to create a musical for Broadway, even though it had been over a decade since there had been a Black musical on Broadway. Caseen Gaines describes this meeting in *When Broadway Was Black*:

> The four men were aware of the long odds but thought that if anyone could bring Black folks back to Broadway, they were the ones. The comedians . . . already had the skeleton of a story; the musicians had a dozen songs they could work into a narrative. With nothing but a handshake agreement in place, the quartet agreed to give it a shot.[16]

The plan was that Miller and Lyles would expand their comic skit "The Mayor of Dixie" into a two-act book about a mayoral election in a fictional Black community in South Carolina, which they dubbed "Jimtown." Sissle and Blake would provide the score which would incorporate several of the surefire hits from their vaudeville act, along with new songs written specifically for the story. In addition, Sissle, Miller, and Lyles would all play leading roles, Blake would conduct the orchestra, and near the end of the show, after the plot wrapped up, Blake would join Sissle onstage to perform a segment of their vaudeville act billed as "A Few Minutes With Sissle and Blake."[17]

As might be expected, this quartet of Black performers, who had never before appeared in, or written, a Broadway show had tremendous difficulty finding a backer who would provide the necessary financing. They finally persuaded white producer John Cort to fund an out-of-town tryout of the show. Following this chaotic and severely underfinanced pre-Broadway tour, *Shuffle Along* limped into New York $21,000 in debt (the equivalent of more than $300,000 today). The only theater the show could obtain was a rarely used, rundown old lecture hall with a wide but extremely shallow stage and a much too small orchestra pit, located on West 63rd Street, more than ten blocks north of the theater district. Nevertheless, with all of this stacked against it, *Shuffle Along* opened there on May 22, 1921, and against all odds, became a massive hit! In fact, after only a few weeks of performances, the street in front of the theater had to be changed to one way to prevent the crowds arriving at the show from bringing traffic in the neighborhood to a complete standstill.

The show attracted a large, diverse, multiracial audience who, to an unprecedented degree, were seated side by side in unsegregated seating. The white stars, cast members, and creative teams of other Broadway shows were so eager to see *Shuffle Along* that a "midnight matinee" (actually 11:30 pm) was instituted on Wednesday nights to accommodate them. Irving Berlin saw the show many times, often sitting front row center so he could cheer on Eubie Blake who stood directly in front of him conducting the orchestra. And there is no doubt that George and Ira Gershwin, Rodgers and Hart, Vincent Youmans, Dorothy Fields, Cole Porter, Noel Coward, and virtually all the other songwriters of the day were influenced by Sissle and Blake's eclectic score. The show's biggest hit, "I'm Just Wild About Harry," has an infectious syncopation—but it didn't start out that way. The story goes that Blake, who was a great admirer of Victor Herbert's music, had composed a waltz for the show in Herbert's signature style. During rehearsals, however, it was decided that a waltz might not be the right fit for the show, so rather than throw out a great melody, Blake transformed the song's original 3/4 time signature into a jaunty 2/4 rhythm.

For more than a century, "Harry" has been performed and recorded countless times, used in dozens of films and television shows, and most notably enjoyed a major resurgence in 1948 when it was used as the official campaign song for candidate Harry S. Truman's successful run for U.S. President.

Shuffle Along's acclaimed dancing also had a tremendous impact on Broadway. Ziegfeld, George White, and other producers soon hired *Shuffle Along*'s dancers and choreographers to teach their white stars and chorus dancers how to move like that. Furthermore, in addition to the show's authors, *Shuffle Along*'s large cast introduced many talented and dynamic Black performers who would become major show business stars, including Adelaide Hall, Florence Mills, Paul Robeson, and Josephine Baker.

"Full of Pep and Syncopation"—Black Broadway in the 1920s (B, W)

Perhaps most importantly, *Shuffle Along*'s immense financial success demonstrated that both white and Black audiences were eager to see talented African American performers onstage in Black-authored shows and would pay top ticket prices to see them. During its nearly fourteen-month, 504-performance run, *Shuffle Along* grossed an estimated $1.5 million, equivalent to over $26 million today.[18] As a result of this achievement, and as the lyrics to the show's title song had recommended, Broadway did indeed "just keep shufflin' along." Over the following decade, at least two dozen musicals written by and starring Black theater artists would open on Broadway. As author Caseen Gaines has noted, "There were more Black folks working on Broadway in 1924 than there are today."[19]

In stark contrast to *Shuffle Along*'s struggle to find financing, white Broadway producers were now eager to open their checkbooks and partner with Black theater artists. For example, the second Black musical of the decade, **Strut Miss Lizzie**, was produced by the Minsky Brothers, otherwise most famous for introducing the striptease to burlesque shows. Billed as "the all Creole revue," *Lizzie* opened in the spring of 1922, just as *Shuffle Along* entered the second year of its run. The show had book and lyrics by **Henry Creamer** (who also staged the show) and music by **J. Turner Lsyton**, a highly successful Black songwriting and vaudeville team who had created the early jazz/blues hit "After You've Gone," and had regularly been contributing songs to the *Ziegfeld Follies* since 1917. Borrowing a page from Sissle and Blake, late in the second act of *Lizzie*, Creamer and Layton also took to the stage to perform "a selection of their hit songs, old and new."[20] It seems the Minskys brought their signature sensibility to *Lizzie* since, according to the *New York Age*, the show featured "gorgeous and attractive costumes" that left "little to the imagination" and were "about the most daring display of female pulchritude, unadorned, that New York audiences have looked on in many a day."[21] However, despite that provocative display combined with dance numbers that critics called "not only fast and furious but uncommonly good,"[22] *Strut Miss Lizzie* lasted only eighty performances.

Meanwhile, jazz music and Black dance styles quickly spread to white Broadway shows. That same month, a "glittering, spectacular" and "resplendent" sixteenth edition of the *Ziegfeld Follies* opened including not only a finale ("Come Along") written by Creamer and Layton, but also Gilda Gray, "the Queen of the Shimmy," leading a chorus of women in a satirical musical number titled "It's Getting Dark on Old Broadway"[23] which wryly commented on the "invasion" of Black shows and performers onto Broadway, not only in mainstem musicals but also in Times Square area cabaret and nightclub revues, which had started booking Black talent in the wake of *Shuffle Along*. As described by critic Gilbert Seldes, at the climax of this number, the stage lights faded, "and radiolight [luminescent paint] picked out the white dresses of the [white] chorus," members causing their hands and faces to "recede into undistinguishable black."[24] (In more recent theatrical terminology, this would be called a "blacklight effect.")

Several shows in this string of Black musicals were, in essence, sequels to *Shuffle Along*, with stories set in the same fictional location, Jimtown, SC. But, interestingly, **Liza**, the first of these to appear, was created by an entirely different team of theater artists, although the book was written by Flournoy Miller's brother, Irvin C. Miller (who also played a leading role), and another Miller brother played a character role, so perhaps it was all in the family. The music and lyrics were by Maceo Pinkard (who later would write the jazz classics "Sweet Georgia Brown" and "Them There Eyes"). *Liza* played the same theater that *Shuffle Along* had put on the map, and critics and audiences received it enthusiastically, with the *New York Age* declaring that "there isn't a dull moment. Verve, vivacity, pep, jazz—all these and others, if I knew them, could be aptly used in describing the efforts of those who make up the *Liza* company." All of which helped *Liza* to run a healthy 172 performances.[25]

Almost exactly a year later, Miller and Lyles (fresh from an acrimonious and litigious falling out with Sissle and Blake)[26] returned to Jimtown and reprised their roles as conmen Sam Peck and Steve Jenkins in the book they wrote for 1923's **Runnin' Wild**. With a score by **Cecil Mack** (lyrics) and **James P. Johnson**, this show was produced by Ziegfeld rival George White, and although its run of 228 performances equaled only half the performance total of *Shuffle Along*, it was still an outstanding run for the period, coming the closest of all the Black shows to replicating *Shuffle Along*'s success. Critic Burns Mantle actually found *Runnin' Wild* to be a "much better entertainment" with "more speed and greater control" than *Shuffle Along* and with a book that was "more wisely edited."

Broadway Dance #4: "The Charleston" (B, W)

The most notable and enduring legacy of *Runnin' Wild* is that this show popularized the 1920s off-beat dance craze, "The Charleston," and introduced the infectious Mack and Johnson song of the same name—a tune that still defines the decade. This first-act finale number was staged by Lyda Webb, who had been one of *Shuffle Along*'s trendsetting chorus girls. With this show, she now became the second Black woman to choreograph a Broadway musical (or at least the second to receive credit for doing so). Almost immediately, the Charleston was copied, replicated, and performed in nearly every 1920s Broadway musical that followed. In fact, in his review of the 1925 operetta *The Vagabond King*, which is set in the fifteenth century, one critic remarked:

> I could scarcely believe I was attending a musical show when I realized that nobody had done the "Charleston." Producers of musical shows have a most uncanny way of working in a "Charleston" number somewhere no matter how inappropriate its inclusion may be.[27]

Once again, a vernacular Black social dance that had evolved from African roots became the center of mainstream Broadway theatrical dance, which then helped to propel it to the center of mainstream international social dancing.

The Charleston is a wild, exuberant, uninhibited dance that perfectly reflected the embrace by urban young people, especially women, of the new social and sexual freedom of the era, as well as their response to the conservative ideology that had imposed Prohibition on America. "Most nice girls were forced by their mothers to wear foundation garments, but the flappers hated them" because they made it difficult to execute this wild new dance and its spin-offs with abandon. Therefore (as echoed in the song "All That Jazz" from *Chicago*), "as soon as girls arrived at parties they rushed into the ladies room and 'parked their girdles.'"[28] Although it may look harmless and cute to us today, at the time, the dance was correctly viewed as being sexually provocative and was considered by those same conservative forces to be "immoral, unspeakable and unworthy."[29] Clergymen called for the appointment of "a national dance censor" who would forbid the dance,[30] and several cities and towns across America "barred the dance from public halls by passing ordinances" against it.[31] Police in Oakland, California, raided a dance at an organization called the Sons and Daughters of Washington, whose members included some of "the city's leading citizens," after "clubwomen reported alleged improper entertainment at the hall." Upon entering, the police found "high school boys and girls . . . dancing the newest dance steps . . . in a way they shouldn't." The young couples had been told by the manager of the club to "stop dancing the Charleston, but they continued."[32] There was a heavy undercurrent of racism in all of these objections to this "negro dance," which was said to "have been poisoned and degraded by immoral influences."[33]

In perhaps its biggest disruption of popular culture, the Charleston introduced elements of breakaway solo improvisation into social dancing, with couples separating at times to, as we would say in the 1960s, "do their own thing." Over the course of the twentieth century, this would expand into a near-total dominance of individual expression on the dance floor, with partnered ballroom dancing reduced to a quaint nostalgic relic of the past.

Despite all objections, the Charleston craze swept ballrooms, dance halls, nightclubs, and living rooms across America and around the world, and Charleston contests became immensely popular, attracting "huge audiences" that "fairly boil over with enthusiasm as the contestants for prizes contort and twist from the waist down."[34] Unfortunately, as might be expected, some white artists tried to take credit for this Black creation.

In a 1926 letter to the editor of the *New York Times*, songwriter Will Marion Cook (a veteran of the first wave of Black musicals) "took exception" to an article from the previous week that had given credit to producer George White for "introducing and popularizing the Charleston" as well as for "originating" the Black Bottom—a sort of Charleston spin-off that was a highpoint of that year's *George White's Scandals*.[35] "I have the greatest respect for Mr. White as an organizer and producer of revues, but why do an injustice to the Black folk of America by taking from them the credit of creating new and characteristic dances?" Cook reasonably asked. And then he set the record straight:

> From "Old Jim Crow" to "Black Bottom," the negro dances came from the Cotton Belt, the levee, the Mississippi River and are African in inspiration. The American Negro, in search of emotional expression, recreated and broadened these dances. Either in their crude state or revised form, in St. Louis, Chicago, or New York, the dance is discovered (?) [sic] by white theatrical producers and sold to the public as an original creation. The Charleston has been done in the South, especially in the little islands lying off of Charleston, SC, for more than forty years, to my knowledge. The dance reached New York five years ago. In Harlem any evening a group of negro children could be seen "Doin' the Charleston" and collecting pennies . . . It is doubtful if Mr. White even saw a "Charleston" until he attended the final rehearsals of *Runnin' Wild*. Similarly, for many years, the "Black Bottom" has been evolving in the South . . .[36]

Cook then went on to note that two years earlier, Josephine Baker had "thrilled all Paris" with her rendition of the Black Bottom.[37] What Cook also likely knew but didn't say is that dancing stars Ann Pennington and Tom Patricola, who had introduced the DeSylva, Brown and Henderson song "The Black Bottom" in the *Scandals of 1926*, had been coached, and likely choreographed, by uncredited Black choreographer Buddy Bradley.

In an exciting and ongoing exchange between the vernacular social dances that came from the streets and dance clubs of Harlem and the theatricalized versions of them as adapted by professional choreographers, both Black and white, for Broadway musicals and nightclub revues, over the following decade many other spin-offs and variations of the Charleston, such as "The Varsity Drag,"[38] followed in quick succession. Then, during the 1930s, the Charleston and its variations evolved and were incorporated into the Big Apple, the Lindy Hop, the jitterbug, and other varieties of swing dancing, all of which remain vital and active elements in the vocabulary of Broadway dance today.

Finally, in the fall of 1924, after a long tryout tour, Sissle and Blake brought their follow-up to *Shuffle Along* to Broadway: ***The Chocolate Dandies***. This musical comedy had a book co-authored by Sissle and comedian **Lew Payton**, who was also the show's star. As Caseen Gaines tells us, in terms of budget and spectacle, this show "was as far from *Shuffle Along* as one could get. The production cost approximately $100,000 to stage and featured a cast of over one hundred people . . . and three live horses." Payton played a racehorse owner who falls asleep and dreams that his horse wins so much prize money that he becomes "the most respected and powerful person in town."[39] The show included "quite a startling scene" during which the horses were "shown on a revolving platform as if they were in a race, the jockeys urging their steeds as if they were nearing the winning post."[40] And although critic Stark Young, writing for the *New York Times*, hailed *The Chocolate Dandies* as "a thoroughly amusing show, equipped with plenty of good comedy and catchy songs" and "undoubtedly one of the best Negro musicals shows that has been seen in New York," most of the other reviews were much more mixed.

It was around this time that a confining and disturbing strain of criticism began to emerge. Black musicals now began to be reproached for being too polished and professional and not rowdy and wild enough. "For all of its costly costumes and scenery . . . there is too much so-called politeness, too much platitudinous refinement, and not enough of the razor-edged. There is, in a word, too much art and not enough Africa."[41] Even Eubie Blake's music was criticized for sounding too much like his idol Victor Herbert's. As Caseen Gaines observed:

> When a show was offered with all of the Broadway trimmings, it was dismissed out of hand for not being sufficiently Black enough, or worse yet, many critics rhetorically asked why the public should spend top dollar to see Black performers do the same thing whites could.[42]

This would not be the last time white critics would suggest that Black artists should stay in their lane. Burdened by its enormous running costs and an unrelenting, ticket-sales-killing heatwave, *The Chocolate Dandies* closed three months later after a disappointing run of only ninety-four performances.

"Sweet And Hot!"—Time Travel Destination #1: September 1925 (♩, ♪, ♫)

In September of 1924, a twelve-month period began in which six smash hit musicals— *Rose-Marie, Lady, Be Good!, The Student Prince, The Garrick Gaieties, No, No, Nannette,* and *The Vagabond King*—all premiered on Broadway, and the two distinct strains of the musical challenged each other for dominance: Romantic Melody vs Sexy Jazz; the Waltz vs the Charleston; the Operetta vs the Musical Comedy and the Revue. And in the process, both styles were vividly and definitively established and solidified. Most musical theater fans have time-travel fantasies, and one of mine is to be able to journey back to the final month of that period—September of 1925—and experience all six of these shows back-to-back!

With music by Rudolf Friml and Herbert Stothart and book and lyrics by Otto Harbach and Oscar Hammerstein II, **Rose-Marie** opened on September 2, 1924, ran for 557 performances, and revitalized the American style of operetta that had been pioneered by Victor Herbert. The story is set in the wild Rocky Mountains of Saskatchewan, populated by hunters, trappers, miners, indigenous people, and a stouthearted chorus of Canadian Mounties. The central characters are Jim Kenyon, a hard-drinking, wild, and wooly miner who has been reformed by his love for the French-Canadian girl, Rose Marie La Flamme. In coming decades, the show's massively popular hit song "Indian Love Call," with its melismatic "When I'm Calling You-oo-oo-oo-oo-oo-oo" refrain, will be ridiculed, parodied, and spoofed endlessly—but there was certainly nothing sappy or campy about it at the time. No, that song was considered the pinnacle of drama and romance and had an effect on its audience much like *The Phantom of The Opera*'s "The Music of The Night" has had on contemporary audiences.

The polar opposite of *Rose-Marie* was **Lady, Be Good!**, which opened two months later. This was the first of fourteen Broadway musicals created by the team of songwriting brothers **George Gershwin** and **Ira Gershwin**, and it established them as an unparalleled team. This show also turned the brother–sister team of **Fred Astaire** and **Adele Astaire** into major Broadway stars. George and Ira's parents were Russian Jewish immigrants, and the brothers grew up on New York's Lower East Side, near the Yiddish Theater district, which greatly influenced them both. Fred and Adele's parents were Austrian-Prussian-(Jewish)[43] immigrants, and the duo had been a headlining Vaudeville act since they were children.

In *Lady Be Good*, the Astaires played penniless orphans Dick and Suzie Trevor. Dick is in love with Shirley, a middle-class girl whom he can't afford to marry, but he is being hotly pursued by Josephine Vanderwater, an amorous wealthy socialite, who (we find out) has arranged for the Trevors to be evicted from their apartment so that Dick will feel that the only financially responsible thing to do is marry her. With the help of various wacky schemes and outlandish disguises, Suzie manages to save her brother from this undesirable fate, and both siblings end up marrying their true loves.

There was a tremendous amount of interest in *Lady Be Good* even before it opened because earlier that year, twenty-six-year-old George Gershwin had premiered his "jazz concerto," *Rhapsody In Blue*, at Carnegie Hall and become an overnight celebrity. Gershwin's songs epitomize the melding of cultural influences, especially the affinity between Black and Jewish music that created the musical language of the Broadway showtune. *Lady Be Good*'s jazz-infused score included the title song, "Little Jazz Bird," "I'd Rather Charleston," and the "Half of It Dearie, Blues," inspired by Bert Savoy's famous catchphrase. However, the show's biggest hit was "Fascinating Rhythm," which captivated audiences with its arrestingly modern sound that perfectly echoed the jagged tempo and unrelenting activity of New York City during the Jazz Age. This "happy combination of clowning song and dance that is never permitted to lag or become stupid" would go on to run for 330 performances.[44]

The very next night, it was back to operettaland with **The Student Prince**. Set in 1860, this show told the bitter-sweet romantic tale of a German prince, Karl-Franz, who, while studying at the university in Heidelberg, falls in love with Kathie, a waitress who works in the beer garden where he and his fellow students gather, drink, and sing after class. With book and lyrics by Dorothy Donnelly (see Box below) and music by Sigmund Romburg,[45] With its triumphant run of 608 performances, *The Student Prince* became the longest-running show of the 1920s as well as an international sensation.

> ### *Golden Days* — Dorothy Donnelly (l, W)
>
> Actress, playwright, librettist, producer, and director **Dorothy Donnelly** was born in New York in 1880 into a theatrical family. Her father was an Irish Catholic immigrant who had established a successful career as an actor and singer before becoming the manager of the Grand Opera House. For about a dozen years, just after the turn of the century, Dorothy was an acclaimed leading Broadway actress before she turned her attention to playwriting. She created the book and lyrics for eight Broadway musicals and operettas, including several blockbuster hits. Her first was ***Blossom Time*** (1921), an operetta based on the life and music of composer Franz Shubert, which opened the same season as *Shuffle Along* and ran just as long! (Again, we have the two forms — musical comedy and operetta — on Broadway side by side.) Over the following two decades, there would be endless road companies of *Blossom Time*, as well as six (!) Broadway revivals. In 1924, Donnelly wrote (book and lyrics) and directed the musical ***Poppy***, in which she created a career-defining role for comedian W. C. Fields. His signature persona — a bogusly elegant conman — was first established in Donnelly's script, and ongoing variations of that character made Fields one of the biggest stars on Broadway in the 1920s and in Hollywood in the 1930s. Next, it was her turn to collaborate with composer Sigmund Romburg when she created the book and lyrics for ***The Student Prince***. This massively popular operetta would also tour for years, be revived on Broadway in 1931 and 1943, and continue to be produced by major theaters worldwide into the 1990s.

The Garrick Gaieties, which opened later that spring, was an irreverent revue that spoofed the plays, stars, and theatrical scene of the day.[46] It was intended only to be a two-performance fundraiser put on by young members of the Theatre Guild (sort of like "the interns are putting on a show"). However, the audience response was so enthusiastic that the run kept being extended and ended up at more than 200 performances, which was significantly longer than nearly any edition of the *Ziegfeld Follies*. Central to the success of this revue were the delightfully smart, witty, and tuneful songs by twenty-three-year-old composer Richard Rodgers and thirty-year-old lyricist Lorenz Hart.[47] One song in particular became an instant smash — "(I'll Take) Manhattan" — and the team of **Rodgers and Hart** became the toast of the town. As Rodgers later remembered it, after six years of struggle and frustration, "Literally overnight, I was lifted from despair."

Rodgers and Hart take Manhattan (the Bronx and Staten Island, too) (I, J, Q)

The Garrick Gaieties was the first of Rodgers and Hart's thirty-one Broadway musicals—all of which debuted during the Silver Age. Their shows were witty, tuneful, and often quite innovative and experimental in their form and subject matter. Out of them came some of the smartest, funniest, most delightful, and most heartbreaking showtunes of all time, dozens of which have become timeless standards.

Richard Rodgers is arguably the most significant composer in the history of the Broadway musical. He was born in New York in 1902 into a prosperous German Jewish family—his father was a doctor. His parents loved music and theater, and as a child, Rodgers was given piano lessons and taken to many musical shows and operas. During his teens, he would spend nearly every Saturday at the matinee of a musical, and "if it were by Jerome Kern, he would see it over and over again."[48] He attended Columbia University, where he became the first freshman to compose the full score for the annual Varsity Show and where he met both Larry Hart and Oscar Hammerstein II. With these two partners (and a few others), over a career that stretched from 1919 to 1979, Rodgers composed the scores of forty-three Broadway musicals and more than 900 songs, many of which are the most performed, recorded, and beloved of all time.

Lorenz (Larry) Hart was born in New York in 1895, the son of German Jewish immigrants. His father's friends included the great Weber and Fields star Lillian Russell, and Larry grew up entranced by the world of show business. He saw every show he could, and he was especially enthralled by Jerome Kern's series of Princess Theatre musicals. In 1914, he entered Columbia University, where, amazingly, among his classmates were two other soon-to-be top Broadway lyricists: Howard Dietz (who would become half the team of Dietz and Schwartz) and Oscar Hammerstein II. Neither Hart nor Hammerstein could have imagined how their future lives would be intertwined. During his early twenties, Hart, who was fluent in German, got a job with the Shubert Bros translating German plays into English,[49] but his true ambition was to become a lyricist, and he actively set out to find a composer to partner with him.

By 1919, seventeen-year-old Richard Rodgers was attending Columbia, and was introduced to Hart by a mutual friend. Rodgers would later recall his first impressions of Hart:

> The total man couldn't have been more than 5 feet tall. He wore frayed carpet slippers, a pair of Tuxedo trousers, an undershirt, and a non-descript jacket. His hair was unbrushed and he obviously hadn't had a shave for a couple of days. All he needed was a tin cup and some pencils . . . He had a handsome face, but it was set in a head that was too large for his body and it gave him a slightly gnomelike appearance.[50]

The two young men hit it off immediately. As Rodgers recalled, "I was enchanted by this little man and his ideas," especially by the older Hart's strong opinions about what Broadway musicals should and could be. "He was violent on the subject of rhyming in songs, feeling that the public was capable of understanding better things than the current monosyllabic juxtaposition of 'slush' and 'mush.'"[51] And Hart instantly responded to Rodgers's music. As Rodgers put it: "That day I left Hart's house having acquired in a single afternoon a career, a partner, a best friend, and a source of permanent irritation."[52]

That irritation came from a number of issues that resulted in a vicious cycle. First of all, Hart hated the way he looked—he was barely five feet tall, and his head was out of proportion to his body. He couldn't stand to look at himself in a mirror. Secondly, he was homosexual. However, unlike many of his Queer contemporaries in the Broadway theater, Hart's particular German Jewish family values caused him to feel tremendously ashamed. He was mortified that he was attracted to men and devastated that he was too ugly (or at least believed he was too ugly) for any of those men to be attracted to him. His solution was to try to drown this circle of shame with booze and possibly drugs, and he would sometimes go off on benders and disappear for days at a time. To make matters worse, as author Gerald Mast suggests, Hart's "deepest, unrequited love" may have been for his partner Richard Rodgers. Understandably, Hart seems to have been most comfortable with his homosexuality during the 1920s, when society was looser and more accepting of all kinds of diversity, and when Rodgers and Hart were first becoming the toast of Broadway. Like Porter, Hart's lyrics often include not-so-hidden Gay innuendos. Even that very first hit song, "Manhattan," contains this reference to the already well-known Gay mecca, Greenwich Village.

> We'll go to Greenwich,
> Where modern men itch
> to be free . . .

As we will see, Hart's struggle with his sexuality became even more of an issue as he moved into the more repressive 1930s.

"I Want To Be Happy"—Vincent Youmans and *No, No, Nanette* (♪, ♩, ♫)

Although *No, No, Nanette* was officially part of the 1925–6 season, that is a bit of a technicality because, by the time this blockbuster musical finally opened on Broadway, it had already been playing for more than a year in Chicago, where what was supposed to have been a pre-Broadway tryout proved so successful that the show just kept running. In addition, two road companies were already touring America, and a hit West End production had been entrancing London audiences for more than six months. As the *Daily News* wryly noted:

> Boston saw it. Philadelphia saw it. Chicago saw it. London saw it, and Guatemala, Medicine Hat, and the Canary Islands have probably seen it as well. But it wasn't until last night that New York saw it and Broadway gave it a hearty approval ... Having heard "Tea For Two" and "I Want To Be Happy" for the 1,876,934th time last night, but this time played officially, we are still firm in our belief that Vincent Youmans is about the best musical comedy composer in town.[53]

This mildly sexy farce was lyricist **Irving Caesar**'s biggest hit. Born Isidor Keiser in NYC in 1895, the son of Romanian Jewish immigrants, Caesar would go on to create lyrics (and sometimes the music and/or the book) for thirty-seven Broadway shows. The show's book was by Otto Harbach and Frank Mandell, and its tuneful hit-filled score was by **Vincent Youmans**.

Although Youmans is not as well known today as many of his colleagues, he was one of Broadway's most famous composers during the Silver Age. Cole Porter even paid tribute to him in "You're The Top'" from *Anything Goes* with the lyric "some gifted humans like Vincent Youmans." Much like Porter, Youmans is an anomaly in the Broadway songwriting world since he, too, was born into a wealthy WASP family and attended Yale. Also, like Porter, several researchers assert that Youmans was Gay or Bisexual. However, if this is true, he left behind very little evidence. He rarely worked with any of his lyricists or bookwriting collaborators more than once and had a reputation for being cold and distant, but I wonder if he was just deeply in the closet and very reticent and afraid of getting too close or revealing too much of his personal life to his colleagues. Tuberculosis and alcoholism forced him to retire from songwriting when he was only thirty-six. Even so, during his short career, he composed the scores for twelve Broadway musicals and one classic movie musical that together introduced many timeless hits, including "I Want To Be Happy," "More Than You Know," "Time On My Hands," "Hallelujah," and one of the most performed and recorded songs of all time: "Tea For Two." This song, beloved by both soft-shoe dancers and jazz musicians, received new chart topping hit recordings in every decade from the 1920s through the 1960s, when it was reinvented as a cha-cha. Then, in 1974 (as detailed in Chapter 11), an unexpected smash hit Broadway revival of *No, No, Nanette*, where the song had originated, propelled "Tea For Two'" back into the cultural zeitgeist and played a central role in engendering the "Nostalgia Craze" of the 1970s and 80s.

Just five days after *No, No, Nanette*'s opening night, ***The Vagabond King***—a "highly colored, richly esthetic, and mellifluously melodic operetta containing a panorama of costumes of such gorgeous plumage as to bankrupt most Broadway producers for the rest of their natural lives"—opened to rapturous notices including from critic Burns Mantle who told his readers, "surely this Nebuchadnezzarian orgy of singing and costumes deserves our young city's patronage."[54] It was an adaptation of a widely read novel, *If I Were King*, by Justin Huntley McCarthy, which back in 1901 the author had adapted into a hit play of the same name that by 1916 had already been revived on Broadway five times. This "picturesque, moving, and poetic operetta"[55] version had a score that was "splendidly suited to the text,"[56] provided "in his own best tradition"[57] by composer Rudolf **Friml**, in collaboration with lyricists Brian Hooker and William H. Post. Set in fifteenth-century Paris, the show's title character was "the most attractive of history's rogues, the most smooth-tongued of scoundrels,"[58] the real-life French poet Francois Villon, played by Dennis King, the star of *Rose-Marie*,[59] who was "as elegantly picaresque and tuneful a person as Villon could have desired to be in a 1925 representation."[60] Although, as was the case with nearly every operetta, the humor of the piece was "quite anesthetic,"[61] audiences who reveled in "beautiful music, real voices, and a perfectly staged production"[62] had something to look forward to in *The Vagabond King* which "had about everything entertainment should have,"[63] including a thrilling and unforgettable climax. As described by critic Arthur Pollock, "François Villon's ragged army of villains came sweeping onto the stage last night chanting Villon's 'Song of the Vagabonds,' as they waved aloft their weapons of staves, sickles, clubs, and spears bringing down the third act curtain with as stirring a finale as there has been heard in years."[64] *The Vagabond King* was played in four acts, and this stirring third-act finale in which the beggars, thieves, and rabble of Paris rise up and march off to take back their city was an event that not been in either the novel or the play and "was purely the invention of the makers of the musical version."[65] It certainly was not the last time a scene of this type would be presented in a Broadway musical.

Flagrant Disguise — Queer Artists of the 1920s (I, J, Q)

While the theater world had long served as a haven for Gay and Lesbian artists, the newfound sexual liberation of the 1920s caused an explosion of Queer culture around the world, in London, Berlin, Paris and especially in New York, where a host of gifted young gay artists began to establish themselves as vital forces on Broadway. However, even during this period of relative acceptance and visibility, some Gay artists struggled with their sexuality while others reveled in it.

The Master Magician of Broadway — Hassard Short

Throughout a career spanning thirty years and fifty Broadway shows, director and designer **Hassard Short** was constantly in demand as one of the most acclaimed "stagers" of both musical comedies and revues. He was called a "genius of stagecraft"[66] and hailed as "the master magician of Broadway."[67] Among the theatrical innovations that Short introduced was the "traveling platform,"[68] and he revolutionized Broadway lighting design by eliminating traditional footlights and replacing them with spotlights mounted on the "balcony rail"—which is still standard practice today.

Hassard Short was born in Lincolnshire, England, and ran away from home at fifteen to pursue a life in the theater. His first stage appearance in London was in 1895. By 1901, he had become successful enough that producer Charles Frohman (see page 58) brought him to New York, where he achieved great success as an actor portraying what he called "silly-ass Englishmen." Apparently, he did this so effectively that these kinds of roles became known as "Hassard Short" parts.[69] Meanwhile, Short began staging special fundraising performances, and it was one of these, an all-star event in support of the Actor's Equity Union strike of 1919, that very quickly led to his first directing job on Broadway: "a play with music" called *Honeydew* (1920), which ran an impressive 249 performances. As a result, Short soon became a key collaborator with Broadway's top talents.

During the 1920s, Short staged three editions of Irving Berlin's *Music Box Revue* (1921, 1922, and 1923); the Kern–Harbach–Hammerstein smash-hit *Sunny* (1925), starring Marilyn Miller; the *Greenwich Village Follies of 1925*; and a show titled *Hassard Short's Ritz Revue*, among many others. His work was regularly singled out by critics as being a significant factor in the success of these shows:

> Given a song, be it ever so simple, Hassard Short does something more than simply stage it. He dramatizes it. Long after you think it is over, new golden curtains open to reveal new stage depths, new stairs, and new figures in towering costumes. Mr. Short is more or less of a pioneer of this particular field. Last night he produced at least four or five striking effects in this way . . .[70]

In *The Gay and Lesbian Theatrical Legacy*, writer Kevin Winkler tells us:

> From the beginning of his career, Short established complete directorial control over his productions and was known for his time-efficient approach to rehearsals. As a "staging director," he mounted the production numbers and "routined" the show, deciding the placement of all scenes, sketches, songs, and production numbers. His multi-faceted contributions were reflected in his billing, which was usually a variation on "Staged and Lighted by Hassard Short" but it was often much grander. For Franz Léhar's *Frederika* (1937) his billing stretched to "Entire production including settings, costumes, and lighting executed under the personal supervision of Mr. Short."[71]

Short was especially acclaimed for his staging of four spectacular revues of the early 1930s. The first two had scores by the songwriting team of Dietz and Schwartz: *Three's A Crowd* (1930), which featured what critics acclaimed as a breathtaking staging of the song "Body and Soul"; and *The Band Wagon* (1931) starring Fred and Adele Astaire, in which Short employed what was reportedly the first revolving stage[72] to outstanding effect. These were followed by two shows by Irving Berlin: *Face The Music* (1932) and *As Thousands Cheer* (1933), which included what critics called "masterpieces of lighting and color control," especially in regard to his staging of the second show's first act finale, "Easter Parade." Short's productions were as lavish and spectacular as any *Ziegfeld Follies* but were designed and executed with such impeccable taste and attention to detail that they "made Ziegfeld's extravaganzas seem old fashioned and garish by comparison."[73]

Short often traveled to Europe with his close collaborators Moss Hart and Irving Berlin (accompanied by Berlin's family) in search of inspiration and new ideas for their productions. Like all major celebrities of the period, their comings and goings were avidly covered by the press in the theater news and gossip columns of the day. But what the reporters declined to mention (even though they most certainly were aware) was that Short was always accompanied by his life partner, William "Billy" Ladd, a slender, bleached-blond former chorus boy who performed in three musicals directed by Short. Regarding their relationship, Mrs. Irving Berlin would later remark, "I disapproved, but as time went by, I couldn't help noticing that theirs was the happiest marriage of the group. Mine excepted, of course."[74] Hassard Short was likely the model for "Julian Marsh," the openly gay, British Broadway director character in Bradford Ropes' 1932 novel *42nd Street*, from which the 1933 film musical and the 1980 stage musical were adapted. And it is clear that Ropes used Billy Ladd as the inspiration for "Billy Lawlor," the character in the novel who is Marsh's bleached blond boyfriend. The homosexuality and relationship of these two characters is made abundantly clear in the novel but was reduced to only a slight subtext for Marsh in the film, and then both characters were reconceived as decidedly heterosexual for the stage version. Julian Marsh's first name, however, is undoubtedly an echo of **Julian Mitchell**, the straight WASP director who was Short's Broadway contemporary and rival. Ropes' biographer, Maya Cantu, suggests that yet another inspiration for Marsh was another early staging genius, showman John Murray Anderson.

The King of Revues—John Murray Anderson[75]

In his 1954 autobiography *Out Without My Rubbers*, director, lyricist, bookwriter, designer, and producer **John Murray Anderson** described himself as a "friendly rival" of Hassard Short,[76] and indeed, both made their Broadway staging debuts less than a year apart. Between 1919 and 1954, Anderson staged thirty-one Broadway revues and musical comedies. He was born in Newfoundland, Canada, in 1886 into an upper-middle-class Scottish–English family. As a child, Anderson was sent to boarding school in Scotland, where he fell in love with all manner of theater, from Shakespeare to Music Hall. After attending college in Switzerland, he returned to the UK to study theater, singing, and dance in London at Beerbohm Tree's Academy of Arts. After moving to New York, Anderson got his initial start in show business as a male "taxi dancer" at the fashionable cabaret Bustonoby's during the ballroom dance craze of the 1910s.[77] That launched him into teaching ballroom dance, and he soon became "one of New York society's favorite dancing masters."[78] Then, after teaming up with dancing partner Genevieve Lyon, she and Anderson set out to become "a leading society dance team [and] compete with the Castles—Irene and Vernon." But, as Anderson acknowledged, "We never quite did, but probably ran them a close second."[79] In 1914, at the height of their success, like many vaudeville and ballroom dance duos, Anderson and Lyon got married. Their career and marriage would be tragically cut short, however, when Genevieve contracted tuberculosis and died just two years later. Anderson lovingly took care of his wife to the end, but judging from his memoir, their marriage seems to have been a very affectionate professional relationship rather than a love match.

By 1918, Anderson was performing at the fashionable Palais Royal cabaret/nightclub on Broadway at 48th Street with a new dancing partner, and it was there that Anderson first began to stage productions that, as he wrote in 1952, "were really the forerunners to the elaborate nightclub shows of today."[80] This led to him being hired to produce, direct, and co-write the book and many of the lyrics for *The Greenwich Village Follies of 1919*. This was the first of this popular revue series, which under his supervision "prospered for six consecutive years and ... graduated from ... the tiny Greenwich Village Theatre in Sheridan Square to the Nora Bayes (Theatre), then to the Shubert Theatre, and finally the Winter Garden"[81] (one of Broadway's largest venues at the time). The following season, Anderson repeated all of those roles on the acclaimed revue *What's In a Name?*, where his work drew the praise of *New York Times* theater critic Alexander Woolcott:

> The ascendant star of John Murray Anderson shines exceedingly bright after the production last night of the successor to his *Greenwich Village Follies* ... It is full of a striving for new things, marked in every episode with a determination not to imitate but rather to differ from the preceding twenty-five musical shows of the season. It is often surpassingly lovely to look upon. A stagecraft of considerable cunning, good taste, and real imagination rules over its preparation. Indeed, *What's In A Name?* marks the most beautiful staging of a musical comedy New York has ever known.[82]

Similar acclaim would follow Anderson throughout his long career. His next show was the 1920 edition of the *Greenwich Village Follies* starring Bert Savoy (see page 60). After three more editions of this revue, Anderson and Hassard Short traded places—Short staged *The Greenwich Village Follies of 1925*, while Anderson staged the fourth and final edition of Irving Berlin's *Music Box Revue*, which had all previously been staged by Short.

Among the musical comedies that Anderson staged and directed were Rodgers and Hart's *Dearest Enemy*, which had a book by Herbert Fields, and Anderson would collaborate with Fields again the following season on *Hello, Daddy*, which featured a score by Dorothy Fields and Jimmy McHugh and choreography by Busby Berkley. By this point, like Hassard Short, Anderson was receiving billing such as "Entire Production Under the Supervision of John Murray Anderson." Revues and extravaganzas were his forte, however, and he memorably staged three late editions of *The Ziegfeld Follies*[83] as well as the massive Hippodrome Theater production of Rodger and Hart's musical, *Jumbo*. In addition to his work on Broadway, Anderson staged seven seasons of the *Ringling Bros. and Barnum and Bailey Circus*, four of Billy Rose's (World's Fair) Aquacades, and "twenty-four elaborate nightclub shows"[84] primarily at Billy Rose's Diamond Horseshoe and Casa Manana nightclubs. He also conceived and directed the 1930 movie musical *King of Jazz* as well as the spectacular aquacade sequences in the 1944 Esther Williams film *Bathing Beauty*.

Anderson's memoir was written in the repressive 1950s, so it's not surprising that he makes no direct reference to his sexual orientation. Beyond his brief early marriage, he never mentions any kind of romantic relationships with either sex. However, throughout his life he was at the center of a close circle of Queer colleagues and friends that included the prolific Broadway set and costume designer Raul Pen DuBois[85]; producers Saint-Subber, Leonard Sillman, and Harry Rigby; songwriters Robert Wright and George Forrest; and choreographers Donald Saddler and Robert Alton, who was Anderson's "protégé."[86]

Remarkably, during the final two years of his life (although no one, including himself, knew this was the case), he staged two triumphant Broadway revues that were among the last of their kind: *Leonard Sillman's New Faces of 1952* (which made stars of Eartha Kitt, Paul Lynde, and Alice Ghostly), and *John Murray Anderson's Almanac* (1953), which starred Hermione Gingold and Harry Belafonte, who received a Tony Award as "Best Featured Actor in a Musical." The *Daily Mirror* described Anderson's final production as "A glittering, tuneful dazzling, and stunningly beautiful show . . . the laughter lusty and the applause deafening."[87] Anderson died of a heart attack at age sixty-seven while his *Almanac* was still running on Broadway.

Hassard Short, Julian Mitchell, and John Murray Anderson were among the first artists to reveal the tremendous impact that dynamic *musical staging* can have on a Broadway musical and to demonstrate how staging and choreography can often be of equal importance to the text and music. They forged a path that a long line of remarkable (and predominantly Gay) directors and choreographers have followed right up to today.

"A Talent to Amuse"—Noel Coward

Noel Coward was one of the most remarkable figures of the twentieth century. He was born in 1899 into a lower-middle-class family in Teddington, a suburb of London, where his father was a rather unsuccessful traveling piano salesman. Young Noel attended only a few years of elementary school before dropping out to become a child actor, but by the time he had turned twenty-five, he was acclaimed in both London and New York as the personification of style, wit, and sophistication.

Coward's first show on Broadway was *Andre Charlot's Revue of 1924* (that amazingly rich theatrical year!). The French impresario, Andre Charlot, was called "London's Ziegfeld," and in 1924 he brought one of his acclaimed shows to New York. "Far more literate than any American revue,"[88] this show marked the Broadway debut of a trio of great British stars—Gertrude Lawrence, Jack Buchanan, and Beatrice Lillie—and included songs by Eubie Blake and Noble Sissle, as well as by another Gay British songwriter and performer, Ivor Novello. Coward contributed only two songs to the revue, but one of them, "Parisian Pierrot," became an enduring hit and made a Broadway star of Gertrude Lawrence. Amazingly, during the following year, Coward would open four more productions on Broadway, including the plays *The Vortex*, *Hay Fever*, and *Easy*

Virtue, along with a second Charlot revue,[89] and for several months, three of those shows were running simultaneously. This quickly and firmly established Coward as one of the defining voices of the 1920s.

During his forty-year career, Coward would go on to achieve significant fame and success as a playwright, composer, lyricist, actor, singer, director, novelist, painter, and filmmaker—which is why he is still often referred to as "The Master." He created the book, music, and lyrics for more than twenty musical shows, including operettas, revues, and musical comedies, out of which came hundreds of brilliantly witty, sweepingly melodic, and expertly crafted songs. In addition, he wrote dozens of plays, several of which have become frequently revived classics.

His impeccably stylish persona and personality infused and informed all of his work. As one of the first modern media celebrities and one of the first stars to turn himself into a personal brand, he was about as open about his sexuality as anyone could be without ever publicly acknowledging it, and his plays and songs were often further "out" than he was. For example, in his smash hit 1929 operetta **Bitter Sweet**,[90] Coward included a party scene set in the 1890s that featured the song, "We All Wear A Green Carnation," described by Coward biographer Oliver Soden as "a daring quartet . . . satirizing the symbol of homosexuality and aestheticism worn by Oscar Wilde and his circle."[91] Unconnected in any way to the plot, "four over-exquisitely dressed young men enter." In his stage directions, Coward identifies them as "a poet . . . a painter . . . a dilettante and . . . a playwright . . . THEY sing:"

> Blase boys are we
> Exquisitely free
> From the dreary and quite absurd
> Moral views of the common herd . . .
> Pretty boys, witty boys, too, too, too
> Lazy to fight stagnation
> Haughty boys, naughty boys all we do
> Is to pursue sensation . . . [and then several choruses later it concludes:]
> And as we are the reason for the "Nineties" being gay,
> We all wear a green carnation.[92]

As Soden notes, the *Oxford English Dictionary* cites this lyric from *Bitter Sweet* as only "the second traceable attestation of 'gay' used to mean homosexual."[93] We might assume that most audience members were oblivious to Coward's sly turn of the then popular nostalgic phrase, "the gay Nineties," but somehow this number still had a strong effect, with critics across America hailing the "eccentrically dressed"[94] "Green Carnation boys foursome"[95] as one of the "most notable"[96] and "clever and amusing"[97] highlights of the show.

Even in the conservative 1950s, when Coward became an unlikely American television personality, he still often included coded gay messages in his songs and performance style that you would think would have made his queerness obvious to everyone. Apparently, 1950s TV audiences saw only what they wanted to see. As his most recent biographer, Oliver Soden, phrased it, Coward didn't so much "hide in plain sight" as he "revealed himself through flagrant disguise."[98]

He Wrote the Book—Herbert Fields

The books for many of the Rodgers and Hart musicals were written by another very significant Gay artist, **Herbert Fields**. He was the son of Broadway star performer and producer Lew Fields (of Weber and Fields) and the brother of lyricist Dorothy Fields and playwright/bookwriter Joseph Fields. Nearly the entire history of the Broadway musical is encompassed within the Fields family's theatrical dynasty. Herbert Fields' career alone spanned the period 1925 to 1960.

Herbie (as he was called by family and friends) was a "slight and sensitive" child with a "quick wit and a love of the stage, dance, music, costumes—anything to do in any way with theater."[99] From early on, he began devising verses, rhymes, and jokes, which led his father to humorously speculate about "having a librettist in the family." This, of course, turned out to be entirely prophetic. Herbert Fields would go on to write or co-write the books for twenty-one Broadway musicals (often in collaboration with his sister, Dorothy), and many of them were the biggest hits of their day. Those musicals include six shows with Rodgers and Hart,[100] seven with Cole Porter, one with Vincent Youmans, one with George and Ira Gershwin, and one mega-hit, *Annie Get Your Gun*, with Irving Berlin.

Herbert Fields' musicals are filled with sight gags, visual comedy, slapstick humor, and racy situations—and although today nearly all of them go unproduced, at the time, his work was acclaimed for its originality and innovation. His songwriting collaborators especially gave him tremendous credit for the success of, not just the shows, but also their songs. I contend that Herbert Fields is one of the key inventors of the musical as we know it. Amazingly, he was also one of those rare talents who were able to successfully navigate the transition from the free-wheeling musical comedies of the Silver Age to the fully integrated post-*Oklahoma!*-style musical comedies of the Golden Age—and indeed have his biggest hit in that new format.

Herbert Fields never married and appears to have lived rather happily and openly as a Gay man—at least within the accepting world of Broadway. In a letter that George Gershwin sent to his brother, Ira, he describes a party he attended and reports that Herbie Fields had also been there "with his sweetheart" (meaning his boyfriend),[101] while his nephew, Armond Fields, described Herbie as a "soul mate" of Larry Hart "whose bohemian lifestyle he tried to emulate."[102] Herbert Fields, however, understood that his openness could only go so far. According to author Frederick Nolan, "Herb was part of the gay scene, but also always maintained the fiction of straightness," and to foster that illusion, "he had a string of statuesque chorus girls for whom he bought immensely ostentatious mink coats."[103] As noted above, Herbert Fields' most frequent collaborator was one of only a handful of Broadway songwriters whose name became world-famous and whose songs and persona were so inextricably linked to each other that they became immediately recognizable brands unto themselves—Broadway's Queer superstar, Cole Porter.

"Let's Do It"—Cole Porter

Even today the name **Cole Porter** conjures up an Art Deco world of glamor, wit, and sophistication. Porter is also on a very short list of Broadway songwriters who created both the words and the music for their songs—and who did it with equally brilliant craftsmanship. Stephen Sondheim believed that, "Technically, in both music and lyrics, no one's better than Porter, and few are his equals."[104] Between 1915 and 1955, he created songs and/or full scores for twenty-eight Broadway musicals, as well as dozens of film musicals, totaling more than 1,000 songs—including more than fifty enduring standards that remain some of the wittiest, most romantic, and most beloved songs of all time.

Cole Porter was born in 1891 in the sleepy little town of Peru, Indiana. His grandfather, J. O. Cole, having amassed a fortune during the California Gold Rush, was the richest man in Indiana. And he had his grandson's life all mapped out: Cole would go east to study law and then return home to join the family business. However, Cole's equally strong-willed mother, Kate, believed that Cole had artistic gifts, and she began his musical training early: violin at six, piano at eight; and with a little help from his mother, Cole even wrote an operetta when he was ten. Cole's father was an unassertive man who played only a minor role in Cole's upbringing, although he was an amateur poet, which may have had some influence.

At fourteen, Porter was sent east to Worcester Academy in Massachusetts. He brought his piano with him and discovered that his skill at entertaining made him quite popular. In 1909 he entered Yale University, where he majored in English, minored in music, and studied French. He was president of the Glee Club and a founding member of Yale's still-famous singing group, the Whiffenpoofs. While at Yale, he wrote over 300 songs, including several football fight songs still sung today, and composed the scores for several musical comedies produced by the dramatic society. Cole quickly formed a close circle of friends who were all rich, gay, and devoted to theater, music, and art—including his lifelong friend and colleague, Monty Wooley (profiled on the next page). As described in the book *Staging Desire—Queer Readings of American Theater History*:

> The homosexual scene at Yale in the teens was typical of the situation in wealthy American circles: faculty, staff, and students knew that there were homosexuals on campus, but they were young men from some of the country's wealthiest and most influential families, and so were fairly immune to criticism or harassment.[105]

> ### "A Perfect Blendship" — Monty Wooley
>
> Cole Porter was frequently aided and abetted both personally and professionally by director and actor **Monty Wooley,** who had a remarkably similar background of wealth and privilege as that of his former Yale classmate. When Porter arrived at Yale, Wooley was already ensconced as a leading force in the Dramatic Association. They quickly became close friends and remained so for the rest of their lives. Today, Monty Wooley is primarily remembered for his brilliant and hilariously acerbic performance as "Sheridan Whiteside" in both the Broadway and film versions of George S. Kaufman and Moss Hart's play *The Man Who Came To Dinner* (1939). But a decade earlier, Wooley directed seven Broadway musicals, all of which were written by the leading Queer artists of the era—Cole Porter, Larry Hart, Herbert Fields, and Moss Hart. These included such hits as *Fifty Million Frenchmen* (1929), *The New Yorkers* (1930), *America's Sweetheart* (1931), and *Jubilee* (1935). Wooley's life partner was another Yale classmate, Cary Abbott, whom the press usually identified as his "courier–secretary–traveling companion."

After graduating from Yale, Porter fulfilled the promise he had made to his grandfather and enrolled in the Harvard Law School—but soon switched to Music. In 1915, two songs he had written for Yale shows were placed in the Broadway musicals *Hands Up!* and *Miss Information*. The following year, he wrote his first full Broadway score for a "patriotic comic opera" entitled *See America First*. Unfortunately, it was a quick flop and closed after only fifteen performances. Porter spent the next year loafing around New York and then went to Paris during World War I, where he worked for a war relief organization. He would later claim that he had joined the French Foreign Legion, but that is likely an exaggeration. While in Paris, Porter met Linda Lee Thomas, a wealthy Kentucky-born divorcee eight years his senior. In her youth, she had been called "the most beautiful woman in America." They were married in 1919. Linda was completely aware of Cole's sexual orientation, but having been brutally abused by her first husband, she was not interested in a sexual relationship. Cole and Linda's partnership was mutually advantageous and provided Cole with a glamorous heterosexual facade. By all reports, there was genuine love and affection between them, and they remained married until Linda's death in 1954.

In 1923, Cole's grandfather died, and because Cole had failed to become a lawyer as promised, J. O. left Cole completely out of his will. Cole's mother, however, inherited more than $4 million (equivalent to $70 million today), and she promptly gave half of it to Cole. Cole and Linda split their time between Paris and Venice, where they lived in a succession of rented palazzos and threw legendary parties (often attended by such emerging Broadway talents as Noel Coward, Rodgers and Hart, and Jack Wilson). Porter seemed to be the man who had everything. But something was missing. As disastrous as *See America First* had been, and as fabulous as his current life was, he still felt his true identity was as a songwriter. So, amid all the parties, world travel, and fabulous high life, Porter continued to study and write music. He studied orchestration and counterpoint at the Schola Cantorum, and, influenced by the music of Stravinsky and Ravel, he began to introduce new, modernist sounds into his work, leaving behind the rather ordinary harmony and melody of his previous songs. Within the limits of the popular song, Porter was a musical modernist, and that can clearly be traced back to his years in Paris. In later life, he would downplay this compositional shift with the glib words, "I realized that to become a success I would have to learn to write Jewish tunes." While this is ridiculously simplistic, it can't be denied that Porter's first hit songs often featured long, sinuous melodies and startling harmonic shifts between major and minor tonalities that are characteristic of Jewish music.

Encouraged by Irving Berlin, Porter reintroduced himself to Broadway in 1928 with a musical appropriately titled *Paris*. Its songs included "Let's Misbehave" and the sexually provocative smash hit "Let's Do It." In his lyrics for this song, Porter's repeated use of the words "do it" is masterful. At first, we think he is referring to sex—but then, at the last possible second, he turns it into "love." And he continues to brilliantly work this delightful deceit over five choruses of the song. Author Mark Fernow asserts that "The song stands as an emblem of Porter's entire way of living: reveling in the raw, erotic power that drives life, then slapping a token mask of convention over this truth before showing it to the world."[106] In many of his early hit songs Porter refers to love as either an "it" or a "thing," including "Let's Do It," "What Is This Thing Called Love?" "You Do Something to Me," "You've Got That Thing"—and he uses both in "It Was Just One of Those Things." I believe that he knew exactly what he was doing. All of those "its" and "things" can be interpreted as either innocent or naughty, either male or female, and either straight or gay. Although Alan Jay Lerner would later describe Porter as "a homosexual who had never seen the closet," Porter was certainly never "out" in any contemporary sense. Instead, he can be seen as "hiding in plain sight" by regularly employing coded language and gay slang in his songs that would only be recognized by those "in the know." Author Mark Fearnow sums him up like this: "Cole Porter reveled in the delightful irony of pretending to satisfy cultural expectations of gender and sexuality while at the same time doing just what he felt like doing behind a shield of what was called good taste and discretion."[107] I would only add that this is entirely representative of the disruptive, subversive, subliminal, and ultimately liberating nature of the Broadway musical.

Noel, Cole, and Jack Wilson

Although **John C. Wilson** (1899–1961) produced and/or directed more than forty Broadway plays and musicals in collaboration with the top tier of Broadway creators and stars, today, he has been largely forgotten, and his significant career is little more than a footnote in most Broadway histories. Only with the 2015 release of his previously unpublished 1959 memoir, *Noel, Tallulah, Cole and Me*,[108] has his story been more fully told. Jack Wilson, as he was generally known, was born into wealth in New Jersey in 1899, and even though there was "no taint of theatrical blood" on either side of his family, he was drawn to the theater at an early age. Young Jack would spend hours in his room cutting out figures and backgrounds from magazines to turn shoeboxes into miniature theaters in which he would present elaborate productions that were, in his words, "a twelve-year-old's version of Dillingham and Ziegfeld combined!" At fourteen, he was sent to Andover prep school and then went to Yale, where he too fell under the sway of the charismatic but waspish drama director Monty Wooley. In 1922, "facing the necessity of the facts of life," he went to work for a major Wall Street brokerage firm.

Three years later, his life took a major turn when, during a trip to London, he was unable to get tickets to the reining hit, *No, No, Nanette*, and instead ended up with front-row seats to the play *The Vortex*, written and directed by, and starring, Noel Coward. "This was dismal news," Wilson recalled in his memoir, "as we had never heard of Coward nor his play." That night, however, Wilson was overwhelmed by "one of the most exciting performances I have ever seen."[109] A few days later, after attending Coward's hit revue *On With The Dance*," he was taken by a mutual acquaintance to meet Coward in his *Vortex* dressing room where "to Jack's delighted consternation," Coward held court "clad only in a pair of silk drawers."[110] The following fall, when Coward came to New York for what would be his breathtaking breakthrough year on Broadway, Wilson and Coward reconnected and, as "Coward doodled in the margins of a notebook, 'We are having a perfectly fizzing time . . . The car broke down and Jack kissed me in the tonneau [backseat].'"[111] According to Coward's biographer, Oliver Soden, this was "the first relationship of Noel's life that can conclusively be called a love affair."[112] By the next year, Wilson was living with Coward in London, acting as his business manager, and becoming, as Coward later stated, "so much a part of our lives that scarcely any decision could be made without him."[113] The British press was soon reporting on "Noel Coward and his ultra-modern" American friend.[114] Through Coward, Jack Wilson was introduced to everyone of theatrical importance in both London and New York and gradually became more and more involved in both the business and creative aspects of the theater. During his career, in addition to Coward, Wilson frequently collaborated with playwright Terrence Rattigan and stars Tallulah Bankhead and Lynn and Alfred Lunt. Among the Broadway plays and musicals he produced are **Tonight At 8:30**, **Set to Music**, **Bloomer Girl**, **The Winslow Boy**, **The Deep Blue Sea**, and **Quadrille**. He directed (and in a few cases also produced) the Broadway productions of **Blithe Spirit**, **The Pirate**, the 1943 revival of **A Connecticut Yankee**, **Present Laughter**, **Kiss Me, Kate**, and **Gentlemen Prefer Blondes**, for which he was acclaimed for having staged "this side splitting comedy"[115] "expertly, in a festive manner"[116] "with memorable skill"[117] and "at a lively clip,"[118] and hailed for having "put everything and everybody in the right place."[119]

Although Jack and Noel would remain close friends and business partners throughout Wilson's life, in 1937, Jack married fashion model, film actress, and actual Russian princess Natalie Paley, with Noel Coward serving as his best man. The Wilson–Paley marriage was "one of companionship and deep friendship if not sexual passion,"[120] similar to that of Cole and Linda Porter, and, in fact, the two couples spent a great deal of time together vacationing in Europe. "Everyone in their circle understood the arrangement and welcomed the two couples into the world of high society. In fact, they were among the most attractive and charming foursomes on two continents."[121]

"Masculine Women, Feminine Men"—Broadway's Drag Superstars, Part 2

Due to his untimely death, Bert Savoy just missed the "Pansy Craze," a phenomenon that he had, no doubt, helped to inspire. However, another "top-notch entertainer" and "premier female impersonator" was at the center of this sudden flourishing of flamboyant, outrageous, overtly Queer performers, songs, and comedy that in the late 1920s and early 1930s created a sensation. Born Georg Francis Peduzzi in Baltimore in 1897, **Karyl Norman** was a vaudeville headliner who the *Oakland Tribune* described in 1925 as bringing to the stage "a youth and a feminine voice that [Julian] Eltinge in his prime did not possess."[122] Norman first made the leap to Broadway as one of the featured stars of *The Greenwich Village Follies of 1924* (featuring songs by Cole Porter and staging by John Murray Anderson). Then, in 1927, Norman was billed above the title of *Lady Do*, a musical created specifically to showcase his exceptional talents, and in which he played several roles, both male and female.

The origins of the so-called Pansy Craze can be traced back to the first of New York's infamous masquerade balls, held in Harlem in 1869. By the 1920s, these drag balls had become so popular that "as many as 7000 people of all colors and classes were attending,"[123] and top Broadway stars and celebrities served as the judges of the costume contests. Meanwhile, throughout the city, Prohibition had given birth to hundreds of wild, vibrant, clandestine speakeasies and nightclubs that catered to a young, hip, adventurous clientele that included an increasingly visible Queer contingent—both on and off the stages. Variety reported in 1930 that "Broadway will have nite [sic] places with 'pansies' as the main draw. Paris and Berlin have similar night resorts, with the queers attracting the lays [laypeople]."[124] Karyl Norman was the headliner at a nightspot called The Pansy Club, on the corner of Broadway and 48th, which featured "a bevy of beautiful girls in 'something different' entitled 'Pansies On Parade.'"[125] Across the street was the Everglades Club where another drag star, **Francis Renault**, headed the floorshow.[126] Just a few blocks away was Club Abbey, where its wisecracking, risqué master of ceremonies, **Jean Malin,** was pioneering a new type of Queer performance that challenged traditional gender expectations. The *Star Gazette* described Malin as "a female impersonator who doesn't bother to put on dresses."[127] Instead of appearing in drag, Malin wore elegant form-fitting men's suits and tuxedos while sporting a wavy crop of elaborately coiffed blond hair and heavy feminine makeup. The effect was that of an outrageous, flamboyant, openly Queer man. The highlight of Malin's performances were the witheringly clever comebacks and put-downs he launched at homophobic hecklers in his audience (who may have been "plants" employed by Malin as part of the act). Instead of punching them in the face, as Julian Eltinge had done, Malin skewered them with his wicked tongue and rapier wit, much to his audience's delight. This soon made Jean Malin the talk of Broadway and "the highest-paid entertainer of 1930."

This fascination with camp culture and Queer identities influenced "main stem" shows as well. Even superstar Eddie Cantor interpolated a song titled "Masculine

Women, Feminine Men" (by Edgar Leslie and James Monaco) into his hit Broadway musical *Kid Boots*,[128] including lyrics that echoed the gender explorations of the era:

> Masculine woman, feminine men,
> Which is the rooster, which is the hen?
> It's hard to tell them apart today. And say,
> Sister is busy learning to shave,
> Brother just loves his permanent wave.
> It's hard to tell them apart today. Hey, hey!
> Girls were girls and boys were boys when I was a tot
> Now we don't know who is who, or even is what?[129]

The Pansy Craze was short-lived, however. In January of 1931, the notorious mobster Dutch Schultz was gunned down and stabbed (but survived) at Club Abbey. The next day, its doors were padlocked, and a few nights later, the Pansy Club and several other queer-themed nightspots were raided by police and shut down. In hindsight, historians now consider this crackdown on LGBTQ visibility to have been much more about homophobia than public safety, with the authorities using the violence as an excuse to close down these centers of Queer gathering and expression. This was part of a conservative turn in society that took place as the Depression deepened and the loose morals of the 1920s were viewed as part of the cause.

As we have seen, LGBTQ artists responded in a variety of ways to shifting attitudes toward homosexuality during the first half of the twentieth century. As we will see in upcoming chapters, Queer men such as Leonard Bernstein, Jerome Robbins, Arthur Laurents, and Stephen Sondheim will find the repressive 1950s an even more challenging period in which to navigate a Broadway career.

"Just *Keep Shufflin'*"—More Black Musicals (I, B, W)

In 1926, as the *New York Times* put it, "Harlem continued its invasion of the Broadway stage," when Flournoy Miller and Aubrey Lyles returned with **Rang Tang**, a musical comedy that for some strange reason had a book written by a Scandinavian immigrant actress-turned-playwright named Kaj Gynt, and a score by Black songwriters **Ford Dabney** (music)[130] and **Jo Trent** (lyrics). Miller and Lyles, "the two stellar comedians," once again portrayed Sam Peck and Steve Jenkins, and *Rang Tang* took these now beloved characters "from Jimtown, USA, to Africa, and back again for a grand finale in a Harlem nightclub."[131] Critics described the show as being so elegant, lavish, and "elaborate in production and trappings'" that "Mr. Ziegfeld would not cast a scornful eye."[132] Once again, however, some critics felt that "in the long run," the spectacular staging worked against the show and that "smothered in scenery," *Rang Tang* became "unqualifiedly sluggish and tedious." The *New York Times* even went so far as to suggest that with its "painstaking reproduction of the [white] Broadway spectacles . . . there was around the entertainment last night the suspicion that it might be . . . passing [as white]," and if that wasn't clear enough the review concluded with the assertion that "*Rang Tang* in its attempt to be refined and gorgeous loses a good deal" of the "distinctive racial quality" that other Black shows possess "through sheer unpretentiousness and a native lack of inhibitions."[133] Instead of being encouraged to develop, evolve, grow, and experiment with the form, style, and content of the Broadway musical alongside their white counterparts, Black musical theater artists were finding themselves boxed into a repetitive pattern of stereotypically "Black" music, dance, and comedy that audiences were already beginning to grow tired of. *Rang Tang,* however, played out a very respectable run of 119 performances.

Originality and experimentation were certainly not at the top of Miller and Lyles' agenda as they quickly assembled their next Broadway musical, which, inevitably, was titled **Keep Shufflin'** (1928). Again, they wrote the book and cast themselves as Peck and Jenkins, who this time owned a Jimtown bank from which they skimmed money. The plot's lightly satirical take on socialism and communism was an intriguingly topical premise. However, much like those late twentieth-century hit movies that spun off way too many sequels, this franchise was beginning to wear thin. *Keep Shufflin*'s producer was veteran white Broadway songwriter Con Conrad, and he engaged a remarkable sextet of first-rate Black songwriters to create the show's score—James Johnson, Thomas "Fats" Waller, Clarence Todd, Andy Razaf, Henry Creamer, and Will Vodery. But even with all of that talent on hand, no enduring songs emerged from a score that critics found to be "pleasant if not memorable." The dancing, however, was "of course, fast and furious."[134] Still, *Keep Shufflin'* managed to run for 104 performances.

The following season, composers **Thomas "Fats" Waller** and **Harry Brooks**, in collaboration with lyricist **Andy Razaf**, had significantly more success with the revue **Hot Chocolates**, "a noisy, high-spirited, fast-moving show" that the *New York Times* found to be "produced with more slickness and competence than any of its immediate predecessors." This was an expanded version of a revue that had originated at the popular Harlem nightclub Connie's Inn. The production grew so big that "alterations" had to be "made to the stage and pit of the Hudson Theater to accommodate the large cast of eighty-nine that ranged in age from three-and-a-half-year-old Boots Miller to sixty-eight-year-old singer Lou Bell."[135] The show's outstanding song was an "entirely pleasant jazz ballad called 'Ain't Misbehavin'" and its rendition "by an unnamed member of the orchestra was a highlight of the premiere." That unnamed singer/musician was jazz trumpet virtuoso, singer, and future entertainment superstar **Louis Armstrong**, making his Broadway debut.

Broadway Dance #5: Mr. Bojangles (B)

In a 1948 article tracing the history of Black dance, historian Marion Hannah Winter wrote that "the repertoire of every current tap dancer contains elements that had been established theatrically" by William Henry Lane known as "Master

Juba" (see page 56).¹³⁶ If this is true, those elements were certainly passed down to the greatest tap dancing star of the Silver Age, **Bill "Bojangles" Robinson**, perhaps the most influential tap dancer of all time. Gene Kelly and Fred Astaire both asserted that if it weren't for Bojangles's, they never would've been the tap dancers they were.¹³⁷ Robinson was born in Richmond, Virginia, in 1878 and was raised largely by his grandmother, who had been enslaved. As a young man, he earned the nickname "Bojangles" for his contentious and cantankerous nature. (He was always amused later when white people perceived this as a cute and endearing moniker.) At the age of five, Robinson began dancing to make money, performing in local beer gardens. By twelve, he was touring with a show called *The South Before the War*. He then teamed up with another dancer named George W. Cooper, and from 1902 to 1914, they were a popular vaudeville duo. Like Sissle and Blake, they refused to wear blackface makeup, which was still customarily used by most Black performers in mainstream vaudeville at the time.

After they split up, Robinson launched a solo career in vaudeville and nightclubs and became one of the few Black performers to headline at New York's prestigious Palace Theatre. "Playing the Palace" was the pinnacle of success for every vaudeville performer. Robinson's signature routine was his "stair dance," which he introduced in 1918.¹³⁸ Extraordinary both for its showmanship and its musicality, each step emitted a slightly different pitch and tone as Robinson tapped up and down each side of the double staircase.¹³⁹ He performed various versions of this routine throughout his career including in his Broadway debut in the "hot, fast, and furious"¹⁴⁰ hit musical revue *Blackbirds of 1928*, the first of five Broadway musicals he would star in. He also appeared in fourteen movies, including four hit films in which he memorably danced with child superstar Shirley Temple, making them the first interracial couple to dance together on screen.¹⁴¹ In Hollywood, Robinson was mostly limited to playing a very narrow range of stereotypically "Black" supporting roles, but the films provided him with steady, lucrative employment and made him world famous. In 1939, at the age of sixty-one, Robinson returned to Broadway to star in *The Hot Mikado*, a jazzed-up adaptation of the Gilbert and Sullivan operetta. He celebrated his sixty-first birthday by dancing down sixty-one blocks of Broadway, cheered on the entire way by adoring crowds.¹⁴² Despite earning millions during his lifetime, Robinson died poor in 1949, at the age of seventy-one, but this was only because he had given away so much of his wealth to various charities prior to his death. His funeral was attended by thousands, including many of show business's biggest stars. In 1989, a joint resolution of the U.S. Congress established May 25 as "National Tap Dance Day," a date chosen specifically because it was Bill "Bojangles" Robinson's birthday.

Nearly every critic compared *Hot Chocolates* (favorably) to the previous season's smash hit revue, **Lew Leslie's Blackbirds of 1928**—a show that became even more popular and successful than *Shuffle Along*. Its over-the-title producer was a Russian Jewish immigrant originally named Louis Lessinsky, who also "staged and conceived" the "entire production." Leslie was completely captivated by African American performers and spent most of his career producing shows featuring all-Black casts. Inspired by the *Ziegfeld Follies*, *Blackbirds of 1928* was a lavish, star-studded musical revue with a cast of 100 headed by Adelaide Hall and Bill "Bojangles" Robinson. It was first performed at a theater in Harlem, then traveled to Paris, and then to London before returning to New York for an astonishing 518 performances on Broadway—a run that would hold the record as the longest-running Black Broadway show until the 1970s. *Blackbirds* also marked the Broadway debut of lyricist Dorothy Fields.

"Ladies Don't Write Lyrics"—Dorothy Fields (I, J, W)

Lyricist **Dorothy Fields**' amazing fifty-year career stretched from the Silver Age to the Modern Era—from the vaudeville era to the age of rock. Utilizing her gift for natural, direct language and her keen ear for slang, Fields wrote some of the best-known standards in the American songbook. She was born into a show business dynasty. Her father was Lew Fields, of the team of Weber and Fields, and her brothers were Herbert and Joseph Fields. After retiring from performing, Lew became one of Broadway's most successful producers. Like many successful Broadway figures of his generation, he did everything he could to keep his children out of show business. However, he made a mistake when he assigned young Dorothy the task of organizing his scrapbooks. At first, she was only interested in reading her father's rave reviews, but soon she became fascinated by what the critics had to say about what makes a show a hit, what material worked, and what didn't. She became obsessed with the inner workings of show business. A short time later, a friend suggested that she try her hand at writing lyrics. After some trial and error, she teamed up with Irish American composer **Jimmy McHugh** to contribute songs for a low-budget revue. Lew Fields attempted to put his foot down, proclaiming that "Ladies don't write lyrics." She responded with a snappy play on her father's most famous punchline,[143] "I'm not a lady, I'm your daughter!"[144] The song was cut before the show reached New York, but undaunted the team took it to producer Lew Leslie who hired them to write the entire score for his *Blackbirds of 1928*. The song was "I Can't Give You Anything But Love," which became one of the biggest hits of that year and one of the most recorded songs of the century. Three other songs from the score also hit big, vividly demonstrating that women could compete with men on Broadway—and as we will see, in the early 1930s, a string of talented female lyricists and composers followed her example.

Another Setback for Black Artists (B)

Again following Ziegfeld's example, Lew Leslie staged multiple editions of his revue, including *Blackbirds of 1930, 1934, 1936,* and *1939,* all featuring great Black stars such as Ethel Waters and Lena Horne. While these revues often provided career-changing opportunities for the Black performers and musicians who appeared in them, they also introduced an unfortunate new trend that would soon come to dominate the Black Broadway musical. From this point on and over the following forty years, nearly every "Black musical" would feature brilliant and amazing Black performers in shows that were written, directed, and choreographed by white artists.

One of the last shows of this period to feature an entirely Black creative team was *Brown Buddies* in 1930. Bill Robinson—whom the *New York Age* called "one of Broadway's leading theatrical favorites . . . internationally conceded as the foremost living comedian of his race" and "recently acclaimed as the greatest tap dancer of all time by the American Association of Dance Masters, during their convention last summer"—was the star and driving force behind this show, whose producers emphasized was "a musical comedy, with a real book, and not a musical revue." This was a very unusual show in that unlike any of the other Black musical comedies, *Brown Buddies* was a period piece that looked back to World War I and told the story of a "company of colored soldiers who left the mud flats of East St. Louis to do their bit for Uncle Sam in the muddy trenches of France" and who are followed there by a group of Black entertainers from "their old home town and a pretty romance develops between the star of the show [played by Adelaide Hall] and top sergeant, Bill Robinson."[145] Six of the show's songs had words and music by songwriter Shelton Brooks, whose earliest songs had bridged the transition between ragtime and jazz and whose hits included "Walkin' The Dog," "Darktown Strutter's Ball," and Sophie Tucker's signature tune, "Some Of These Days." Again, some reviews criticized the show for being too much like white shows and, even more problematic, for not being Black enough, or as one critic put it, "What is an 'all-colored show' without a couple of tons of good, vivid Negro color?"[146] Even so, it ran for a respectable 111 performances.

"Life is Just a Bowl of Cherries"—De Sylva, Brown, and Henderson (I, J)

Toward the end of the decade, another of the 1920s most successful songwriting teams emerged: **DeSylva, Brown, and Henderson**. Born DeSylva, Brownstein, and Brost, this Portuguese, Russian Jewish, and German trio of collaborators was a cultural melting pot unto themselves, coming together somewhat by accident. George Gershwin and DeSylva had collaborated on most of the songs for *George White's Scandals of 1922,* '23, and '24, but when Gershwin decided to leave revues behind and team up with his brother to write musical comedies, George White, who "had the keenest musical ear of all revue producers"[147] wanted to team up De Sylva with composer Ray Henderson, but he was already paired with lyricist Lew Brown. Not one to let details like this stand in his way, "White bunched the three together," and it turned out that the songs the trio wrote for the *Scandals of 1925* and *1926* "were better than the ones De Sylva had written with Gershwin,"[148] including two major hits, "The Birth of the Blues" and their follow up to "The Charleston"—"The Black Bottom." The new team then embarked on a series of wacky musical comedy hits, all with plotlines and subject matter ripped from the latest headlines and cultural fads of the day.

Their most enduring show is **Good News** (1927), which they set at fictional Tate College. Prior to World War I, only the children of the very wealthy went to college—and they were almost exclusively male. The prosperity of the 1920s, however, produced a huge surge in middle-class college enrollment that included a significant number of women. By 1926, coed college life, especially college football, had become national topics of interest, and DeSylva, Brown, and Henderson set out to capitalize on this development. After all, this setting provided a chance to fill a Broadway stage with young, attractive, horny college kids. The lyric of the opening number set the tone:

> Students are we of dear old Tait College
> Learning, learning, learning, every day!
> Filling our minds with jewels of knowledge . . .
> Learning how to sin—not how to think,
> How to mix our gin right in the sink!
> We spend our days having romances.
> We spend our nights hoofing at dances . . .
> Learning, learning, learning, all the time!

Good News introduced the hit songs, "The Best Things in Life Are Free," "Just Imagine," and the dance craze "The Varsity Drag"—another variation of the Charleston. With its remarkable run of 557 performances, *Good News* was the first of four consecutive DeSylva, Brown, and Henderson smash hit musical comedies that typified everything that was stylish and racy on Broadway in the late 1920s.

The plot of **Hold Everything!** (1928) revolved around the sport of boxing, and the show made a star of comedian Burt Lahr, and introduced the song "You're the Cream in My Coffee." **Follow Thru** (1929) was subtitled "A musical slice of country club life," and its story involved a women's golf tournament. This show made a star of dancer Eleanor Powell and introduced "Button Up Your Overcoat." Record-setting airplane pilots Charles Lindberg and Amelia Earhart were, of course, front page news in the late 1920s, so it's not surprising that DeSylva, Brown, and Henderson's final show was set in the world of aviation and titled **Flying High** (1930). Together and separately, Buddy DeSylva, Lew Brown, and Ray Henderson created dozens of Broadway musical comedies and revues, including an enduring catalog of classic hit songs.

Life on the Mississippi—The Arrival of *Show Boat* (I, J, B, W)

Good News and *Lew Leslie's Blackbirds* both opened during the 1927–8 Broadway season, which was the all-time peak year for the Broadway musical, at least with regard to the number of productions. A record fifty-nine musicals opened that season, including a show that is arguably the most significant musical of the Silver Age and one of the most influential of all time—***Show Boat***—produced by Florenz Ziegfeld, with music by Jerome Kern, book and lyrics by Oscar Hammerstein II, and based on the bestselling novel of the same name by Edna Ferber. Like the novel, the musical told the epic tale of three generations of Mississippi River show-folk, beginning in the 1890s when floating theaters brought plays and variety acts from town to town along America's waterways, and ending with a scene set in the present day (1927), featuring the youngest characters dancing the Charleston. *Show Boat* was groundbreaking in myriad ways: it was the very first musical to intertwine the stories of both Black and white characters who shared equal importance in the book and score. It also featured a large multiracial cast with white and Black actors sharing the stage side by side for the first time. Perhaps most importantly, it demonstrated how musicals could embrace important, consequential subject matter—especially issues of equity, social justice, and inclusion—and from *Show Boat* on, these have been among the principal themes of the Broadway musical. On top of its groundbreaking subject matter, Kern and Hammerstein's songs were woven tightly into the story and specifically tied to its captivatingly flawed, complex characters with an unprecedented level of seamless integration. Critic Brooks Atkinson hailed it as "the most beautifully blended musical show we have had in this country."[149] (Note: The legacy and themes of *Show Boat*, as well as the controversies surrounding it, are explored further in Chapters 7 and 13.)

Show Boat became a true smash hit. After running on Broadway for 572 performances, it toured extensively for years and returned to Broadway in a hit revival only five years after its premiere. All of which provided significant employment for large numbers of Black performers. However, its success and popularity, coupled with that of *Blackbirds of 1928* and *Porgy and Bess* in 1935, unintentionally reinforced the sidelining of Black writers, directors, choreographers, and producers. Then, just a year later, the stock market crash of 1929 and the Great Depression that followed made the economics of producing any kind of Broadway musical extremely challenging, and for Black theater-makers, it proved even more disastrous. By the mid-1930s—the darkest days of the Depression—Black songwriters, bookwriters, directors, and choreographers had, in effect, again been exiled from Broadway. They would not find significant opportunities there again until the 1970s.

Many of their white colleagues, however, fared somewhat better, and despite the tremendous hardship and struggle of the Depression (or perhaps because of it), the 1930s engendered an extraordinary period of artistic advancement and continuing development of the Broadway musical, precipitated by the arrival of a host of new, young masterminds of musical theater.

CHAPTER 6
"OLD MAN TROUBLE, I DON'T MIND HIM"—THE SILVER AGE OF THE BROADWAY MUSICAL, PART 2: THE 1930S (I, J, Q, B, W)

The Great Depression had a devastating impact on Broadway. Many of the leading producers, including Ziegfeld and the Shuberts,[1] went bankrupt in the aftermath of "Black Tuesday" (October 29, 1929), when the New York Stock Exchange lost $14 billion in one day, and then dropped another $26 billion over the following two weeks. Compared to the sixty-one musicals that had opened during the peak season of 1927–8, only twenty-seven musicals opened in 1932–3.[2] Of course, it wasn't just the pool of producers and investors that shrunk—the audience quickly dwindled as well. Many Broadway theaters sat empty or were repurposed as movie theaters because almost simultaneously with the onset of the Depression, movies had begun to talk—and sing—and audiences could now see Al Jolson for only a quarter. Nearly one-third of all New Yorkers were unemployed, and at least 20,000 of them were theater artists and craftspeople. Throngs of New York actors, singers, dancers, producers, directors, choreographers, designers, and other production personnel began fleeing to Hollywood.

Gradually, the economic damage rippled across the entire country. By the end of 1932, virtually the entire U.S. banking system had collapsed, and one-quarter of the American workforce was out of a job. This incapacitated the market for Broadway touring and sent vaudeville into a death spiral. In 1925, approximately 1,500 vaudeville theaters had been spread across America, but by 1930 only 300 were still in operation.[3] At the lowest point, during the 1936–7 season, only thirteen new musicals opened on Broadway.

The Hollywood film musicals of the 1930s are often described as frivolous, lightweight entertainments designed to soothe a Depression-weary audience that was eager to escape the grim realities of life. Meanwhile, a surprising number of Broadway musicals from that same decade endeavored to reflect and comment on what really was happening to the people of America. In his book *Ring Bells, Sing Songs—Broadway Musicals of the 1930s*, writer Stanley Green notes that even "the most opulent, extravagant, and unabashedly commercial form of theater—could not hide from what was going on." Of course, Broadway also provided relief from reality by offering "evenings of mirth and hilarity," but at the same time, it "showed a growing awareness of its own unique ability to make telling comments on such issues of the day"—not just the Depression but also "the folly of war, municipal corruption, political campaigns, the workings of the federal government, the rising labor movement, the dangers of both the far right and the far left, and the struggle between democracy and totalitarianism." Broadway's leading creative artists and performers discovered that "a song lyric, a tune, a wisecrack, a bit of comic business, a dance routine, could say things with even more effectiveness than many a serious-minded drama simply because the appeal was to a far wider spectrum of the theater-going public."[4]

"Brother Can You Spare A Dime?" (♩, ♪)

A prime example is the classic song "Brother Can You Spare A Dime?," written for a 1932 Broadway revue, *Americana*. Its haunting music was created by composer **Jay Gorney**, who was born Abraham Jacob Gornetsky in 1896 in Bialystok, Russia, where in 1906, he and his parents fled a pogrom and emigrated to Detroit, Michigan. Gorney paid his way through the University of Michigan by working as a pianist. His musical talents eventually led him to New York, where between 1923 and 1950, he contributed songs to fourteen Broadway musicals, most of them revues. Gorney maintained that he had based the melody line of "Brother Can You Spare A Dime?" on a lullaby his mother had sung to him as a child in Russia.[5] As Gorney recalled In a 1974 interview, "I didn't want to write a song to depress people. I wanted to write a song that would make people think."[6]

The ideal partner to help him accomplish that was lyricist **E. Y. "Yip" Harburg**. He was born Isidore Hochberg in 1898 to Russian Jewish immigrant parents in New York's Lower East Side. As a child, he was nicknamed "Yipsle"— which means squirrel in Yiddish—and a slightly shortened version of that name stuck with him for the rest of his life. The Yiddish theater had "a profound effect" on him, and its "deft blend of humor, fantasy, and social commentary left an indelible mark on his work."[7] Yip attended high school with Ira Gershwin, where the two budding lyricists bonded over their shared passion for the witty wordplay of W. S. Gilbert (and Sullivan), and it was Gershwin who introduced Harburg to Jay Gorney. The powerful lyrics that Harburg wrote for "Brother, Can You Spare A Dime?" perfectly aligned with his lifelong activism and advocacy for progressive politics, which later during the McCarthy Era resulted in him being blacklisted from working in film, television, and radio from 1950 to 1962. The blacklist had little power on Broadway, however, and Harburg created lyrics for twenty-two musicals and revues.

The challenge of the revue format is that since there is no ongoing plot or set of characters to tie the material together, each song has to function as a one-act, mini-musical all on its own. As the curtain goes up on each song and scene, the writers and stagers of the revue need to instantly establish a new setting, a new situation, and new characters that the audience can immediately understand and identify with. And even if there is no actual event or story, they still have to establish some kind of dramatic tension. In a production photo of "Brother Can You Spare A Dime?" as performed in *Americana*, ten men dressed in dark, rumpled, mismatched work clothes are grouped on a bare stage—some sitting, some standing. At the center of the group, one man, presumably the leading singer, straddles a wooden chair. All of them stare (accusingly?)

straight out at the audience.[8] It looks strikingly spare and modern, especially in contrast to the vibrant spectacle of most revue numbers, and it's not hard to imagine the powerful impact this song must have had in this staging. However, nothing other than the music and lyrics is necessary for us to appreciate what great musical dramatists Harburg and Gorney were—are! Somehow, they are able to condense all of the pain, suffering, injustice, and heartbreak of the Great Depression into one unforgettable song.

Girl Crazy—"Who Could Ask For Anything More?"

In the 1930s, several of the brightest lights of the previous decade now reached full wattage, including Cole Porter, Rodgers and Hart, Kay Swift, and the Gershwin brothers who kicked off the decade with the "sensational"[9] *Girl Crazy* (1930), which was acclaimed as "just about the perfect musical show"[10] and had "everything that all good musical comedies should have, and quite a number of things many of them have not." Several critics commented on the show's speed, noting that "a musical show demands pace from beginning to end, and *Girl Crazy* never slows down for a moment."[11] The marquee stars were comic Willie Howard,[12] Ginger Rogers, and Allen Kearns (who played the romantic lead in three Gershwin musicals), who headlined a show loaded with gags, girls, cowboys, and the soon-to-be smash hit songs "Embraceable You," "But Not for Me," and "Bidin' My Time." The book by Guy Bolton and John McGowan tells the story of "a New York playboy who drives west in a taxi and soon becomes the owner of a modernistic dude ranch" located on the Arizona–Mexico border, where he then proceeds to bring "the gaiety of Broadway to the plains and everyone, including the audience." Amazingly, *Girl Crazy*'s orchestra was led by "Red" Nichols and included future Big Band superstars Benny Goodman, Gene Krupa, and Glenn Miller. "The standout attraction,"[13] however, was "a vivid new personality in musical comedy" named Ethel Merman, who made her Broadway debut in the "hard-boiled role of Kate from the Barbary Coast" and brought the first act to a soaring climax by belting out "I Got Rhythm" and stopping the show cold "with her new and almost hypnotic method of singing."[14] (For more on Merman's debut, see page 230.) *Girl Crazy*'s legendary opening night came just one month after the Broadway debut of George Gershwin's professional and romantic partner, Kay Swift.

"The Sunny Side of the Street": Women of the Silver Age (I, J, W)

Kay Swift was born Katherine Faulkner Swift in NYC in 1897 to British American parents. She was educated at the Vetlin School for Girls and then trained as a classical musician at the Institute of Musical Art (today's Juilliard School). In 1925, she met and began a long-term romantic relationship with George Gershwin, who encouraged her to focus her talents on popular music. As a result of this astute advice, in 1930, Kay Swift became the very first woman to compose the music for the full score of a Broadway musical. The show was a musical comedy called *Fine and Dandy*, and its title song became a jazz standard. *Girl Crazy* and *Fine and Dandy* were the two biggest hits and longest-running shows of that season, and people who were "in the know" about George and Kay's relationship dubbed them the "Golden Couple of Broadway." Swift was Gershwin's closest musical associate, and her handwritten notes and suggestions can still be seen in his original manuscript of *Porgy and Bess*. After his untimely death in 1937, it was Swift who completed many of Gershwin's unfinished works.

Another romantic partner of George Gershwin was composer and lyricist **Ann Ronell**. She was born Ann Rosenblatt in 1905 in Omaha, Nebraska. She attended Radcliffe College, where she trained as a composer, and after interviewing Gershwin for her college newspaper, she became determined to become a Broadway songwriter herself. With Gershwin's help and encouragement, Ronell soon began working as a rehearsal pianist and vocal coach for several Broadway shows, including Gershwin's 1928 musical *Rosalie*. Her first hit song, "Let's Go Out in the Open Air," was written in collaboration with songwriter Muriel Pollack and was featured in the 1931 Broadway revue *Shoot The Works*. A decade later, in 1942, Ronell became the first woman to create both music and lyrics for the full score of a Broadway musical, the wartime-themed musical comedy *Count Me In*. Today, her best-known songs are "Who's Afraid of the Big Bad Wolf?" (written with Frank Churchill for the classic Disney animated short, *The Three Little Pigs*) and the great jazz standard "Willow, Weep for Me," for which she wrote both words and music in 1932. She dedicated that song to Gershwin, and because its style was so similar to his own blues-inflected compositions, there were sexist insinuations that he had actually written the music. The reality, however, is that Ann Ronell was just very much in tune with Gershwin's style and methods and simply wrote her own "Gershwin-esque" melody. And who knows to what degree Gershwin was influenced by her?

Meanwhile, lyricist Dorothy Fields continued to produce an amazing string of hits with composer Jimmy McHugh, including "On the Sunny Side of the Street," which they wrote for *Lew Leslie's International Revue* (1930), where it was introduced by yet another son of Russian Jewish immigrants to become a big Broadway star—song and dance man **Harry Richman**.[15]

Several female choreographers thrived during the Silver Age, including **Gertrude Hoffmann** (see page 66), who, in the mid-1920s, retired from performing and reinvented herself yet again by forming "The Gertrude Hoffman Girls," which consisted of several troupes of rigorously trained young women who performed Hoffmann's very athletic and acrobatic choreography, including kicks, leaps, and even aerial gymnastics, in productions around the world, including three sexy Shubert revues—*Artists And Models* (1925), *A Night in Paris* (1926), and *A Night in Spain* (1927).

Closely following Hoffmann's lead was the amazing **Albertina Rasch**, who choreographed thirty-three Broadway shows, including many of the biggest hits of the 1920s and 1930s. Born in Vienna in 1891 to a Polish Jewish mother and Russian father, when she was just seven years old she began studying at Vienna's Imperial Ballet and joined that company as a professional dancer while still in her teens. At eighteen, Rasch was engaged to come to New York to be a leading dancer at the gigantic Hippodrome Theater. Known for its spectacular, monumental productions, with 5,000 seats the Hippodrome claimed to be the largest theater in the world. After dancing there and with various other productions in New York and Europe, in 1923, she opened the Albertina Rasch Dance Studio, offering private and group lessons in ballet and interpretive dance. Rasch's strict regimen of body alignment and breathing exercises set her students apart from the typical vaudeville and Broadway hoofers. The studio became wildly successful and led to the formation of her own troupe, "The Albertina Rasch Girls," who performed her own unique style of dance which she called "New World Ballet." Combining classical ballet with modern American jazz dance styles, it became her signature. By 1925, Rasch had 150 dancers performing under her name on vaudeville stages all across America.

Her Broadway career began when a troupe of twenty of her dancers was engaged to appear in *George White's Scandals of 1924*. Evidently, that went well because the following year Rasch was engaged to choreograph five Broadway musicals, including *The Ziegfeld Follies of 1927*, McCarthy and Tierney's *Rio Rita*, Victor Herbert's *Mlle. Modiste*, and the musical comedy *Show Girl*, for which she choreographed a ballet set to George Gershwin's brand-new, jazz-infused orchestral piece *An American in Paris*—twenty years before Gene Kelly's version in the classic MGM film musical. Most notable was her work on three legendary musical revues of the 1930s—*Three's A Crowd*, *Flying Colors*, and *The Band Wagon*. That last show starred Fred and Adele Astaire and included Rasch's staging of the Dietz and Schwartz song, "Dancing in the Dark," which one critic described as a "choreographic feast." Rasch frequently collaborated with staging wizards Hassard Short and Moss Hart, and that trio's outstanding partnerships include Irving Berlin's *Face The Music*, Cole Porter's *Jubilee*, and the landmark musical *Lady In The Dark*. Rasch also had a very successful career in Hollywood, where she choreographed more than a dozen film musicals.

There are two interesting side notes to Rasch's career: she was married to Dimitri Tiomkin, one of the greatest film composers in the history of Hollywood; and she was involved in launching the famous New York restaurant, The Russian Tea Room, which for several years was billed as the "Albertina Rasch Russian Tea Room."

As the Silver Age reached its climax, Albertina Rasch's choreography set the stage for the entrance of Agnes DeMille, a dynamic force of nature who would lead Broadway dance into the Golden Age (see page 174).

Cole Porter and "The Set That's Smart" (♩)

Broadway's diminished Depression audience was, of course, made up of only the people who could still afford Broadway's ticket prices (top prices of $4 to $5 would be the equivalent of $80 to $90 today). This world-weary crowd wanted stylish, racy, and sophisticated entertainment and, with his upscale background, Cole Porter was the ideal songwriter to serve it to them. As we have seen, Porter's music and lyrics often combined a glamorous, sensual, classy sophistication with risqué, sexually provocative humor, and the cognoscenti clamored for his satiric, ironic, irreverent, sometimes cynical view of a world that seemed to be falling apart. And often, they saw themselves reflected back in the characters onstage. In 1930, Porter teamed up with two other leading Gay artists of the period, bookwriter Herbert Fields and director Monty Wooley, to create a show titled *The New Yorkers*, which they subtitled "A Sociological Musical Satire."

The New Yorkers took its audience on a scandalous tour of New York life, both high and low, with stops on Park Avenue, a street in Harlem, a bootleg gin factory, the prison at "Sing Sing," and a speakeasy where dancing star Ann Pennington and bandleader Fred Waring and his Pennsylvanians cavorted with the raucous nightclub entertainers **Jackson, Clayton, and** (Jimmy) **Durante**. One of the show's songs, "Love For Sale," proved to be quite controversial and pushed the boundaries of taste even on broad-minded Broadway. On opening night, a very young-looking, "pink and white," blond singer named Kathryn Crawford played the role of a "lily of the gutter,"[16] a streetwalker who sang that sinuous musical inner monologue as she plied her trade on a set designed to look like a section of Park Avenue just outside the then quite fashionable Reuben's Restaurant.

Love for sale
Appetizing young love for sale.
Love that's fresh and still unspoiled,
Love that's only slightly soiled,
Love for sale.[17]

Some critics and audience members found the song to be distasteful, even immoral, and lobbied for it to be cut from the show. After a few weeks of this hullabaloo, Black singer **Elizabeth Welch**, who had already been performing the song in a nightclub, was hired to take over the role. In a 1980 interview, she recalled that the only change that was made in the show was to repaint the street sign from "Park Avenue" to "Lennox Avenue" and change "Reuben's" to "The Cotton Club."[18] For some, no doubt, racist reason, it was considered less disturbing to depict a Black sex worker in Harlem than a white one on Park Avenue. The song made Elizabeth Welch a star, but Porter's lyrics were not permitted to be broadcast on radio (and later television) until the 1960s. Only the sinuous tune could be heard. Silver Age Broadway musicals were created almost exclusively for adult audiences who expected them to be racy and sophisticated. Cole Porter made them even more so.

The next five years were among Porter's most creative. In 1932, he wrote the score for what would be Fred Astaire's final Broadway musical, **Gay Divorce**, another show that lightly rocked the establishment boat with its comic critique of the absurd legal difficulties of obtaining a divorce at that time—especially for women. Although the word "gay" hadn't yet acquired its modern meaning (for most people, it still just meant "happy"), the show's title proved controversial in a different way. When the musical was filmed two years later, the title had to be changed to *The Gay Divorcee* because, according to the Hollywood Production Code, a divorced woman could be happy, but a divorce could not. This was Astaire's first show without his sister Adele, and in it, he introduced what became Porter's best-known and most-performed song, "Night and Day"—one of many Porter songs that in both words and music hauntingly dramatizes an unrelenting, almost obsessive kind of infatuation and desire.

Anything Goes—"A Rowdy, Naughty, Subversive Masterpiece"

In Porter's 1934 musical ***Anything Goes***, Ethel Merman belted out a score loaded with hits, including a title song that perfectly captured the era's spirit. The show was the brainchild of producer Vinton Freedley, who had been financially devastated by the stock market crash. To escape his creditors, he abandoned his New York residence and began living onboard a fishing boat in the Pacific. That's where he got the idea for the setting of his next show, which was originally titled *Hard To Get*. It would take place aboard a transatlantic ocean liner whose passengers would be a madcap collection of debutantes, gangsters, missionaries, sailors, and nightclub performers. Despite his shaky finances, Freedley managed to sign three of the biggest stars of the day—**William Gaxton**, **Ethel Merman**, and **Victor Moore**. And to guarantee success, he engaged the hottest songwriter—Cole Porter. Musicals in this era were often written incredibly quickly. From concept to creation to opening night might happen over only two or three months, and occasionally even less. The songwriters often worked from just a brief, rough outline of the plot and frequently wrote songs that later had to be shoehorned into the story. What mattered most were the songs, the stars, and the jokes. To create the book, Freedley engaged a couple of seasoned pros: Guy Bolton and P. G. Wodehouse, who were renowned for the Princess Theater musicals (see page 36). They submitted their script and went home—Wodehouse to France and Bolton to England. Bolton had planned to return to New York for rehearsals, but was struck with burst appendix and was unable to travel.[19]

Now, there's a famous story about *Anything Goes* that's been told and retold in dozens of books over the years: it reports that the original storyline of the show revolved around a shipwreck that was treated in a madcap, intended-to-be-hilarious fashion. But then about a month before rehearsals were scheduled to begin, a real cruise ship, the S.S. *Morro Castle*, returning from a seven-day cruise to Havana, was passing the beach at Asbury Park, NJ, when it suddenly burst into flames. Hundreds of beachgoers watched in horror as the ship was engulfed by fire and sank with a loss of more than 125 lives. It was by far the worst maritime disaster of the 1930s, so it was clear to everyone involved that the Wodehouse–Bolton book could no longer be used. And since the original authors were overseas and unavailable for rewrites, Freedley asked the show's director, **Howard Lindsay**, to take over the bookwriting duties. Lindsay determined that he would need a partner to get the rewrites done in time, and eventually **Russell Crouse**, a press agent for the Theatre Guild with very little previous playwriting experience, was hired for the job.

There's just one problem with this story. It isn't true. Researchers have uncovered the original script, and guess what? There's no shipwreck. The truth, which has been confirmed by letters and telegrams, is that the original Wodehouse–Bolton book was found to be unfocused, unfunny, and made little sense—even by Silver Age standards. And the entire "can't have a shipwreck in the show" story was apparently made up by Freedley to explain the sudden change of authorship and to give Wodehouse and Bolton a face-saving exit.[20] Working around the clock, the new partners quickly rewrote *Hard To Get*, throwing out most of the previous book, keeping the basic plot, a few of the characters and, of course, the ocean liner setting.[21] **Lindsey and Crouse** would go on to become one of Broadway's top writing teams, with a thirty-year career that included the long-running plays *Life With Father* and *Arsenic and Old Lace*, and smash hit musicals such as *Call Me Madam* and *The Sound of Music*. Less than six weeks after throwing out the script, Freedley called the cast to rehearsals for the new show—still named *Hard To Get*. He was hoping for a new title as well, and the creative team racked their brains trying to come up with one. Finally, one day during rehearsals, as leading man William Gaxton was entering the theater "he plaintivy demanded of the stage-doorman, "What are we going to call this musical hash, anyway?" The doorman "shrugged, grinned, and respnded, Well you know Mr. Gaxton, anything goes." And Cole Porter, knowing a "money title" when he heard one, rushed out to compose a title song.[22] The next morning, he came in with the catchy tune and brilliant lyrics we know and love today.

Anything Goes opened in November of 1934 and was an immediate and resounding success. Porter's score was loaded with hit tunes that monopolized the radio and dance band repertoire for months afterwards. Despite the Depression, the show ran for 420 performances—the second longest run of the decade. Today, it is one of only two or three musicals from the entire Silver Age that is regularly revived on Broadway and frequently seen in professional and amateur productions. Why has this show lived on in the canon? It's not just because of that sensational score. Dozens of shows from this period are loaded with great songs. *Anything Goes* is still viable because Lindsey and Crouse's book is more solidly constructed and involving than most others from this period, and its characters are truly memorable. Yes, the book has undergone various revisions over the years, and songs from other Cole Porter musicals have been interpolated into it—but the plot, characters, and situations remain largely unchanged, as does most of the dialogue and jokes. And as is evident in the video capture of the 2021 West End production starring Sutton Foster,[23] twenty-first-century audiences continue to revel in *Anything Goes*' madcap humor. Most, however, are likely unaware that the show sharply satirizes a number of topical issues, personalities, and ripped-from-the-headlines events of the 1930s.

For example, one of Lindsey and Crouse's most significant contributions to the show was Ethel Merman's character, Reno Sweeny, who they purposely conceived as an ironic, improbable cross between the world-famous evangelist Aimee Semple McPherson and the equally notorious nightclub hostess Texas Guinan. Aimee's visit to Guinan's speakeasy in 1927 had made worldwide front-page news. *Anything Goes* also lampooned the

Prohibition era's celebrity worship of gangsters. Just months before the show opened, John Dillinger, the FBI's Public Enemy No. 1, had gone on a violent crime spree, robbing banks and killing ten men, before dying in a shoot-out with government agents. In the musical, when the leading male character, Billy Crocker, is mistakenly identified as gangster Snake Eyes Johnson (the show's fictional Public Enemy No. 1), he is mobbed by the ship's passengers who are thrilled to finally have "a real celebrity onboard" the not so subtly named, "S.S. *American*." Author Scott Miller describes *Anything Goes* as "a rowdy, naughty, subversive masterpiece of musical comedy" and a "stinging satire of Americans' quirky habit of turning religion into show business, and criminals into celebrities."[24] Today, the show still produces huge laughs like clockwork, and audiences still revel in Porter's sparkling wit and tuneful, perfectly crafted songs.

"Broadway Baby": Moss Hart (J, Q)

In a thirty-year career stretching from the 1930s to the 1960s, **Moss Hart** served as the playwright, bookwriter, and/or director for twenty-nine Broadway musicals and plays. He was born in 1904 on E.104th Street in a working-class tenement neighborhood that was a sort of uptown outpost of NYC's Lower East Side. The grandson of impoverished Jewish British immigrants, at fifteen, Moss was forced to drop out of high school to support his parents and younger brother. He would later chronicle his improbable rags-to-riches rise from office boy in a theatrical booking office to world-famous playwright in *Act One*, his bestselling (if somewhat fictionalized) book that *Time* magazine called "one of the best memoirs of this or any other theatrical generation." His first big success came in 1930 with *Once in a Lifetime*, the first in a series of plays he co-authored during a ten-year partnership with playwright/director George S. Kaufman that included *Merrily We Roll Along* (1934),[25] *You Can't Take It With You* (for which they received the 1937 Pulitzer Prize for Drama), and *The Man Who Came to Dinner* (1939).

Hart worked extensively with nearly all of the major theatrical figures of the Silver Age, including Irving Berlin, Cole Porter, Rodgers and Hart, Monty Wooley, Hassard Short, Robert Alton, and George M. Cohan. And, as we will see, Hart will continue to be a significant force in the Golden Age as well (see page 172).

Hart is one of the most complicated artists to pin down in regard to his sexuality. He alternated back and forth between phases of being relatively out and open about his attraction to men and periods of feeling deeply ashamed, tormented, and determined to assert and demonstrate his heterosexuality. Much of this depended on which psychoanalyst he was working with at the time. For many years he was under the sway of celebrity psychiatrist Dr. Lawrence Kubie, who espoused that homosexuality was pathological but curable and subjected Hart to an early version of conversion therapy. (At that time, homosexuality was still a criminal act and was officially classified as a mental disorder.) Dr. Kubie would

> screw up the lives of quite a few Queer theater artists before the American Psychiatric Association finally removed homosexuality from its list of mental disorders in 1973.[26]

Cole Porter teamed up with Moss Hart for his next show, the "brilliant musical comedy"[27] *Jubilee* (1935). This, again, was a very topical show that took a satirical look at a mythical European royal family in which the King, Queen, and young adult Prince and Princess are so eternally bored with their lives in the palace that when facing the threat of an impending revolution they jump at the chance to abdicate and escape into the real world for a wild series of amorous adventures. Critic Burns Mantle described it as:

> ... perhaps the smartest musical comedy, and the most satisfying that has been produced ... within the length of trustworthy memories. It does for musical comedy what *As Thousands Cheer* did for the revue. It sets new standards and provides new satisfactions. First, an intelligent and perfectly consistent book. For years and years, you have been reading of those new musical comedies in which the music was pleasant but the book was terrible. You will not read that about *Jubilee*. And if you should, don't believe it. Moss Hart has here provided so gorgeously fantastic a story framework on which to hang music cues and lyrical interruptions that your clever sons who are now in college and hope to be librettists one day will be having it held up to them as a model for years to come ... There is going to be a good bit of raving about *Jubilee*. Well, there should be when old forms are broken, and new standards are created in a reborn theatre.[28]

A few days later, Mantle doubled down with a second rave notice that declared the show to be "the most notable contribution to the American theatre this generation has had a chance to welcome." In addition, director Hassard Short was hailed for having "staged the show with resource and imagination," and Albertina Rasch was said to have "designed the dance numbers with amazing skill."[29] Despite receiving rave reviews and introducing "Just One of Those Things" and "Begin The Beguine," two of Porter's most enduring and unconventional songs, *Jubilee* ran for only a modest 169 performances, which suggests that it may have been just a tad too sophisticated for a general audience.

The following season, Porter again joined forces with bookwriters Lindsay and Crouse for the musical comedy **Red, Hot and Blue!** (1936), another vehicle for Ethel Merman, "that high priestess of Cole Porter melodies ... at her best."[30] This time, Merman co-starred with **Jimmy Durante**, "serving in his inimitable fashion as chief clown,"[31] and soon-to-be entertainment superstar **Bob Hope**.[32] This show was "not as amusingly plotted as *Anything Goes*,"[33] and much less sophisticated than *Jubilee*. The plot revolved around a national "Love Lottery" to find a bride for Bob Hope's character (a plot device many critics noted was perhaps too similar to the First Lady love contest that "swept the country" in the 1931 Gershwin musical *Of Thee I Sing*). In this case, the winner would be the person who could locate a woman who, as a child, had accidentally sat on a red hot waffle iron which left an identifying burn mark on her bottom. Even though, as the *New York Times* put it, "the ghost of *Anything Goes* has been haunting the makers of *Red, Hot and Blue!* to their disadvantage,"[34] both audiences and critics ultimately concluded, "What did it matter if the story was loosely assembled and quite silly" when there were "Porter tunes, smart dance routines [by George Hale], and ribald comedy bits that rush to the rescue."[35] Ethel Merman's remarkable "artistry was poured full strength into such persuasive songs such as "Down in the Depths on the Nineteeth Floor." "Ridin' High,'"[36] and her showstopping duet with Hope, "It's De-Lovely." These very classy songs clearly demonstrate Porter's penchant for mixing highbrow and lowbrow aesthetics.

"Wintergreen for President!"—Political Satire on Broadway (I, J, Q, B, W)

The Gershwins moved even further in the direction of social and political satire with three sharp, witty, and ambitious musical comedies: *Strike Up The Band* (1930), *Of Thee I Sing* (1931), and *Let Them Eat Cake* (1932)—all three with books by **George S. Kaufman** and **Morrie Ryskind**, who were both the children of Jewish immigrants. The most successful was their "stinging satire of national politics,"[37] *Of Thee I Sing*, which tells the story of candidate John P. Wintergreen and the shady backroom deals, intrigues, and publicity stunts that get him elected President of the United States. The show's pointed targets include corrupt congressmen, pandering political platforms, the nebulous role of the Vice President, the dubious decisions of the Supreme Court, and a presidential sex scandal that results in an impeachment. Clearly, not much has changed over the past ninety years. Most importantly, *Of Thee I Sing* marked a significant advancement in the development of the Broadway musical. Critic Brooks Atkinson wrote that it "substituted for the doddering musical comedy plot a taut and lethal satire" that was "funnier than the government and not nearly so dangerous." The show's topsy-turvy humor and structure reflected Ira and George's early affection for the operettas of Gilbert and Sullivan. They broke from the standard scene/song format and instead employed extended and complex musical sequences that encompass large sections of the story.

That year, for the first time in the history of the Pulitzer Prize, the "drama committee surprised the world by selecting the musical comedy *Of The I Sing* as the prize-winning play."[38] This was not without controversy, especially since Eugene O'Neil's drama, *Mourning Becomes Electra*, was passed over in favor of it. In an article headlined "Pulitzer Play Vulgar," and in a tone that wavers between admiring and scandalized, Ruth Faxon Macrae of the *Chattanooga Daily Times* wrote:

> This play is ultra-modern and very naughty, every page teeming with outrageous remarks and bald vulgarity. One is amazed at the extraordinary impudence of the entire theme, and after reading it one comes to the conclusion that it is the most

daring bit of satire and vapid naughtiness ever written for the stage. It smacks of the Gilbert and Sullivan lampoons plus a modern lack of respect for everything in the world . . . It has been the musical comedy hit of the season, but musical comedy and drama are not usually synonymous . . . How it ever won the Pulitzer Prize is a puzzle to the most up-to-date and hardened musical comedy fans.

The judges on the committee held firm, however: "This award may be unusual, but the play is unusual. Not only is it coherent enough to class as a play, aside from the music, but a biting and true satire on American politics and the public attitude toward them. Its affect on the stage promises to be considerable."[39] The Pulitzer was shared by bookwriters George S. Kaufman and Morrie Ryskind and lyricist Ira Gershwin, but composer George Gershwin was not deemed eligible to receive a literary prize.

The Great Collaborator: George S. Kaufman

George S. Kaufman was one of the most successful playwrights, bookwriters, and directors in Broadway history. Beginning with his first hit play, *Dulcy*, in 1921 (written in collaboration with Marc Connolly), Kaufman had at least one hit show on Broadway in every season through 1945—and often several hits running simultaneously. He applied his talent for sharp wit and satire to at least forty-five productions, including eighteen Broadway musicals.[40] Kaufman was born in 1888 into a middle-class German Jewish family in Pittsburg, PA. He began his career as a columnist and drama critic and became famous as one of the founding wits of the Algonquin Roundtable.[41] As a playwright, Kaufman is best known for his collaborations with Edna Ferber on *The Royal Family* (1927), *Dinner At Eight* (1932), and *Stage Door* (1936); and with Moss Hart on *Once In A Lifetime* (1930), the Pulitzer Prize-winning *You Can't Take It With You* (1936), and *The Man Who Came To Dinner* (1936). Kaufman's musical credits include the books for two shows created as vehicles for the Marx Brothers: ***The Coconuts*** (1925) and ***Animal Crackers*** (1928); the Dietz and Schwartz revues ***The Band Wagon*** and ***Flying Colors*** (1932); Rodgers and Hart's ***I'd Rather Be Right*** (1937);[42] and the trio of political satires in collaboration with the Gershwins: ***Strike Up The Band***, ***Of Thee I Sing***, and ***Let Them Eat Cake***.[43] Kaufman continued to have major successes well into the Golden Age, most notably as the director of the landmark hit ***Guys and Dolls*** in 1950 and as the director and co-bookwriter[44] of Cole Porter's final musical, ***Silk Stockings***, in 1955.

"Dancing in the Dark"—Dietz and Schwartz and the Intimate Revue

The smaller, more elite Broadway audience of the Depression era also inspired an evolution in the musical revue—known as *the intimate revue*. This new iteration was more focused, streamlined, cohesive, and sophisticated than the extravagant *Ziegfeld Follies*, *George White's Scandals*, and *Earl Carroll's Vanities* style of "girly show" revues of the previous decades. Instead of just a grab-bag of incongruent (if often terrific) material from a multitude of writers, these new-style revues often utilized themes (a cruise around the world,[45] sections of a newspaper),[46] or a strong point of view (pro-labor,[47] progressive politics)[48] to unify their songs, dances, and comedy sketches, all of which were created by a single small team of writers (as had become standard practice in musical comedies). The intimate revue first started to take shape with a series of **Irving Berlin's Music Box Revues** that he created annually between 1921 and 1924 for his new, intimate Music Box Theatre. These productions automatically had a stronger unity than most other revues because all of the songs were "written and conceived" by Berlin, and three of the four productions were staged by Hassard Short. However, it was the Jewish American songwriting team of **Howard Dietz and Arthur Schwartz** who became the virtuosos of this form, with a string of smart, stylish, and extremely topical revues that included *Three's A Crowd* (1930), *The Band Wagon* (1931), *Flying Colors* (1932), and *At Home Abroad* (1935), all produced by Max Gordon[49] and all filled with major stars, hilarious sketches, and hit songs.[50]

In a very similar vein, Irving Berlin and Moss Hart's 1933 revue, **As Thousands Cheer** (also staged by Hassard Short), was literally ripped from the headlines of the day. It employed a newspaper format as its unifying theme, with news headlines projected on a screen above the stage (one of the earliest theatrical uses of projection technology), followed by songs, dances, and comedy sketches that dramatized those headlines with high comedy, biting satire, and even pathos. The show began with front-page news: a comedy sketch about the recent inauguration of President Franklin Delano Roosevelt. It then moved on through the weather report with the song "(We're Having A) Heat Wave," satiric comedy sketches about the birthday of millionaire John D. Rockefeller and the impending celebrity divorce of Hollywood stars Joan Crawford and Douglas Fairbanks, Jr. Next, the "funny pages" sprang to life in a ballet (choreographed by modern dance pioneer Charles Weidman) in which dancing superstar **Marilynn Miller**, dressed as a little girl, romped with all the most popular comic strip characters of the day. Then a spectacularly designed, sepia-toned, first-act-finale nostalgically looked back to the 1880s by presenting an illustrated society page "rotogravure section" in which debonair song and dance man **Clifton Webb**[51] and an ensemble of fashionably dressed New Yorkers promenaded down Fifth Avenue as they introduced the song "Easter Parade." The second act opened with a sequence spoofing the Metropolitan Opera, but then a headline flashed on the screen reading: "Unknown Negro Lynched By Frenzied Mob." Out of the darkness below emerged the great African American singer and actress **Ethel Waters**, dressed as a poor, young sharecropper's wife, struggling to hold her life together as she desperately tries to cope with her loss. She sings, "Suppertime ... I should set the table 'cause it's suppertime ... somehow I'm not able, cause this man o'mine ain't comin' home no more ..."[52] As many in the audience would have been well aware, in 1933, twenty-eight Black men were reported to have been lynched in eleven states (and undoubtedly there were many more that went unreported). Irving

Berlin wrote this song especially for Waters, and it should be noted that this was four years before Billie Holiday introduced the similarly themed song, "Strange Fruit." After devastating the audience, the revue then flipped back into high comedy mode with satirical depictions of Mahatma Gandhi, the Cuban revolution, Noel Coward, Josephine Baker, and the British Royal Family. The final headline read, "Supreme Court Hands Down Important Decision." The judges' edict was that, henceforth musical revues were forbidden from ending with reprises of their previous songs—so the cast performed a new one.[53]

This was the power of the revue—the ability to turn on a dime from comedy to drama and even, on occasion, tragedy, and then instantly pivot back to satire, glamor, and romance. The most important element of a revue was the running order—the sequencing of the songs and sketches—and the creators would go to great lengths and much trial and error to ensure that their shows were programmed for maximum impact.

"Heat Wave": Ethel Waters (B, Q, W)

Superstar **Ethel Waters** was born into extreme poverty in Pennsylvania in 1896. She began singing as a teenager, and following a very successful early career in vaudeville, nightclubs, and recording,[54] she made her Broadway debut as the star of the short-lived revue *Africana* in 1927. Waters' performance in *Africana* brought her to the attention of Irving Berlin, who became even more captivated by her when she introduced the Harold Arlen/Ted Koehler song, "Stormy Weather," at Harlem's Cotton Club in 1933. This led directly to Berlin engaging her as one of the four principal stars of *As Thousand Cheer*.[55] During her long career, in addition to starring in nine Broadway musicals and two plays, Waters achieved major stardom in nightclubs, radio, film, and television and became one the highest-paid performers in show business—white or Black. Fortunately for us, she recreated her acclaimed stage performances in the musical *Cabin in the Sky* (1940) and the play *The Member of the Wedding* (1951) in the subsequent film versions. Offstage, Waters was married three times but was also well-known in Harlem's Lesbian circles. Perhaps her most significant relationship was with dancer Ethel Williams. During the 1920s, they lived together and toured in a vaudeville act called "The Two Ethels." However, like virtually every other Gay and Lesbian star prior to the 1970s, Waters herself never made any public statements or acknowledgment regarding her sexuality.

Interestingly, two years after the opening of *As Thousands Cheer*, the WPA's Federal Theater Project (1935–9)[56] was established, and one of its most acclaimed and popular programs was its "living newspaper" unit. These innovative, often radical productions also took their inspiration from the newspaper headlines of the day by dramatizing social, economic, and racial issues and imploring their audiences to go out and enact change. It is not clear if *As Thousands Cheer* had any direct influence on those productions, but it does demonstrate that Irving Berlin had an incredible ability to anticipate and respond to the social issues, concerns, and styles of the moment and to remain relevant throughout the many decades of his Broadway career.

Going Hollywood — Broadway Heads West (I, J, Q, B, W)

Nearly simultaneously with the onslaught of the Depression, the movies began to talk, and, of course, sing, and suddenly the Hollywood movie studios suddenly needed a lot of songs. As a result, virtually every successful white Broadway songwriter was enticed to go west by the promise of big money and mass exposure for their work. None of the Black songwriters, however, were offered this opportunity—no matter how successful they were. This was for the same reason that no Hollywood studios would purchase the film rights to Black musicals: movie theaters in the South refused to show films with Black leading characters, and the studios didn't want to make movies they would be unable to distribute to thousands of Southern theaters. This is why none of the popular Black musicals of the 1920s, including the mega-hit *Shuffle Along*, ever received a film adaptation. This crystal-clear example of institutionalized racism put Black Broadway creators at a severe financial disadvantage compared to their white counterparts. In contrast, Irving Berlin; Dorothy Donnelly, George and Ira Gershwin; De Sylva, Brown, and Henderson, and most of their colleagues all achieved significant success and reaped enormous financial rewards from writing songs for early movie musicals and/or having their stage hits adapted into films.

Dorothy Fields arrived in Hollywood in 1930 and began writing with various composers, including Jerome Kern. Most famously, they collaborated on the score for the classic Fred Astaire/Ginger Rogers film *Swing Time*, which included the Academy Award-winning song "The Way You Look Tonight." Dorothy was now, without a doubt, one of the top lyricists in show business. Among her biggest hits was a song titled "I Feel a Song Comin' On," but in various appearances and interviews,[57] she later admitted that she didn't "believe a word of it! A song just doesn't come on! I've always had to tease it out—squeeze it out." And she emphasized repeatedly that "Lyric writing is hard work, partly because it's so condensed—you have to express an original thought in a very few words. Elizabeth Barrett Browning could write a poem two pages long. Try taking that to a music publisher!" Like most of her colleagues, Dorothy Fields did not stay in Hollywood long because, as historian Laurence Maslon has noted, Hollywood couldn't offer Broadway songwriters what they most desired—creative freedom:

> In addition to the interference of studio chiefs and tone-deaf line producers, Hollywood had its own form of self-censorship. The Production Code, better known as the Hays Code, was introduced in 1934. Even if film producers wanted

sophisticated Broadway material reproduced intact . . . the Hays Code made that impossible. The most benign lyrics were tweaked with idiotic regularity by inane sensibilities.[58]

On Broadway, however, they "were much freer to write more adult, more sophisticated, and often more sexually explicit lyrics for more sophisticated New York audiences."[59] By the end of the decade, Dorothy had returned to New York and Broadway, where she teamed up with her brother, Herbert Fields, and during the war years, they wrote the books for three hit Cole Porter musicals: ***Let's Face It*** (1943), ***Something for the Boys*** (1944), and ***Mexican Hayride*** (1945). *Something for the Boys* was a vehicle for Ethel Merman, who had become Broadway's biggest female star. Ethel and Dorothy became great friends, and soon Dorothy came up with the idea for another musical they could work on together—a show that would catapult them both into the Golden Age of the Broadway musical.

Meanwhile, Cole Porter had also found huge success writing songs for film musicals, including such enduring hits as "Easy to Love," "I've Got You Under My Skin," and "In the Still of the Night." And Porter loved the Hollywood lifestyle, especially its wild underground Gay scene, which he jumped into with great enthusiasm. Linda, however, grew more and more concerned that Cole's homosexuality would be exposed and wreck both his career and their marriage, and this led to one of the few serious rifts in their relationship. Although much has been written about Porter's considerable appetite for casual sexual encounters with soldiers, sailors, chorus boys, and rent boys, he also had several very loving, passionate, and sometimes tortured, long-term relationships with male lovers, including the Russian dancer and ballet librettist Boris Kochno, architect Ed Tausch, dancer and choreographer Nelson Barclift, director John Wilson, and longtime friend Ray Kelly, whose children still receive half of the royalty income from Porter's songs and shows.[60] Many of Porter's best and most romantic songs were written with these specific men in mind.

Cole and Linda would soon reconcile, but only after a tragic and catastrophic event. In 1937, while riding at a Long Island country club, Porter's horse reared, fell to the ground, and rolled over on top of him, crushing both of his legs. Linda immediately rushed back from Paris to take care of him. Porter was hospitalized for seven months, and his doctors told him that his right leg would have to be amputated, and possibly the left one as well, but he refused—he just couldn't face the prospect of being pitied as the legless songwriter. That choice, however, meant that he would remain in nearly constant pain for the rest of his life. In spite of this enormous setback, Porter was determined to somehow rise above it and get back to work. And he did. However, as we will see, his musicals in the late 1930s and early 1940s were a very mixed bag. The accident had clearly affected his work—he still created hit shows and hit songs, but it was clear that he had lost much of his spark. By the end of the decade, offers to write came few and far between, and many believed that Porter's career was over.

Broadway Dance #6: Queer Choreographers of the Silver Age (Q, l)

The stereotype that most male dancers and choreographers are homosexual is even more of a cliché than the idea that all Gay men love Broadway musicals. However, it does seem to be true that, throughout history, the male contingent of Broadway dancing ensembles has been predominantly made up of Gay men. There are, of course, no official statistics, but the reality of this is made abundantly clear in a number of period sources including Bradford Ropes' trio of backstage novels[61] inspired by his own experiences as a Gay dancer on Broadway in the 1920s, as well as an unpublished memoir by Queer theater producer John Kenley, who started out as an acrobat and chorus boy in the 1920s. Theater critics during the Silver Age would often comment on the noticeable effeminacy (if not directly the sexual preference) of Broadway chorus men, in their reviews, and actress and playwright Mae West hired forty chorus boys to appear in her 1927 play, *The Drag*, later contending that "All of the chorus boys [in those days] were Gay. But the producers never gave speaking parts to homosexuals. So I helped a lot of gay boys along,—I gave them parts."[62] And when casting their 1928 show, *Present Arms*, set near a U.S. Marine base at Pearl Harbor, Rodgers and Hart, Herbert Fields, and choreographer Busby Berkeley "were in agreement that the show would be different in at least one respect from most musical comedies: there would be no effeminate young men in the chorus."[63] These homophobic reactions only confirm that this is a stereotype based in reality, and one that seems to be equally valid for musical productions in London, Paris, and Berlin during the same period. This, of course, poses the eternal chicken or egg question: Are Queer people drawn to the "theatrical milieu" because they somehow intuitively sense that even if it is not an entirely safe haven, it will, at least, "offer them more tolerance than most workplaces?"[64] Or can it be that, for some reason, performing artists, especially male dancers, are just more likely to be Queer? Whatever the case, chorus dancers often grow up to be choreographers, so the overwhelming majority of male Broadway choreographers (with a few notable exceptions) have been Gay.

"I have exactly six minutes in which to raise the customer out of his seat. If I cannot do it, I am no good."—Robert Alton[65]
Robert Alton was born in 1902 in Vermont. He "fell in love with show business at an early age," but after his dream of becoming a circus contortionist was "dashed by his parents, he began seriously studying dance and eventually made his professional début with Mikhail Mordkin's ballet company." Alton made his Broadway debut as a dancer in the chorus of the *Greenwich Village Follies of 1924*, where he became a protege of John Murray Anderson, who eventually hired him to create "additional choreography" for *The Ziegfeld Follies of 1934*. From there, Alton went on to choreograph twenty-eight Broadway shows, which included five Cole Porter

musicals (including *Anything Goes*), four Rodgers and Hart musicals (including *Pal Joey*), one show by Jule Styne (*Hazel Flagg*), and one by Rodgers and Hammerstein (*Me and Juliet*), as well as two late editions of the *Ziegfeld Follies* (1936 and 1943).

According to author Brent Phillips, Alton's choreography amounted to an "active redesign of musical comedy dancing," in which he "rejected old-style line patterns" and instead "flooded the Broadway stage with movement, 'jiving' ballet, refining tap and swinging modern dance in the process."[66] Anticipating Agnes De Mille's approach, Alton "revolutionized Broadway show dancing by replacing the precision routines of the chorus line with dances for soloists and small groups, always elegantly staged and with unusual attention to stylistic details."[67] In an interview with Phillips, the two-time Tony Award-winning choreographer Donald Saddler insisted that "Everything we know about staging a musical number comes from the work of Robert Alton."[68]

The "dream ballet" that Alton created to close the first act of *Pal Joey* in 1940 was a key precursor to the ballets that Agnes DeMille and Jerome Robbins created just a few seasons later for *Oklahoma!* and *On The Town*. When *Pal Joey* was revived on Broadway in 1952, *New York Times* dance critic John Martin noted that although Alton had "been in Hollywood most of the time since the New Era had set in for dancing shows," he had nevertheless still "played an important role" in bringing that new era into being:

> Just how important we might not have remembered but for this happy restoration of "Joey." Though [Alton] could always handle a "routine" with the best of them, it was characteristic of his choreography then as now that it was beautifully integrated into the show itself. It is interesting in the light of the *Oklahoma!* revolution of Agnes de Mille, how plainly Alton's ballet "Joey Looks Into The Future" prepared the way for Miss De Mille's "Laurey Makes up Her Mind." They are vastly different, of course, in content and form but there is nonetheless an undeniable link between them in function.[69]

Although Alton was briefly married to his dance partner, Marjory Fielding, and fathered a son with her, his same-sex relationships were well known within the industry, and he was involved in a long-term relationship with another noted Broadway and Hollywood dancer and choreographer, **Charles Walters**.[70] During the 1950s, Alton primarily worked in Hollywood, where he died of a kidney ailment in 1957 at fifty-three. His legacy, however, has lived on through the dozens of iconic dances and musical numbers that he created for a string of classic film musicals such as *The Harvey Girls*, *Easter Parade*, *White Christmas*, and *There's No*

Business Like Show Business, which have had a tremendous influence on several generations of Broadway choreographers.

Choreographer **Charles Weidman** is known as one of the innovators of American modern dance. He was born in Nebraska in 1901, where he studied dance as a child. By age nineteen, he received a scholarship to the Denishawn school in New York City, where he worked closely with modern dance pioneers Ruth St. Denis and Ted Shawn. Soon he became a leading Denishawn dancer, partnering Martha Graham and replacing Shawn in important roles. In 1928, Weidman joined forces with Doris Humphrey to form their own Humphry–Weidman dance school and company, which became another leading force in the modern dance movement. In addition, between 1932 and 1958, Weidman choreographed fifteen Broadway revues and musical comedies, including ***Americana*** (1932), ***As Thousands Cheer*** (1932), ***Life Begins At 8:40*** (1934), ***I'd Rather Be Right*** (1937), ***New Faces of 1943***, ***Sing Out Sweet Land*** (1944), and ***Portofino*** (1958). Weidman had a long romantic relationship with another modern dance pioneer, the Mexican American dancer and choreographer **Jose Limón**, who was a member of the Humphrey–Weidman Company and a featured dancer in *Americana* and *As Thousands Cheer*. Limón also choreographed the hit 1933 musical *Roberta*.

Dancer and choreographer **Jack Cole** is one of Broadway's most significant but perhaps least-known choreographers outside of the dance world. Over his four-decade career working in nightclubs, stage, film, and television, he developed a unique and distinctively American style and vocabulary of dance by combining ballet and modern dance with a variety of multicultural world dance forms and then melding them together into a movement language often referred to as "theatrical jazz dance." Cole himself preferred to call it "urban dance." He never hid his sexuality, and by modern standards, he would likely be considered to have been openly Gay at a time when virtually no one else was.

Cole was born in New Jersey in 1911 to Irish and German immigrant parents. He left home as a teenager to study at the Denishawn School, where he was invited to join the company after only six weeks of classes. He was a charter member of Ted Shawn's groundbreaking all-male dance troupe, Ted Shawn and his Men Dancers, and then joined the Humphrey–Weidman group. During this time, Cole became interested in many styles and forms of ethnic dance. He studied Indian dance with master instructor Uday Shankar.[71] He hung out in the dance clubs of Harlem, where he immersed himself in the Lindy Hop and other Black vernacular jazz dances. Later he traveled to various Caribbean islands and Brazil to study their indigenous dances in person. Cole was always passionate about doing dance research, and while preparing to choreograph the Broadway musical *Kismet* (1953), he reportedly traveled to Baghdad, where its story was set.

In 1937, Cole formed a nightclub act called "Jack Cole and His Dancers," and soon they were headlining the top clubs in New York and across the country. Cole's sexy mix of East Indian and American swing dance styles became a sensation. Critics incorrectly dubbed it "Hindu Swing," but, indeed, it was difficult to categorize. It wasn't pure Indian dance, authentic jazz dance, or classic modern dance, but rather a new hybrid of all three. This juxtaposition of cultures gave birth to Cole's unique style and brand. On Broadway in the *Ziegfeld Follies of 1943*, he borrowed from the uptown culture of Black and Spanish Harlem for a number titled "The Wedding of a Solid Sender." His choreography was often very challenging and rigorous. In his club act, during "Sing, Sing, Sing," an all-male cast would strut, leap, and slide on their knees to the blaring horns of Benny Goodman's classic tune. Dancer Buzz Miller remembered that the first time they danced that challenging number, Cole "came bouncing off the stage, but everyone else was in the corner throwing up."[72] The Jack Cole Dancers were then hired to appear in a Betty Grable movie, which led to Cole being hired to create the choreography for nearly thirty Hollywood films. He had an amazing talent for coaxing dynamic performances out of actors who were not trained dancers, as exemplified by Marilynn Monroe and Jane Russell in the film version of the Broadway hit *Gentlemen Prefer Blondes*. It's important to note that, in addition to creating the choreography, Cole also directed the camerawork and supervised all aspects of the musical sequences of those films.[73] However, "his highly individual dance style emphasized the sensuality of his stars and usually caused trouble with the film censors. More than one of his dance numbers ended up on the cutting-room floor."[74]

Today, those films constitute the most tangible record of Cole's work. But, throughout all of his Hollywood success, he relentlessly pursued what he most desired—a signature musical on Broadway. He choreographed twelve Broadway shows, including the considerable hits **Kismet** (1953), ***A Funny Thing Happened on the Way to the Forum*** (1962), and **Man of La Mancha** (1965). Of those, only *Kismet* included extended dance sequences (which Cole recreated in the 1955 film version), and it was the closest he would come to having his choreography memorably and inextricably linked to a musical in the way that Agnes De Mille, Jerome Robbins, and Bob Fosse achieved with *Oklahoma!*, *West Side Story*, and *Sweet Charity*.

Within the theater world, however, Jack Cole is acknowledged as one of the key innovators of Broadway dance. Every choreographer since has been influenced by his work—most directly Jerome Robbins, Michael Kidd, Gower Champion, Peter Gennaro, Michael Bennett, and, especially, Bob Fosse. Today, Fosse's name is synonymous with Broadway jazz dance, and Cole's is only a footnote. But there would be no "Fosse style" without the heavy influence of Jack Cole on his work.

"Our Little Den of Iniquity"—*Pal Joey* and the Beginning of the End (♩, ♪, ♩)

Rodgers and Hart also had success in Hollywood during the 1930s, and Larry Hart also got swept up in the wild underground Gay scene there, but unfortunately, a somewhat seedier version of it than Cole Porter got involved in. Like most Broadway songwriters, Rodgers and Hart got fed up with not having more control over their work and the use of their songs and eventually returned to New York, where society was becoming progressively more conservative and intolerant of homosexuality. Hart's benders and disappearances began to occur with increasing frequency, and Rodgers would sometimes have to resort to locking Hart in a room to ensure that he would finish the lyrics for an upcoming show. It's a sad story. Hart does not appear to have ever had any kind of substantial romantic relationship. Even though he was constantly throwing parties and surrounding himself with crowds, he was always lonely. Singer Mabel Mercer described him as "the saddest man I ever knew."[75] While it is easy to focus on the pain and sadness in Hart's life, it was also, without a doubt, a life filled with creativity, including the lyrics (and sometimes the books) for twenty-nine Broadway musicals. That kind of creativity always brings joy—at least to some extent. And since no one's life can be painted in just one color, I prefer to think of Larry Hart the way Oscar Hammerstein II described him:

> I think of him always as skipping and bouncing. In all the time I knew him, I never saw him walk slowly. I never saw his face in repose, I never heard him chuckle quietly. He laughed loudly and easily at other people's jokes and his own too. His large eyes danced, and his head would wag. He was alert and dynamic and fun to be with.[76]

During the 1930s, Rodgers and Hart created ten Broadway musicals and continued to lift the form to new heights with shows such as ***Jumbo***, ***On Your Toes***, ***Babes in Arms***, ***The Boys From Syracuse***, and ***I'd Rather Be Right*** (whose central character was Franklin D. Roosevelt, played by George M. Cohan). The peak of their partnership came in 1940 with their musical ***Pal Joey***—a show that marked a major step forward in the evolution of the loosely assembled musical comedies of the Silver Age into the more cohesive and unified structure that would soon revolutionize the musical. And one of the principal driving forces behind this revolution was *Pal Joey*'s producer, director and (uncredited) bookwriter, George Abbott.

Broadway's Longest Running Hit: Mr. Abbott

George Abbott is one of the major exceptions to the central premise of this book—he was a straight, WASP male—and he is also one of the single most important figures in the history of Broadway. He certainly had the longest theatrical career of the twentieth century. In the course of his long life (he lived to 107!), George Abbott was involved as the director, and/or writer, and/or producer of more than 120 Broadway productions. *New York Times* journalist Gilbert Millstein once wrote that "on the basis of sheer frightening volume alone, an argument can be drummed up that no living individual, or possibly even dead, has contributed more to the Broadway theater than George Abbott."[77] That was written in 1954, the fortieth year of Abbott's career, and he still had fifty years of work ahead of him. Most of Abbot's career was devoted to directing plays. He didn't tackle his first musical until 1935, when he co-directed Rodgers and Hart's circus extravaganza, *Jumbo*. Over the next twenty-seven years, he staged twenty-six musicals—twenty-two of which became major hits. He wrote and directed the musicals as if they were plays—with integrity and respect for the logic of their stories and the believability of their characters. And he directed the plays like musicals—with vibrant pacing and breakneck speed.

By the late 1930s, Abbott had garnered such a high level of reference and respect that even his closest friends and colleagues stopped using his first name and began to call him "Mister Abbott." And there was much talk of the "Abbott Touch." Like the legendary King Midas, it was thought that Abbott's directorial touch turned a play or musical into gold. When asked to explain the "Abbott Touch," he would scoff and respond, "I make them say their final syllables." And indeed his directing method has often reductively been characterized as simply: "Louder, Faster, Funnier." But clearly, there was much more to it than that. Abbott emphasized the importance of clarity in the story. "Sometimes if you fix the writing, you fix the directing," he said. "I've seen so many plays bore the audience because the story is muddy." And he instructed his actors to always approach comic situations very seriously: "If you play comedy for laughs it won't work; if you play it for real, it will."

Pal Joey, with music and lyrics by Rodgers and Hart and choreography by Robert Alton, was based on a series of short stories by **John O'Hara** that had first appeared in the *New Yorker* magazine. The musical's central characters are Joey Evans, a young, ambitious, cheap but crudely charismatic small-time nightclub entertainer, who becomes the willing boy toy of a glamorous, sophisticated, middle-aged, married high-society matron, Vera Simpson, who funds Joey's dream of opening his own nightspot.[78] For both of these characters, Hart wrote lyrics that I think come very close to expressing his own jaded, world-weary, but at the same time, heartfelt view of love and relationships, especially in his lyric for the score's most famous song, "Bewitched, Bothered and Bewildered":

After one whole quart of brandy,
Like a daisy, I awake.
With no Bromo-Seltzer handy,
I don't even shake.
Men are not a new sensation,
I've done pretty well, I think:
But this half-pint imitation
Puts me on the blink.

I'm wild again!
Beguiled again!
A simpering, whimpering child again!
Bewitched, bothered and bewildered am I . . .
Couldn't sleep
And wouldn't sleep
Until I could sleep where I shouldn't sleep.
Bewitched, bothered and bewildered am I![79]

Pal Joey's cynical, provocative storyline and amoral anti-hero brought a darkness and toughness to the Broadway musical that had not been seen before. It was also wildly entertaining, with a hit-filled score, remarkable choreography by Robert Alton, and a thrilling star-making performance by Gene Kelly in the title role.

Pal Joey was both the pinnacle and the beginning of the end for Rodgers and Hart's stellar partnership. Although two more hit shows would follow it, by the early 1940s, Hart was disappearing for weeks at a time, and his drunken binges were becoming more and more disturbing. When the team received an offer from the Theatre Guild to turn the play *Green Grow The Lilacs* into a musical, Rodgers made an offer to Hart, "I want you to have yourself admitted to a sanitarium, and I'll get myself admitted, too. We'll be there together and work together. But you've got to get off the street."[80] Hart made it clear that this was not going to happen. There was no way he was checking himself into any sanitarium—and in fact, he was on his way to Mexico. Rodgers finally gave him an ultimatum: "Larry, if you walk out now, someone else will do the show with me." "Anyone in mind?" Hart asked. Rodgers replied, "Oscar Hammerstein will write the lyrics." "There's no better man for the job," replied Hart, "I don't know how you put up with me all these years. The best thing would be for you to forget about me." With that, Hart walked out of their meeting, leaving Rodgers—and the show that would become *Oklahoma!*—behind. Larry Hart attended the opening night of that epoch-changing musical and, afterward, hugged Rodgers and told him it was "the best show he had ever seen!" But less than a year later, Hart died of pneumonia after losing his coat during an all-night bender on the icy cold streets of New York.

Hart was too smart not to have seen the writing on the wall. After all, he had in no small way helped to usher in the major disruption that was about to take place. The loose, sometimes ramshackle, but wildly funny, tuneful, and entertaining Rodgers and Hart-style musical comedies of the Silver Age would soon be almost entirely replaced by the story-driven, character-rich, perfectly crafted, and cohesive *musical plays* of Rodgers and Hammerstein—a form Hammerstein had pioneered back in 1927 with *Show Boat*. These new, groundbreaking works would usher the Broadway musical into its Golden Age.

Fig. 5: The vaudeville team of Harrigan and Hart were among the first theatrical artists to create what were at least embryonic versions of the Broadway musical. Between 1873 and 1893, Edward Harrigan (right), in partnership with Tony Hart (left, in drag), produced, directed, and co-starred in forty-one not-quite-yet-musicals featuring a revolving cast of ethnic character types from the streets of New York—Irish, Germans, Italians, Jews, and African Americans. Smith Collection / Gado / Getty Images.

Fig. 6: Classically trained Irish immigrant composer Victor Herbert pioneered a new, distinctly American form of operetta. Among his principal collaborators was Rida Johnson Young, who between 1910 and 1924 wrote the book and lyrics for eleven musicals and operettas, including Herbert's greatest success, *Naughty Marietta* (1910), which introduced the hit song, "Ah, Sweet Mystery of Life." M. Witmark & Sons.

Fig. 7: Left to right, star Eddie Cantor, producer Florenz Ziegfeld, Jr., songwriter Irving Berlin (at piano), director-choreographer Sammy Lee, and the Ziegfeld Girls rehearse for *The Ziegfeld Follies of 1927*. Bettmann / Contributor.

Fig. 8: Composer Will Marion Cook contributed songs to thirteen Broadway musicals, including *Clorindy, or The Origin of the Cakewalk* (1898), *The Casino Girl* (1900), *In Dahomey* (1903), *Abyssinia* (1906), *Bandana Land* (1908), and *The Ziegfeld Follies of 1910*. Will Marion Cook.

Fig. 9: Lyricist, bookwriter, director, producer, and performer Bob Cole (seated) and composer, lyricist, and performer J. Rosamond Johnson created songs for at least twenty Broadway musicals (often in collaboration with Rosamond's brother James Weldon Johnson), including Weber and Fields' *Whoop-De-Doo* (1903), *Humpty-Dumpty* (1904), *The Shoo-Fly Regiment* (1907), and *The Red Moon* (1909). Bob Cole and John Rosamond Johnson.

Fig. 10: Top vaudeville and Broadway stars Bert Williams and George Walker flank the "Queen of the Cakewalk," choreographer and performer Aida Overton Walker, in their 1904 musical *In Dahomey* (music by Will Marion Cook, lyrics by Paul Dunbar, book by Jesse Shipp). Williams would later become the first Black star of *The Ziegfeld Follies*. Wisconsin Center for Film and Theater Research.

Fig. 11: In 1921, the songwriting and vaudeville team of Noble Sissle and Eubie Blake kicked Broadway into the Jazz Age with their smash hit musical comedy *Shuffle Along*. This dynamic, long-running show helped to spark the Harlem Renaissance and initiated a vibrant second decade of Black musicals on Broadway that included their follow-up musical, *The Chocolate Dandies* (1924). JP Jazz Archive / Contributor.

Fig. 12: Broadway, vaudeville, and film star, Bill "Bojangles" Robinson, perhaps the most influential tap dancer of all time, celebrated his sixty-first birthday by dancing down sixty-one blocks of Broadway, cheered on the entire way by adoring crowds. Afro Newspaper / Gado / Contributor.

Fig. 13: Irving Berlin and Moss Hart's 1933 "sophisticated" revue, *As Thousands Cheer*, staged by Hassard Short, employed a newspaper format as its unifying theme. In Act One, Broadway star Ethel Waters electrified the audience with the weather report, "Heat Wave" (pictured here), choreographed by Charles Weidman, and then, in the second act, she devastated the audience with the dramatic song "Supper Time." Performing Arts Images / ArenaPAL.

Fig. 14: Producers Charles Frohman (left) and Charles Dillingham (right) were a Queer Broadway power couple who, during the earliest decades of the Broadway musical, were remarkably visible, even in the press, as unusually close friends and business partners. Together and separately, they helped launch the careers of many of the Queer theater artists who played significant roles in inventing the musical. New York Public Library.

Fig. 15: One of the most popular and highest-paid stars of the Genesis Period was Julian Eltinge. Between 1905 and 1915, he starred in five Broadway musicals created especially for him by top talents such as Cohan, Berlin, Harbach, and Kern to showcase his extraordinary talents for "female impersonation." In this trick photo, Eltinge appears as both the groom and the bride. Studio of Luther S. White.

Fig. 16: Queer director, choreographer, and lighting designer Hassard Short, whose thirty-year career included fifty Broadway shows, was constantly in demand as one of the most innovative and acclaimed "stagers" of musical comedies and revues. Theodore C. Marceau.

Fig. 17: Between 1925 and 1943, Richard Rodgers (music) and Lorenz Hart (lyrics) created the scores for thirty-one witty, tuneful, and often quite innovative and experimental Broadway musicals. However, the loose, ramshackle, yet wildly entertaining Rodgers and Hart-style musical comedies of the Silver Age would eventually be replaced by the story-driven, character-rich, impeccably crafted, and cohesive musical plays of Rodgers and Hammerstein. Bettmann / Contributor.

"Old Man Trouble, I Don't Mind Him"

Fig. 18: Actor, playwright, composer, lyricist, and director Noel Coward with Broadway director and producer John (Jack) Wilson on the deck of a ship. The pair frequently traveled the world together as creative, business, and romantic partners. Copyright – The Noël Coward Archive Trust. With thanks to the Noel Coward Foundation.

Fig. 19: Director Josh Logan (center, in chair) and choreographer Robert Alton (right), on the stage of a Broadway theatre, in rehearsal for the 1942 Rodgers and Hart musical *By Jupiter*, with stars Constance Moore and Ray Bolger. New York Public Library.

Fig. 20: From left, director Agnes De Mille, producer Saint-Subber, songwriter Cole Porter, and choreographer Hanya Holm in rehearsal for the 1950 musical *Out of this World*. New York Times Co. / Contributor.

"Old Man Trouble, I Don't Mind Him"

Fig. 21: Prolific bookwriter Herbert Fields and his equally prolific sister, lyricist, and bookwriter Dorothy Fields, photographed by *Vogue* magazine in 1943, presumably backstage at *Something for the Boys*, the hit Cole Porter musical for which they collaborated on the book. Together and separately, they were central to the creation of dozens of hit Broadway musicals. Luis Lemus / Contributor.

Fig. 22: Actress, playwright, librettist, producer, and director Dorothy Donnelly was a leading Broadway actress before she turned her attention to playwriting. Between 1916 and 1927, she created the book and lyrics for eight Broadway musicals and operettas, including the blockbusters *Blossom Time* and *The Student Prince*. *Cosmopolitan*, Vol. 48.

Fig. 23: Choreographer and star dancer Gertrude Hoffmann was the first woman to be credited with the "dance direction" of a Broadway show (although other uncredited women, including Aida Overton Walker, likely preceded her). Between 1903 and 1927, Hoffmann designed the dances for fifteen Broadway musical comedies and revues. Nickolas Muray / Contributor.

Fig. 24: Polish-Russian-Jewish immigrant Albertina Rasch choreographed thirty-three Broadway shows, including many of the biggest hits of the 1920s and 1930s, such as *The Ziegfeld Follies of 1927*, *Rio Rita*, and *Mlle. Modiste*; the legendary Dietz and Schwartz musical revues: *Three's A Crowd*, *Flying Colors*, and *The Band Wagon*; and the landmark 1941 Moss Hart/Kurt Weill/Ira Gershwin musical *Lady in the Dark*. Maurice Goldberg / Contributor.

Fig. 25: In her choreography for nine Broadway productions, including *Cabin in the Sky*, in which she starred as the temptress "Georgia Brown," the extraordinary dancer, choreographer, and anthropologist Katherine Dunham created highly theatrical evocations of indigenous dances from around the world, all derived from her anthropological research. She also mined the rich history of African American dance, from the cakewalk to the hot swing dances of the 1940s. Annemarie Heinrich.

Fig. 26: Actor Bobby Watson (flanked by co-stars Gladys Miller and Eva Puck) was acclaimed for his performance as the flamboyant "male modiste Madam Lucy" in the 1919 smash hit musical *Irene*. Twenty-two years would go by before audiences would see another overtly Queer principal character in a Broadway musical. Frank A. Munsey Company.

INTERMISSION

Figs. 27, 28, 29, 30: The Broadway musical as a craft and artform has been passed down directly from one artist to the next, generation to generation. One of the most direct and significant examples of this kind of "legacy chain" is the connection between (clockwise from top left) Otto Harbach, Oscar Hammerstein II, Stephen Sondheim, and Lin-Manuel Miranda. GAB Archive / Contributor (Fig. 27); Z Arthur (Fig. 28); Michael Hardy / Stringer (Fig. 29); Joan Marcus / ArenaPAL (Fig. 30).

CHAPTER 7
"BY YOUR PUPILS, YOU'LL BE TAUGHT": A BROADWAY LEGACY CHAIN FROM HARBACH, TO HAMMERSTEIN, TO SONDHEIM, TO MIRANDA (🎵, 🎶, 🎵)

In the Introduction to this book, I described the Broadway musical as an art and a craft that has been passed down directly from one artist to the next, generation to generation—almost like in a medieval craft guild. One can directly trace the first-hand connections between composers, lyricists, bookwriters, directors, producers, and performers from the earliest days of the musical right up to their counterparts working more than a century later on Broadway today. This chapter will highlight one of the most direct and significant examples of this kind of "legacy chain" by tracking the knowledge, insight, and skills that flowed from Otto Harbach to Oscar Hammerstein II to Stephen Sondheim to Lin-Manuel Miranda.

At first glance, it might seem that Otto Harbach's loosely constructed Silver Age musical comedies and operettas would have only a limited relationship to Hammerstein and Rodgers' tightly woven, story-driven musical plays, or that Sondheim's edgy, ironic, sardonic musicals would have much to do with the open-hearted Hammerstein shows that preceded him or with Lin Manuel-Miranda's rap music-influenced shows that followed. However, a closer look reveals a very direct connection—and together, the combined works of these four musical theater giants encompass nearly the entire history of the Broadway musical.

Otto Harbach wrote the book and/or lyrics for forty-five Broadway musicals. He was born in 1873 and grew up in Salt Lake City, where his Danish immigrant parents worked on a farm. His family was very poor, but somehow Otto worked his way through Knox College in Illinois and then received a Master's in English at Whitman College in Washington State.

Meanwhile, in 1895, **Oscar Hammerstein II** was being born into a theatrical dynasty in New York. His father, William, was one of America's most successful theater managers. He ran Hammerstein's Victoria Theatre, New York's most popular vaudeville house at that time. Oscar's uncle Arthur was a successful Broadway producer of musical comedies and operettas. His grandfather was the German Jewish immigrant Oscar Hammerstein I, the flamboyant showman profiled in Chapter 1, whose name and face were continually in the public eye as he made and lost fortunes, built twelve theaters, and ran several opera companies. As author Laurie Winer relates, "Oscar II grew up at the epicenter of a cultural mashup unlike anything that had come before." He recalled going to his father's theater "every Sunday where the performers taught him everything he needed to know about comedy and pacing," and just like his grandfather, he fell hopelessly in love with musical theater.[1]

It was around this time that Otto Harbach arrived in New York with the intention of getting a Ph.D. from Columbia University. But when his failing eyesight made intense reading too challenging, he dropped out to take a job in advertising. Then, in 1906, after attending a performance of George M. Cohan's *Forty-Five Minutes From Broadway*, he instantly became fascinated by the possibilities of musical theater. Just two years later, he made his Broadway debut, writing the lyrics for the musical *Three Twins* (1908), which introduced one of the most popular songs of the era, "Cuddle up a Little Closer, Lovey Mine" (music by Karl Hoschna).[2] Over the following twelve years, Harbach worked on seventeen Broadway musicals. Most of them were hits, and many were produced by Oscar's uncle, Arthur Hammerstein.

As Oscar's passion for theater deepened, his father, who hated show business, grew very concerned and, on his deathbed, made Oscar swear to become a lawyer and never, ever go into the theater! Three years later, in 1912, Oscar dutifully entered Columbia University. But ironically, it was there that he became permanently hooked on theater after becoming involved in Columbia's annual varsity shows. He contributed his first known lyric to the 1916 edition, and then in 1917, he co-wrote the book and all of the lyrics for a show entitled *Home, James*—and played the comic lead as well. The next year, when the United States entered World War I, Hammerstein was eager to enlist but was turned down when he was classified as underweight. Despondent, he quit Columbia and, after much persuasion, finally convinced Uncle Arthur to take him into the family business. He began first as a gopher—what we would call an intern today. He would later write that he was "an office boy and play reader by day, stage manager by night, and an eager kibitzer at the rehearsals of new shows." His uncle soon gave him a chance to try his hand at contributing lyrics to a musical he was producing called *Furs and Frills* (1917). The show was not a success, but Oscar now had his first song in a Broadway musical.[3]

Then, Uncle Arthur decided to team Oscar up with Otto Harbach to write the book and lyrics for a musical comedy titled **Tickle Me**, so that Hammerstein could really learn his craft. Although Harbach was twenty-two years older than Oscar, he was more than willing to take him on as a sort of junior partner. As author Todd Purdam notes,

> It was a fateful collaboration. Harbach, a kind and generous mentor, insisted that Oscar, whose instinct was to write quickly, slow down and think seriously about his goals before putting words on paper. He likened the construction of a musical play to building a fire, in which all the elements—logs, kindling, matches, a good flue—had to come together.[4]

Tickle Me would go on to run for an impressive 207 performances. Inspired by Otto Harburg, Hammerstein began to envision a kind of show in which the songs would be a more integral part of the story and in which both the songs and the story would be more meaningfully expressive of human life and emotion. This intention was achieved only haltingly and infrequently at first—but eventually, this idea would change the structure and the very nature of the Broadway musical. Harbach and Hammerstein partnered on the book and lyrics for ten musical comedies and operettas, working with top composers such as Rudolf Friml, Vincent Youmans, Sigmund Romberg, and Jerome Kern, including the smash hits **Rose-Marie**, **Sunny**, and **The Desert Song**.

Then it was time for Hammerstein to go off on his own, and in 1927, Jerome Kern asked him to join him in adapting Edna Ferber's acclaimed bestselling novel **Show Boat** for the musical stage. Most of their colleagues thought this was a crazy idea. Ferber's plot dealt with alcoholism, gambling addiction, and spousal abandonment, but, most significantly, the center of the story was focused on the issues of racism and interracial marriage (or miscegenation, as it was called at the time)—none of which had ever before been dramatized in a musical. Furthermore, the staging of this story would require bringing the first fully integrated cast to Broadway, with large numbers of Black and white performers sharing the stage, including the three principal African American characters who were central to the plot and score. Hammerstein and Kern, however, had vision and courage, and to an extraordinary degree, especially for the time, they did not shy away from the novel's provocative themes and events. The result was one of the most groundbreaking, acclaimed, and popular musicals of the twentieth century. It is also a show that was inevitably burdened by the pervasive internalized racism, prejudices, stereotypes, and social constructs of the period in which it was written.

As insightfully laid out by Warren Hoffman in his book *The Great White Way—Race and the Broadway Musical*—today, nearly a century after its debut, *Show Boat* is viewed in two very divergent ways. In the first instance, *Show Boat* is considered by many to be a timeless "theatrical classic" that not only "revolutionized the form, structure, and content of the American musical as we know it" but also "charted new territory by addressing serious themes," and "advanced race relations by featuring a racially integrated cast to dramatize the difficult plight of African Americans in the United States." Simultaneously, however, in the view of many others, *Show Boat* is "a racist musical that demeans and stereotypes African Americans" through its depictions of Black characters who are forced to speak in an offensive Black dialect, show "no character development over the course of the three-hour musical . . . and are merely background servants who help the white characters achieve all they can in the decades-spanning work." They view *Show Boat* not as a classic but rather as "a travesty of the American stage that should be forgotten and never revived lest it continue to propagate Black stereotypes."[5]

A strong argument can be made for both of those viewpoints. What should we do when we encounter acclaimed works of art from the past that contain elements we today consider to be sexist, racist, or problematic in other ways? What obligation do we have to try to understand the historical context, as well as the point of view and intentions of the authors at the time they were creating the show? This is especially perplexing with a musical like *Show Boat*, which we know was intended to be anti-racist. After all, what is the so-called "miscegenation scene" if not a scorching indictment of the structural racism and ludicrous racist laws of the Jim Crow South? *Show Boat* was both praised and criticized for its progressive themes at the time, but now it is often perceived to be hopelessly stuck in past ways of thinking. Should it be canceled? Should it be revised and rewritten to eliminate the offending elements? Or should it be presented as it was originally created? Any and all of that is now possible since on January 1, 2023, the copyright of *Show Boat* expired, and its

A Broadway Musical Leg

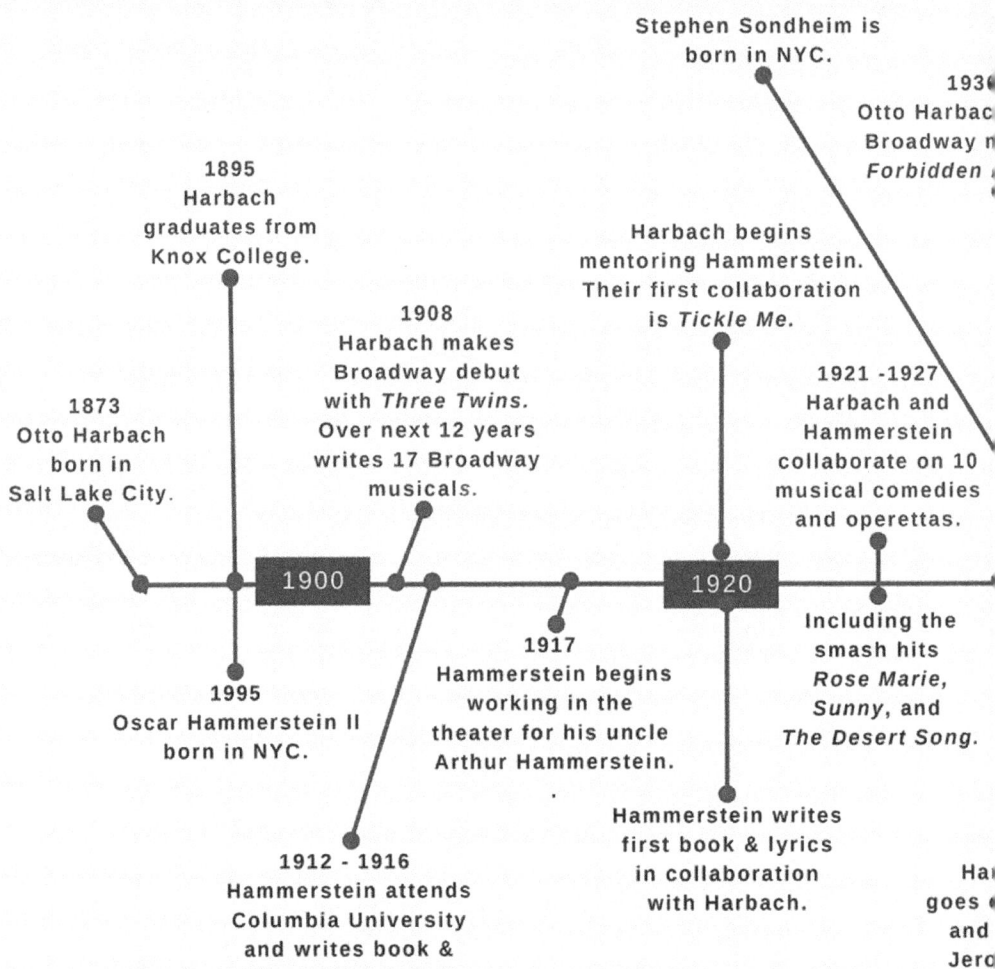

- **1873** Otto Harbach born in Salt Lake City.
- **1895** Harbach graduates from Knox College.
- **1995** Oscar Hammerstein II born in NYC.
- **1908** Harbach makes Broadway debut with *Three Twins*. Over next 12 years writes 17 Broadway musicals.
- **1912 - 1916** Hammerstein attends Columbia University and writes book & lyrics for two varsity shows.
- **1917** Hammerstein begins working in the theater for his uncle Arthur Hammerstein.
- Harbach begins mentoring Hammerstein. Their first collaboration is *Tickle Me*.
- Hammerstein writes first book & lyrics in collaboration with Harbach.
- Stephen Sondheim is born in NYC.
- **1921 -1927** Harbach and Hammerstein collaborate on 10 musical comedies and operettas.
- Including the smash hits *Rose Marie*, *Sunny*, and *The Desert Song*.
- **193(** Otto Harbac(Broadway n *Forbidden*

"By Your Pupils, You'll Be Taught"

cy Chain: The Harbach/

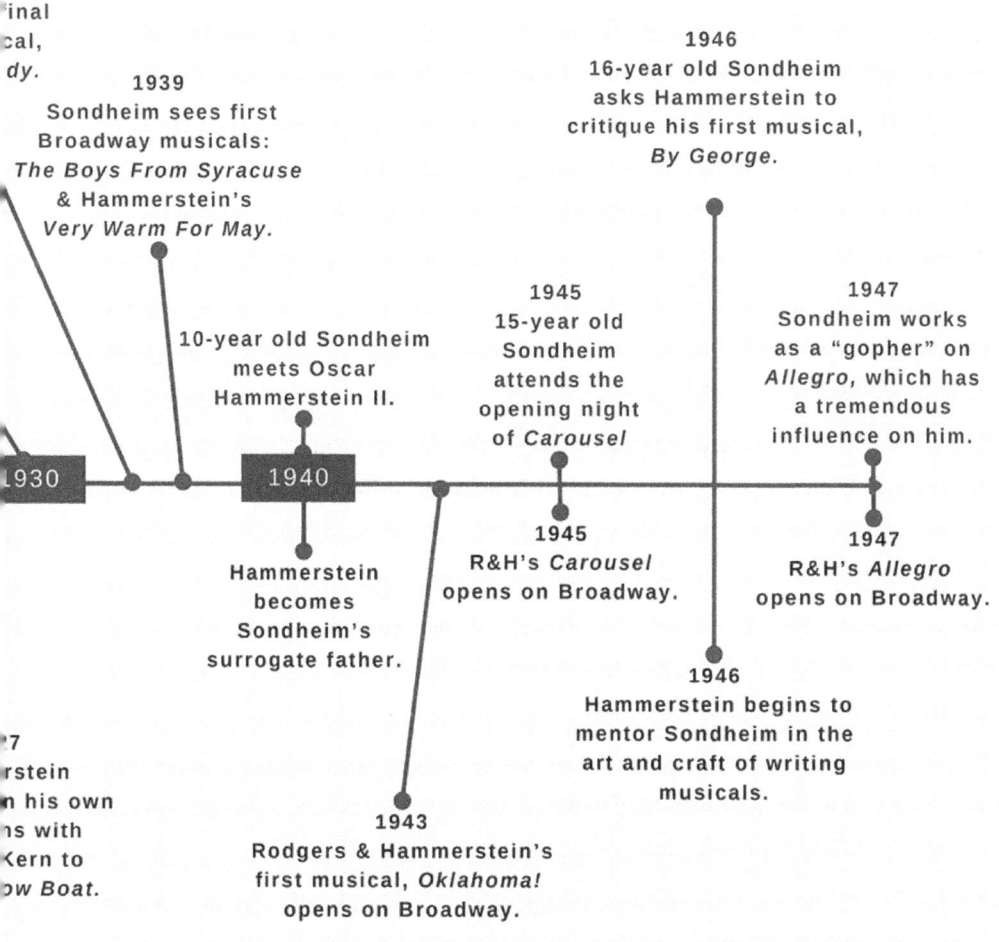

book, music, and lyrics all fell into the public domain. This is an unprecedented development for a major Broadway musical, and it will be fascinating to see what happens. (The legacy and themes of *Show Boat* are further explored in Chapter 13.)

On March 22, 1930, three years after the premiere of *Show Boat*, **Stephen Sondheim** was born in New York City, the only child of a prosperous German Jewish dress manufacturer named Herbert Sondheim, and his wife and chief fashion designer known to all by the nickname Foxy. Sondheim's father would frequently entertain out-of-town buyers by taking them to the latest Broadway musicals, and since he was a "natural" amateur musician, he was able to return home and play the hit tunes from those shows on the family's piano from memory— much to his son's great delight. The youngster soon began taking piano lessons "like any nice upper-class Jewish boy."[6] Among the first Broadway musicals that Sondheim remembered being taken to were Rodgers and Hart's *The Boys from Syracuse* (1938) and Kern and Hammerstein's *Very Warm for May* (1939). Though not a success, the latter show introduced the classic ballad, "All The Things You Are," which Sondheim credited as one of the songs that inspired him to want to become a composer. Just two years later, Hammerstein himself would become an integral part of young Sondheim's life.

On a summer's day in 1941, a friend of Sondheim's mother, Dorothy Hammerstein, arrived for a visit with her ten-year-old son, Jimmy, in tow. The boys bonded instantaneously, and by the end of that first visit, they informed their mothers that Steve would be coming to spend the weekend at the Hammerstein's house in Bucks County, Pennsylvania.[7] Sondheim ended up staying the rest of the summer there and soon became more a part of the Hammerstein family than his own. Jimmy's father was, of course, Oscar Hammerstein II. He was forty-six years old at the time and had not had a hit show in almost ten years. He was, however, just beginning what would become his historic collaboration with Richard Rodgers.

Sondheim says he "osmosed" into the Hammerstein household: "They were my surrogate family. My mother was a difficult lady, and I had a difficult time with her."[8] This seems to be something of an understatement. Sondheim's mother was, according to Jimmy Hammerstein, "the worst mother I have ever seen ... [Steve] adopted us, and if you prized your mental health, it was a sensible emotional position to take. And Dad always had time to talk to Steve." As a child, Sondheim was filled with rage, anger, and pain, but as Susan Hammerstein remembered, "[Oscar] seemed able to bypass that and got to some other place with him."[9] His relationship with Oscar Hammerstein would come to shape and inspire Sondheim's life. As he frequently stated, "I wrote for the theater in order to be like Oscar. I have no doubt that if Oscar had been an archeologist, I would have become an archeologist." Of course, if Sondheim had not had the talent and drive that was necessary to follow in Hammerstein's footsteps, he would likely have switched to another field of endeavor. But due to a remarkable quirk of fate, the man who was on the verge of becoming, in my estimation, the most significant individual in the history of the Broadway musical, took on the role of "surrogate father" and direct mentor to the second most important individual in that history.

Away We Go!—The Revolution of *Oklahoma!*

Meanwhile, Hammerstein made a tremendous comeback with *Oklahoma!*—a musical even more groundbreaking than *Show Boat* because, this time, the innovations spread to other shows and creators and eventually completely changed the landscape of Broadway. What was it that made this show so revolutionary? When this new team of Rodgers and Hammerstein decided to adapt a moderately successful little play called *Green Grow The Lilacs*, they didn't set out to break all the rules or throw away all the conventions of the musical comedy. They simply allowed the source material and subject matter to dictate the ways in which they would musicalize the story. If that meant instead of bringing the curtain up on a bevy of "chorus cuties" kicking up their heels in a lively opening song and dance number, as was standard operating procedure at the time, they would have it rise to reveal just one middle-aged farm woman slowly churning butter as a lone cowhand begins singing offstage and acapella "Oh, What a Beautiful Morning"—then that's what they would do. If the story required forty minutes of the show to go by before the chorus girls even entered—well, that was alright, too. And even if it meant including the violent death of one of the major characters—practically unheard of in musicals of the day—then okay, they would adapt the musical to the story at hand. Because of this uncompromising approach, the show's lead producers, Theresa Helburn and Laurence Langer, had tremendous difficulty raising money to fund its production—nobody thought it would work. When producer Mike Todd was solicited to invest, he allegedly dismissed the show with the now classic quip: "No gags, no girls, no chance!" Very few people have ever been proven so completely wrong.

From the very first out-of-town try-tryout performance in New Haven, it was clear that the creators of *Away We Go!*, as it was titled at the time, were onto something special. During the second pre-Broadway tryout in Boston, several changes were made to the show: one song was cut, and the show was fitted with a new title when what had been a duet was transformed into a big rousing chorus number. *Oklahoma!* opened on Broadway in March of 1943 and ran for more than five years—2,212 performances. This was twice as long as any previous Broadway musical, and touring productions crisscrossed America for ten years. The show's many innovations were noticed and lauded right from the start. In his opening-night review, critic Burns Mantle stated that:

> *Oklahoma!* really is different—beautifully different. With the songs that Richard Rodgers has fitted to a collection of unusually atmospheric and intelligible lyrics by Oscar Hammerstein 2nd, *Oklahoma!* seems to me to be the most thoroughly and attractively American musical comedy since . . . *Show Boat* was done by this same Hammerstein . . .[10]

Note that Mantle refers to the show as a "musical comedy" even though it was billed as "a musical play" on its posters and in its playbill. It would take a while for this new(ish) term to catch hold. Another innovation was *Oklahoma*'s *Original Cast Recording*, the first complete recording of a Broadway musical, which sold over a million copies and has never gone out of print. Because of the popularity of that cast album, millions of people who never got to see *Oklahoma!* onstage were still able to experience the story, bond with the characters, and fall in love with the songs.

The success of this new kind of musical was so overwhelming that soon virtually every other creator of Broadway musicals felt the need to emulate it. It became clear that there was no turning back. From this point on, even musical comedies would need to have dimensional characters and coherent storylines—and utilize its songs to tell that story.

In 1946, during his sophomore year at a prep school called The George School, Sondheim wrote his first musical, a satire of campus life entitled *By George!* Sondheim thought the show was "pretty terrific," and with visions of "being the first fifteen-year-old to have a show on Broadway," he asked Hammerstein to read it and critique it "as if it were just a musical that crossed your desk as a producer." In his 1993 book, *Sondheim*, Martin Gottfried dramatized what occurred the next morning when Hammerstein telephoned to suggest that the youngster come over to hear his assessment:

> "Now you really want me to treat this as if it were by somebody I don't know?"
> "Yes, please," the boy urged.
> "Well, in that case," Oscar said, "it's the worst thing I ever read in my life."
> That could bring tears to an adolescent's eyes, and nearly did.
> "I didn't say it wasn't talented," Hammerstein hastily added. "I said it was terrible and if you want to know why it's terrible, I'll tell you."
> With that, the famous Broadway librettist-lyricist who had written *Show Boat* and *Oklahoma!* analyzed every aspect of *By George!*, beginning with the first stage direction . . .[11]

Sondheim always credited that afternoon with changing his life. As he worked his way through the script, Hammerstein began passing on his knowledge to young Stephen Sondheim, showing him, in Sondheim's words:

> . . . how to structure songs, how to build them with a beginning and a development and an ending . . . how to introduce a character, what related a song to a character . . . four hours of the most packed information. I dare say, at the risk of hyperbole, that I learned more that afternoon than most people learn about songwriting in a lifetime. I was getting the distillation of [Hammerstein's] experience. And he did indeed treat me as if I were a professional.[12]

As Gottfried observed:

> It was, of course, an extraordinary stroke of luck for him, both professionally and personally . . . A young man, growing up in love with Broadway musicals, was being foster-fathered and now tutored by the theater's most successful lyricist-

librettist, Oscar Hammerstein II... who was dedicated to two basics in all of life, progress and teaching. And his one and only student was Steven Sondheim.[13]

Starting that day, Hammerstein laid out a course of study for Sondheim involving four assignments. The first was to write an entire show—book, music, and lyrics—based on a successful, well-made play. Second was to write a musical adapted from a play that had serious flaws in its construction. The third was to base a show on source material not written for the stage, such as a novel or short story. Finally, Sondheim was to write an original musical that was not an adaptation of any previous story. Over the following years, Sondheim would tackle each of these assignments, and each would be reviewed and critiqued by Hammerstein.

Meanwhile, after the overwhelming, unprecedented success of *Oklahoma!*, Rodgers and Hammerstein had to figure out what their next show would be. As Rodgers put it, "Whatever we write next—whatever anyone writes next—will be compared to *Oklahoma!*, and probably unfavorably." Movie mogul Samuel Goldwyn offered Rodgers some unsolicited advice:

Goldwyn: "This is such a wondeful show ...You know what you shoud do next?"
Rodgers: "What?"
Goldwyn: "Shoot yourself!"[14]

Eventually, Rodgers and Hammerstein determined that their second collaboration would be based on Ferenc Molnár's dark, bittersweet play titled *Lilliom*, which blended fantasy with stark reality, and once again, their commitment to stay true to the story and world of their play led them to new heights of innovation. **Carousel** (1945) significantly increased the level of seamless integration of book, music, lyrics, and choreography beyond what the team had achieved in *Oklahoma!*, especially in a musical sequence near the top of the show that has come to be known as "the Bench Scene"—a masterful tour de force of dialogue and song interwoven into a bed of continuous music.

As a fifteen-year-old, Stephen Sondheim attended the opening night performance of *Carousel* and found it to be an overwhelmingly emotional experience,[15] and he often identified the Bench Scene as "probably the singular most important moment in the evolution of contemporary musicals." (For further analysis of the Bench Scene, see page 191.) We can observe the influence of this groundbreaking creation in subsequent musicals by Rodgers and Hammerstein and nearly every other musical theater writer, including Sondheim's extended musical sequences in *Sweeney Todd* and *Into the Woods* and Lin-Manual Miranda's in *Hamilton* and *In the Heights*. Sondheim also singled out *Carousel*'s "Soliloquy" as being equally game-changing and influential because it "pioneered the plot-and-character defining internal monologue song."[16] Its influence can clearly be seen in "I've Grown Accustomed To Her Face" in *My Fair Lady*, "Rose's Turn" in *Gypsy*, *Jesus Christ Superstar*'s "Gethsemane," *Sweeney Todd*'s "Epiphany," and "Javert's Suicide" in *Les Misérables*, to name only a few. The "Bench Scene" and "Soliloquy" are what Hammerstein had been working toward since *Show Boat*, and as Sondheim noted, "they led the way to sophisticated improvements and experimentation that, happily, are still taking place today."[17]

In addition to his priceless one-on-one apprenticeship with Hammerstein, Sondheim was soon given the opportunity to witness the production of a Broadway musical firsthand. In the summer of 1947, following his freshman year at Williams College in Massachusetts, he was offered a job as a "gofer" on Rodgers and Hammerstein's third musical, *Allegro*. As he described it, the seventeen-year-old's job was "assistant vice president in charge of retyping and getting Danish and coffee." Still, he found this opportunity to hang around rehearsals and travel with the show to New Haven for its out-of-town tryout to be "a seminal influence on my life . . . it showed me a lot of smart people doing something wrong."[18] *Allegro* was a very unconventional musical, somewhat similar in form and spirit to Thornton Wilder's 1938 play *Our Town*. Due to the tremendous drawing power of Rodgers and Hammerstein at that time, the show ended up having a respectable 315-performance run—but it was not a success, either financially or artistically. It did, however, introduce several bold, innovative, and even experimental concepts to the Broadway musical, which had a profound effect on Sondheim: "Right away I accepted the idea of telling stories in space, of skipping through time, and using gimmicks like the Greek chorus. All the stuff that's in *Allegro*." In fact, Hammerstein's "gimmick" of turning the usual Broadway singing and dancing chorus into a Greek chorus who commented on the action of the play and voiced the inner thoughts of the main characters would be borrowed and employed by Sondheim throughout his career, especially in *A Little Night Music*, *Pacific Overtures*, and *Sweeney Todd*. Sondheim would later recognize that he had spent most of his career "trying to fix *Allegro*"—in other words, trying to take the bold concepts Hammerstein had introduced in that musical and finally make them work and affect an audience (the way Hammerstein had intended) in his own musicals. During the summer between his sophomore and junior years, Sondheim completed the first of Oscar's assignments, *All That Glitters*—a musical adaptation of a George S. Kaufman comedy. It was produced at his college, but Hammerstein was unable to attend because he was in rehearsals for **South Pacific** (1949).

"You've Got to be Taught"—The Ethos of *South Pacific*

Rodgers and Hammerstein's fourth musical was based on *Tales of the South Pacific*, James Michener's 1947 Pulitzer Prize-winning collection of short stories drawn from his own experiences serving in the U.S. Navy during World War II. With this musical, Hammerstein again put issues of race and social justice front and center. Both of the musical's parallel love stories hinge on racial prejudice—and at the climax of the plot, the central character, Nellie Forbush, must face up to her own internalized racism in order to bring the show to its enchanting conclusion. Virtually every song in the score became a hit: "Some Enchanted Evening," "I'm in Love With a Wonderful Guy," "Nothing Like A Dame," "I'm Gonna Wash That Man Right Out of My Hair," "Bali Hai," and more. But at the center of the score is "You've Got to be Carefully Taught," a song that identified and condemned internalized and systematic racism decades before those concepts were named. During the show's out-of-town tryout, "a group of experienced theater people" strongly suggested to Rodgers and Hammerstein that they should cut that number from the show. The authors reportedly replied that the song represented the main reason they wanted to do the play and that even if it meant the show would fail, the song was going to stay in.[19] The song continued to elicit strong reactions throughout the show's run: One early audience member wrote to Hammerstein imploring him to "Please eliminate that song . . . it is not necessary to carry the point or 'message' of the play (if you insist on having a 'message' in it) and it seems out of place." And he went on at length to complain that "this theme is wearing thin" and that "people go to a musical to be entertained—not harangued to." Hammerstein replied:

> Please forgive me for not agreeing with you. I am most anxious to make the point not only that prejudice exists and is a problem but that its birth lies in teaching and not in the fallacious belief that there are basic biological, physiological, and mental differences between races . . . You say "the theme is wearing thin," but in spite of this, I see progress being made only very slowly.[20]

Later, during *South Pacific*'s national tour, two Georgia legislators denounced the show as propaganda and vowed to introduce legislation that "would outlaw movies, plays, and musicals having 'an underlying philosophy inspired by Moscow.'" And they emphasized that their charge of propaganda referred specifically to "Carefully Taught" because it "urged justification of interracial marriage," and they concluded with the disturbing assertion that "in the South, we have pure bloodlines, and we intend to keep it that way."[21]

Despite any controversy, *South Pacific* was an absolute triumph! It received rapturous reviews hailing it as "A show of rare enchantment . . . rich in dramatic substance and eloquent in song" and "the ultimate modern blending of music and modern theater to date," as well as "an utterly captivating work of theatrical art." Audience response was even more enthusiastic. Tickets became nearly impossible to obtain, with $8.00 top-price tickets being sold for as much as $200.00 (equivalent to $102.95 and $2,568.83, respectively, today!) At the fourth annual Tony Awards in the spring of 1950, *South Pacific* swept every major category, winning ten awards—a record that would remain unbroken until *The Producers* in 2001. Among the recipients was **Juanita Hall**, who became the first Black woman to win a Tony Award (see page 213). A few weeks later, the show's authors received the Pulitzer Prize for Drama, and unlike what had happened to George Gershwin and *Of Thee I Sing*, this time, Richard Rodgers was included as an official recipient of the award. When the show's cast album was released, it quickly rose to the top of the *Billboard* charts, where it stayed at No. 1 for a record-breaking sixty-three weeks, an "astounding achievement unmatched for a decade."[22] During its nearly five-year, 1,925-performance run, *South Pacific* reigned as a massive social and cultural phenomenon at the very center of American culture. It was the *Hamilton* of its day. (For further analysis of *South Pacific*, see Chapters 14 and 15.)

Sondheim now plunged into Hammerstein's second assignment: adapting a flawed play. For this, he chose Maxwell Anderson's *High Tor*, and would later remember that "It taught me something about playwriting, about structure, about how to take out fat, and how to make points." Sondheim selected *Mary Poppins* for his third assignment: musicalizing a novel or short story. This was more than a decade before the Disney movie musical version, and he found it difficult to structure a play out of a group of short stories and "wasn't able to accomplish it." It was nevertheless an instructive exercise, as he would later remark, "As a result of Oscar, I think I probably knew more about writing musicals at the age of nineteen than most people do at the age of ninety."[23] By the time he completed that show, he was graduating (magna cum laude) from Williams College with the class of 1950 and being awarded the Hutchinson Prize, the school's highest honor in the arts.

Meanwhile, Hammerstein and Rodgers were working on what would become the smash hit ***The King and I*** (1951). Officially based on Margaret Landon's 1943 novel, *Anna and the King of Siam*, the musical also closely follows the screenplay of the 1946 film of the same name—both of which were inspired by the memoirs of Anna Leonowens, in which she presents a somewhat exaggerated account of the years she spent working as a tutor to the children and wives of the King of Siam during the 1860s. Again, Rodgers and Hammerstein tackle big issues and themes in this musical: colonialism, imperialism, globalism, human rights, and the conflicts between traditional cultures and the modern world (all of which are further explored in Chapter 15). When *The King and I* opened, *South Pacific* was still going strong, and for the next three years, both musicals played simultaneously on Broadway. Twenty-five years later, *The King and I*'s subject matter, themes, staging, and point of view would be responded to and critiqued by Stephen Sondheim and his collaborators in their 1976 musical, *Pacific Overtures*.

At a dinner party in 1952, Oscar introduced Sondheim to screenwriter and playwright George Oppenheimer, who was searching for an assistant to help him write a television series. "Steve needs a job," Hammerstein said. "Why don't you show him some of your stuff, Steve?" Sondheim got the job, and within weeks he was at work in Hollywood. Although he had never written a professional script and considered himself much more of a composer and lyricist than a playwright, his first professional job was as a writer of half-hour television scripts for a sitcom based on the *Topper* movies.

While working on *Topper*, Sondheim finished his final assignment, an original musical called *Climb High*, and mailed it to Hammerstein, believing it had commercial possibilities. "At that point," Sondheim later admitted, "I was still imitating Oscar in terms of emotion. At that age, I didn't have a lot of insight into lives that weren't like mine." And Hammerstein pointed out Sondheim's poetic Hammerstein-style lyrics. He said, "That's not what you feel. Don't write what I feel. Write what you feel." Sondheim would later say, "Oh! It had never occurred to me to write what I felt. And Oscar was the one who taught everyone to do that."[24] Sondheim returned to New York, and eager to make a name for himself in the musical theater, he played his scores for anyone who would listen.

Sondheim's first big break came when he was hired to write the music and lyrics for an adaptation of a play by Phillip and Jules J. Epstein, the authors of the movie *Casablanca*. The musical was to be called *Saturday Night*, but the producer died before the show went into production, and the musical remained unproduced until thirty years later. Next, he was asked to create the lyrics for a musical with a book by Arthur Laurents and music by Leonard Bernstein. Sondheim told Hammerstein that he really didn't want to write only lyrics. His goal and his ambition was, first and foremost, to be a composer. But Hammerstein convinced him that the show would offer him the chance to get started on Broadway and, most importantly, to work with top professionals. Sondheim accepted the job, and, of course, the show turned out to be *West Side Story*. Sondheim was still showing his lyrics to his mentor, but the relationship was changing: "I started to become argumentative when we discussed the songs I was writing ... *West Side Story* changed Oscar's attitude toward me. It was like seeing a bird fly for the first time. He was no longer protective."

Hammerstein also encouraged Sondheim to sign on when a second job as a lyricist was offered because the star of the show was Ethel Merman, and Hammerstein felt that it would be an invaluable experience for Sondheim to again work with top-tier Broadway writers (Jule Styne and Laurents) on a show that was being specifically tailored for a star performer and personality. (For more on this, see page 232.) This show became *Gypsy*, a musical that many consider one of the greatest and most perfectly crafted of all time, as well as a pinnacle of the Rodgers and Hammerstein-style *musical play*.

During this period, Rodgers and Hammerstein created two more hit musicals, **Flower Drum Song** and **The Sound of Music**. Interestingly, they tailored this last show specifically for Merman's only rival for Broadway stardom, Mary Martin. Oscar Hammerstein died in 1960 at the age of sixty-five. If he had lived just two years longer, he would have been able to see Stephen Sondheim achieve his dream of writing both lyrics and music for a Broadway musical, *A Funny Thing Happened on the Way to the Forum*, which received the 1963 Tony Award for "Best Musical." In his introduction to a biography of Hammerstein, Sondheim summed up his mentor with these words:

> He was a giant. He changed the texture of the American Musical Theater forever. There may be librettists and lyricists whose work is more admired, but there are none greater. He taught me not only everything I know, but everything I needed to know in order to write for myself and not for him. But then he taught everybody: he sang for us all. He understood everything about teaching because that's what he was[,] a teacher[,] and what he liked best about it was—as he wrote in the verse to "Getting to Know You" in *The King and I*—"it's a very ancient saying—but a true and honest thought—that if you become a teacher—by your pupils you are taught.[25]

Stephen Sondheim would go on to become "the theater's most revered and influential composer-lyricist of the last half of the 20th century, if not its most popular, and the driving force behind some of Broadway's most beloved and celebrated shows."[26] His adventurous and diverse string of nineteen musicals include **West Side Story, Gypsy, A Funny Thing Happened on the Way to the Forum, Anyone Can Whistle, Company, Follies, A Little Night Music, Pacific Overtures, Sweeney Todd, Merrily We Roll Along,**

Sunday in the Park with George, *Into the Woods*, *Assassins*, *Passion*, *Road Show*, and the posthumously produced *Here We Are*. He received Tony Awards for the scores of seven of those musicals, and five of them were awarded "Best Musical."

Sondheim's shows and songs have now inspired and influenced several generations of writers, just as Rodgers and Hammerstein inspired and influenced Sondheim's generation. And in the spirit of his relationship with Hammerstein, Sondheim has personally encouraged and mentored a number of aspiring Broadway songwriters during the early stages of their careers, especially the late Jonathan Larson (as dramatized in the film version of Larson's musical *Tick, Tick . . . Boom!*), as well as Jeanine Tesori, Jason Robert Brown, and Lin-Manuel Miranda.

"Lights up on Washington Heights"

Lin-Manuel Miranda was born in 1980 in Inwood, the neighborhood on Manhattan's far Upper West Side where his musical *In the Heights* is set. His mother was a clinical psychologist, and his father a consultant for the Democratic Party; and while growing up, Miranda spent summers with his grandparents in Puerto Rico. He was taken to only three musicals on Broadway during his childhood—*Cats*, *Les Misérables*, and *The Phantom of the Opera*—which he calls "the holy trinity!"[27] His mother and father, however, were big fans of movie musicals. His Mom "loved Shirley Temple movies," and his father loved "*Sound of Music*, *My Fair Lady*, and anything with Debbie Reynolds."[28] Miranda inherited this love of musicals, and his passion grew even stronger when he was cast as Bernardo in a sixth-grade production of *West Side Story*. "My mother rented the movie so we could watch it together. When the song 'America' started and it was about whether to live in Puerto Rico or live in the U.S . . . I was like, 'Holy shit! *West Side Story* is about Puerto Ricans?!'"[29] Then, during his senior year of high school, he directed a production of the show himself, and his relationship with *West Side Story* would continue into his professional career.

Miranda studied theater and film at Wesleyan University in Connecticut, where he met Tommy Kail, who would become his closest collaborator and the director of both *In the Heights* and *Hamilton*. Miranda wrote the earliest draft of *In the Heights* during his sophomore year, and the musical received a full staging at Wesleyan the following year. He graduated with the class of 2002 and immediately set his sights on getting the show to Broadway.

Following several years of development, including a well-received off-Broadway production, ***In the Heights*** opened on Broadway in 2008, receiving four Tony Awards, including "Best Musical" and "Best Score," and ran for 1,184 performances. This directly led to Miranda being engaged by Sondheim to create the Spanish translations for several of his lyrics in ***West Side Story***. For this 2009 Broadway revival, ninety-two-year-old Arthur Laurents revised his original book so the Puerto Rican characters spoke in Spanish, at least among themselves, which he felt gave "the Sharks infinitely more weight than they've ever had."[30] Sondheim, who had on many occasions voiced his dislike of his own lyrics for the show, told Miranda that he could use whatever imagery he wanted. His only concern was "that Lin observe the rhyme schemes." So, "I Feel Pretty" became "Siento Hermosa," and "A Boy Like That" became "Un Hombre Así." "It was the hardest bilingual crossword puzzle I've ever done," Miranda told the *New York Times*.[31]

The following season, Miranda joined the songwriting team of the Broadway adaptation of the cheerleading film ***Bring It On!***.[32] In the fall of 2017, when Hurricane Maria devastated Puerto Rico, Miranda asked Sondheim for permission to sample the song "Maria" from *West Side Story* and incorporate it into a star-studded pop recording and music video titled "Almost Like Praying," which raised funds in support of relief efforts. Meanwhile, throughout all of this, Miranda was working on *Hamilton*, often sending sections of it to Sondheim for his insight and feedback:

> Sondheim was one of the first people that I told about my idea for a piece about Alexander Hamilton, back in 2008. I'd been hired to write Spanish translations for a Broadway revival of *West Side Story*, and during our first meeting he asked me what I was working on next. I told him "Alexander Hamilton," and he threw back his head in laughter and clapped his hands. "That is exactly what you should be doing. No one will expect that from you. How fantastic." That moment alone, the joy of surprising Sondheim, sustained me through many rough writing nights and missed deadlines. I sent him early drafts of songs over the seven-year development of *Hamilton*, and his email response was always the same. "Variety, variety, variety, Lin. Don't let up for a second. Surprise us."[33]

Originally conceived as a concept album, *The Alexander Hamilton Mixtape*, Miranda's musical began to create a buzz in the Broadway world from its earliest readings and workshops. Much of this was due, of course, to its unlikely, incongruous source material: Ron Chernow's massive and scholarly 2004 biography of Alexander Hamilton, "the 10-dollar founding father without a father," as Miranda's lyric describes him. This was all kicked off by Miranda's visibly nervous but ultimately triumphant performance of an early version of the show's opening number as part of "An Evening of Poetry, Music and Spoken Word" at the White House in 2009, which included a standing ovation from President Barack Obama and Michelle Obama.

Hamilton was first produced downtown at the Public Theatre, where, like those previous landmark hits, *Hair* and *A Chorus Line*, it became an impossible-to-get-tickets-for-must-see event. And its audacious concept, as described here by author Kat Sherell, became the talk of the town:

> Acknowledging no disconnect between its sound and its setting, *Hamilton* bypasses the self-consciousness of anachronism . . . [and] convinces us that hip-hop and its generic cousins embody the cocky, restless spirit of self-determination that birthed the American independence movement. Like the early gangsta rap stars, the founding fathers forge rhyme, reason and a sovereign identity out of tumultuous lives.[34]

Its cast of predominantly Black and Latinx actors "looks like America looks now, and that's certainly intentional," Miranda said. "It's a way of pulling you into the story and allowing you to leave whatever cultural baggage you have about the founding fathers at the door."

What it was not, however, was a game-changing revolution in the form of the Broadway musical. As might be expected from an author whose touchstone musicals include both *Fiddler on the Roof* and *Les Misérables*, in essence, *Hamilton* is an expertly crafted, traditional book musical which employs a poperetta-style sung-through format. According to Sherell, this is "directly in line with the aspirations of artists like Kern and Hammerstein: song flowing from story flowing from character."[35] It is also not the first musical to use hip-hop/rap music as a significant aspect of its score—Miranda's own *In the Heights* and *Bring It On* preceded it, as did 2014's short-lived *Holler If Ya Hear Me* and 1996's *Bring in the Noise, Bring in the Funk*. Even Andrew Lloyd-Webber's *Starlight Express* featured a rap song back in 1987. Still, in his meticulous crafting of *Hamilton*'s eclectic book, music, and lyrics, Miranda pays tribute in equal measure to hip-hop and pop music artists such as Beyoncé, DMX, Nicki Minaj, and Eminem, and musical theater artists from Gilbert and Sullivan, to Boublil and Schönberg, to Jason Robert Brown, including specific references to Rodgers and Hammerstein's "You've Got To Be Carefully Taught," Notorious BIG's "Ten Crack Commandments," and, inevitably, "Sit Down, John" from Sherman Yellen's *1776*.

In the wake of the phenomenal success of *Hamilton*, Lin-Manuel Miranda has been sought after to work in nearly every aspect of the entertainment industry. As a songwriter, he created songs for the Disney animated films *Moana Encanto*, and *Mufasa: The Lion King*, and the live action version of *The Little Mermaid*. As an actor, he starred in Disney's *Mary Poppins Returns*. He executive produced the FX miniseries *Fosse/Verdon*, co-produced the film version of his own *In the Heights*, and directed the film adaptation of Jonathan Larson's *Tick, Tick . . . BOOM!*. All of this before the age of forty-five.

Stephen Sondheim died on November 26, 2021. His obituary in the *New York Times* hailed him as, "A titan of the American musical" and "one of the great artists of any art form of the twentieth century," as well as "an artistic genius on the level with Shakespeare."[36] Three days later, hundreds of members of the Broadway community, including the casts of Broadway shows past and present, gathered at noon on the landmark red steps behind the statue of George M. Cohan in the center of Times Square to celebrate Sondheim's life and art. Lin-Manuel Miranda briefly addressed the crowd, reading a passage from Sondheim's book *Look, I Made A Hat* and quoting a line from the book of *Sunday In the Park With George*: "A blank page. His favorite. So many possibilities." He then joined Broadway songwriters Stephen Schwartz, Sara Bareilles, Tom Kitt, and Marc Shaiman and the massive chorus that had assembled in singing that show's thrilling first-act finale.

> It's hard to overemphasize Sondheim's influence on American musical theater . . . Sondheim built on Hammerstein's innovations by experimenting relentlessly with subject matter and form: from his early lyrics . . . to more than 50 years' worth of scores that have pushed the boundaries and subject matter of musical theater in

every conceivable direction. He is musical theater's greatest lyricist, full stop. We now talk about his work the way we talk about Shakespeare or Dickens or Picasso—a master of his form, both invisible within his work and everywhere at once.[37] [Lin-Manuel Miranda]

To sum all this up, Otto Harbach (later aided and abetted by Oscar Hammerstein II) had a vision, or at least an inkling, of a greater artistic potential for the Broadway musical, and the high level of structural integrity that it could achieve. This vision was then substantially realized by Oscar Hammerstein and Jerome Kern, and then to an even greater degree by Hammerstein and Richard Rodgers. Their game-changing disruption instituted a new model and standard for creating musical theater that was then inherited, copied, imitated, rejected, embraced, and absorbed by Stephen Sondheim, Lin-Manuel Miranda, and everybody else.

ACT III
THE GOLDEN AGE

Fig. 31: In Rodgers and Hammerstein's Pulitzer Prize-winning musical *South Pacific* (1949), both of the show's parallel love stories hinge on issues of internalized racism and social justice. In the emotional final scene, American nurse, "Ensign Nellie Forbush" (originally played by Mary Martin), joins hands with French planter, "Emile De Becque" (Ezio Pinza), as his mixed-race children (Barbara Luna, Michael or Noel De Leon) welcome him home.

CHAPTER 8
"SOMETHING'S COMING, SOMETHING GOOD"—THE GOLDEN AGE OF BROADWAY, PART 1: THE TRANSITION BETWEEN *OKLAHOMA!* AND *CAROUSEL* (I, J, Q, B, W)

Of course, no revolution happens overnight. Even though the critics recognized *Oklahoma!* as a game changer, it should not be surprising that it took a considerable amount of time for Broadway's established creative class—its producers, writers, directors, and choreographers—to jump on board with this new way of making musicals. It would also take time for the taste and expectations of the Broadway audience to evolve as well. After all, they needed to see *Oklahoma!* in order to understand what other shows were lacking, and it was nearly impossible to get tickets! And, of course, quite a few Silver Age-style shows were already moving through the Broadway pipeline, oblivious to the major disruption that was about to take place. So, for the eighteen months following the March 31, 1943 premiere of *Oklahoma!*, it would remain the only fully realized new-style *musical play* on Broadway, while an oddly vibrant transition period ensued during which many Silver Age-style musicals and revues continued to thrive unabated.

In fact, the very next night, April 1, the ***Ziegfeld Follies of 1943*** opened to rave reviews ("The new *Ziegfeld Follies* is a knockout!") and became one of the most successful editions ever of that famed revue series.[1] Florenz Ziegfeld had died nearly a decade earlier, but his brand-name value was still strong. This new edition was produced by the Shuberts, who had been Ziegfeld's arch-rivals during his lifetime, and it starred comedian Milton Berle, movie stars Ilona Massey and Arthur Treacher, "100 Gorgeous Ziegfeld Girls," and Jack Cole and his dancers performing the kind of "inspired, angular dancing for which he is quite properly renowned."[2] It would go on to run for a very healthy 553 performances. It was quickly followed by several more successful "old school" shows including the bawdy musical comedy ***Early to Bed***.[3] Remarkably, this show's creative team included both Black and white collaborators as well as a racially integrated cast. The choreography was by Robert Alton, and the swinging music was composed by "the great 'Fats' Waller,"[4] who just six months into the show's run died at the age of only thirty-nine. This is another tragic case of "what great songs and musicals did he not live to write?"

"Out of Your Dreams"—The Innovations of *Lady in the Dark*

Not all of the credit for bringing about the revolutionary leap into the Golden Age can be given to Hammerstein and Rodgers. Composer Kurt Weill and his collaborators were on an alternate but parallel track, and two of his musicals contributed significantly to the sea change that was taking place. The first was ***Lady in the Dark***, which actually began its initial Broadway run in 1941, more than two years before *Oklahoma!* Then, following its national tour, *Lady in the Dark* returned to Broadway and played concurrently with the Rodgers and Hammerstein hit. So, during three months of 1943, there were two groundbreaking shows shaking things up on Broadway.

Lady in the Dark was unlike any musical that had come before—or even after. The book was the brainchild of Moss Hart, who was obsessed with Freudian psychoanalysis, which was very trendy at the time but still controversial and somewhat mysterious. Hart had suffered a nervous breakdown and credited psychoanalysis for his recovery, and for much of his life thereafter he went every day to a therapy session to work on his various issues—especially his acceptance (or at times rejection) of his homosexuality. Considering the dominant position that psychoanalysis had in his life, it is not surprising that he would write a show about a character who undergoes psychotherapy. The complex character he created—the "lady in the dark"— is Liza Elliot, the high-powered editor of a swanky fashion and beauty magazine (sort of a 1940s forerunner to *Vogue* editor Anna Wintour). And Hart conceived this role specifically for the glamorous British superstar **Gertrude Lawrence**.[5]

"This is New": Kurt Weill in America (♩, ♪)

During the late 1920s Weimar period in Berlin, composer **Kurt Weill** (another son of a cantor!) had become world famous for his collaborations with playwright Bertolt Brecht, especially *The Threepenny Opera*, an unclassifiable musical theater piece that became an international hit but had flopped on Broadway in 1933. Along with thousands of other Jewish, leftist refugees from Hitler's Germany, Weill fled to NYC in 1935. He was accompanied by his wife and muse, actress and singer Lotte Lenya, who had starred in most of the Brecht/Weill works in Germany (and would later have a role created specifically for her in the original Broadway production of *Cabaret*). Weill came to America determined to reinvent himself as a Broadway composer. Two early musicals—the antiwar parable *Johnny Johnson* (1936) and the political satire *Knickerbocker Holiday* (1938)—failed to establish him strongly on Broadway or open doors in Hollywood, where producers told him he "wasn't American enough." "The most American composer, Irving Berlin, is a Russian Jew," he responded, "and I'm a German Jew, that's the only difference."[6] Following the success of *Lady in the Dark*, Hollywood was a bit more receptive.

The entire creative team of *Lady in the Dark* was first class. Ira Gershwin wrote the lyrics (his first show after the tragic early death of his brother George), with Hassard Short staging "one of the most lavish plays ever produced on Broadway,"[7] and Albertina Rasch as the choreographer. The team actually went in the opposite direction of trying to seamlessly integrate all of the elements of a musical—instead, they separated them. Half of *Lady in the Dark* is, in essence, a straight play containing scenes in which we see Liza working at her office at *Allure* magazine and dealing with the mounting pressures of her professional and personal lives, alternating with scenes of Liza in her psychiatrist's office undergoing psychoanalysis. None of these scenes include songs or even music of any kind—until, as part of her therapy, Liza is encouraged by her analyst to remember and recount her dreams—which then vividly come to life in three elaborate, expressionistic, and surreal "mini-musicals," which in great contrast to the rest of the show are filled with non-stop song and dance. In these extended musical sequences, the significant characters from Liza's real life reappear as manifestations and reflections of her subconscious feelings, conflicts, and desires. During the penultimate dream sequence, Liza finds herself on trial for both not being able to make up her mind about which illustration to use on the cover of the magazine (the circus cover or the Easter cover), and not being able to decide which of the men in her life she should choose. And bizarrely, this entire trial sequence takes place within the context of a circus.

Given the high-profile, "must-see" status of *Lady in the Dark*, it seems reasonable to assume that these elaborate dream sequences dramatizing the psychological conflicts of a leading character had at least some influence on Agnes DeMille's dream ballet in *Oklahoma!* (which coincidentally (?) had originally been conceived by Hammerstein as a circus dream).[8] Gertrude Lawrence famously stopped her show cold with the central song of *Lady*'s trial/circus sequence, "The Saga of Jenny," which concludes with the lyric, ". . . don't make up your mind!" Is it merely another coincidence that *Oklahoma!*'s first act reaches its climax when Laurey's song, "Out of my Dreams," leads into an elaborate, expressionistic, surreal dream sequence titled "Laurey Makes Up Her Mind," during which she struggles to decide which man she should choose? I can find no references to confirm any connections between them, but the parallels are striking! *Lady in the Dark* was not the first musical to explore the psychological implications of dreams, but it was certainly the first to deal with mental health issues in a serious way.

Among its other innovations, *Lady in the Dark* also included the first Gay principal character to appear in a Broadway musical since *Irene*'s Madam Lucy in 1919. This character, a fashion photographer named Russell Paxton, is similarly flamboyant, especially as originally played in a star-making performance by Danny Kaye. Paxton's sexuality is made abundantly clear right from his first entrance when, having just finished shooting photos of a sexy, rugged, cowboy movie star for the magazine, he exclaims to his co-workers: "Girls, he's God-like! I've taken pictures of beautiful men, but this one is the end—the *end*! He's got a face that would melt in your mouth . . ."[9] Broadway musicals won't see another openly Queer character until *Hair* in 1968.

Legend has it that *Lady in the Dark* is the only show in Broadway history to be entirely sold out at every single performance, but unfortunately, despite its great score, the show has not aged well and has rarely been revived. Primarily, this is because of the show's final scene in which Liza finally does make up her mind, but in a way that modern audiences just can't get behind. She chooses to give up her high-powered career, turn her job over to a man, and devote herself to being a traditional wife. It's hard to read in the script, much less see it played out on the stage. I suspect, however, that if Moss Hart had opened this show just one year later after America was thrust into World War II and when American women were being urged to go to work, he might have devised a very different ending for *Lady in the Dark*.

This period's second Kurt Weill musical was the classy musical-comedy-fantasy *One Touch of Venus*.[10] Produced by Cheryl Crawford, the show starred Mary Martin as the goddess Venus, whose statue magically comes to life and completely disrupts the life of a typically modern New York man. Although largely conceived in a standard issue Silver Age musical comedy style, this show had a freshness, sophistication, and "adult manner"[11] that made it feel "smart, new-fangled and glossy,"[12] and critics perceived it to be breaking "sharply away from the pattern and accepted routine."[13] And clearly there was a yearning at the time for the routine pattern to be broken. With music by Kurt Weill, lyrics by Ogden Nash, and a book by Nash and S. J. Perlman, "which while not perfect throughout was better than those of most musicals."[14] Choreographer Agnes DeMille, following up on her dance creations for *Oklahoma!*, which had set New York "on its ear,"[15] was now considered to be "the most sought-after choreographer on Broadway."[16] She received near unanimous praise for her "striking and imaginative dance numbers,"[17] including two ballets that were thought to "rival in originality and skill . . . her *Rodeo* and *Oklahoma!*" and display "her highly developed and individual comedy sense." And even though critic Willella Waldorf[18] in the *New York Post* voiced prophetic concern that "if she [DeMille] goes on staging dances hereabout people may grow tired of her style, which is distinctive," she had to admit that with this show, DeMille was "top grade" and "at her peak."[19] In a follow-up article a few days later, the *New York Times* added, "In truth, *One Touch of Venus* is not another *Oklahoma!* although it may well be the best new musical to have opened since that time."[20]

Broadway Dance #7: Agnes DeMille and the Dancing Ladies of the Golden Age (I, J, B, W)

Agnes DeMille is arguably the most important woman in the history of the Broadway musical. She was born in NYC in 1905 and grew up in an extended theatrical family. Her father and grandfather were playwrights, and her uncle was the famous film director Cecil B. DeMille. From a young age, she was determined to be a dancer and studied in New York and London. Unable to find work, she began choreographing solo works for herself to perform. Her big breakthrough came in 1942 when she created the ballet *Rodeo* (and danced the leading role) for the Ballet Russe de Monte Carlo. That ballet's Western setting and uniquely vibrant Americana spirit led producer Teresa Helburn and Rodgers and Hammerstein to select her to create the dances for *Oklahoma!* Drawing on her ballet and modern dance background, DeMille pioneered a dramatic story-based approach to choreography that delved deeply into the emotions and psychology of the characters and ushered in a new era of Broadway dance. Her sixteen Broadway musicals included the major hits ***Oklahoma!*** (1943), ***One Touch of Venus*** (1943), ***Bloomer Girl*** (1944), ***Carousel*** (1945), ***Brigadoon*** (1947), and ***Gentlemen Prefer Blondes*** (1949). At one point in 1945, DeMille had four hit musicals running on Broadway simultaneously and was featured on the cover of *LIFE* magazine. With Rodgers and Hammerstein's musical *Allegro* (1947), she became the first woman to both direct and choreograph a Broadway musical. Unfortunately, that show's limited success was a setback for her career and damaged her relationship with Rodgers and Hammerstein. Even so, she is, without a doubt, one of the most significant and influential Broadway creators of all time.

As might be expected, DeMille's tremendous success inspired Broadway producers and writers to seek out other choreographers from the concert dance world, and she was followed to Broadway by three talented colleagues. **Hanya Holm** is considered one of the "Big Four" founding mothers of American modern dance. She was born Johanna Eckert in Germany in 1893. As a teenager, she became a disciple of the expressionist dancer, choreographer, and teacher Mary Wigman, who renamed her Hanya Holm. Eventually, Holm became chief instructor at Wigman's dance school in Dresden. Then, after touring America with Wigmam's dance company, Holm emigrated to New York in 1931 to establish an American branch of Wigman's school, which eventually became the Hanya Holm School of Dance.[21] In addition to her many acclaimed modern dance works, during the Golden Age of Broadway, Holm choreographed ten Broadway musicals, including the legendary hits ***Kiss Me, Kate*** (1948), ***My Fair Lady*** (1956), and ***Camelot*** (1960).

Another modern dance pioneer was **Helen Tamiris**. Between 1930 and 1945, Tamiris choreographed 135 modern dance works, many of which reflected her concerns about the political and social inequities of the time.[22] She was born Helen Becker in NYC in 1902 to Jewish parents who had fled Russia. According to the *Jewish Women's Archive*, "early in her career, she took the name of Tamiris, a ruthless Amazonian queen of Persia who overcame all obstacles."[23] At age eight, Tamiris began studying "free movement" (Isadora Duncan-style dance) at the Henry Street Settlement, and by the age of fifteen, she was dancing professionally with the Metropolitan Opera Ballet. She made her Broadway debut as a featured dancer[24] in Irving Berlin's *Music Box Revue of 1924*,[25] and would go on to choreograph thirteen Broadway musicals, including ***Annie Get Your Gun*** (1946), ***Up in Central Park*** (1947), ***Fanny*** (1954), and ***Plain and Fancy*** (1955).

Onna White was born in Nova Scotia, Canada in 1922. She began studying dance at twelve and made her professional debut as a dancer with the San Francisco Ballet while still in her teens. She danced in the Broadway musicals *Finian's Rainbow, Guys and Dolls*, and *Silk Stockings*, often also working as the assistant to choreographer Michael Kidd. This inspired White to try her own hand at choreography. During her more than forty-year career, she choreographed sixteen Broadway musicals for which she received eight Tony Award nominations. Among her biggest hits were ***The Music Man*** (1957), ***Mame*** (1966), and ***1776*** (1969), and she adapted her stage choreography for all three of their film adaptations. White choreographed a number of other major film musicals as well, including *Oliver!*, for which she received a special Academy Award.

The extraordinary dancer, choreographer, anthropologist, and social activist **Katherine Dunham** was born in Chicago in 1909. Her father, who ran a dry-cleaning business, was a descendant of enslaved Africans from Madagascar and West Africa. Her French Canadian Native American mother died when Katherine was four years old, and she was raised by her stepmother, a schoolteacher from Iowa. Early on, Dunham became interested in dance, theater, and writing, and at fifteen she shocked neighbors when she announced she was going to stage a "cabaret party" to raise money for her church. She was the "producer, director, and star of the entertainment."[26] Later, she confessed that she had scarcely known what the word "cabaret" meant.

Dunham received her bachelor's degree from the University of Chicago, where she also earned her doctorate in anthropology. Meanwhile, she studied various styles of dance, including Spanish, East Indian, Javanese, Balinese, early modern, and classical ballet with Russian dancer Ludmilla Speranzeva (one of the first ballet teachers to accept Black dancers), who helped Dunham establish the Chicago Negro School of Ballet and a dance company, the Negro Dance Group, which eventually evolved into the Katherine Dunham Dance Company. Dunham's distinctive dance technique and choreography originated out of the anthropological fieldwork that she did as a graduate student in the Caribbean in 1935, after receiving a fellowship to study the traditional dances of Jamaica, Martinique, Trinidad, and Haiti.

Dunham and her company moved to New York and made their Broadway debut in 1939 when she was invited to create a new dance for the long-running labor-themed revue *Pins and Needles*. She used her salary from that show to finance a dance concert of her choreography. Titled *Tropics and Le Jazz Hot: From Harlem to Haiti*, the show was first presented on a "dark" Sunday night at the theater where *Pins and Needles* was playing. It received rave reviews and was repeated every Sunday for the following thirteen weeks.[27] This led directly to Dunham being engaged to play the principal role of Georgia Brown in the 1940 Broadway musical *Cabin in the Sky*, and she insisted that her entire dance company be engaged to perform in the show with her. During rehearsals, director and choreographer George Balanchine periodically asked Dunham to assist him with various aspects of the choreography. Eventually, her contributions to *Cabin in the Sky* grew to such an extent that she had co-choreographed the show with Balanchine. Then, one week before opening night, the producers fired Balanchine, who, according to cast member Talley Beaty, was "removed from the choreographic scene, and Dunham had to reset all of the dances" except for one. Balanchine, however, retained sole credit as the choreographer of the show, even though "he didn't choreograph it."[28] The show was acclaimed by the *New York*

Times as "a rare evening of theatrical delight," noting that "throughout the evening it is Miss Dunham's chief business to sizzle . . ." Following the Broadway run, Dunham and her dancers went on the road with the touring company of *Cabin in the Sky*, winding up in Los Angeles, where Katherine choreographed and/or appeared with her dancers in the film musicals *Star Spangled Rhythm* (1942), *Pardon My Sarong* (1942), and *Stormy Weather* (1943).

Dunham returned to Broadway in 1943 with a show of her own titled *Tropical Revue*. As "choreographed and staged by Katherine Dunham," the first two acts of this show consisted of her dramatic and highly theatrical evocation of indigenous dances and songs from around the world, including Cuba, Haiti, Mexico, Brazil, the South Pacific island of Rara Tonga, and more, all derived from her anthropological work. The third act then traced the history of African American dances from the cakewalk right up to the boogie-woogie, barrelhouse, and hot swing dances of the 1940s.[29] Audience and critical response was sensational. While some critics appreciated the artfulness and esthetic significance of what Dunham was trying to do with *Tropical Revue*, describing it as "a careful, intelligent, handsome show" and hailing her as "one of our finest entertainers" whose "dance conceptions offer color, variety, and exuberance, as well as unusual human warmth," others responded more viscerally to Dunham's innate showmanship, as well as the sheer entertainment value and sex appeal of much of the material that she presented, with sensational quotes such as "Broadway Wows With A Sizzling Show, " "Sex In The Caribbean Is Doing Alright," and "Likely to send thermometers soaring to the bursting point. Tempestuous and torrid, raffish and revealing."[30] As a result, *Tropical Revue*'s original two-week engagement extended into a three-month run of eighty-seven performances, followed by a national tour. Dunham and her company returned to Broadway seven times between 1944 and 1955 in a series of special concert presentations of her works.

In 1944, she opened the Dunham School of Dance and Theater, where, through 1957, students could receive training from master teachers in dance (ballet, tap, and modern, including Dunham's signature technique), acting, design, playwriting, and theater history. Among the aspiring performers and theater-makers who studied there were Chita Rivera, Eartha Kitt, Arthur Mitchell, James Dean, Marlon Brando, Jose Ferrer, and future choreographer Peter Gennaro. In fact, Gennaro's deep immersion at the Dunham School in Caribbean and Latin dance styles directly influenced his choreographic contributions to *West Side Story* (see page 209).

In 1963, Dunham became the first African American to choreograph at the Metropolitan Opera since 1934, "startling audiences with her lusty dances" for a production of Verdi's *Aida*. *New York Times* critic Allen Hughes described her choreography: "There is modern in it, belly-dancing, the foot-stamping and hip-and-shoulder shaking of primitive African dancing and much more. All pure Dunham."[31] Over the next thirty years, Dunham would continue to teach, perform, and tour with her now-renowned dance company throughout the U.S. and to more than fifty countries worldwide. "Judging from reactions," she once said, "the dancing of my group is called anthropology in New Haven, sex in Boston, and in Rome—art!" In 1988, Dunham received a Kennedy Center Honor which was presented to her by Agnes DeMille, who hailed Dunham as:

> ... the first to investigate, exploit, [and] develop, the culture of the Blacks in the Western hemisphere that wasn't tap dancing or vaudeville dancing, because she was an anthropologist, among other things, and she had the hound-dog instinct of a real hunter . . . Oh, she's given much to her people, but she's given so much more to us, all of the other artists in every field. Because she told us what art really is—communication. The direct speech from the heart that goes way beyond reason. And she's been able to do this because of her great love and her great understanding of humanity.[32]

The Music That Made Them Dance—Trude Rittmann and the Unsung Art of the Broadway Dance Arranger

A crucial partner of every Broadway choreographer is the *dance arranger*, a profession that was largely invented by the Jewish German immigrant **Trude Rittmann**, who between 1943 and 1989 worked in close collaboration with many of Broadway's top choreographers and composers, arranging and composing dance music, choral music, and incidental music for at least thirty-five musicals, including *One Touch of Venus*, *Carousel*, *Finian's Rainbow*, *Brigadoon*, *South Pacific*, *Gentlemen Prefer Blondes*, *Peter Pan*, *The King and I*, *My Fair Lady*, *The Sound of Music*, and *Camelot*. As the *New York Times* described it, "Ms. Rittmann's was an unsung art, performed mostly behind the scenes, with no Tonys and little public notice until fairly recent years."[33]

What exactly does a dance arranger do? On most shows, the dance arranger is responsible for all of the music in the show that is not sung, including incidental music that is used to underscore and augment the dialogue scenes as well as whatever transition music might be needed to propel the show from one scene into the next.[34] Most significantly, as the job title indicates, they compose the music that accompanies the show's dance sequences. This could include everything from the dance breaks of vocal numbers, such as the jaunty "whistle chorus" dance section of "Wouldn't it be Loverly" that Rittmann created in conjunction with choreographer Hanya Holm for *My Fair Lady*, all the way to the mammoth "Small House of Uncle Thomas Ballet" she created with Jerome Robbins for *The King And I*. Although a large part of the dance arranger's job is to adapt melodies and themes from the composers' score and weave them into the dance and incidental music,[35] they will also often compose original music of their own.

Why doesn't the show's composer write the dance and incidental music? On most shows, they simply do not have enough time. Once a Broadway musical is greenlighted for production, it typically must come together very quickly. During the "five weeks you rehearse and rehearse" that Cole Porter wrote about,[36] which is still fairly standard, a big Broadway musical, will often have multiple rehearsals going on simultaneously. In one room (the stage of the theater during the Silver and Golden Ages) the principal and supporting actors will be working with the director, composer, lyricist, and music director on the show's book scenes and main songs. A second space (often the theater's lower lobby or ladies' lounge) will serve as the home of vocal music rehearsals. Meanwhile, in a third room (possibly a dance studio across town) the chorus dancers and singers are working with the choreographer and dance arranger on the dances and choreography. All three of these spaces may be brimming with activity eight hours a day, six days a week—with performers shuttling between them as needed. Even if a composer possesses the musical skills necessary to create dance arrangements, they generally don't have the bandwidth or patience to sit in the dance rehearsal eight hours a day devising them. Instead, they need to be working with the director, music director, and leading performers on any changes, adjustments, edits, and additions that are needed for the book and score and be available to write new songs overnight, if necessary. As a result, this often tedious work is "sub-contracted" to dance arrangers like Trude Rittmann.

Rittmann was born in Germany in 1908, where she began piano lessons at six and quickly proved to be a child prodigy. After graduating from the Cologne Conservatory, she started on a very promising career as a concert pianist and was even hailed as "Germany's most brilliant woman composer."[37] But with the rise of the Nazis, and Jewish heritage in her family, Rittmann was forced to flee Germany in 1933. By 1937, she had found her way to NYC, where she quickly fell in with the top tier of New York's classical music world, working with choreographer George Balanchine and his American Ballet Caravan (a forerunner to the New York City Ballet), where she adapted and shaped music by Aaron Copland, Virgil Thompson, Mark Blitzstein, and Leonard Bernstein. This led to her collaboration with Agnes DeMille on several concert dance works and then, in 1943, to her first Broadway show, *One Touch of Venus*—the first of eight Broadway musicals that Rittmann and DeMille would work on together during their twenty-five-year creative partnership.

Their second Broadway show was Rodgers and Hammerstein's *Carousel*, for which Rittmann created extensive dance music, and it is believed that she contributed musical underscoring for some of that show's dramatic scenes as well.[38] A large part of the dance arranger's job is to serve as a dramatist, creating music that evokes the mood of the scene and conveys the emotions and feelings of the characters. A prime example of this is Rittmann's scoring for *Carousel*'s second act ballet, which has to inform both the audience and Billy Bigelow about what's been happening with his now teenage daughter, Louise, during the fifteen years that have transpired during intermission. Dance arrangers also have to possess a great deal of showmanship, including the ability to create musical impact and excitement for its own sake. When creating the big sailor's hornpipe dance in *Carousel*, Rittmann had to take Richard Rodgers' purposely simple faux sea shanty, "Blow High, Blow Low," and, through extensive variations and elaborations of that basic tune, transform it into a series of show-off, bravura dance specialties that built to a thrilling climax. Agnes DeMille contended that Rodgers could never have written that dance music himself and emphasized that not only was it Rittmann who created it, but that she was the only one who *could* have created it.[39]

It is evident that Richard Rodgers highly valued Trude Rittman's contributions to *Carousel*, because he included her as a key member of the creative teams of five of his subsequent shows. Their second show together was *South Pacific*, and because this show included very little overt dancing or choreography, Rittmann now took on a new role. Her job was to "work hand in glove with Josh Logan" (the show's director, musical stager, and co-bookwriter) to amplify the drama and "heighten the cinematic style"[40] of the show. As author Todd Purdam described it, "For *South Pacific*, Rittmann would write lush underscoring for the most intense dialogue scenes, going off at night to elaborate on themes from Rodgers's tunes and then rehearsing over and over with Logan until the music was set." Perhaps the most explicit example of this occurs in the show's first scene at the end of the song "Twin Soliloquies," during which the central characters, Nellie Forbush and Emil DeBeque, stand on opposite sides of the stage and alternate singing their inner thoughts. As originally written by Rodgers, the music consisted of just the very simple tune we still hear repeated six times. But in his autobiography, Logan described how, in an early rehearsal, when the song finished, he felt like, "Well, we need more. The scene can't end there." So, he began sketching out some action to follow the song that would progress the relationship of the two unlikely lovers by bringing them physically together. The staging Logan created that day can still be seen on YouTube in the complete recording of the original 1952 London production of *South Pacific*: Emile (played by Wilber Evans) slowly crosses and hands a large Brandy snifter-type glass to Nellie (Mary Martin), who watches closely as he drinks from the odd glass. Apparently, she has never drunk from one before.[41] Meanwhile, on the piano, Rittmann began improvising a dramatic extension of the song to accompany this action, which would eventually have its own name in the published score: "Unspoken Thoughts." As Nellie and Emile sip their drinks, lower their glasses, and stand face to face, Rittmann builds Rodgers's tune into a huge, almost Wagnerian climax, during which, as described in the original stage directions, "One is made aware that in this simple act of two people who are falling in love, each drinking brandy, there are turbulent thoughts and feelings going on in their hearts and brains."[42] Logan would later state that he thought this was the moment "where the show became great." Almost every scene in *South Pacific* is underscored in a similar manner with music that reveals the emotions of the characters, even when they themselves don't fully understand what they are feeling. This technique, very similar to movie scoring, is quite unusual for a Broadway musical, and Rittmann did it brilliantly. Most people at the time, however, knew nothing about Trude Rittmann, much less understood her important contributions to *South Pacific*. Even if audience members did happen to notice her name in the show's playbill, they would have seen her credited there as "Assistant to Mr. Rogers," which sounds like she was following him around fetching him coffee and sharpening his pencils.

Trude's greatest contributions to Rodgers and Hammerstein's musicals were made in collaboration with choreographers Jerome Robbins and Joe Layton. The brilliant "Small House of Uncle Thomas Ballet" in *The King and I* is the centerpiece of that show's second act and a major turning point in its story. While this self-contained, one-act mini-musical does include a few sections adapted from Rodgers' songs, the "great bulk of the music in the fifteen-minute ballet was hers alone, even if the name on the published score was Richard Rodgers."[43] Rittmann worked in yet another role on *The Sound of Music*. She had created vocal arrangements here and there for previous Rodgers and Hammerstein shows, but for their final show together, she created all of the vocal arrangements. As befits the show's title, the extensive music for nuns and the von Trapp children adds up to a tremendous amount of choral singing. In addition, most people would be surprised to learn that not all of this show's music was created by Richard Rodgers—especially in regard to the iconic song, "Do, Re, Mi." Again, the song itself is remarkably simple, but its function in the story is crucial, both as a device for Maria, on a prosaic level, to teach the children the fundamentals of music, and on an emotional level, to awaken their hearts to the beauty of music and the joy of singing together. However, it still needs to seem fairly realistic that Maria is improvising this lesson as she goes along and that the children are learning (quite quickly!) to do something they have never done before. On top of all of that, "Do, Re, Mi" has to function as a "production number." Since this show has no real chorus (other than the nuns), the children have to fulfill that role and provide the show with that kind of dynamic impact. The assistant conductor of *The Sound of Music*'s original production was **Peter Howard**[44] (who would go on to become another of Broadway's great dance arrangers) and he described how the entire middle section of "Do, Re, Mi," was created in rehearsal. Howard remembered that the sort of "Swiss bell-ringing sequence"—which begins with "Do-Mi-Mi / Mi-So–So / Re-Fa-Fa / La-Ti-Ti" and then goes into double-time and builds to the final grand marching chorus—came out of a combination of music that Trude Rittmann had worked out at home the night before, and the action that Layton improvised with the actors that day on the spot. "When we started doing the staging of it, Joe took over. He asked Trude for certain parts to be repeated, certain embellishments," and the number evolved from there. Howard also recalled that Richard Rogers was thrilled with it: "Rogers allowed Trude to do whatever she liked." And, at least on this show, her billing read, "Choral arrangements by Trude Rittman."

None of this is meant to take anything away from Richard Rodgers. He was certainly a great musical dramatist—arguably the greatest ever. At the same time, his greatness is somewhat diminished by his unwillingness to share credit with Rittmann and other people who helped to make his shows so effective. In more recent decades, the Rodgers and Hammerstein Organization has made a determined effort to set the record straight and ensure that Trude Rittmann is remembered and acknowledged for the many significant artistic contributions she made to these shows.

Other leading Broadway songwriters also wanted Trude Rittmann on their team. She made major contributions to all three of Lerner and Lowe's signature musicals, and she worked on multiple shows with composers Jule Styne, Burton Lane, and Harold Rome, and on individual shows with Cole Porter, Dietz and Schwartz, Mary Rodgers, Kurt Weill, and Sigmund Romberg. In addition to the choreographers mentioned above, Rittmann worked with Michael Kidd, Helen Tamiris, and Onna White, and on three musicals with Hanya Holm. All of these top Broadway artists chose Trudy Rittman Weill as a key creative partner because they wanted to ensure that their shows would be the best they could possibly be. This put Trude in great demand and often resulted in her working on multiple musicals simultaneously, such that producers would sometimes schedule the rehearsal dates of their shows around Trude's availability because they didn't want to do the show without her!

Trude Rittmann was, of course, not the only great dance arranger of the Golden Age, and not even the only great female dance arranger of the Golden Age. Following in the trail that Trude blazed, there was also **Genevieve Pitot**, who worked on twenty-one Broadway musicals, including *Kiss Me, Kate, Call Me Madam, Can-Can, Lil' Abner*, and *Milk and Honey*; and **Betty Walberg**, who created the dance arrangements for seven Broadway shows including, *Gypsy, A Funny Thing Happened on the Way to the Forum*, and *Fiddler on the Roof*.

A month after the opening of *One Touch of Venus*, even Richard Rodgers was back in Silver Age musical comedy mode with a revival of the 1927 Rodgers and Hart show, *A Connecticut Yankee*. Theater critics had been disparaging and dismissing the books of Broadway musicals from the very beginning of the form but in this post-*Oklahoma!* period, they seemed to have even less patience for the usual musical comedy silliness. Herbert Fields had expanded and updated his original book to bring the modern elements of *A Connecticut Yankee*'s story into the 1940s, but *The New York Times* still found it to be "not the show's best feature." And ignoring the shining example of *Oklahoma!* which was enthralling audiences just a block away, critic Lewis Nichols noted that even though director John C. Wilson had "not always disguised the fact that the book is feeble," he concluded that it was unimportant since in musicals the "books lead only into dances, choral singing, and parodies. . .that is likely all that matters."

Carmen Jones (I, J, Q, B)

Then, just ten months following *Oklahoma!*'s premiere, Hammerstein opened another "simply superb" smash hit show that further solidified his reputation as "the best lyric writer in the business"[45] and further advanced his vision of what a Broadway musical could be. ***Carmen Jones*** was advertised as a *musical play*, but it was really a "transliteration"[46] of the classic opera *Carmen* in which Hammerstein kept most of composer Georges Bizet's original music intact but re-envisioned the story and characters for an all-Black cast. As one critic described it:

> It makes its people Black, instead of Spanish; its time is shifted from the never-never time of grand opera to this moment [1943]; its locales are changed from a cigarette factory to a [defense plant] parachute factory; from a bullring to a prize [-fight boxing] ring; from smuggler's retreat to a barbecue house. And not once is *Carmen Jones* wrong.[47]

Right up to the show's opening night, there was erroneous speculation in the press that the show was going to be a "swing version" of *Carmen*, a confusion no doubt inspired by two jazzed-up versions of Gilbert and Sullivan's *The Mikado* featuring Black casts that had played on Broadway simultaneously in 1939.[48] However, critics and audiences soon discovered that the music in *Carmen Jones* was "not boogie-woogie," or at least "not more so than Bizet wrote it at the time."[49] No, Hammerstein's version was "not a parody but a parallel,"[50] and "still *Carmen*, straight and pure,"[51] with Bizet's music performed in its original operatic style by "Negro voices better than any I ever heard at the Met[ropolitan Opera]."[52]

The racism and discrimination of the era had meant that prior to *Carmen Jones* there had been very few job opportunities for classically trained Black singers either in opera companies or on Broadway. As a result, Hammerstein and producer **Billy Rose** struggled to find professional Black performers who were able to take on leading roles that were so vocally demanding that they had to be double-cast so that no singer was required to perform more than four performances a week. After months of auditions and endless casting calls, the widely acclaimed Black artists who ended up starring in *Carmen Jones* included a "checker in the Philadelphia Navy Yard" and "a New York cop on leave,"[53] both making their professional debuts.[54] In a recurring theme, another critic reported that they made "the Metropolitan [Opera] look anemic."[55]

In its original version, the opera *Carmen* included extended sections of spoken dialogue, so to a certain degree, it was already a "musical play." Hammerstein's adaptation closely followed the opera's tragic plot line but re-envisioned the title character as a contemporary "Rosie The Riveter" World War II era factory worker, and the men in her life were changed from the Spanish Army corporal Don Jose to just plain [GI] Joe, and from bullfighter Escamillo to boxing champ Husky Miller—a transformation that was considered to be "a triumph for all concerned from Billy Rose to Bizet." That kind of acclaim extended to every department, with critics hailing the show as "a dazzling extravaganza, stunningly staged"[56] "with a skill that does not falter"[57] by Hassard Short, who "becomes more firmly entrenched as a master craftsman with his staging, lighting, and color schemes,"[58] which perfectly complemented some of the "most riotously beautiful costumes ever seen on a Broadway stage."[59] As was now expected, *Carmen Jones* included several extended dance sequences (choreographed by Eugene Loring) filled with "boundless humor and invention" and acclaimed for being "remarkable even in a season of remarkable ballets." The lion's share of the praise, however, went to Hammerstein, whose "incandescent imagination sets your own afire with the first number . . . and keeps it aglow until the final curtain." To a great extent, *Carmen Jones* was seen as a masterful encore to Hammerstein's most recent achievement: "No more praiseful rockets have been sent up in the Broadway sector since *Oklahoma!*"[60]

It is extremely difficult today to comprehend the tremendous impact and influence that *Carmen Jones* had on Broadway during the thirteen months (505 performances) that it played alongside *Oklahoma!* Although this show has received a handful of successful revivals (most notably Simon Callow's production at London's Old Vic in 1991 and John Doyle's at the Classic Stage Company in 2018), for most of us, the only opportunity to experience this show has been through Otto Preminger's 1954 film version which, at least in my view, is a poorly paced, overly long, and a much too literal presentation of a work that, by all reports, was wonderfully imaginative and theatrical in its original stage incarnation. Therefore, it is hardly surprising that many people now view *Carmen Jones*, at best, as a weird hybrid of opera and Broadway musical or, at worst, a problematic period piece burdened (at least on the page) by Hammerstein's heavy-handed use of dialect which writer James Baldwin said made its Black characters sound "ludicrously false and affected, like antebellum Negroes imitating their masters."[61] It is clear from the acclaim and popularity *Carmen Jones* received in its day, however, that its unique combination of dazzling, state-of-the-art staging techniques and production values, coupled with its dynamic Black cast and the tragic dimensions of its storyline (including the violent death of its title character) greatly expanded critics' and audiences' view of the potential scope and range of a Broadway musical, and the serious subject matter they could encompass.

Follow the Girls to the *Mexican Hayride* (I, J, Q, B, W)

Just a month later, Herbert Fields was back on Broadway, this time in partnership with sister Dorothy, with their book for Broadway's next hit musical comedy: Cole Porter's *Mexican Hayride*. This show was created as a vehicle for the wild and wacky comedian Bobby Clark, who, although almost entirely forgotten today, was a major Broadway star. Between 1920 and 1950, Clark appeared in nineteen Broadway musical comedies and revues, and always sporting his trademark look: round black eyeglasses painted right onto his face! Assessments of *Mexican Hayride*'s book were all over the place, ranging from "the book is harmless" with "a plot which is practically nothing, thank goodness," all the way to "there is a book by Herbert and Dorothy Fields, that is inspired, contemporary, satirical, logical in development, and full of ingenious incidents to draw Bobby Clark on the stage." Hassard Short did "his usual slick job of staging and lights" and Cole Porter was said to have "turned out a satisfactory score with one very excellent song and the rest good enough for their purpose."⁶² (Porter was immersed in a decade-long period of hit shows containing lackluster songs that he would not emerge from until he, too, embraced the new paradigm.)

We also now start to see a pattern of resistance from some critics, and no doubt many audience members, to Broadway's shift toward the *musical play*, and Bobby Clark's wild antics in *Mexican Hayride* were cheered for "upholding the tradition of Broadway comedy." It's clear, however, that the show's creators were fully aware that Rodgers and Hammerstein were shaking things up a few blocks away. At one point, Bobby Clark's character is accused of being "wanted in five states," but Clark protests that it's "only four." And when the accuser insists that it is, indeed, "Five! You forgot Oklahoma!" Clark scoffs, "I couldn't get tickets!"⁶³ Overall, most critics, and presumably most audience members based on its run of 481 performances, agreed with the reviewer from the *World-Telegram*, who found *Mexican Hayride* to be "a dream world of splendor, mirth, melody, and enchantment," and with the *Brooklyn Citizen* who proclaimed it to be "one of the most delightful trips into the world of make-believe this department has experienced in more than a quarter century of theatergoing."

An even bigger hit was **Follow the Girls**, a "pleasant enough but not distinguished musical comedy . . . In the Broadway tradition of color and noise, of dance steps, familiar comedy and songs, it is big and always active." This show was the product of a much less distinguished team of creators.⁶⁴ Their only top-tier member was co-bookwriter Guy Bolton, but he doesn't appear to have elevated the writing of this show very much. As the *New York Times* put it, "The book is banal of course, and Guy Bolton and Eddie Davis, who wrote it, should go stand in a corner." The show's plot, "if any, is about a burlesque queen in a serviceman's canteen and is so bad they simply throw it away and do vaudeville for the greater part of the second act." It was the polar opposite of *Oklahoma!* but that didn't prevent it from running for 888 performances; when it closed in 1946, it was the second longest-running show on Broadway!⁶⁵ Running nearly as long was the smash hit **Song of Norway**, an unlikely return to operettaland based on the life and music of Edvard Grieg, with songs derived from his classical compositions by the Queer songwriting team of **Robert Wright and George Forrest**, who specialized in this sort of thing.⁶⁶

"The Indivisibility of Human Freedom"—Yip Harburg and *Bloomer Girl* (I, J, B)

A few weeks later came **Bloomer Girl**, written by Yip Harburg and **Harold Arlen**. The previous year, Harburg had become intrigued by an idea for a musical that he described to a colleague as having "the freshness of [the blockbuster hit play] *Life With Father* and the brashness of *Of Thee I Sing*. "Also," he continued, "it is away from *Oklahoma!* which has spurred a new race of men all megalomaniacally bent on duplicating same." In hindsight, this is a puzzling and ironic statement because (as Harburg's son and biographer pointed out) today, *Bloomer Girl*, the musical Harburg was then conceiving, might best be remembered as "the first post-*Oklahoma!* musical to consolidate and build upon the formal revolution that *Oklahoma!* had begun."⁶⁷

Even if Harburg and Arlen were not consciously trying to duplicate Rodgers and Hammerstein's success, artistically, they were very much on the same wavelength, as is evident from their score for the 1939 movie musical *The Wizard Of Oz*, in which every song is purposefully and seamlessly integrated into a storyline that, in addition to his role as lyricist, Harburg played a big role in plotting and shaping. In the view of musical theater historian Stanley Green, no other writer understood and appreciated the growing importance of the book and the bookwriter more than Yip Harburg, so "when *Oklahoma!* broke through, Yip was ready—and by the decade's end, he stood second only to Hammerstein among those who had transformed the American musical stage."⁶⁸

With *Bloomer Girl*, Harburg took full command of the show, selecting and guiding the bookwriters (Fred Saidy and Sig Herzig), writing the lyrics, and staging the production himself. And like Hammerstein, Harburg had a lot to say. His strongly leftist political views and his passionate advocacy for social justice and equal rights were irrepressible. But unlike Hammerstein, Harburg always mixed a strong dose of comic satire into his work—and with *Bloomer Girl*, he found the perfect vehicle for his full agenda. The musical's story revolves around and ties together themes of both women's liberation and racial justice, or as Harburg put it, "the indivisibility of human freedom."⁶⁹ Set just before and during the American Civil War, *Bloomer Girl*'s central character is Evelina Applegate (played by Celeste Holm, *Oklahoma!*'s original Ado Annie), a hoop skirt manufacturer's daughter who has fallen under the sway of her feminist and abolitionist aunt, Dolly Bloomer (inspired by the real-life Amelia Bloomer). As dramatized in the jaunty activist march, "If it was Good Enough for Grandma," Dolly and Evelina incite the women of Cicero Falls, NY, to throw off the inhibiting bondage of antebellum corsets and hoop skirts and embrace the freedom and liberty of wearing bloomers:

> When Grandma was a lady,
> She sewed and cleaned and cooked,
> She scrubbed her pots
> And raised her tots,
> The dear old gal was hooked.
> She stitched her little stitches,
> Her life was applesauce.
> The thing that wore the britches
> Was boss.
> She had no voice in gov'ment
> And bondage was her fate.
> She only knew what love meant
> From eight to half-past eight.
> And that's a hell of a fate
> It was good enough for Grandma,
> That good old gal,

With her frills and her feathers and fuss.
It was good enough for Grandma,
Good enough for Grandma,
But it ain't good enough for us!

Meanwhile, Evelina, who is also active in the Underground Railroad, is being courted by one of her father's leading salesmen, Jeff Calhoun, a Kentuckian whose escaped slave Evelina and Dolly just happen to be hiding. The enslaved man, Pompey (portrayed by Dooley Wilson, who played Sam in the film *Casablanca*), celebrates his newfound freedom with "The Eagle and Me," which authors Harold and Ernie Harburg describe as "the first theater song of the fledgling civil rights movement."[70]

In addition to Celeste Holm and its Americana ambiance, *Bloomer Girl* borrowed several other elements from the Rodgers and Hammerstein megahit. The secondary female lead, Daisy, was played by Joan McCracken, who as a featured dancer in *Oklahoma!* had become famous as the comic "Girl Who Falls Down." Most significant, however, and perhaps *Bloomer Girl*'s strongest asset, was choreographer Agnes DeMille, whose "Civil War Ballet" became one of the show's highlights. *Bloomer Girl* tackled big important themes, but essentially it was a *musical comedy*. However, near the end of the second act, this "serious ballet about women's emotions in war" single-handedly shifted *Bloomer Girl* into the realm of the *musical play*. And, of course, the fact that every woman in the audience at that time was having their own personal experience of living through a war imbued De Mille's ballet with an intense and immediate impact.

Nearly every critic compared *Bloomer Girl* to *Oklahoma!*, including Arthur Pollock of the *Brooklyn Daily Eagle*, who wrote, "As everybody knows by now, New York has in addition to *Oklahoma!* another phenomenon named *Bloomer Girl*, that will make theatergoers happy, when they can buy tickets, for years to come." Nearly all of the critics recognized the high quality and innovation of this new kind of musical, even if, like Pollock, they were very confused about what exactly to call them:

> Both [shows] are so curious as musical comedies that it has become necessary to describe them as something more high-toned than that, so they are often spoken of as folk opera. Whatever the definition, they are musical comedies developed to a better level than ever before anywhere [and are] . . . farther along in the process of evolution . . .[71]

And while Pollock agreed with the general consensus that the creators of *Bloomer Girl* had not quite equaled the achievement of Rodgers and Hammerstein, unlike most other critics he did not ignore the big themes underlying the show and prophetically recognized the tremendous social impact that Broadway musicals were now capable of:

> Probably *Bloomer Girl* is a trifle less smooth, silken, leisurely, and assuaging than *Oklahoma!* It's a little jumpy now and then. But it does a remarkable thing. It

actually has a meaning, something to say. It's a kind of new, amusing cry for freedom, hooking up the freedom of women with the freedom of the Negro and, by inference, with freedom of all kinds. It's big and beautiful, rich in songs and lyrics, expertly played in all respects, a musical comedy masterpiece . . . Broadway's power is at last harnessed and put to work for a better world.[72]

Even though *Bloomer Girl*, for all of its popularity and acclaim, never entered the canon of classic, enduring Broadway musicals, its significance in engendering the Golden Age of Broadway should not be underestimated.

Next, the manic comedy team of Olsen and Johnson boomeranged Broadway back into anything-for-a-laugh-style musical comedyland with their rough and rowdy revue, **Laffing Room Only**, which the *New York Daily News* declared had "practically everything," including

> . . . shotguns, pretty girls, brassieres, seltzer siphons, a piano with boxing gloves, a man with rabbits . . . a race between a soldier and a sailor trying to put on women's underthings and then run around the house, some more siphons of seltzer, and the general pretense of busting a gut in the hope that you might bust one of your own in appreciation.

Ole Olsen and Chic Johnson's previous shows included *Hellzapoppin* (1938), a wild, surreal, raucous hodgepodge of skits and songs that, at 1,404 performances, was the longest-running show in Broadway history until *Oklahoma!* broke its record. *Laffing Room Only* was more lavish and elaborate than their previous shows, "with attractive settings and, just when you least suspect it, there is a beautiful chorus doing some really excellent dancing . . . choreographed by the ubiquitous Robert Alton . . . who for my money is one of the stars of the show." Again, a number of the critics were thrilled to see this kind of Silver Age-style show return to Broadway and alluded to shows like *Carmen Jones* and *Bloomer Girl* with comments such as "The songs by Burton Lane are just corny enough to be catchy—and I prefer them to many I have heard in this season's pretentious and arty musicals."[73]

"A Helluva Town!" (J, J, Q, W)

And there was yet another exciting group of innovative collaborators on a parallel track with Rodgers and Hammerstein. All four of them were under thirty years old, all four were Jewish, and two of them were Queer. And all of them, together and separately, would go on to have a substantial and enduring impact on the Broadway musical. It began in 1944 when **Jerome Robbins**, a young dancer with what is now American Ballet Theatre, choreographed his first ballet for the company, *Fancy Free*, created in collaboration with up-and-coming composer Leonard Bernstein. Their goal was to bring real contemporary life to the ballet stage, so for their subject matter, they decided to focus on characters who, in the middle of World War II, could be seen every day on virtually every street in NYC: rowdy, horny, lonely sailors on shore leave in search of fun and girls. This was part of a movement in the ballet world of the time toward distinctly American subject matter.

Broadway Dance #8: Americana and the Musical

Fancy Free was only one of a series of acclaimed "Americana" ballets that emerged in the late 1930s and 40s as young choreographers endeavored to move away from the swans, fairies, princes, and cavaliers of nineteenth-century story-ballets and instead bring American stories and characters to the stage by combining classical ballet technique with more natural, vernacular styles of movement. First was ***The Filling Station*** (1937), choreographed by Lew Christensen and with music by Leonard Bernstein's mentor, Virgil Thompson. The leading role of the sexy gas station attendant was danced by **Eugene Loring**, who was then inspired to choreograph ***Billy the Kid*** (1938) with music by another of Bernstein's mentors, Aaron Copland. Loring would go on to choreograph three Broadway musicals, including Oscar Hammerstein II's *Carmen Jones* and Cole Porter's *Silk Stockings*, as well as several classic movie musicals, for which he was noted for "successfully fusing ballet, modern dance, and jazz dance to create lively production numbers."[74] The title role of *Billy The Kid* was first danced by future Broadway choreographer Michael Kidd (who also later danced in *Fancy Free*).[75] In 1942, inspired by *Billy The Kid*'s Western ambiance, Agnes DeMille choreographed and starred in ***Rodeo*** (again with music by Copeland), and that ballet served as a large part of the inspiration for the choreography in *Oklahoma!* In 1948, DeMille further explored this style in her ballet ***Fall River Legend***, with music by Morton Gould and inspired by the story of Lizzie Bordon. Many of these works sought to redefine the image of male dancers by focusing on characters who were icons of strong masculinity. In that regard, as well as their subject matter and choreography, these Americana ballets had a tremendous influence on Broadway dance in the Golden Age.

Fancy Free's premiere has become legendary, with reports of the audience demanding dozens of curtain calls from the stunned cast and creators, quickly followed by rave reviews from the critics. Incredibly, only eight months and ten days later, **On The Town** opened on Broadway. The musical expanded the basic premise of the ballet: three sailors on shore leave in New York, New York, with "one day and not another minute" to pack in a lifetime of fun, romance, and excitement before they ship off to war. As was typical of stories written and set during the war, the three women the sailors encounter are all strong, dynamic, independent working women: an anthropologist, a professional dancer, and a taxicab driver. And the show was very lucky to have an equally strong, dynamic, independent working woman to bring them to life. She was one half of the writing team of **Comden and Green**.

Betty Comden was born Basya Cohen in Brooklyn, NY, in 1917. Both of her parents were Russian Jewish immigrants. **Adolph Green** was born in the Bronx in 1914, and his parents were Hungarian Jewish immigrants. After finishing high school, Adolph worked as a runner on Wall Street while he tried to break into show business. Meanwhile, Betty studied drama at NYU, and they met around the time of her graduation in 1938. They teamed up as nightclub performers, but they were too poor to pay for material, so they started writing their own. The result was a witty act called *The Revuers* that featured lots of topical humor. Their good friend Leonard Bernstein would often show up at their gigs and take over the piano playing. So, when the idea was being floated of adapting *Fancy Free* into a full musical, Lenny insisted that Comden and Green be hired to write the book and lyrics, as well as play two of the leading roles.

Guided by the show's director, the venerable Mr. Abbott, the musical the quartet came up with is a wild, sexy, madcap mashup of musical comedy gags and swinging tunes interspersed with extended sequences of Bernstein's angular, arty, edgy, modernist music that in Comden and Green's estimation provided the show with "a symphonic texture unlike any musical before or since."[76] That music accompanies large sections of the story told only through dance. *Oklahoma!* had opened just eleven months earlier, and it feels to me as if Jerome Robbins was responding to Agnes DeMille's instantly acclaimed dream ballet by choreographing three elaborate dream ballets of his own for *On The Town*." On the surface, *On The Town* is all youthful joy and exuberant hijinks, but underneath lies a heartbreaking subtext: the audience and characters themselves are well aware that one, or conceivably all three, of the sailors might not come back from the war. *On The Town* marked the Broadway debut of all four of its twenty-something creators—Robbins, Bernstein, Comden and Green—and it immediately transformed them into major forces on Broadway.

"A Perfect Relationship": Betty Comden and Adolph Green (I, J, W)

In a remarkable career that began at the dawn of the Golden Age and thrived well into the Modern Era, Betty Comden and Adolph Green wrote the script and/or lyrics (usually both) for seventeen Broadway musicals. Working in collaboration with several of Broadway's greatest composers (including two shows with Leonard Bernstein, nine with Jule Styne, and two with Cy Coleman), Comden and Green created a series of hit shows such as **On The Town, Wonderful Town, Peter Pan, Bells Are Ringing, Applause, Lorelei, On the Twentieth Century**, and **The Will Rogers Follies**. Meanwhile, they wrote the screenplays for several classic MGM film musicals, including what is widely considered to be the greatest movie musical of all time, *Singin' in the Rain*.

Unchallenged as "the longest-running act on Broadway," Comden and Green were in a category all their own.⁷⁷ Many people assumed they were married—and they were, just not to each other. For six decades, they met every morning and set to work. As Comden described it in 1977, "We meet, whether or not we have a project, just to keep up a continuity of working . . . We have a theory that nothing's wasted, even those long days of staring at one another." Their belief was that "you had to go through all that to get to the day when something did happen."⁷⁸ Green attibuted the team's success to Betty. "She was always unforgivably responsible," he told the *New York Times*. "She is always on time for everything, while I am late for anything. I have lived for years in the shadow of an overwhelming suspicion that all our collaborations have, in reality, been solo efforts written by Betty alone. Without her, I'm nothing."⁷⁹ Comden, however, insisted that "Everything is together. We don't divide the work up. We develop a mental radar, bounce lines off one another," and she added that she could not imagine life without their collaboration.⁸⁰ All of the musicals that Comden and Green created feature strong female characters that, much like Betty herself, are all vibrant transgressive women who break the rules and defy the conventions of their day.

"Round in Circles"—Rodgers and Hammerstein's *Carousel* (J, J, W)

Finally, two years after the premiere of *Oklahoma!*, Rodgers and Hammerstein opened their second collaboration, ***Carousel*** (1945). It was based on *Liliom*, a dark, moody play by Hungarian Jewish playwright Ferenc Molnar. This was in no way a safe or obvious choice as source material for a musical—but it was a challenge that Rodgers and Hammerstein were excited to take on. The idea had actually come from producer **Theresa Helborn**, the dynamic Jewish American producer of more than fifty Broadway plays and musicals who had also suggested that Rodgers and Hammerstein turn the play *Green Grow The Lilacs* into *Oklahoma!* With *Carousel*, the team significantly increased the level of seamless integration of book, music, lyrics, and choreography beyond what they had achieved in *Oklahoma!*—especially in a sequence near the beginning of the show that has come to be known as "the Bench Scene."

The Bench Scene: "The Singular Most Important Moment in the Evolution of Contemporary Musicals"

That's how Stephen Sondheim described the so-called "Bench Scene" in Rodgers and Hammerstein's *Carousel*, and it is an assertion that certainly gets your attention. But what is it about this sequence that made it such a game-changer? To kick off the love story of a Silver Age musical comedy, the show's writers might also have had a boy and girl meet on a bench in a park, and on the surface, the action of that scene might be very similar to the scene in *Carousel*. The leading couple, who have been thrown together by a quirk of fate, now have their first real conversation and are drawn to one another. The boy is brash and boastful. The girl is reserved and a bit standoffish. To cap off this dialogue scene, the boy woos the girl with a song, and by the end of the scene, they know they are in love. In those earlier shows, this sequence would have been built around a single stand-alone song consisting of a functional verse that established whatever story points the audience needed to know, followed by a melodic refrain with lyrics general enough that they could be sung outside of the show. In fact, the 1927 musical *Good News* has a scene set on a park bench almost exactly like that, which leads into the song "The Best Things in Life are Free." But Hammerstein and Rodgers wanted to do something quite different.

As author Barry Kester noted in his book, *Round in Circles—The Story of Rodgers and Hammerstein's Carousel*, Hammerstein greatly admired Ferenc Molnar's original version of this scene in his play, *Liliom*, and "thought that Molnar's writing was too tight and beautiful to change in any significant way and that it would lend itself to a beautiful musical number."[81] He became determined to "keep as close to the original text as possible and make changes only when necessary."[82] So, how could he and Rodgers stay true to the source material and still set this lengthy dialogue scene to music? Of course, opera librettists and composers had been musicalizing dialogue for several centuries using a technique called "recitative." This declarative style of musical composition attempts to imitate the phrasing and rhythms of natural speech, but in practice, the result is often dramatically dull, musically monotonous connective material, filling space between the big arias. Rodgers and Hammerstein did not want to replicate that either. As Richard Rodgers later asserted, "When the script calls for recitative, I write melody instead."[83]

So, they created the Bench Scene in a unique way by employing a deftly interwoven series of what my colleague, Albert Evans, has dubbed "songlets." Even though these short passages of music and lyrics are only eight to sixteen bars long, they are as dramatically and musically satisfying as full songs and often just as memorable. In form, the seven songlets that Rodgers and Hammerstein fold into the Bench Scene are somewhat like advertising jingles—engaging, self-contained mini-songs that instantly become locked in our brains. In this case, however, these earworms are deeply resonant, character-revealing, musical building blocks that the writers combine with brief passages of spoken dialogue and spread over a bed of nonstop orchestral underscoring. The underscoring provides the twelve-minute sequence with remarkable unity and also expresses emotions that Billy and Julie themselves are unaware they are feeling or are trying to suppress. Each of the scene's songlets is used more than once. They include a reprise of the main theme of the previous full song, "You're a Queer One"; the purposely monotonous "When I worked in the mill/Kind of scrawny and pale" songlet;[84] the "Never gonna marry/Couldn't take my money" songlet; and, most significantly, the "Two little people" songlet. Rodgers and Hammerstein employ this technique again later in the show in the eight-minute tour de force solo, "Soliloquy," and, to a much lesser extent, in "This was a Real Nice Clambake." As Kester points out, "Where *Carousel* differs from most of its predecessors is the extent to which it uses extended musical sequences through which the story is told." He estimates that the musical content of *Carousel* is "some seventy-five percent of the show, compared with the norm at the time of around fifty percent."[85] This is what makes this show and this scene so revolutionary.

Like those Silver Age shows, the Bench Scene builds to two soaring renditions of "If I Loved You," a big, extractable ballad that has, indeed, become wildly popular outside of the show. This is one of Hammerstein's "conditional" love songs—a strategy he developed to allow him to place a passionate love song early in a show, even though the leading romantic couple who sing it have just met. "If I Loved You," however, goes far beyond the playful flirting of *Show Boat*'s "Only Make Believe" or *Oklahoma!*'s "People Will Say We're in Love" and gets to something much deeper. Billy and Julie already intuit that their love is doomed, and the song is so compelling that we don't realize it's one big spoiler—it gives away the entire rest of the story. Billy will soon leave her and go off in the midst of day.

"Time and again . . . Round in circles . . ." *Carousel* is about repetition, going in circles —yes, like a carousel. It's about life as a journey that gets you nowhere. Most significantly, it's about abusive and destructive patterns that repeat and persist for generations, and the timidity and shame that keep us from breaking them. Billy and Julie's tragedy is that they will indeed let their golden chances to say those simple words "I love you" pass them by until it is (almost) too late.[86]

For almost two years, *Oklahoma!* and *Carousel* played to packed houses in theaters across the street from each other in the heart of the Broadway theater district. This signaled loudly and clearly that there was no turning back—there was no longer any possibility of returning to the lively but ramshackle musicals of the Silver Age. From this point on, this new level of depth, invention and expert craft was what audiences and critics would expect from a Broadway musical.

CHAPTER 9
"ANOTHER OP'NIN', ANOTHER SHOW!"—THE GOLDEN AGE OF BROADWAY, PART 2: THE 1940S AND 1950S (I, J, Q, W)

In the mid-1940s, following the end of World War II, this new, integrated style of musical theater began to totally dominate Broadway, and soon, another major writing team emerged who would not only follow the lead of Rodgers and Hammerstein but ultimately rival them at their own game.

The Street Where They Lived—Lerner and Loewe

Frederick Loewe (always called Fritz) was born in Berlin in 1901 to Austrian parents. His father was a famous operetta tenor who originated the leading male role of Danilo in the first production of *The Merry Widow* in 1905. As a result, young Fritz grew up in a home that was filled with music and art. He was a musical prodigy who, at thirteen, became the youngest piano soloist ever to play with the Berlin Philharmonic. Just two years later, he composed the music for a song called "Katrina," which reportedly sold over one million copies of sheet music. Prior to World War I, the Loewe family was relatively prosperous, but then, with inflation rising to unimaginable heights, money became worthless, and the family fortune simply evaporated (including, one supposes, the royalties from "Katrina") and like most Berliners, Fritz and his family suffered from poverty and hunger for several years. Then, in 1924, Fritz's father got an offer to sing in New York, and Fritz, now in his early twenties, decided to go with him with a plan to stay and establish himself as a Broadway composer. However, because of cultural and language barriers, it took quite a few years before Loewe was able to break into the theater, first as a pianist in Broadway pit orchestras and, by the 1930s, by placing a few songs into several not-very-successful Broadway shows.[1]

Meanwhile, **Alan J. Lerner** was growing up in New York City. Born in 1918 (seventeen years after his future partner), he was the grandson of Russian and German Jewish immigrants whose three sons had founded the Lerner Shops, an immensely successful national chain of women's dress stores. Alan was raised in a seventeen-room apartment on Park Avenue and was educated at the best schools, including Choate in New Hampshire, where he co-edited the yearbook with future American president John F. Kennedy. He then went to Harvard, where he wrote sketches and lyrics for several *Hasty Pudding* shows, and during summer breaks, studied musical composition at Juilliard.[2]

In 1942, Lerner met Loewe, but their new partnership got off to a rocky start. During the first four years of their collaboration, they created three musicals, all written in Silver Age musical comedy style—and all of them flopped. However, in 1947, following the examples of *Oklahoma!* and *Carousel*, the team adopted the musical play format. The result was **Brigadoon**, a romantic fantasy about a disillusioned American ex-serviceman who stumbles by chance on a quaint Scottish village that, as the result of a miracle, comes into existence for only one day every 100 years. Like Hammerstein, Lerner wrote all of the words—book and lyrics—which provided all of their shows with a great deal of cohesion. In addition, on *Brigadoon* they collaborated closely with choreographer Agnes DeMille to tell large segments of the story primarily through dance. Critics, who had now begun to assess shows based on how "brilliantly integrated" they were, took note: "To the growing list of major achievements on the musical stage add one—*Brigadoon*," Brooks Atkinson wrote for the *New York Times*. "For once, the modest label 'musical play' has a precise meaning. For it is impossible to say where the music and dancing leave off and the story begins in this beautifully orchestrated Scottish idyll."[3] *Brigadoon*'s tuneful score spun off several major song hits, resulting in a substantial success that, in its original production, ran for nearly 600 performances, followed by multiple Broadway and West End revivals.

"The Show of the Century": My Fair Lady

In 1956, Lerner and Lowe scored their biggest hit with **My Fair Lady**, one of the most successful and acclaimed musicals of all time. *My Fair Lady* was an immediate success, hailed as "the world's greatest musical,"[4] "the perfect musical play,"[5] and "the show of the century." Many critics and theatergoers still regard it as an unsurpassable model of drama, melody, elegance, and wit. But this was by no means a foregone conclusion.

The source material was George Bernard Shaw's 1913 play *Pygmalion*, an intellectual comedy that, like most of Shaw's plays, was written to prove a thesis: that class differences are entirely artificial and based only on surface elements such as manners, deportment, appearance, and above all, speech. To dramatize this, Shaw invented two unforgettable characters: Eliza Doolittle, a poor, bedraggled, but defiant cockney flower girl, and Henry Higgins, a brilliant but irascible professor of phonetics. The story begins when Higgins bets his sidekick, Colonel Pickering, that in six months' time, he can pass Eliza off as "a duchess at an embassy ball" simply by teaching her upper-class speech and behavior. He eventually wins his bet, but his transformed pupil, Eliza, proves not nearly as grateful as he had expected. During his lifetime, Shaw turned down several proposals to musicalize *Pygmalion*. He did, however, write the screenplay of a hit 1938 film version which opened up the action to include scenes that were only spoken about in the play, and he even added (or at least allowed) a hint of romance in the final scene. All of which proved crucial to the success of the eventual musical version.[6]

When Shaw died in 1950, his estate became receptive to the idea of a musical *Pygmalion*. Several writers were approached, including Cole Porter, Dietz and Schwartz, Yip Harburg, Noel Coward, and Rodgers and Hammerstein—but all of them decided that as great as the play was, there were just too many obstacles to transforming it into a musical.[7] There was almost no romance, and most of the action took place entirely in small interior rooms. How could you work in a large singing and dancing chorus, which was considered to be a crucial element of any mid-century Broadway musical? In 1952, the project was offered to Lerner and Loewe,[8] but they also struggled to find ways to make the show sing. They abandoned the project but then returned to it a few years later. In the meantime, Lerner had had two revelations: (1) the play had already been "opened up" in Shaw's own screenplay, which had added the "scenes between the scenes"—such as the Ascot races and the Embassy Ball, and (2), instead of adapting Shaw to the conventions of the musical, why not adapt the musical to Shaw? So what if there's no principal love story and no secondary comic couple? Shaw's play had enchanted audiences for decades—why not trust it?[9]

My Fair Lady, starring Rex Harrison and Julie Andrews, directed by Moss Hart and choreographed by Hanya Holm, opened on March 15, 1956, to rapturous reviews. Critic John Chapman called it

> ... as fine a piece of work, of its kind, as our stage can be asked to give us. Not since *Guys And Dolls* have all the elements of a big musical production—the stars and the chorus, the sets and the costumes, the dances and the plot, the melodies and the lyrics—been blended so artfully and so enjoyably.[10]

It was another "*Hamilton* of its day"—sold out for months, and impossible to get a ticket. It would go on to run for six years, and at 2,717 performances, *My Fair Lady* became the show that finally broke *Oklahoma!*'s record, making it "the longest-running musical of all time"—a title it would hold for nearly a decade.

In addition, the unprecedented success of *My Fair Lady*'s original cast album would make Lerner and Loewe's hit-filled score known to everyone, including those who never set foot in a theater. It's hard to convey the cultural impact of this album, especially because we consume music so differently today. Within a month of its release, the record zoomed to No. 1 on the *Billboard* chart of bestselling LP albums, where it stayed for eight consecutive weeks. It then returned to the No. 1 spot seven additional times over the next four years. As Laurence Maslon relates in his book *Broadway to Mainstreet: How Showtunes Enchanted America*, the *My Fair Lady* album stayed "on the Top 10 chart for 173 weeks (a record by 57 weeks); in the Top 40 for 292 weeks (another record and double the next runner up); and charted for a total of 480 weeks—more than nine years."[11]

The Time of King Arthur—The Trials and Tribulations of Camelot

In 1960, Lerner and Loewe, Moss Hart, and Hanya Holm joined forces again for **Camelot**, a musical about the legendary King Arthur based on *The Once and Future King*, a massive fantasy novel comprising four individual books. The events of the first book, *The Sword in the Stone*, about Arthur's youth, were only briefly referred to in *Camelot*, but three years later, they were musicalized in Disney's animated film of the same name. However, the remaining three books are so packed with characters, incidents, locations, battles, and supernatural events, that trimming the story down to a manageable size for the musical proved to be a daunting and never fully accomplished task. The casting, however, was sensational, with Richard Burton as Arthur, Julie Andrews as Guenevere, Robert Goulet (in his Broadway debut) as Lancelot, and Roddy McDowell as the antagonist Mordred. However, on its pre-Broadway opening night in Toronto, *Camelot* ran nearly four hours long, inspiring Noel Coward to quip that it was "longer than the Ring Cycle and not nearly as funny." With so much work to be accomplished, there could not have been a worse time for both Alan Lerner and Moss Hart to end up in the hospital—Lerner with a bleeding ulcer and Hart with his second heart attack. Somehow, more than an hour of material had been hacked out of the show by opening night on Broadway. The reviews the next day were very mixed, and the fate of the show was in question. But then a few weeks after the opening, several extensive excerpts from the show were presented on *The Ed Sullivan Show*, an enormously popular television variety show. In this condensed format, *Camelot* came off as one of the most dazzling musicals ever. The next day, ticket sales soared, and soon, the box office achieved an unprecedented advance sale of three and a half million dollars. Then, during her first interview following the assassination of President John F. Kennedy, his widow, Jackie Kennedy, revealed that *Camelot*'s original cast album had been the favorite bedtime listening at the White House and that President Kennedy's favorite lines were in the final number: "Don't let it be forgot, that once there was a spot, for one brief, shining moment that was known as Camelot."[12] This tiny tidbit of personal information drew enormous attention to the show and forever linked the musical with John F. Kennedy.[13]

Musical Comedy 2.0

The rise of the *musical play* did not, however, bring about the demise of the *musical comedy*, but it did mean that musical comedies now had to join the revolution. Even if the sole reason for a show to exist was to make the audience laugh, tap their toes, and delight in the great performers strutting their stuff while belting out hit tunes—those shows also had to have well-structured plots with songs that emerged out of, and helped to tell, that story. Perhaps most importantly, from this point on, a majority of those songs would now be used to breathe life into captivating three-dimensional characters.

Very few characters from the previous eras of the Broadway musical achieved any kind of currency beyond the star performers who played them. Audiences responded to the persona and charisma of the star, not the character. But now, in the Golden Age, virtually every hit musical (play or comedy) would introduce unforgettable, dynamic, fully dimensional characters who seemed to live above and beyond the musicals that contained them. This is one of the most notable innovations of the era and one of the main distinctions of the Golden Age. What was it that made these characters so vibrant? Broadway songwriters now began to create character-defining songs—often called "I want" or "I am" songs—that crystallized exactly who the character was and what they desired. Among the best and earliest example are *Oklahoma!*'s "I'm Just a Girl Who Can't Say No," and "Lonely Room." Songs like these caused the audience to deeply identify with and emotionally embrace these characters and the situations and conflicts they were involved in. As audience members, we experience what they experience; we want them to achieve their goals and we participate emotionally in the challenges that stand in their way and the resulting choices they make as they move through the story.

These songs vastly deepened and improved the musical comedy—and made them funnier as well. Unexpectedly, it was four of the least likely suspects—Irving Berlin, Cole Porter, and Dorothy and Herbert Fields—the oldest of the old school—who would pioneer this new phase of the revolution and provide us with four of the greatest comeback stories in theater history.

"Doin' What Comes Naturally"—Irving Berlin, Herbert and Dorothy Fields, and *Annie Get Your Gun* (I, J, W, Q)

When last we encountered Dorothy Fields, she was trying to dream up a project to showcase the unique talents of her friend Ethel Merman. As Fields told the story, "Sometimes an idea for a show drops down from God's hands into yours." The idea was, "Wouldn't it be marvelous to have Ethel Merman as (the legendary real-life sharpshooter) Annie Oakley?"[14] In Dorothy's original vision, the show was to have a book by Herbert and Dorothy Fields, lyrics by Dorothy, and music by Jerome Kern. Tragically, just as that illustrious team was to begin work on what seemed like a surefire hit, Kern suffered a massive stroke and died. The show's producers were Rodgers and Hammerstein, who, in addition to writing, had branched out into producing plays and musicals by other writers. After the shock of Kern's death subsided, Rodgers and Hammerstein suggested that the team should try to coax Irving Berlin out of semi-retirement to compose the score. However, they pointed out that even if they were to succeed in persuading him, there was another problem—Berlin always wrote his own lyrics. So, Dorothy gracefully agreed to relinquish that job and concentrate on the book.

By 1945, Irving Berlin was already fifty-seven years old, and thirty-five years after his Broadway debut, he was very reluctant, and probably frightened, to try his hand at this new format Rodgers and Hammerstein had created—which Berlin called "a situation show."[15] He told them he didn't know how to write songs for a story and wasn't sure he wanted to try. Rodgers and Hammerstein, however, convinced him that it was actually easier to write this way, and Berlin finally agreed to give it a try. He took a draft of Herbert and Dorothy's book with him to Atlantic City for the weekend and came back just a few days later with four wonderfully entertaining, expertly integrated, soon-to-be classic showtunes that still serve as models of how to tell a story and define characters through song: "Doin' What Comes Naturally," "You Can't Get a Man With a Gun," "They Say it's Wonderful," and a song destined to become a ubiquitous show biz anthem, "There's No Business Like Show Business."[16] With direction by Joshua Logan and choreography by Helen Tamiris, the original production of *Annie Get Your Gun* ran for 1,147 performances and expertly demonstrated how musical comedies had to be crafted in this new era.

Powerhouse: Joshua Logan (Q)

As described by Richard Rodgers, director/writer/producer/choreographer **Joshua Logan** was a "big hulk of a man with a flamboyant personality."[17] He was born in 1908 in Texarkana, Texas, and grew up in Mansfield, Louisiana. He was eight years old when he saw his first professional play, and as he wrote in his 1976 autobiography, *Josh*, it was a case of "love at first sight." He attended a military academy in Indiana during his late childhood and teens, and the day he entered his first drama class there, he said, "I felt my life swerve and suddenly steady itself."[18] At Princeton University, Logan was elected president of the Triangle Club and helped found the University Players, a noted summer stock company on Cape Cod, with fellow students Henry Fonda, James Stewart, and Margaret Sullivan. During his senior year, he obtained a scholarship to study acting with Konstantin Stanislavsky at the Moscow Art Theatre in Russia, where he observed the famed acting teacher direct an opera with the goal of achieving a "total integration of acting and music."[19] After graduating, Logan pursued work as an actor and stage manager and appeared in two short-lived Broadway plays.

Much more successful was his directing career, which kicked into high gear in 1938, when at twenty-nine years old, he vaulted to the front ranks of Broadway directors with three hit shows: the play *On Borrowed Time*,[20] Kurt Weill/Maxwell Anderson's musical **Knickerbocker Holiday**, and Rodgers and Hart's musical comedy, *I Married an Angel*. This was the first of seven Broadway shows he worked on with Richard Rodgers, whom he described as "the person who meant more to my professional life than any other."[21] From the beginning, Logan established himself as one of Rodgers' key collaborators. The songwriters had written the book for *I Married an Angel* themselves, and Rodgers later recalled that after the first week of rehearsal, "Josh . . . came to Larry and me and told us he was upset with the way things were going."[22] That night, the three men met in Hart's apartment to "thrash things out." After listening to Logan's assessment of the show and his many ideas for improving it, Rodgers and Hart "decided to start immediately on a thorough rewrite." With Logan's prodding, they "threw out about a third" of what they had written, "adding new dialogue and situations, even entire scenes . . . At six in the morning, we finally had a script that worked." The show, in Rodgers's view, "turned out to be our biggest hit in about ten years."[23] Logan directed two additional Rodgers and Hart musicals: **Higher and Higher** (1940), which was based on an idea that came from Logan,[24] and the racy musical comedy **By Jupiter** (1942), the biggest hit of the three. Logan was then offered the opportunity to direct *Oklahoma!*, but he had already enlisted in the U.S. Army Air Corp Combat Intelligence Division to serve in World War II.[25]

Immediately after the war, in 1945, Logan married actress Nedda Harrigan (daughter of Edward Harrigan of Harrigan and Hart) and quickly reestablished his directing career with three hit Broadway shows: the musical *Annie Get Your Gun* (1946), and the plays *Happy Birthday* (1946)[26] and *John Loves Mary* (1947)[27]—all of which were produced by Rodgers and Hammerstein. Then, in 1948, Logan scored his biggest hit yet when he co-wrote and directed the long-running play *Mister Roberts* (starring his former classmate Henry Fonda) and received his first three Tony awards for "Best Director," "Best Author," and "Best Play."

It was Logan who suggested to Rodgers and Hammerstein that James A. Michener's story collection, *Tales of the South Pacific*, might be interesting source material for a musical.[28] This led to him directing, choreographing, co-producing, and co-writing the book for **South Pacific**, which brought him four additional Tony Awards and the 1950 Pulitzer Prize for Drama. Nothing could top the success of that show, but Logan was still able to follow it up with a string of significant hits, including directing the plays *Picnic* (1953),[29] for which he received his eighth Tony, and *The World of Suzie Wong* (1958).[30] He also directed and wrote the books for the musicals **Wish You Were Here** (1952) and **Fanny** (1954).[31] At one point, he had four hit shows running on Broadway simultaneously.

Although Logan is not usually remembered as a director-choreographer, in addition to directing *South Pacific*, he created all of its "musical staging," and he directed and staged the dances for the musical *Wish You Were Here* as well.[32] Both shows were acclaimed for their seamless movement and fluid transitions from scene to scene. *South Pacific* was especially groundbreaking in this regard. Harold Prince recalled being grilled by his mentor George Abbott about why that show's opening night (which they had both attended) was such an important event. As Abbott explained to his protege, "For the first time, a musical had moved without interruption, had flowed as if it were a film."[33] This kind of cinematic flow would become the hallmark of the great director-choreographers and move the Broadway musical into a new dimension.

Logan's staging of *South Pacific* also added to his self-described reputation as "the nudity king of Broadway."[34] Unusually, however, nearly all of the musicals and plays he directed featured copious displays of hunky, half-naked male performers rather than the usual scantily clad chorus girls. That Logan was Gay (or perhaps Bisexual) was an open secret within the industry, and although he never came out publicly, this may have been a way for him to express his sexuality while still remaining in the closet. It also may just have been a product of his show business savvy that anticipated the changes taking place in Broadway's core audience as it shifted from the proverbial "tired businessmen" to women and gay men purchasing the bulk of the tickets. In the Modern Era of Broadway, "beefcake" has more often provided musicals with the kind of sexual charge that "cheesecake" offered during the Silver and Golden ages.

Logan was also one of the rare Broadway directors who achieved nearly equal success in Hollywood, directing hit movies such as *Mister Roberts*, *Picnic*, *Bus*

Stop, Sayonara, and *South Pacific.* But as his career moved into the 1960s, he struggled through a series of unsuccessful shows and films, most notably the high-profile Broadway flops *Mr. President* (1962) and *Look to the Lilies* (1970) and the film adaptations of *Camelot* and *Paint Your Wagon.*

"Brush Up Your Shakespeare"—Cole Porter and *Kiss Me, Kate* (I, J, Q, W)

Cole Porter couldn't have helped but take notice of the huge success of *Annie Get Your Gun.* After all, he was close friends with Irving Berlin and had collaborated with Herbert Fields on seven hit musicals and with Dorothy on three of those. And he desperately needed a hit. The songs in Cole's recent string of girls-and-gags wartime shows had evidenced a sharp falling-off in his wit and inspiration.[35] Then, two outright flops nearly ended his career.[36] By 1948, Porter was in a deep depression, feeling washed up and uninspired. Then the phone rang. A not-very-famous producer wanted him to write the score for a musical based, in part, on a play by Shakespeare. This didn't seem like a very viable idea to Cole, but no one else was calling, and he was hungry for a project. So, reluctantly, he agreed. It was the best decision of his life.

That producer was a Gay man named Arnold Subber.[37] Born into a Jewish family in New York in 1918, he was the son of Broadway ticket brokers, and he grew up immersed in the theater. After studying at NYU, Subber broke into the business in 1938 as an assistant stage manager on the long-running revue *Hellzapoppin'.* He then became a protege of John Murray Anderson, assisting him on several productions, including the *Ziegfeld Follies of 1943*. It was while working on a 1940 production of *The Taming of the Shrew* (starring the famous acting duo Alfred Lunt and Lynn Fontaine) that Subber conceived the idea of a musical about a married couple feuding backstage while performing in Shakespeare's comedy.[38] Eight years later (in collaboration with co-producer and scenic and costume designer Lemuel Ayers) that idea evolved into *Kiss Me, Kate.* Eventually adopting the name **Saint-Subber**, he went on to produce twenty-five Broadway musicals and plays, including Cole Porter's *Out of This World* (1950), *The Grass Harp* (1952), *House of Flowers* (1954), **and** *1600 Pennsylvania Avenue* (1976), as well as the original productions of seven of Neil Simon's plays, including *Barefoot in the Park* (1963), *The Odd Couple* (1965), and *Plaza Suite* (1968).[39]

The musical that Subber envisioned was to be a knockabout comedy that was also sophisticated and sexy, with an undertone of deep feeling. At first, Porter was frightened. Could he adapt to this new style? And yet, the show seemed designed with him in mind. It would take place in a world Porter knew well: a backstage drama of putting on a Broadway show with high stakes for all concerned. And the stakes couldn't have been higher for Porter—if this show flopped, he might be finished in show business.

Amazingly, the score that Porter produced was "one of his all-time best."[40] Not only was it "studded with hits,"[41] according to the *New York Times*, but the Italian setting gave

"Mr. Porter an opportunity to poke beyond Tin Pan Alley into a romantic mood. Without losing his sense of humor, he has written a remarkable melodious score, with an occasional suggestion of Puccini, who was a good composer, too."[42] Virtually every song in the score became a hit, and as usual, the lyrics were loaded with hidden, and not-so-hidden, sexual and Queer undertones, "some of which would shock the editorial staff of the police gazette."[43] This is especially true of *Kiss Me, Kate*'s second act opener, "Too Darn Hot," which prominently included a ripped-from-the-headlines reference to the *Kinsey Report*. That landmark study of sexual behavior in the human male had been published just a few months prior to the show's opening, and it had sent shockwaves through mid-century America.[44] Kinsey armed the early gay rights movement with compelling research that would eventually transform American society's view of homosexuality.[45] While Porter could not have foreseen any of that, he clearly was well aware of the bombshells the report contained and he knew that referencing it would be provocative, at the very least.

Kiss Me, Kate, starring Alfred Drake and Patricia Morrison, opened on Broadway in December of 1948 and quickly became a smash hit. Director John C. Wilson kept the "complicated show sliding hitchlessly along" and "toned the performances with a smooth ease" that made "the rambunctious plot all the more effective." Hanya Holm's dances were "individual and effervescent" and had "the rare gift of making each dancer look as if he has a purpose to what he does."[46] At the 1949 Tony Awards, the show received the very first Tony ever awarded for "Best Musical," as well as "Best Book" for Bella and Sam Spewack, and "Best Score" for Cole Porter. With a run of 1,077 performances, *Kiss Me, Kate* became Porter's longest-running show and most-produced musical.

Newly reinvigorated, Cole Porter followed up *Kiss Me, Kate* with two more substantial hits: *Can-Can* in 1953 and *Silk Stockings* in 1955, both of which produced top-drawer hit songs that have become standards.[47] But following the deaths of his beloved mother in 1952 and his wife Linda in 1954, Porter's right leg was finally amputated in 1958. Although this provided him with some much-needed relief from the constant pain, it also drove him into virtual seclusion for the last six years of his life. And he never wrote another song.

Cole Porter died in 1964, aged seventy-three, but his work has certainly lived on. In the twenty-first century, Porter's two most enduring musicals, *Anything Goes* and *Kiss Me, Kate*, have kept his star shining bright with multiple revivals on Broadway, in the West End, and around the world. And dozens of his greatest songs continue to be performed and recorded by contemporary artists and rediscovered by new audiences. Stephen Sondheim declared Cole Porter to be:

> ... the easiest of the major lyricists to imitate because his style is so extreme in its distinction. The list songs are such a gallimaufry of pop culture references, the salacious songs are so heavy with double entendre, the love songs and out-of-love songs are so outrageously extravagant that they verge on, and often cross over into camp. The unique thing about Porter though, even at his most camp, is that the lyrics are genuinely felt. When he writes "A trip to the moon on gossamer wings" [in "Just One of Those Things"], you believe it because he believes it.[48]

And Sondheim adds that Porter was "too smart not to have been aware of what his writing style conveyed. He and Larry Hart are the two acknowledged gay lyricists in the American pantheon, but Hart's style conceals his homosexuality, Porter's parades it."[49]

Irving Berlin's *Annie Get Your Gun* and Cole Porter's *Kiss Me, Kate* would inspire a new wave of writers, directors, choreographers, and producers who, over the next several decades, would create a seemingly endless stream of finely crafted, new-and-improved Golden Age-style musical comedies.

New Kids on the Block: Styne, Loessor, Adler and Ross (♩, ♪)

Composer **Jule Styne** was born Julius Kerwin Stein in 1905 in the immigrant slums of London's East End, to which his Russian Jewish parents had emigrated from Ukraine. When he was only three years old, his parents took him to see British music hall star Harry Lauder, and little Julius created a sensation when he jumped onto the stage and began singing along in the middle of a song. After the show, Lauder recommended that this clearly talented kid be given piano lessons. Jule's parents couldn't afford to buy a piano but were able to arrange for him to take lessons and practice on a rented piano. In 1912, at eight, Jule moved with his family to Chicago, where he soon enrolled in the Chicago College of Music. By age ten, he was winning piano competitions and performing with the Chicago, St. Louis, and Detroit symphony orchestras. He joined the musician's union at sixteen and started playing with various dance bands and in the pit at the Haymarket Burlesque Theater in Chicago—an experience that would significantly inform the creation of his most acclaimed musical, *Gypsy*. Styne's songwriting career began in Hollywood, where during the late 1930s and '40s he wrote hundreds of songs for all kinds of films, dozens of which became huge chart-topping hits. However, like most composers, Styne considered Broadway to be the pinnacle of achievement for a songwriter, and in 1947 he jumped at the chance to compose the score for *High Button Shoes*, with lyrics by his main Hollywood collaborator, Sammy Cahn. Directed by George Abbott and choreographed by Jerome Robbins, this musical was a vehicle for comedy star Phil Silvers and became a substantial hit, running for two and a half years (727 performances).

Over the next several decades, Styne would team up with various lyricists, such as Leo Robin, Comden and Green, Bob Merrill, and Stephen Sondheim, on twenty-one Broadway musicals, including **Gentlemen Prefer Blondes**, **Peter Pan**, **Bells Are Ringing**, **Gypsy**, and **Funny Girl**. In the process, he created a series of show-stopping songs and career-defining roles for many of Broadway's greatest female stars—Carol Channing, Mary Martin, Judy Holliday, Ethel Merman, Leslie Uggams, and Barbara Streisand. He also became a significant Broadway producer. As a composer, Styne had a genius for melody, and over his nearly seventy-year career, he wrote 2,000 songs, of which an incredible 200 became substantial hits. When asked about the difference between writing for the movies and the stage, he often replied, "In Hollywood, you're just a songwriter, but in New York, you're a composer."

Composer and lyricist **Frank Loessor** was born in NYC in 1910. Although he never studied music formally, he grew up surrounded by music. His parents had come from the

German state of Prussia in the 1880s, both of them Jewish, but not religious in any way. Although they were a middle-class family, they had very highbrow and intellectual tastes. His father, Henry, was a classical piano teacher, and his older brother, Arthur, was a child piano prodigy who became a renowned concert pianist and music critic. But Frank was a rebel from the beginning—he refused to speak German (the family's language at home) and refused to study classical music. He was interested in pop music, which his father and brother abhorred. Frank taught himself to play the harmonica and the piano while in his early teens and styled himself after the Jewish songwriters who flourished on Tin Pan Alley by cultivating a brassy New York accent sprinkled with Yiddish flavor and expressions. He attended City College but had to drop out when his father died suddenly. Frank had always loved wordplay and now began writing lyrics, sketches, and radio scripts. By 1936, he was singing and playing piano in nightclubs and had contributed five songs to the Broadway revue *The Illustrators' Show*. The show was a quick flop but it led to Frank finding work in Hollywood, primarily under contract with Paramount Studios. During this period, he wrote songs for sixty films, at first working only as a lyricist in collaboration with many different composers (including Jule Styne). Eventually, Loessor began writing both the words and the music. After serving in World War II, he returned to Hollywood for a while until a young Broadway producing team, Cy Feuer and Ernest Martin, convinced him to come to New York to write the score for their 1948 musical *Where's Charley?*, based on the popular farce *Charley's Aunt*. Featuring a legendary performance by Broadway and Hollywood star Ray Bolger (best known as the Scarecrow in the 1939 film *The Wizard of Oz*), the show became a hit and proved that (like Styne) Loesser was much more than just a Hollywood pop tune writer. Although he wrote only four major musicals—**Where's Charley?**, **Guys and Dolls**, **The Most Happy Fella**, and **How to Succeed in Business Without Really Trying**—the brilliant craft, incredible variety, and theatrical genius of these shows thrust him forever into the top tier of Broadway creators. Like Rodgers and Hammerstein, Loessor established his own publishing company, branched out into producing, and actively nurtured and developed new talent. Two of his most promising mentees were the young songwriting team of **Adler and Ross**.

Richard Adler was born in NYC. Like Loessor, his father was a renowned pianist and music teacher whose students included Aaron Copeland, one of America's great classical composers. Adler graduated from the University of North Carolina and served in the Navy in World War II. After the war, he teamed up with **Jerry Ross**, who was born in the Bronx to Russian Jewish immigrant parents. As a child, Ross worked as a professional actor and singer in Yiddish Theater productions. He attended New York University but dropped out to pursue songwriting. Soon after Adler and Ross joined forces in 1950, they came to the attention of Frank Loesser and became his protégés. During this period, they wrote several pop hits, including "Rags to Riches," which became a No. 1 song for Tony Bennett. Their first Broadway score was for the 1953 revue *John Murray Anderson's Almanac*, and several songs they wrote for that show also became pop hits. Based on this success, Loessor decided the team was ready for a full book musical. The show was *The Pajama Game*, and it introduced Adler and Ross and Bob Fosse as significant new voices on Broadway. The director was George Abbott, who co-wrote the book with Richard

Bissell, the author of *Seven and a Half Cents*, the bestselling novel about a conflict between labor and management in a midwestern pajama factory that the musical was adapted from. The original production ran for 1,063 performances and received the Tony Award for "Best Musical," while its biggest hit song, "Hey, There," was recorded by Rosemary Clooney and became the No. 1 song of 1954.

Adler and Ross's second show, **Damn Yankees**, opened in 1955 and became an even more acclaimed hit. It also had book and direction by George Abbott and choreography by Bob Fosse. Based on the popular comic novel *The Year the Yankees Lost the Pennant*, by Douglass Wallop, the story revolves around a middle-aged baseball fan who sells his soul to the devil for the chance to be transformed into the hot young slugger who can lead his favorite perennially losing team to finally win the championship. Gwen Verdon played the devil's sexy henchwoman, Lola, a role that transformed her into a top Broadway star. **Damn Yankees** played 1,019 performances and won the Tony Award for "Best Musical."

Tragically, this was the last musical Adler and Ross would ever create. Jerry Ross died that same year at the age of twenty-nine from complications related to a lung disease. Richard Adler continued to write musicals and songs with other collaborators but was never able to create another hit show. Both *The Pajama Game* and *Damn Yankees* received faithful and effective film adaptations (although with a good deal of their original sexiness censored or toned down). Abbott directed both films, which include an unusually large percentage of their original Broadway casts recreating their stage performances, including the Tony Award-winning performances of *The Pajama Game*'s featured actress, Carol Haney, and *Damn Yankees*' stars Ray Walston, Russ Brown, and Gwen Verdon. And both movies recreated the Tony Award-winning choreography of Bob Fosse.

Broadway Dance #9: Jerry Robbins and Company (Q, I, J, W)

Director-choreographer **Jerome (Jerry) Robbins** was born Gershon Wilson Rabinowitz in NYC in 1918. His parents were Jews who had emigrated from Poland in 1904. Young Jerry showed an early aptitude for dance, music, and theatrics. He attended New York University intending to study either chemistry or journalism, but had to drop out during the Depression because his family could no longer afford the tuition. Unwilling to work in his family's corset factory, he was inspired by his sister, who was already a professional dancer, to try to find work in show business. In his early years, he danced and performed with ballet troupes, Yiddish theater productions, and in the chorus of several Broadway musicals. Then, he was invited to join what became American Ballet Theater, where he danced roles in works choreographed by Agnes DeMille and the company's founder, George Balanchine. Soon Robbins became eager to choreograph his own ballet and came up with the idea for *Fancy Free*. The success of this short work led quickly to it being expanded into the hit musical *On The Town*, both with music by Leonard Bernstein. Robbins would go on to choreograph and/or direct sixteen Broadway musicals, including **High Button Shoes, Call Me Madam, The King and**

I, *Peter Pan*, *West Side Story*, *Gypsy*, and *Fiddler on the Roof*, for which he received five Tony Awards. After *Fiddler*, Robbins stopped working on Broadway and instead devoted all of his time to New York City Ballet, where he had been appointed the Associate Artistic Director. For NYCB and other dance companies, he created sixty ballets, many of which are still regularly performed worldwide.

Robbins' controversial interactions and relationships with his colleagues are still points of contention. Like many young, idealistic, Jewish theater artists drawn to various peace and social justice movements and liberal causes in the 1930s and '40s, Robbins had briefly joined the Communist Party, then quickly became disillusioned with it and moved on. Then, in 1953, at the height of the McCarthy Era and its Communist witch hunts, Robbins stunned the theatrical community when he agreed to appear before the House Un-American Activities Committee, during which he admitted to having been a member of the Communist Party and named eight friends and colleagues who had also been members (seven of whom had previously been named by others). What has only been fully revealed in recent years, and what no one knew at the time, is that the HUAC was blackmailing Robbins by threatening that if he did not testify and name names, they would publicly reveal his homosexuality, which, of course, would have ruined his life and career. But the theater world only saw him as a traitor. As author Misha Berson relates:

> The people Robbins named, and many of his other colleagues, were horrified by his caving to the HUAC. Some shunned or avoided him for the rest of his life. Robbins also faced the ignominy of being identified, in virtually every historical account of the McCarthy Era blacklists, as one who named names.[50]

In addition, Robbins acquired a notorious reputation for being a cruel and unrelenting perfectionist and an uncompromising taskmaster and for taking that out on the dancers who worked for him. As a young dancer, future Tony Award-winning Broadway star Helen Gallagher[51] performed in two musicals choreographed by Robbins: *Billion Dollar Baby* (1945) and *High Button Shoes* (1947). Forty years later, I had the pleasure of directing her in an off-Broadway musical. During a conversation over lunch one day, Helen recalled an event that has become legendary in theatrical lore—although exactly when and on which show it happened has often been in dispute. Helen, however, distinctly remembered being seated onstage with her castmates in the large dancing and singing chorus of *High Button Shoes*, receiving notes from Robbins following that evening's dress rehearsal, and, in his "ruthlessly mean" signature style, he had begun viciously skewering each cast member, one by one. Gallagher recalled that he had an uncanny ability to expertly hone in on each performer's vulnerabilities and deepest insecurities. Meanwhile, he was entirely unaware that he was slowly inching backward toward the lip of the stage and the orchestra pit looming just inches behind him. Astoundingly, the entire cast silently watched as Robbins took that one last step backward and plummeted into the pit. Not one of the dozens of cast members warned Robbins that he was about to fall, and as Gallagher described it, many of them took some grim glee in what had happened. "We didn't want him to die or be seriously injured," she said, "but we were happy to see him get hurt." However, Helen immediately countered that Robbins was a genius and that she would have worked on any show he asked her to do.[52] This exactly mirrors Stephen Sondheim's statement that

> . . . as difficult as it was to work with Robbins—and he could be really mean and an awful man—I would work with him any time. It's worth it. The end product is worth it. He does get—not only the best out of you—some of his invention rubs off on you. You get more inventive when you work with Jerry Robbins.[53]

Sondheim also frequently described Jerry Robbins as "the only genius" he had ever worked with.

Bob Fosse was born in Chicago in 1927. His mother had emigrated from Ireland, and his father was Norwegian American. He started working professionally while still in his early teens, performing a tap-dancing act in nightclubs and burlesque theaters, whose main attractions by this time were the striptease acts. After serving in World War II, he moved to New York with the intention of becoming "the new Fred Astaire." He got jobs dancing in two Broadway musicals, and on several early TV variety shows. He then got a contract with MGM in Hollywood, where he played supporting dance roles in several films, most notably as one of the "three suitors" in the 1953 film version of *Kiss Me, Kate*—a role that would alter the course of his life and career. The film's choreographer was Hermes Pan, but Fosse was granted permission to choreograph his own short duet with dancer Carol Haney. It was only a one-minute segment of a lengthy dance sequence, but it became a standout moment in the film and it put Fosse on the map as a promising young choreographer with his own distinct style. The following year, he was hired to choreograph *The Pajama Game*. That show's standout dance number, "Steam Heat," introduced Fosse to Broadway and established much of what would come to be known as the "Fosse style." He would go on to choreograph twelve Broadway musicals (six of which he also directed), including *Damn Yankees*, *Bells Are Ringing*, *Redhead*, *How to Succeed in Business Without Really Trying*, *Little Me*, *Sweet Charity*, *Pippin*, *Chicago*, and *Dancin'*, for which he received nine Tony Awards. In 1973, Fosse became the only person ever to win a Tony Award (for directing the Broadway musical *Pippin*), an Emmy Award (for directing the television special *Liza With a Z*), and an Academy Award (for directing the film *Cabaret*) all in the same year.

Gwen Verdon was born in 1925 in Culver City, CA. Her parents, who had emigrated from Britain, were "showpeople." Her father was an electrician at MGM Studios, and her mother had danced in Vaudeville with the Denishawn dance troupe and was a dance teacher. As a toddler, Verdon had rickets (softening of the bones) which left her legs so badly misshapen that she was called "Gimpy" by other children and spent her early years wearing orthopedic boots and rigid leg braces. Her mother put the three-year-old in dance classes to strengthen her legs. By the time she was eleven, she was already dancing onstage and in films, and at fifteen, she was cast in a 1940 Los Angeles revival of *Show Boat*. Early on, Verdon got a job as the assistant to choreographer Jack Cole. During her five-year employment with Cole, she played small "specialty dancer" roles in movie musicals that Cole choreographed, and coached and trained major movie stars to dance his choreography, including Betty Grable and Marilyn Monroe.

After moving to New York, Verdon danced in the choruses of several Broadway shows. Her breakthrough role came when choreographer Michael Kidd cast her as the second female lead in Cole Porter's *Can-Can* (1953). During the musical's out-of-town tryout, Gwen's performance proved to be such a hit that the show's leading lady, French star Lilo, became furious and insisted that Verdon's part be cut down to just three numbers. Even so, Verdon became a sensation, stopping the show cold on the opening night in New York and winning a Tony Award for "Best Featured Actress in a Musical." With *Damn Yankees* she began a forty-year professional and personal relationship with Bob Fosse, whom she would marry in 1960. During her thirty-year career on Broadway, Verdon starred in six Broadway musicals, several of which were written especially for her, including *Sweet Charity* and *Chicago*. She dominated the Tony Awards during the 1950s with wins in 1954, 1956, 1958, and 1959.

Choreographer **Michael Kidd** was born Michael Greenwald in Brooklyn, NY, in 1915. His parents were both Russian Jewish immigrants. While still in High School, he attended a modern dance performance and became immediately infatuated. Kidd attended the City College of New York, intending to be a chemical engineer, but left in 1937 when he received a scholarship to the School of American Ballet. Soon, he became a member of the dance company called Ballet Caravan and toured the country dancing many roles, including the lead in *Billy the Kid*. From 1942 to 1947, Kidd was a soloist with what is now the American Ballet Theater. While there, he was given the opportunity to create his own ballet, titled *On Stage!* His first Broadway show as choreographer was *Finian's Rainbow*, which led to him working on seventeen more Broadway musicals. He received Tony Awards for five of those shows, including *Finian's Rainbow* (1947), *Guys and Dolls* (1951), *Can-Can* (1954), *Li'l Abner* (1957), and *Destry Rides Again* (1960). Kidd also found significant success in Hollywood as choreographer of the classic MGM movie musicals *Seven Brides for Seven Brothers* and *The Band Wagon*. His primary focus for any dance number was the story and the characters. Kidd said, "I always write a scenario first, even if it is a scenario for an emotion."

Jerome Robbins frequently worked with dance specialists and associate choreographers on his shows, such as Michiko and Yuriko on *The King and I*, but perhaps the most significant was his collaboration with dancer/choreographer **Peter Gennaro** on *West Side Story*. Born in Louisiana in 1919, as a child, Gennaro's Sicilian-born mother often entered him in local Charleston contests, which he usually won. As a teenager, he studied tap, danced in nightclubs in New Orleans, and participated in that city's Jazz Funeral second lines. During World War II, Gennaro served as part of an entertainment unit and afterward moved to NYC to study at the Katherine Dunham School on the GI Bill. There, he studied ballet, modern dance, and dance styles of the African diaspora, including Afro-Cuban and Afro-Caribbean.[54] By the early 1950s, Gennaro was dancing in a series of four Broadway musicals, working for Michael Kidd (*Arms and the Girl* and *Guys and Dolls*), Bob Fosse, and Jerome Robbins (*The Pajama Game* and *Bells Are Ringing*). Meanwhile, he made his own choreographic debut with the short-lived 1955 musical **Seventh Heaven**. Robins initially asked Gennaro to be his assistant on *West Side Story*, but Gennaro would only agree if he could be co-choreographer. Drawing on the significant training in Latin dance he had acquired at the Dunham School, Gennaro choreographed virtually all of the dancing of the Shark characters in *West Side Story*, including their sections of the "Mambo" and the show-stopping "America." He also appears to have played a significant role in the overall staging of the show, but only in recent decades, following Robbins' death, has Gennaro's unique contribution to *West Side Story* has begun to be fully acknowledged. Between 1955 and 1989, Peter Gennaro choreographed thirteen Broadway musicals, including **Fiorello!**, **The Unsinkable Molly Brown**, and **Annie**. Simultaneously, he established a major career as a choreographer and star dancer on television.

Designing Women—Jean Rosenthal, Peggy Clark, and Tharon Musser Invent Broadway Lighting Design (I, J, Q, W)

As we might expect, from the earliest days of the Broadway musical, many of the most prominent and acclaimed Broadway costume designers have been women, such as Lucinda Ballard, Irene Sharaff, Patricia Zipprodt, Florence Klotz, Theoni Aldredge, Willa Kim, Katherine Zuber, Anne Hould-Ward, and the unusual female design collective known as Motley, to name only a few. A handful of women have also distinguished themselves as Broadway scenic designers, especially in recent decades. However, what we might not expect is that women dominated the field of Broadway lighting design for most of the twentieth century.

Thomas Edison's invention of the practical incandescent lamp in 1879 ushered in the modern era of stage lighting—which, from the very beginning, was linked to musical theater. The world's first electric theatrical lighting system was installed in London's Savoy Theatre, the home base of Gilbert and Sullivan, and it was first used at a performance of their comic operetta *Patience* in December of 1888. The next day, *The Times* reported:

> The success of this new mode of illumination was complete, and its importance for the development of scenic art can scarcely be overrated. The light was perfectly steady throughout the performance, and the effect was pictorially superior to gas, the colours [sic] of the dresses—an important element in the 'aesthetic' opera—appearing as true and distinct as by daylight.[55]

Almost exactly one year later, Gilbert and Sullivan's *Iolanthe* opened Boston's new Bijou Theatre, where Edison had personally supervised the installation of America's first electric stage lighting, and the reviews were similarly enthusiastic: "Never have we seen a steadier and softer light in a theatre than that given by Edison's incandescent burners," the *Boston Globe* reported.[56] So, when theaters began springing up in Times Square at the turn of the century, in addition to their brilliantly lit exteriors, the stages of the "Great White Way" were also illuminated by electric lights. Those lights, however, were mounted in much the same positions as earlier gaslights had been, and while that certainly improved the overall visibility of the actors and scenery, it did not allow much opportunity for artistic variation or creative design.

This is why, during the first four decades of the twentieth century, the task of lighting a Broadway play or musical was the responsibility of the theater's staff electrician, who would endeavor, as best he could (and yes, it was always a man), to fulfill the vision of the production's scenic designer, director, and/or producer. However, even within these limitations, several theater artists, including director Hassard Short, set designer Jo Meilziner, and early lighting expert Abe Feder, were able to make significant advances in the field of stage lighting design. But it was a woman who would transform a technical craft into an art form, elevate lighting design to the status of a profession, and pave the way for other women to thrive in a highly technical field that had been dominated by men.

Jean Rosenthal was born in 1912 in New York City, the daughter of Romanian Jewish immigrants. Both her parents were physicians who regularly attended the theater and exposed young Jean to a wide range of art and culture.[57] After briefly studying acting and dance at the Neighborhood Playhouse in the late 1920s, Jean began working as a technical assistant to modern dance pioneer Martha Graham, who was a member of the Playhouse's dance faculty. This began

Rosenthal's lifelong association with Graham and her dance company.[58] After three years of studying theater history and design at Yale, she returned to New York and got a job as a technical assistant with the WPA Federal Theatre Project (where she worked with Abe Feder), and one of her first Broadway credits was as Production Manager of the FTP's fabled production of Marc Blitzstein's *The Cradle Will Rock*. The first Broadway show for which Rosenthal received credit as Lighting Designer was the operetta *Rosalinda* in 1942. Between then and her death in 1969, Jean Rosenthal designed the lighting of eighty-five Broadway plays and musicals, most notably **West Side Story**, **The Sound of Music**, **A Funny Thing Happened on the Way to the Forum**, **Hello, Dolly!**, **Fiddler on the Roof**, and **Cabaret**. And with each production, she continued to advance the technology and artistic potential of stage lighting design by adding new elements and innovations to the lighting designer's toolbox and vocabulary, such as saturated color washes of backlight and side light.

Another lighting design pioneer was **Peggy Clark**, who was born in 1915 in Baltimore.[59] Like Rosenthal, Clark's parents were involved in the medical sciences and shared a deep passion for theater, which they instilled in their daughter. Clark went to Smith College to study acting but soon switched to set and costume design. She then went to Yale, where she developed an interest in stage lighting. Her first professional jobs involved working as an assistant to several scenic designers and eventually taking over the lighting of their shows because, as she later recalled, "Very few scene designers really knew about lighting or really cared awfully much about it . . . and I did!"[60] Clark worked especially closely with Oliver Smith, one of the greatest set designers of the Golden Age.[61] Her first Broadway credits as Lighting Designer were for Duke Ellington's 1946 musical **Beggar's Holiday**, followed just ten weeks later by Lerner and Loewe's **Brigadoon**. Over the next three decades, she designed more than sixty Broadway productions, including **High Button Shoes**, **Gentlemen Prefer Blondes**, **Paint Your Wagon**, **Wonderful Town**, **Kismet**, **Peter Pan**, **Bells Are Ringing**, **Flower Drum Song**, **Bye Bye Birdie**, and **The Unsinkable Molly Brown**.

Midway through her career, Jean Rosenthal became the mentor of another dynamic woman who would further define the profession. **Tharon Musser** was born in Virginia in 1925, and often recalled, ironically, that her family was so poor they couldn't afford electricity, so she grew up mostly with candles and gaslights.[62] Unlike Rosenthal and Clark, Musser had no exposure to the arts as a child but became seriously interested in working in the theater when she attended Berea College in Kentucky. She then went on to Yale, where her focus turned to lighting design. After working as Rosenthal's assistant, Musser moved on to her own career. Between 1956 and 2006, she designed the lighting for 122 Broadway productions, including **Mame**, **Applause**, **Follies**, **A Little Night Music**, **The Wiz**, **A Chorus Line**, **Pacific Overtures**, **Dreamgirls**, **The Secret Garden**, and **42nd Street**. Musser also brought groundbreaking technological and artistic contributions to the field. Most significantly, in 1975, for her landmark design of *A Chorus Line*, she became the first designer to use a computerized electronic lighting control board on Broadway. By 1981, every Broadway show was using one. The complexity and consistency of today's elaborate and spectacular Broadway lighting designs would be impossible to achieve without them.

Jean Rosenthal died in 1969, Peggy Clark in 1989, and Tharon Musser in 2009, but their legacy certainly lives on. They opened the door to a veritable parade of outstanding female lighting designers, including Musser's life partner, **Marilyn Rennagel**, as well as **Jennifer Tipton**, **Marcia Madeira**, **Pat Collins**, **Peggy Eisenhour**, **Beverly Emmons**, and **Natasha Katz**, to name only a few.

"Colorful" — Black Broadway in the Golden Age (B)

Black performers and Black stories maintained a reduced yet still significant presence on Broadway during the Golden Age, especially during the 1960s, when the achievements of the Civil Rights Movement began to be felt throughout American culture. But almost all of these "Black musicals" were written, directed, and choreographed by white artists.

The major exceptions to this were two of the earliest musicals of this period, both of which involved writers who had risen to prominence during the 1920s Harlem Renaissance. The 1947 musical *Street Scene* had a book by Elmer Rice (adapted from his 1929 play), music by Kurt Weill, and beautifully crafted lyrics by the Black writer and poet **Langston Hughes**. Featuring a multi-racial cast, this near-operatic work ran for only 148 performances. The previous season's musical, *St. Louis Woman*, had a book by Black writers **Arna Bontemps** and **Countee Cullen.** Based on Bontemps' 1931 novel, the musical was set in a low-life world of gamblers, loose women, jockeys, and horse racing. The show was plagued with problems from the start. First the head of the NAACP[63] accused the show of "offering roles that detract from the dignity of our race," which caused the show's intended star, Lena Horne, to drop out. Then co-author Cullen died two days before rehearsals were to begin. During the rehearsals the show's original director and choreographer were both fired and director Rouben Mamoulian (fresh from his triumphs with *Oklahoma!* and *Carousel*) and choreographer Charles Walters were brought in as late replacements during the show's pre-Broadway tour. Composer Harold Arlen and lyricist Johnny Mercer's score was largely dismissed at the time, but it contained at least three songs that have become enduring standards.[64] Overall, the show was considered by critics to be "a hybrid affair,"[65] stuck somewhere between an old-school *musical comedy* and a modern *musical play*, and it ran for only 113 performances. However, in addition to providing leading roles for the Nicholas Brothers and Rex Ingram, who were already established Black stars, *St. Louis Woman* also introduced two dynamic Black women who would become Tony Award-winning stars.

Juanita Hall (1901–68) made her Broadway debut as a replacement in the chorus of the original production of *Show Boat* and also sang in the ensembles of the long-running play-with-music *Green Pastures* (1930) and the 1944 "Salute to American Folk and Popular Music" *Sing Out, Sweet Land*. After moving up to a key supporting role in *St. Louis Woman*, Hall's breakthrough performance came three years later when she created Bloody Mary, a Tonkinese character, in Rodgers and Hammerstein's *South Pacific*, for which she received the Tony for "Best Featured Actress in a Musical," making her the first Black performer to win a Tony Award. In addition to her appearances in eight Broadway plays, Juanita Hall created leading roles in two additional Broadway musicals: 1954's *House of Flowers* and Rodgers and Hammerstein's *Flower Drum Song*, in which she played the Chinese character Madam Liang, and Hall recreated her performances in the film versions of both *South Pacific* and *Flower Drum Song*.[66]

St. Louis Woman also introduced the charismatic nightclub singer **Pearl Bailey** to Broadway, who stopped the show cold with both of her numbers and became the most celebrated aspect of the show. She returned to Broadway in 1950 with featured roles (and similar impact!) in two short-lived shows: the musical comedy ***Arms and the Girl*** and the revue ***Bless You All***. By 1954, it was time for Bailey to star in a show of her own—*House of Flowers*—where she was supported by an (almost) entirely Black cast that featured an astonishing group of emerging young dance-theater artists, including **Alvin Ailey**, **Carmen de Lavallade**, **Geoffrey Holder**, **Louis Johnson**, **Donald McKayle**, **Mary Louise**, and **Arthur Mitchell**. It was producer Saint-Subber's idea to create a musical based on Truman Capote's novella, which is set on an island in the West Indies and involves the rivalry between the Madams of two competing bordellos. The musical's book, unwisely written by Capote himself, was loaded with color and atmosphere but contained only the tiniest whisp of a plot. The calypso-infused score, however, with music by Harold Arlen and lyrics by Capote and Arlen, introduced several of the most radiant theater songs ever created. This very bawdy and racy show also had a rocky road to Broadway, with both its original director, Peter Brook, and choreographer, George Balanchine, being replaced by Herbert Ross along the way. Once again, Pearl Bailey walked off with the show, no doubt because, as one critic observed, "Nobody in the theater has her deadly aim or deceptive relaxation. To that, add the haunting voice and the good looks of the dame, and you have a star."[67] Juanita Hall scored strongly as the rival Madam, and the show also marked the Broadway debut of a "plaintive and extraordinarily appealing ingenue" named **Diahann Carroll** (1935-2019), who introduced several of the score's "most evocative songs," including "A Sleepin' Bee" and "I Never Has Seen Snow," which "this engaging actress" delivered "with serious eyes and the enthusiasm of a newly hatched bird." Although *House of Flowers* received largely favorable reviews, even its greatest admirers noted that Capote's story evaporated in the second act, and the show only managed to run for 165 performances.

Meanwhile, four other charismatic Black nightclub performers were working their way to Broadway. **Eartha Kitt** (1927–2008) first appeared on Broadway in 1945 as a member of Katherine Dunham's dance company in the short-lived "all-Negro variety show" *Blue Holiday*. While touring the world with Dunham's troupe, Kitt began singing in cabarets in Paris, Istanbul, London, and, eventually, New York, which brought her to the attention of producer Leonard Sillman, who featured her in his **New Faces of 1952**. Her "sultry song style" and show-stopping performances in that hit revue quickly established her as "one of the exciting new stars of the year."[68] Over the next fifty years, Kitt would return to Broadway in six additional musicals and plays, including the all-Black revisal of *Kismet*, retitled ***Timbuktu!*** (1978), ***The Wild Party*** (2000), and the 2003 revival of ***Nine***.

The first Black man to win a Tony Award was **Harry Belafonte** (1927–2023), who began making actual calypso music wildly popular in the early 1950s through his hit records and appearances in New York nightspots and on television. Then in 1953, he starred in the Broadway musical revue ***John Murray Anderson's Almanac***, where his performance was hailed as the show's "high point in theatrical artistry"[69] and earned him the Tony for "Best Featured Actor in a Musical," adding another dimension to his long career as a chart-topping recording artist, film star, and civil rights leader. The following year, the multi-talented **Sammy Davis Jr.** (1925–90) made his Broadway debut. Davis had begun performing at the age of three with his father, Sam Sr., in a vaudeville troupe run by entertainer Will Mastin. Eventually, after vaudeville died, a scaled-down version of the act became a major nightclub attraction. Now billed as "The Will Mastin Trio, starring Sammy Davis Jr.," it served as a dynamic showcase for his many talents.[70] In 1956, Davis starred in ***Mr. Wonderful***, a loosely biographical Broadway musical produced and conceived by Jule Styne and written especially for Davis, with a book by Joseph Stein and Will Glickman, and a score by Jerry Bock, Larry Holofcener, and George David Weiss. The show's negligible plot focused on an aspiring nightclub performer, much like Sammy himself, and the second act culminated in a replication of his acclaimed nightclub act. Despite receiving universally disdainful reviews, two hit songs that emerged from the score,[71] along with Davis's star power, virtuosity, and unflagging promotion of the show, kept *Mr. Wonderful* running for a full year (383 performances).[72]

Another headlining nightclub entertainer of the postwar era was MGM movie star **Lena Horne**.[73] She first appeared on Broadway in 1934 in the short-lived musical *Dance With Your Gods*,[74] and aside from an equally brief run in *Blackbirds of 1939*, Horne did not return to Broadway until 1957 when, following a triumphant engagement in the Empire Room at the Waldorf Astoria, she became the over-the-title star of the musical ***Jamaica***. Set on "Pigeon Island, a mythical island off Jamaica," the show had originally been conceived by its lyricist and co-bookwriter,[75] Yip Harburg, as a pointed social/political satire of colonialism, consumerism, and the capitalist rat race of modern life—and as a star vehicle for Harry Belafonte, who had grown up in Jamaica. But when Belafonte withdrew, the show was revamped for Lena Horne and another MGM star, the Mexican American actor **Riccardo Montalbán**. In the process, producer David Merrick insisted that the satirical commentary had to be toned down or eliminated, and he brought in bookwriter Joseph Stein to accomplish that task.[76] This caused Harburg to become so distraught that he refused to attend the show's opening. However, as a showcase for "a hurricane named Lena," the final version of the show was an unqualified success. Her performance was hailed as "hypnotic . . . incandescent . . . alluring, sinuous, and magnetic,"[77] and the large (mostly) Black cast that supported her included **Ossie Davis**, **Josephine Premice**, and **Adelaide Hall**, who had starred in both *Shuffle Along* and *Runnin' Wild* back in the 1920s. Future dance legend Alvin Ailey also appeared in this show as choreographer Jack Cole's leading dancer. As *Jamaica*'s delightful original cast album demonstrates, Yip Harburg and Harold Arlen provided the show with another captivating, swinging, calypso-infused score that still managed to slip in some social significance with songs such as the comic anti-nuclear warning, "Leave the Atom Alone." With a run of 555 performances, *Jamaica* was a solid financial success. Horne, Montalbán, Davis, and Premise all received Tony nominations, and the show itself was nominated for "Best Musical," but in a season that included both *The Music Man* and *West Side Story* (see page 218), all of them went home empty-handed.

In 1962, Diahann Carroll triumphantly returned to Broadway with her Tony Award-winning performance in **No Strings**, Richards Rodgers' first Broadway musical following the death of Hammerstein, and the only Broadway show for which Rodgers wrote both music and lyrics. With stylish, inventive staging by director-choreographer Joe Layton, the show was set in contemporary Paris and focused on a sophisticated, adult romance between a glamorous Black fashion model (Carroll) and a white expat writer, played by Richard Kiley. While Rodgers went to great lengths in pre-opening interviews to make it clear that the show was not about "race relations" and that Carroll's role "could be played by a white girl without a line being changed," the mere act of placing an interracial couple at the center of a big mainstream "Richard Rodgers" Broadway musical during the Civil Rights era was in itself a political statement, and the decision to set the story in Paris because, as Rodgers pointed out, "such a situation is completely acceptable there," only underlined the fact that interracial relationships and marriages were not acceptable, and still illegal, in much of the U.S. The show became a major box office hit, running for 580 performances and winning Tony Awards for Carroll ("Best Actress in a Musical"), Layton (Best Choreography), and Rodgers (Best Score).[78]

Two years later, Sammy Davis Jr. returned to Broadway in a much more ambitious musical created especially for him—**Golden Boy**. Based on Clifford Odets' acclaimed 1937 play of the same name about a young Italian American violinist who gets pulled into the world of championship boxing, its original Depression era immigrant/class-struggle-themed story was updated and reset in the present day, with the story reworked to reflect the racial equity and civil rights issues of the time, including an interracial love story that prompted frequent death threats and bomb scares throughout the musical's run. This show had encountered numerous difficulties and setbacks during its long development process and pre-Broadway tour. Odets, who wrote the first drafts of the musical's book himself, died of cancer just before the show premiered in Philadelphia, and playwright William Gibson, whom Odets had mentored, was brought in to complete the book. The original director, Peter Coe (*Oliver!*), clashed with both Davis and Gibson and was replaced by Arthur Penn. The impressive, wide-ranging score by Charles Strouse and Lee Adams is arguably their best work, even if some of their songs did not ultimately fit into the show's constantly changing storyline. Davis was paid $20,000 a week, which at that time made him the highest-paid performer in Broadway history,[79] and his high octane, non-stop performance dominated the show. As one critic noted, he was "given a chance to do everything but play the tuba—he dances, sings, and acts brilliantly,"[80] even if by opening night, his voice was showing signs of exhaustion. He appeared in eleven of *Golden Boy*'s seventeen musical numbers, which (at Davis's urging) did not shy away from including biting, satirical, and even confrontational social commentary regarding America's systemic racism and injustice. The show climaxed in an exciting and visceral prizefight sequence choreographed by **Donald McKayle**. Overall, *Golden Boy* received mixed-to-positive reviews and garnered four Tony Award nominations, including "Best Actor in a Musical," "Best Choreography," and "Best Musical," but lost all of them to *Fiddler on the Roof*. *Golden Boy* made history by becoming the first musical to run for more than 500 performances and not pay back its investment,[81] which reflected the changing economics of Broadway in the Golden Age's final decade.[82] In 1968, Davis starred in a West End production of *Golden Boy* at the London Palladium, where the musical was much more critically acclaimed, and its originally scheduled engagement had to be extended for an additional six weeks.

The ambitious concept musical **Hallelujah, Baby!** (1967) was created by an extremely high-profile and high-powered team of leading white Broadway theatermakers: Arthur Laurents (book), Betty Comden and Adolf Green (lyrics), and Jule Styne (music). Their intention was to dramatize the epic struggle of Black people in America from the turn of the twentieth century up to the current day through the story of a young Black woman striving for a career in show business, and who remains the same age throughout the sixty-year time-frame. The central role was conceived and written for Lena Horne, but when she turned it down, it was reworked for **Leslie Uggams**, who had become nationally famous as a singer on the popular early 1960s TV show *Sing Along With Mitch*. Despite the clearly positive and progressive intentions of the show's authors, *Hallelujah, Baby!* came off as being woefully tone-deaf and outdated, especially in the wake of the protests and civil unrest that swept America following the Watts rebellion of 1965.[83] The 1967–8 Broadway season was an extremely weak one for musicals, so, even though it had closed three months prior to the Tony Awards,[84] *Hallelujah, Baby!* won "Best Musical" and "Best Score,"[85] while Leslie Uggams won "Best Actress in a Musical."

That same year, David Merrick took the bold step of closing down his smash hit production **Hello, Dolly!** three years into its run, and reopening it a month later with a new, all-Black cast headed by Pearl Bailey, whose performance was declared "a Broadway triumph for the history books."[86] As future Broadway director Sheldon Epps remembered it:

> Her Dolly was Thornton Wilder's, Jerry Herman's, Gower Champion's, and somehow completely Pearl's all at once. She brought to the role the same humor,

charm, and vivacity of previous Dollys but added her own indescribable finesse and quite profound soulfulness to the role in a way that made her Dolly simply soar off the stage.[87]

The supporting cast included jazz great **Cab Calloway** as Horace Vandergelder, **Clifton Davis**, **Ernestine Jackson**, and **Morgan Freeman** (!) as Rudolph, the headwaiter. At a time in history when "integration" was one of the principal goals of Civil Rights leaders, there some criticism, especially prior to the opening, of this all-Black casting of the show, which, as *New York Times* critic Clive Barnes wrote, "sounded too much like 'Blackbirds of 1968', and too patronizing for words." But Barnes, and virtually everyone else, were "overwhelmed" by the actual impact of that cast in that show and conceded that "Maybe Black Power is what some other musicals need."[88] Bailey and company played *Dolly* on Broadway for twenty-five months and then took the show on a wildly popular national tour.[89]

1958: *West Side Story* vs *The Music Man* (♩, ♪, ♫)

The decade of the 1950s was crowned by four legendary musicals that went head-to-head for the "Best Musical" prize at the Tony Awards. During the 1957–8 season, it was *West Side Story* vs *The Music Man*, and the 1959–60 season brought *Gypsy* vs *The Sound of Music*. There are Broadway fans today who are still upset about which of those shows won and which of them, in their view, was robbed of the award. As a group, these four shows exemplify the Golden Age Broadway musical at its zenith.

The story behind **West Side Story** begins in 1949 when composer Leonard Bernstein, choreographer Jerome Robbins, and bookwriter Arthur Laurents first began talking about creating an updated musical version of Shakespeare's *Romeo and Juliet*. Since both Robbins and Bernstein were Russian American Jews, their first idea was to set their story on the Lower East Side during the Easter/Passover season and use contemporary conflicts between Catholics and Jews to explain the violent hatred between the Capulets and Montagues, and their working title for that version was "East Side Story."[90]

However, after much discussion, that idea was shelved because it sounded too much like a musical version of the 1922 hit play *Abie's Irish Rose*, a sentimental comedy about a secret marriage between a Jewish boy and an Irish Catholic girl. Though enormously popular, it was despised by most critics, and its title had become something of a punchline over the years. A lyric in Rodgers and Hart's first major hit song, "Manhattan," expressed the feelings of many sophisticated theater-makers, who were disgruntled that such a schmaltzy show had become the longest-running play in history: "Our future babies / we'll take to Abie's Irish Rose / I hope they'll live to see it close . . ." In 1955, Bernstein and Robbins picked up the idea again when they were both working in Los Angeles on separate projects and met at the Beverly Hills Hotel. Deborah Jowitt describes this meeting in her book *Jerome Robbins, His Life, His Theater, His Dance*:

> Dangling their legs in the pool, they gradually drifted to the subject of "East Side Story" and the current newspaper headlines about violence between juvenile gangs

of Chicanos and Anglos. Eureka! Robbins readily agreed that ethnicity rather than religion should be the crux of the conflict, and that gangs rather than families, the antagonists.[91]

In the final result, the musical's dramatic plotline would be ripped from the headlines of New York's daily newspapers. In 1956, the *New York Times* reported that "five youths displaying their prowess before a gang of fifteen girls critically wounded a boy on the west side last night." Another article a year later stated that "four youths were arrested last night in the aftermath of a teenage gang fight in which one youngster was fatally stabbed." This, coupled with national news about juvenile delinquency and growing racial conflict in America, convinced the authors that the most effective central conflict for their show would be a turf war on the Upper West Side of NYC between the Sharks, a Puerto Rican gang, and the Jets, a motley mix of white, Polish, Italian, and Irish immigrant stock. As the Sharks ironically point out in the show, the Jets, who are the children and grandchildren of actual foreign immigrants, are the ones who want the Puerto Ricans to go back "where they came from" and, of course, where the Puerto Ricans came from was America. It was the growing accessibility and affordability of air travel that had led to what is now known as "the Great Migration," a massive wave of Puerto Ricans that poured into New York City during the 1950s, and Puerto Ricans were the very first Latinx group to move to New York City in large numbers.

The original plan was for Bernstein to write both the music and the lyrics, but it soon became clear that his classical conducting schedule would make that impossible to accomplish, so young Stephen Sondheim was brought on board to take over the lyric writing. This now completed a very Queer creative team. All four of the principal creators of *West Side Story* were both Jewish and Gay, or Bisexual. Other Queer creative team members included set designer Oliver Smith, lighting designer Jean Rosenthal, and costume designer Irene Sharaff.

For a brief while, the show seemed like it would be saddled with the unfortunate title of "Gangway." But finally, the team landed on a slight variation of their original title and named it *West Side Story*. In her book *Something's Coming, Something Good, West Side Story, and the American Imagination*, author Misha Berson relates:

> The topicality of the theme, and the prospect of weaving Latin musical motifs into his score, excited Bernstein. "I hear rhythms and pulses, and—most of all—I can sort of feel the form," he wrote in his journal. He adored Latin music, which he sought out on numerous visits to Latin America and South America. (His actress wife, Felicia Montealegre Bernstein, hailed from Chile.)

Berson goes on to state that in the, end, Bernstein's score for *West Side Story*

> ... is distinguished by its dance-driven urgency and its broad sonic palette of musical modes, from Wagnerian leitmotifs to Latin dance music to big band blues and American avant-garde music. It constantly shifts rhythms and keys and

confounds the then-circumscribed categories of "show music" and "long hair" music with agility.[92]

However, even with all this incredible musical variety, the score, and in fact, the entire show, has amazing unity. It all works and feels as if it came from one voice, one theatrical vision. A large part of this unity can be attributed to Bernstein's use of a much-talked-about musical device, as described on my podcast by Albert Evans:

> Bernstein's score for *West Side Story* is shot through with a jarring sound that was previously rare in theater music. It's a musical interval called the tritone. An interval is the distance between two notes. In this case, the two notes are three whole tones apart. Those notes can be played separately, as part of a melody, or together, as a harmony. Think of the first two notes of the song "Maria": E–flat and A. That's a tritone. In the Middle Ages, the tritone was called "diabolus in musica"—the Devil in music—not, as later imagined, because anyone actually believed Satan dwelt in its notes, but because it was devilishly hard to sing and harmonize. Nevertheless, its sinister reputation lasted for centuries, and it was thought best to avoid it. In the Romantic era, composers who wanted to create a diabolic sound were quick to employ the "wicked" tritone. Saint Saëns, in his "Danse Macabre," uses the tritone to represent the sound of the devil playing a fiddle next to the bed of a dying man, and there are countless other examples. In the Rock era, heavy metal bands like Black Sabbath adopted it as a surefire satanic flourish.
>
> The tritone is at the heart of at least half the songs in *West Side Story*. The very first notes we hear in the score are a tritone variation on a Jewish shofar call. The shofar is an ancient instrument fashioned out of a ram's horn, and its loud voice has been used for millennia to call the people to assemble or to prepare for war. Bernstein bent the tones of the traditional shofar call to his own purposes, altering a note to announce his story of an unstable world and call the slum gangs to battle. From then on, the score is filled with tritones. We hear them in "The Jet Song," as well as in the opening phase of "Something's Coming." Then, in the "Dance at the Gym," the tritone begins to take on a gentler tone as a cha-cha, which in the next scene morphs into the hyper-romantic "Maria"—a love song with a warning hidden in its melody. It turns up again, hyped-up and edgy, in "Cool," then mocking and sardonic in "Officer Krupke." Finally, the show ends with a haunting tritone as the Jets and Sharks come together to carry Tony's body away.
>
> The show's creators were uncertain how audiences would react to its unusual score, and at first, the response was very mixed—everything from raves to walkouts. A few critics even called the music "tuneless." Maybe their ears just weren't accustomed yet to the Devil's interval. By the time the movie version came out in 1961, the music of *West Side Story* had won over America and the world and was recognized as a landmark of the musical theater. It also made the tritone a

standard item in the theater composer's toolbox, almost even a cliché. Since then, we have heard it everywhere—in dozens of musicals, in Michael Jackson videos, and even in the theme song from *The Simpsons*.

Contrary to many reports, the original Broadway production of *West Side Story* was financially successful and, to a great extent, critically acclaimed as "a work of art,"[93] "a bold new kind of musical theater . . . extraordinarily exciting . . . the manner of telling the story is a provocative and artful blend of music, dance, and plot,"[94] and "[p]ooling imagination and virtuosity, they [the authors] have written a profoundly moving show that is as ugly as the city jungles and also pathetic, tender and forgiving."[95] However, it was not universally embraced. The story was too dark, abrasive, and "repugnant"[96] for many people, and, as noted above, the score was too discordant and "astringent"[97] for some critics and audience members. Even so, *West Side Story* was nominated for six Tony Awards, including "Best Musical," and won the Tonys for "Best Choreography" and "Best Scenic Design." The original production ran for a very respectable, if not spectacular, 732 performances. Then less than a year after it had closed,[98] the national tour came back to Broadway[99] and played an additional 249 performances.[100] But it is certainly true that this show, its staging, and its score were truly ahead of their time. Audiences caught up quickly, however, because in 1961, the blockbuster film version of *West Side Story* won ten Academy Awards, including "Best Picture," and, in tandem with its chart-topping soundtrack album, this turned *West Side Story* into one of the most acclaimed and beloved musicals of all time.

A Dancer's Life: Chita Rivera

Chita Rivera literally leapt to stardom in 1957 as the original Anita in ***West Side Story***. Born Dolores Conchita Figueroa del Rivero in Washington, D.C., in 1933, her father had been born in Puerto Rico and her mother was of Scottish, Irish, Puerto Rican, and African American descent. Chita began studying dance as a child and moved to New York as a teenager when she was awarded a scholarship to the School of American Ballet. After graduating from high school, she was cast in the national tour of the Irving Berlin musical *Call Me Madam*, choreographed by Jerome Robbins. After ten months on the road, Rivera made her Broadway debut when she replaced Onna White as the principal dancer in *Guys and Dolls*, choreographed by Michael Kidd, which led to her being hired by Kidd as a replacement in *Can-Can*, where she first met and worked with her future *Chicago* co-star Gwen Verdon. Encouraged by Verdon to seek out roles beyond the chorus, Rivera eventually landed a featured part in ***Mr. Wonderful*** (1956), starring Sammy Davis Jr. The following year, she electrified audiences in *West Side Story*, dancing the mambo in the gym, leading the Shark women in "America," and with her powerful and heartbreaking duet with Carol Lawrence, "A Boy Like That/I Have a

Love." In 1960, she was cast as Rosie in *Bye Bye Birdie*, a role that the show's authors reconceived and rewrote to showcase her personality, ethnicity, and talent. Rivera's fifteen starring roles on Broadway include creating the murderous floozy Velma Kelly in **Chicago** (1975), her Tony Award-winning performances in both *The Rink* (1984) and **Kiss of the Spider Woman** (1993), and her 2005 career retrospective, **Chita Rivera: The Dancer's Life**. In 2018, in honor of her extraordinary sixty-five-year Broadway career, she was awarded a special Tony for "Lifetime Achievement." Chita Rivera died in 2024 at the age of ninety-one.[101]

The Music Man is one of the only hit musicals in history to have its book, music, and lyrics all written by the same person, **Meredith Willson**.[102] The story was inspired by his own experiences growing up in Mason City, Iowa, where his mother was a music teacher, and the character of Winthrop is, in many ways, a stand-in for Willson himself in his youth. He learned to play the flute and piccolo as a child, and in high school he performed in the marching band. Then, at seventeen, with his battered piccolo in his pocket, he took a train to New York City and enrolled in the Institute of Musical Art, which today is the Juilliard School of Music. By now, Willson was a highly trained musician, and he soon got a job playing First Piccolo in John Philip Sousa's renowned concert band at the height of its fame—so he's the one audiences would have heard playing that virtuoso piccolo counterpoint in "The Stars and Stripes Forever." Next, while still in his early twenties, he joined the New York Philharmonic under the autocratic leadership of Arturo Toscanini, the most famous conductor of the day. There, "his experiences of playing the latest avant-garde concert works," as author Dominic McHugh points out, "provided him with the tools to create the kind of complex harmonic language and forms that he would later develop and exploit in parts of *The Music Man*, most notably in 'Marion The Librarian.'"[103]

During the next phase of his career, Willson became the music director for various radio networks (all of whom fielded their own symphony orchestras), wrote movie scores, and became a celebrity himself by hosting and conducting his own radio shows. That's where Harold Hill's unique "rap" style was born. One radio program had to keep broadcasting during a musician's strike, which meant there could be no musical accompaniment for what were supposed to be singing commercials. Undaunted, Willson wrote a rhythmically chanted, tuneless advertising jingle, which was so well received that the stunt was repeated even after the musicians returned. In 1950, Frank Lesser encouraged Willson to turn a memoir about his childhood,[104] which he had written the previous year, into a musical comedy. That seemed like a great idea, but it would take him eight years and thirty revisions to complete the show, and he had to write more than forty songs to arrive at the nineteen that actually ended up in the final version.

When asked how he had created *The Music Man*, Willson would always say, "I didn't have to make anything up. All I had to do was remember."[105] However, the plot of *The Music Man* is far from the nostalgic, wholesome, apple-pie-slice of Americana that it may appear to be at first glance. As Scott Miller writes:

The script and score are expertly constructed, savagely funny, occasionally touching, and filled with wonderfully eccentric characters. Along the way, the show takes gleeful potshots at most of what Americans hold dear: Small town generosity, family values, representative government, education, the Fourth of July, Caucasian Americans' view of Native American culture, classical Western culture, and the great and often misplaced hope of so many parents that their child might have the talent to play a musical instrument.[106]

Harold Hill (originally played by Robert Preston) arrives in River City with only one intention: to con the townspeople out of as much of their hard-earned cash as he possibly can through his bogus scheme to create a boy's band—and then skip town with the cash before they find out it's a scam. As insurance, he will try to seduce Marian, the librarian and local piano teacher (originally played by Barbara Cook) to make certain she doesn't see through his lack of musical ability and expose him as a conman. And yet, the audience loves Harold Hill and roots for him to succeed, from his very first line and through to the final curtain.

Why do audiences love this scoundrel? Because Meredith Willson deftly establishes a town that, prior to Harold Hill's arrival, is close-minded, isolationist, dysfunctional, and emotionally shut down. In author Raymond Knapp's view, "[River City] is full of separate individuals who are distrustful of one another and prone to gossip and scapegoating, and it is continually undermined by youthful rebellion, bickering leadership, and the perceived threat of outsiders."[107] And Knapp goes on to point out that every one of those traits was mirrored in the post-Korean War, Cold War, McCarthy Era of the 1950s. (Just like *West Side Story*, *The Music Man* closely reflected the issues of its day.) Harold Hill, despite his chicanery, is the "life force character" that River City in 1912 (and America in 1957 or even today) desperately needs to save it from itself and, as Knapp contends, "to goad it out of its lethargic smugness, its summer doldrums, into recognizing the energizing power of community-based feeling and activity."[108]

It's perhaps no coincidence that *The Music Man*'s Queer director, **Morton da Costa**, also directed the previous year's big hit Broadway play, *Auntie Mame* (and directed the terrific film versions of both shows as well). The characters of Mame Dennis and Harold Hill share much of the same theatrical DNA. Both are vibrant, charismatic disruptors who advocate for art, freedom, and progressive values and who, during the course of their stories, vanquish the intolerant, conformist, conservative beliefs that stand in their path. Mame's famous battle cry is, "Live! Live! Live! Life is a banquet, and most poor sons-of-bitches are starving to death!"[109] In a very similar vein, Harold Hill tells Marion, "My dear little librarian—pile up enough tomorrows and you'll find you've collected nothing but a lot of empty yesterdays."[110]

The underlying message of *The Music Man* is that there is music everywhere if you just open your heart to it: "There were bells on the hill, but I never heard them ringing . . ." And one of the reasons *The Music Man* is so effective, as Knapp observes, is that each of its story problems and plot complications "is solved specifically through music."[111] At every turn, Harold Hill uses the power of music to galvanize River City into becoming a genuine, functioning community. The result, in Scott Miller's words, "is a real American myth and one that George M. Cohan would be very proud of."[112]

To complete the comparison, here is Albert Evans's analysis of Meredith Willson's brilliant structure and conception for the score for *The Music Man*:

> In 1957, the Tony Award for "Best Score" went to *The Music Man* instead of the season's other outstanding musical, *West Side Story*. Sometimes people are surprised by that. They have the impression that *Music Man*'s score is a simple affair made up of simple tunes, but that is far from the truth. Yes, Meredith Willson's score is very accessible, in the best sense of that word. No audience member was ever baffled or turned off by its complexity or strangeness. From his years as a radio music director, Willson knew exactly how to reach the public and tickle their ear, and he knew exactly how far he could indulge and, if necessary, disguise his own taste and training for musical complexity. With Willson, all that high-brow conservatory stuff is under the hood, so to speak. In the very first scene, Willson surprises us—the opening number is chanted, not sung, by a railroad car full of traveling salesmen. Without sound effects or musical accompaniment, the salesmen's words evoke the sound of a train, starting up slowly, picking up speed, rolling along the tracks, then braking and grinding to a halt. Willson's masterstroke comes soon after but usually goes unnoticed by the audience—although surely they feel it subliminally. Marian's first song, "Goodnight My Someone," is a beautiful wish-on-a-star waltz. In the very next scene, Harold Hill works his pied piper magic on the townspeople with the intoxicating march, "Seventy-six Trombones." Although Marian has taken an instant dislike to Professor Harold Hill, these two songs tell us that they are destined to be together. How? Because both songs share the same melody. Finally, let's consider Willson's virtuoso use of counterpoint. On two occasions, Willson employs his exceptional musical technique to create moments of theater magic by introducing seemingly independent songs that are then sung simultaneously and blend together perfectly: "Pick a Little Talk a Little"/"Goodnight Ladies" and, most memorably, "Lida Rose"/"Will I Ever Tell You?"

The Music Man was hailed as "a knockout," "a whopping hit," "a triumphant musical," and "one of the few great musical comedies of the last 26 years."[113] The show became a massive hit, winning five Tony Awards, including "Best Musical," and ran for a remarkable 1,375 performances (nearly twice as long as *West Side Story*), while the show's original cast album received the first Grammy ever awarded for "Best Musical Theatre Album" and spent 245 weeks on the *Billboard* charts.

West Side Story is clearly a *musical play*, and in fact, it's one of the Broadway musical's only tragedies. Still, the overall feeling of the show is vibrantly exciting and kinetic because Jerome Robbins was able to tell so much of the story through dynamic, breathtaking dancing that conveyed multiple levels of feeling and emotion that the otherwise inarticulate characters are unable to express. (As a result, *West Side Story* has one of the briefest, tersest scripts in musical theater history.) Also, following Shakespeare's lead, the authors expertly deepen the tragedy by including large measures of irreverent, insightful, and show-stopping comic relief. On the other hand, *The Music Man* is unequivocally a *musical comedy*, but one with a fully engaging and involving story, fascinatingly complex characters, and important and serious underlying themes. On the surface, these two shows may seem very different, but they actually share a lot in common.

Both musicals are about a community in crisis. Both involve issues of prejudice and intolerance. And, as we have seen, both reflect specific social issues and problems of the 1950s. Both feature a dance at the gym where star-crossed young lovers come together. Although it's only one of several subplots, the *Music Man* features its own Romeo and Juliet story involving the dancing juveniles Zanita Shinn, the mayor's daughter, and Tommy Djilas, the tough young hoodlum and gang leader. In fact, in the dance section of "Marian, The Librarian," they are discovered cuddled together reading a large tome of Shakespeare's famous play (at least they do that in the movie version, and it seems to have also been part of Onna White's original Broadway staging). In a later scene, in response to her father forbidding her to see Tommy again, Zanita responds, "Papa, please, it's Capulets like you who make blood in the marketplace. Ye gods!" So, the allusion to Romeo and Juliet couldn't be more explicit. In addition, the main reason the Mayor disapproves of Tommy has to do with cultural, and perhaps even racial, prejudice. The boy's last name is "Djilas," the only non-Anglo Saxon character name in the show. Mayor Shinn brands Tommy a "wild kid" and describes his father as "one of them day laborers that live south of town." Even today, day laborers are often associated with immigrants, and in a line added for the film version, Shinn even refers to Tommy as being "Nithelanian." Presumably, the malaprop-prone Mayor means Lithuanian. Once again, the issue is immigrants who won't stay where they belong. And as Willson said, he "just had to remember" because, in fact, between 1910 and 1920, thousands of Eastern Europeans emigrated to northern Iowa, and the countries they came from included Serbia, Yugoslavia, Croatia, and Lithuania. And indeed, Djilas is a common surname in that part of the world, and, as discussed in Chapter 3, even as late as 1912, when *The Music Man* is set, immigrants from Eastern Europe were often not considered to be entirely "white." Harold Hill's belief in Tommy and the investment of time, attention, and trust that he accords to the young lad is exactly what the juvenile delinquents of *West Side Story* will never get. Yes, Tommy and Zanita's entire story probably takes up less than fifteen minutes of total stage time, and within that, much of their story is told through dance rather than dialogue or song. And, yes, unfortunately, in many productions, Tommy is played by a not-very-dangerous-looking young dancer, which seriously dilutes the impact of this storyline. But even so, the intention behind this subplot is clearly delineated in the text.

The other strong strain of prejudice in the show is directed at Marion herself. She is the victim of vicious, small-minded gossip and is ostracized from the community because she is an independent single woman and because of her advocacy for art, music,

"Another Op'nin', Another Show!"

and literature. Like many librarians today, she is accused of advocating for "dirty books." Both communities, the Upper West Side slums of Manhattan and River City, demand conformity from their inhabitants. Finally, both shows employ complex musical scores that include a great deal of foreshadowing and cross-referencing. Chord progressions and melodic motifs from one song are echoed or hidden in another. And all of this creates a remarkable sense of unified design and cohesion.

By *The Music Man*'s final curtain, the town of River City has been healed, and art, love, and music have triumphed. But in *West Side Story*, bigotry, hate, and prejudice have prevailed, and the community is left devastated, with only a small final glimmer of hope that out of this tragedy, some good may come. Without a doubt, the 1957–8 Broadway season produced two of the greatest musicals of all time. So, which show should have won the 1958 Tony Award for "Best Musical?" For me, it's a toss-up. The two musicals are equally brilliant, equally moving, and equally deserving of their classic status.

"Here's To Us!"—Women Writers of The Golden Age (I, J, W)

Bookwriter, playwright, and screenwriter **Bella Spewack**[114] was born in Romania in 1899. Her Jewish parents were already divorced when Bella and her mother emigrated to New York in 1902. Like so many of the inventors of Broadway, she grew up in the crowded tenements of the Lower East Side, but she managed to graduate from high school and, in 1913, found a job as a reporter for a small newspaper. In 1922, she married Sam Spewack, a foreign correspondent for the *New York World*. They spent a few years together as news correspondents in Moscow before returning to the States and settling down just outside NYC, where Sam wrote novels and Bella and Sam collaborated on writing plays. Their first big hit was *Boy Meets Girl* (1937), a satire about a Hollywood screenwriting team searching for the secret to success. In that play, they seem to have invented the now-legendary plot formula: "boy meets girl, boy loses girl, boy gets girl." They then went on to apply that formula to several Hollywood screenplays that they wrote, mostly for B-movies. Then, in 1938, the Spewacks made their Broadway musical debut with their book for the hit Cole Porter musical comedy hit, ***Leave It To Me!****,* the satirical tale of a reluctant American Ambassador in Stalinist Russia.

The Spewacks had a famously turbulent relationship and were not speaking to each other in early 1948 when they were approached to write the book for another Cole Porter musical, based on Shakespeare's *The Taming of the Shrew*. In fact, Bella initially began working on the show alone but finally agreed to bring Sam on board to help with the plot. Sam had always been the story partner of the team, while Bella had a genius for character and dialogue. Together, they completed the book—sometimes communicating only through intermediaries—and in spite of, or perhaps because of, their marital conflicts (given the subject matter), *Kiss Me, Kate* became a giant hit, and the Spewacks won Tony Awards for "Best Author" and "Best Musical." In 1953, they wrote another hit play, *My Three Angels*, that was adapted into the Humphrey Bogart film *We're No Angels*. *Kiss Me, Kate*, however, was by far the highest point of their career. Bella did, however, leave another lasting legacy: while working as a publicist for the Girl Scouts, it was she who came up with the idea of raising funds by selling cookies.

Mary Rodgers was the daughter of Richard Rodgers and a gifted composer in her own right. She made her Broadway debut in 1959 with **Once Upon a Mattress**, a fractured fairy tale starring the young Carol Burnett. *Mattress* had a healthy run, and "Sixty years on, it remains one of the most popular titles in the musical theater catalog, performed hundreds of times a year by schools and amateurs and revived regularly by professionals."[115] It has also been presented on television in three different productions. After a couple of other not-so-successful on- and off-Broadway musicals, she turned to the more manageable career of writing children's fiction so that she could concentrate on raising her six children. Both endeavors proved very successful. Among her books was the bestseller, *Freaky Friday*, and among her six children is **Adam Guettel**, the Tony Award-winning composer and lyricist of the musicals *Light in the Piazza* (2005), *Days of Wine and Roses* (2023), and *Floyd Collins* (1996 and 2025).

Among the best Broadway lyricists of the 1950s and '60s was **Carolyn Leigh**. Her first Broadway job was contributing lyrics for the musical version of ***Peter Pan***, starring Mary Martin. She then teamed up with jazz pianist Cy Coleman on several very sophisticated pop hits such as "Witchcraft" and "The Best is Yet to Come," both of which were famously recorded by Frank Sinatra. Coleman and Leigh then collaborated on the scores for two Broadway musicals, ***Wildcat*** (starring Lucille Ball) and ***Little Me*** (book by Neil Simon and direction and choreography by Bob Fosse), and her final show was ***How Now Dow Jones*** with composer Elmer Bernstein. Unfortunately, none of these musicals proved to be more than moderately successful, but remarkably, they all produced big hit songs. Leigh's most enduring show has been *Peter Pan*, which has been revived on Broadway five times. Her lyrics for that show enchanted the nation when, as the very first Broadway musical to be adapted for television, it was broadcast live in 1955 and watched by an incredible sixty-five million people.[116]

Meanwhile, **Dorothy Fields** continued writing in top form through the 1950s, including two notable hits, ***A Tree Grows in Brooklyn*** (music by Arthur Schwartz) and the musical murder mystery ***Redhead*** (music by Albert Hague), which starred Gwen Verdon, was directed and choreographed by Bob Fosse, and received the 1959 Tony Award for "Best Musical." Then, for the first time, Dorothy's career hit a lull. In 1965, she turned sixty and started to think of herself as "retired against her will." Then one night at a cocktail party, composer Cy Coleman asked Dorothy if she'd like to collaborate with him on a new show. She grabbed his arm and whispered, "Thank God! I thought I was dead." The show turned out to be *Sweet Charity*—a hard-edged, absolutely up-to-the-minute story of a dance hall girl looking for love. Dorothy was once again working with top collaborators—Gwen Verdon, Bob Fosse, and Neil Simon—and the lyrics she created for the show astonished everyone. She had certainly not lost her ear for contemporary speech. Phrase after hip-phrase perfectly captured the zeitgeist of the Swingin' Sixties. Seven years later, Coleman and Fields teamed up for one final show: *Seesaw*, a musical adaptation of the hit play *Two for the Seesaw*. It got mixed reviews but enjoyed a healthy run and included some terrific songs. Sadly, Coleman and Fields' partnership was cut short the following year by Dorothy's death at the age of sixty-eight. But what an amazing career! For nearly a half-century, from the 1920s to the 1970s, Dorothy Fields' smart, conversational, and beautifully crafted lyrics captivated Broadway audiences.

1960: *Gypsy* vs *The Sound of Music* (and Mary vs Ethel) (I, J, Q, W)

Now let's jump to the 1959–60 Broadway season, which brought the debuts of both *Gypsy* and *The Sound of Music*. Spoiler alert!—there was a tie for the "Best Musical" Tony Award that season, and if you don't already know what happened, it probably didn't turn out the way you may think it did. As with our previous pairing, there are still Broadway mavens who remain outraged over which show won and which musical was, in their view, denied its rightful award.

Surprisingly, *The Sound of Music* and *Gypsy*—a lyrical musical play about a nun and a brassy musical comedy about a stripper—also have a lot in common. Both shows were star vehicles created specifically to showcase the talents and personalities of Broadway's two greatest stars, Mary Martin and Ethel Merman, both of whom (as detailed in previous chapters) had made star-making Broadway debuts in Silver Age-style *musical comedies* in the 1930s and then successfully navigated the tricky transition into the Golden Age, which brought them to even greater heights of stardom. However, unlike most other star vehicles, both *Gypsy* and *The Sound of Music* have lived on without their original stars and become centerpieces of the musical theater canon. And one of them, by many estimates, has become the most popular musical of all time. In addition, both shows feature children in significant roles, and the plotlines of both musicals revolve around the upbringing, education, and welfare of those children. And both musicals shared a dynamic producer named Leland Hayward.

In contrast to the majority of writers, directors, choreographers, designers, and performers who are profiled in this book, many Broadway producers came from very WASPy and privileged backgrounds because, of course, that's where the money was. **Leland Hayward** was born in Nebraska in 1902 into a wealthy and illustrious family. After dropping out of Princeton, he kicked around aimlessly for a few years and then fell into show business almost by accident. He was hanging out at a New York nightclub in

1926 when the owner, who was a friend of Hayward's, began complaining that business was terrible and that he would pay serious money to an entertainer who could really pull in the crowds. Hayward leapt at the challenge. He rushed over to the Liberty Theater, where Fred and Adele Astaire were starring in the Gershwin musical *Lady, Be Good!* and recruited that famous couple for a twelve-week engagement at the club. It was a very lucrative deal, not just for the Astaires but for Hayward as well, and this inspired him to pursue a career in the entertainment industry. In short order, he became one of the most powerful agents in Hollywood, where, in addition to Fred Astaire, he represented Ginger Rogers, Greta Garbo, and Judy Garland. Then, in 1945, at the height of his power and success as an agent, he sold his talent agency and became a Broadway producer. Again, he had almost immediate success, producing and co-producing a string of Broadway blockbuster plays and musicals, including Rodgers and Hammerstein's *South Pacific*, starring Mary Martin, and Irving Berlin's *Call Me Madam*, starring Ethel Merman, and in 1959 he would work with both stars on *The Sound of Music* and *Gypsy*.

A few years prior, however, Hayward was hired by the Ford Motor Company to produce a two-hour live television spectacular to celebrate Ford's 50th anniversary. In the 1950s, Ford was at the center of American culture, and this event, one of the very first "television specials," was scheduled to be broadcast simultaneously on CBS, NBC, ABC, and Dumont, the only four television networks that existed at that time. The stature of this event required engaging entertainers who were equal to Ford in their prestige and importance to American culture. And in the 1950s, that meant Broadway. So, for the centerpiece of the show, Hayward persuaded the two women who personified Broadway at its highest level, Ethel Merman and Mary Martin, to perform together for the very first time. In her autobiography, Martin fondly recalled that Hayward had talked her into doing the show by telling her that Merman had already agreed, and as she subsequently discovered, he had told Merman the same thing, thereby tricking them both into saying yes. The idea was that first they would each sing several of their signature hits and then partner on a twelve-minute medley of old standards tracing fifty years of American popular music. Hayward engaged Jerome Robbins to stage the sequence, and Robbins wisely determined that with these two powerhouse stars onboard, nothing else was needed except for some simple stools for the ladies to perch on.

Many Broadway wags had predicted there would be conflict between these two great divas of the stage, but Martin and Merman had a ball rehearsing the show and got along wonderfully. Ethel Merman even used her old secretarial skills to type up the daily revisions that were made in the medley. On June 15, 1953, *The Ford 50th Anniversary Show* was watched live by a phenomenal sixty million viewers, a larger audience than Merman and Martin would perform to in all of their Broadway shows combined. And forever after, star performers on television would sit side-by-side on stools and perform medleys of hit songs just like Mary and Ethel. If you've never seen a video of this performance, I encourage you to track it down. It's a rare chance to see these two great stars at the height of their power and just a few years before their two greatest triumphs.

"Another Op'nin', Another Show!"

A few years later, in 1957, Gypsy Rose Lee, the renowned striptease artist turned unlikely mainstream celebrity and media star, published a memoir in which she recalled her early years touring in vaudeville with her child-star sister, June; her own later success in burlesque; and most vividly her ferociously driven stage mother, Rose, who was determined to turn her girls into stars. The book became a bestseller, and producer David Merrick quickly acquired the stage rights.

"The Abominable Showman": David Merrick (J)

David Merrick, arguably the most famous Broadway producer after Ziegfeld, was born into a Jewish family in St. Louis in 1911. He would go on to produce more than eighty plays and musicals on Broadway, including ***Gypsy***; ***Hello, Dolly!***, ***Oliver!***, ***Promises, Promises***, and ***42nd Street***. Due to his ruthless producing style and competitive Machiavellian manner, he acquired the nickname, "the abominable showman." He once boasted that his guiding philosophy was, "It is not enough that I should succeed—others should fail." He was, however, a marketing genius and a virtuoso of the publicity stunt. His best-remembered scheme was cooked up to try to save the failing 1961 Jule Stein/Comden and Green musical *Subways are for Sleeping*. Merrick located seven New York residents who had the exact same names as the seven leading New York drama critics and persuaded each of these seven imposter critics to contribute a short but glowing review for the show, which Merrick included in a full-page newspaper advertisement. (Merrick had actually been planning this stunt for many years, but he had to wait for the critic, Brooks Atkinson, to retire since he could never have found a match for that name.) The ad was quickly spotted as a hoax and pulled from most newspapers, but the stunt became a giant news story, the talk of the town, and generated enough ticket sales to allow *Subways are for Sleeping* to run almost long enough to recoup its capitalization.

"A Pioneer Woman Without a Frontier"—Curtain up on Gypsy (L, J, Q, W)

Merrick first engaged Betty Comden and Adolph Green to create the book and lyrics for *Gypsy*, and their frequent collaborator Jule Styne to compose the music. But Comden and Green stepped away from the project to write the screenplay for *Auntie Mame*, and *Gypsy* sat dormant for nearly a year until Merrick joined forces with Leland Hayward to get the show back on track, now with Ethel Merman as its intended star.

Greatest of All Time: The Merm (W)

Ethel Merman was born Ethel Zimmerman in Queens, New York, in 1908, into a working-class family of German and Scottish ancestry. Her father was an accountant, and her mother was a teacher. From childhood through high school, on Friday nights, the Zimmerman family would take the subway into Manhattan to see that week's vaudeville show at the Palace Theater. There, Ethel saw Fanny Brice, Sophie Tucker, and Nora Bayes and, back at home, tried to emulate their singing. Through this process, she discovered her own distinctive vocal style. Meanwhile, she enrolled in a secretarial course at her high school. After graduating in 1924, Merman was hired as a stenographer and, eventually, a personal secretary. During this period, she also began appearing in nightclubs and vaudeville shows. She decided that Zimmerman was too long to fit on a theater marquee, so she shortened it to "Merman." She made her Broadway debut in 1930 in the George and Ira Gershwin musical comedy *Girl Crazy*, in which she had a featured role that included three songs. Her second song was "I Got Rhythm," and during the second chorus, Merman hit and held a belted "C" for sixteen bars and, according to all reports, unleashed pandemonium. As Stacy Wolf relates in her book, *A Problem Like Maria*:

> Merman's stardom burst forth from that long, long, note and from a legendary intermission conversation with Gershwin, who according to Merman said, "Do you know what just happened to you?" She had become a star in one night. And the story goes that he also told her to never take a singing lesson. Merman was one of those rare Broadway singers to belt, to use what is called the chest voice rather than the head voice like a classical singer. Sophie Tucker had belted, and she had modeled her "Red Hot Mama" persona on African American blues singers like Bessie Smith.[117]

From that point on, Broadway songwriters all wanted to write songs and shows, especially for her. Merman, however, acknowledged that she was not always the easiest person in the world to write parts for. She said her roles had to be built to emphasize "the brassy side, with lots of oomph, something with guts and sock songs, not sweetness and light." And as Stacey Wolfe goes on to note, "Merman never played ingenue romantic heroines. She always played women who defied gender expectations in some way."

Between 1931 and 1966, Ethel Merman starred in fifteen Broadway musicals, most of which were created especially for her, including two shows by Irving Berlin and five by Cole Porter, and in the process, she became a legend in her own lifetime. Referred to by friends and colleagues as "the Merm," stories about her brash, straightforward, down-to-earth manner and bawdy humor abound. She cursed like a sailor and loved telling dirty jokes. There are dozens of legendary and very racy anecdotes about her, including one that Stephen Sondheim loved to tell. As the story goes, Ethel was engaged to be a guest star on the 1950s television show *The Loretta Young Show*. Young was a glamorous Hollywood star who was famously religious and did not allow anyone to curse in her presence. This was, of course, a challenging position to take in show business, where colorful language is not just tolerated but often relished. So, Young kept a "curse jar" handy on the set of her show, and anyone caught using foul language had to put a quarter in the jar for each infraction. The money was sent to some Catholic charity or other. Well, Ethel shows up for the first day of rehearsal, and not even five minutes go by before she says, "Where's the damn prop!" Loretta immediately grabs her jar and says, "Naughty, naughty, Ethel, now you have to put a quarter in the jar," and Ethel begrudgingly gave her a quarter. A few minutes later, Ethel exclaims, "Goddammit!" over some new frustration, and Young makes her contribute another quarter. Just minutes after that, Ethel fumbles a prop and exclaims, "For Christ sake!" But before Loretta can even pick up the jar, Ethel shouts, "Look, Loretta, here's ten bucks—now go fuck yourself." That story may indeed be apocryphal, but as Stephen Sondheim said, "I like to believe it is true of Ethel—because it is profoundly true of Ethel."[118]

Gypsy would end up being the highest point of Ethel Merman's monumental career—but first, the producers needed a book and score that would be worthy of their star. They engaged Arthur Laurents to write the book and Jerome Robbins to direct, both still basking in the success of *West Side Story*. First, Cole Porter and then Irving Berlin were asked to write the songs, but Porter's health was failing, and Berlin did not envision himself writing songs for a story about a stripper. Cy Coleman and Carolyn Leigh wrote a few songs as an audition but did not get the job. Next, the producers approached Stephen Sondheim, who said he would do it only if he could write both the lyrics and the music. Merman, however, vetoed that idea. Her most recent Broadway musical, *Happy Hunting*, had a score written by new, inexperienced songwriters that critics had labeled "third rate."[119] Ethel told the producers that Sondheim could write the lyrics, but she wanted Jule Stein to write the music, "He knows my style, and he writes great showtunes!" Sondheim again went to Hammerstein for advice. His mentor insightfully predicted that the experience Sondheim would gain from writing for a famous star would prove invaluable and far outweigh any negatives. As Sondheim later described it:

> Instead of writing for Madame Rose, you write for Madame Rose as played by Ethel Merman. This turned out to be very useful because when I wrote Joanne for *Company*, I wrote Joanne as played by Elaine Stritch. I wrote Mrs. Lovett as played by Angela Lansbury . . . It's not so much that you tailor the material, but you hear the voice in your head whether you want to or not.[120]

And Sondheim goes on to suggest that this is why so many hit songs have been written during the out-of-town tryouts for so many shows: "Because by that point in the process, you know the person who's playing the character. You know their strengths and weaknesses, and whether it's conscious or not, it filters into what you write."[121]

Now, many reports claim that once this now full team of collaborators set to work, Arthur Laurents came up with the idea of shifting the focus of the story away from Louise (Gypsy Rose Lee) and making her mother, Rose, the leading character, but that doesn't make any sense to me. The show was already being written specifically for Ethel Merman, and it's impossible to believe that anyone expected that Merman would play a supporting role. Having Rose as the story's central focus must surely have been the plan by the time she came on board.

Styne and Sondheim were both worried that they would have a rocky and difficult collaboration—Broadway's established old guard in conflict with the cocky, brash, young, new generation. Their partnership, however, turned out to be highly successful, with each of the gifted collaborators pushing the other to do brilliant work. Late in the process, the team had still not figured out what to do for Rose's climactic moment of revelation that the entire story was building to. Jerome Robbins' original idea had been to create a nightmare ballet (another dream ballet!) that would echo and reprise moments and images from Rose's past in order to dramatize her emotional breakdown. But after spending a week trying to stage it, Robbins decided that it was simply not going to work and abandoned the concept. This key moment in the story was intended to be accomplished with a song—and that song would have to bring the show to its dramatic and emotional climax.

Sondheim described the night that "Rose's Turn" was created as "fulfilling every Hollywood fantasy" he ever had. *Gypsy* was rehearsing in the rundown, decrepit, but very picturesque and evocative former roof garden of the New Amsterdam Theatre, where Ziegfeld's *Midnight Frolic* shows had been staged thirty years earlier (and where Disney Theatricals offices are located today). At the end of rehearsal one night, Jerry Robbins said to Sondheim, "Why don't you stay, and we'll talk about the number?" Sondheim proposed an idea of taking all of the songs connected to Rose and mashing them up in a similar way to what Robbins had been planning for the staging of the nightmare ballet. Sondheim later recalled that night as:

> ... one of those things that you dream about when you're a kid. You write a song with a star, only it was Jerry Robbins as the star. He started moving, performing a strip, sashaying back and forth on the stage. And I started to ad-lib at the piano with the tunes that were already written.[122]

A few days later, after refining the number with Jule Styne, the authors presented this dramatic musical monologue to Ethel Merman. Sondheim performed it with Styne accompanying him on the piano. By all reports, it was a thrilling performance. And after Sondheim belted out Rose's final defiant, "... for me!" Merman, with tears streaming down her face, rushed to embrace the songwriters exclaiming, "It's a goddamned aria!"

Gypsy opened on Broadway in May of 1959 and played for 702 performances. Since then, in a series of high-profile revivals, the musical theater's greatest female stars have risen to the challenge of playing the indomitable Rose: Angela Lansbury in 1974,

Tyne Daly in 1989, Bernadette Peters in 2003, Patti LuPone in 2008, Imelda Staunton in London in 2015, and went to press in the winter of 2024, a fifth Broadway revival starring Audra McDonald, whom the *New York Times* declared "our leading musical tragedienne" and "a star who has to be seen in this role," opened to mostly rave reviews.[123] The critical acclaim lavished on *Gypsy* started high and has only grown over the years. Walter Kerr called the original production "the best damn musical I've seen in years."[124] In 1974, Clive Barnes said, "*Gypsy* is one of the best of musicals."[125] In 1989, Frank Rich declared it his "favorite Broadway musical," and in 2003, he wrote that "*Gypsy* is nothing if not Broadway's own brassy, unlikely answer to King Lear." In 2008, Ben Brantley enthused that "It may be the greatest of all American musicals," and in 2024 Jesse Green concurred declaring it "one of the greatest American musicals" and "one of the great works of mid-century American drama."[126] Many theater professionals consider *Gypsy* to be the best-written, most brilliantly crafted musical of all time and certainly one of the pinnacles of the cohesive Golden Age *musical play* style that was invented by Rodgers and Hammerstein. So, it is somewhat ironic that at the 1960 Tony Awards, *Gypsy* would go head-to-head with the final musical written by Rodgers and Hammerstein themselves.

"Let's Start at the Very Beginning"—The Sound of Music (📖, 🎵, 👁, 🎬)

The initial idea for ***The Sound of Music*** came from its eventual director, Vincent J. Donahue, who had seen a German film called *The Trapp Family*, which had been a success in Europe and South America and which told the life story of Baroness Maria von Trapp. "In many ways it was amateurish," he said, "but I was terribly moved by the whole idea of it, almost sobbing." He immediately saw it as a perfect vehicle for Mary Martin, and sent the film to Martin and her husband, who was one of Donahue's closest friends. They both loved it. Martin later said, "The idea was irresistible, a semi-Cinderella story." Soon, producer Leland Hayward joined the team, and Howard Lindsay and Russel Crouse were engaged to write the book. Initially, the show was envisioned as a dramatic play featuring authentic Austrian folk songs and, ideally, one new song that would be written by Rodgers and Hammerstein. Then, as Rogers recalled in his autobiography, *Musical Stages*:

> Oscar and I saw the picture and agreed that it had the makings of an impressive stage production but disagreed with their concept. If they wanted to do a play using the actual music, fine, but why invite a clash of styles by simply adding one song. Why not a fresh score? When I suggested this to Leland and Mary, they said they'd love to have a new score, but only if Oscar and I would write it. We had to explain that we would be tied up with the *Flower Drum Song* for a year, but they came back with the two most flattering words possible. We'll wait![127]

"A Cockeyed Optimist": Mary Martin (Q, W)

Mary Martin was born in Texas in 1913. Her mother was a violin teacher, and her father was a lawyer. She got hooked on performing right from the start: "Give me four people, and I'm on," she said. "Give me four hundred, and I'm a hundred times more on." After working in vaudeville and radio on the West Coast, she made her Broadway debut in Cole Porter's 1938 musical *Leave it to Me!*. Sophie Tucker was the show's star, and Martin had only one song. But luckily for her, that song was "My Heart Belongs to Daddy." The contrast between the twenty-five-year-old Martin's naive manner and Porter's suggestive lyrics, accompanied by Robert Alton's faux striptease staging, turned the number into a triumphant success. The *New York Times* wrote that "Martin's mock innocence made 'My Heart Belongs to Daddy' the bawdy ballad of the season." With one song, Martin became a star overnight. Employing her unique combination of feminine softness and tomboy playfulness, she would go on to star in ten more Broadway shows, originating the roles of Nellie Forbush in *South Pacific*, the title role in *Peter Pan*, and Maria Rainer (von Trapp) in *The Sound of Music*.

Mary Martin's personal life was complicated. In 1941, she married Richard Halliday, an upper-class, closeted Gay man who became her manager, and often, producer. Martin also was Queer and had close relationships with several women over the years, including film actress Janet Gaynor.

Rodgers and Hammerstein became co-producers with Halliday and Hayward, and because Lindsay and Crouse had already been signed as the bookwriters, *The Sound of Music* became one of the few productions for which Oscar Hammerstein contributed only the lyrics. It's notable that these four great writers, who had all been young breakthrough stars of the Silver Age, now came together to create one of the Golden Age's crowning achievements. Hammerstein's more limited role, however, turned out to be for the best because, just as rehearsals got underway, he was diagnosed with incurable cancer. Hammerstein accepted his fate with equanimity and told his wife and Rodgers that he intended to go on working as long as he possibly could.

With Joe Layton now on board as choreographer,[128] *The Sound of Music*'s rehearsals and out-of-town tryouts went smoothly, and advance ticket sales for New York broke records. The only issue was the final concert sequence with which Rodgers was still not satisfied. He felt that one more song was needed—a solo for Captain von Trapp. Hammerstein, who had been too ill to attend the Boston preview performances, was able to make it there for the opening night, and agreed with Rogers about the song. Six days later, "Edelweiss" was put into the show—it was the last lyric that Oscar Hammerstein would ever write.

The Sound of Music opened on Broadway in November of 1959. Overall, the reviews were positive, but some critics found the story to be corny, sentimental nonsense and, as they would do forever after, described the show using adjectives such as "sugary, sickly-sweet, and saccharine." Even so, *The Sound of Music* became an immediate smash hit. It ran for nearly four years on Broadway (1,443 performances) and was an even bigger success in London. The original cast album spent sixteen weeks at No. 1 on the album charts and stayed in the charts for 276 weeks. There was still no Cast Album chart—these were the sales charts for all LP albums.

Then, in 1965, the blockbuster movie version lifted *The Sound of Music* to even greater heights. Driven by unprecedented repeat viewings, the film quickly became the number one box office movie in America, a position it held for thirty out of the next forty-three weeks. And at the 1966 Academy Awards, *The Sound of Music* received five Oscars, including "Best Picture," while the film's soundtrack album became one of the most successful in history. Incredibly, as Laurence Maslin states in his book *Broadway to Main Street—How Showtunes Enchanted America*, "in an era marked by the rise and triumph of Beatlemania, the ascension of Motown, and the beachhead of the British Invasion, the two most dominant LPs [albums] of the mid-1960s were far and away the soundtracks to *Mary Poppins* and *The Sound of Music*." The reviews for the film version were even worse. Most famously, critic Pauline Kael dubbed it "the sugar-coated lie that people want to eat."[129] Nonetheless, the film became a worldwide sensation and one of the highest grossing movies of all time. As Richard Rodgers once remarked, "the only smart people in show business are the audience."[130]

The popularity of both the stage and film versions of *The Sound of Music* has only grown over the decades. Those repeat viewings of the film have continued unendingly, as the movie has made its way to television, video, and streaming and has been re-released for anniversaries and popular "Rocky Horror Picture Show"-style audience participation singalongs that feature cosplay costume contests. Meanwhile, Broadway and London revivals of the stage show, along with live television broadcasts and countless regional, stock, community theater, and high school productions, continue to draw large and enthusiastic audiences.

For whatever reason, *The Sound of Music* has proven to be incredibly moving, inspiring, and meaningful to mass audiences around the world who want to see this story replayed over and over, time and time again. And one naturally has to wonder, why? What makes *The Sound of Music* so incredibly popular? It is, of course, easy and often fashionable to criticize both the show and the film, and indeed, many critics and theater professionals despise them. However, I don't believe that a work of art can become so universally loved, achieve such a major cultural impact, and capture the public's imagination on such a global scale unless it has the power to deeply connect with its audience on an emotional, conscious, and subconscious level. What is it about this story that causes such an impact? Mary Martin described the show as "a Cinderella story," and that folk tale has certainly lost none of its mythic power over the centuries. Author Ethan Mordden calls *The Sound of Music* "a fairy tale with all the power to move us that we find in *The Wizard of Oz*," summarizing its plot as follows:

> A prince who is under an enchantment that has frozen his heart, meets a young woman of an order of healers who frees him. Monsters overrun the land, but the

healer's people open up a hidden portal of escape. It's almost a parable of dueling magics, the magic of the spirit versus the magic of destruction, and music does the healing.[131]

I would propose that the story of *The Sound of Music* is an epic, if picturesque, battle between the forces of good and evil. The antagonist is the greatest villain of all time, Adolf Hitler, and the specter of the Nazi regime and its evil philosophy hangs over the musical on stage and film, even if they are only rarely mentioned or alluded to. We never see any direct depiction of their ruthless persecution of Jews, homosexuals, Roma, or other minorities. And in fact, the one character who might be Jewish and/or Gay is funny Uncle Max, who is presented as a lovable, but decadent and amoral collaborator, too weak and too much in love with his access to wealth, privilege, and position to stand up to the Nazis. He is presented as a cautionary tale: when the next wave of fascists comes—don't be like Max! The von Trapp family itself is a metaphor for the rescuing of Austria, Germany, and the world from Hitler's grasp. Raymond Knapp points out that, prior to Maria's arrival, the Trapp family is basically a mini-Fascist state,

> ... run by an autocratic, militaristic Captain blind to the individual needs of his own children ... It is above all the children that are at stake in this family's saga, for they not only represent the quintessential family unit ... that will surely be destroyed by totalitarianism, but they also, and more basically, represent the future. They are "tomorrow"—to borrow and invert the language of *Cabaret*—and the show is about who they will belong to.

The children are, in Knapp's words, "an empty page that the world is about to write on." Maria represents "the key to rescuing the family ... and it is remarkable how much of an idealized American she is." She has the courage to stand up to the captain, and "courage was then widely seen as what the 'good' Europe lacked in the 1930s, the courage to stand up to Hitler and Mussolini early on, before it was too late." In contrast,

> [Maria] is in touch with nature; she loves freedom too much to accept life as a nun, despite her devotion; she pays attention to the children and is immediately more mother than governess ... she's resourceful, able to turn curtains into play clothes; and of course, she has music, specifically the music that will make you one with nature.[132]

As in *The Music Man*, music solves all of the problems and conflicts in *The Sound of Music*. (Chapter explores one of the principal and most ubiquitous themes of the Broadway musical: "Transgressive Women," like Maria and Rose, who refuse to follow the rules or live the life that society and the patriarchy have set out for them.)

So, what happened at the 1960 Tony Awards? Five musicals were nominated for "Best Musical" that year: *Take Me Along, Fiorello!, Gypsy, The Sound of Music,* and *Once Upon a Mattress*.[133] *Gypsy* was nominated in eight categories, including "Best Actress," "Best

Supporting Actor and Actress," "Best Director," "Best Scenic Design," and "Best Musical," but Ethel Merman and all of the other nominees went home empty-handed. *The Sound of Music* was nominated for six awards and won four: "Best Actress," "Best Supporting Actress," "Best Scenic Design," and "Best Musical." However, as noted above, there was a rare tie that year, and **Fiorello!** also received a Tony for "Best Musical." With a score by Bock and Harnick and a book by George Abbott and Jerome Weidman, *Fiorello!* was a musical biography of New York's beloved Depression-era mayor, Fiorello LaGuardia. It must have been a terrific show because it also received that year's Pulitzer Prize for Drama, but it never entered the musical theater canon, probably because it connected most strongly with a New York audience who remembered and revered LaGuardia. So, you could say that *Gypsy* came in third! From our perspective today, it's easy to get at least a little outraged over that. However, in 1960, there were no separate categories for "Best Book" or "Best Score," and if there had been, it's possible that *Gypsy* might have made it into the winner's circle. Privately, Merman was deeply disappointed with the outcome, but in public, she just shrugged it off, wisecracking, "How you gonna buck a nun!"

Which show do I think should have won "Best Musical"? Although I admire *The Sound of Music* tremendously and always enjoy seeing it, *Gypsy* is one of my favorite musicals of all time, and perennially in the list of my "Top Five." I find it to be brilliantly crafted, endlessly fascinating, and deeply moving and affecting—so that's where my vote would go.

CHAPTER 10
"OPEN A NEW WINDOW"—THE GOLDEN AGE OF BROADWAY, PART 3: THE 1960S (♪, ♩, ♫)

As the 1950s came to an end, Broadway musicals were at the very center of American culture. Because of their chart-topping original cast albums, the songs, stories, and characters of hit Broadway musicals were known and loved from coast to coast, and individual Broadway showtunes were the biggest pop singles of the day, recorded by the top singers and bands. Hit musicals, along with their creators and stars, were often featured on the covers of national magazines such as *Life* and *Time* and were showcased on the highest-rated television programs. Meanwhile, many of the hit musicals of the 1940s and early '50s were being transformed into immensely popular major motion pictures, which expanded the Broadway audience even more. Then, in 1960, as if on cue, two immensely popular musicals kicked off the decade, foreshadowing several of the major changes that were about to take place in American culture—changes that would dramatically affect the Broadway musical and by the end of the decade leave its future in doubt.

"I Can See It!"—*The Fantasticks* and the Rise of the Off-Broadway Musical (♫)

While Broadway was at its zenith in terms of prestige and influence, down in Greenwich Village, the off-Broadway theater movement was emerging as a disruptive counter-cultural alternative to mainstream musical theater. It was kicked off in 1954 by a revival of Kurt Weill and Bertolt Brecht's *The Threepenny Opera*, which, in its Broadway debut twenty-one years earlier, had closed after only twelve performances. This new translation by Marc Blitzstein, however, ran for an amazing 2,704 performances, and in the wake of this success came a wave of small, quirky, off-beat musicals that would never have flown on Broadway—most notably *The Fantasticks*.

Tom Jones, who wrote the book and lyrics, and his Queer collaborator, **Harvey Schmidt**, who composed the music, began working on the *The Fantasticks* while they were still at college in Texas. Although they had originally conceived it as a full-scale, Rodgers and Hammerstein-style musical play, circumstances led them to enlist their college classmate, director **Word Baker**, to help them reinvent it as a small cast, small stage, bare-bones production. *The Fantasticks* is based on Edmund Rostand's 1894 French play, *Les Romanesques*, and its plot is kind of a reverse 'Romeo and Juliet' story in which two fathers pretend to hate one another in order to trick their defiant children into falling in love. If they forbid it, the teenagers will naturally want to do it.

"Open A New Window"

The Fantasticks premiered in the intimate 153-seat Sullivan Street Playhouse, where the show's simple platform set and thrust stage created an intimate and engaging effect. Word Baker's highly stylized direction and staging was an inventive combination of traditional musical theater, French mime, Commedia dell'Arte, Kabuki, Noh, and other world-theater and avant-garde theater techniques. In addition, *The Fantasticks'* captivating and delightful score, which produced several popular hit songs, is both refreshingly unconventional and reassuringly traditional at the same time. The impact of this show was so strong that the original off-Broadway production ran for an incredible forty-two years—from 1960 to 2002—and its grand total of 17,162 performances made it the world's longest-running musical, a title it still holds.[1] During that long New York run, *The Fantasticks* was also produced in virtually every city throughout the U.S., and in at least sixty-seven other countries around the world, all of which earned the show's original backers a more than 240 percent return on their investment. As author Scott Miller writes:

> *The Fantasticks* was a musical born of one of the most fascinating periods in American history: the 1950's. When traditional domesticity was being challenged, when organized religion was being challenged, when the unquestioned authority of parents and other experts was being questioned, and when young Americans were becoming obsessed with individuality, with rebellion, with freedom, with art as a means to criticize social and political structures, and most disconcerting of all, with modern jazz. All of this would find full bloom in the 60s but the seeds were here in the 1950s with the beat writers when composer Harvey Schmidt and writer Tom Jones, two young turtlenecked bohemians in 1950s Manhattan, were creating this masterpiece.[2]

The Fantasticks is, indeed, a masterpiece. However, the show became so widely popular, and its avant-garde style became so integrated and absorbed into mainstream theatrical culture that its radicalness and innovations are now often overlooked.

"The Other Generation": The Boomers and *Bye Bye Birdie* (♩, ♪)

That same year, the satirical musical comedy ***Bye Bye Birdie*** became the first Broadway show to include any kind of rock 'n' roll music in its score and, along with *The Fantasticks* and Rodgers and Hammerstein's *Flower Drum Song* (1958), it was also one the first to dramatize the impact the post-war Baby Boom generation (the largest in history) was beginning to have on American culture, and the resulting "generation gap" that the dominance of the baby boomers was starting to create.

It was only four years earlier that Elvis Presley had burst onto the national music scene and brought rock 'n' roll music into the mainstream through a series of hit records and television appearances that culminated in his legendary first appearance on *The Ed Sullivan Show*, seen by approximately sixty million viewers. (Rock 'n' roll's fascinating origin story is also a uniquely American saga of how the merger and intermingling of Black and white music revolutionized an artform—but, unfortunately, that is beyond the scope of this book.) Because Pressley's suggestive dance moves and pelvic gyrations were considered much too provocative to be seen on national television, the cameras were mostly restricted to showing Elvis only from the waist up. The audience in the studio, however, could see all of him, and nearly every phrase of every song was punctuated by the wild screaming of his adoring fans.[3] All of which turned Presley into a superstar. Then, in 1958, Elvis was abruptly forced to put his singing career on hold when, much to the dismay of teenage fans, he was unexpectedly drafted into the U.S. Army.

Inspired by these real-life events, the creators of *Bye Bye Birdie* invented a fictional knockoff named Conrad Birdie who was "just like Elvis Pressley, only more so,"[4] and devised a satirical story about what might happen if a sexually provocative young rock 'n' roll star was suddenly dropped into the lives of a typical, middle-class, all-American family in a small midwestern town they named "Sweet Apple, Ohio." They then took every opportunity they could find to lampoon mid-century American values, mores, society, and culture. (Unfortunately, much of the show's pointed satire was severely watered down for the 1963 film version.)

Bye Bye Birdie became the surprise hit of the 1960–1 season. The *New York Daily News* called it "the funniest, most captivating, and most expert musical comedy one could hope to see in several seasons of show-going."[5] The show not only launched Dick Van Dyke and Chita Rivera into major stardom, but also launched the careers of four men in their early thirties who would have a tremendous impact on the Broadway musical during the final decade of the Golden Age and into the Modern Era.

Composer **Charles Strouse** was born in New York City in 1928 to middle-class Jewish parents who worked in the tobacco business. He began taking piano lessons at ten, and at fifteen he entered the Eastman School of Music at the University of Rochester. He then studied classical music composition in Paris with the famous teacher Nadia Boulanger and returned to the United States to study with composer Aaron Copeland. Strouse met lyricist **Lee Adams** at a party in 1949, and a long and successful musical partnership was born. The duo started out contributing songs to numerous revues. Then, in 1958, Edward Padula, an experienced stage manager turned novice producer, was auditioning songwriting teams for a new musical about teenagers, which at that point was titled "Let's Go Steady." Strouse and Adams got the job, and over the following year, they wrote more than fifty possible songs for the show. Because no one associated with the show had any significant Broadway experience, Strouse and Adams had to pitch the show and perform their songs at more than seventy-five "backers auditions" in order to raise the financing needed to produce the show. To the surprise of nearly everyone, *Bye Bye Birdie* (as it was retitled) became an enormous hit and won four 1961 Tony Awards, including "Best Musical"— and this was in a season that included musicals by Jule Styne and Comden and Green,[6] and Meredith Willson,[7] as well as Lerner and Loewe's *Camelot*. That certainly got Broadway's attention and put the new songwriting team on the map. Over the next thirty years, in partnership with Lee Adams and other lyricists, Charles Strouse would compose the scores of thirteen more Broadway musicals, including two additional "Best Musical" Tony winners: *Applause* (1970) and *Annie* (1977).

Birdie's young bookwriter was **Michael Stewart**. Born in New York City in 1924, Stewart was both Gay and Jewish. He told friends that he made the decision to write for the musical theater at ten years old when he was taken by his family to see the Cole Porter musical *Anything Goes*. After attending Queens College and the Yale School of Drama, during the early 1950s he began contributing comedy sketches to various off-Broadway revues. Following the success of *Bye Bye Birdie*, he went on to write the books (and occasionally the lyrics) for fifteen more Broadway musicals, including the long-running hits **Carnival**, **Hello Dolly!**, **I Love My Wife**, **Barnum**, and **42nd Street**. Stewart often complained that bookwriters were not accorded the same kind of appreciation that composers and lyricists received: "I don't understand why any bright person would want to be a book writer," he told the *New York Times* in 1979. "You're scorned by critics, you get no recognition from the public, and the money isn't that good either. I feel that I've written two classic American musicals, *Bye Bye Birdie* and *Hello Dolly!*, but both of those books got terrible reviews."[8] Apparently, he had forgotten the rave reviews he received for *Birdie*, including from the *Daily News*, which stated that Stewart and director Gower Champion had "jam packed" the show "with humor and light-hearted imagination." His colleague, Wakefield Poole, described Stewart as "the first completely out-of-the-closet writer I knew in the theater, which was unheard of at that time. I guess if everyone had Michael's success, there would be more courageous people."[9]

Broadway Dance #10: The Rise of the Director-Choreographer (J, Q)

Bye Bye Birdie, along with two musicals that came just before it—*West Side Story* and *Gypsy* (both directed and choreographed by Jerome Robbins)— heralded another new phenomenon on Broadway: the rise of the **director-choreographer**. These productions demonstrated that when the tasks and responsibilities of these two related but disparate jobs are combined into the job description of one uniquely talented and gifted individual it can vastly elevate the overall effect and impact of a show. The best director-choreographers infuse a show with a level of cohesion and a unity of vision that, up to this point, was unprecedented. Even though this was "his first crack as staging a book musical,"[10] Gower Champion's vibrant, seamless, and inventive direction and choreography of *Bye Bye Birdie* immediately established him as one of those rare gifted individuals.

Gower Champion was born in Illinois but grew up in Los Angeles and attended Hollywood's Fairfax High School (known as the 'high school of the stars' because so many movie stars had graduated from there). During his junior year, Gower won an amateur dance contest with his first dance partner, Gene Tyler, and soon they were dancing professionally in Los Angeles area nightclubs. They made their Broadway debuts in 1939 as featured performers in the revue *Streets of Paris*, starring Brazilian singer Carmen Miranda. During World War II, Champion served in the Coast Guard and toured in a military musical show, *Tars and Bars*. He returned to show business in the star-studded 1946 film *Till the Clouds Roll By* (based on the life and music of Jerome Kern) and then formed a new dance team with Marjory Belcher (the daughter of his teacher, legendary Hollywood dance instructor, Earnest Belcher). Marge and Gower married in 1947. Champion made his stage directing debut with the 1948 hit revue **Lend an Ear**, for which he received his first Tony Award. However, despite this early Broadway success, Marge and Gower Champion then spent most of the 1950s back in Hollywood, appearing in a string of MGM movie musicals, including the 1951 version of *Show Boat*. They also became popular guest stars on early television variety shows, and even had a series of their own, *The Marge and Gower Champion Show*, in 1957. Gower then came back to Broadway to direct and choreograph **Bye Bye Birdie**, which brought him his second and third Tony Awards. He followed that success with **Carnival** and then the megahit **Hello Dolly!**, which earned him another pair of Tonys. Although they weren't blockbusters on the level of *Dolly*, his next two Broadway musicals brought him honors as well. In 1966, he was Tony-nominated for his direction of **I Do! I Do!**, and then won two more Tony Awards for his staging of **The Happy Time** in 1968. Throughout all of this, **Marge Champion** was his uncredited and unacknowledged collaborator, working closely with Gower on the choreography for all of those musicals.

The next decade was challenging for Gower, with several flops and missteps in both his professional and personal life. Then, in 1979, he learned that he had a very rare form of blood cancer. Against his doctors' advice, he signed on to direct and choreograph **42nd Street**, a new stage adaptation of the classic 1933 film musical. That show's Broadway opening night has become legendary.[11] During the exuberant curtain call that followed the triumphant opening night performance, producer David Merrick unexpectedly appeared on the stage and tried to quiet the audience's tumultuous applause. Finally, the crowd calmed down, and Merrick grimly informed the audience, cast, opening night press, and television cameras that Gower Champion had died earlier that day. Pandemonium broke out as cast members began to scream and cry. The audience was stunned and the curtain was quickly brought down. Merrick had actually known about Champion's death all day but had withheld the information from everyone until after the opening night performance was completed, which is likely what Gower Champion, the consummate showman, would have wanted him to do. The high drama of this incredible mix of triumph, tragedy, and showbiz savvy created front-page news around the world and has become an enduring Broadway legend. After receiving two Tony Awards—"Best Musical" and a posthumous eighth Tony to Gower

Champion for "Best Choreography"—*42nd Street* would go on to an eight-year Broadway run of 3,486 performances.

Director-choreographer **Joe Layton** was one of the pioneers of a more intimate, smaller scale, smaller cast, reduced orchestra style of staging Broadway musicals that began to emerge in the 1960s and is standard practice today. He was born Joseph Lichtman in Brooklyn, NY, in 1931. As a child, he studied singing and dancing and performed in school plays, local theater, and at resorts in the Catskill Mountains. At sixteen, he landed his first job on Broadway as a dancer in *Oklahoma!* and met Richard Rodgers, who would become an important ally in his career. This was also where he first worked with Agnes DeMille, whom he would later dance for in *Gentlemen Prefer Blondes*. Layton also danced for Jerome Robbins in both *High Button Shoes* and *Miss Liberty* and for Donald Saddler in *Wonderful Town*. He made his own choreographic Broadway debut in 1959 with his much lauded musical staging for ***Once Upon a Mattress***. This led directly to "the 28-year-old wonder" being hired to choreograph Rodgers and Hammerstein's *The Sound of Music* that same season.[12] Two years later, in 1962, Layton made his debut as a director-choreographer with ***No Strings***, the first musical Richard Rodgers wrote after the death of Hammerstein. As part of his acclaimed direction of this show, Layton employed "movie techniques, including crossfades and dissolves"[13] as well as a myriad of other notable innovations:

> The staging, under imaginative Joe Layton, who is also the choreographer, attempts and brings off effects the musical theater had never seen before. The musicians are not in the pit but on the stage, sometimes seen, most of the time not ... Players move sets and props themselves in many instances. Layton's employment of his dancing chorus lays as much stress on groupings and atmospheric movement as it does on dancing. Not a second is lost in moving from scene to scene ... the effects are spectacularly different and beautiful.[14]

Layton won his first Tony Award for his choreography for this show.

All in all, between 1959 and 1990, Layton directed and/or choreographed twenty-four Broadway musicals, including the significant hits ***George M!*** (1968), for which he received a second Tony for choreography, and ***Barnun*** (1980), for which he was praised for the "non-stop,"[15] "eye-popping opulence" of his "whiz-bang direction. Layton's staging is simply dazzling, both manic and precise."[16] He also had tremendous success directing and staging television, film, and concert appearances for stars such as Bette Midler, Barbara Streisand, Diana Ross, and Cher.

Joe Layton was married to dancer Evelynn Russell and fathered a son with her while at the same time being involved in various same-sex relationships, including with his frequent collaborator—the choreographer and filmmaker Wakefield Poole.[17]

"A World Outside of Yonkers"—Jerry Herman and *Hello, Dolly!* (I, J, Q, B, W)

Without a doubt, the highest point of both Champion and Stewart's careers was ***Hello, Dolly!*** The history behind this landmark musical is long, involved, and very Queer. In 1838, playwright John Oxenford wrote a short farce called *A Day Well Spent*, which was adapted into a full-length play by Austrian playwright Johann Nestroy in 1842. Then, in 1938, Gay playwright Thornton Wilder Americanized Nestroy's version and titled it *The Merchant of Yonkers*, but it was a dismal failure and ran for only thirty-nine performances on Broadway. Seventeen years later, Wilder extensively rewrote his play, transforming the rather minor character of Dolly Gallagher Levi into the leading role. Retitled *The Matchmaker*, this new version became a smashing success on Broadway in 1954, as well as a popular film four years later. David Merrick had produced the play, and it was his idea to turn it into a musical.

The original production of *Hello Dolly!* (1964) was a triumphant "pot wallowing hit,"[18] that received unanimous rave reviews and an unprecedented demand for tickets. Howard Taubman, writing for the *New York Times*, called it "A musical shot through with enchantment" and noted its "qualities of freshness and imagination that are rare in the run of our machine-made musicals."[19] In the *Herald Tribune*, Walter Kerr described the show as "[a] musical comedy dream" and "a marvelous chunk of entertainment, a bizarre and brilliantly colorful tumble of eccentrics, and its musical numbers are solid gold brass."[20] "The only problem now is how to get tickets. At last report, the line starts in Yonkers."[21] And just four months after its opening, *Hello, Dolly!* became the first show to match *South Pacific*'s unprecedented ten Tony Awards, a record it would hold for thirty-seven years until *The Producers* won twelve in 2001. Gower Champion's "dazzling choreography and overall staging"[22] played a tremendous part in securing that success. As critic John Chapman noted, "*Hello, Dolly!* is at its ebullient best when director Gower Champion turns loose the finest Broadway dancers in the most exciting numbers I have seen since Jerome Robbins staged *West Side Story* . . . Merrick was very smart in picking Champion to stage *Hello, Dolly!* It is really Champion's show."[23] Absolutely every other critic was in fervent agreement: "Champion is practically a genius when it comes to staging a musical . . . and he has done wonders with this one . . . Even when there are no dance numbers, and there are some dandies, he has a way of seeming to make both the actors and the scenery move in a smooth manner akin to choreography."[24] "Seldom has a corps of dancers brought so much style and excitement to a production . . . and he [Champion] has certainly created a whole new career for Carol Channing."[25]

The role of Dolly Levi had been written expressly for Ethel Merman, but after *Gypsy* she decided to focus on film and television projects rather than commit to another long-running Broadway production. Dolly was then offered to Mary Martin, who also turned it down. Eventually, the part went to **Carol Channing**, the star of the 1949 hit musical *Gentlemen Prefer Blondes*, who "in sassiest stellar form"[26] was "glorious"[27] and "a complete delight"[28] in the role and "the most outgoing woman on the musical stage today—big and warm, all eyes and smiles, in love with everybody in the theater and possessing a unique voice ranging somewhat upward from basso profundo."[29] Champion launched Channing into major stardom with his staging of what has become one of Broadway's most iconic musical sequences: "a pair of curtains part and Miss Channing comes down a long stairway, red on red, to begin the evening's title song. It is the beginning of musical madness that is likely to linger until your ears wear out." "Resplendent in scarlet gown embroidered with jewels and a feathered headdress and looking like a gorgeous, animated kewpie doll, she sings the rousing title song with earthy zest and leads a male chorus of waiters and chefs in a joyous promenade around the walk that circles the pit."[30] "It is difficult to describe the emotion that [Channing] produces. Last night the audience tore up the seats ... It is a whale of a tribute to the personal appeal of Miss Channing and the magical inventiveness of Mr. Champion's staging."[31] For the next fifty years, Carol Channing would remain one of Broadway's most distinctive and indelible stars.

When Channing left the show, David Merrick adopted the unusual tactic of engaging even bigger stars to replace her—and because this was a role written for a middle-aged woman, there was a parade of major movie stars from the 1930s and '40s who were eager to follow her down that staircase, including Ginger Rogers, Martha Ray, Betty Grable, Pearl Bailey (with an all-Black cast), stand-up comedian Phyllis Diller, and in the touring productions: Mary Martin, Eve Arden, Yvonne De Carlo, and Dorothy Lamour—all of which proved that the biggest star of all was the show itself. Finally, in 1970, Merrick persuaded Ethel Merman to come out of semi-retirement to be the seventh and final Dolly Levi of the show's original run and then to extend her contract so that the show could break *My Fair Lady*'s record as the longest-running musical in Broadway history.

In 2002, the original cast recording of *Hello, Dolly!* was inducted into the Grammy Hall of Fame, in part because of its remarkable success in challenging the mid-60s pop music dominance of the "Fab Four." In early June of 1964, that record rose to No. 1 on the *Billboard* album chart but was bumped down to No. 2 the following week by jazz great Louis Armstrong's new album, which was also titled *Hello, Dolly!* and featured Armstrong's No. 1 hit single of the show's title song.[32] The OCR of *Funny Girl* held the No. 3 spot, followed by *The Beatles' Second Album* and *Meet the Beatles* in spots 4 and 5.

Hello, Dolly! has become one of the most enduring musical theater hits, with four Broadway revivals, dozens of international productions, and a miscast overblown 1969 film. Most recently, the 2017 Tony Award-winning Broadway revival of *Hello, Dolly!*, starring Bette Midler, amassed the biggest advance ticket sales in Broadway history, and in 2024, Imelda Staunton led an acclaimed revival at the London Palladium.

"Tune The Grand Up"—Jerry Herman (J, Q)

The composer and lyricist of *Hello, Dolly!* was **Jerry Herman**. He was born in New York in 1931 and raised in New Jersey. His middle-class Jewish parents loved music, art, and theater, and the family frequently attended Broadway musicals. Seeing Ethel Merman in *Annie Get Your Gun* was a seminal event for Herman, and years later he would write the score of *Hello, Dolly!* with Merman's distinctive voice in his head. Young Jerry discovered at an early age that he could instinctively play piano by ear. His parents both worked in Jewish summer camps and Catskill mountain resort hotels, much like the hotel in the movie *Dirty Dancing*. Eventually, they took over the management of one of those camps. Herman spent all of his summers there from age six to twenty-three, and it was there that he first became heavily involved in putting on theatrical productions. Later, he studied theater at the University of Miami, where he wrote, produced, and directed his first musical.

After graduation, Herman moved to New York and produced several revues made up of his original songs, each more successful than the one before it. His work began to be noticed by Broadway producers, one of whom engaged Herman to create the score for his first Broadway musical, ***Milk and Honey*** (1961). The show's story takes place in the year it was produced and revolves around a tour group of lonely American widows hoping to find husbands while on a trip to Israel—and set against that country's struggles to establish itself as a brand new, independent nation. The star of the show was the great Yiddish Theater performer Molly Picon, who played sort of a matchmaking precursor to both Dolly Levi and *Fiddler on the Roof*'s Yente (whom Picon would later play in the film version of that show). Though not technically a hit, *Milk and Honey* was well received and ran for more than 500 performances, with Herman earning rave reviews and a Tony nomination. This brought him to the attention of David Merrick, who, as Herman would later recall, "summoned" him to his office and presented him with Michael Stewart's early draft of *The Matchmaker* musical and asked him to write a few songs as an audition to prove that he was up to the task of creating an entire score. As Herman later wrote, Merrick only gave him the weekend to accomplish the task:

> I produced those four songs in two days of the wildest, most intensive writing binge of my life. I was like a crazed person, pacing up and down in the middle of the night, scribbling down lyrics and popping candy in my mouth. But I was young, I was full of energy, and I wanted this happy, brightly colored American musical score more than anything in the world.[33]

Herman arrived at Merrick's office with completed versions of four songs: "Call On Dolly," "I Put My Hand In," "Dancing," and "Put On Your Sunday Clothes"—"exactly as it is heard in the show." He had enlisted a singer to help him perform the songs. "It was like a scene from a movie. Merrick, who is supposed to be pretty dour, stood up with a big smile after we finished singing and said, 'Kid, the show is yours.'"

The unprecedented success of *Hello, Dolly!* was quickly followed two years later by the triumph of *Mame*, and together they firmly established Jerry Herman as an example of that rare Broadway breed: the composer/lyricist. Like Irving Berlin, Cole Porter, Noel Coward, and Frank Loessor, Herman could create "rich melodies with powerful lyrics that stopped shows, dazzled critics, kept audiences returning for more, and paved Broadway with gold for producers and performers."[34]

Only two months after *Dolly*'s opening night, another star-making musical arrived on Broadway: **Funny Girl**. With a book by screenwriter Isobel Lennart, music by Jule Styne, and lyrics by Bob Merrill, *Funny Girl* was a bio-musical dramatizing the early life and career of Silver Age superstar Fanny Brice. The show encountered big problems during its pre-Broadway out-of-town tryout engagements and postponed its Broadway opening several times until Jerome Robbins could be persuaded to come on board and "supervise" the production. By this time, Robbins had inherited Mr. Abbott's mantle as the most sought-after "show doctor," and by opening night in New York, Robbins had whipped *Funny Girl* into a crowd-pleasing hit, mostly by making sure **Barbara Streisand**, the show's vibrant and idiosyncratic new star, was "at stage center almost all the time."[35]

"She's The One!"—The Big Transgressive Lady Shows (I, J, Q, W)

Hello, Dolly! and *Funny Girl* solidified another hallmark of the Golden Age: musicals that theater historian Ethan Mordden has dubbed "Big Lady Shows." This trend was probably first established by musicals that were created to showcase Ethel Merman, especially *Gypsy*, and the retooled 1966 revival of *Annie Get Your Gun*. Building on Mordden's idea, I call these shows the "Big Transgressive Lady Shows." These are musicals that center on dynamic, larger-than-life female protagonists who entirely dominate their shows in every way. Most importantly, they are characters who refuse to do what mid-century American society thinks women should do—and fascinatingly, mid-century American audiences worshiped and adored them! (For more on this, see Chapter 14.) Another musical of this type is the 1966 musical **Mame**, Jerry Herman's smash hit follow-up to *Hello, Dolly!*, with a book by **Jerome Lawrence** and **Robert E. Lee**, the prolific and very successful gay/straight writing team of many hit plays and musicals. *Mame* was based on their play, *Auntie Mame*, which had itself been adapted from the comic novel of the same name by Queer novelist Patrick Dennis. As the irrepressible center of a bestselling book, hit Broadway play, hit movie, and hit Broadway musical, the character of Mame Dennis became one of the signature Gay icons of Queer men who came of age in the 1950s and '60s.[36]

Broadway Goes Avant-Garde (J, Q, W)

The Fantasticks was not the only show of this period to fold experimental theater techniques into mainstream musical theater. During the 1960s, a number of Broadway musicals began incorporating writing, staging, and design elements inspired by the work of avant-garde European theatermakers such as Bertolt Brecht, Jerzy Grotowski, Antonin Artaud, Joan Littlewood, Peter Brook, and others, including four musicals that originated in London and were imported to Broadway by producer David Merrick. The first was the 1960 musical ***Irma La Douce***, which, indeed, was directed by Peter Brook himself and choreographed by Onna White.[37] Next was the crowd-pleasing smash hit, ***Oliver!*** (1962), with book, music, and lyrics by Jewish and Queer British songwriter **Lionel Bart**. In addition to Bart's hit-filled score, *Oliver!* featured a groundbreaking revolving "unit set" (by designer Sean Kenny) and "epic staging" (by Peter Coe) that would provide major inspiration for the direction and scenic design of dozens of later musicals—especially Trevor Nunn and John Caird's original staging of *Les Misérables*.

That same year, British songwriters Leslie Bricusse and Anthony Newley collaborated on the book and score for ***Stop the World—I Want to Get Off*** (1962) and were back on Broadway three years later with ***The Roar of the Greasepaint—The Smell of the Crowd*** (1965)—two very unconventional musicals that featured Newley as both star and director. Both shows were high-concept allegories so specific to their moment in time that it's nearly impossible to revive them today (or frankly even to understand what they were trying to say). Despite their extreme quirkiness, both shows became hits, and both produced multiple chart-topping songs, including the still much recorded and performed, "Feelin' Good." In between, in 1964, visionary British director **Joan Littlewood**, "London's formidable distaff specialist at daring stagecraft,"[38] brought her anti-war documentary musical collage, ***Oh, What A Lovely War!***, to Broadway. This innovative London hit, which Littlewood had created with her acclaimed Theatre Workshop company, was what we would classify as a "devised" theater piece today, and with it, she became the first woman ever to be nominated for a Tony Award for "Best Director of a Musical." The pioneering use of neo-vaudeville, mime, circus, and other physical theater techniques in all of these productions anticipated and influenced later Modern Era musicals such as *Hair*, *Godspell*, and *Pippin*.

Most significant was the American-made 1966 "Best Musical" Tony Award-winner, ***Man of La Mancha***—another blockbuster that became a truly international sensation. *La Mancha*'s revolutionary design, staging, and overall meta-theatrical concept would not seem all that groundbreaking to audiences today—but this is only because its many notable innovations have been so thoroughly absorbed into the fabric of contemporary musical theater writing and staging.

"Miracle of Miracles": *Fiddler on the Roof* (♩, ♪)

The final decade of the Golden Age was jam-packed with truly great musicals, including one of the most perfectly realized of all time: the 1964 mega-hit, **Fiddler on the Roof**. It was created by **Jerry Bock** (music), **Sheldon Harnick** (lyrics), and **Joseph Stein** (book), and directed and choreographed by Jerome Robbins—all of whom were the children or grandchildren of Eastern European Jewish immigrants. Initially, the authors struggled to find a producer willing to take a chance on this show. The general consensus was that its story of an orthodox Jewish milkman struggling to eke out a life in a village in the Pale of Settlement in 1905 would have appeal only to Jewish theatergoers. But from *Fiddler*'s first performance, it was clear that its story, characters, and themes resonated with all kinds of audiences. The show immediately became a sold-out-for-months blockbuster success and swept the Tony Awards with wins for score, book, direction, choreography, costumes, leading actor and actress, and producer, crowned by "Best Musical." It would go on to break all box office records, racking up 3,242 performances and eventually overtaking *Hello, Dolly!* as the longest-running show in Broadway history.[39] Over the following decade, *Fiddler* was presented in two dozen countries around the world, including Australia, Finland, France, Germany, Holland, Mexico, Yugoslavia, and South Africa, and its themes of generational conflict and the challenges of maintaining traditions in a modern world proved to be universal.[40] The show has been especially popular in Japan, where since its debut there in 1967, it has been produced hundreds of times. Bookwriter Joseph Stein loved to tell the story of a Japanese producer who was baffled at how Americans could understand a story that was "so Japanese."[41] A 2015 article in *The New Yorker* described the show's cultural impact:

> Anticipating—and helping to sow—the "roots movement" that burgeoned in the following decade, *Fiddler* helped audiences respond to the turbulent change gathering force in the early 1960s. The show's rebellious daughters carried a flame of women's liberation; its decrial of bigotry reverberated with the civil-rights movement; its offering of a plucky Ashkenazi origin story correlated with a shift toward a national self-definition of the United States as a country of immigrants.[42]

To date, *Fiddler* has received five Broadway revivals plus a hit off-Broadway revival performed in Yiddish, as well as countless professional and amateur productions worldwide.

In addition to its universal themes, much of this show's success must be credited to its brilliant craft and construction. As *New York Times* critic Howard Taubman noted,

"Compounded of the familiar materials of the musical theater—popular song, vivid dance movement, comedy, and emotion—it combines and transcends them to arrive at an integrated achievement of uncommon quality."[43] Ironically, if *Fiddler on the Roof* is the prime example of a perfectly crafted, fully realized, Golden Age-style story-driven musical, in at least one significant way it sowed the seeds of a rebellion that over the following decade would launch the Broadway musical in an entirely different direction (see page 270).

ACT IV
THE MODERN ERA

Fig. 32: The original London cast of *Hair* (1968), book and lyrics by Gerome Ragni and James Rado, musical by Galt MacDermit, directed by Tom O'Horgan, choreographed by Julie Arenal. Central Press / Stringer.

CHAPTER 11
"LET THE SUNSHINE IN"—THE MODERN ERA OF BROADWAY, PART 1: THE MULTIPLE REVOLUTIONS OF THE 1970S (J, Q, B, W)

Time Travel Destination #2: April 1968

Another of my top time travel fantasy destinations would be the week of April 22, 1968, because it would provide an exceptional opportunity to witness a key turning point in Broadway history. I would start that week by seeing the two great Jerry Herman musicals back-to-back: *Mame*, choreographed by Onna White and now starring Janis Page on Monday night, and *Hello, Dolly!*, directed and choreographed by Gower Champion and starring Pearl Bailey and Cab Callaway on Tuesday. On Wednesday, I'd catch most of the original cast of *Cabaret*, directed by Harold Prince and choreographed by Ron Field, at the matinee (there will be more on that show and its creative team soon), and that night, I'd see *Cabaret*'s already departed Tony-winning star Joel Grey play "The Father of the Musical Comedy" in the bio-musical *George M!*, directed and choreographed by Joe Layton. On Friday, I'd attend Jones and Schmidt's big Broadway hit, *I Do! I Do!*, also staged by Champion and now starring Gordon McCrea and Carol Lawrence. Then on Saturday, I'd start with the matinee of *Man of La Mancha* and catch *Fiddler on the Roof* at the evening performance. Broadway shows didn't play on Sundays back then, but off-Broadway shows did, so that day, I would venture down to the Village to see the matinee of Jones and Schmidt's original off-Broadway hit, *The Fantasticks*, now in its eighth year. Then, to top this all off, I would stick around 1968 for one more day to attend the Broadway opening night of the "American tribal love-rock musical," **Hair**. In just eight days, I would experience eight of the prime examples and crowning achievements of the Golden Age m*usical play* and *musical comedy* at its peak and then witness the shocking and abrupt jump cut to what I call the Modern Era of the Broadway musical.

The dawn of the Modern Era coincided with a period of disruption and cultural revolution in American society that included vibrant social justice and liberation movements that (though not using these current terms) advocated for BIPOC rights, racial equity, women's rights, LGBTQ rights, economic realignment and more—all of which were reflected in, and had a significant impact on, the Broadway musicals of the era. This chapter will explore five concurrent and interrelated Broadway "rebellions" that rethought, reshaped, remade, and disrupted the form, content, and structure of the Broadway musical during the tumultuous decade of the 1970s. They include the rise of the (pop)Rock Musical; the return of the Black Musical, the Nostalgia Craze phenomenon;

Broadway Nation

the advent of the Concept Musical; and the emergence of Queer themes and characters on Broadway.

Hair and the Rise of the (pop)Rock Musical (J, Q)

As described by the magazine *The Advocate*:

> *Hair* is the outrageous, groundbreaking, influential, and very bisexual rock musical that altered the social and sexual landscape in America, changed the modern musical, and helped turn public opinion against the Vietnam War. It was the first rock musical on Broadway, the first Broadway show to feature full nudity, and the first to feature a same-sex kiss.[1]

As this description might indicate, *Hair* created a major disruption to the system of Broadway. At first glance, it seemed to be a near-total break from, and even a betrayal of, the traditions, conventions, and craft standards of the Broadway musical. It certainly felt that way to many of the established creators of Broadway at the time—Jule Styne, Stephen Sondheim, Jerome Robbins, Agnes DeMille, Comden and Green, and Lerner and Loewe—and was presumably even more disturbing to those Silver Age artists who were still active, such as Irving Berlin, Dorothy Fields, and Richard Rodgers. It was also a shock to established Broadway producers because this show, and its whole new team of young creators, had mainly come from outside the Broadway system. In hindsight, however, I would argue that *Hair* and the so-called "Rock Musicals" that followed it, along with the other disruptive new forms of musical theater this chapter will explore, were all part of the ongoing evolution of an art form that has always closely reflected what was going on in American culture.

Hair's co-creators, **James Rado** and **Gerome Ragni**, were both successful mainstream actors who had appeared on Broadway. They met in 1964 when they performed together in an off-Broadway play. Rado loved acting but had always wanted to create a musical. "That's where my real heart lay creatively," he said, "that was the ultimate to me!"[2] In addition to mainstream theater, Ragni had been involved with two seminal experimental theater companies, The Living Theatre and The Open Theater, and in 1966 he played a leading role in the latter's anti-war play *Viet Rock*. This inspired Ragni and Rado to begin work on a musical about hippie culture. As research, they started hanging out with a group of young people in New York's East Village who, in the lingo of the era, "were turning on, tuning in, and dropping out" by experimenting with psychedelic drugs, rejecting consumerist values, opposing the Vietnam War, and dodging the draft. As Rado recalled, "There was so much excitement in the streets and the parks and the hippie areas, and we thought if we could transmit this excitement to the stage, it would be wonderful ... We hung out with them and went to their Be-Ins and let our hair grow."[3] So, they moved into a small apartment together in Hoboken, NJ, and began writing *Hair* in every spare moment—either in longhand or on a typewriter they'd borrowed from their landlord. "We were great friends," Rado remembered. "It was a passionate kind of relationship that we directed into creativity, into writing, into creating this piece. We put the drama between us on stage."[4] An agent then introduced Rado and Ragni to Canadian composer **Galt McDermot**, who joined them to write the show's score. MacDermot's personal life was in great contrast to that of his co-creators: he had short hair, a wife and four children, and lived on suburban Staten Island. "I never even heard of a hippie when I met Rado and Ragni," he would later recall. For the most part, they worked independently: Rado and Ragni would write lyrics and mail them to MacDermot, who completed the first version of the score in just three weeks. That first batch of songs included "Hair," "I Got Life," "Ain't Got No," and "Where Do I Go?," all of which would become highlights of the eventual Broadway production.

To a great extent, *Hair* is a thematic revue—the theme being "hippie culture"—made up of a series of songs and sketches, each of which take on a topic of urgent concern to the "Tribe" of young people who were the characters in the show. These include opposition to the Vietnam War and the military draft, sexual liberation, civil rights, the Black Power movement, the women's liberation movement, concern for the environment, the legalization of recreational drugs, and, in general, critique and rejection of the values of the establishment. You could say that each segment of *Hair* is ripped from the headlines of its day, much as the songs and sketches in Irving Berlin's revue *As Thousands Cheer* had been thirty years earlier. In other ways, *Hair* echoes the Rodgers and Hammerstein template. It even has a sort of dream ballet: late in the second act, Claude experiences a bad drug trip and hallucinates a series of whacked-out scenes in which he finds himself interacting with George Washington, Sitting Bull, and other figures from American history, including a minstrel show-inspired sequence that includes a Black woman playing Abraham Lincoln.

Hair includes frequent critiques like this of the era's racial inequity. Perhaps the most pointed and provocative is the song "Colored Spade," in which the character, Hud, a militant Black activist, proudly proclaims himself to be every racial slur and negative stereotype ever used to demean Black people. The intention was to commandeer and co-opt these slurs much in the way that the word "queer" was later rebranded by LGBT activists. Today, however, I suspect this song makes many people very uncomfortable. But it was the show-stopping song sequence "Black Boys/White Boys" that made people uncomfortable back in 1968, with its depiction of sassy young Black and white women singing joyfully and lustfully about their interracial sexual desires.

At the center of *Hair*'s startlingly pansexual tribe is a bisexual love triangle between the leading characters of Berger, Sheila, and Claude, which intentionally mirrored the sexual revolution and social changes that were taking place at this time. As Rado explained it, "To have intimations of these kinds of other relationships on stage, rather than just boy meets girl, that was just very organic to what we were writing about: the hippie scene. It was truly about men loving each other as opposed to fighting each other."[5]

Hair was first produced downtown as the inaugural production of Joseph Papp's Public Theater, and then, based on that success, it moved to a discotheque called The

Cheetah. This is when experimental Queer director **Tom O'Horgan** was brought on board to restage the show, and over the following three months, *Hair* was completely overhauled for its Broadway opening. With years of experience in the downtown avant-garde theater scene, O'Horgan had been the authors' first choice to direct the Public Theater production, but he had been unavailable at the time. Under his guidance the creative team now created thirteen new songs, including "Let the Sun Shine In," which was added to make the ending of the show more uplifting. In addition, Rado and Ragni now took over the central roles of Claude and Berger, the characters they had based on themselves, and which constitute the central love relationship in the musical. However, it wasn't until an interview in 2008 that Rado, for the first time, publicly described himself as "omnisexual" and spoke openly of being Ragni's lover: "It was a deep, lifelong friendship and a love of my life," and he added that *Hair* had "made a point of the love between two men—not only two men . . . we also have other things happening. Girls with girls, boys with boys as part of the tribal behavior and . . . with all people in the tribe there was affection and physicality. And that was something very, very new: that kind of behavior on a stage."[6] As *The Advocate* noted:

> The bisexuality in *Hair* was not a 1960s cover for being homosexual. It was the true expression of Ragni and Rado who, although able to respond to more than one gender [Ragni was married and had a son before meeting Rado], were engaged in a love relationship with each other based on profound friendship and deepened by professional collaboration.[7]

Although their relationship was never publicly acknowledged at the time, it certainly was not hidden from their co-workers, cast mates, or friends.

There was, however, something else that Rado and Ragni did keep secret from nearly everyone—their true ages. During this period of youth rebellion when "Don't trust anyone over thirty" was a much-believed and often repeated mantra, by the time the show opened on Broadway, Rado and Ragni were already in their mid-thirties. To fit in with the young cast surrounding them, many of whom were teenagers, they trimmed nearly a decade off of their actual ages. They certainly did not want it known that they were too old to be drafted to fight in Vietnam—an issue that was central to the plot of *Hair* and of immediate concern for the younger male Tribe members. As Diane Paulus (who directed the 2009 Broadway revival of the show) pointed out, "What was so radical about 'Hair' is, it was reflecting exactly what was happening in real-time in the street, to the point that cast members in the show would get draft notices delivered to the stage door."[8]

Hair became notorious for its famous "nude scene" which, despite being extremely brief and very dimly lit, became the most talked about aspect of the show. The authors believed the nudity was vital to the show's spirit of defiance and its celebration of freedom. The scene was inspired by an actual event they witnessed during a "Be-In" in Central Park, which had attracted a crowd of 10,000 participants. As Rado remembered it:

These two guys in the midst took their clothes off, and everybody was just amazed and astounded, just like an audience. It sent them into this incredible place they had never been before. [Then apparently, a plainclothes policeman rushed out to inform the mounted policemen who were circling the crowd.] Thirty policemen on 30 horses moved in on the crowd to arrest somebody. But the crowd turned to the policemen and started chanting, "We love cops, we love cops." As they were chanting this, the two guys who had taken their clothes off, disappeared into the crowd and put their clothes on. So there was no one arrested. It was the perfect hippie happening, and we felt it had to be in the play.[9]

There is no doubt that the widespread notoriety of the nude scene helped to make *Hair* a box office sensation. From early previews on, the Broadway production played to near capacity and eventually ran for 1,750 performances. Meanwhile, nine other productions of the show were playing simultaneously in other U.S. cities. At its peak, there were nineteen productions of *Hair* running worldwide, including the London production which opened in 1968, its original cast including Richard O'Brien, who would later write the book, music, and lyrics for **The Rocky Horror Show**, and Tim Curry, who would star in that show.

Hair was one of the last Broadway musicals to generate multiple "Top 10" recordings. At one point in 1969, hit singles from *Hair* dominated the top four spots on *Billboard*'s Top 40 chart: "Aquarius / Let The Sunshine In" by The Fifth Dimension was No. 1; "Hair" by The Cowsills was No. 2; "Good Morning Starshine" by Oliver was No. 3; and "Easy To Be Hard" by Three Dog Night claimed the No. 4 spot. And the immense popularity of *Hair*'s music was universal—that same year, "Aquarius / Let the Sunshine In" became the No. 1 song in the world.[10]

The next few years brought a wave of musicals to Broadway that shared the same DNA as *Hair*—some were emulating it, and others were the work of creators simply having the same kind of ideas at the same time. As we have seen, big cultural changes often take place on multiple fronts—even if those innovators have little or no contact with one another. It's all just part of the zeitgeist. And in hindsight, under the surface of many 1960s Golden Age musicals, we can sense a yearning for something new. Broadway was already starting to change, with multiple creators introducing aspects of avant-garde and experimental theater into mainstream musicals. Why did this change take place? I think it was because the Golden Age *musical play* format was so mature, so developed, so powerful—and with musicals such as *My Fair Lady*, *Gypsy*, and *Fiddler on the Roof*, so perfect—that it didn't leave anywhere to go. If you were a young person just out of college in the late 1960s and interested in making your mark in musical theater, you no doubt loved and admired those shows, but you also intuitively understood that there was little room left for you to bring anything to it that hadn't already been done. The same thing was happening in pop music at this time. The Tin-Pan-Alley-Great-American-Songbook era that was established in the 1890s and had evolved and continued into the 1960s had taken that form of music about as far as it could go, as well. Then, if you add a gigantic new generation of young people who, like all generations, want to, and need to, rebel against their parents and the previous generation—they will want to create something that is the opposite of what came before. They will seek out something of their own that will set them apart—even if that means borrowing elements from their grandparents' or great-grandparents' pop culture—which is exactly what occurred in this period.

A perfect example of this is this re-embrace of the *revue*. This form, which had its heyday during the Silver Age, now made a major comeback in the Modern Era. *Hair* led the way, but as we will see, this trend was not confined to *(pop)rock musicals*. Later in this chapter, we will explore how the revue form underlies the *concept musical* as well. What made this antique brand of theatrical presentation—only one step removed from vaudeville—so attractive to a new generation of creators and audiences? In part, it was because the revue's fast-paced, disjointed, disconnected, non-linear style seemed to reflect the chaotic pace and feel of modern life more accurately than linear storytelling. But more tellingly, I think they were drawn to the revue format because it was a direct about-face from the "integrated" well-made musicals of the previous era. The *revue* was the polar opposite of the *musical play*. Either deliberately or subconsciously, they were trying to get as far from the Golden Age model as they could get as part of their rebellion against the status quo!

"The Beat Goes On"—More (pop)Rock Musicals

At least a dozen (pop)rock musicals followed in the wake of *Hair*—some even written by Rado and Ragni. However, only three of those shows achieved significant success. *Jesus Christ Superstar* and *Godspell* both opened in 1971, both retold the last seven days of the life of Christ, using contemporary music, modern dress, and of-the-moment "downtown" theater techniques—and both marked the debut of gifted young songwriters who would go on to major Broadway careers and create multiple blockbuster hits.

Jesus Christ Superstar was written by composer **Andrew Lloyd Webber** and lyricist **Tim Rice**. They originally conceived it as a stage musical but, unable to find a producer who would take a chance on what seemed to be an outrageous idea, the first incarnation of *Superstar* was as a "concept album"—a kind of long-form rock/pop album that was very popular at the time. In 1969, both the Beatles' *Sgt. Pepper's Lonely Hearts Club Band* and the Who's *Tommy* had been released and become wildly popular. Those albums, however, were by world-famous rock bands, whereas **Webber and Rice** were entirely unknown at the time. The authors dubbed it a "rock opera," and it was released as a two-record set (86 minutes of music) in the fall of 1970 in the UK. Surprisingly, as Rice told the *New York Times*, "there the album sunk like a stone," but eight days later, when it was released in the U.S., "it took off like a bullet," as it soon did in other countries. Eventually, *Jesus Christ Superstar* became the top-selling album of 1971 in America, even outselling Carol King's massive hit *Tapestry*. Record sales and popularity on that scale made a Broadway production inevitable, and almost exactly one year after the release of the album, a stage version of the show, flamboyantly and outrageously staged by Tom

O'Horgan (the director of *Hair*, who now had three shows running concurrently on Broadway),[11] opened on Broadway and ran for more than 700 performances.

Nearly simultaneously, the musical **Godspell** was being incubated. It started out as bookwriter and director **John-Michael Tebelak**'s[12] master's thesis at Carnegie Mellon University, where it was first performed in 1970. Tebelak's innovative conception and non-traditional staging drew heavily on a variety of improvisational and physical theater techniques, including mime and clowning. After an off-off-Broadway premiere at Café La MaMa, the show's producers engaged twenty-three-year-old Stephen Schwartz, another Carnegie Mellon graduate, to write a new set of songs for the show. "They called me and said, 'Would you look at this show?'" he later recalled. "'We want to move it off-Broadway, but we think it needs a new score.'"

Stephen Schwartz was born in 1948 into a Jewish family in New York City. His mother was a teacher, and his father a businessman, and he grew up in a suburban home on Long Island. He started piano lessons at age seven, and during his high school years, he studied piano and composition at the Juilliard School. Up to this point, Schwartz "was only interested in classical, or show music, and folk music." But then, in 1964, in college, he had a seminal experience: "[M]y roommate had a Supremes record, and the Motown sound changed my life and my writing. I got very interested in that music, and then the Beach Boys, Burt Bacharach, the Beatles, the Mamas & the Papas, Jefferson Airplane, Judy Collins, James Taylor."[13] Schwartz drew heavily on those key musical influences in his breakout score for *Godspell*, which he composed in a wide variety of musical styles, including rock, pop, folk, gospel, and even Silver Age-style showtunes.

Prior to his involvement, the show included pop songs that had been interpolated into it and traditional hymn lyrics that the cast themselves had set to music, including the song "By My Side," which would remain in the show. Of the thirteen songs in *Godspell*, Schwartz wrote new lyrics for only five of them. "A lot of the Godspell score is basically re-setting of Episcopal hymns," Schwartz noted, "which is one of the reasons I was able to write it so quickly because I didn't have to write very many lyrics . . . and lyrics are what, at least for me, take a lot of time—music happens pretty quickly."[14] So, as he described it, Schwartz would take the lyrics of a particular hymn that he and Tebelak had identified for a certain spot in the script and, "I'd put them up on the piano, and I would sit there and look at them—and just start to play—and that's how most of it got written."[15] Those new songs included the score's breakout hit, "Day by Day," which spent fourteen weeks on the *Billboard* Hot 100 chart, peaking at No. 13. That song certainly helped *Godspell* become a long-running off-Broadway sensation, which the *New York Times* hailed as "a fidgety, color-splattered, jubilant and most enjoyable new rock musical."[16] After five years off-Broadway, *Godspell* transferred uptown to Broadway for a total run of 2,651 performances. In spite of their enormous popularity, both *Godspell* and *Superstar* were condemned and picketed by religious groups who considered them to be blasphemous, heretical, and/or antisemitic—and both musicals were criticized for not clearly depicting or including the resurrection of Jesus.[17]

On the personal front, in 1980, thirty-five years prior to the legalization of Gay marriage in the United States, John-Michael Tebelak was involved in a legal dispute with a former partner that was an early effort to define the rights of cohabiting same-sex couples.[18]

The third (pop)Rock hit was the 1971 Tony Award-winning "Best Musical," ***Two Gentlemen of Verona***—an "up to date and sexy"[19] adaptation of Shakespeare's play of the same name. It had book and lyrics by Gay playwright John Guare[20] who had, according to *New York Times* critic Walter Kerr, "perfectly insinuated himself into the small rift that exists between Shakespeare's sensibility and our own."[21] This show marked the return to Broadway of composer Galt MacDermot who had "tapped so many vitalizing streams" of contemporary music and "seized the opportunity to fill his score with a kaleidoscopic series of styles and rhythms drawn for Latin and Black music . . . Gospel, calypso, soul, sambas, those doo-bee-doo vocal quartets of the fifties, suggestions of a mariachi or a conjunto—one comes tumbling after another in a . . . performance that is bubbling with rhythm."[22] The result, critics felt, was "more subtly shaded and more variegated than his score for Hair."[23] Performed by a sensational young, multi-racial cast who frolicked on designer Ming Cho Lee's influential multi-level, "monkey bar" set, the play's original Renaissance Italy setting was somehow "translated into [1970s] New York's own melting pot of ethnic juices and verbal babble,"[24] and the adaptation brought out the contemporary resonance in Shakespeare's gender-bending comedy.

In an outcome that is still controversial, *Two Gentlemen of Verona* won the 1972 "Best Musical" Tony Award over the Stephen Sondheim/James Goldman/Harold Prince musical *Follies*, a show that everyone I have ever met who saw it describes as one of the peak theatrical events of their life. To add insult to injury for Sondheim fans, at 614 performances, *Two Gents* also ran 100 performances longer than *Follies*. I, unfortunately, did not get to see the original production of *Follies*, but I did see the national tour of *Two Gentlemen of Verona* when it came to Cincinnati when I was in high school—and found it to be entirely delightful and have vivid memories of the dynamically kinetic staging by director Mel Shapiro and choreographer Jean Erdman.

Stephen Schwartz's success and acclaim from *Godspell* led directly to **Pippin** (1972), a musical that he had begun writing in college. Like Galt McDermott had done with *Two Gents*, with this score, Schwartz expanded the scope of a "rock musical" by folding in elements of pop, rock, folk, gospel, Motown, Latin jazz, and Broadway showtunes. Bob Fosse directed and choreographed *Pippin* and, in the process, ended up bringing so much of his own sensibility and distinctive style to the show that it became at least as much his creation as it was that of Schwartz and bookwriter Roger O'Hirson. *Pippin* came at the height of Fosse's career and at the time, many observers considered his masterful direction of the show to be a triumph of dazzling conceptual staging over weak material. Critics have never given Stephen Schwartz much credit, in spite of, or perhaps because, of his enormous success and popularity. Having been dazzled by the original production on more than one occasion, I personally believe that all three of this show's creators did top-notch work and are equally responsible for *Pippin* becoming a long-running smash and an era-defining hit.

In a similar way, the success of *Jesus Christ Superstar* led to Webber and Rice's blockbuster hit, **Evita**. Having first found success as a concept album and then onstage in London the previous year, by the time the show opened on Broadway in 1979, it was already a pre-sold hit. Somehow, despite its title character being a very unsympathetic protagonist, the writers were able to turn the true-life story of Argentina's notorious first lady, Eva Peron, into a thrilling and captivating piece of theater. Webber and Rice created both *Superstar* and *Evita* as "sung-through" musicals, meaning that there is virtually no spoken dialogue, and the entire story is told through lyrics and music. This is the legacy of the "Bench Scene" taken to the ultimate degree, and it established the pattern for nearly all of the British mega-musicals of the 1980s. And like *Pippin* and *Two Gents*, the principal musical language used in *Evita* is pop rather than rock music. Over the following years, both Schwartz and Lloyd Webber would move even further away from rock music and simply do what Broadway composers had always done: fold the pop music of the day into an eclectic mix of musical styles best suited to the particular story and characters they are dramatizing. Rock music, in its purest form, is actually not very well suited for musical theater storytelling. Its musical, rhythmic, and lyric forms are too limited and repetitive. The most successful so-called "rock musicals," from *Hair* to *Rent*, are actually "rock-flavored musicals" that employ a wide variety of pop and traditional styles of music.

"Everybody Rejoice!"—The Return of the Black Musical (J, Q, B, W)

The 1970s also brought a return of the *Black musical* (or at least the predominantly Black musical). For the first time since the 1920s, a succession of musicals opened on Broadway that not only centered on Black characters and performers but, most importantly, were primarily created by Black writers, directors, choreographers, and producers. These musicals paralleled the *(pop)Rock musical* by bringing contemporary rhythm and blues, gospel, and soul music to the Broadway stage. They were, in part, a product of the Civil Rights movement and Black activism of the 1950s and '60s, and it all kicked off in 1970 with **Purlie**. With a book by Black playwright and actor Ossie Davis (adapted from his 1961 play *Purlie Victorious*) and a score by Jewish songwriters Peter Udel and Gary Geld, *Purlie* is a satirical musical comedy about the conflict between a dynamic young Black, "new-fangled preacher man" named Purlie Victorious and Ol' Capt. Cotchipee, a white plantation owner in the Jim Crow South. In his *New York Times* review, critic Clive Barnes declared:

> *Purlie* is victorious ... From the opening number—a smashing crash of gospel singing and great jazz dancing [by Black choreographer Louis Johnson]—to the end, the musical blends a fine mixture of humor and passion. This is by far the most successful and richest of the Black musicals, chiefly I think for the depth of the characterization and the salty wit of the dialogue.[25]

It is difficult to understand exactly which "Black musicals" Barnes was referring to since Black-created musicals had been entirely absent from Broadway for more than forty years (except for a disastrous 1952 revival of *Shuffle Along* that closed after only four performances). One can only assume he was referencing white-created musicals with Black casts and subject matter, such as 1964's *Golden Boy* or 1967's *Hallelujah, Baby!*

Purlie launched nearly all of its leading actors (including Clifton Davis and Sherman Hemsley) into film or television stardom, especially as part of the wave of Black sitcoms like *The Jeffersons* that emerged and flourished during the following decade. And the show's leading lady, Melba Moore (who had been featured in *Hair*), "made the kind of Broadway debut people talk about years afterward,"[26] and scored a hit single with a recording of her show-stopping solo, "I Got Love."

The following season brought a much grittier, provocative, and confrontational look at Black life to Broadway with ***Ain't Supposed to Die a Natural Death*** (1971)—a revue-like, free-form collage of spoken word poetry interwoven with songs and music that ranged from jazz to funk to soul to R&B. With book, music, and lyrics all written by **Melvin Van Peebles**, the show was subtitled "Tunes From Blackness," and the playbill identified its setting simply as, "Place: Here. Time: Now." It was staged by director **Gilbert Moses** on an abstract platform set with a dynamic ensemble cast of eighteen each playing multiple roles that included a junkie, a pimp, a hooker, a drag queen, a death row inmate, and a giant dancing rat. The overall effect was as if the Black cast members from *Hair* now had an entire show to themselves and were determined to make sure that their message of social justice was heard. As described by author Ben West, *Ain't Supposed to Die a Natural Death* was "a violent, unforgiving, and aggressively human portrait of African American life in the modern-day ghetto."[27]

Two years later, the success of *Purlie* directly inspired ***Raisin*** (1973), which was also based on a play by a noted Black playwright, in this case, Lorraine Hansbury's acclaimed *A Raisin in The Sun*. *New York Times* critic Clive Barnes found that the book by **Robert Nemiroff** (Hansberry's former husband) and **Charlotte Zaltzberg** retained "all of Miss Hansbury's finest dramatic encounters, with the dialogue as cutting and honest as ever, intact."[28] And yet, at the same time, the inventive staging by director-choreographer Donald McKayle, and the dynamic, modern, jazz-infused score by Jewish songwriters **Judd Woldin** (music) and **Robert Brittan** (lyrics), somehow managed to excitingly explode Hansbury's "once tightly knit, four-walled, close-quartered play, plucking the walls away, and spilling the action onto the streets . . ."[29]

Donald McKayle had been a friend of Hansbury's since she was a teenager and he was rightly given much of the credit for successfully transforming the play into a musical. He was born in Manhattan in 1930 to parents who had emigrated from Jamaica. As a child, he attended performances by the modern dance pioneers Katherine Dunham, Martha Graham, and Pear Primus, as well as the Broadway musical *Finian's Rainbow*, and those experiences inspired him to become a dancer. In 1947, he received a scholarship to study with the New Dance Group, and by 1950, he was dancing in his first Broadway show, the musical revue *Bless You All*, choreographed by Helen Tamiris. A year later,

McKayle choreographed the first of a series of concert dance works that wove the African American experience into modern dance, including the acclaimed "Rainbow 'Round My Shoulder."[30] On Broadway, he first served as Bob Fosse's Associate Choreographer on the musical *Redhead* and then went on to choreograph seven Broadway musicals, including **Golden Boy** and **Raisin**. With *Raisin*, McKayle became the first Black man to direct and choreograph a Broadway musical and the first to receive Tony Award nominations for both of those roles.

Clive Barnes hailed McKayle's direction, staging, and choreography for *Raisin* as "among the best in years" and compared him to Jerome Robbins, who, like "McKayle comes to the musical as a ranking choreographer, but also like Mr. Robbins, his skill with actors must now be unquestioned. The performances blaze—not just one, or two, but every single one of them."[31] Among those blazing performances were leading actors **Joe Morton**, **Ernestine Jackson**, **Debbie Allen**, and especially **Virginia Capers**, who received the Tony Award for "Best Actress in a Musical" for her searing performance as the matriarch of the family. *Raisin*, which Barns said "warms the heart and touches the soul," received the 1974 Tony Award for "Best Musical" and ran for 847 performances.

The year 1975 brought another Black "Best Musical" Tony Award winner: ***The Wiz***. This contemporary retelling of L. Frank Baum's classic children's novel *The Wonderful Wizard of OZ* was subtitled "The Super Soul Musical" and featured a sensational all-Black cast. And except for William F. Brown, the show's white bookwriter, *The Wiz* was the creation of an all-Black creative team as well, all of whom received Tony Awards for their contributions, including composer and lyricist **Charlie Smalls**[32] and director **Geoffrey Holder** (who also designed the show's wildly imaginative Tony Award-winning costumes). In the view of critic Howard Kissell, what "really gave the show drive" was "**George Faison**'s excellent choreography," Kissell finding the entire show to be "wonderfully alive with movement," including the "dancing tornado" that flew Dorothy from her native Kansas to Oz embodied by "a chorus in black with upturned umbrellas and tortured dance steps; even the yellow brick road is a foursome with oversized yellow shoes constantly in motion."[33] In the view of scholar Douglas R. Jones, Jr., this new cultural framework that *The Wiz* gave to this classic story represented "Black theater-makers grasping on to something that was dear to Americans and saying, 'This is ours too.'"[34] Although *The Wiz* was produced with a "very evident and gorgeous sense of style," it received very mixed reviews, and the show's Black producer, **Ken Harper**, considered closing the show soon after its Broadway opening. But the audience reaction and word of mouth were so positive that instead, he decided to invest in a publicity campaign that included a television commercial featuring footage of the show's stars **Stephanie Mills**, **Hinton Battle**, **Tiger Haynes**, and **Ted Ross** singing "Ease On Down The Road," which started to get ticket sales moving. Meanwhile, a single of that song recorded by the disco group Consumer Rapport became a Top 40 hit, and soon the show was selling out. Harper's gamble certainly paid off, considering that *The Wiz* went on to a four-year Broadway run of 1,672 performances.

Two dynamic women were also central to this resurgence in Black musical theater. In 1972, the "brightly polished, enormously spirited"[35] hit gospel revue ***Don't Bother***

Me I Can't Cope opened on Broadway, and more than one critic described it as "the Black man's *Hair*."[36] Although this was intended positively, it perhaps was not the most accurate summary since the show had been conceived and "staged with style and vigor" by actor, playwright, producer, and director **Vinnette Carroll,** the first Black woman to direct a show on Broadway, as well as the first to be nominated for a Tony Award for "Best Director." In addition, the show's "infectious"[37] score, which the *Daily News* credited with "expressing the Black condition with pride and exuberance,"[38] was by **Micki Grant**, the first Black woman to write the entire score—both music and lyrics—and the book of a Broadway musical. Grant was also one of the show's leading performers. With dynamic dances created by George Faison (in his Broadway choreographic debut), *Don't Bother Me I Can't Cope* ran for an amazing 1,065 performances. Six years later, Vinnette Carroll (whom Micki Grant hailed as "the great mother of us all")[39] was back on Broadway as the director and bookwriter of *Your Arms Too Short to Box With God* (1978). Billed as "a soaring sensation in song," this gospel retelling of the biblical Book of Matthew had music and lyrics by Alex Bradford and additional songs by Micki Grant. After a year-long, 429-performance run on Broadway, *Your Arms Too Short* toured sixty-six American cities, returned to Broadway in 1980, and then came back again in 1982 in a production starring pop stars Patti LaBelle and Al Green.[40]

"Everything Old is New Again"—The (so-called) Nostalgia Craze

Meanwhile, amid this vibrant contemporary wave of pop, rock, gospel, and soul-infused new musicals, the biggest, most unexpected, and most unlikely hit of the 1971-2 Broadway season was a revival of *No, No, Nanette*—the Otto Harbach/Irving Caesar/Vincent Youmans musical comedy that had introduced the mega-hit "Tea For Two" way back in the Silver Age (see page 89). The star of this revival was **Ruby Keeler**, whose most recent appearance on Broadway had been in the 1929 musical *Show Girl*, produced by Ziegfeld and with songs by the Gershwins. Soon after that show closed, Ruby went off to Hollywood, where in the early 1930s she became a major movie star in a series of hit film musicals, many of which featured elaborate kaleidoscopic dance sequences created by director and choreographer **Busby Berkely**, such as *42nd Street*, *Gold Diggers of 1933*, and *Footlight Parade*. By 1970, Keeler had been retired from show business for many years, but a Gay producer named **Harry Rigby** persuaded her to come back to Broadway. With a heavily reworked book, sparkling new musical arrangements and orchestrations, and a striking Art Deco-inspired set and costume design, this reincarnation of *No, No, Nanette* became a smash hit.

Most significantly, *Nanette* fanned a growing mania for anything and everything that recalled the music, style, and glamour of the 1920s, '30s, and '40s. The media dubbed this phenomenon the "Nostalgia Craze," and it quickly spread into every aspect of American life. Suddenly, Tiffany lamps, Mickey Mouse watches, vintage comic books, Kit Kat Klocks, and old Coca-Cola signs became coveted collector's items. Original Art Deco furniture, sculpture, and artworks became high-priced antiques, and much of 1970s–'80s contemporary fashion, architecture, and interior and graphic design began to echo the Art Deco period.

Over the following decades, this phenomenon would continue to have a profound effect on Broadway, which in some respects is still ongoing. Before I review that history, I want to explore the artistic, social, and cultural forces that came together to bring about this unlikely phenomenon. Although later critics have sometimes interpreted the Nostalgia Craze as a reactionary response against the youth rebellion of this period, I believe it can more accurately be seen as yet another way in which young people rebelled against the status quo.

This phenomenon had its origins in the 1960s, when young people began to notice and point out the similarities between their own era and the freewheeling, rebellious spirit of the Jazz Age. Both were eras in which skirts got scandalously shorter, the use of illegal mind-altering substances became popular and widespread, and young people rejected the social conformity and sexual hang-ups of their parents' generation. As a result, most '60s rock bands and singers (both American and British) included vintage vaudeville/ music hall songs in their repertoire, such as Herman's Hermits' No. 1 hit, "I'm Henry The Eighth, I Am" (written in 1910), or The Mamas & the Papas' Top 10 hit, "Dream a Little Dream of Me" (written in 1931), or wrote new songs that sounded like vintage songs, such as The Beatles' "When I'm Sixty Four." They also ransacked thrift stores and their grandparents' attics to find vintage fashions to go along with those songs. The baby boomers' parents, who had actually lived through the Jazz Age, the Depression, and World War II, wanted nothing to do with any of this—at least in the beginning. Simultaneously, old movies from the 1930s and '40s—a majority of which had been unseen for decades—now became a central programming component of local television stations across the U.S. and were rediscovered by hip young film critics and "art house" movie theaters and became wildly popular with college campus film societies. This was especially true of those Busby Berkley musicals because, with their fantastical and surreal musical numbers—which were already extremely "trippy"—students considered them to be the perfect films to view when experimenting with "mind-expanding" drugs.

Meanwhile, and for similar reasons, a new generation of young Gay theater artists, working off- and off-off-Broadway, began mounting their own alternatives to mainstream Broadway and the status quo of the Golden Age *musical play*. This had started back in the late 1950s with small-scale revivals of Sliver Age hits such as *Leave it to Jane* (1959), *Anything Goes* (1962), *Best Foot Forward* (1963), and *The Boys From Syracuse* (1963). There were also new musicals like Rick Besoyan's **Little Mary Sunshine** (1959), which spoofed classic operettas, especially their 1930s film versions starring Jeanette McDonald and Nelson Eddy. In London, Sandy Wilson was on a similar track with his valentine to 1920s-style musical comedies, *The Boy Friend* (1954).[41] This movement had its biggest impact with the campy off-Broadway musical spoof, **Dames At Sea**, which was first staged in 1964 at the Café Cino, founded by Joe Cino, an openly Gay dancer of Scillian heritage. This tiny Greenwich Village coffee house opened in 1958 and soon became a venue for short, experimental, avant-garde plays, many of which dealt with Queer themes and were written by young emerging Gay playwrights such as Doric Wilson, Lanford Wilson, and Tom Eyen. As a result, the cafe became something of a haven for the LGBT community.[42] With book and lyrics by George Haimsohn and Robin Miller and music by Jim Wise, *Dames at Sea, or Golddiggers Afloat* was presented first as a fifteen-minute sketch that was quickly expanded into a fifty-minute one-act version starring eighteen-year-old **Bernadette Peters** in her first major role. She played Ruby, a girl from the Midwest who, on her first day in New York, gets cast in the chorus of a big Broadway musical. Then, when the star of the show becomes incapacitated, Ruby is promoted to the leading role and becomes an overnight star. Performing to packed houses over a three-month period, the show had the most success of any Cino production ever. In 1969, an expanded two-act version of *Dames at Sea* opened off-Broadway,[43] where it would run for 575 performances and make Bernadette Peters a star. Along with its wry and hilarious book and delightful pastiche score, the central comic engine of the show is its conceit of re-creating a lavish and spectacular Busby Berkeley-style movie musical (which typically featured hundreds of dancers) on a postage-stamp-size stage, with makeshift scenery, and a cast of six. In his *New York Times* review, Clive Barnes found "this little gem of a musical" to be "informed by a genuine love and knowledge" for the period, "even when it is mocking it. Today you don't have to have lived through the 30s to have loved them. In fact, it is probably better not to have. For the real lovers of the 30s are the people who have absorbed them through that new time machine called the late-night movie on television."

Over the following decade, *Dames at Sea* was produced to wild acclaim in virtually every city in America, and this played a major role in the spreading of "camp" sensibility, style, and humor from downtown Gay culture into the American mainstream during this period. This is why I believe the media misnamed and misunderstood the "Nostalgia Craze." The young, often Gay, people who initiated and drove the resurrection of these songs, films, shows, and styles were too young to have experienced them in their heyday, so it had nothing to do with nostalgia for their own childhoods or past. It was instead, another form of counter-cultural rebellion. Ironically, by championing these works of art, pop culture, and kitsch that their parents, the previous generation, had rejected and dismissed, they pushed them into mainstream rediscovery and celebration.

It's difficult to convey the tremendous impact the revival of *No, No, Nanette* had on American culture at the time. As one reporter noted, "From the moment the curtain went up, the audience went wild ... laughing, applauding, and shouting their love over the footlights."[44] There was no "Best Revival" Tony category in 1971, but "The New 1925 Musical," as it was billed, received Tony Awards for "Best Choreography," "Best Costume Design," "Best Actress in a Musical" (for Golden Age Broadway star **Helen Gallagher**), and old-time movie star, **Patsy Kelly,** was awarded "Best Featured Actress" for her first appearance on Broadway since 1932. The show inspired front cover articles and multipage spreads in national magazines such as *Life* and *Time*. In addition, after years of being almost entirely absent from Broadway, *Nanette* brought tap dancing back into fashion in a major way.

The "craze" continued in 1973 with a successful revival of the 1919 musical *Irene*, starring 1950s movie star **Debbie Reynolds**, followed by hit revivals of the 1915 Jerome

Kern "Princess Theater" musical ***Very Good Eddie*** (1975); the 1930s style Burlesque revue ***Sugar Babies*** (1979*),* starring classic movie stars **Mickey Rooney** and **Ann Miller**; a stage adaptation of the movie musical ***42nd Street*** (1980); a lightly pop-infused production of Gilbert and Sullivan's *The Pirates of Penzance* starring **Linda Ronstadt** and **Kevin Kline** (1981); a revival of Rodgers and Hart's 1936 musical ***On Your Toes*** (1983); and a revival of the Gershwin musical *Funny Face*, starring **Tommy Tune** and **Twiggy**, that was so heavily revised it was given a new title: ***My One and Only*** (1983).

I would even include the 1980 blockbuster *Annie* in this category. Although it was an entirely new musical, it certainly played on nostalgia for the Depression-era comic strip and radio show that inspired it: *Little Orphan Annie*. And it smartly used that time period to echo the recession of the 1970s that was still lingering when the show opened. A musical based on an old comic strip character seemed like a very bad idea, and the show was viewed with enormous skepticism before it opened. In its original production, however, *Annie* proved to be a wonderfully joyous theatrical experience, whose authors accomplished something that seemed impossible at the time. They created a brand new, entirely captivating, traditional Golden Age-style musical comedy at a time when that form was largely considered to be dead and buried. *Annie*'s three Jewish authors were lyricist **Martin Charnin**, who was the driving force behind the production; composer **Charles Strouse**, whose music for the show was a very savvy mix of 1970s pop and traditional show tunes; and bookwriter **Tom Meehan**, who said he saw Annie as "a metaphorical figure standing for innate decency, courage, and optimism in the face of hard times, pessimism and despair." *Annie* ran for 2,377 performances, and in addition to its motion picture and television adaptations, it has returned to Broadway in two revivals and continues to be one of the most popular and widely produced musicals of the Modern Era.

"Greased Lightnin'"—The 1950s Nostalgia Wing

Almost exactly one year after the opening of the *No, No, Nanette* revival, the musical *Grease* made its New York debut, first off-Broadway and then quickly moving to Broadway.[45] As directed by Queer director **Tom Moore** and choreographed by **Patricia Birch**, the original 1972 version of the show was very different in tone and content from either the movie version or the family-friendly stage productions we see today. In its original conception, *Grease* was aggressively raunchy, irreverent, and rather subversive. Its script and lyrics, by **Jim Jacobs and Warren Casey**, reveled in the vulgarity and rebellious anti-social behavior of its working class, ethnic characters. Quite unexpectedly, *Grease* became wildly popular and ended up running for eight years on Broadway (2,377 performances), eventually even passing *Fiddler on the Roof* to become the longest-running musical of all time.[46] And the enormous success of *Grease* soon inspired a widespread 1950s wing of the Nostalgia Craze (in this case, it was actual nostalgia since every adult had lived through the 1950s) that included both the fairly gritty hit movie *American Graffiti* (1973) and the enormously popular, bubbly-gummy TV show, *Happy Days*, which premiered in 1974.

The watering down of *Grease* began with the 1978 movie adaptation, which transferred the location of Rydell High School from gritty urban Chicago to sunny California and substantially sanitized the original script in the process. However, some of the stage show's overtly sexual content still survives in the lyrics and in Birch's staging of such songs as "Greased Lightnin.'" Next, each of *Grease*'s two Broadway revivals cleaned up and diluted the content even further. Today, the show's licensing company won't even allow professional theater companies to produce the original version of the script—only a censored version of the show in which even the racy lyrics that were retained for the movie have been expurgated of anything deemed inappropriate for children. In its original incarnation, however, *Grease* can be seen as sort of a reaction to *Hair*, in which the older siblings of that show's Tribe, who had been pushed aside by the dominance of the baby boom generation, bring their own earlier counter-cultural rebellion to the forefront shouting, "don't forget us—we led the way!"

"It Don't Mean a Thing if it Ain't Got That Swing"—The Black Nostalgia Craze (Q, B, W)

Simultaneously, a "Black Wing" of the Nostalgia Craze further demonstrated the renewed vitality of the revue format. At its center was a series of wonderfully entertaining and highly theatrical "songbook revues" that paid tribute to the great Black songwriters of the Silver Age. The first was **Bubbling Brown Sugar** (1976), a musical revue conceived by actor and producer **Rosetta LeNoire.** This show had a thin thread of a book by Black playwright and theater historian **Lofton Mitchell** that led its audience on a tour of New York during the Harlem Renaissance, but the show's principal appeal was its dynamic multi-generational cast performing "a dandy succession of songs and dances vibrantly staged by **Billy Wilson**, whose swinging 'choreography and musical staging' are altogether delightful."[47] The show featured both classic and rediscovered songs by Duke Ellington, Eubie Blake, Count Basie, Cab Calloway, and Fats Waller, as well as several new songs tied to the narrative. *Bubbling Brown Sugar* received a Tony nomination for "Best Musical" and ran for 766 performances.

This success led to composers Ellington, Blake, and Waller each being honored with full revues of their own. *Ain't Misbehavin'* (1978) was devised from the songs of composer/performer **Fats Waller**, who had contributed songs to *Hot Chocolates* and other Broadway shows during the 1920s and was a star on radio and film into the early 1940s. Conceived and directed by **Richard Maltby**, with thrilling choreography by **Arthur Faria**, this was one of the most artfully put-together revues of all time. As the *New York Times* declared, it had "a first act that will knock your ears off, and a second that will come back for the rest of you."[48] With its sensational five-member cast—**Andre De Shields, Charlaine Woodard, Armelia McQueen, Ken Page**, and soon-to-be major television star **Nell Carter**—*Ain't' Misbehavin'* became the most popular of all of the Black shows of this period and ran for 1,604 performances.

Broadway Dance #11: Black Choreographers Take Centerstage (B, Q)

In addition to **Donald McKayle** (see page 262), the 1970s brought a host of brilliantly talented Black choreographers to Broadway. **Billy Wilson** was born in 1935 in Philadelphia, where he received his early dance training. At fifteen, he received a scholarship to study classical ballet with Antony Tudor, artistic director of the Philadelphia Guild Ballet School and Company. At nineteen, Wilson made his New York debut, dancing in the 1956 City Center revival of *Carmen Jones* (choreographed by Onna White), and quickly went on to dance in the original Broadway productions of *Bells Are Ringing* (choreographed by Jerome Robbins and Bob Fosse), and *Jamaica* (choreographed by Jack Cole). Wilson then left America to join the London cast of *West Side Story*, which led directly to him being invited to join the National Ballet of Holland[49] as a soloist. He returned to America four years later, to head the dance department at Brandeis University and founded his own company, the Dance Theater of Boston. In 1976, Wilson created the choreography and musical staging for *Bubbling Brown Sugar*, receiving a Tony Award nomination for "Best Choreography," and in 1978, he received a second Tony nomination for *Eubie!*, which he co-choreographed with Henry LeTang. He went on to choreograph *The Little Prince*, *Merlin*, *Dance A Little Closer*, and the 1978 revival of *Stop The World I Want To Get Off*, starring Sammy Davis Jr. Most notably, Wilson directed and choreographed "with sure, suave smoothness" the 1976 all-Black revival of *Guys And Dolls*.

Famed tap dance teacher and choreographer **Henry LeTang** was born in Harlem in 1915, to which both of his parents had emigrated from the Caribbean island of St. Croix. He began studying tap at ten with Harlem dance teacher Ella Gordon and choreographer Clarence "Buddy" Bradley. By the age of sixteen, LeTang was touring as a dancer with vaudeville and Broadway star Sophie Tucker and being mentored by the great rhythm tap dancer John Bubbles.[50] By seventeen, LeTang had opened a dance studio and quickly become known as "the teacher of the stars." His students included Billie Holiday, Betty Hutton, Lena Horne, Chita Rivera, Debbie Allen, and the Hines Brothers: Gregory and Maurice. LeTang had a long but sporadic career on Broadway. He made his debut in 1943 as the assistant to choreographer Felicia Sorel[51] on a musical comedy called *My Dear Public*. The following year he collaborated with choreographer George Balanchine on the musical fantasy *Dream With Music*, where his billing was "Tap Routines Directed By . . ." But after serving as the sole choreographer of a short-lived revival of *Shuffle Along* in 1952, twenty-six years went by before LeTang returned to Broadway. During that period he was very active teaching tap and staging club acts and specialty dances for stars such as Milton Berle, Lola Falana, Flip Wilson, Ben Vereen, Leslie Uggams, and Bette Midler.[52] LeTang returned to Broadway as a crucial part of the success of the Black Nostalgia revues, receiving Tony Award nominations as the co-choreographer of both *Eubie!* (1978) and *Sophisticated Ladies* (1981). In 1989, he finally won the Tony for "Best Choreography" for *Black and Blue*, in tandem with co-choreographers

Cholly Atkins, Frankie Manning, and Fayard Nicholas. During this period, LeTang also staged the tap dance sequences for the films *The Cotton Club* (1984) and *Tap* (1989), and the 2001 television biopic, *Bojangles*.

George Faison choreographed seven Broadway musicals, including *The Wiz*, for which he became the first Black choreographer to win a Tony Award. He was born in 1945 in Washington, D.C., where he began to study dance during high school. Two years after entering Howard University (where he planned to qualify to become a dentist) he attended a performance by the Alvin Ailey American Dance Theater and within a week decided to move to New York and become a professional dancer. He trained at the School of American Ballet and then joined the Ailey company in 1967. Three years later, he left to establish his own company: the George Faison Universal Dance Experience. After dancing in the ensemble of *Purlie*, in 1970, for Black choreographer Louis Johnson, Faison made his Broadway choreographic debut with the long-running hit, *Don't Bother Me I Can't Cope*, and went on to choreograph *Via Galactica*, *1600 Pennsylvania Avenue*, *The Moony Shapiro Songbook*, and a 1983 revival of *Porgy and Bess*. He also created choreography for many musical groups and entertainers, including Aretha Franklin, Earth, Wind and Fire, Dionne Warwick, Patti LaBelle, and Stevie Wonder. With his life partner of fifty years, Tad Schnugg, in 1997, Faison established the Faison Firehouse Theater as a cultural center for the Harlem arts community.[53]

That same year, *Eubie!*—a revue devised from the songs of Eubie Blake—introduced the sensational tap-dancing brothers Gregory and Maurice Hines to Broadway. It was directed by Julianne Boyd and choreographed by Billy Wilson, and many of the songs came from Sissle and Blake's 1921 musical, *Shuffle Along*. Eubie Blake was nearly 100 years old at the time but still very spry and active, and his numerous interviews and TV appearances helped to promote the show to a 439-performance run.

The last in this series was 1981's *Sophisticated Ladies*, which featured the music of jazz and theater composer Duke Ellington. This was the most challenging of these revues to put together because much of Ellington's signature compositions were orchestral or not inherently theatrical. However, with its swinging onstage big band, thrilling choreography by Michael Smuin, Donald McKayle, and Henry Le Tang, and spectacular dancing by a dynamic cast, again led by Gregory Hines, the show ran for nearly two years, playing 767 performances.

"Next!"—Hal Prince and the Concept Musical (♩, ♪)

The key figure in the development of what is called the *concept musical* is Harold Prince. Over the course of his more than sixty-year career, Prince produced and/or directed more than forty Broadway productions and, in the process, won a record twenty-one

Tony Awards—more than any other single individual. What exactly is a *concept musical*? In the beginning, nobody knew. It was something that had to be discovered.

Harold Prince, known to friends and colleagues as Hal, was born in New York City in 1928. His adoptive father was the child of Polish Jewish immigrants, and his mother was from a Jewish Canadian family. At an early age, he was taken to Broadway shows by his theater-loving parents and discovered a lifelong calling. After graduating from the University of Pennsylvania at nineteen, Prince was eager to find a way to break into the theater. His first job was working as an unpaid intern in the office of producer and director George Abbott, where he eventually worked his way up to becoming the Assistant Stage Manager of the hit Broadway musical *Call Me Madam* (written by Irving Berlin and starring Ethel Merman), working under Stage Manager Bobby Griffith. Prince served briefly in the Korean War and then returned to Abbott to stage manage the Broadway production of the Joe Fields, Leonard Bernstein, and Comden and Green musical *Wonderful Town*. Then, with Abbott's blessing, Prince and Griffith formed their own production company and together produced the next three musicals that Abbott wrote and directed, which included two smash hits: *The Pajama Game* and *Damn Yankees*. Emboldened by that success, the team then produced *West Side Story*. Following that triumph, Griffith largely retired and, branching off on his own, Prince then produced a string of classic musicals: *A Funny Thing Happened on the Way to the Forum*, *Fiorello*, and *Fiddler on the Roof*. Amazingly, he was still in his thirties and considered the "boy wonder" of Broadway—but Hal was not satisfied. Producing was great, but his true ambition was to be a director. This turned out to be more difficult than he anticipated, and after one moderate hit and several high-profile flops, he was about to give up. But then, in 1966, Prince achieved a major success as both the producer and director of the groundbreaking musical **Cabaret**, a show considered by many to be the first *concept musical*—although I would give that credit to *Hair*.

The thinking behind the *concept musical* actually began in the Golden Age with Jerome Robbins and *Fiddler on the Roof*. During that show's development, Robbins (its director and choreographer) kept pushing the writers to uncover a unifying theme that would bring focus to the entire production. Lyricist Sheldon Harnick remembered it like this:

Working with Robbins was like working with the world's greatest district attorney, asking us question after question, probing—What is the show about? – and not being satisfied by the glib answers we were giving. We kept saying, "it's about a dairy farmer and his daughters and trying to find husbands for them." He'd say, "No, that's not what gives these stories their power." Ultimately we said, "Oh for God sakes, Jerry, it's about tradition isn't it?" And Jerry said, "That's it! Write that!"[54]

As the show's producer, Hal Prince was involved in this entire process, and he later credited that event with having "unlocked everything that the show needed." Now that *Fiddler*'s unifying theme had been identified, Robbins relentlessly insisted that it guide every aspect of the show. Harnick remembered that Robbins "would say again and again, 'Well, if that's what the show's about, why isn't it in this scene, why isn't it in that scene? Why don't we see it in this character or that character?'"[55] Robbins also made sure that his staging and choreography were always in the service of this central idea as well. One memorable example is in the wedding sequence when Tevye, after being challenged by Perchik, breaks with tradition and publicly dances with his wife. Robbins' relentless pursuit of this unifying idea—or concept—resulted in *Fiddler* becoming one of the most cohesive and effective musicals ever. Hal Prince picked up this technique and ran with it, and over the following decade, he found the ideal collaborators to help him bring the idea to a new level.

First, there was the songwriting team of **Kander and Ebb**—both of them Gay and Jewish. They would go on to write sixteen Broadway musicals, including two mega hits—*Cabaret* and *Chicago*—as well as dozens of classic songs for stage and screen, including "(The Theme From) New York, New York." Composer **John Kander** was born into a Jewish family in Kansas City, Michigan, in 1927. His father worked in his father-in-law's egg and poultry business. His parents loved the arts and regularly took their two sons to local theater and orchestra concerts, and once a year, treated them to a theater trip to New York. After serving in World War II, Kander studied music at Oberlin College and earned a master's degree from Columbia University. He then began music directing and conducting the orchestra at various summer stock theaters which led to him being hired as the rehearsal pianist for the original production of *West Side Story*. He must have impressed Jerome Robbins because he then hired Kander to write the dance arrangements for *Gypsy*.

Lyricist **Fred Ebb** was born one year after Kander, in 1928, to a Jewish family in NYC. Unlike almost every other theater artist profiled in this book, Ebb told an interviewer that there was no music in his house growing up: "Nobody played the radio. Nobody sang. I developed a love of music independently." He first fell in love with theater when he saw Al Jolson perform in the Broadway musical *Hold Onto Your Hats* in 1940. Ebb said, "I loved the fact that it was live—that it was real, even though it was all illusion."[56] After working his way through college, he graduated from NYU with a bachelor's degree in English literature and then a master's in English from Columbia. Both Kander and Ebb found some early success writing with other partners, but after being matched up by their music publisher, they were hired by Hal Prince and George Abbott to write the score for *Flora the Red Menace*, which starred nineteen-year-old Liza Minelli in her Broadway debut. The show was not a success, but it led both to their long association with Minnelli and to Hal Prince asking them to create the score for *Cabaret*.

Concept 1: Life is a Cabaret

Cabaret is another musical with a very Queer history and creative team. In addition to both Kander and Ebb and choreographer **Ron Field**, the show's book was created by Gay writer **Joe Masteroff** and based on works by two other Gay writers—*The Berlin Stories* by Christopher Isherwood and the hit play that was adapted from them, *I am a Camera* by John Van Druten.

Cabaret tells the story of a young American named Cliff who travels to Berlin during the Weimar Republic and becomes entangled in the wild bohemian life of a charismatic second-rate cabaret star named Sally Bowles, as, meanwhile, the Nazi party rises to power around them. *Cabaret* is a landmark show, but because it came so early in the development of the concept musical, it is also a somewhat flawed one. In many ways, it's a transitional piece comprised of two different kinds of musicals that sort of alternate with one another. One is a traditional Golden Age-style *musical play*, with a linear story centered on two couples and using songs that emerge from that story and define the characters. The other is a non-linear *concept musical* consisting of revue-like cabaret songs that break the fourth wall, exist outside the story, but still reflect and comment on it. These cabaret songs are performed primarily by a metaphorical character identified only as the Emcee, and it is that seductive and disturbing character who ties the two disparate musicals together. When seen in performance today, the original version of *Cabaret* can feel very disjointed—again, like two separate musicals that have been grafted together, and not in an entirely satisfying way. But this is only because we are seeing it in hindsight and have experienced the much more tightly conceived *concept musicals* for which *Cabaret* paved the way. The brilliant 1972 Oscar-winning film adaptation of *Cabaret*, directed by Bob Fosse, tried to address this issue by eliminating all of the "book songs" and keeping only the acknowledged songs. Since the release of the film, *Cabaret* has been revived on Broadway four times, and in each of those productions, the director and choreographer, in collaboration with the original authors and rights holders, have reworked, reconceived, and revised the show in an effort to bridge that gap.[57]

At the time of its original production, however, *Cabaret* was both a critically acclaimed and enormously popular success that received eight Tony Awards, including "Best Musical," "Best Score," "Best Direction," and "Best Choreography," and its run of 1,165 performances put Kander and Ebb on the map and established Hal Prince as one of Broadway's most brilliantly innovative and visionary directors.

Concept 2: Life is Company

Following up on this success, Prince teamed up with Stephen Sondheim and George Furth to create the landmark musical **Company**. The idea of the *concept musical* was now beginning to come into much clearer focus, and *Company* is one of the best examples of the form because it is so clearly dramatizing an idea or concept rather than a traditional story. In this case, the concept is *marriage*. Many people have called *Company* "the first plotless musical," but I believe it is more accurate to say that with this show, Prince and the authors revived the revue format of the Silver Age and reinvented it for the Modern Era. Each of the show's scenes and songs explores an aspect of marriage in a manner nearly identical to the comedy sketches and musical numbers in a classic revue. You can imagine the creators saying, "We are going to create a revue that is all about marriage in the modern world, and we'll look at it from every angle and explore the pros and cons, the ups and downs, the funny and the sad, the fantasy and the reality, as well as the place of marriage in modern society." And that, indeed, is what happened, but in a sort of roundabout way.

Company started out as a series of unrelated one-act plays written by George Furth that he gave to Hal Prince to read in hopes that he might want to produce them. Prince found them interesting and noticed that several of them were about marriage—different takes on marriage—and he thought something along the lines of "What if we take those marriage plays, and write a few more also about marriage, and get Steve Sondheim to write some songs about marriage, and then combine all of that into a show." And they could have just done exactly that—created a revue of unconnected songs and sketches all about marriage. But they went a step further and created the character of Bobby, along with a thin but crucial story thread to tie it all together. Eventually, they settled on a cast of characters composed of five married couples, their best friend Bobby, and his three girlfriends. Into this mix, the show's creators folded a collage of the cultural and social issues spinning through NYC (and other big cities) in 1970. If *Hair* was about baby-boomer/hippies and their counter-cultural lifestyle down in the East Village, *Company* was about their older siblings—a thirty-something crowd of young professionals who live in glass and steel high-rise apartment buildings on the Upper East Side and "find each other in the crowded streets and the guarded parks."[58] They have also been affected by the increasingly fast pace of urban life, the sexual revolution, recreational drug use, and a general questioning of traditional values. *Company* is about a desperate need for connection in a world that is making people increasingly disconnected. Again, this was all part of the Modern Era shift away from Golden Age-style integrated musical play and towards more unconventional, non-linear kinds of storytelling.

Company was only the first of six extraordinary musicals that Prince and Sondheim would create together. It would be followed by *Follies, A Little Night Music, Pacific Overtures, Sweeney Todd,* and *Merrily We Roll Along*. Three of those six (*Company, Night Music,* and *Sweeney*) received the Tony Award for "Best Musical." And a great deal of the success of the first two of those shows must be attributed to choreographer Michael Bennett.

"I Can Do That"—Michael Bennett

He was born Michael Bennett DeFiglia in Buffalo, NY, in 1943. His mother's side of the family were Russian Jews, and his father's side had emigrated from Sicily. His mother put him into dance lessons at age two, even though his father was highly resistant to the idea. His mother said she could tell Michael was "different" from the time he was a baby: "He didn't act like, you know, normal, always moving, bouncing, struggling, like."[59] During High School, Bennett convinced his parents to let him spend his summers in NYC studying dance, where he was profoundly influenced by seeing the original productions of *The Pajama Game, Damn Yankees,* and *Guys*

And Dolls. "I always knew what I wanted to do," he would later say. "I really wanted to become Jerry Robbins. I wanted to become this brilliant choreographer/director in the 'theatahh.'"[60]

Bennett dropped out of High School to play the role of Baby John in a European tour of *West Side Story*, then danced in the chorus of four Broadway shows[61] and got a few jobs choreographing summer stock productions. Eventually, this all led to him being hired to create the choreography for two Broadway musicals, both of which were flops, but with acclaimed choreography,[62] and one big hit, **Promises, Promises**—and all three shows garnered Bennett Tony Award nominations. Those shows got him noticed, especially by Hal Prince, who invited him to work on **Company**. Bennett's staging of the show's musical numbers was spectacular, acclaimed, and highly conceptual. Like his idol Robbins had done with *Fiddler*, Bennett found imaginative ways to illustrate the themes of *Company* using potent choreographic metaphors and images. Prince and Sondheim were, of course, eager to have Bennett choreograph their next show, **Follies**, as well. But, much like Prince had felt just a few years prior, Bennett was itching to become a director-choreographer and told Prince that he would only agree to choreograph *Follies* if he could also be the co-director. Since it would be a big, elaborate, highly conceptual show in which the choreography would be crucial, Prince agreed.

Concept 3: Life is a Ziegfeld Follies

The inspiration behind the 1971 musical **Follies** epitomizes the idea of the *concept musical*. It was prompted (at least in its final form) by a *Life* magazine photo of vintage movie star Gloria Swanson standing amid the ruins of the demolished Roxy Theatre dressed in a glamorous black gown and red feather boa—her arms reaching to the sky in classic show biz style, as if she is saying, "Everything I love is gone, but I'm still here." A metaphor, rather than a story, now becomes the basis of a show. Smart theatermakers like Sondheim and bookwriter William Goldman, however, know that you can't build a musical only on a metaphor. The structure of *Follies* is an event: a reunion party of *Ziegfeld Follies*-like showgirls and performers played out in real-time on the bare stage of an abandoned theater that is haunted by ghosts and memories of lost youth and destined to be torn down the following day. Although, like *No, No, Nanette*, the cast of *Follies* included show biz stars from days gone by, such as Alexis Smith, Gene Nelson, Dorothy Collins, and Yvonne DeCarlo, in most ways, the show was an unromantic, anti-nostalgia musical that separated critics and audiences into to two camps: those who found it to be the most breathtakingly brilliant theatrical event of their lifetime, and those it left baffled and depressed, some of whom actually snuck out of the theater halfway through.

Sondheim's score and Prince and Bennett's staging, however, were spectacular and brilliantly conceived throughout. The standout moment was "Who's That Woman?," a song-and-dance number that virtually everyone who saw the original production, including Stephen Sondheim, has vociferously declared to be "the most brilliantly staged number in Broadway history."[63] Despite the disparity in its reception, *Follies* received Tony Awards for "Best Score" (Sondheim), "Best Actress" (Smith), and for its scenery, costumes, and lighting.[64] It also brought Michael Bennett his first Tony Award for "Best Choreography," and both Bennett and Prince received Tonys for "Best Director."

Concept 4: Life is an Audition

It was Michael Bennet who brought the concept musical to its highest peak with his 1975 musical, *A Chorus Line*, which he conceived, directed and choreographed. The show's book, by Nicholas Dante and James Kirkwood, and its songs, by composer Marvin Hamlisch and lyricist Edward Kleban, are based on the real-life stories and verbatim accounts of actual Broadway dancers. To a great extent, it can be described as the "first reality show"—decades before that genre became a staple of television.

It began with a group of dancers who had all worked together in a flop show,[65] and had come away from the experience feeling abused and powerless. Two of them, Michon Peacock and Tony Stevens, decided to get a bunch of the dancers together to just talk in a sort of "consciousness-raising session," as was popular at the time, and they invited Michael Bennett to be a guest. That first night, they met late, after the working members of the group had finished performing in their Broadway shows. They started with a dance class, drank some wine, and then just started to talk. Luckily, they had a tape recorder running. Michael Bennet was very taken with stories that emerged from these sessions and encouraged the dancers to meet several more times, with Michael now asking specific questions about their lives and their art. No one, including Bennet, was sure exactly where this was headed. Eventually, he approached producer Joe Papp to ask if he would provide him with some space at the Public Theater to explore some staging and script ideas that might come out of these personal stories. This would initiate a way of working that had never before been used in the creation of a Broadway musical but would soon be widely adopted. For the first time, a show was created in a workshop setting by a group of theater makers working together and with the performers being actively involved from the beginning of the process. Eventually, under Bennet's inspired guidance and over the course of multiple workshops, the actual words and real-life stories of Broadway dancers were crafted into *A Chorus Line*.

Both *Company* and *A Chorus Line* are frequently referred to as plotless musicals, and certainly, both of them employ a thematic revue format. But *A Chorus Line* has a highly charged dramatic situation at its core—a dance audition for a Broadway musical. Anticipating by decades the ubiquitous reality show contests that have dominated television in the twenty-first century, *A Chorus Line* functions in a similar way to a sporting event, with the underlying dramatic question being: who is going to win? Like *Follies*, *A Chorus Line* is set and performed on the bare stage of a theater, and the action plays out in real-time, including multiple diversions into the minds, pasts, and unspoken thoughts of its characters. There is dramatic tension throughout because we know that only eight of the eighteen smart, talented, funny, flawed, and extremely brave characters that we have come to know and love will get the job at the end of the show.

When *A Chorus Line* opened off-Broadway at the Public Theater, word quickly spread that something very special was happening downtown, and it became nearly impossible to get a ticket. Even so, Bennett and company kept working on the show, adding nuances and tweaks, so that by the time it opened on Broadway in 1975, it was universally acclaimed as one of the greatest musicals of all time. *A Chorus Line* received nine Tony Awards, including "Best Book," "Best Score," "Best Direction," "Best Choreography," and "Best Musical." It was also awarded the 1976 Pulitzer Prize for Drama. It would go on to play fifteen years on Broadway (6,137 performances), nearly doubling *Grease*'s run to become the longest-running show in history, a record that *A Chorus Line* would hold for fourteen years until it was broken by its doppelganger, *Cats* (see below).[66]

Concept 5: Life is a (sleazy) Vaudeville Show

In the musical **Chicago**, Kander and Ebb (in collaboration with director-choreographer and co-bookwriter Bob Fosse) recycled several of the conceptual techniques they had pioneered in *Cabaret*, but now took them even further. The show was created as a vehicle for **Gwen Verdon**, who had always wanted to star in a musical based on this source material, a 1926 play of the same name by Maurine Dallas Watkins. What they were able to achieve was a musical set in the Jazz Age that alluded to, and cynically commented on, the Watergate era. Its overriding concept is that the story of Roxy Hart and her murder trial is presented in the format of a vaudeville show, with each of its show-stopping musical numbers written in a presentational style modeled on specific 1920s stars such as Helen Morgan ("Funny Honey"), Ted Lewis ("All I Care About is Love"), Bert Williams ("Mr. Cellophane"), Sophie Tucker, ("When You're Good to Mamma"), and Eddie Cantor ("Me and My Baby"). All of this was presented by Fosse in a sexy, sleek, and very modern neon and Art Deco-infused staging. What is truly remarkable about this show is that the creators were able to tell this very cynical story, with its irredeemably amoral characters, and still delight, amaze, entrance, and thoroughly entertain us. Contrary to many reports, the original 1975 production of *Chicago*, co-starring **Chita Rivera** and **Jerry Orbach**, was a substantial hit that ran for nearly 1,000 performances, even if it was overshadowed and shut out of the Tony Awards by the gargantuan success of *A Chorus Line* that same season. If *Chicago* had opened one season earlier or later, it likely would have won every award. However, the 1996 revival of *Chicago*, presented in a modern dress concert-style staging, opened at the exact right moment. In the waning days of the British megamusical, this revival's dynamic cast of triple-threat performers (including **Ann Reinking**, **Bebe Neuwirth**, **James Naughton**, and **Marsha Lewis**), knocking 'em dead in classic old-school Broadway style, suddenly made *Chicago* feel vital and new. Still playing at the time of writing, after nearly 11,000 performances and twenty-nine years, this revival has become the second longest-running show in Broadway history.

Concept 6: Life is a Jellicle Ball

Although it may not be evident at first glance, Andrew Lloyd Webber's musical **Cats** (1982) was inspired by *A Chorus Line*, as well as by the real-world impact that show had on the dancers of London's West End. Prior to *A Chorus Line*, musical theater dancers in London, with rare exceptions, were not up to the same high standards as those on Broadway, especially in regard to having the training and skills to sing, dance, and act in relatively equal measure. After conducting extensive auditions, it was determined that the initial London cast of *A Chorus Line* would have to be entirely imported from the U.S. However, according to the rules of the British Actors' Equity, the Americans would only be permitted to stay in the show for six months, after which time they would have to be replaced by British performers. This inspired an entire generation of UK performers to study and train so that they could take over and perform in what became a three-year run of *A Chorus Line* in London. Inspired by this sudden increase in dance ability, Lloyd Webber decided to write a show specifically to showcase this new British crop of "triple threat" performers. The result was *Cats*.

Based on a book of poems by T. S. Elliott, **Cats** has no specific story or dialogue. It is simply a series of musical numbers in which each of the cat characters comes forward to perform their particular "I am" song-and-dance routine. In other words, *Cats* is a paraphrase of *A Chorus Line*. Using a similar thematic-revue-style format, a stage full of dancers (this time pretending to be cats) relate their individual stories to a powerful authority figure as they compete to be chosen and rewarded by him with a chance to move on to the next phase. In *A Chorus Line*, that means getting a job dancing in a Broadway show, and in *Cats*, it means ascending into the "Heavy Side Layer"—whatever that is.

With innovative and dynamic staging by director **Trevor Nunn** (some of it borrowed from his landmark staging of *Nicholas Nickleby*) and evocative, wall-to-wall choreography by **Gillian Lynne**, what seemed to many to be a ridiculous idea for a musical became one of the world's most popular shows, running twenty-one years in London, and eighteen years on Broadway. Ironically, as noted above, with its unprecedented run of 7,485 performances, *Cats* shattered *A Chorus Line*'s record as Broadway's longest-running musical!

5, 6, 7, 8!—The Dance Explosion

A Chorus Line, *Chicago*, and *Cats* were at the center of another cultural phenomenon of the late 1970s and early '80s: "The Dance Explosion"—as the media dubbed it at the time.[67] For the first time, classical ballet and modern dance stars such as Rudolf Nureyev, Mikhail Baryshnikov, and Twyla Tharp crossed over into pop stardom and hit films such as *The Turning Point*, *Saturday Night Fever*, *All That Jazz*, *Fame*, *Flashdance*, and *Footloose* all featured dancers and extended dance sequences at the center of their stories. The Broadway wing of this phenomenon included almost all of the previously discussed Nostalgia Craze shows (both Black and white), along with many of the concept musicals and three final hits from Bennett, Champion, and Fosse.

Bob Fosse's Dancin' (1978) was in every aspect an unadulterated revue: no book, no story, no characters—just a cast of phenomenal performers executing a series of dynamic new dances (and a few songs) choreographed in Fosse's distinctive signature style and set to an eclectic selection of classical, pop, and Broadway music that ranged from Bach to George M. Cohan to Benny Goodman to Neil Diamond. The show played for 1,774 performances and earned Fosse his seventh Tony Award for "Best Choreography."[68] (Much of that choreography would be recycled into the 1998 hit Broadway revue *Fosse*.)

The 1980 hit musical **42nd Street**, produced by David Merrick and directed and choreographed by Gower Champion (see page 241), was part of both the Dance Explosion and the Nostalgia Craze. Based on the 1933 film musical, this show uses a very minimal, streamlined book by Michael Stewart and Mark Bramble[69] to string together a series of spectacular production numbers and retell the iconic "song and dance fable of Broadway" about a young, inexperienced chorus girl who, by a stroke of fate, becomes an instant Broadway star. In a thrilling *coup de théâtre*—that most certainly was Champion's direct response to Bennett's opening sequence in *A Chorus Line*—*42nd Street* began with the curtain slowly rising (at first only to thigh height) to reveal a giant stage jam-packed with dozens of eager chorus kids all tap dancing their hearts out as they audition to be in a big Broadway show.[70] This initial production of *42nd Street* ran for more than 3,486 performances (eight years), and its 2001 revival would rack up another 1,524 performances.

Michael Bennett would have one more blockbuster hit, the 1981 musical **Dreamgirls**, a show that brought together nearly all of the hallmarks of this era: it was a (Pop)rock musical, a Black musical, and a dance musical, and it nostalgically looked back to 1960s Motown girl groups like the Supremes. And although in form it was, more or less, a conventional *musical play*, Bennet's staging of the show was highly conceptual, featuring an extraordinary design in which all of the elements danced—not just the actors, but also the scenery and lighting—and even the costume changes magically took place centerstage, propelling the story forward.[71] *Dreamgirls* would go on to run for 1,521 performances and win six Tony Awards, including **Tom Eyen** for "Best Book" and Michael Bennett and co-chorographer **Michael Peters** for "Best Choreography."

The period between *A Chorus Line* and *Dreamgirls* marked an extraordinary rebirth of the Broadway musical, during which it once again returned to very near the center of American culture. Soon, however, an emerging health crisis would cast the future of Broadway into serious doubt.

"I Am What I Am"—Gay Liberation on Broadway (J, Q)

Legend has it that the inciting incident of the Gay Liberation movement, the Stonewall Uprising, was sparked by a musical theater-related event that took place earlier that same day, June 22, 1969, the first of the three nights of civil disobedience that began as a protest against a police raid on the Stonewall Inn, a Gay bar in New York's Greenwich Village.

That morning, 20,000 fans had jammed the streets of the Upper East Side, where singer and actress Judy Garland's funeral was being held. Garland had a tremendous Gay following, and the theory is that the Gay community's grief over her untimely death later that night fed their anger and incited their resistance to the latest episode in a long history of police violence and harassment against the Gay community. Some historians dispute this idea, asserting that the Queer street youth who were at the center of the rebellion were more likely to have been into "rhythm and blues" and pop music than be fans of Judy Garland's showtunes. However, I doubt that the separation between those two musical worlds was as rigid at the time as later historians might assume. Whatever the case may be, Judy Garland is certainly tied in a multitude of ways to the Gay rights movement, as is most evident from its symbol, the "Rainbow Flag," which was at least, in part, inspired by Garland's signature song "Over The Rainbow."

The Stonewall Uprising brought Gay issues into the mainstream, and its first-year anniversary inspired the first Gay rights marches in New York and Los Angeles, which eventually led to Gay Pride parades and celebrations being held nationwide and around the world. By the early 1970s, LGBTQ people began to feel comfortable being "out, loud, and proud" in significant numbers. And, of course, it was probably inevitable that this new visibility and feeling of liberation would be felt on Broadway, where there had always been a large representation of Queer people. As a result, Queer characters and stories soon began appearing on Broadway in both plays and musicals. I detailed some of the extensive pansexual content of *Hair* earlier in this chapter, and remarkably, that show actually opened on Broadway more than a year before the Stonewall Uprising, *Hair*, however, was so shocking and controversial in so many ways that its abundant Queer content was, and still is, largely overlooked.

Just six months after Stonewall, actor **Rene Auberjonois** received a Tony Award for playing the role of Sebastion Baye, a flamboyantly Gay fashion designer, in the high-profile musical ***Coco***, with book and lyrics by Alan J. Lerner, music by André Previn, and starring movie star Katherine Hepburn as legendary designer Coco Chanel. This was the first openly Gay character of the Modern Era, and he was remarkably similar to the role that Danny Kaye had played in *Lady in the Dark* thirty years earlier—the last time there was a clearly identifiable Queer character in a musical. This time, however, the character was the story's antagonist, and even in 1970, some denounced the role as a demeaning stereotypical caricature. Today, with so many Queer characters in the media, I doubt anyone would be offended by either this character's flamboyance or because the Gay character was the villain.

Three months later came the 1970 smash hit ***Applause***, with a score by Strouse and Adams, and a book by Comden and Green that was based on the classic film *All About Eve*. *Applause* featured openly Gay actor **Lee Roy Reams** as Duane, the Gay best friend, hairdresser, and confidante of Broadway star Margo Channing, played by movie star **Lauren Bacall**. In contrast to *Coco*, this was a very positive depiction of an out Gay man, and perhaps most importantly, it was included in a hit, mainstream, Tony Award-winning, Big (Transgressive) Lady Musical. As part of the leading character's establishing "I Am" song, "But Alive," the show's authors boldly had the Gay character, Duane, escort Margo out for a night on the town at a Gay bar in the Village. Less than a year after the Stonewall Rebellion, mainstream Broadway audiences would witness an entire production number set in a Gay bar, much like the Stonewall Inn itself. *Applause* became the big hit musical of the season, winning four Tony awards, including two for its Queer director-choreographer, **Ron Field**, and during its more than two-year run, it played for 896 performances.

Three years later, **Tommy Tune** won his first Tony Award as "Best Featured Actor" in the musical ***Seesaw*** (1973) for his portrayal of another Gay best friend character—this time a dancer with big dreams of becoming a Broadway choreographer. This was truly a case of art reflecting life, since Tommy Tune himself would soon become one of Broadway's most accomplished and acclaimed director-choreographers. *Seesaw*, based on the hit play *Two for the Seesaw*, was another high-profile show (though not a major hit), with direction and choreography by Michael Bennett, music by Cy Colman, and lyrics by the incredible Dorothy Fields in her final show, forty-five years after her Broadway debut!

Both *Applause* and *Seesaw* featured subplots involving the trials and tribulations of Broadway chorus dancers that, in many ways, were precursors to the 1975 Broadway smash ***A Chorus Line***. That show, of course, marked another giant step forward in Queer visibility and representation by placing (at least) three talented, intelligent, funny, accomplished, and empathetic openly Gay male characters centerstage and presenting them to an enormous mainstream audience. The progressive social impact of *A Chorus Line*'s fifteen-year, 6,137-performance run on Broadway, along with its multiple decades-long-running national touring productions, international productions, Broadway revivals, stock, amateur, and high school productions, cannot be underestimated.

Then, in 1979, a small four-character musical called *In Trousers* debuted off-Broadway. It was not well received, but it did introduce a quirky character named Marvin, who would continue to struggle with his sexuality in two later musicals that were combined to become a major hit. Most importantly, it marked the debut of Queer composer and lyricist **William Finn**. Born in Boston in 1952 into a conservative Jewish family, Finn majored in music at Williams College, and like a previous alumnus, Stephen Sondheim, he received the Hutchinson Prize for musical composition. In 1981, in collaboration with director James Lapine, Finn brought Marvin back in a one-act musical called *March of Falsettos*, in which he leaves his wife and son and begins a stormy relationship with a Gay man named Whizzer. The show became a critically acclaimed off-Broadway hit, running for 265 performances. This would not be the last we would see of Marvin, Whizzer, and Finn.

"The Best of Times is Now"—La Cage Aux Folles (♩, ◎)

Like nearly every other Golden Age theater artist who was still in the game, Jerry Herman and Arthur Laurents struggled mightily to find their place in the rapidly changing landscape of Broadway. Herman suffered through the pain and humiliation of three very high-profile flops in a row,[72] and Laurents had not created a hit show since *West Side Story*. However, in 1983, both achieved giant comebacks with **La Cage aux Folles**. Herman created the music and lyrics, Laurents directed, and they brought an exciting young Queer playwright named **Harvey Fierstein** on board to write the book. Based on a hit French play and its hilarious blockbuster French film adaptation[73] (which later was remade as *The Birdcage*), the musical is set in a nightclub in the south of France that features drag entertainers. For the very first time, the central characters and romantic leads of a Broadway musical were a Gay male couple involved in a long-term relationship. This was in a big, brassy, mainstream "Jerry Herman musical" that received eight Tony Awards, including "Best Score," "Best Book," and "Best Musical," and ran for four years (1,761 performances) on Broadway. Its thrilling first-act-finale, "I Am What I Am," quickly became an international chart-topping disco hit, as well as an enduring gay anthem. *La Cage* has been revived twice on Broadway (in 2004 and 2010), and both productions received the Tony Award for "Best Revival of a Musical." Again, the impact of all this on American society should not be understated.

"Something Bad is Happening"—The AIDS Crisis and Broadway

Meanwhile, even as *La Cage* was in its planning stages, Gay men in New York and Los Angeles were beginning to get horribly sick and then die quickly of an unknown cause. This mysterious "gay plague," as it was called, was first mentioned in the *New York Times* in 1981 in an article headlined, "Rare Cancer Seen in 41 Homosexuals." It would soon be officially called AIDS (Auto Immune Deficiency Syndrome).[74]

The full shameful history of AIDS is, of course, beyond the scope of this book, but some context is necessary. Even as hundreds and eventually thousands of people were dying in New York and other major cities across America, the epidemic was willfully ignored by much of mainstream society. President Reagan refused to even mention it until 1985, by which time more than 12,000 people had died. Meanwhile, much of the Gay community was also in denial because it rightly feared that identification of disease with Gay men would negatively affect the giant strides that had been made over the previous decade in achieving increasingly greater levels of tolerance and acceptance.

During the 1980s and '90s, AIDS had a devastating effect on Broadway. In June of 1987, an article on the front page of the *New York Times* was headlined, "Creative Arts Being Reshaped By The Epidemic," and went on to detail how AIDS was "increasingly causing death and illness in the worlds of art and entertainment." The exact number was unknown because "AIDS-related deaths go unreported as such because of the stigma that is just beginning to fade." The devastated reactions of several key figures in the world of theater were included:

> Joseph Papp, producer of the New York Shakespeare Festival, commented: "I have had so many people around me dying of this, I don't even want to talk about it. It's too painful." "We realize we are losing, first of all, friends," said Colleen Dewhurst, an actor who also is president of the Actors' Equity Association, the union of professional actors and stage managers. "But then, too, we are losing some of the great creative minds and some of the coming creative minds." . . . The impact of AIDS can be discerned in the work not accomplished, as well as in obituaries.

Michael Bennett, one of the most influential Broadway directors and choreographers of his generation, withdrew as director of the musical "Chess" in January 1986 when, according to information confirmed by The New York Times, he was stricken with the illness. He has been in Tucson, Arizona, since December, battling the disease that has prevented him from working for more than 18 months ... Vincent Liff, a Broadway casting director, said his agency contended with the consequences of AIDS every day. "I must confess that it's horrifyingly widespread in the community we're dealing with on a day-to-day basis," he said. "The sheer quantity of losses is stunning and ever-growing all through the industry. I would easily say that over the past four years, 150 performers we have known, been in our shows or auditioned for us over the years, are dead. We work a great deal in the musical theater, and an astounding number of them have died ... Michael Callen, a 32-year-old singer and songwriter who has been battling AIDS since 1981, has met illness head-on, often with a macabre humor that comes through in conversation and in his work, as well. Mr. Callen interrupted an interview last Thursday to take a telephone call. Returning, he reported the death of Joseph Foulon—an actor. "That's my day," he said, his voice still betraying weariness from a trip to Washington earlier in the week, where he was in a group of people arrested in a protest against what activists regard as a sluggish response to the AIDS epidemic. "I tremble every time the phone rings. I keep a file of cards I've taken off my Rolodex. There are about 40 of them."[75]

The major Broadway creators who died of AIDS include:

Howard Ashman, 40, bookwriter/lyricist/director of *Little Shop of Horrors* and the primary force behind the "Disney Renaissance."
Michael Bennett, 44, director-choreographer of *A Chorus Line*, *Dreamgirls*, *Follies*, *Company*.
Warren Casey, 53, co-author of the book, music, and lyrics of *Grease*.
Christopher Chadman, 47, assistant to Fosse on *Pippin* and *Chicago* and choreographer of the 1992 hit revival of *Guys and Dolls*.
Nicholas Dante, 49, bookwriter of *A Chorus Line*.
Tom Eyen, 50, bookwriter and lyricist of *Dreamgirls*.
Ron Field, 54, director-choreographer of *Applause*, choreographer of *Cabaret*.
Larry Kert, 61, actor, original Tony in *West Side Story*, and Bobby in *Company*.
James Kirkwood, 58, bookwriter of *A Chorus Line*.
Joe Layton, 63, director-choreographer of seventeen Broadway musicals, including *The Sound of Music*.
Michael Peters, 46, co-choreographer of *Dreamgirls*, choreographer of Michael Jackson's "Thriller" video.
Billy Wilson, 59, director-choreographer of *Bubbling Brown Sugar*, *Eubie*, and six other Broadway musicals. His companion of eighteen years, Broadway performer Chip Garnett, died just a few months before him.

And in 1985, **Jerry Herman** was diagnosed with AIDS. He, however, was one of the fortunate few able to survive until advanced drug therapies could be developed to successfully manage the disease. Although he would live until 2019, his long illness largely derailed his career, and *La Cage Aux Folles* was the last new musical he would bring to Broadway.

In addition to these industry leaders, AIDS claimed the lives of **hundreds of actors, singers, musicians, stage managers, production assistants, designers, company managers, general managers, and producers**—as well as many young dancers who had worked for and been trained by Bennett, Fosse, Champion, and Tune and might have become the next generation of talented directors and choreographers.

It was only natural that the impact of the AIDS epidemic would be reflected onstage, and in 1990, William Finn and James Lapine brought Marvin and his family back in a second hit one-act off-Broadway musical, **Falsettoland**. As in their earlier piece, *March of the Falsettos*, the catchy, tuneful score was "sung-through," but not in the British poperetta style. Instead, Finn employed his own quirky style of comic and heartbreaking pop-inflected show tunes along with extended musical sequences that again demonstrate the legacy of the "Bench Scene." This time, they added two additional characters: the "lesbian couple that live next door." The duel focus of the story is Marvin's son's Bar Mitzvah and Wizzer's diagnosis and ultimate death from AIDS.

Then, in 1992, *March of the Falsettos* and *Falsettoland* were combined into the Broadway musical **Falsettos**, for which William Finn received Tony Awards for both "Best Book" and "Best Score." The show went on to run for 487 performances and was revived on Broadway in 2016.

The theater community has also been at the forefront of AIDS activism and caregiving. In response to the epidemic, in 1987, the Actors' Equity Association founded **Equity Fights AIDS**, and in 1988, the Producers' Group instituted **Broadway Cares**. The two groups merged in 1992 to form **Broadway Cares/Equity Fights AIDS**, and since then, through a series of fundraising events that utilize the talents and resources of the Broadway community, the organization has raised more than $300 million for essential services for people nationwide who are living with HIV/AIDS, or facing other critical illnesses.[76]

An entire generation of creative talent was wiped out or sidelined by this devastating disease, and during this same period, both Bob Fosse and Gower Champion also died prematurely of other causes, and Jerome Robbins abandoned Broadway to work at the New York City Ballet. This sudden vacuum of talent opened the door to a new wave of musicals from Great Britain that would soon come to dominate Broadway.

CHAPTER 12
"DO YOU HEAR THE PEOPLE SING?"—THE MODERN ERA OF BROADWAY, PART 2: CAMERON MACKINTOSH AND THE BRITISH INVASION (♩, ♪)

By this time, the midtown Broadway theater district was hitting rock bottom. In part, this was a result of a severe financial crisis that had hit NYC in the mid-1970s and lingered into the 1980s. The streets around Times Square were rundown, dirty, and sometimes dangerous. A 1981 *Rolling Stone Magazine* article declared West 42nd Street to be "the sleaziest block in America."[1] Most out-of-town tourists, and even many New Yorkers, felt unsafe walking in the area after dark. It's hard to imagine today, when, even post-pandemic, thronging crowds in and around Times Square make it almost impossible to get from dinner to a show on time. But back in the 1980s, those same streets were often deserted because so few shows were playing at any one time. Many Broadway theaters sat dark and unoccupied for months at a time, with the logos of shows that had closed months ago still looming large on their marquees. A blockbuster hit like *The Wiz* or *A Chorus Line* could still entice audiences to venture into Times Square, but overall, it was not a healthy situation, and it was made worse by the incredible power of the *New York Times* theater critic to make or break a show. At that time, a negative review from the *Times* could trigger the producer of a show to close it immediately. This, in tandem with some very outdated methods of producing and marketing shows, meant that in every season, several high-profile new musicals would open, receive negative reviews from the *Times*, and quickly close after playing only a handful of performances, losing their entire investment in the process. Then came the invasion.

Cats (1982) is often categorized as the first British *mega-musical*, but as discussed above, it is actually a 1970s-style *concept musical*. Still, its massive popularity had clearly demonstrated that Andrew Lloyd Webber was a theatrical force to be reckoned with— even without his former partner Tim Rice.[2] And, *Cats* did introduce several elements that would become hallmarks of the *mega-musical*: it featured innovative scenic, lighting, and sound designs that required remarkably advanced, sophisticated, and expensive technical elements and equipment—all of which would then come together to create an unforgettable, gasp-inducing, signature stage effect that was central to that show's impact. In this case, it was the giant tire that, in the climax of the show, blasts Grizabella into the heavens. *Cats* also featured a frequently "pre-prised" and reprised centerpiece ballad built on a lush, sweeping, operatic melody that its leading lady can belt into the stratosphere and that the full orchestra can echo in a Puccini-like manner. Perhaps most importantly, *Cats* demonstrated the lucrative effect that cutting-edge, global brand marketing techniques can have on the sales and longevity of a Broadway musical.

All of those elements were carried over into the trio of spectacular, bombastic, and unprecedentedly popular "Brit Hits" that dominated Broadway during the 1990s—*Les Misérables* (1987), *The Phantom of the Opera* (1988), and *Miss Saigon* (1991)—all produced first in London's West End before arriving on Broadway as much-anticipated, pre-sold smash hits.

"Music of the Night"—The Unexpected Return of the Operetta

Perhaps the most unlikely aspect of these wildly popular shows is that they brought the *operetta* back to Broadway in a major way—proving, I suppose, that eventually, everything old is indeed new again. If the 1970s brought back the revue and tap dancing, the late 1980s resuscitated an even more antique form of musical theater. No doubt, the fact that operettas had been almost entirely absent from Broadway for decades helped to make these shows feel new and different. Yes, the scores of these British invasion shows do (to varying degrees) all include frequent infusions of (pop)Rock musical flavoring to make them feel up to date, but the big romantic duets at their center, such as "A Heart Full of Love" from *Les Misérables*, "Sun and Moon" from *Miss Saigon*, and *Phantom*'s "All I Ask of You," are virtually indistinguishable from "Ah, Sweet Mystery of Life" from *Naughty Marietta*, "Indian Love Call" from *Rose-Marie*, or "Only a Rose" from *The Vagabond King*. And *Lez Miz*'s "Drink With Me" could have been lifted right out of *The Student Prince*. The time periods, costuming, and subject matter of these musicals also strongly echo the operettas of the past. And these "Poperettas," as they have (I think) very appropriately been dubbed, all had one other major element in common: openly Gay producer Cameron Mackintosh.

At the height of his success, **Cameron Mackintosh** was described by the *New York Times* as the "most successful, influential and powerful theatrical producer in the world."[3] He is perhaps most notable for his transformation of "the musical" into a truly global brand. He was born in London in 1946 and started his theatrical career as a stagehand and stage manager before moving into producing. He achieved only moderate success, however, until he took a chance on a show called *Cats*. Then, in 1983, a friend gave him an audio recording of a concert production of a musical based on Victor Hugo's classic (and massive) novel *Les Misérables* written by an unknown French songwriting team— **Boublil and Schönberg**.

Lyricist and book writer **Alain Boublil** was born into a Jewish family in Tunisia. He emigrated to France at eighteen to work in the pop music industry. "And . . . so did Claude-Michel," he told the *Los Angeles Times* in 2019, "we both come from the pop songwriting world . . . until I discovered my own attraction for musical theater, and that was like a disease."[4] The disease took hold of him while attending a touring production of *West Side Story* that came to Paris sometime in the late 1960s or early '70s, and he remembers thinking, "'This is what I've been wanting to do all my life.' Watching the first musical of my life, watching the geniuses of Leonard Bernstein, Jerome Robbins, and

"Do You Hear the People Sing?"

Stephen Sondheim accomplish an update of 'Romeo and Juliet.' I thought . . . How do you do that?'" Then, in 1973, after seeing *Jesus Christ Superstar* on Broadway, Boublil became determined to create the first French rock opera with the French Revolution as its subject matter:

> I came back to Paris and told about all my discoveries to my friends with whom I used to write pop songs, and I could see in their eyes both the curiosity and also thinking that I was going mad. But in the end, they said, "Why not?" And so the composer I used to work with said, "But what you are asking is too complicated for me on my own. Let's call Claude-Michel, who is a mad opera fan."[5]

Composer **Claude-Michel Schönberg** was born in France to Hungarian Jewish parents. His father was an organ repairer, and his mother was a piano tuner. The musical that Boublil, Schönberg, and two other songwriters joined forces to create, *La Révolution Française*, became an enormous success in France—first as a concept album and then as a theatrical concert staged at the Palais des Sports in Paris. While their other collaborators went back to pop songwriting, Boublil and Schönberg wanted to keep making musicals. It was at a production of *Oliver!* in London a few years later that Boublil found his next inspiration. When he saw the character of the Artful Dodger, it immediately made him think of the boy, Gavroshe, in Victor Hugo's novel:

> Little by little, I started to really see two shows on that stage. One was "Oliver," playing in front of me, and . . . on the stage of my head . . . I was seeing Valjean, Javert, Cosette. I was lucky the day after to find a copy of the novel in the library in Old Compton Street . . . There was a chapter called "J'avais rêvé d'une autre vie," and I thought, "That's a song." And it became in English the song "I Dreamed a Dream."[6]

The team immediately quit their jobs to work full time on **Les Misérables**, and within two years they had written, recorded, and staged it—again at the Palais des Sports. It was a tape of that production that Mackintosh fell in love with in 1983 and decided to produce after hearing only four of the songs. Mackintosh knew, however, that a great deal of work would need to be done before the show would be ready for a full West End production—at this point, the show's book was extremely sketchy and still written in French. It would take years of development, and the contributions of several other writers to create a version of the show that Mackintosh was finally ready to bring to the stage.

Les Misérables opened in London in 1985 to blisteringly bad reviews. Critics called it "witless and synthetic entertainment" and "the reduction of a literary mountain into a dramatic molehill." But the following day, ticket buyers overwhelmed the box office. The public adored the show from its first performance. By opening night in New York, *Les Misérables* had racked up the largest advance sale in Broadway history: $11 million. It would go on to run for more than sixteen years (6,680 performances) in New York, and nearly forty years later, it is still running in London. Undisputedly, it is one of the world's most popular musicals, seen by over 130 million people worldwide, performed in fifty-three countries, and translated into twenty-two languages, with no end in sight.[7] Remarkably, Cameron Mackintosh's next show would receive equally negative reviews but achieve even greater success.

The gothic backstage melodrama ***The Phantom of the Opera*** was composed by **Andrew Lloyd Webber**, with lyrics by **Charles Hart** and **Richard Stilgoe**. Stilgoe and Lloyd-Webber collaborated on the book, which they officially adapted from a French novel by Gaston Leroux, but they actually modeled the show more closely on its 1925 silent film adaptation. All three versions relate the story of a physically deformed musical genius, the Phantom (originally played by **Michael Crawford**), and his mad obsession with transforming a beautiful young corps de ballet dancer, Christine Daaé (**Sarah Brightman**), into an opera star.

By opening night in New York in 1988, *Phantom of the Opera* was already an Olivier Award-winning "Best Musical" smash hit in London and had racked up a record $17 million Broadway advance sale and was sold out for months. And since history is written by the victors, it may be pointless to note that it was lambasted by critics like Jacques Le Sourd, who called it

> ... the emblematic show of the late '80s, expensive, flashy, and completely second rate—from its plastic-guilt sets to its knockoff score by Andrew Lloyd Webber, the Donald Trump of the theater, and a lot of people seem to be dazzled by him—as a success story, if not as an artist.[8]

And critic Frank Rich warned prospective ticket buyers not to "let the hype kindle the hope that *Phantom* is a credible heir to the Rodgers and Hammerstein musicals that haunt Andrew Lloyd Webber's creative aspirations and the Majestic Theater as persistently as the evening's title character does." *Carousel* and *South Pacific* had both premiered at the Majestic, but what Rich now found there instead was "a characteristic Lloyd Webber project—long on pop professionalism and melody, [but] impoverished of artistic personality and passion." Rich and most other reviewers, however, heaped praise on Hal Prince's "brilliantly directed" production, and the lush and spectacular "consummate stagecraft" of Prince and choreographer Gillian Lynne. And in contrast to "plastic guilt sets," most critics and audience members found the physical production to be "stunningly and sumptuously designed and costumed by Maria Bjornson, [and] dazzling lighted by Andrew Bridge."[9]

The Phantom of the Opera received seven 1988 Tony Awards, including for direction, scenic design, costume design, "Best Actor in a Musical" (Crawford), "Best Featured Actress in a Musical (**Judy Kaye**), and "Best Musical." The Tonys for "Best Score" and "Best Book," however, went to Stephen Sondheim and James Lapine for *Into the Woods*. But Lloyd-Webber's position, power, and significance in the Broadway pantheon was made abundantly clear when, with the opening of *Phantom*, he became the first composer since his idol Richard Rodgers to have three musicals running simultaneously on Broadway, the other two being *Cats* and his second paraphrase of *A Chorus Line*, **Starlight Express** (1987). *Phantom* was the first of several "Beauty and the Beast" themed stories that would be adapted into stage and film musicals over the following decade, including *Disney's Beauty and The Beast*, DreamWorks' *Shrek*, Disney's *The Hunchback of Notre Dame*, and *King Kong*.

After an unprecedented thirty-five-year, 13,982-performance run on Broadway, *The Phantom of the Opera* finally closed in 2023 as the longest-running musical in Broadway history, a record that may prove impossible for any show (even *The Lion King* or *Wicked*) to ever break. Meanwhile, *Phantom* has been seen by more than 100 million people worldwide, and as this book went to press, productions were playing or were scheduled to play in London, Antwerp, Mumbai, Vienna, Singapore, Belgrade, Prague, Ljubljana, Madrid, Budapest, and Vienna.

Like the operettas of the past, the Brit hits all feature romantic, melodramatic, and often tragic storylines but offer very little humor or comic relief. And, like those Silver Age operettas, even what little comedy these musicals do include is usually not very successful. In my view, *Les Miz*'s "Master of the House" duet may be the least funny comedy song of all time. And because the mega-musicals took themselves so seriously, they often became prime targets for ridicule, especially from the long-running off-Broadway revue **Forbidden Broadway**. Just as Weber and Fields had done eighty years earlier, *Forbidden Broadway*'s inspired creator **Gerard Alessandrini** took aim at the biggest hits of his day by burlesquing their grandiose, overblown, and pretentious aspects unmercifully. And to his great credit—even though the revue memorably skewered him as the merch-mad "Napoleon of Broadway"—Cameron Mackintosh was one of *Forbidden Broadway*'s biggest fans.

In 1991, Boublil, Schönberg, and Mackintosh were back on Broadway with another direct from London hit: **Miss Saigon**. This time, they took the basic storyline of the classic opera *Madame Butterfly* (which itself was based on a popular play) and transposed it to the Vietnam War era. This time it was Schönberg who had the inspiration for the show when he saw a photo in a French news magazine of a Vietnamese woman saying goodbye to her young daughter at an airport during the fall of Saigon. As Schönberg later wrote, "This photo was for Alain and I, the start of everything . . ."[10]

> The little Vietnamese girl was about to board a plane for the United States where her father, an ex-GI she had never met, was waiting for her. Her mother would never see her again. Was that not the most moving, the most staggering example of the ultimate sacrifice, as undergone by the title character in Madame Butterfly—giving up her life for her child?[11]

The team played tapes of some early songs for Cameron Mackintosh, who was a bit thrown. "The subject matter was completely unexpected," he later recalled. "It was contemporary, and contemporary musicals don't usually work. And it was on a topic that had brought America to the brink. I had to think about it."[12] Ultimately, he did decide to produce the show "despite and perhaps because of the extraordinary challenge that it represented." Mackintosh suggested that Boublil and Schönberg partner with lyricist **Richard Maltby** to create the English lyrics.

Miss Saigon opened in London in 1989, where it became an enormous hit and ultimately ran for more than ten years. However, when the show was announced for Broadway, a giant controversy erupted. Cameron Mackintosh intended to bring over the show's two acclaimed West End stars: **Lea Salonga,** the dynamic young Filipino singer and actress whom Mackintosh had discovered during an extensive worldwide talent search, and **Jonathan Pryce**, the white British actor who played the mixed-race French-Vietnamese character called "The Engineer." In London, Pryce had worn "eye prosthetics and bronzer"[13] to play the role, which does not seem to have been remarked upon there. But the Actors' Equity Association, the union of professional actors in the U.S., threatened to deny permission for Pryce to work on Broadway. Their position was that an Asian American actor should play the role because making up a white man to look Vietnamese was "an affront to the Asian community," and casting an actual Asian actor would help to "break the usual pattern of casting Asians in minor roles."[14] This was one of the first high-profile protests concerning issues of racial equity, "yellowface," and color-blind and color-conscious casting. Mackintosh, however, became furious and threatened to cancel the entire New York production and all the jobs that went along with it. After much controversy and a considerable delay, Equity backed down, and Pryce was allowed to open the show (not wearing eye prosthetics or makeup). Amid continued protests, the show became a hit, and Pryce won the Tony Award for "Best Actor in a Musical." However, every actor who has played that role since then, during *Miss Saigon*'s nearly ten-year run on Broadway and in its many tours and revivals, has been of Asian heritage. Most importantly, that controversy jump-started some crucial discussions and necessary reassessment that Broadway and the theater world at large are still grappling with.

There is one American composer who achieved a measure of success adopting the "international style," poperetta model—**Frank Wildhorn**. He was born to Jewish parents in New York City in 1959, where he spent his early childhood before moving with his family to Florida when he was fourteen. As a teen, Wildhorn played in and wrote music for several bands that ranged from rock 'n' roll to R&B to jazz. And as he told a reporter, he continues to write in a wide variety of musical styles today:

> I just love music. I'm a composer. When I work in the theater, I'm a theater composer. When I'm writing for Whitney Houston or Kenny Rogers or Natalie Cole, I'm a pop composer. I've been commissioned by the Bolshoi to do a full-length ballet, so I'm a classical composer when I'm doing that . . . depending on the medium I work in, that's what I am that day.[15]

Wildhorn's biggest Broadway hit was his 1997 musical *Jekyll and Hyde*.[16] This adaptation of Robert Louis Stevenson's famous gothic horror novel ran for four years on Broadway (1,543 performances) and featured several soaring ballads that have been widely performed. Later that same year, Wildhorn followed it up with the era's only comic poperetta, *The Scarlet Pimpernel*, based on another classic novel. Then, in 1998, when his song cycle (revue) *The Civil War* opened in New York, Wildhorn joined Stephen Schwartz and Andrew Lloyd Webber in that elite group of composers who have had three musicals running on Broadway simultaneously—even if *The Civil War* lasted only sixty-three performances. Despite their sometimes substantial runs, none of Wildhorn's musicals have been financially successful on Broadway; however, several of those shows and other Wildhorn musicals have become extremely popular long-running hits in Europe and Asia.

"Look, I Made a Hat"—Sondheim Just Keeps Moving on

In addition to Harold Prince, there was at least one other American theater artist from the Golden Age still standing and still having a tremendous influence on Broadway during the period of the British Invasion—Stephen Sondheim.[17] In a very strange coincidence, Sondheim shares a birthday with Andrew Lloyd Webber: March 22.[18] But in great contrast to Lloyd Webber's bombastic, large-scale, sweeping *mega-musicals*, Sondheim chose to focus on a series of much smaller scale, artsy, *concept musicals* that he created in collaboration with a new partner—playwright and director **James Lapine**. These were musicals that still felt arrestingly modern and sophisticated, even though they chose to stick with the traditional Broadway "book-musical" format of spoken dialogue leading in and out of the songs, rather than the sung-through, continuous music, "international style" of the Brit hits.

Sunday in the Park with George, with music and lyrics by Sondheim and book and direction by Lapine, was inspired by the French pointillist painter Georges Seurat's monumental work, *A Sunday Afternoon on the Island of La Grande Jatte*, which depicts a crowd of nineteenth-century Parisians relaxing by the river on their day off. The first act is set in Paris in 1884 and revolves around George, a fictionalized version of Seurat himself, obsessively struggling to complete that complex painting while at the same time trying to maintain his relationship with his muse, model, and lover, Dot. She loves George deeply but is understandably fed up with continually being ignored and neglected in favor of his art, and she reluctantly comes to the conclusion that George will never change. So, just before the end of Act One, Dot leaves George to marry a baker and move to America. Then, in Sondheim's shimmering and majestic first-act finale, "Sunday," George is finally able to create harmony out of chaos as the painting comes together in a thrilling and unforgettable tableau. In the second act, the story leaps forward 100 years to New York in 1984, where a contemporary conceptual artist, also named George (and maybe the great-grandson of Dot and Seurat), is struggling to find the inspiration to move on to his next work. Somehow, the dramatic tensions, emotional conflicts, and romantic complications of the first act are resolved through (almost) entirely different characters in Act Two. It shouldn't work, but somehow it does, and for me, quite movingly—although not all audience members are willing to make the necessary leap of faith. Perfectly cast with stars **Mandy Patinkin** and **Bernadette Peters**, backed by an expert ensemble, *Sunday in the Park with George* opened on Broadway in 1984 to mixed reviews. It was nominated for ten Tony Awards but received only two—for its scenic and lighting design. Somewhat controversially, the Tonys for "Best Musical" and "Best Score" that year were won by *La Cage Aux Folles* and Jerry Herman, who in his acceptance speech pointedly declared that "the simple, hummable show tune" was once again "alive and well" on Broadway.[19] *Sunday in the Park*, however, received the 1985 Pulitzer Prize for Drama, and has received two acclaimed Broadway revivals in 2008 and 2017.

Into the Woods (1987), again with music and lyrics by Sondheim, and book and direction by Lapine, intertwines the plots of several classic fairy tales ("Jack And The Beanstalk", "Rapunzel," "Cinderella", "Little Red Riding Hood", etc.) as related in the often gruesome versions collected by the Brothers Grimm, and at the end of the first act, each of the storylines concludes with a happy ending. Then, in Act Two, the musical goes on to explore what happens after "happily ever after"—much in the same way the off-Broadway musical *The Fantasticks* had done back in 1960. In the same season in which *The Phantom of the Opera* swept almost every Tony Award category, including "Best Musical," Sondheim and Lapine received awards for "Best Score" and "Best Book." The sparkling ensemble cast was headed by **Bernadette Peters**, **Chip Zien**, and **Joanna Gleason**, who received the Tony for "Best Actress in a Musical." *Into the Woods* has been revived twice on Broadway, adapted into a hit film in 2014, and become Sondheim's most frequently produced work, especially popular with educational theater programs because of its *Into the Woods, JR.* version.

Sondheim and Lapine's third musical was 1994's **Passion**, adapted from the Italian film *Passione d'Amore* and a novel titled *Fosca*. Set in nineteenth-century Italy, the plot centers on the unlikely relationship between a handsome young soldier named Georgio, and Fosca, his commander's homely, sickly cousin who falls fiercely, passionately, and obsessively in love with him and pursues him relentlessly. Despite receiving very mixed critical and audience response, *Passion* won the 1994 Tony Awards for "Best Musical," "Best Score," "Best Book," and "Best Actress in a Musical" for **Donna Murphy** for her performance as Fosca.

The original productions of all three Sondheim/Lapine musicals (including the stellar performances of their brilliant original casts) have been beautifully preserved in video captures that originally aired on the PBS series *American Playhouse*. It is evident from viewing them, however, that they did have one striking thing in common with the Brit hits of this era—the near total absence of dance. With the exception of *Miss Saigon* (choreographed by Bob Avian), none of the musicals outlined in this chapter featured significant choreography or dancing of any kind, and only in very limited ways did they use dance as a storytelling device. In the mega-musicals, and to a lesser extent in Lapine-directed shows, it was the scenery that moved in spectacular ways and assisted in telling the story. This was, of course, because, as previously discussed, by this point, nearly all of the great director-choreographers had died or abandoned Broadway. This left Tommy Tune as "the only game in town in his field"[20] to demonstrate the kinetic power and artistry that inspired staging and choreography could instill in a Broadway musical.

"Famous Feet"—Tommy Tune (♫)

Tommy Tune (Thomas James Tune) was born in Texas in 1939. His father was of British ancestry, and his mother was part Shawnee Indian. He spent his childhood studying tap and acrobatic dance and organizing the neighborhood children to perform backyard "Patio Revues." "I've always been putting on shows," he would later say.[21] His dream of being a ballet dancer was dashed, however, when a painful growth spurt as a teenager eventually caused him to shoot up to six-foot-six (or "five-foot-eighteen," as he often quipped). His obsession with theater and dance only deepened in high school and college, and in 1960, he made his professional debut as a dancer in the chorus of *Redhead* at Dallas Summer Musicals.

On his very first day in NYC after moving there in 1963, he attended his first audition and was hired to dance in a twenty-two-week tour of the musica*l Irma La Douce*. From then on, he worked constantly as a dancer and choreographer, especially on the thriving summer stock theater circuit. Tune made his Broadway debut dancing in the chorus of *Baker Street* (1965), choreographed by Lee Becker Theodore and directed by Hal Prince. He then danced in *A Joyful Noise* (1966), choreographed by Michael Bennett, and *How Now Dow Jones* (1967), choreographed by Gillian Lynne and show-doctored by Bennett, and who now became Tune's mentor. When Bennett took over the direction and choreography of the struggling musical **Seesaw**, he hired Tune as his associate choreographer and eventually moved him into a key performing role in the show, for which Tune staged his own show-stopping 11 o'clock spot production number: "It's Not Where You Start, It's Where You Finish." This resulted in Tune's first Tony Award for "Best Featured Actor in a Musical" (see page 281). Because he was playing an openly Gay character in the show, Tune was warned not to take his boyfriend, dancer Michael Stuart, as his date to the Tony Awards ceremony. But never one to hide his sexuality, Tune ignored that advice, and later contended that the television cameras did not show him sitting in his seat because he was sitting next to another man.

Despite his Tony win, Tune had trouble finding suitable roles as a performer but gained great acclaim as a director-choreographer for his clever, innovative staging of *The Club*, a small off-Broadway musical featuring an all-female cast who portrayed the chauvinistic members of an all-male social club. This led to Tunes' choreography and co-direction of the long-running[22] hit ***The Best Little Whorehouse in Texas*** (1978), which included a series of innovative and satiric crowd-pleasing production numbers involving a sex doll drill team halftime show, a shirtless beefcake clog-dancing football team, and a sidestepping Governor of Texas. Then, with his dazzling Tony Award-winning staging of the half Hollywood-nostalgia-revue/half Marx-Brothers-pastiche-musical-comedy, *A Day in Hollywood/A Night in the Ukraine* (1980), Tune advanced "to the top of the class with such choreographer/directors as Michael Bennett, Bob Fosse, Joe Layton, and the incomparable Jerome Robbins."[23]

Following Bennett's example, Tune used extended workshops to develop both the musicals **Nine** (1982) and **Grand Hotel** (1989), and, as author Kevin Winkler observes, "Like Bennett . . . he established himself as the primary architect of his shows, reshaping the work of writers and composers to conform to his vision, and directing the work of designers to illustrate that vision."[24] This auteur approach to both shows in tandem with his brilliant conceptual staging garnered him three additional Tony Awards, and amid great controversy, *Nine* won the award for "Best Musical" over Michael Bennett's *Dreamgirls*. Eager to re-establish himself as a performer, in between those shows Tune starred with Twiggy in "the new Gershwin musical," **My One and Only** (1983). When that show, under the leadership of avant-garde director Peter Sellars, proved to be a disaster, Tune had no choice but to take over the direction himself. During a grueling extended pre-Broadway tour, he was able to reshape and revamp the show into a substantial hit that earned him two more Tonys—for "Best Actor in a Musical" and "Best Choreography."

In contrast to the sleek, stylized minimalism of *Nine* and *Grand Hotel*, Tune's production of **The Will Rogers Follies** (1991) was appropriately his most lavish and opulent. Subtitled "A Life in Revue," this *concept musical* presented the life and career of the famous radio, movie, and Ziegfeld star as a series of Follies-style routines and production numbers, all staged on a massive, illuminated staircase. Tune was again awarded Tonys for both his direction and choreography. This triumph was followed by a disastrous flop: **The Best Little Whorehouse Goes Public**. Unfortunately, the quick demise of this sequel to his earlier hit, along with the ill-fated *Busker's Alley*, which never made it to Broadway, and an announced but abandoned stage adaptation of the film *Easter Parade*, has resulted in a thirty-year absence of Tune from Broadway as director, choreographer, or performer. Since, as of this writing, Tune is in his mid-eighties, it is unlikely that we will see another Tommy Tune production. In 2015, however, in "celebration of his extraordinary accomplishments" and in "acknowledgment of his legacy as the last link in a celebrated chain of Broadway director-choreographers," Tommy Tune was presented with a special tenth Tony Award for Lifetime Achievement.[25]

CHAPTER 13
"DEFYING GRAVITY"—THE MODERN ERA OF BROADWAY, PART 3: BROADWAY IN THE TWENTY-FIRST CENTURY (J, Q, B, W)

As the Broadway musical entered its second century, it was again changing and evolving in new and significant ways. This was accomplished by a new generation of Broadway creators who (as usual) revitalized the musical by reclaiming, recycling, and reinventing many of the established forms and traditions of the past and by inventing at least one new(ish) kind of musical. Perhaps most surprisingly, this generation re-embraced both the traditional *musical play* and the *musical comedy* and re-established them in ways that likely would have made Rodgers and Hammerstein, Irving Berlin, Cole Porter, and Comden and Green very proud.

"You Can't Stop the Beat"—The Musical Comedy Strikes Back! (J, Q, W)

Back in May of 1991, there were two "Best Musical," Tony Award-winning *musical comedies* running on Broadway: the recently opened smash-hit, *The Will Rogers Follies*, and the still-running hit from the previous season, *City of Angels*—both of which might be considered late extensions of the Nostalgia Craze, at least in terms of subject matter. But then, nearly ten years would go by before another new, original *musical comedy* opened on Broadway. In fact, during that time—the era of the Brit hits and the Sondheim/Lapine musicals—there was a strong belief that the *musical comedy* was dead and buried, with the only possible exceptions being revivals of classic musicals from an earlier, and presumably more naive, time period. As John Kenrick wrote in 1996:

> The great musicals of the 20th Century were products of a basically optimistic mindset. Today's darker entertainments reflect the increasing pessimism of our time. The wit of Porter and the heart of Hammerstein seem to no longer have a place in a culture that musically celebrates vicious violence. It breaks my heart to admit it, but the classic Broadway musical is dead. We can revive the best of them, but successful new musicals in that tradition are simply not to be.[1]

However, as Kendrick suggested, in the midst of that humorless decade, some glimmers of fun did start to break through with revivals of some of the best musical comedies of the twentieth century—or at least parts of them.

The first was billed as "a new Gershwin musical comedy." It had started out as a revival of the 1930 hit, *Girl Crazy*, but during its development it underwent so many plot and character changes, and so many songs from other Gershwin musicals were interpolated into its score, that it was given a new title: *Crazy for You*. The final result featured a fresh and hilarious book by **Ken Ludwig**, expert comic direction by **Mike Okrent**, and in her Broadway debut as choreographer, sensational, show-stopping dances by **Susan Stroman**—a vibrant, new, young talent who it was instantly clear could finally provide Tommy Tune with some competition. *New York Times* critic Frank Rich could not have been more prescient when he wrote:

> When future historians try to find the exact moment at which Broadway finally rose up to grab the musical back from the British, they just may conclude that the revolution began last night. The shot was fired at the Shubert Theater, where a riotously entertaining show called "Crazy for You" uncorked the American musical's classic blend of music, laughter, dancing, sentiment and showmanship with a freshness and confidence rarely seen during the "Cats" decade.[2]

Crazy For You was followed just a few months later by a revival of ***Guys and Dolls***, directed by **Jerry Zaks**, choreographed by Fosse protege **Christopher Chadman**, and featuring star-making performances by **Nathan Lane** and **Faith Prince**. It, too, opened to rave reviews, including from the then all-important *New York Times* critic Frank Rich, who described it as "an enchanting rebirth of a show that defines Broadway dazzle." The following day, as recounted by Michael Riedel in his book *Singular Sensation: The Triumph of Broadway*, the line to buy tickets at the theater's box office stretched down the block and "by close of business, *Guys and Dolls* had taken in $396,709.50, shattering by more than $35,000 the single-day record that had been set by *Phantom [of the Opera]* in 1988."[3] These two shows, plus the 1996 revival of *Chicago*,[4] were produced and performed with a freshness and effervescence that vividly and viscerally demonstrated what Broadway had been missing—*musical comedy*, which, according to the musical *42nd Street* are "the two most glorious words in the English language!" The triumphant return of new, original musical comedies to Broadway would soon be initiated by the back-to-back double-whammy of two shows that opened just months apart during the 2000–1 season: *The Full Monty* and *The Producers*.

Broadway Dance #12: Daughters of DeMille—Dancing Ladies of the Modern Era (W)

Following (sometimes literally) in the footsteps of Agnes DeMille, five remarkable women have had a tremendous impact on Modern Era Broadway as choreographers and director-choreographers. Like their Golden Age predecessors, most of these women gravitated to Broadway from the concert dance world. Between them, since 1970, they have choreographed seventy-five Broadway musicals, including a number of the most popular and acclaimed shows of all time.

Five-time Tony nominee **Patricia Birch** was born in New Jersey in 1934 and made her Broadway debut dancing for Agnes DeMille in the 1957 revival of *Brigadoon*. Two years later, Jerome Robbins cast Birch as Anybodys in the First National Tour *West Side Story*, and she continued in the role when the show came back to Broadway in 1960. Birch spent much of the next ten years as a soloist in Martha Graham's Dance Company. "I loved it, and I loved her," Birch later said, "but I found I loved musicals as much or more than the pure dance world . . . and I wanted to do something more accessible."[5] The twenty-two Broadway musicals that Birch went on to choreograph include *The Me Nobody Knows* (1970), *You're A Good Man Charlie Brown* (1971), *A Little Night Music* (1973), *Candide* (1974), *Over Here!* (1974), *Pacific Overtures* (1976), *They're Playing Our Song* (1979), and, most notably, the long-running, record-breaking smash-hit *Grease* (1972). "[That] was when I really began to realize what great things you can do with actors who move," Birch said. "What I really like doing is storytelling, finding the body language that is necessary for the story. And when I'm doing it, and it's working, I'm thrilled."[6] Birch later recreated and adapted her Broadway choreography for the blockbuster film version of *Grease* and directed the movie *Grease 2*.

Graciela Daniele was born in 1939 in Argentina, where she began taking ballet lessons at age seven because a doctor told her parents it would help to correct a malformation in the arch of her foot. Dance became her passion and her career, eventually taking her to Paris, where she continued to dance and study classical ballet technique but became somewhat disenchanted with the form. "There was not enough plot," she said, "there was not enough acting." Her life changed when, in 1957, she saw a European touring production of *West Side Story* and realized, "Oh my God, this is what I want to do! I want to be able to tell a story through dance. I want to be like these people. But I didn't know the language—the jazz [dance] language. So, I came to New York to study."[7] Within a month, she was dancing in the chorus of the 1964 musical *What Makes Sammy Run?*, choreographed by the great theatrical jazz dancer Matt Mattox. After dancing in two musicals for Michael Bennett (*Promises, Promises* and *Coco*), he asked her to be his assistant on *Follies* (1971). Then, in 1975, she served as the dance captain on Bob Fosse's original production of *Chicago*. Those experiences of using her "creative mind, as opposed to using just the performing side," led Daniele to become a choreographer. "Bennett and Fosse . . . were very encouraging. They thought that I had the creativity for it, so they not only inspired me but sort of pushed me towards trying it. You always have to have that person who says, 'You can do it.'"[8] Since 1978, Daniele has choreographed eighteen Broadway musicals, including *The Pirates of Penzance* (1981), *The Mystery of Edwin Drood* (1985), *Ragtime* (1998), and *The Visit* (2015). Six of those shows she also directed, including the 1999 revival of *Annie Get Your Gun* and the original production of *Once on this Island* (1990). Most recently, in 2023, Daniele conceived, directed, and co-choreographed (with Alex Sanchez) the tango-infused off-Broadway musical *The Gardens Of Anuncia*, written by her longtime collaborator, Michael John LaChiusa,[9] and inspired by her own childhood experiences growing up in Buenos Aires during the 1940s under the shadow of the Perón regime. Graciela Daniele is the recipient of ten Tony Award nominations, and in 2020, she was awarded a special Tony for Lifetime Achievement.

Gillian Lynne was born near London in 1926. She was a very hyperactive child and when she was eight, her mother took her to a doctor to seek help. As Lynne described the scene, the doctor, who had been watching little Gillian very closely, turned on some music on the radio and asked her mother to leave the room with him. "Of course, the minute they'd gone, I started to dance. I lept up on his desk and lept up on the settee and lept all over the place." Meanwhile, her mother and the doctor had been observing all of this surreptitiously. The doctor declared, "This child is not sick . . . It's just she's a born dancer," and prescribed that she immediately be enrolled in a dance class.[10] "The minute I got to dance [class] . . . I felt at home."[11] By her teens, Gillian was a soloist with the prestigious Sadler Wells Ballet.[12] During the 1950s, as Lynne was transitioning from ballet to musical theater, London's West End was dominated by American musicals featuring the choreography of Agnes de Mille, who had a major influence on Lynne: "She was a goddess to me. I would fall to the pavement . . . I adored her."[13] Soon, her life would change when the choreographer of a revue she was dancing in suddenly quit. "I jumped right in," she later recalled, "One minute, I *wasn't* a choreographer, and the next minute, I *was* the choreographer. I was dropped in the pot."[14] Her early work in London got her noticed by producer David Merrick, who in 1965 brought Lynne to New York to choreograph *The Roar of the Greasepaint and the Smell of the Crowd*, the first of seven Broadway musicals she would choreograph, including two of the most popular and longest running musicals of all time: **Cats** (1982) and **Phantom of the Opera** (1988). With its revue-like, *concept musical* format, *Cats* relied heavily on Lynne's extensive choreography for its impact, and she also served as its Associate Director. In 2019, just a month before she died at age ninety-two, the theater where *Cats* had originally opened[15] was renamed the Gillian Lynne Theater, making history as the first West End venue to be named after a woman.

Five-time Tony Award winner **Susan Stroman** was born in Delaware in 1954. The Stroman house was filled with music, and she began taking dance lessons when she was five. She majored in theater at the University of Delaware and, after graduating in 1976, moved to New York City, where she soon found work as a dancer, including in the national tours of *Chicago* (starring Gwen Verdon and Chita Rivera) and in the Broadway revival of *Whoopee*. Her first big breaks as a choreographer came with two off-Broadway shows, both directed by Scott Ellis and involving the songwriters John Kander and Fred Ebb—a 1987 revival of their early flop, **Flora, the Red Menace**, and a hit 1999 revue of the team's song titled **And the World Goes Round**. The following year, Stroman collaborated with British director Mike Okrent (whom she would marry in 1995) on "the new Gershwin musical," ***Crazy For You***, a spectacular dance-filled, "Best Musical" Tony-winning success for which she received her first Tony Award for "Best Choreography." Then, in 1994, Harold Prince invited Stroman to collaborate with him on a revival of ***Show Boat,*** which he said he wanted "to dance more" than any previous version of the show.[16] In response, she invented several memorable dance montages that used changing dance styles and fashions to fill in the jumps in time in *Show Boat*'s epic story, as it moves from the 1880s to the 1920s. Stroman's choreography, which also dynamically illustrated the effects of Black dance forms on American culture, earned her a second Tony Award. She won an Oliver Award for her choreography for the 1991 National Theatre production of ***Oklahoma!*** (directed by Trevor Nunn), where she met the considerable challenge of honoring the original concepts and dances of Agnes DeMille, which are among the most iconic in Broadway history, while still succeeding in creating captivating new choreography that was entirely her own. Critic Michael Coveney of the *Daily Mail* hailed Stroman's choreography as "perhaps the biggest star of the night."

Then, in the spring of 2000, she received four more Tony Award nominations for directing and choreographing the revival of ***The Music Man*** and for her direction and choreography of her dance-play ***Contact***, which she also conceived. *Contact* won the Tony for "Best Musical," and Stroman earned her third Tony for the show's wall-to-wall choreography. Meanwhile, for several "glorious months," Okrent and Stroman worked with bookwriters Mel Brooks and Tom Meehan to bring Brook's cult classic film *The Producers* to the stage. The plan was for Okrent to direct and Stroman to choreograph, as they had done on both *Crazy For You* and ***Big—The Musical.*** But when Okrent was diagnosed with leukemia, all work on the show stopped, and just eighteen months later, Okrent was dead, leaving Stroman heartbroken and bereft. Eventually, Brooks and Meehan approached Stroman and told her they wanted her to direct *The Producers*. "I didn't know what to say," she later wrote:

> I couldn't speak. To be honest, I was already drained of any emotion...My first thought was to say no ... Then Mel Brooks said to me, "If you want to feel alive again, you will do this. You will wake up every morning and cry, and you will go to sleep every night and cry. But in between, you will laugh. I will make you laugh."[17]

Stroman agreed, and as a result, she became the director and choreographer of the most-awarded musical in Broadway history, including two more Tonys for her direction and choreography. To date, Stro, as she is called by her friends and colleagues, has directed and/or choreographed fifteen Broadway musicals, including ***Steel Pier***, ***Thou Shalt Not***, ***The Frogs***, ***Young Frankenstein***, ***The Scottsboro Boys***, ***Big Fish***, ***Bullets Over Broadway***, ***The Prince of Broadway***, and ***New York, New York***.

Kathleen Marshall was born in Wisconsin in 1963. Her parents were academics who took her and her older brother, Rob (see page 308), to all kinds of performances, ballet, operas, symphonies, plays, and musicals, but Kathleen didn't start dancing until she was thirteen. As she described it, "We were fans [of the performing arts] before we ever thought we could participate in it." By the time she finished high school, she was dancing with a semi-professional ballet company in Pittsburg and "doing lots of musical revues."[18] At Smith College, Marshall majored in English but was heavily involved in theater and dance, studying ballet and musical theater dance with Broadway dancer Gemze de Lappe, who, as a disciple of Agnes DeMille, was the foremost authority on remounting the choreography of *Oklahoma!* and other DeMille shows. "She ran really tough ballet classes, and she did musical theater choreography classes," Marshall recalled. "We did the *Carousel* ballet as a dance concert. She was really influential."[19] For Marshall, it was "exactly the kind of dance I wanted to study."[20] After college, she moved to New York, danced in and served as the dance captain for the National Tour of *Cats*, and then began assisting her brother, who had already begun to establish himself as an up-and-coming choreographer. As Marshall has explained:

> Choreography is an apprenticeship career, and I got my brother's hand-me-downs. You start as a dancer; then, if you're interested in the whole, people pick up on that, and you become a dance captain or an assistant choreographer. Then someone you're assisting gets an offer he can't do, and suddenly you're a choreographer.[21]

Marshall's first Broadway show as choreographer was the 1995 revue *Swinging on a Star*, while she made her debut as director-choreographer with the revival of *Wonderful Town* (2003), starring Donna Murphy. The majority of Marshall's twelve Broadway musicals (and biggest hits) have been revivals and period pieces, including, as choreographer, *1776* (1997), *Kiss Me, Kate* (1999), *Follies* (2001), *Little Shop of Horrors* (2003); and as director-choreographer, *The Pajama Game* (2006), *Grease* (2007), *Anything Goes* (2011), and *Nice Work if You Can Get it* (2012). "I'm the vintage girl," Marshall laughingly told a reporter, but noted that, even though a show might be a revival, she approached it,

> ... as if it were a new show—to make it our own, in a way ... The folks who wrote these original musicals were real showmen. They knew they were creating this as popular entertainment ... I love theater that challenges and provokes, but I also think there's a place in the world for theater that entertains and transports. And I think you can do that with intelligence.[22]

"Let It Go!" — *The Full Monty* (J, Q, B)

The sea change on Broadway was not lost on the critics of the day, as is evident from the first paragraph of critic Michael Kuchwara's review of *The Full Monty*:

> Ok, when was the last time a brash, crowd-pleasing musical with nothing more on its mind than good fun found its way to Broadway? In the 1950s and '60s, shows like *Bells Are Ringing, Lil' Abner, Bye Bye Birdie,* and *Do Re Mi* were staples. Today they are practically extinct. Now comes along . . . a musical that restores one's faith in frivolous entertainment.[23]

Openly Gay playwright **Terrence McNally**,[24] smartly adapted a charming, low-budget 1997 British film that turned into a giant international hit by transplanting the story from economically depressed Sheffield, England to equally down on it heels Buffalo, NY, where the steel plants have closed and a diverse group of "irresistibly endearing"[25] misfit, blue-collar workers, "a microcosm of male insecurity,"[26] hatch a desperate plan to make some quick cash by becoming male strippers. The show's "winning, ear-catching pop score" was by newcomer **David Yazbek**, another of those rare talents who can create both words and music, and, as staged by the dynamic team of director **Jack O'Brien** and choreographer **Jerry Mitchell,** this "good-natured salute to the human spirit" remained "as fresh, bouncy and downright delightful" as the movie had been, even as at the same time it was transformed it into "into a full-fledged dance musical, albeit one that clings to the quaint Old-fashioned notion of retaining a story."[27] Mitchell's "ingenious choreography" managed to "create compelling production numbers using only the movements you might expect from a bunch of steel workers just learning to dance."[28]

Something Different — The Songs of David Yazbek

Writer, composer, lyricist, and recording artist David Yazbek was born in NYC in 1961. His father was of Arab Lebanese descent, and his mother was of Jewish Italian ancestry. He began music lessons on the cello in grade school and took up the piano as a teenager. While attending Brown University, he wrote an original musical and directed a production of *Hair*. After graduating from college in 1982, Yazbek got a job writing for television's *The Late Show with David Letterman*, and in 1996 won an Emmy Award along with the rest of the show's writing team. He then left to focus on his music career, and between 1987 and 1989, he wrote advertising jingles, released five rock albums, and co-wrote the theme song to the animated children's series *Where in The World is Carmen Sandiego?* In 2001, Yazbek was engaged to write the score for *The Full Monty* when his former bandmate, composer Adam Guettel (Richard Rodgers's grandson), turned the job down and recommended Yazbek.²⁹ ***The Full Monty*** ran for two years, and Yazbek received the 2001 Drama Desk Award for "Outstanding Music" and a Tony Award nomination for "Best Score." In a review of ***The Full Monty***'s original cast album, music critic Michael Phillios noted that Yazbek's "best pop hooks, and brash, gleefully crude lyrics owe equally honorable debts to Frank Loessor. [The song "Scrap" recalls the waitresses' lament in *The Most Happy Fella*] and the grinning-satyr Brit-pop of XTC [a band with whom Yazbek has worked]. But just as effectively as his rousers, Yazbek delivers two honestly felt ballads . . ."³⁰

The Full Monty led to four additional Broadway musicals with music and lyrics by Yazbek: ***Dirty Rotten Scoundrels*** (2005), ***Women on the Verge of a Nervous Breakdown*** (2010), ***Tootsie*** (2019), and, most notably, ***The Band's Visit*** (2017), which received the 2018 Tony Awards for "Best Musical" and "Best Book" (by Itamar Moses), and for which Yazbek received the Tony for "Best Score." As this book went to press, following its acclaimed off-Broadway premiere in 2024, *Dead Outlaw*, another musical comedy with music and lyrics by David Yazbek (in collaboration with Erik Della Penna) and a book by Itmar Moses was announced to open on Broadway in the spring of 2025.

Yazbek's Favorite Musicals

In David Yazbek's view:

> Every song in *Guys and Dolls* is a winner, and funny. And *West Side Story*, because the music is so spectacular, and because of the dancing. I really love great dance, and you don't see it anymore. And there's individual Sondheim songs that I can psych myself up with when I'm having trouble getting to work, like "Please Hello" from *Pacific Overtures*. I think Sondheim has written some of the best single lines in musical theatre. And when I listen to the end of "Ladies Who Lunch," I'm like oh, fuck, that's just devastating. That's something to aspire to as a songwriter . . . I think *The Music Man* is pretty close to perfectly structured, and *Pajama Game* has a lot of great stuff . . . But Frank Loesser is my guy, in terms of musical theatre.³¹

When *The Full Monty* opened in the fall of 2000, the *Guardian* declared it "the hottest ticket on Broadway,"³² and it seemed as if it would be the hit of the season, win every award, and, as the *New York Times* suggested, run "for a long, long, time." And indeed, the show did run for almost two years (770 performances). It was nominated for an impressive nine Tony awards, including "Best Direction," "Best Choreography," "Best Book," "Best Score," and "Best Musical," and if it had opened the previous season, it would likely have won all of them. But that spring, another new musical comedy blitzkrieged into town, stole much of *The Full Monty*'s thunder, and walked off with every single one of those Tony Awards.

"It's Good to be the King" (of Broadway)—Mel Brooks and *The Producers* (I, J, Q, W)

That show was a "sublimely ridiculous spectacle"[33] called *The Producers*, and it was the brainchild of comedian, writer, actor, director, and producer **Mel Brooks**, who was seventy-five years old when his first hit Broadway musical opened on Broadway. He was born Melvin James Kaminsky on his family's kitchen table in Brooklyn, NY, in 1926.[34] His parents were both Jewish immigrants: his mother, Kitty, was from Ukraine, and his father, Max, who died when Brooks was only two years old, was a German Jew from Poland. Life during the Depression was challenging, of course, for a poor single mother, and Kitty had to take in garment piecework to support Brooks and his three older brothers. At nine, young Melvin was taken by an uncle "one fateful night" to see his first Broadway show: Cole Porter's *Anything Goes*, starring Ethel Merman. As he vividly recalled eighty-seven years later:

> That show changed me and changed my life. My hands stung from screaming and applauding so much after it was over, and I remember going back in Uncle Joe's cab, and I remember saying as he was driving me back home to Williamsburg, "Uncle Joe, Uncle Joe! I want to be part of that show. I want to be in show business!"[35]

Brooks knew, "then and there," that he was not going to go into the garment industry like the rest of his family. He "was not going to be pushing a rack of clothes to the post office," but would be instead, "an arrow heading for show business!"[36] Brooks began playing drums as a teenager, taking lessons from a classmate of his brother who would become jazz great Buddy Rich, and learned to play well enough to get some paying gigs, but it was while serving in the Army during World War II that he started getting into comedy. After the war, he eventually worked his way up the show business ladder to a job as a "tummler" (a sort of entertainer-in-chief) at Grossinger's Resort in the Catskill Mountains.[37] This led to work in the emerging new field of television variety shows, most significantly as a staff writer on Sid Caesar's *Your Show of Shows*.[38] During the 1950s and early '60s, Brooks also worked on three Broadway musicals, only one of which was a hit: the revue *New Faces of 1952*, for which he wrote a burlesque of the play *Death of a Salesman*.[39] But it was the failure of his third musical, *All American* (1962),[40] that got Brooks wondering, "What would happen if someone tried to produce an intentionally awful musical?"[41]

The result was his 1968 film, *The Producers*, which became an instant cult classic and won Brooks an Academy Award for "Best Original Screenplay." Then, during the 1970s, Brooks wrote, directed, and often starred in a series of hit films that outrageously burlesqued classic Hollywood genres: *Blazing Saddles* (westerns), *Young Frankenstein* (horror movies), *High Anxiety* (Hitchcock films), *History of the World, Part 1* (historical epics), and *Silent Movie*—several of which are included on many lists of the greatest film comedies of all time. But even though each of those films featured prominent songs with music and lyrics by Brooks, when the Broadway musical adaptation of *The Producers* was announced in 1999, the idea was met with a great deal of skepticism—especially regarding Brooks' ability to compose the music for a full Broadway score. The recent track record of famous Hollywood film and music industry figures trying to duplicate their success on Broadway had not been good.[42] But with the expert assistance of musical arranger Glen Kelly, who helped Brooks to get the tunes he heard in his head down on paper and fully fleshed out, the end result was a hilarious, tuneful, and very effective score that purposefully echoed the classic sounds of Broadway's Golden Age.

The plot of *The Producers—The New Mel Brooks Musical* was essentially the same as in the original film but backdated to 1959, the heart of the Golden Age. It told the story of a washed-up Broadway producer, Max Bialystock (played by **Nathan Lane**), and a timid accountant, Leo Bloom (played by **Matthew Broderick**), who dream up the ultimate Broadway scam: find a musical that is so ineptly written, and so offensive, that it couldn't possibly succeed. Then, to guarantee failure, hire the worst, most inappropriate cast and most incompetent director you can find. Finally, and most importantly, raise a lot more money than you actually need to mount the show so that when it flops, you can fly off to Rio with the remaining loot. Max and Leo believe they have hit gold when they uncover a musical titled "*Springtime for Hitler*—a gay romp with Adolf and Eva at Berchtesgaden," written by an unhinged Nazi, and they hire the outrageously flamboyant director Roger De Bris (**Gary Beach**) to stage the show. Of course, in the end the unintentionally comic musical becomes a massive hit, and our duo of misfit heroes are carted off to jail.

From the moment that *The Producers* opened its pre-Broadway tryout in Chicago, it was clear that the show was "a triumph" for Mel Brooks and his principal collaborators, **Thomas Meehan** (who co-wrote the book) and **Susan Stroman**, who was hailed for her "magnificent direction and choreography," and by the time of its Broadway opening, the show was already sold out for the following six months.[43] The response of the critics was equally ecstatic: the show was hailed as "a grand, old-fashioned Broadway musical fashioned with a sharp modern attitude,"[44] and again both audience and critics were excited to see the return of "the real thing: a big Broadway book musical that is so ecstatically drunk on its powers to entertain that it leaves you delirious, too."[45]

The show's "almost non-stop hilarity,"[46] was its most acclaimed aspect. It was hailed as a "demented, deliriously funny evening" that was packed "as full of gags, gadgets, and gimmicks as an old vaudevillian's trunk,"[47] and described as a show "that comes at you like a supersonic train from its first scene" and "sweeps away years of dreary . . . noncomedies—including the entire glum Stephen Sondheim era and all these somber Andrew Lloyd-Weber-type shows—to bring the American musical back to its original roots, which had to do mostly with wisecracking fun."[48] Brooks was celebrated for being

... shameless in his pursuit of laughs. No joke is too low, no pun too broad, no situation too silly, especially if it will get a giggle—and there are plenty of giggles, not to mention outright guffaws ... But then *The Producers* is in the grand and honorable tradition of zany mayhem and outrageousness that stretches back to burlesque and beyond.[49]

"In one fell swoop," Mel Brooks had "revived musical comedy and driven a stake through the heart of political correctness on Broadway."[50] This theme was echoed in virtually every review of the show, with one critic admiringly describing it as "an orgy of bad taste ... Loud, crass, foolish, and happily defiant about the thinning skins of political correctness,"[51] and another pointing out that the show "served up a banquet of insults for whites, Blacks, Jews and gay people, old ladies, and young bimbos—not to mention, of course, the Nazis—that work brilliantly for one reason: They are screamingly funny."[52] "We call it an equal-opportunity offender," joked one of the musicals actual producers.[53] This kind of "bad-taste" humor had always been part of Mel Brooks's brand of comedy, and in this show, he certainly did not "give in to political correctness in presenting [its many] Gay characters," which included the flamingly effeminate Roger De Bris; his "common-law assistant," Carmen Ghia (**Roger Bart**); and "a household full of every gay male stereotype imaginable ... along with a glum lesbian" lighting designer. But as the critics consistently noted, "all of this is done with such a big wink—and without an ounce of malice—that it comes off as the kind of impudent, unfettered fun that the show is all about." Indeed, the Broadway musical version of *The Producers* had much more heart than the more abrasive original film, making it clear that the "Brooklyn boy who grew up in the age of Cole Porter and Busby Berkeley" was "totally, giddily in love with the showbiz mythology" he was sending up.[54] A few weeks after it opened, *The Producers* won a record twelve Tonys, still the most ever awarded to any one show, and it would go on to a six-year run of 2,502 performances.

The Full Monty and *The Producers* had several elements in common. Both employed a boldly audacious, irreverent, in-your-face style of modern comedy style that Mel Brooks had pioneered in his films, which included a mix of high and low comedy, vulgar language, and frank sexual references, and as a result, both shows were criticized by some critics for their crudeness. Both also featured significant Gay characters, although the tone of presentation of those characters was drastically different. In a sub-plot expanded from the movie, the nerdy Gay couple in *The Full Monty* is presented in a warmly comic manner and provided with a lovely, touching love song, "You Walk With Me." In contrast, in a musical in which every character is presented as a broadly comic stereotype, in both the showstopping production number, "Keep It Gay," and Roger DeBris-as-Hitler's hilarious spin on Judy Garland's "Born in a Trunk" sequence from *A Star Is Born*, the Gay characters in *The Producers* are presented as flamboyantly campy characters in the tradition of *Irene*'s Madam Lucy, *Lady in the Dark*'s Reginald Paxton, Bert Savoy, and the stars of the "Pansy Craze."

Most importantly, both musicals demonstrated that there was a vast audience clamoring for modern musical comedy. Some observers have speculated that this renewed hunger for comic musicals was a result of the psychological effects of 9/11—that in the aftermath of that tragedy, audiences were seeking fun and distraction. However, both *The Full Monty* and *The Producers* had opened and established themselves as hits many months before 9/11. Like all trends, however, this one might soon have faded if another immensely popular and joy-filled musical comedy hadn't come along quickly to seal the deal.

"Mama, I'm a Big Girl Now"—Post-Modern Musical Comedy and *Hairspray*

Hairspray is a musical that is very dear to my heart because, in 2002, it received its world premiere at The 5th Avenue Theatre in Seattle, where, at the time, I was serving as the Producing Artistic Director. This provided me with a one-of-a-kind inside view of the creation and development of that show from its first draft and early demo recordings through its staged readings, rehearsal period, pre-Broadway tryout in Seattle, and onto its thrilling opening night on Broadway.

I want to emphasize what an unlikely hit *Hairspray* appeared to be at the time. First of all, it was based on a quirky, only moderately well-known film whose writer and director was John Waters—best known for making shockingly provocative cult films purposely intended to attack and offend middle-class values. Secondly, only one of the show's writers, co-bookwriter Tom Meehan, had ever written a Broadway musical before, and the only cast member of note was Harvey Fierstein, and even he had only a limited profile outside of New York at that time. And confusingly for potential ticket buyers, Fierstein would be playing one of the leading female roles. Finally, *Hairspray* is a wild, wacky, irreverent comedy that revolves around some very serious issues, including body image, fat shaming, agoraphobia, racial prejudice, segregation, interracial relationships, class discrimination, and female empowerment—a combination that did not necessarily make it seem likely to become a major hit.

The driving force behind the show was its lead producer, Margo Lion, who in several interviews, related the genesis of *Hairspray*:

> I wanted to do a musical about young people that had a lot of dance—as a result of the 80s, when there hadn't been a lot of dance. Because the British musicals didn't dance and I was looking around for something. I was home, and I had a cold or flu or something, and I had a bunch of movies, one of which was *Hairspray*, and a few minutes into the movie, I thought, "I want to do this." It had all of the ingredients that one wants for a show. It had a larger-than-life character who wanted something—who had obstacles to overcome.[55]

Still, Lion never imagined that a musical derived from a John Waters movie could ever become a massive mainstream hit, but a series of developmental staged readings of the book and score for invited audiences made it clear that the creators had tapped into something special and quickly started a feeding frenzy among potential investors. This optimism was confirmed at the first preview performance in Seattle when the audience screamed its approval after every number. And at the unforgettable third preview, with 300 members of the Seattle Men's Chorus in attendance, even after the final curtain call was over and the cast had exited the stage, the audience refused to leave the theater. They just kept cheering and applauding until Harvey Fierstein finally came down from his dressing room in a robe for one more triumphant bow. It felt like a scene from a cheesy backstage movie musical—but it was absolutely real. I was there. And ever since, audiences have gone wild for *Hairspray*.

The show's (almost) entirely Gay creative team consisted of director Jack O'Brien, choreographer Jerry Mitchell, bookwriter Mark O'Donnell, and songwriters Marc Shaiman and Scott Whitman. Only co-bookwriter Tom Meehan was straight. *Hairspray* opened on Broadway in August of 2002, won eight Tony Awards, including, "Best Score," "Best Book," "Best Director" and "Best Musical" the following spring, and proceeded to run for nearly six and a half years (2,642 performances). It was adapted into a hit motion picture in 2007 and a live television musical in 2016. The *New York Times* review perfectly captured the essence of how *Hairspray* and virtually all the other twenty-first-century musical comedies that have followed it have been able to accomplish this reinvention:

> *Hairspray* succeeds in recreating the pleasures of the old-fashioned musical comedy without seeming old-fashioned. Think of it as a postmodern musical. It's a work that incorporates elements of arch-satire, kitsch, and camp, all those elements that have ruled pop culture for the past several decades. But it does it without the long, customary edges of jadedness and condescension.[56]

Together, *Hairspray*, *The Full Monty*, and *The Producers* inspired a vibrant stream of new-fashioned, twenty-first-century musical comedies that, as this list below makes evident, shows no signs of letting up:

> **Twenty-first Century Musical Comedy**
>
> *Thoroughly Modern Millie, Avenue Q, Monty Python's Spamalot, Dirty Rotten Scoundrels, Legally Blonde, The 25th Annual Putnam County Spelling Bee, The Drowsy Chaperone, Curtains, The Book of Mormon, Kinky Boots, A Christmas Story, A Gentleman's Guide to Love and Murder, Elf, Aladdin, Something Rotten, The Prom, Beetlejuice, Mean Girls, Pretty Woman, Back To The Future, Some Like It Hot, Shucked, and Death Becomes Her.*

All of these are traditional "book musicals" much closer in form to the *musical comedies* of the Golden Age, like *Guys and Dolls* or *Damn Yankees*, than they are to the *concept musicals* of the 1970s or the *poperettas* of the 1980s and '90s. However, they are very different from the musical comedies of the past in one very significant way—almost all of them use (pop)Rock musical scores to tell their stories.[57]

Broadway Dance #13: Queer Choreographers of the New Millennium (Q)

In the final decade of the twentieth century, as the devastation of AIDS finally began to recede, a new generation of Queer choreographers and director-choreographers (all of whom were born between 1959 and 1973) graduated from the dancing ensembles of Broadway musicals and picked up the mantle of Robbins, Bennett, and Tune. The first to emerge were three Midwesterners, all of whom were born in 1960.

Rob Marshall, the brother of Kathleen Marshall (see page 300), made his Broadway debut as a dancer in *Cats* in 1982 and went on to perform in three subsequent musicals, all of which were choreographed by Graciela Daniele. Then, in 1993, he burst onto the scene with his vibrant choreography for the Kander and Ebb/Hal Prince musical *Kiss of the Spider Woman*, starring **Chita Rivera**, and his inventive and hilarious "musical staging" for a revival of *She Loves Me*. Marshall followed those up the next season with a hit revival of *Damn Yankees*, giving him three hit shows running simultaneously—all three of which earned him Tony Award nominations for "Best Choreography." He would choreograph five more Broadway musicals, mostly revivals, including the 1998 smash hit revival of *Cabaret*, which he also co-directed with Sam Mendes. Then, in 2002, the success of his direction and choreography of a television adaptation of the musical *Annie* led to him being hired to direct the film version of *Chicago*, which became a major box office hit, won the Academy Award for "Best Picture," and earned Marshall an Oscar nomination for "Best Director." He followed this up with big screen versions of the Broadway musicals *Nine* and *Into the Woods*, the live-action version of Disney's *Little Mermaid*, and the original film musical *Mary Poppins Returns*. Marshall's husband, **John DeLuca,** choreographed *Dr. Seuss' How the Grinch Stole Christmas!* on Broadway and has worked closely with Marshall as a producer and creative partner on "every second, every frame," of these films.[58]

Jeff Calhoun became a protégé of Tommy Tune after Tune hired him to dance in the national tour of *The Best Little Whorehouse in Texas*. Then, after Calhoun made his Broadway debut as one of the brothers in the 1981 stage production of *Seven Brides for Seven Brothers*, Tune hired him to perform as his standby in *My One and Only*. Next, Tune engaged Calhoun to serve as his Associate Choreographer on *The Will Rogers Follies* and then as the Choreographer of *The Best Little Whorehouse Goes Public* (1994), which Tune directed. This was the first of ten Broadway musicals that Calhoun has choreographed and/or directed, including the hit revivals of *Grease* (1994), *Annie Get Your Gun* (1999), and Deaf West Theater's production of *Big River* (2003), and the new musicals *Grey Gardens* (2006) and *Newsies* (2012).

Jerry Mitchell performed in six Broadway musicals, beginning in 1983, dancing first for Michael Bennett as a replacement in *A Chorus Line*, then for Agnes DeMille in a revival of *Brigadoon*, Joe Layton in *Barnum*, Donald Saddler in a revival of *On Your Toes*, Tommy Tune in *The Will Rogers Follies*, as well as serving as Jerome Robbin's assistant on *Jerome Robbins' Broadway*. To date, Mitchell has choreographed thirteen Broadway musicals, including *The Full Monty* (2000), *Hairspray* (2002), *La Cage aux Folles* (2004 revival), and *Dirty Rotten Scoundrels* (2005); directed and choreographed *Legally Blonde* (2007), *Kinky Boots* (2013), *On Your Feet* (2015),[59] and *Pretty Woman* (2018); and received two Tony Awards for his choreography of *La Cage* and *Kinky Boots*. At the time of writing, Mitchell is scheduled to bring **BOOP! The Betty Boop Musical** to Broadway in the spring of 2025.

Then, during the first decade of the new century, several more talented young men joined their ranks. **Rob Ashford** made his Broadway debut dancing in the 1987 revival of *Anything Goes*, the first of eight musicals in which he either performed, dance captained, and/or assisted choreographers Michael Smuin, Liza Gennaro, Susan Stroman, Rob Marshall, Kathleen Marshall, and Patricia Birch. He received a Tony award for his very first Broadway show as choreographer, 2002's *Thoroughly Modern Mille*, and thus far he has followed that up with nine more, including the hit revivals of **Promises, Promises** (2010), **How to Succeed in Business Without Really Trying** (2011), and **Evita** (2012), and the new musicals **The Wedding Singer** (2006), **Curtains** (2007), and **Frozen** (2018).

Sergio Trujillo, who was born in Columbia in 1963, made his Broadway debut as a dancer in *Jerome Robbins' Broadway* (1989), followed by appearances in the 1992 revival of *Guys and Dolls* and *Fosse* (1999). He has created the choreography for a very eclectic group of thirteen Broadway musicals, including **Jersey Boys** (2005), **Next to Normal** (2009), **Memphis** (2009), **The Adams Family** (2010), **On Your Feet** (2015), and **Ain't Too Proud** (2019), for which he received the Tony Award.

Andy Blankenbuehler made his Broadway debut replacing Sergio Trujillo dancing in that 1992 revival of *Guys and Dolls*, and then, in 1999, Blankenbuehler and Trujillo performed together in the original cast of *Fosse*. Blankenbuehler has gone on to choreograph nine Broadway musicals, most notably **In the Heights** (2008), **Hamilton** (2015), and **Bandstand** (2017), which he also directed, and he received the Tony Award for "Best Choreography" for all three of those productions.

Following his debut as a replacement in the original Broadway run of *Cats*, **Christopher Gattelli** went into *Fosse* as a replacement. Since 2006, he has created the choreography for seventeen Broadway shows, including the acclaimed revivals of **Sunday in the Park with George** (2005), **South Pacific** (2008), and **My Fair Lady** (2018). In 2012, he received a Tony Award for his dynamic choreography for **Newsies**, and as this book was going to press Gattelli was receiving wide acclaim for his direction and choreography of the Broadway musical **Death Becomes Her**.

Four talented young men from the United Kingdom have also had a significant impact on Broadway choreography over the past two decades. **Warren Carlyle** began his choreographic career as Susan Stroman's Associate Choreographer on the 1998 West End revival of *Oklahoma!* He then served in that same role on the Broadway premiere of *The Producers* (2001) and the 2002 Broadway revival of *Oklahoma!* Carlyle then immediately made the jump to director-choreographer with the short-lived *A Tale of Two Cities* (2008), the first of fourteen Broadway productions he has choreographed, which include the revivals of *Follies* (2011), *On the Twentieth Century* (2015), *She Loves Me* (2016), *Hello, Dolly!* (2017), *Kiss Me, Kate* (2019), and *The Music Man* (2022), as well as the new musical *A Christmas Story* (2012). And he both directed and choreographed the 2009 revival of *Finian's Rainbow* and the new musicals *Chaplin* (2012), *After Midnight* (2017), and *Harmony* (2023). Acclaimed ballet choreographer **Christopher Wheeldon** has directed and choreographed two hit Broadway musicals: 2015's *An American in Paris* and 2022's *MJ The Musical*, and was awarded a Tony for "Best Choreography" for both shows. **Peter Darling** has choreographed four musicals, including 2013's *Matilda* and his first Broadway show, *Billy Elliot*, for which he received the Tony Award for "Best Choreography." The odd man out in this group is **Steven Hoggett,** who, unlike his colleagues, has not come from a musical theater dance background. Instead, he came from the world of devised performance/physical theater, and as a result, he has created choreography for just as many Broadway plays as he has musicals, thirteen in total, including a string of hits: *American Idiot* (2010), *Once* (2012), *The Curious Incident of the Dog in the Night-Time* (2014), *Harry Potter and the Cursed Child* (2018), *A Beautiful Noise, The Neil Diamond Musical* (2022), and the 2023 revival of *Sweeney Todd*.

Finally, **Casey Nicholaw**'s extensive Broadway performing career connected him to nearly every leading choreographer of the Modern Era. In his first Broadway show, he danced for Susan Stroman in the original cast of 1992's *Crazy For You* and worked for her again in 1997's *Steel Pier*. He also danced for Jeff Calhoun and Tommy Tune in *Best Little Whorehouse Goes Public*, Rob Marshall in *Victor/Victoria*, Kathleen Marshall in *Seussical*, and Rob Ashford in *Thoroughly Modern Millie*. Nicholaw then made a spectacular debut as the choreographer of *Monty Python's Spamalot*, and the next season made his director-choreographer debut with *The Drowsy Chaperone*. Since then, he has directed and choreographed eight additional Broadway musicals, including *Elf* (2010 and 2012), *The Book Of Mormon* (2011), for which he received the Tony Award for "Best Director of a Musical," *Disney's Aladdin* (2014), *Something Rotten* (2015), *Mean Girls* (2018), *The Prom* (2018), and *Some Like It Hot* (2022), for which he received his second Tony Award for "Best Choreography."

"A Whole New World"—Disney on Broadway (J, Q, B, W)

The Walt Disney Company's relationship with Broadway begins back in 1989 with the release of *The Little Mermaid*, the first in a series of musical films that revitalized Disney's animated film business and initiated a ten-year period known as "the Disney Renaissance." The score of *The Little Mermaid*, as well as those of the blockbuster hits *Beauty and the Beast* and *Aladdin* that followed it, were the creation of the young songwriting team of **Howard Ashman and Alan Menken**. In 1982, they had scored a tremendous long-running hit with the off-Broadway musical *Little Shop of Horrors*, a perfectly crafted traditional musical comedy featuring an infectious 1960s pop-flavored score; modern, irreverent humor; and a campy B-movie horror story that made it feel hip, fresh, and contemporary. Impressed by this success, Disney hired Ashman and Mencken to help them find a way to reboot their animated musical films.

These two young writers were steeped in the traditional styles, forms, and structures of the Broadway musical and brought that deep understanding with them to Hollywood. As a result, their string of Disney films closely follow established Broadway models in how songs are used to define the characters, move the story forward, and expand emotional moments. As the *New York Times* noted in 1991:

> With *Beauty and the Beast* . . . Disney has done something no one has done before: combine the latest computer animation techniques with the best of Broadway. Here, in the guise of furthering a children's fable, is the brand of witty, soaring musical score that is now virtually extinct on the stage. "The Little Mermaid" was similarly a showcase for the extraordinary songwriting talents of Alan Menken and Howard Ashman, but this time the music is even more central. Broadway is as vital to this film's staging and characterizations as it is to the songs themselves.[60]

And at the end of the year when Frank Rich, chief theater critic of the *New York Times*, declared that "the best Broadway musical score of 1991" had been written, not for Broadway, but for the animated *Beauty and the Beast*[61]—and this was in a Broadway season that included *Miss Saigon*, *Once on this Island*, *The Secret Garden*, and *The Will Rogers Follies*—it was probably inevitable that Disney would begin to transform its series of animated films into live Broadway musicals, beginning with *Beauty and the Beast* in 1994.

Although not enthusiastically received by critics, the powerful Disney brand, along with lavish costumes and impressive (if clunky) stagecraft and special effects, made the Broadway adaptation immensely popular with family audiences who were becoming less afraid of venturing into a newly cleaned-up and sanitized Times Square. *Beauty and the Beast* ran for a remarkable 5,462 performances (more than thirteen years), and this was only the beginning of Disney's conquest of Broadway.

Disney's next and greatest success was *The Lion King*, which opened in 1997. In great contrast to the extremely literal "recreate the movie onstage" approach that was taken for the design and staging of *Beauty and the Beast*, the Broadway incarnation of *The Lion King* features imaginative, innovative, and highly stylized theatrical staging by the maverick avant-garde director and designer, **Julie Taymor,** and Jamaican American modern dance choreographer **Garth Fagan**. This is perhaps best exemplified by the breathtaking "Circle of Life" sequence, during which the creators employ a wide range of timeless world theater and puppetry techniques (most notably Bunraku), blend them with traditional African music, dance, and masks, and combine it all with cutting-edge stage lighting and technology. The result is a shimmering, wonderous, transcendent opening number that, unfortunately, in my estimation, the rest of the show never quite equals. But even though several of the show's comedy scenes and comic characters remain trapped in a clunky, cartoon version of the show, Taymor and her team repeatedly find ways to dazzle, move, and delight us with her distinctive artistic vision. *The Lion King* received six 1998 Tony Awards: for choreography, scenic design, costume design, lighting design, and "Best Musical," while Julie Taymor made history when she became the first woman to win a Tony for "Best Direction of A Musical."

The popularity and financial success of *The Lion King* is unprecedented. So far, as a result of its twenty-seven-year, nearly 11,000-performance run on Broadway, and its twenty-seven spin-off productions worldwide, the show has been seen by more than 112 million people and has grossed nearly $10 billion.[62] This makes the Broadway stage version of *The Lion King* not only the most successful musical in history but also the highest-grossing entertainment property of all time![63] The second highest-grossing entertainment property in history is also a Broadway musical, *The Phantom of the Opera*, which has grossed over $6 billion worldwide. To put this in perspective, both of these Broadway stage musicals have grossed more than the film *Avatar* ($2.8 billion) and more than all of the *Star Wars* films combined.[64]

Disney Theatricals hit some unexpected speed bumps, however, with their Broadway adaptations of *Tarzan* (2006) and *The Little Mermaid* (2008), both of which were major flops.[65] But they recovered their hit-making mojo with *Mary Poppins* (2006), *Newsies* (2012), and especially *Aladdin* (2014), which I'm happy to say also had its world premiere at the 5th Avenue Theatre during my tenure and has become another long-running, worldwide hit.

We certainly have to give Disney credit for bringing millions of new audience members to Broadway-style musicals—many experiencing live professional theater for the very first time. This has vastly expanded the current and future audience for musical theater in New York and around the world.

"Money Makes the World Go Around"—The Perilous Economics of Modern Broadway

The mammoth economic success of shows such as *The Lion King*, *The Phantom of the Opera*, *Wicked*, and *Hamilton* can grossly distort the expectations of financial success on Broadway. The reality is that that most Broadway musicals lose money.

Only one in five shows ever recoup their production costs, much less turn a profit. Why? Because creating a Broadway musical is among the most difficult and unpredictable endeavors known to humankind. Even an entity with the creative talent, power, and enormous financial resources of Disney will fail at least as many times as they succeed. For example, Disney's most recent Broadway musical, its 2018 adaptation of the blockbuster animated film *Frozen*, was assumed by nearly everyone to be a surefire hit. But for some reason it failed to catch on with audiences and after running for only 825 performances, Disney decided not to reopen it following the pandemic. As the old saying goes, "You can't make a living on Broadway—but you can make a killing."

"I've Heard That Song Before"—The Jukebox Musical (W)

At the dawn of the twenty-first century, a new kind of musical emerged—*the jukebox musical*. These shows have become enormously popular and also somewhat controversial. What exactly is a jukebox musical? I define it as a musical that tells its story using pre-existing songs rather than new songs written specifically for that show. In most cases, these are pop songs that were not originally conceived to be part of a narrative. One of the motivating factors behind the creation of these musicals, and certainly behind their popularity, is (actual) nostalgia. Jukebox musicals provide a chance for its audience to re-experience the songs of their youth in a new theatrical context. Under that definition, there are actually two quite different kinds of jukebox musicals. First, there are *biographical jukebox musicals* that dramatize the life and times of a legendary performer, songwriter, band, or singing group, with the show built around the songs they created and/or made famous. Hit shows in that category include **Jersey Boys**, **Beautiful**, **Tina**, **A Beautiful Noise: The Neil Diamond Musical**, **Hell's Kitchen**, and **MJ**. The second category comprises *fictional jukebox musicals*, such as **Mamma Mia!**, **Moulin Rouge!**, and **& Juliet**. These shows usually employ a specific catalog of pop songs to tell a new fictional story. Musical shows that, in my estimation, should *not* be classified as jukebox musicals are songwriter revues such as *Jacques Brel is Alive and Well and Living in Paris*, *Oh Coward!*, *Smokey Joe's Café*, or *Ain't Misbehavin'*. These highly entertaining shows display great theatricality, but like all revues, they do not try to tell an overall story. The defining factor for a jukebox musical of either kind is that it uses pre-existing songs to support a narrative. And as experience has shown, this is not easy to pull off.

Thrilling shows like *Jersey Boys* make the *biographical jukebox musical* seem relatively simple to create. After all, the songs are already chart-topping hits that the audience comes into the theater humming, and a large group of fans already idolizes the story's central character(s). Therefore, it might seem that all you need to do is include enough "behind the music" plot points to keep the hit parade marching along. However, a very long list of flop shows based on the life and music of luminaries such as John Lennon, Ellie Greenwich, John Denver, Gloria Estefan, Donna Summer, and Cher clearly demonstrates that this is not so simple. Biographies are often messy and difficult to shape into compelling narratives, and pop song lyrics can be static, repetitive, and lacking in character and drama.

Even more difficult to pull off are those shows that try to weave pre-existing hit songs into a new, fictional story. Only a handful of shows have made this formula work. More often than not, the creators find themselves missing pieces they need to tell the story effectively. So far, only *Mamma Mia!*, *Rock of Ages*, *Moulin Rouge*, *& Juliet*, and *Hell's Kitchen* have made this work successfully on Broadway. However, none of these impediments to success seem to discourage anyone from trying to create the next big jukebox hit.

Dancing Queens—The Women Behind *Mamma Mia!*

It was British producer **Judy Craymer** who came up with the idea for what would eventually become *Mamma Mia!* She then had to convince Björn Ulvaeus and Benny Andersson, the songwriters behind the pop group ABBA, to entrust her with their multi-million-dollar song catalog, which she told them was not going to be used in a "tribute show" or to tell the AABA story, but rather as part of a "truly original 'book' musical." They weren't "100% convinced at the time," she later recounted, "but they didn't absolutely close the door, so I took hope." She next commissioned playwright **Catherine Johnson** to write the book, and briefed her with these instructions: no lyrics could be changed, the story needed to be "a contemporary, ironic, romantic comedy," and if she "listened carefully to ABBA's songs, she'd notice how they fell into two different generations: the slightly younger, playful songs like 'Honey, Honey' ... and the more mature, emotional songs such as 'The Winner Takes It All.'" Out of that observation came the show's cross-generational mother–daughter story. Meanwhile, Craymer persuaded **Phyllida Lloyd**, whose background was "serious theater" and opera, to come on board as the show's director. The three women soon discovered that they all shared the same birth year and "firmly bonded."[66]

It was quite unusual, if not unheard of, for three women to be the creative forces behind what was to become such a tremendous commercial success. Appropriately, *Mamma Mia!* features three strong women, Donna, Tanya, and Rosie, at the center of its story. Author Grace Barnes describes them as clearly being "products of the Women's Rights movements of the 1960s and 1980s":

> They are all single with sexual histories that have been formed through the choices they have actively made ... Neither Tanya nor Rosie has children or (current) husbands, which can be read as a further rejection of the conformist societal pressure on women. The three women demonstrate agency in all areas of their lives, and we assume have jobs which give them sufficient

> financial security to be able to afford holidays on a Greek island . . . A close reading of *Mamma Mia!* . . . [reveals] a feminist agenda which utilizes an unashamedly female-centric show as an, albeit mild, call to arms.[67]
>
> *Mamma Mia!* premiered in the West End in 1999, where it is still running. It opened on Broadway in 2001 and ran for nearly fourteen years (5,758 performances). In addition to the smash hit film version (directed by Lloyd and with a screenplay by Johnson), Judy Craymer has gone on to produce fifty productions of the show in sixteen languages around the world.

It's interesting to note that while this genre of musical is relatively new to Broadway, both kinds of jukebox shows have a long history in Hollywood. Since the 1930s, dozens of biographical backstage film musicals have told the (often highly fictionalized) stories of songwriters such as George M. Cohan, Rodgers and Hart, George Gershwin, Jerome Kern, and Cole Porter (in two movies), as well as famous entertainers from Al Jolson, Ruth Etting, and Billie Holiday, right up to Loretta Lynn, Johnny Cash, Ray Charles, Freddie Mercury, Selena, Elvis, Aretha Franklin, and Elton John. Even more significantly, several of the most acclaimed and revered movie musicals of all time are fictional jukebox musicals built on established hit song catalogs, such as *An American in Paris* (Gershwin), *The Band Wagon* (Dietz and Schwartz), and *Singin' in the Rain* (Freed and Brown).

Now, back to the controversy I alluded to earlier. On Broadway, *jukebox musicals* have often been derided by critics, who view them as just lazy, cynical attempts by big music corporations to exploit their back catalogs—in other words, to make further profits from songs they already own. And often, those critics have been correct. However, whatever the initial motivation, truly engaging musicals cannot be faked or mandated by decree. It's simply too difficult an art form. When a musical succeeds in captivating a large and ongoing audience, it is only because somewhere along the way, an artist or group of artists became inspired to tell that particular story and created a dynamic and unique way of bringing it to the stage. That is certainly what happened with the best of the jukebox musicals.

"Good News!"—The Return of the Musical Play

This brings us to the *musical play*. Despite all of the experimentation with plotless musicals and the revue format during the 1970s and '80s, the creators of twenty-first-century musicals whose goal is to make us feel something, rather than just make us laugh (not that that is easy to do), have largely returned to the durable format Rodgers and Hammerstein invented back in the 1940s. But folded into these traditionally structured, story-driven musical plays are a variety of major influences carried over from late twentieth-century musicals. First and foremost, the current era's shows often emulate the darkness, moral ambiguity, expert craftsmanship, and extended musical sequences found in Sondheim's shows, such as *Sweeney Todd* and *Into the Woods*. Equally impactful has been the scope and ambition of the musical *Ragtime* (a show whose influence on the field far outweighs its critical acclaim and popularity). Also widely adopted has been the musical sweep and pomposity of the Lloyd Webber and Boublil and Schonberg megamusicals that this current generation of creators grew up on—but notably, not their sung-through, all-music format. Perhaps most significantly, nearly every new millennium musical has followed the example of *Rent*.

"One Song Glory"—Jonathan Larson and the Enduring Legacy of *Rent*

The 1996 smash hit musical **Rent**, with book, music, and lyrics by **Jonathan Larson**, is very loosely based on the plot and characters of Giacomo Puccini's *La Bohème*. Like that classic opera, *Rent* tells the story of a diverse group of impoverished young artists struggling to survive and create a life, in this case in Lower Manhattan's bohemian "Alphabet City" neighborhood during the AIDS crisis. Tragically, thirty-five-year-old Larson died suddenly of an aortic dissection the night before the show's off-Broadway premiere. Everyone involved, including Larson's parents, agreed that despite the tragedy, the show had to go on in his honor. *Rent* became an impossible-to-get-a-ticket-to, off-Broadway sensation—especially after the *New York Times* declared it "an exhilarating, landmark rock opera."[68] After transferring to Broadway, *Rent* won Tony Awards for "Best Book," "Best Score," and "Best Musical." Its enormous popularity and twelve-year, 5,123-performance run, along with its many long-running national tours and international productions, would continue well into the new century, where it has had a tremendous effect on the musicals that *have* come after it. Thirty years after *Hair*,[69] the enormous success of *Rent* finally solidified the use of rock and pop-influenced music in Broadway musicals, and nearly every musical since has employed a (pop)Rock score that blends contemporary rhythms and styles with traditional show tune structures and strategies.

> At the center of the reinvigoration of the *musical play* is four-time Tony Award nominee **Michael Greif**, one of the most successful Broadway directors of the twenty-first century. He was born into a middle-class Jewish home in Brooklyn, NY, in 1959, located in an economically mixed community, which he says "made him sensitive to the inherently dramatic conflicts of the 'over and underprivileged.'"[70] As he told the *Los Angeles Times*, the feeling of alienation and dislocation that is often expressed in his work, and of being what he called "the other," came from "growing up gay. That can really give you a strong perception of the threat a political system can

perpetrate on an individual—whether you're talking about Jews or gays or women or people of color." After directing musicals in high school, Greif pursued an acting and directing career at Northwestern University, where he studied under Broadway directors Frank Galati (*Ragtime*) and Des McAnuff (*Tommy, Big River, Jersey Boys*). Since Greif's own Broadway debut in 1996 with the smash hit **Rent**, he has directed nine additional Broadway musicals, including **Grey Gardens** (2006), **Next to Normal** (2009), and **Dear Evan Hanson** (2016). In 2024 Greif became the first director in history to open three new musicals all in the same season, when **Days of Wine and Roses**, *The Notebook*, and Alicia Keys autobiographical musical, **Hell's Kitchen**, all opened within weeks of each other. As historian Jennifer Ashley Tepper noted, "Since directing a new musical often requires more in-depth developmental work *and* more involved levels of production work than directing a revival or a straight play, this is particularly notable."[71]

The Wizard and Stephen (J, W)

The first twenty-first-century *musical play* to establish this hybrid style was **Wicked**. With music and lyrics by **Stephen Schwartz** and a book by **Winnie Holzman**, it was adapted from Gregory Maguire's bestselling 1995 novel *Wicked! The Life and Times of the Wicked Witch of the West*, itself a revisionist riff of Frank L. Baum's classic novel *The Wonderful Wizard of Oz* and its beloved MGM movie musical adaptation. Starring **Idina Menzel** and **Kristin Chenoweth**, the show opened on Broadway in 2003 to very mixed reviews but has since become one of the biggest Broadway hits of all time. (The story and themes of *Wicked* are explored further in Chapter 14). In 2023, *Wicked* celebrated its twentieth anniversary on Broadway and passed *Cats* to become the fourth longest-running Broadway musical. At the time of writing, six additional companies are playing worldwide, including sit-down productions in London, Australia, Germany, and Japan. More than 65 million people have seen *Wicked*, and since movie versions tend to boost the audience for still running stage productions, there is no end in sight. Within weeks of its opening at the end of 2024, the first instalment of the two-part film adaptation established itself as a pop culture juggernaut passing *Mamma Mia!* to become the highest-grossing Broadway musical film adaptation of all time[72] and one of the top fifty highest grossing movies in history.[73] As a result, during Christmas week of 2024, the New York production of *Wicked* became the first show in Broadway history to bring in more than $5 million in ticket sales in one week.[74]

Wicked has been followed by a string of vibrant, popular, and acclaimed musical plays that do not shy away from tackling significant and provocative subject matter. These include the following.

> ### Twenty-first Century Musical Plays
>
> *The Color Purple, Spring Awakening, The Light in the Piazza, Gray Gardens, In the Heights, Billy Elliot, Next to Normal, Memphis, Once, Fun Home, Hamilton, Waitress, Dear Evan Hansen, The Great Comet, The Band's Visit, Kimberly Akimbo, The Days of Wine and Roses, The Notebook, Water for Elephants, Suffs, The Great Gatsby, Maybe Happy Ending,* and *The Outsiders.*

Second Wave — Twenty-First Century Concept Musicals

Amid the new millennium's re-establishment of the traditional book musical, four vibrant and successful concept musicals emerged as popular, award-winning hits. Like their influential predecessors, all of these shows employ non-linear stories and revue-like formats, and each of them seems to be modeled, at least in part, on specific concept musicals from the 1970s and '80s. For example, 2017's remarkable **Come from Away**, with book, music, and lyrics by **Irene Sankoff and David Hein**, forgoes traditional story structures and even a central protagonist and instead employs an intricate mosaic-like format similar to, but more complex than, Tommy Tune's *Grand Hotel* (1989),[75] and bookwriter Peter Stone and songwriter Maury Yeston's *Titanic* (1997). Like the latter team, Sankoff and Hein also took on the challenge of dramatizing an actual historical event, including characters based on specific real-life people or, in some cases, composites of several people. (For more on *Come from Away*, see Chapter 16.)

Then in 2019, the Tony Award for "Best Musical" went to **Hadestown**, with book, lyrics, and bluesy, Americana-infused music by singer-songwriter **Anais Mitchell**. As staged by director Rachel Chavkin and choreographer David Neumann, the show is set in a New Orleans-style jazz joint quite similar to the Greek nightclub setting of the 1968 Kander and Ebb/Joseph Stein musical *Zorba*, as originally staged by Hal Prince and Ron Field. In the opening numbers of both shows, a master of ceremonies-like narrator steps up to a microphone and begins singing a story about "life" to the diverse group of patrons seated around them, who then are soon drawn into acting out the tale. This concept, of course, echoes Prince and Field's own staging of *Cabaret*, and *Hadestown*'s narrator/storyteller character, Hermes, is clearly a spin-off of *Zorba*'s Leader, *Cabaret*'s M.C., and *Pippin*'s Leading Player.

With book, music, and lyrics by **Toby Marlow and Lucy Moss,** the 2021 musical *Six* is presented in a "reality competition show" format,[76] quite similar to that of *A Chorus Line* and *Cats*, and the show's Tony Award-winning songs and costumes, as well as the performance styles of each of Henry VIII's six wives, are based on specific contemporary pop divas. According to Marlow and Moss, Catherine of Aragon's look and music are based on Beyoncé; Anne Boleyn is styled after Avril Levine; Jane Seymour references Adele; Anne of Cleves incorporates elements from both Rihanna and Niki Minaj; Catherine Howard is a mix of Ariana Grande and Britney Spears; and Catherine Parr is based on Alicia Keys.[77] This closely parallels how Kander and Ebb's songs in *Chicago* are each based on the signature songs and performance styles of 1920s vaudeville stars, such as Sophie Tucker, Helen Morgan, and Eddie Cantor.

Even more high concept is the 2022 Tony and Pulitzer Prize-winning musical *A Strange Loop*, which its author, **Michael R. Jackson** (who wrote the book, music, and lyrics), has described as "a musical about a fat, Black gay man, who is writing a musical about a fat, Black gay man, who is writing a musical about a fat, Black gay man, who is writing a musical about a fat, Black gay man, who is trying to change himself." The leading character is named Usher, and when he is not trying to write a musical, he works as an usher at the Broadway theater where *The Lion King* is playing, which in real life is where Jackson worked while he was writing the show. Somewhat like *Company*, this entire show takes place inside the mind of Usher, the only "human" character in the show, and the six other actors in the cast all play the various thoughts and voices inside of his head.

Also in 2021, *Company* itself made a startling comeback in a reworked gender-swapped adaptation that was the brainchild of British director **Marianne Elliott**. She said she loved the original show but wanted to bring it into the present day and felt it would have more potency with a female central character because, as she told The *New York Times*:

> Today, a male Bobby, who is turning 35 and who has clearly got a lovely life, lots of friends, lots of girlfriends, obviously doing quite well, an apartment in the city—nobody's going to be pushing him into getting married. They'd probably just slap him on the back and say, "Have a great time." But for a woman at 35, obviously, it's quite a threshold. There's going to be a lot of pressure on her from her friends to make a wish that she will actually "sort her life out" and settle down and get married and have a family, maybe.[78]

Eventually, Elliott was able to convince an initially skeptical Sondheim to work with her to make the necessary rewrites and changes, and in that process, they switched the genders of several other characters in the show as well. This was the final Broadway production that Stephen Sondheim would work on. Originally scheduled to open on his ninetieth birthday in 2020, after nine preview performances this new *Company* and all of Broadway went into lockdown because of the Covid 19 pandemic. The production finally resumed performance on November 15, 2021, with Sondheim in attendance. He died just eleven days later. The production would go on to win five Tony Awards including "Best Director" for Marianne Elliot and "Best Revival of a Musical."

"Who Tells Your Story?"—Record-Breaking Broadway Herstory

The 2023–4 Broadway theater season smashed a number of records regarding women directing Broadway musicals. When **Schele Williams** made a double Broadway debut as both the director of the revival of *The Wiz* and co-director (with Michael Grief) of *The Notebook*, she became only the second Black woman to ever direct a Broadway musical. While this is certainly a landmark to be celebrated, the first was Vinnette Carroll, who directed *Don't Bother Me I Can't*

Cope in 1972, *But Never Jam Today* in 1979, and *Your Arms Too Short to Box With God* in 1976 and 1980. This means that in the entire history of Broadway, only six musicals have ever been directed by Black women—and only two Black women have ever been given the opportunity to direct a Broadway musical.

In addition, for the first time ever, four out of the five 2024 Tony nominations for "Best Director of a Musical" went to female-identifying directors: Maria Friedman for *Merrily We Roll Along*, Leigh Silverman for *Suffs*, Danya Taymor for *The Outsiders*, and Jessica Stone for *Water for Elephants*, who received her second consecutive nomination.[79] In the end the award was won by Danya Taymor, who became the sixth woman to win this award. The first was her aunt, Julie Taymor, who received it in 1998 for her direction of *The Lion King*.[80]

"Never Mind a Small Disaster"—What's Next for the Broadway Musical?

In the winter of 2025, as this book goes to press, Broadway continues to struggle from the lingering effects of a global pandemic that in April of 2020 forced a total shutdown of all forty-one Broadway theaters and an unprecedented closure of all Broadway shows that lasted a year and a half. Several significant changes in audience behavior resulted from this, which have caused a considerable drop in ticket sales. The persistence of hybrid work means there are fewer commuters in Manhattan each day looking for entertainment after hours, and even though international and national tourism to NYC has started to rebound, suburban theatergoers have not come back in their previous numbers. In multiple ways, the pandemic seems to have broken the theater-going habit for a large number of people. As one Broadway producer put it, "It is not a secret that we are still missing a core part of our audience."[81]

On the positive side, twenty-one musicals opened during the 2023–4 Broadway season, including sixteen new musicals and five revivals.[82] Notably, these productions were created by the most diverse group of creative artists in Broadway history. Sixteen of those musicals included women as members of their core creative teams (book, music, lyrics, direction, choreography), ten were helmed by female directors, and two include women in all five of those key creative positions. In addition, eight of this season's musicals included artists of color in their core creative teams, including history-making Shelle Williams (see Box above). This evolution is also being reflected in the audience, which reportedly is "younger and more diverse than it had been before the pandemic."[83] So, in that regard, the future looks bright.

Also, on the positive side, what has not changed is that three principal themes continue to dominate the *musical plays*, *musical comedies*, and *concept musicals* of post-pandemic twenty-first-century Broadway: The Trials and Triumphs of Transgressive Women; Equity, Social Justice, and Inclusion; and The Crucial Importance of Community. As Chapters 14, 15, and 16 will demonstrate, these have been the most ubiquitous and prevalent themes of the Broadway musical throughout its history and have contributed significantly to what has made this art form so powerful, popular, and subversive.

Fig. 33: Set just before and during the American Civil War, the central character of *Bloomer Girl* (1944) is Evelina Applegate (Celeste Holm), a hoop-skirt manufacturer's daughter who has fallen under the sway of her feminist aunt, Dolly Bloomer (Margaret Douglass, left), who is also active in the Underground Railroad. Here, Pompey (Dooley Wilson, center), a runaway slave, is delivered to Bloomer's office, where she is assisted by Daisy (Joan McCracken, right). Although *Bloomer Girl* never entered the canon of classic, enduring Broadway musicals, it was a highly influential show in its day. Eileen Darby.

Fig. 34: In the original production of *Annie Get Your Gun* (music and lyrics by Irving Berlin, book by Herbert Fields and Dorothy Fields, direction by Joshua Logan, choreography by Helen Tamiris), sharpshooter Annie Oakley (Ethel Merman) shows off her chest full of championship medals to her rival and fiancé Frank Butler (Ray Middleton). Wide World Photos, New York.

Figs. 35, 36: Three pioneering women have dominated the history of Broadway lighting design: Jean Rosenthal (left), Peggy Clark, and Tharon Musser (right). Billy Rose Theatre Division, The New York Public Library for the Performing Arts.

Fig. 37: The *West Side Story* creative team: (left to right) Stephen Sondheim (lyrics), Arthur Laurents (with his hand on his shoulder—book), Hal Prince (producer), Robert Griffith (producer—seated), Leonard Bernstein (music), and Jerome Robbins (director and choreographer). University of Bristol / ArenaPAL.

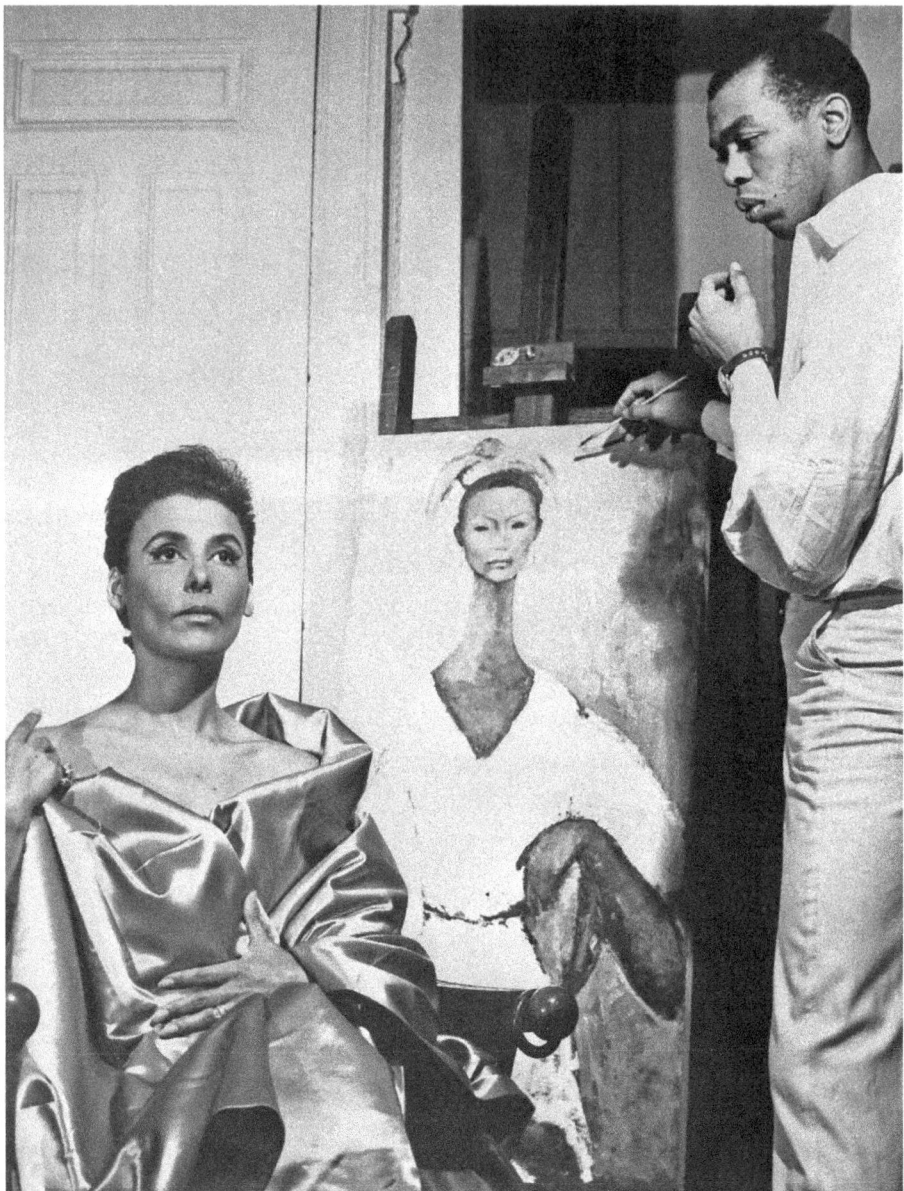

Fig. 38: Lena Horne, star of the 1957 Broadway musical *Jamaica*, sits for a portrait painted by Geoffrey Holder, who, eighteen years later, would win two Tony Awards for his direction and costume design of *The Wiz*. Bettmann / Contributor.

"Defying Gravity"

Fig. 39: *No Strings* (1962) was Richard Rodgers's first Broadway musical after the death of Hammerstein and the only show for which Rodgers wrote both music and lyrics. Featuring stylish, inventive direction, and choreography by Joe Layton, the musical was set in Paris and focused on a romance between a glamorous Black fashion model (Diahann Carroll) and a white expat writer (Richard Kiley). It became a major box office hit, running for 580 performances and winning Tony Awards for Carroll, Layton, and Rodgers. Bettmann / Contributor.

Fig. 40: Crowds flood into the Majestic Theatre to see Sammy Davis Jr. in the 1964 Broadway musical *Golden Boy*. With a book by Clifford Odets and William Gibson (based on Odets' 1937 play), and an often-thrilling contemporary score by Charles Strouse and Lee Adams, the musical climaxed in an exciting and visceral fight sequence choreographed by Donald McKayle. Michael Ochs Archives / Stringer.

Fig. 41: The blockbuster 1964 "musical comedy dream," *Hello, Dolly!*— produced by David Merrick, with book by Michael Stewart, music and lyrics by Jerry Herman, and direction and choreography by Gower Champion—applied the unusual tactic of following its original Tony-winning star, Carol Channing, with a series of even bigger stars: Ginger Rogers, Martha Raye, Betty Grable, Phylis Diller, Pearl Bailey, and Ethel Merman. Herman (center) appeared at the 1969 Tony Awards with two of his Dollys: Pearl Bailey (left) and Carol Channing (right). Ron Galella / Contributor.

"Defying Gravity"

Fig. 42: In 1960, choreographer Joe Layton had three shows running on Broadway simultaneously: *Once Upon a Mattress*, *Greenwillow*, and *The Sound of Music*. He would go on to choreograph and/ or direct more than twenty Broadway shows, including *No Strings* and *George M!*, both of which earned him Tony Awards for "Best Choreography," and the long-running hit musical *Barnum*. Jack Mitchell / Contributor.

Fig. 43: The West End stars of the musical *Hair* with the show's creative team. From left, actor Oliver Tobias, co-authors James Rado and Gerome Ragni, actor Paul Nicholas, and director Tom O'Horgan. Larry Ellis / Stringer.

Fig. 44: The 1970 Tony-winning "Best Musical" *Applause* (book by Betty Comden and Adolph Green, score by Charles Strouse and Lee Adams, direction and choreography by Ron Field) featured Lee Roy Reams (center) as "Duane," one of the first openly gay characters seen in a Broadway musical since 1941's *Lady in the Dark*. Here, he escorts the show's central character, "Margo Channing," played by Lauren Bacall (left), out for a night on the town at a Greenwich Village gay bar, where they encounter dancer Sammy Williams (right), who, five years later, received a Tony for his performance as the groundbreaking gay character, "Paul," in *A Chorus Line*. Bettmann / Contributor.

Fig. 45: With her staging of the 1972 hit gospel revue *Don't Bother Me I Can't Cope* (book, music, and lyrics by Micki Grant), Vinnette Carroll became the first Black woman to direct a Broadway musical, as well as the first to be nominated for a Tony Award for "Best Director." In 1978, she directed and wrote the book for another long-running hit, *Your Arms Too Short To Box With God* (music and lyrics by Alex Bradford, and additional songs by Micki Grant). Jack Mitchell / Contributor.

Fig. 46: Left to right, Tony nominee Vivian Reed, Newton Winters, and Lonnie McNeil stopped the show cold with their performance of "Sweet Georgia Brown" (choreographed by Billy Wilson) in *Bubbling Brown Sugar* (1976), the first of a series of Black songwriter revues that captivated Broadway during the "nostalgia craze" of the 1970s and early '80s that included *Ain't Misbehavin'*, *Eubie*, and *Sophisticated Ladies*. Afro Newspaper / Gado / Contributor.

Fig. 47: Director-choreographer and star performer Tommy Tune won the third of his ten Tony Awards for his direction of the 1982 musical *Nine*, which was also awarded "Best Musical." Here, Tune clowns with classic Broadway and Hollywood stars Ann Miller and Milton Berle at the awards ceremony. Bettmann / Contributor.

Fig. 48: Gillian Lynne, seen here working in her West London home in 1971, choreographed seven Broadway musicals, including two of the longest-running hits of all time: *Cats* and *The Phantom of the Opera*. Chris Ware / Stringer.

Fig. 49: Another Broadway songwriting "legacy chain": (left to right) Stephen Schwartz (*Godspell, Pippin, Wicked*) poses with Kristen Anderson-Lopez (*In Transit, Frozen*) and Robert Lopez (*Avenue Q, Book of Mormon, Frozen*) at the Dramatists Guild Foundation's Celebration Concert honoring Schwartz's 70th birthday in 2018. Walter McBride / Contributor.

Fig. 50: The dynamic trio of women behind the international mega-hit jukebox musical *Mamma Mia!*: (left to right) director Phyllida Lloyd, producer Judy Craymer, and bookwriter Catherine Johnson on the red carpet at the 2014 Laurence Olivier Awards. David M. Benett / Contributor.

Fig. 51: Director-choreographer Jerry Mitchell (right) with bookwriter Harvey Fierstein (left) and composer-lyricist Cyndi Lauper (center), in rehearsal for a touring production of their 2013 Tony Award-winning "Best Musical" *Kinky Boots*. Walter McBride / Contributor.

Fig. 52: Since 1992, five-time Tony Award winner Susan Stroman has directed and/or choreographed eighteen Broadway musicals and plays, including *Crazy For You*, the 1994 revival of *Show Boat*, *Contact*, and *The Producers*. Walter McBride / Contributor.

"Defying Gravity"

Fig. 53: Director-choreographer Casey Nicholaw (center) joins the creative team and cast of *Disney's Aladdin* on stage during the show's opening night curtain call. Front row, left to right, music supervisor Michael Kosarin, dance arranger Glen Kelly, bookwriter/lyricist Chad Beguelin, (Nicholaw), composer Alan Menken, scenic designer Bob Crowley, and lighting designer Natasha Katz. Second row, left to right, Jonathan Schwartz, Brandon O'Neil, Brian Gonzales, James Monroe Iglehart, Adam Jacobs (hidden behind Mencken), Courtney Reed, and Jonathan Freeman. Walter McBride / Contributor.

ACT V
THE PRINCIPAL THEMES

Fig. 54: The original cast of the 2017 musical *Come From Away* (book, music, and lyrics by Irene Sankoff and David Hein, direction by Christopher Ashley, musical staging by Kelly Devine, musical supervision by Ian Eisendrath). This musical demonstrated very effectively that, even within the financial limits and reduced cast sizes of twenty-first-century Broadway, inspired creative teams can still find effective ways to continue the Broadway musical's long tradition of bringing entire communities to life on stage. Photo by Mathew Murphy.

CHAPTER 14
"GOODBYE TO BLUEBERRY PIE!"—THE TRIALS AND TRIUMPHS OF TRANSGRESSIVE WOMEN (I, J, Q, B, W)

When you consider the demographics of the inventors of the Broadway Musical—the Immigrant, Jewish, Queer, and Black men and women highlighted in this book—it should be no surprise that the three main themes that these outcast inventors have dramatized most frequently are

- Transgressive Women and their impact on society.
- Equity, Social Justice, and Inclusion.
- The vital importance of forming and maintaining a healthy, functioning Community.

Nearly every musical, both classic and modern, is centered on one of these three themes, and many shows tackle two or even all three of them. This chapter focuses on what is perhaps the most pervasive and ubiquitous theme: Transgressive Women. For at least 125 years, an overwhelming majority of Broadway musicals have centered on stories about the trials and ultimate triumphs of transgressive women who go to battle against a patriarchal society. What exactly do I mean by "Transgressive"? For our purposes, the term can be defined in three ways. The first two are:

1. Involving a violation of accepted or imposed boundaries, especially those of social acceptability.
2. Someone who breaks the rules—a sinner by some people's way of thinking.

In nearly all of those Broadway musicals, the central female character embodies both definitions. This is not how musicals are generally perceived, however. Most people would not readily identify transgressive women as the most prevalent central characters in musicals, and I believe this disconnect reveals a crucial aspect of the Broadway musical's subversive power. We experience these ubiquitous, underlying themes subliminally, which is why musicals themselves can be considered to be transgressive as defined in a third meaning of the term:

3. Relating to fiction, theater, film, or art in which orthodox cultural, moral, and artistic boundaries are challenged by the representation of unconventional behavior and the use of experimental forms.

In the introduction to her book *Changed for Good: A Feminist History of the Broadway Musical*, author Stacy Wolf describes the impact of the song "Defying Gravity":

> At the end of Act 1 of *Wicked*—Stephen Schwartz and Winnie Holzman's 2003 blockbuster hit—Elphaba, the misunderstood, green-skinned witch-heroine separates from her dear friend and co-conspirator, Glinda, to pursue her passion as an activist and truth seeker . . . As she levitates 20 feet above the stage floor, and most crucially belts out a loud and long "me," Elphaba tells the audience that this show is hers.[1]

This song is only one in a long line of what Wolf identifies as a recurring convention of the Broadway Musical: "the belted act 1 finale of female assertion." This useful and often thrilling trope has been repeated and reproduced in dozens of musicals, including Fanny Brice's "Don't Rain On My Parade" in *Funny Girl*, Dolly Levi's "Before The Parade Passes By" in *Hello, Dolly!*, Effie White's "And I'm Telling You I'm Not Going" in *Dreamgirls*, and what in Wolf's view "might be the most terrifying and enthralling display of confidence" ever experienced on a Broadway stage, Mama Rose's "Everything's Coming Up Roses" in *Gypsy*. While each of these songs is a unique and specific creation, at the same time, their authors are honoring, echoing, and responding to what is at least a nearly seventy-year-old musical theater tradition. As Wolf points out, these act-one-finales-of-female-self-assertion can only come at the end of the first act after the audience has formed a relationship with the central character, and "witnessed the forces that conspire against her, which she must defy." Wolf concludes her Introduction with this assertion: "*Wicked* uses the tools and conventions of traditional musical theater—the musicals of Rodgers and Hammerstein from the 1940s and 50s, from *Oklahoma!* to *The Sound Of Music*—to craft a feminist and queer musical."[2] And that is just Wolf's jumping off place for what is a very fascinating and provocative book.

However, as the early chapters of this book have demonstrated, the Broadway musical's Transgressive Women can be traced back to long before Rodgers and Hammerstein. Chapter 4 profiled such early Genesis Period rule-breaking superstars as Lydia Thompson, Nora Bayes, and Fanny Brice—dynamic women who called the shots on both their art and their careers before women even had the right to vote. However, those charismatic star performers were acclaimed primarily for their own distinctive personas and personalities rather than for any of the characters they may have played.

As we have seen, the advent of the *musical play* and Golden Age *musical comedy* brought vibrant, dynamic, unforgettable principal characters to the musical stage, and it is those characters (rather than the performers who played them) that live on so vividly in our collective memories—and a great number of those characters are Transgressive Women. I find it useful when talking about these characters to divide them into several categories of "character types." Both Glinda and Elphaba are twenty-first-century examples of an age-old type of female character—the ingenue or young leading lady.

"Don't Rain on my Parade"—Rebellious Ingenues and Feisty Leading Ladies

Right from the beginning, the earliest musical comedies established a particular spin on the ingenue that has endured for more than 100 years. The *rebellious ingenue*, or *feisty leading lady* of the Broadway musical, is almost always an unmarried, working girl—at least until the end of the story. This is quite different from the way women were depicted in film and later television narratives during most of that same time span. In those media, young women were almost always defined by their relationship to the central male character—as girlfriends, daughters, and wives. But not in Broadway musicals.

In the long-running smash hits *Irene* (1919) and *Sally* (1920), the title characters were Irene O'Dare, a plucky Irish immigrant girl who works in an upholstery shop, and Sally Rhinelander, an orphan dishwasher who dreams of being a dancer. Both characters were created as stand-ins for the thousands of young women entering the workforce in New York and other cities during the decade following World War I. Even the lyric soprano leading ladies of American operettas were working girls, such as Kathie, the beer garden waitress in *The Student Prince*, and the frontier saloon singer who is the title character of *Rose-Marie*, both produced in 1924. As outlined in Chapter 5, the 1920s also saw the emergence of the "Flapper"—in real life and onstage. We see them represented in the college coeds, female golf pros, and "jazz babies" of DeSylva, Brown, and Henderson's series of hit musical comedies, as well as in the title character of *No, No, Nanette* and her friends, who in that show's opening number introduce themselves by singing:

> Flappers are we, flappers are we,
> Flippant and fly, and free!
> ... Puritans knock us
> Because the way we're clad
> Preachers all mock us
> Because we're not sad ...
> Most flippant young flappers are we![3]

Nannette herself rebels against her parents, her boyfriend, and even her circle of friends, and their reaction to her transgressive behavior is dramatized in the show's title song. Where was it that these flappers, both real and fictional, had first been exposed to wild jazz dancing?—in *Shuffle Along* and that vibrant wave of Black musicals that followed it, especially *Runnin' Wild*, the show that officially introduced "The Charleston" (staged by Broadway's first credited Black female choreographer, Lyda Webb, as discusssed on page 81). *Shuffle Along*'s vibrant female chorus was hailed for performing with "wild abandon," and criticized for being "unladylike," but the dance steps and style of those vibrant young Black women were soon copied and replicated by nearly every white ingenue and leading lady in every 1920s Broadway musical, as well as by millions of real-life young women in nightclubs, ballrooms, and living rooms across America.

The Great Depression of the 1930s brought a more worldly-wise, independent, and sexually sophisticated leading lady to Broadway, as epitomized by a young and sexy Ethel Merman in roles such as Reno Sweeney in *Anything Goes* and Nails O'Reilly in *Red, Hot, and Blue!* As we know, Merman firmly established "belting" as Broadway's signature female singing style. The act of "belting out a song" exudes a sense of power and confidence that is equal to any man, and all of the expressions related to it are assertive and aggressive: you "belt it out to the back wall"—you "murder the audience"—you "knock 'em dead."

"I Wanna be Bad"—The Sexual Mavericks

Those early Merman roles overlap with another category of transgressive female characters—the *sexual mavericks*. These are sex-positive, sexually liberated women who are unashamed to express a desire for sex, which they view as casual, uncomplicated fun. We see them in characters like Babe, the second female lead in the 1927 hit *Good News*, and Angie in 1929's *Follow Thru*, whose defining song is "I Wanna be Bad."

> If it's naughty to rouge your lips
> Shake your shoulders and twist your hips
> Let a lady confess, I wanna be bad!
> If it's naughty to vamp the men
> Sleep each morning till after ten
> Then the answer is, yes, I wanna be bad!
> This thing a being a good little goody is all very well,
> But what can you do when you're loaded with plenty of heal-th and vigor?
> When you're' learning what lips are for
> If it's naughty to ask for more
> Let a lady confess, I wanna be bad![4]

An older, more powerful, and sophisticated version of the sexual maverick is Vera Simpson in *Pal Joey* (highlighted in Chapter 6), a strong, jaded, confident woman who calls all the shots, both sexual and financial, in her relationship with her boytoy, Joey Evans. Then, in the 1940s, World War II brought six million women into the American workforce and sparked a new era of independence and liberation, as dramatized by all three of the feisty young leading ladies of *On the Town*: Claire, a scientist; Ivy, a professional dancer; and Hildy, a lusty female taxicab driver who clearly demonstrates that she is unafraid of expressing and pursuing her sexual desires in that show's comic duet "Come Up To My Place."

Rodgers and Hammerstein continued to employ these long-established character types in their classic series of musical plays, but they infused them with progressively greater levels of depth and complexity. Right from the start, the women of *Oklahoma!* are feisty, strong, and independent. Rebellious ingenue Laurey and her Aunt Eller own and run their own farm. There are no husbands or fathers on the scene, and neither of them seems to be desperate for one to come along. In fact, in the verse to Laurey's "I Am" song, "Many A New Day," she states emphatically that she will never be one of those women who "blubber liked a baby if her man goes away" or think the man she loses "is the only man among men." Instead, she will buy a new dress, scrub her neck, brush her hair, and "start all over again."[5] And we have no reason not to believe her.

Meanwhile, Aunt Eller appears to be the leader and most important person in the show's community. She is consulted and deferred to by the men on every decision. She is the one chosen to run the auction to ensure that the money needed to build the schoolhouse gets raised. She is the one who imposes order when a fight breaks out, and she is the one who makes the final decision on the validity of Curley's impromptu trial. Aunt Eller falls into another character category that I have dubbed *Wise Women and Caretakers*.

"Don't be Afraid of the Dark"—Wise Women and Caretakers

Rodgers and Hammerstein include one of these in each of their five major shows: Aunt Eller in *Oklahoma!*, Nettie Fowler in *Carousel*, Bloody Mary in *South Pacific*, Lady Thiang in *The King And I*, and Mother Superior in *The Sound of Music*. They usually function as mentors and advisors to the rebellious ingenue or feisty leading lady and provide her with crucial, life-changing advice and encouragement at a key turning point in the story—which, in most cases, is expressed in a big anthemic song of inspiration such as "You'll Never Walk Alone" and "Climb Ev'ry Mountain."[6]

Ado Annie is *Oklahoma!*'s sexual maverick character, and her "I Am" song defines this category. She can't say no—and doesn't think she should have to. Her guiding principle is that sex is fun—so enjoy it—and she feels no guilt or shame about it. She knows she "oughta" feel shame, but she doesn't! Among the many sexual maverick characters that followed Annie in the Golden Age are Meg Brockie in *Brigadoon*, Daisy in *Bloomer Girl*, Dorothy in *Gentlemen Prefer Blondes*, Lola in *Damn Yankees*, Nancy in *Oliver!*, and Charity Hope Valentine in *Sweet Charity*.

"There'll Be Some Changes Made"—The Disruptors

This brings us to another category that I've labeled the *Disruptors*. These are women who actively unsettle and challenge the status quo in even more overt ways than their sisters in the other categories. This character type goes back at least as far as Liza Elliott, the powerful fashion magazine editor in *Lady in the Dark*, and Lilli Vanessi, the high-powered Broadway and Hollywood star in *Kiss Me, Kate*, and continues through the title characters of *Bloomer Girl*, *The Unsinkable Molly Brown*, *Annie*, and all the way to Elphaba in *Wicked*. Only one of those women is "tamed" at the end of her story—Liza Elliott. All the others end in transgressive triumph.

Dorothy and Herbert Fields brought this character type vividly to life in their book for *Annie Get Your Gun*, which in turn inspired Irving Berlin to write his most character-revealing score. Their vibrant, gender-defying personification of real-life sharpshooter Annie Oakley is loud, coarse, crude, unrefined, smart, funny, competitive, uncompromising, and, most of all, "unladylike"—except when she wants to be—and, in the words of Berlin biographer Laurence Bergreen, "charged with the sexual implications of a woman who used her phallic gun with mastery."[7] As the world champion of a stereotypically male sport, Annie is a one-woman assault on the patriarchy. The musical climaxes in a raucous battle-of-the-sexes challenge duet titled "Anything You Can Do, (I Can Do Better)," during which Annie and her archrival and fiancé, the hypermasculine Frank Butler, compete in a series of contests, the results of which are surprisingly unbalanced—Annie wins all of them, which Frank begrudgingly acknowledges.

The final moments of the show, however, can be troubling for modern audiences because Annie decides to purposely lose the final championship shooting match in order to "get her man." This has been tempered in most recent productions with winks and nods added between Frank and Annie to make it clear that he is fully aware she is letting him win. But even in the original version, it always seemed clear to me, and I assume to most audiences, that Annie is finding a solution that will work for both of them. She understands that in the male-dominated, early twentieth-century world in which they live, Frank will be made a laughingstock if he loses this shooting match to a woman. Annie knows she can't change the world, so, in essence, she is protecting him. It's sort of like a wedding present. From the beginning of the story, it's been perfectly clear that Annie and Frank love each other and are exasperated by one another with equal passion. They're in constant conflict when they're together and despondent when they're apart (what Larry Hart described as "the lovely loving and the hateful hates"). As such, their relationship is a metaphor for all relationships. Every couple shares some aspect of this—hopefully to a much lesser degree than Annie and Frank. But if we listen and watch closely, we understand that their final act is to agree to stop trying to change one another and instead accept each other's limitations without limiting themselves. Annie knows that she's the best at sharpshooting and pretty much everything else—and she knows that Frank knows it, too. We have just seen her beat the pants off him in every other kind of contest that Irving Berlin could dream up. And Frank and the audience understand that Annie will not be dominated by him—only two songs earlier, we heard her loudly and definitively assert that she will "love and honor" but "NOT obey!" him.[8] And, of course, in performance, her dominance is made even clearer just a few minutes later when it is Annie Oakley, and not Frank Butler, who takes the final bow. In fact, the entire finale and curtain call are purposely designed and structured to build up to Annie's triumphant final re-entrance with the entire company, including Frank, as her adoring supporting cast. She owns the show.

South Pacific's leading lady, Nellie Forbush—yet another unmarried, independent working woman—owns her show as well. And what a fascinating character she is. Some audience members today are put off by the internalized racism Nellie discovers within herself during the course of the story, which causes her to turn down Emile De Becque's proposal of marriage. However, I would encourage them to look closely at what ultimately takes place in the story, which reveals what the story is actually about.

What does Nellie decide to do in the final scenes of *South Pacific*? And what do we imagine she will decide to do after the curtain falls? Or, more tellingly, what will she decide *not* to do? Presumably, Nellie decides not to return to her family and former life in the racially segregated American South of Little Rock, Arkansas,[9] and instead, marries Emile and lives out her life on a small island on the other side of the world as the loving stepmother of two dark-skinned, mixed-race children. In the mythic story structure of *South Pacific*, it is the woman, Nellie, who is strong enough and open enough to both recognize and confront her own internalized racism and then change, grow, and evolve as a person. This is in stark contrast to Lt. Joe Cable, the male warrior figure, who is too weak, too afraid, and too tied to the status quo to be able to break away from his family's racist attitudes—at least until it is too late. This is why, from a metaphoric story perspective, Cable must die in the war. Nellie, however, chooses life.

This takes us into the 1950s, that famously buttoned-down and repressive period in American history. The traditional "nuclear family" was central to the ethos of this era because, following the disruption of the war, traditional family values were seen as the stabilizing force the United States needed to protect it from "un-American activities," such as communism and homosexuality. In response, during the '50s, the range of principal female characters on film and television became even narrower, with women nearly always depicted as stay-at-home wives and mothers or their non-working ingenue daughters. But again, not on Broadway. In great contrast to the culture at large, Broadway musicals still overwhelmingly focused on independent, single, working women such as Marian the librarian and piano teacher, Eliza the flower seller, Adelaide the hard-working nightclub performer, Sarah Brown the missionary, Babe the pajama factory worker and union official, and Anna the single mother and teacher of dozens of the children and wives of the King of Siam. Even Maria in *The Sound of Music* is a transgressive woman. She starts off as a rebellious tomboy—"a problem" that must be solved. Then, she takes on the extremely difficult job of serving as the governess to seven children, ages five to sixteen. Both at the abbey and in the Captain's household, Maria continually defies all authority and breaks every rule and restriction that's put in front of her. All of which is exactly what allows her to triumph in the end, especially when all that time she spent out climbing mountains instead of inside the abbey praying is what provides her with the knowledge and skills she needs to lead her family to safety and outfox the Nazis.

The Broadway musicals of the 1960s went even further in this direction, no doubt because of the women's liberation movement that was just emerging at the time. *Fiddler on the Roof* (1964) is practically a feminist tract! Its plot can be summed up as follows: one by one, each of Tevye's three ingenue daughters rebels against the sexist, patriarchal traditions of her father and her society, and in the process, each of these young women becomes a groundbreaking change agent for herself, her family, her community, and, by extension, the world.

"Life is a Banquet!"—The Forces of Life

The musicals of the 1960s were dominated by another category of female characters—*forces of life*. Most of these characters are vibrant, dynamic middle-aged women in their forties or early fifties (usually portrayed by vibrant, dynamic women of the same age or a bit older). These are the "Big Transgressive Lady Shows" discussed in Chapter 10, in which not only the story of the musical but also the overall structure of the show itself is designed to reinforce the star lady's importance and dominant position in the proceedings. The entire show is created and staged to showcase this character's vibrant transgressive personality and actions. These characters—Dolly Levi, Fanny Brice, Mame Dennis, and, in her own misfit way, Charity Hope Valentine—are smarter, funnier, and more resourceful than everyone else in the story. They are also more capable, more dynamic, and more filled with life! Even darker versions of this character type—such as Rose in *Gypsy*, Eva Peron in *Evita*, or Mrs. Lovett in *Sweeney Todd*, characters whose behavior and actions often horrify us—are still *forces of life* who we end up admiring, identifying with, and even rooting for. Why? Because we are in awe of their resourcefulness, their moxie, and their determination. Unlike us, they won't let anything stand in their way—and we would like to have at least a small piece of that for ourselves. Of course, we are aware that these characters have flaws—*big* flaws! But they are *her* flaws. And she owns them—just as each of these characters owns their show.

The *sexual mavericks* continued into the 1960s but grew a bit darker, with characters such as Sally Bowles (*Cabaret*) and Aldonza (*Man of La Mancha*). In the Modern Era, the advent of the sexual revolution brought us Rizzo (*Grease*), Roxie and Velma (*Chicago*), and a bit later, Shug Avery (*The Color Purple*).

The three leading ladies of *Dreamgirls*—Deena, Lorelle, and Effie—embody multiple Transgressive Women character types. They are all *rebellious ingenues, disruptors*, and, to some extent, *sexual mavericks*. Only one of them, however, will become a *force of life*: Effie White. During this show's unforgettable act-one-finale-of-female-self-assertion, the rage that Effie feels from being betrayed by her lover and manager, Curtis, and then unjustly thrown out of "The Dreams" (the girl group that she initiated) is unleashed in the heart-wrenching pop aria, "And I Am Telling You (I'm Not Going)." With this defiant, searing anthem of emotional pain and righteous anger, Effie hits rock bottom, so that by the end of the story, as the result of several very satisfying twists and turns, she can ascend to new heights of triumph, justice, and even forgiveness.

Hairspray brings almost all these categories together in one character—Tracy Turnblad. She is a *rebellious ingenue*, a *disruptor*, and a *force of life*. In fact, Tracy is so dynamic and confident that it is easy for audiences to discount her character's significant level of marginalization within the world of the story. She is so vibrant and proactive and so rarely lets the prejudice she faces get her down that her actual degree of disenfranchisement is often in danger of being overlooked. That is why her mother, Edna, is almost a co-protagonist in the story. Edna and Tracy are positioned as parallel characters so that we can fully comprehend their low status. Edna not only makes it clear just how disadvantaged these poor, underclass, undereducated, and overweight (at least in the standard view) characters are, but also dramatizes the effect this can have on self-esteem and mental health. At the beginning of the show, Edna is so filled with shame about her "current weight" and the economic status of "people like us" that she has become agoraphobic. She hasn't left the house "since Mamie Eisenhower rolled her hose and bobbed her bangs" way back in the early 1950s. One of the major events of *Hairspray*'s first act is when Tracy persuades Edna to venture out into the world in the showstopping production number, "Welcome to the 60s." Tracy, who has already confronted these issues and (at least partly) overcome them, now inspires her mother to "throw away her old-fashioned fears," let go of the past, and release her shame—and in the process, through the magic of musical theater, Edna is instantly transformed into a *disruptor* and a *force of life* character herself.

Just two scenes later, *Hairspray* puts its own spin on "the act-1-finale-of-female-self-assertion" by handing that song spot over to the musical's *wise woman and caretaker* character: Motormouth Maybelle, the Black DJ and record shop owner. (This is the first of two key moments in the show in which Motormouth incites and inspires a major turning point in the story.) This number, "Big, Blonde and Beautiful," brings together all of the musical's central issues and intersectional themes. First and foremost are the body image issues. This song is a tutorial on how to combat the kind of discrimination that comes at us from society—along with the shame we are made to feel—when our bodies do not conform to the standard ideas of beauty. It is also a song of protest against racial inequity and economic injustice. All three of these issues are of equal importance in *Hairspray* (see page 355). Motormouth inspires Tracy and Edna to flaunt their differences and demand their equal rights. Big is beautiful. Black is Beautiful. And if a Black woman wants to be blonde, well, that's beautiful, too. The song lays out the central thematic statement of *Hairspray*: everyone is beautiful. In addition, in its own wacky way, the message of this song and the protest march that results from it suggests the actual power that could be harnessed—and the major transformations in society that could finally be realized—if all of the disenfranchised people—poor, BIPOC, and big—would join forces, sing in unison, and work together to fight for systematic change.

Other Hit Musicals that Center on Transgressive Women Include:

& Juliet, A Chorus Line, A Little Night Music, Aida, Bells Are Ringing, Bye Bye Birdie, Camelot, Carousel, City Of Angels, Come From Away, Company, Death Becomes Her, Follies, Fun Home, Hadestown, Hamilton, Hell's Kitchen, In the Heights, Into the Woods, Kimberly Akimbo, Legally Blonde, Little Me, Mamma Mia, Memphis, Miss Saigon, On the Twentieth Century, Once on this Island, Once Upon a Mattress, Porgy and Bess, Promises, Promises, Ragtime, Rent, SIX, Suffs, Sunday in the Park with George, Sunset Boulevard, The Secret Garden, Suffs, The Wiz, Wonderful Town

In order to create vibrant, moving, and unforgettable characters like these, bookwriters, composers, and lyricists must fully inhabit the minds, thoughts, and emotions of their characters. They have to immerse themselves in their characters' hopes, fears, and dreams; and vividly imagine the outside obstacles and inner limitations that will stand in the way of their characters achieving what their hearts desire. In essence, a writer must play every role themselves in order to create the book, music and lyrics that they will eventually hand over to the actors.

A significant number of the musicals discussed in this chapter, or included in the box on the previous page were written by women, including *Funny Girl* (book by Isabel Lennart); *Kiss Me, Kate* (book co-written by Bella Spewack); *Annie Get Your Gun* and *Sweet Charity* (both co-written by Dorothy Fields); *On The Town, Wonderful Town, Bells Are Ringing, On the Twentieth Century* (all co-written by Betty Comden); *Little Me* (lyrics by Carolynn Leigh); *In the Heights* (book by Quiara Alegría Hudes); *Ragtime* (lyrics by Lynn Ahrens); *Once on this Island* (book and lyrics by Lynn Ahrens); *Legally Blonde* (book by Heather Hatch; music and lyrics co-written by Nell Benjamin); *The Secret Garden* (book and lyrics by Marsha Norman; music by Lucy Simon); *Fun Home* and *Kimberly Akimbo* (both with music by Jeanine Tesori), and *Suffs* (book, music, and lyrics by Shaina Taub).

This means, however, that the majority of these shows, including their Transgressive Women characters, were written by men. Why were these men, most of whom were Jewish and/or Queer, inspired to create these leading female characters and the musicals that center around them? And how were they able to render them so authentically and effectively? Was it their own levels of marginalization that enabled them to depict these women in such rich and complex ways? And if so, does that mean that a straight, WASP male writer would not be able to accomplish this? Of course not. There are no limits to what a talented and inspired writer can imagine or create, and there are countless examples of male writers who were able to create fully and perfectly realized female characters—and the reverse, of course, is also true. However, I do believe that being Queer, Jewish, or both did make these men more disposed to create these characters and more drawn to telling their stories. Much like themselves, these women are compelled to break the rules of traditional society, battle with the status quo, and fight back against prejudice, inequity, and marginalization.

CHAPTER 15
"MAKE THEM HEAR YOU"—EQUITY, SOCIAL JUSTICE, AND INCLUSION (I, J, Q, B, W)

From the very beginning, issues involving equity, diversity, social justice, and inclusion have been at the center of America's story and its many attempts and recurring failures to fulfill and achieve its founding principle and what was truly a revolutionary idea: that all people are created equal. Since Broadway musicals so often dramatize and reflect America's story, these issues have also continually been at the center of Broadway musicals. Again, many people are surprised by this assertion. They don't think of musicals in that way. To a great extent, this is because they don't differentiate between Broadway and film musicals, the overwhelming majority of which do not deal in these themes (unless they started out as stage musicals). However, as the box below demonstrates, at least thirty-five hit Broadway musicals have explicitly dealt with issues of Equity, Social Justice, and Inclusion.

> **Thirty-five Musicals Dealing with Equity, Social Justice, and Inclusion**
>
> *1776, A Strange Loop, Allegiance, As Thousands Cheer, Avenue Q, Bloomer Girl, The Book of Mormon, Cabaret, Carmen Jones, Caroline or Change, Come From Away, Dreamgirls, Fiddler on the Roof, Finian's Rainbow, Golden Boy, Hair, Hairspray, Hamilton, Hell's Kitchen, In the Heights, Lost in the Stars, Miss Saigon, No Strings, Once on this Island, Pacific Overtures, Passing Strange, Porgy and Bess, Purlie, Raisin, Show Boat, South Pacific, Suffs, The King and I, West Side Story,* and *Wicked.*

Overwhelmingly, the creators of Broadway were visionary individuals and inspired creative teams who were way ahead of their time in understanding these issues. Of that, it is clear. But were they so far ahead that all of their work can be held up to all of today's progressive standards? Of course not. No artist from any period in the past can be expected to have fully visualized how society would evolve over the decades and centuries that followed them, and they could not help but be influenced and affected by the racist, sexist, and patriarchal societies and times in which they lived. Just as no artist of today can be expected to understand the full potential of human liberation that will come after our time. The musicals of today and tomorrow will undoubtedly be seen by future generations as containing dated and problematic elements, much as has already happened with *The Book of Mormon, Dear Evan Hanson,* and *Hamilton* to varying degrees. But I don't believe that these limitations should take anything away from the great shows of the past. Instead, I believe we should celebrate and marvel at how forward-thinking these shows were for their time and how much they still speak to the concerns and issues of today—despite whatever faults and limitations they may contain.

In Chapter 2 and Chapter 5, we looked at the first two waves of musicals created by Black artists—the first of which spanned from 1889 to 1910 and the second which coincided with the 1920s Harlem Renaissance. Although, on the surface, elements of equity, justice, and inclusion don't seem to have figured directly in the stories of these musicals, they were certainly big social statements in and of themselves. Black writers, directors, choreographers, producers, and performers, almost all with parents or grandparents who had been enslaved, now claimed their right to an equal place on Broadway right alongside George M. Cohan, Victor Herbert, Irving Berlin, and the Gershwins. And by creating Black characters who were college students, war heroes, businessmen, and politicians and presenting those characters in serious romantic relationships, they were challenging the view of the white establishment as well. The musical from that first decade that I am most fascinated by is **The Red Moon**, which opened in 1909 (see page 51). With book and lyrics by Bob Cole and music by J. Rosamond Johnson, and in wording that we might disapprove of today, it was billed as "a sensation in red and black." This suggests that if we could go back in time and see this show, we might find it riddled with racist ideas and attitudes toward both African Americans and Native Americans, at least in our contemporary view.[1] However, if we think of what Cole and Johnson were trying to accomplish, I would hope that we could celebrate their obvious anti-racist intent and not let their failure to see what we can now see negate their real achievements.

Another aspect of these early Black musicals that I would love to know more about is the impact and influence they had on the other Broadway writers of that time. What interactions, conversations, and exchange of ideas went on between the Black and white creators? Unfortunately, almost all of the early Black Broadway artists died very young— another legacy, no doubt, of slavery, segregation, and inequity in health care that we are still experiencing today. Because of this, their careers, lives, and connections to their Broadway colleagues are woefully undocumented and underreported. But I can't help but wonder what affect shows like *In Dahomey*, *The Red Moon*, and *Shuffle Along* had on Oscar Hammerstein and Jerome Kern and how that might have influenced their creation of *Show Boat*, which included a song called "In Dahomey," and, of course, placed issues of racial justice at the very center of its story.

"While the White Folks Play"

As discussed in Chapter 5, **Show Boat** was the first integrated musical in both senses of the word. It was the first Broadway show to have both Black and white principals and ensemble members performing side by side in the same scenes and musical sequences, and with *Show Boat*, Hammerstein and Kern more fully and seamlessly integrated the book, music, and lyrics than had ever been done previously. Today, *Show Boat* remains inspiring and clearly progressive in many ways, and at the same time, it includes some very troubling elements. Throughout history, many pioneering progressive movements and individuals have also had anti-progressive blind spots. As the musical *Suffs* relates, some of the suffragettes of the teens and 20s made tremendous strides for women's rights but resisted including women of color in their movement. And even today, some civil rights groups resist extending those same kinds of rights to Queer people.

Despite their lack of agency, the most memorable characters in *Show Boat* are the Black characters, Julie and Joe. The role of Joe was written for the great Black actor and singer Paul Robeson,[2] and that dynamic combination of character and casting inspired Hammerstein and Kern to create "Old Man River," one of the greatest showtunes of all time. Critic James Ferguson insightfully described the character and the song:

> . . . a weary stevedore who admonishes the oblivious, implacable river, yet envies its freedom, a freedom he's unlikely to know, trapped as he is beneath the upstairs glitter of the floating Cotton Palace. He rails against his world of relentless drudgery, where black workers toil "while the white folks play." The song itself reflects this duality; it has a beautiful, rousing tune, flowing in the opposite direction to the words, which sink deeper and darker, as though fed by tributaries of tribulation.[3]

"Old Man River" offers a vivid example of what an "I Am" character-establishing song can do. In less than five minutes, this song creates a fully three-dimensional portrait of Joe and positions him as the heart and soul of the musical. Although he is never central in the plot of *Show Boat*, his multiple reprises of this song tie the entire show together. Joe is the embodiment of the life force of the river, and as the musical makes very clear in the second half of its story, the further the characters get away from the river, the more problems they encounter. Like the river, Joe is a survivor—he just keeps rolling along.

In contrast, Julie is a tragic figure: an African American woman who is passing as white. Even with her limited stage time, she is central to *Show Boat's* story. Everything that happens in the plot is set in motion by what is called the "miscegenation scene"— that dramatic sequence during which Julie's Black heritage is exposed, and she and her white husband, Steve, are forced to leave the showboat. When Julie reappears in the middle of Act Two, her marriage has fallen apart, and she is performing in a Chicago nightclub called the Trocadero, battling alcoholism and barely hanging on. It is appallingly clear that the events of the first act and the systematic racism of that era, even in the North, have ruined Julie's life and marriage. By this point, Magnolia, the show's rebellious ingenue and leading lady, is also living in Chicago. She now has a young child, and her marriage is also falling apart. After great initial success, her husband Gaylord Ravenal's career as a professional gambler has gone disastrously wrong, and he runs away in shame that he can't support his family. He is shown to be a weak man, and Magnolia is revealed as the braver, stronger person who understands that *she* must now provide for her daughter. So, she goes to audition for a singing job at the Trocadero, not having any idea that Julie works there. Unseen by Magnolia, Julie witnesses her old friend Magnolia's audition and tells the club's owner to hire her and then disappears from the club and the musical—we fear that she is going off on a bender. Magnolia never knows that Julie "gave her" the job which will eventually lead to her becoming a big Broadway star. Yes, the white character benefits from the fall of the black character. Truly tragic. And it is clear that the show's authors believed this to be a great injustice that they wanted the audience of 1927 to experience viscerally.

In Chapter 6, I profiled Irving Berlin and Moss Hart's 1933 hit revue **As Thousands Cheer**. Overall, the show was a wildly entertaining series of hilarious, satirical, and very topical comedy sketches literally ripped from the headlines of the day and intermixed with lavishly staged songs and dances performed by several of the biggest stars of the 1930s, including the great Ethel Waters, who was billed above the title along with her three white co-stars. That in itself was a social statement. Then, in the midst of all that show's frivolity and high spirits, Berlin very purposely created one devastatingly serious song especially for Ethel Waters to perform, the heartbreaking "Supper Time"—a song that called out the series of murders taking place that year when twenty-eight Black men were lynched in eleven states. Why did Berlin choose to do this? I would suggest that it was a savvy combination of social activism and showbiz know-how. He wanted to make a statement, and he knew that he had the right star and the perfect framing for it to have a tremendous impact. No one who saw it would ever forget it, and we are still talking about it ninety years later.[4] Other hit shows of the '30s and '40s that explored these themes include *Porgy and Bess*, *Carmen Jones*, and *Bloomer Girl*, whose extraordinarily progressive plotline I detailed in Chapter 8. This then brings us to Rodgers and Hammerstein's *South Pacific*.

Tales of the South Pacific

Racial issues and cultural conflicts are at the center of many of the original nineteen short stories contained in James Michener's semi-autobiographical *Tales of The South Pacific*—especially the two that Rodgers, Hammerstein, and Josh Logan selected to adapt for the two main plotlines of *South Pacific*.[5] In order to use them, however, the team had to break a long-standing musical theater tradition. *Show Boat*, *Oklahoma!*, and *Carousel* had all employed the musical comedy and operetta format of a central plot built around a serious, romantic leading couple paired with a secondary plot featuring a comic (often dancing) supporting couple. Now, for the first time, Rodgers and Hammerstein gave both couples serious plotlines, and they would continue to use this formula in all of their future shows. In *South Pacific*, the couples are Nellie and Emile and Cable and Liat and both plotlines hinge on issues of systemic and internalized racism.[6]

While Hammerstein had strong feelings about injustice in America and the world, and supported and worked for a number of anti-fascist groups and causes, he was especially concerned with racial injustice because it had affected his family personally. His sister-in-law was married to a Japanese man who had been placed in an internment camp during the war and then, even after his release, could not find a job until Hammerstein's wife, Dorothy, hired him to manage the business side of her interior design firm.[7] In the end, Hammerstein, Logan, and Rodgers dramatized these issues so effectively that *South Pacific* received the Pulitzer Prize for Drama and was a massive critical and popular success.

"A Puzzlement"—Anna and the King of Siam

In *The King and I*, Rodgers and Hammerstein tackled a series of world-shattering themes: colonialism, imperialism, globalism, dictatorship vs. democracy, women's rights, and universal human rights. For me, one of the most subversive elements of this story is the central relationship between Anna and the King. There is clearly a strong connection between them and even a very evident sexual tension. However, it is also clear that in that time and place, it would be impossible for them to act on these feelings. From either of their points of view, or the views of both Western and Thai society, there could never be a romantic or sexual relationship between them, no matter how connected and engaged they are on an intellectual and emotional level. And this, at least subliminally, makes us ask, why? Why can't they be together? As audience members we absolutely want them to be together, and as we follow the progression of their relationship, our minds and bodies are emotionally, and even physically, engaged in willing this to happen. By the time we get to the climatic number "Shall We Dance?" the tension is palpable! All of this, of course, makes us question the rules and conventions of not just the time period the characters are living in but also our own. The King has a lot in common with Tevye. He, too, is tasked with the obligation of maintaining the cultural norms and traditions of his society (including upholding the patriarchy) while at the same time, somehow keeping up with a rapidly changing modern world. And, even as we disapprove of many of the King's beliefs and actions, Rodgers and Hammerstein engender tremendous empathy for his dilemma, especially with the song "A Puzzlement."

In recent years, *The King and I* has been criticized for presenting Western culture as superior and more evolved than Thai culture. However, if we take a closer look, I think we will see that Hammerstein is instead pitting feminine, democratic, and humanistic values against masculine, dictatorial, and authoritarian values. The negative aspects of the King don't represent Thai or Asian culture so much as they represent a male-centered, patriarchal power imbalance. Even though the authors depict the King as being incredibly smart, resourceful, charismatic, and dynamic, they also present him as sharing the same inhumane values that (at that exact same moment in history) America was fighting the Civil War over. The "barbarians" in this story are the men—both American and Thai—who believe in slavery.

To illustrate this, Rodgers and Hammerstein again give the second couple of *The King and I* a serious, tragic storyline: Tuptim, an enslaved young woman, has been sent by the King of Burma as a gift to the King of Siam to become another of his many concubines. Tuptim, however, is in love with Lun Tha, a Burmese scholar who was sent to the court of Siam at the same time. Tuptim becomes one of Mrs. Anna's best students, and Anna encourages her to read Harriet Beecher Stowe's anti-slavery novel *Uncle Tom's Cabin* (which was a worldwide sensation at that time) and to create a dance-play based on it to present before the King when the British envoy comes for a state visit. Tuptim's creation is brilliantly and vividly realized in Jerome Robbins's ballet, "The Small House of Uncle Thomas." This elaborate sequence, which directly leads to the climax of the story, boldly underlines that the principal theme of *The King and I* is "anti-slavery"— the fundamental right to freedom of all people.

The musical ends with a complex mix of sadness for the death of the King, for whom both Anna and the audience have developed great affection despite his many flaws, coupled with the great hope we feel for the future of Siam under the new King, Chulalongkorn, who we immediately see begin to bring freedom and democratic values to his people. Anna has literally been the new King's teacher (at least within the semi-fictional story of the musical), and it is clear that she has played a key role in bringing this change about—not, however, because she represents Western culture, but rather because she is a woman who represents freedom and democracy. The story ends with feminine, democratic, and humanistic values triumphing over masculine, dictatorial, and authoritarian values. Still, today, the optics of *The King and I* can make us very uncomfortable. A white woman represents democracy, and authoritarianism is embodied by an Asian man, making it so easy to misconstrue the message. This may be a fatal flaw in this musical because it distorts and obscures what the show is really about.

"A Place for Us"

West Side Story certainly can't be left out of this discussion. The anti-racist themes and messages of this powerful musical are not subliminal—they are front and center. This show's brilliant quartet of Jewish and Gay creators—Arthur Laurents, Stephen Sondheim, Leonard Bernstein, and Jerome Robbins—were clearly making a statement. Every character in the story is marginalized by poverty and prejudice, and two key songs, "America " and "Gee, Officer Krupke," do a remarkably insightful and expert job of encapsulating, exposing, and indicting structural racism and systematic economic injustice decades before those terms came into general use.

Two great musicals from the 1960s both deal with anti-Semitism. *Fiddler on the Roof* was part of that era's "Roots" movement, a counter-reaction to the cultural homogenization of the 1950s. America's ethnic, racial, and cultural origins and history now began to be embraced and celebrated in a sort of "coming out" for ethnicities and identities of all types. *Fiddler* dramatizes life in "The Pale of Jewish Settlement," which for more than 100 years was the only area of the Russian Empire in which Jews were permitted to live and which included all of current-day Belarus, Lithuania, Moldova, and much of Poland and Ukraine. *Fiddler* is set during the final period around the turn of the twentieth century when a series of violent pogroms (organized anti-Jewish riots) swept the region and drove millions of Jews from Eastern Europe to America. The musical *Cabaret* (by another

Jewish and Gay creative team) is set in Berlin thirty years later and uses a charming/heartbreaking story of star-crossed middle-aged lovers to dramatize the tragic effect that the rise of the Nazis had on European Jews and to warn us to keep a vigilant lookout for fascism in our own times.

"And They Called It, Ragtime"

Many musicals in the Modern Era continued to grapple with these issues, including *Hair*, *Purlie*, *Raisin*, *Pacific Overtures*, *Dreamgirls*, *Once on This Island*, *Parade*, and especially **Ragtime**. With a book by Terrence McNally, lyrics by Lynn Ahrens, and music by Steven Flaherty, *Ragtime* masterfully dramatizes the full spectrum of these issues within its multiple central characters and storylines, including white privilege and white supremacy; overt, internalized, and systematic racism; and anti-Semitism. In its epic opening sequence, three very separate and segregated groups of New Yorkers are introduced. The White Anglo-Saxon Protestant Establishment is confronted by both newly arrived Eastern European Jewish Immigrants as well as by an emerging middle class of African Americans, and in choreographer Graciela Daniele's brilliant and unforgettable staging, the three groups circle each other warily. Of course, these groups cannot remain apart, and over the course of the musical, their lives and stories converge in ever deeper and more dramatic ways. The show's final image presents a utopian vision that would have been very unlikely to occur during the actual Ragtime era: a multiracial/multicultural family is formed and the Jewish husband/father, WASP wife/mother, Jewish little girl, and Black little boy join hands and walk off into the future together. They represent what America must become: a family in which all of its members are embraced, valued, and represented equally. *Ragtime*'s moving ending has undoubtedly affected the hearts and minds of the millions of theatergoers who have seen it. Still, I believe its greatest impact has been on the current generation of theater-makers who grew up in love with this show and deeply moved by its message.

"A Struggle We Have Yet to Win"

Integration, equality, equity, and social justice for African Americans are also at the center of *Hairspray*'s storyline, which is set in racially divided Baltimore in 1962, when the Civil Rights movement was reaching its peak.[8] Some people have criticized the show for having a "white savior narrative," which is often a challenge with storylines set in past eras when Black characters would historically have had limited agency within the racist social constructs of the time. Perhaps instinctively, since the term was not in general use at the time, the creators of *Hairspray* at least partially mitigated this concern by transferring two key song spots that are usually reserved for a show's protagonist to a key Black character: Motormouth Maybelle. As discussed in the previous chapter, the first is the "act-1-finale-of-female-self-assertion," "Big, Blonde and Beautiful." Then, fulfilling her function as the musical's "Wise Woman and Caretaker" character, Motormouth also delivers *Hairspray*'s climactic 11 o'clock spot, "I Know Where I've Been." This song affectingly acknowledges the long road of struggle that African Americans have had to contend with and the price they have had to pay to achieve even minimal equity. Simultaneously, Motormouth's souring gospel-infused anthem supplies the encouragement and inspiration that both the Black and White characters need to continue fighting for their dream of a better future and sets in motion everything else that happens in the story.

As in *West Side Story*, nearly all of *Hairspray*'s main characters are disenfranchised and marginalized: Tracy, Edna, Wilber, Penny, Seaweed, and Motormouth. They are poor, fat, Black, and undereducated, and there is a Queer subtext as well. Nearly all of the show's creative team were Gay—both songwriters, the director, the choreographer, one of the two bookwriters, and John Waters, who wrote and directed the original film on which the musical is based. In that movie, the role of Edna Turnblad was created by Divine, a male drag performer. That casting convention was then carried over into the musical. Harvey Fierstein originated the role in the Broadway production and John Travolta played Edna in the movie version, and this has remained a central aspect of the show through thousands of professional, amateur, and high school productions worldwide. What does it mean to have Edna played by a male actor? What effect does that have on the audience? I believe it is a captivatingly subversive way of questioning and undercutting traditional binary views of gender. Even though the role and its effect are wildly hilarious, it is not written or intended as a joke. No matter how outrageous their performance, the actors playing Edna always end up bringing a great deal of heart and even heartbreak to the role. The audience fully believes in Edna as both Tracy's mother and Wilber's wife. They quickly come to empathize and identify with this character, and they see themselves and their own relationships reflected back to them through her. Edna is just like them. And their relationships with their mother, daughter, wife, or husband are much the same as those depicted in *Hairspray*. Even though there are no identifiably Queer characters in *Hairspray*'s storyline, somehow, the musical still advocates for Gay rights and Gay liberation and pulls the entire audience into its Queer worldview.

This focus on Equity, Justice, and Inclusion shows no signs of letting up in the twenty-first century. So far, we have had *Avenue Q*, *Caroline, Or Change*, *Memphis*, *In the Heights*, *Allegiance*, *The Band's Visit*, *Hamilton*, *Come From Away*, the revival of *Parade*, and, of course, Stephen Schwartz and Winnie Holzman's musical blockbuster *Wicked*. With its transgressive, green-skinned, anti-fascist heroine, *Wicked* is another show that incorporates all three of the Broadway musical's main themes – Racial Justice, Transgressive Women, and the focus of the next chapter, Community.

What we still don't have enough of is musicals written by non-white artists—but hopefully, that is starting to change. The winner of the 2020 Pulitzer Prize for Drama, as well as the 2022 Tony Awards for Best Book, Best Score, and Best Musical, was the Black/Queer writer Michael R. Jackson for his musical *A Strange Loop* (see page 319). In his review, *Los Angeles Times* critic Charles McNulty captured the effect of this show:

"Jackson liberates us from the homogeneity that deadens our theaters and leaves so many of us feeling alone. For those searching for reflections of themselves in culture, 'A Strange Loop' offers the balm of community. Broadway has never felt so expansively welcoming."[9]

In addition, South Korean writer Hue Park created the lyrics, and co-wrote the book (with composer Will Aronson), for the hit musical *Maybe Happy Ending*, which opened in 2024.

The musicals discussed here, as wildly different as they are in form and content, all do the same thing—they find a potent, compelling way to dramatize the fallacy of what human rights activist and journalist Nava Ghalili calls "the great lie," which she contends we have collectively been telling ourselves for centuries:

[The great lie is] that somehow you and I are inherently different—that your pain hurts differently from my pain. And that if you hurt, it won't affect me. This lie is the culprit behind our complete lack of awareness to the fact that humankind is actually ONE. And that the suffering of one will eventually catch up to the rest of the world and be the suffering of all.

Ghalili proposes that if people could understand this simple fact and live by this law of nature, then these problems would slowly be eliminated.

I believe that the great artists who invented and sustained the Broadway musical inherently understood this—both consciously and unconsciously—and have woven that idea into the very fabric of the Broadway musical.

CHAPTER 16
"WE KNOW WE BELONG TO THE LAND"— THE VITAL IMPORTANCE OF COMMUNITY (I, J, Q, B, W)

One of the singular strengths of the Broadway musical form is its effectiveness at dramatizing and bringing to life entire communities of people—and in many musicals, the community itself becomes a major character in the drama. As a result of this natural ability, dozens of Broadway musicals—including many of the most popular, acclaimed, and influential—focus nearly as much on the triumphs and tribulations of the community in the story as they do on those of the individual central characters. In fact, in these musicals, the fate and fortunes of the heroine or hero are closely tied to and dependent upon the ability of the community to thrive and function—and visa-versa.

Collectively, Broadway musicals strongly advocate for the vital importance of humans coming together and forming harmonious, well-functioning communities—even if that means we have to compromise or give something up to achieve it. In fact, I would argue that musicals most often are telling us that we *must* give something up to achieve that goal, for the greater good of all concerned. In the context of the polarization and violent conflicts of today's world, "a healing compromise" might be hard to imagine—much less possible to achieve anytime soon. But, as always, I find that that these "frivolous Broadway musicals" are actually profoundly inspiring works of art that still have much to teach us.

It was probably inevitable that *community* would become one of the principal themes of the musical because the central dynamics of a community are baked into the process, form, and structure of musical theater. Choral singing, group dancing, and playacting are natural, indigenous, universal communal activities that, throughout human history, have been tied to meaningful events in the life of a community: the changing of the seasons, the harvest, marriages, and all manner of civic rituals and religious celebrations. This makes those events ideal vehicles for musical theater writers to draw on and tap into when they want to insightfully reflect and reveal the feelings and values of a community.

This was especially true during the Golden Age, when it was not uncommon to have fifty or even eighty people in the cast of a musical. Those huge casts became actual communities of their own, so it was very natural, effective, and potent for them to portray the community in whatever story the musical was telling. Because of this, Golden Age musicals were brilliantly effective at depicting entire towns, villages, neighborhoods, or subcultures within a community. As author Jeffrey Sweet has noted, "The members of the Chorus (in a traditional musical) represent a community that shares words. This community sings lyrics in unison because it shares values."[1] They also share music, which immediately puts them "in tune" with one another, and they often sing in harmony—and harmony is the perfect metaphor for a community that is able to work and function well together. In fact, one of the definitions of harmony is "to be in agreement or concord." Broadway choruses also often move and dance in unison and in synchronized and interconnecting patterns. To pull this off, they must work as a team—a cohesive unit. Right there, we have all the elements of a well-functioning community reflected and embodied in the chorus's performance of the show's music, lyrics, and choreography.

The dynamic dramatizing of a community is aided and abetted by another of musical theater's key dramatic strengths—the way music and lyrics can be artfully employed to take the audience inside the thoughts and feelings of the show's characters—even multiple characters simultaneously. Think of "Hello Twelve, Hello Thirteen, Hello, Love" in *A Chorus Line*, that kaleidoscopic sequence in which the characters look back on and share their experiences of going through adolescence and puberty. The effect of this in performance is that we feel like we are hearing the inner thoughts of all eighteen characters simultaneously. Or consider both the "Tonight Quintet," the thrilling almost First Act finale of *West Side Story*, and the sequence that was clearly inspired by it, *Les Misérables'* arguably even more thrilling actual First Act finale, "One Day More." Both numbers place all of their story's central characters and groups onstage at the same time, even though, in the story, they are in different locations—all over the neighborhood in *West Side Story* and all over Paris in *Les Miz*. In both numbers, the audience is able to experience and understand what each character and group is feeling and thinking as they prepare for and anticipate the big events that are about to take place.[2] This kind of writing goes hand in hand with another strength of musical theater—its frequent use of stylized, non-realistic, abstract staging. In a film or play, it is very awkward to portray multiple characters thinking different thoughts and having various feelings simultaneously. However, a musical can expand and condense time and space to reveal all of the characters' individual thoughts and perspectives. This is why I contend that musicals can often be "more real than real," because the conventions of musical theater are more adept at illustrating the actual multiple layers of reality than are other, more naturalistic forms of drama.

Fiddler on the Roof is a perfect embodiment of all of the above. The village of Anatevka is brought to life and established as a principal character in the story through a series of dynamic musical numbers. In the show's opening, "Tradition," the shared beliefs and values of the entire Jewish community of Anatevka are made clear, and the looming conflict with factions of the greater community is also introduced. Then, in "To Life," during a celebration of an engagement of marriage, we see those conflicting factions—the Jews and the Russians—briefly come together harmoniously to sing and dance. The two groups start out very wary of one another, but then, in a vision of what their shared future could and should be (brilliantly staged by Jerome Robbins), they find a way to maintain their own cultures and identities and yet still dance together in interconnected and intersecting patterns. *Fiddler*'s first act ends with the wedding celebration (although with a different groom), and the wild, intense joy of a community that unexpectedly finds itself embracing liberating change is suddenly swept away by violence and destruction. And, of course, in the show's heartbreaking finale, we see the community being driven away from Anatevka as its members disperse and go their separate ways.

Even that very brief summary of *Fiddler* reveals two very important things: first, the power of ritual in these community-themed musicals. Since the performance of a play or musical is itself a kind of ritual that evolved from religious and community celebrations, it is only natural that community rituals and celebrations, especially weddings, should figure so frequently and prominently in the stories of Broadway musicals. As we will see, the obstacle to the marriage—and there has to be an obstacle, or there is no story—is almost always some kind of cultural mismatch; something woven into the very fabric of the community that is keeping the two lovers apart. Weddings almost always symbolize the resolution of conflict between the factions of the community that the lovers represent and the promise of a brighter future that will come as a result of healing that rift.

Secondly, *Fiddler* illustrates how—since stories are driven by conflict—if you are telling a story about a community, you will need to include characters that are in conflict with the community. Often, this is someone who is a dissenter and/or outcast from the community—and they become the antagonist. Or you might have subgroups of the community in conflict with each other. Rodgers and Hammerstein brilliantly employed all of these elements in *Oklahoma!*

"Territory Folks Should Stick Together"

What exactly is the central conflict within the community of *Oklahoma!*? What is the cause of the tension and disagreement? For audiences today, this can often be hard to grasp, even though it is clearly stated in the text, and there's an entire song spelling it out for us. That song, "The Farmer and The Cowman," can seem like just a lighthearted hoedown intended only to get the second act off to a lively start. But a well-thought-out production of *Oklahoma!* will help the audience understand that there is much more to it than that. This song is actually laying out the central theme of the entire show. The "range wars" that took place across the western United States around the turn of the century were intense and sometimes violent conflicts over the use of the land. As the song tells us, the cowmen wanted wide open ranges where their cattle could roam free and easily be driven to market. The farmers, however, wanted the land to be fenced in and controlled so that their crops would be protected from being eaten or trampled. In an agrarian society—which America certainly was in 1906 when the story of *Oklahoma!* takes place, and to a great extent, still remained in 1943 when the musical was first produced—these are make-or-break, life-and-death issues.

This is one of the most difficult aspects of the show to convey to modern audiences, but it is crucial to the storytelling. Dramatically, the farmers and the cowmen represent opposing values. The farmers represent *civilization*—the settlement of the land and the establishment of schools, churches, and families. The picnic basket auction that figures so prominently in *Oklahoma!*'s plot is being held to raise money to build a new schoolhouse. This is not arbitrary—the playwrights made that choice on purpose in order to underline this issue. The cowboys, on the other hand, represent *untethered freedom* and a very American ideal of self-reliance and self-determination. Cole Porter, in spite of being the least likely person ever to write a cowboy song, captured this idea perfectly when he wrote, "Oh, give me land, lots of land under starry skies above, / don't fence me in. / Let me ride through the wide-open country that I love, / don't fence me in."[3] The cowboys represent what have traditionally been seen as "masculine values," and the farmers represent traditional "feminine values" and concerns. We could also define this conflict as being between *libertarian values* and *communitarian values*. Libertarians seek to maximize political freedom and autonomy, emphasizing freedom of choice—another very American philosophy as exemplified by the early American flag and motto: "Don't tread on me." Communitarian beliefs are also very American, with the basic principle being that "we are all in this together." This conflict is at the heart of *Oklahoma!*, and the musical dramatizes how these conflicting values can come into balance.

What happens at the end of *Oklahoma!*? Two couples, Laurey and Curly and Ado Annie and Will Parker—each comprised of a female farmer and a male cowman, and, as such, embodying both sides of the conflict—join together in the partnership, collaboration, and compromise of marriage. In his book *The American Musical and the Formation of National Identity*, author Raymond Knapp puts it this way: "Both cowman and farmer have just claims to the land, and we are made to understand that their shared love of it will end up mattering more than their differences."[4] In other words, their shared love of that land will bring an end to the range wars. The two groups will still have differences, but they will find ways to compromise and work together for the sake of the community and the land that they love. In the show's title song, only one lyric line reoccurs three times: "We know we belong to the land / and the land we belong to is grand."

"Sit Down, You're Rocking the Boat"

We see this story of two opposing segments of a community that ultimately find a way to come together dramatized (with similar symbolic undertones) in many other musicals, including *Guys and Dolls*, which also ends with two weddings. One very unique aspect of this musical is that, although it retains the age-old format of a serious romantic couple juxtaposed with a bickering comic couple, in this show, it's impossible to say which are the leading characters and which is the secondary couple. Both plotlines hold equal weight and importance. The wedding of Adelaide and Nathan, the showgirl and the gambler, represents another classic compromise between traditional feminine and masculine values. And the marriage of Sarah and Sky symbolizes a merger of conservative evangelical Christian values with liberal, broad-minded, permissive (Jewish?) values. The Damon Runyon stories that serve as the basis for *Guys and Dolls* were originally written and set in the 1920s, just after the intense conflict between conservative rural small-town America and freethinking big urban cities had led to the disaster of Prohibition. This conflict was just as pertinent in 1950, during the McCarthy era, when *Guys and Dolls* debuted, and is clearly a social divide that we are still grappling with today.

The Pajama Game ends with the marriage of Babe and Sid, which brings the community of the Sleep-Tite pajama factory into harmony by uniting labor and management. However, Tony and Maria's lovely and very moving, improvised marriage in the dress shop in *West Side Story* only brings further conflict and destruction, which, of course, defines the essential difference between comedy and tragedy.

The Outsiders

Let's now turn our attention to that other source of dramatic conflict: the dissenter, nonconformist, or outcast from the community. *Oklahoma!* has one of those as well—the groundbreaking character of Jud Fry. As we have noted previously, *Oklahoma!* was a new invention—a musical play as opposed to a musical comedy or operetta—and Jud Fry has a lot to do with that. Without him, the dramatic stakes of the story and its thematic depth would be greatly diminished. What does Jud represent to this community? The most recent Broadway revival of *Oklahoma!* in 2019 was extremely controversial—people either loved it or hated it. Wags quickly dubbed it "Wokelahoma," because, as directed by Daniel Fish, that stripped-down, modern dress production was seen by many as trying way too hard to reframe and reinterpret (or perhaps misinterpret?) the show for a contemporary audience. And I would have to agree. However, one thing that production got exactly right was its depiction of Jud. He was portrayed as an "incel"[5]—a young, misogynistic, heterosexual man who feels so frustrated by his lack of sexual experience and romantic success and so alienated and shut out from society that he becomes an angry, disgruntled, and violent threat to his community. And it was immediately clear that this was who Jud had always been. Jud is neither a farmer nor a cowman but rather a hired hand who comes into the community as a stranger. He does not belong to the land. None of that would necessarily be a problem—a different person coming into the same situation could presumably have become integrated into the community and possibly even ended up marrying Laurey. But not this guy. He has serious mental and emotional issues. There is something dark and twisted about him. He starts off creepy and grows more and more unhinged. But, amazingly, early in the show, Rodgers and Hammerstein give him an "I Am/I Want song" in which he reveals his interior world and deepest feelings—his pain at feeling outcast, inadequate, rejected, and trapped inside his own mind—his "Lonely Room," as the song is titled. This song engenders surprising empathy from the audience for Jud. We really feel for him. But that only goes so far, because in the scene just prior to that song, Jud seemed to have boasted about killing an entire family ("burned up the father, mother and daughter")[6] on another farm where he worked after finding the girl "in the hayloft with another fellow."[7] Or, at the very least, he expressed his great admiration for the hired hand who did kill them. Then, in Act Two, we witness Jud's intense anger and threatening words after Laurey rejects his sexual advances and, depending on how it is staged, thwarts his attempted rape:

JUD (*standing quite still, absorbed, his voice low*): Said yer say! Brought it on yerself. (*In a voice harsh with an inner frenzy.*) Cain't he'p it. Cain't never rest. Told you the way it was. You wouldn't listen—[8]

The question that *Oklahoma!* then poses is, what does society do with a person like that? How do we help them? Can they somehow be integrated into society? And if not, what do we do then?

At the climax of the show, with our very own eyes, we see Jud pull out a knife and violently attack Curly, who is forced to fight back in self-defense. They struggle violently, Curly "succeeds in throwing him" and, as Hammerstein's stage directions clearly state, "JUD falls on his own knife."[9] *Oklahoma!*, of course, opened in the middle of World War II, when America, and much of the world, was being forced to fight back in self-defense against the violent aggression of the Axis powers. I do not think this is a coincidence. This was art reflecting life. And it is not at all a stretch to view Hitler as the ultimate incel. Throughout the first two and a half years of *Oklahoma!*'s original run, the allied forces, led by America, were having to do battle with elements who did not want to be part of the world community and who were, in fact, violently trying to break up and destroy that community. Sometimes, the community has no choice but to fight back to save itself.

From *Oklahoma!* on, conflicts between an outcast and their community have been at the center of many, many musicals, and have played out in a number of different ways. In Lerner and Loewe's 1947 musical fantasy, *Brigadoon* (see page 195), the dark and brooding young rebel, Harry Beaton, is in love with the leading lady's sister, Jean, but she has chosen to marry someone else, and Harry becomes angry, disgruntled and increasingly alienated from the rest of the town—but does not go quite as psycho as Jud Fry. Still, at the end of Act One, during Jean's wedding, Harry's disappointments and frustrations boil over, and he declares, "I'm leaving Brigadoon. 'Tis the end of all of us. The miracle is over."[10] He then dramatically rushes offstage, sending the town into a panic because if he succeeds in escaping the boundaries of Brigadoon, the spell will be broken, and the village and all its inhabitants will disappear forever. Harry Beaton also represents libertarian values. He believes that his personal freedom is more important than whatever will happen to the community as a result of his actions. The villagers chase after him, literally carrying torches, and he ends up dying—also by accident—when he trips and falls, smashing his head against a rock. This is classic mythic storytelling: the character who is against the community and endangering its existence has to die. To save the community, the threat has to be vanquished.

Stephen Sondheim and James Lapine would grapple with this same dynamic many years later in *Into the Woods* and brilliantly illuminate the moral dilemmas and complications that come with it. To save the community of this show, The Giant's Wife must be killed. But as Sondheim and Lapine make sure to remind us, there are always two sides to every story: "Witches can be right, giants can be good. / You decide what's right, you decide what's good."[11]

In other musicals it's the story's protagonist/central character who is the outsider. Both Billy Bigelow in *Carousel* and Harold Hill in *The Music Man* are prime, if very different, examples of this dynamic. From the very beginning of *Carousel*'s story, the carnival barker, Billy Bigelow, is in opposition to the conservative small-town values of the New England community in which he has landed. His main job is to be a sexy, charismatic hunk of beefcake that will entice young women to buy tickets and ride the carousel. After meeting Julie, he recklessly and impulsively abandons his rootless, promiscuous, traveling carnival life and marries into her community. Rodgers and Hammerstein don't show us whatever attempts Billy made (if any) to fit in or settle down. When we pick up the story, Julie and Billy are already married—and he is unable or unwilling to find any kind of job. Billy is not only feeling unsure about the choice he made to leave the carnival but also feels trapped in his marriage and stifled by the community whose values he does not share. This has resulted in Billy physically taking out his frustrations on Julie, at least once, and the talk of the town is that he beats his wife.

Story-wise, this situation cannot continue—the community cannot remain in conflict. Either the protagonist must discover a way to fit into the community, or they must be removed from the community, either by banishment or death. *Carousel* sort of has it both ways. After he discovers that Julie is pregnant, Billy becomes so desperate to support his family that he takes part in an armed robbery. When it all goes wrong, and he's about to be hauled off to jail, Billy removes himself from the community in the only way that seems bearable—he commits suicide. But that's not the end of the story. After he dies, Billy is taken up to heaven, or somewhere on the other side, where the heavenly Starkeeper gives him the chance to return to earth and redeem himself. It's a bit like a therapy session in which Billy has to confront his past behavior and then learn, grow, and heal from the process. When he returns to earth (where fifteen years have gone by), he finds that it is now Julie and their daughter Louise who are in conflict with the community. After screwing things up several more times, Billy finally figures out a way to help his family, and in the show's final moments, Billy joins in singing "You'll Never Walk Alone" with Louise and Julie (the first and only time Billy and Julie sing together). Somehow, his wife and daughter sense his presence, and somehow it helps them to enter into harmony with their community.

In contrast, at the end of *The Music Man*, the outsider protagonist, Harold Hill, for the first time in his life "gets his foot stuck in the door." He is such a brilliant con man that he cons himself and falls under his own spell, as well as Marion's. He will now join the community of River City and presumably become fully integrated into it. (For more on *The Music Man*, see page 221).

Even several of the seemingly plotless revue-like musicals of the Modern Era follow this template. In the very slight but potent main story thread of *Hair*, we see Claude struggle to fully join the Tribe—the community of young people who have dropped out of mainstream society. All of his friends are willing, able, and eager to burn their draft cards and shed their clothes during the big "be-in" at the end of *Hair*'s first act, but for some reason, Claude just can't bring himself to do it. He wants to be part of the group but ultimately can't commit to all of their non-conformist values. By the end of the show, he has been drafted and shipped off to Vietnam where he will die. In the show's finale, the Tribe mourns for Claude and yearns for a day when everyone will be able to break free of the shackles of conformity and "Let The Sun Shine In." In *Company*, it is Robert who is the outsider of that show's community of "crazy married people." In the final scene, when he fails to show up at his own birthday party, we understand that Robert has come to the realization that he must separate himself from the community in order to truly be alive. We see another variation of this with Cassie, in *A Chorus Line*. She left her community of Broadway chorus dancers to try to make it big in Hollywood but now wants to be allowed back in to rejoin her Tribe. Famously, during early previews of *A Chorus Line* at the Public Theater, Cassie did not get the job at the end of the show because Michael Bennett felt strongly that this was what would happen in real life. She was indeed too special to go back into the chorus. However, after seeing one of those performances, actress Marsha Mason called Bennett and begged him to change the ending: "You are saying to us that if we don't make it, we can't go back. You can't take starting again away from people." Bennett took her advice, and from then on, Cassie (and therefore all of us) got a second chance.[12] This is in contrast to Zach, the show's director-choreographer character, who also left the community and now functions in many ways as its antagonist. In the paraphrase of *A Chorus Line*, *Cats*, it is Grizabella, the faded, glamor cat who is the outcast figure in opposition to her community. Some people have suggested that this show is a metaphor for our society's struggles and failures in dealing with our unhoused population. I don't know if the show's creators would agree, but you certainly could say that much the way New York City attempted to solve its "homeless problem" during the 1980s, the solution that the *Cats* community comes up with at the end of the show is sending Grizzabella off with a one-way ticket to the "Heavy-Side Layer."

"There's a Hole in the World Like a Great Black Pit"

A small handful of musicals are set in communities that are broken, failed, and corrupt. *West Side Story* is certainly one of them. *Urinetown* is another, and I would add *Pippin* to that list, at least in regard to *Pippin*'s framing story in which a starry-eyed young man (we don't know his name) is seduced by a dazzling troupe of players who promise him magic, intrigue, romance, sex, illusion, and the glory of war if he will join their company and take on the title role in their dramatization of Charlemagne's son, Pippin. But at the end of the performance, when he discovers that what they actually want him to do is provide them with a sick thrill by setting himself on fire, he rejects this sinister, evil community and settles for the compromises of ordinary, everyday life. And then there is *Sweeny Todd—The Demon Barber of Fleet Street*. The events of this story take place in a community that has completely broken down and is rife with inequity and injustice—a community in which a "privileged few" keep the majority of people disenfranchised, destitute, and starving, where the "cruelty of men is as wondrous as Peru . . . and it goes by the name of London."

One of the many fascinating and remarkable aspects of *Sweeny Todd* is that it simultaneously functions as three different genres of theater. On the one hand, it is a perfectly structured thriller—a tightly constructed, carefully calculated mechanical invention designed to shock, horrify, and astound its audience with spine-tingling plot twists and thrilling reversals of fortune. Like every "external genre" of storytelling, thrillers cannot be organically created. They have to be mapped out, plotted, and engineered in a way that will best manipulate their audience. *Sweeney Todd* is also written in a style called "Grand Guignol," after a famous theater in Paris in the late nineteenth and early twentieth century that specialized in graphic and bloody horror story plays that were precursors to modern-day "slasher films." Finally, the show's original director, Hal Prince, layered a "production concept" over the top of this musical play. The sets, costumes, and staging used the Industrial Revolution and the emergence of the factory system as a metaphor for the inequality and injustice of a modern world in which the common people are just "cogs in a wheel" serving the corrupt ruling class. So, at least in its original production, *Sweeny Todd* was a *musical play* presented in the trappings of a *concept musical*.

At the center of the story, we have another outcast—a direct descendant of Jud Fry, and this time even more of a psycho. But again, the authors create tremendous empathy for him. His backstory is so compelling, and the injustices he has suffered are so heartbreaking that, even throughout his escalating series of murderous rampages, we somehow stay on his side and continue to root for him. Why? Because the Judge, the Beadle, and the society they rule are so corrupt and so evil, Todd remains the moral center of the story. He is the only one seeking justice, even if we don't agree that he has the right to enforce it himself.

And then there is the amoral Mrs. Lovett—whom audiences adore. Why? Because, like Brecht's Mother Courage, in his play of the same name, Mrs. Lovett has discovered the key to surviving: just do whatever you need to do—and never look back. In some primal way, we would all like a piece of that. Watching her, we start to think how much simpler life would be if we had no conscience, no sense of right and wrong, and could be just like Nellie Lovett—even as we are horrified by what she feels so free to do. Despite our deep empathy for Sweeney, the final message of this musical is very clear: revenge doesn't pay; it only leads to even more death and heartbreak. In the end, Sweeney removes himself from the community, although it seems unlikely that any healing of this community will be possible.

Sweeney Todd inspired a series of musicals featuring dark anti-hero protagonists who are in conflict with their societies, including *The Phantom of the Opera*, Disney's *Beauty and the Beast*, *Little Shop of Horrors*, and *The Hunchback of Notre Dame*.

"Welcome to the Rock"

Over the last forty years or so, the economics of Broadway have changed drastically, and creative teams have had to figure out how to tell their stories with increasingly smaller casts and orchestras. In the Golden Age, a show like *Brigadoon* might have twenty singers who didn't have to dance very much and twenty dancers who didn't really have to sing. In recent years, however, most new musicals have had less than twenty people in the entire cast. In the process of this downsizing, what used to be called "the chorus" is now called "the ensemble."

This change, however, was not driven only by economics. As we have seen, as the musical entered the Modern Era, the forms and styles of musical theater changed as well, and much of that had to do with the rise of the director-choreographer. Robbins, Fosse, Bennett, Layton, and Tune all wanted the entire cast to be able to dance, at least to some degree, and wanted movement to flood the entire show and be central to the storytelling. Often, they wanted chorus members to be able to play specific characters as well. *West Side Story* was a major turning point in this regard. Every performer in that show played just one named character, and all of them had to dance, act, and sing. This gave the show an unprecedented level of cohesion and integration that soon spread to other musicals and led to significant changes in the way performers were trained. Musical theater actors now had to be "triple threats," who could sing, dance, and act in as close to equal measure as possible. Fewer performers were now necessary to perform all of the roles in a show, and roles that used to be given to supporting principal actors were now given to members of the chorus/ensemble.

In the twenty-first century, cast sizes have shrunk even more, which has seriously affected how communities can be dramatized and often diminished the ability of musicals to depict communities at all. Musicals that might have benefited from including the community as a significant presence in the story have simply not had enough actors in the cast to do so.

At least one twenty-first-century musical, however, was able to crack the code. What is truly remarkable about **Come From Away** (2017) is that with only twelve hard-working cast members plus a small onstage band, this show is able to bring not just one but two fully realized communities to life: the townspeople of Gander, Newfoundland, and the "come-from-aways"—the Plane People" who find themselves stranded "somewhere in the middle of nowhere." These two communities start out very wary and even afraid of one another, and how they eventually come together is a truly captivating and inspiring story, especially because it's true. The remarkable achievement of *Come From Away* is made possible by those inherent attributes of musical theater to bring communities to life and to transcend time and space—and also by a gifted creative team[13] that figured out how to put them to use so effectively within the production's limited resources. *Come From Away* ends not with a union but a reunion, in which the Plane People return to Gander to commemorate their shared experience ten years earlier, and the musical itself can be seen as an extension of that celebration. Of course, the underlying message of this show is that the Newfoundlanders and the "come from aways" should be friends.

Once again, we can connect the dots in the ongoing continuum of the Broadway musical from *Oklahoma!* to *Come From Away*, with each team of creators, whether they realized it or not, having been inspired by the musicals and creators who preceded them.

NOTES

Introduction

1. Carl Zimmer, "Delving into the Archeology of Music," *New York Times*, May 21, 2014, D10.

Overture: What is a Broadway Musical?

1. Julie Bloom, "Lin-Manuel Miranda on 'Mary Poppins Returns' and Movie Musicals," *New York Times*, November 2, 2018, https://www.nytimes.com/2018/11/02/movies/lin-manuel-miranda-mary-poppins-returns.html.
2. In the 1920s there were close to eighty "legitimate" Broadway theaters.
3. The bookwriter is also often referred to as the "librettist," a term borrowed from the opera world.
4. Any two, or even all three of these tasks can be combined under one individual.
5. Which often may be the same person working as the director-choreographer.
6. One individual might be responsible for several of these jobs.
7. Sometimes called the Scenic Designer.
8. One individual may be responsible for two or more of these positions.
9. Includes actors, singers, dancers, understudies and standbys.
10. Includes stagehands, prop crew, lighting and sound technicians, wardrobe crew and dressers.
11. For example, much of Jerome Robbins' choreography from *West Side Story* has been adapted into a suite of dances that is now in the repertory of several major ballet companies, and a number of Broadway dances by Bob Fosse, Agnes DeMille, and others have been performed outside of the musicals they originally came from.
12. In many cases the Music Director also creates many or all of the show's vocal arrangements.
13. Derek McLane and Eila Mell, *Designing Broadway: How Derek McLane and Other Acclaimed Set Designers Create the Visual World of Theatre* (Running Press Adult, 2022).
14. Ruthie Fierburg, "In the Producers Office," *BroadwayNews*, February 12, 2024, https://www.broadwaynews.com/in-the-producers-office-kevin-mccollum-on-producing-two-new-musicals-in-one-season/.

Prologue: Before Broadway

1. In today's terminology we would call him a lyricist.
2. Oscar Gross Brockett, *History of the Theatre* (Allyn and Bacon, 1974), 287.

Notes

3. William Eben Schultz, Oliver Baty Cunningham Memorial Publication Fund, and Elizabethan Club (Yale University), *Gay's Beggar's Opera: Its Content, History and Influence* (Yale University Press, 1923), 109.
4. Local iterations of the Zarzuela became quite popular around the world in most of the regions that were colonized by Spain, including Cuba, Central America, South America, and the Philippines.
5. Robert C. Toll, *On with the Show: The First Century of Show Business in America* (Oxford University Press, 1976), 173.
6. Toll, *On with the Show*, 173.
7. The Academy of Music
8. Toll, *On with The Show*, 173.
9. Toll, *On with The Show*, 175.
10. Toll, *On with The Show*, 175.
11. Larry Stempel, *Showtime: A History of the Broadway Musical Theater* (National Geographic Books, 2010), 45–6.
12. Toll, *On with The Show*, 177.
13. Toll, *On with The Show*, 177.
14. Toll, *On with The Show*, 177.
15. Toll, *On with The Show*, 179.
16. February 1877 program from Niblo's Garden, Jules Verne.ca, https://julesverne.ca/index.html.
17. Toll, *On with The Show*, 179.
18. David Maxine, "Musical of The Month: A Production History of The Wizard of Oz," New York Public Library, December 15, 2011, https://www.nypl.org/blog/2011/12/15/musical-month-production-history-1903-oz.
19. Toll, *On with The Show*, 215.
20. *New York Herald*, January 26, 1867.
21. *New York Herald*, October 23, 1866.
22. Joseph Whitton, *Wags of the Stage*, 1902, 259, https://docs.google.com/document/d/1w_HdhedLAA391GhBdeY8uSypnz7NpBpdo-oFpPku_Xw/edit.
23. "From New York," *Iowa State Register*, November 3, 1867.
24. Known as variety in its earliest forms and closely related to the British music hall.
25. Gerald Carson, "The Piano in the Parlor," *American Heritage* 17, no. 1 (December 1965).
26. Yiddish is the traditional language of Jews who lived in Central and Eastern Europe, and is a hybrid of Hebrew and medieval German. A century ago, Yiddish was understood by an estimated 11 million of the world's 18 million Jews and was the primary language for many of them.
27. Quoted in Alan Hyman, *The Gaiety Years* (Weidenfeld and Nicolson, 1975), 64.
28. Eubie Blake interviewed by Harry Reasoner on *60 Minutes*, https://www.youtube.com/watch?v=0Mu4L7G9fkM

Notes

Chapter 1

1. Daniel Okrent, *Last Call: The Rise and Fall of Prohibition* (Simon and Schuster, 2010), 236.
2. Matt Artz, "European Immigration and Defining Whiteness (1910–1920)," *Understanding RACE*, January 27, 1910, https://understandingrace.org/history/government/european-immigration-and-defining-whiteness-1910-1920/.
3. Kevin Kenny, "Irish immigrant Stereotypes and American Racism," *Picturing United States History*, https://picturinghistory.gc.cuny.edu/irish-immigrant-stereotypes-and-american-racism/.
4. Samual G. Freedman, "What Musicals and Comedy Owe to Harrigan and Hart," *New York Times*, January 27, 1985, Section 2, 1.
5. https://legacy.chass.ncsu.edu/jouvert/v4i1/onkey.htm.
6. Broadway would not see integrated casts onstage for more than forty years.
7. Lauren Onky, "'A Melee and a Curtain': Black Irish Relations in Ned Narrigan's Mulligan Guard Ball," https://legacy.chass.ncsu.edu/jouvert/v4i1/onkey.htm.
8. Freedman, *New York Times*, January 27, 1985, Section 2, 1.
9. Freedman, *New York Times*, January 27, 1985, Section 2, 1.
10. Nick Maloney, lecture recorded at the Library of Congress in 2009.
11. David Belasco (1855–1931) was one of the leading Broadway producers and playwrights of the late nineteenth century.
12. As Elizabeth T. Craft states in her 2024 biography of Cohan, "his birthdate has been a matter of dispute." Although Cohan's first biographer, Ward Morehouse, uncovered a baptismal record citing Cohan's birthday as July 3, his second biographer, John McCabe, argued that there is reason to believe this was a "clerical error," and that "almost certainly" his true birthdate was the fourth as his family had "always celebrated." By 1918, when Cohan listed his birthdate as July 4 on his draft registration, as Craft states, "few remembered that he had actually been born before and not after midnight." Elizabeth T. Craft, *Yankee Doodle Dandy: George M. Cohan and the Broadway Stage* (Oxford University Press, USA, 2024), 160-2.
13. Rick Benjamin, *You're A Grand Old Rag: The Music of George M. Cohan* (New World Records, 2008.)
14. Benjamin, *You're A Grand Old Rag*.
15. According to Rick Benjamin, "Young George Cohan idolized Harrigan, and in many ways patterned himself after the veteran showman. Late in 1907 Cohan began work on a new musical . . . entitled *Fifty Miles from Boston*, it opened in the Garrick (formerly Harrigan's) Theatre on February 3, 1908. The cast included a character named "Harrigan" who was based on the comic roles that the real Harrigan had played in his own shows decades before . . . when Ned Harrigan himself was eventually coaxed to his old theater to see the show, bittersweet tears streamed down his face as he heard "Harrigan" sung for the first time. Cohan, after his hero's passing some time afterward, made this testament: "Edward Harrigan was a fine artist, a great writer of human comedies and one of the grandest men it has ever been my pleasure to meet . . . I live in hopes that someday my name may mean half as much to the coming generation of American playwrights as Harrigan's name has meant to me." Benjamin, *You're A Grand Old Rag*.
16. Cohan's distinctive dancing style is replicated in the 1942 film biography *Yankee Doodle Dandy*. Throughout rehearsals and filming, the movie's star, James Cagney, worked closely with dancer/choreographer John Boyle to perfect Cohan's style and routines. Boyle had both performed onstage with Cohan, and staged dances for him, in the *Cohan Revue of 1916*.

17. The first song from a Broadway musical to sell over a million copies of sheet music. "You're A Grand Old Flag," Song-Collection, Library of Congress, https://www.loc.gov/item/ihas.200000026.
18. Benjamin, *You're A Grand Old Rag*.
19. See page 63.
20. "'THE MERRY WIDOW' PROVES CAPTIVATING: WINS INSTANT APPROVAL IN AMERICAN DEBUT AT THE NEW AMSTERDAM THEATRE. REPEATS FOREIGN SUCCESS MISS ETHEL JACKSON PLAYS THE WIDOW WITH SPIRIT—FAMOUS WALTZ CHARMS LARGE AUDIENCE," *New York Times*, October 22, 1907, https://www.proquest.com/historical-newspapers/merry-widow-proves-captivating/docview/96725092/se-2.
21. Larry Stempel, *Showtime: A History of the Broadway Musical Theater* (W. W. Norton, 2010), 173-4.
22. Based on a comic play by Henri Meilhac which had premiered in Paris in 1861.
23. "'THE MERRY WIDOW' PROVES CAPTIVATING"
24. The production was "Staged" by George F. Marion (1860–1945), who between 1900 and 1930 directed, staged and choreographed more than fifty Broadway musicals.
25. Stempel, *Showtime*, 175.
26. Philip Furia, *Irving Berlin: A Life in Song* (Schirmer Trade Books, 1998), 6.
27. Laurence Bergreen, *As Thousands Cheer: The Life of Irving Berlin* (Da Capo Press, 1996), 17–18.
28. Bergreen, *As Thousands Cheer*, 27.
29. Bergreen, *As Thousands Cheer*, 27.
30. Bergreen, *As Thousands Cheer*, 57.
31. This was likely the first musical with Mormon characters, although certainly not the most famous.
32. "They Didn't Believe Me: Steyn's Song of the Week," SteynOnline, https://www.steynonline.com/10837/they-didnt-believe-me.
33. Gerald Bordman, *American Musical Theater: A Chronicle* (Oxford University Press, 2001), 330.
34. Stanley Green, *The World of Musical Comedy* (Da Capo Press, 1984).
35. Unattributed, "Musical Comedy of Irene a Great Hit," *Los Angeles Times*, June 12, 1921, 27.
36. McElliot, "Irene Scores Happiest of Hits at Vanderbilt," *Daily News*, November 20, 1919, 14.
37. McElliot, "Irene Scores Happiest of Hits at Vanderbilt," 14.
38. Irene's record was finally broken by the raucous revue *Hellzapoppin* (1938), which ran for more than twice as long, ending with 1,404 performances.
39. "'Irene' is Greatest Musical Success of Them All," *Central New Jersey Home News*, April 17, 1921.
40. Unattributed, "At The Theatres," *Standard Union*, October 4, 1921, 14.
41. Zayda Glover, "When the Curtain Rises in Gotham," *Pittsburg Press*, February 29, 1920, 67.
42. Unattributed, "Amusements, Poli's Irene," [DC] *Evening Star*, November 10, 18.
43. Unattributed, "At The Theaters This Week," *Washington Times*, November 10, 1919.
44. McElliot, "Irene Scores Happiest of Hits at Vanderbilt," 14.
45. Unattributed, "Delightful Irene Casts Spell Here," *New York Herald*, November 19, 1919, 10.
46. Unattributed, "At The Theaters This Week," *Washington Times*, November 10, 1919.

Notes

47. Haywood Broun, "Irene Has Plot, Good Music, and Pace in Plenty," *New York Tribune*, November 19, 1919, 13.
48. Richard L. Stokes, "First Night Audience Pleased with Irene," *St. Louis Dispatch*, April 11, 1921.
49. Unattributed, "Irene Presented At Parsons House," *New Britain Herald*, October 12 1920, 15.
50. Unattributed, "Irene Presented At Parsons House," 15.
51. Unattributed, "Pugilistic Star Plays Role of Male Modiste," *Boston Globe*, January 15, 1922, 58.
52. Unattributed, "At The Theatres," *Standard Union*, October 4, 1921, 14.
53. Unattributed, "Pugilistic Star Plays Role of Male Modiste," 58.
54. Unattributed, "The Stage," *Wisconsin Leader-Telegram*, September 30, 1921.
55. Unattributed, "Irene Proves Comedy Offering of Song Hits," *News-Herald*, October 18, 1921, 12.
56. Unattributed, "Irene, Clean, Wholesome, Sweet, Registers Bullseye," *Punxsutawney Spirit*, October 11, 1921, 1.
57. Unattributed, "Musical Comedy of Irene a Great Hit," 27.

Chapter 2

1. Stewart F. Lane, *Black Broadway: African Americans on the Great White Way* (Square One Publishers, 2015), 7.
2. "The History of Blackface: Unmasking the Racism Re-Ignited by Megyn Kelly Controversy," *CBS News*, October 28, 2018, https://www.cbsnews.com/news/history-of-blackface-unmasking-the-racism-reignited-by-megyn-kelly-controversy/.
3. Carla L. Peterson, "City Room, Answers about Black Life in 19th-Century New York, Part 2," New York Times, February 17, 2012. https://archive.nytimes.com/cityroom.blogs.nytimes.com/2012/02/17/answers-about-black-life-in-19th-century-new-york-part-2/#:~:text=New%20York's%20black%20population%20declined,in%201840%20at%20about%2016%2C300.
4. "The History of Blackface: Unmasking the Racism Re-Ignited by Megyn Kelly Controversy," CBS News, October 28, 2018, https://www.cbsnews.com/news/history-of-blackface-unmasking-the-racism-reignited-by-megyn-kelly-controversy/.
5. Vereen stated this several times in several similar versions, including in a presentation at the City College of New York in February 2012, and in an episode of *Tony Brown's Journal* in 1982.
6. Interestingly, it has long been speculated that Foster was homesexual, and indeed he is included in the "biographical dictionary," *The Gay and Lesbian Theatrical Legacy*. However, as contributor Stephen Berwin notes, as is the case with many nineteenth-century figures, Foster's sexuality "disappears behind the limits that Victorian propriety placed on discussions of physical intimacy."
7. Rikomatic, "The Cakewalk—A Dance of Black Resistance and Celebration," http://www.yehoodi.com/blog/2020/6/14/the-cakewalk-a-dance-of-black-resistance-and-celebration.
8. Advertizement for Sam T. Jack's Creole Burlesque Company, Loc's Public Domain Archive https://loc.getarchive.net/media/sam-t-jacks-creole-burlesque-company-3?zoom=true.
9. Camile F. Forbes, *Introducing Bert Williams* (Basic Civitas, 2008), 78.
10. "The Great Migration, (1910-1970)," National Archives. https://www.archives.gov/research/african-americans/migrations/great-migration.

11. Forbes, *Introducing Bert Williams*, 100.
12. "Dahomey On Broadway," *New York Times*, February 19, 1903, 9.
13. "Dahomey On Broadway," *New York Times*, February 19, 1903, 9.
14. *Boston Post*, September 23, 1902, 4.
15. *Standard Union*, October 14, 1902.
16. "New Williams and Walker Show," *The Sun*, February 21, 1906, 8.
17. "New Williams and Walker Show," *The Sun*, February 21, 1906, 8.
18. "New Williams and Walker Show," *The Sun*, February 21, 1906, 8.
19. "'Abyssinia,' Williams and Walker Make a Hit with New Comedy," *New York Age*, February 22 1906, 1.
20. "'Abyssinia,' Williams and Walker Make a Hit with New Comedy," *New York Age*, February 22 1906, 1.
21. Quote in display ad in the *New York Age*, March 5, 1908, 6.
22. The Old Homestead was a play by Denman Thompson and George W. Ryer that between 1877 and 1913 received ten Broadway productions.
23. "The Theaters," *Brooklyn Daily Eagle*, April 21, 1908, 26.
24. "An Afro-American Success," *Minneapolis Journal*, February 16, 1908, 46.
25. "A Memorable Event," *New York Age*, March 5, 1908, 6.
26. The performers who refused to share the stage with Williams and Walker were James J. Morton, who was just about to open in a musical comedy titled *The Merry Go Round*, and a singing group known as "That Quartet."
27. Equivalent to more than $170,000 today.
28. "Controversy Over W. and W.," *New York Age*, March 5, 1908, 6.
29. *The Routledge Companion to African American Theatre and Performance* (Taylor and Francis, 2018).
30. Allen L. Woll, *Black Musical Theatre: From Coontown to Dreamgirls* (Louisiana State University Press, 1989), 24.
31. At least ten editions of the *Ziegfeld Follies* from 1910 to 1924 featured songs by Black songwriters.
32. A "Jonah Man" was a long established expression for someone who is considered unlucky, like the character of Jonah in the Bible, and it was the title of an earlier Williams/Rodgers song from *In Dahomey*.
33. Eddie Cantor, *As I Remember Them* (Duell, Sloan, and Pearce, 1963), 50.
34. J. A. Rogers, *World's Great Men of Color, Volume II* (Touchstone, 1996), 380.
35. Paul Magriel, *Chronicles of the American Dance—From Shakers to Martha Graham* (DaCapo Press, 1978), 40.
36. Agnes DeMille, *America Dances* (Macmillan, 1980), 13–14.
37. DeMille, *America Dances*, 14.
38. DeMille, *America Dances*, 14.
39. Charles Dickens, *American Notes for General Circulation* (Chapman and Hall, 1842), 80–3.
40. Marshall Stearns and Jean Stearns, *Jazz Dance: The Story of American Vernacular Dance* (Da Capo Press, 1994), 46.

Notes

41. Magriel, *Chronicles of the American Dance*, 47.
42. Tyler Anbinder, *Five Points: The Nineteenth-Century New York City Neighborhood* (Simon and Schuster, 2012), 175.
43. Marian Hannah Winter, "Juba and American Minstrelsy," in *Chronicles of the American Dance* (Da Capo Press, Inc., 1948), 39.

Chapter 3

1. Patrick McGilligan, *George Cukor: A Double Life* (St. Martin's Press, 1991), 115.
2. George Chauncey, *Gay New York: Gender, Urban Culture, and the Making of the Gay Male World, 1890–1940* (Basic Books, 2008).
3. Elisa Rolle, "George James Hopkins," *Queer Places*, http://www.elisarolle.com/queerplaces/fghij/George%20James%20Hopkins.html.
4. Kim Marra, *Strange Duets: Impresarios and Actresses in the American Theatre, 1865–1914* (University of Iowa Press, 2009), 88.
5. Marra, *Strange Duets*, 87.
6. Marra, *Strange Duets*, 87.
7. Andrew L. Erdman, *Beautiful: The Story of Julian Eltinge, America's Greatest Female Impersonator* (Oxford University Press, 2024), 28.
8. C. S. Voll, "The Man Who Became the Ideal Edwardian Woman," *Medium.com*, November 20, 2020.
9. Erdman, *Beautiful*, 45.
10. Frank Cullen, Florence Hackman, and Donald McNeilly, *Vaudeville Old and New: An Encyclopedia of Variety Performances in America* (Psychology Press, 2007).
11. Some sources list Savoy's birth as 1876.
12. O. O. McIntyre, *The Buffalo Enquirer*, August 9, 1919, 8.
13. O. O. McIntyre, *The Buffalo Enquirer*, August 9, 1919, 8.
14. Eve Golden, "Queen of the Dead: Bert Savoy," *Daily Mirror*, October 30, 2012.
15. Hassard Short's *Ritz Revue* (1924), *Artists and Models* (1925), *A Night in Spain* (1927), *A Night in Venice* (1929).
16. Arthur Pollack, "Plays and Things," *Brooklyn Daily Eagle*, June 25, 1925, 7

Chapter 4

1. Anne Caldwell, *Songwriters Hall of Fame*, https://www.songhall.org/profile/Anne_Caldwell.
2. The exact details of her early life are difficult to tie down as she gave conflicting stories to the press over the years.
3. Sarah Whitfield, "Spotlights on Women Composers in Early Broadway History: Nora Bayes," Maestramusica.org.
4. Levi Branson, "Musical of the Month: Night Boat," *New York Public Library Blog*, January 31, 2013, https://www.nypl.org/blog/2013/01/31/musical-month-night-boat.

Notes

5. Kurt Ganzl, *Lydia Thompson: Queen of Burlesque* (Routledge, 2014), 87.
6. Ganzl, *Lydia Thompson*, 91.
7. Ganzl, *Lydia Thompson*, 87.
8. Ganzl, *Lydia Thompson*, 87.
9. Ganzl, *Lydia Thompson*, 106 –7.
10. Ganzl, *Lydia Thompson*, 2.
11. http://operetta-research-center.org/lydia-thompson-father-drag-kings/
12. Ganzl, *Lydia Thompson*, 107.
13. Ganzl, *Lydia Thompson*, 107.
14. John Kenrick, "History of Burlesque Part I," *Musicals101.com*, 2003, https://www.musicals101.com/burlesque.htm.
15. Kenrick, "History of Burlesque Part I."
16. Forbes, *Introducing Bert Williams*, 66.
17. Ganzl, *Lydia Thompson*.
18. Sunny Stalter-Pace, *Imitation Artist: Gertrude Hoffmann's Life in Vaudeville and Dance* (Northwestern University Press, 2020), 1.
19. Max Hoffmann was born in Prussia in 1873 and emigrated as a child to Wisconsin. He would go on to work for Hammerstein, Ziegfeld, and the Shuberts as the composer and/or music director for at least eighteen Broadway musicals and revues.
20. Stalter-Pace, *Imitation Artist*, 27.

Chapter 5

1. https://www.history.com/news/flappers-roaring-20s-women-empowerment.
2. The ammendment had been ratified in 1919.
3. Jerome Charyn, *Gangsters and Gold Diggers: Old New York, the Jazz Age, and the Birth of Broadway* (Thunder's Mouth Press, 2003).
4. Shellie Clark, "The Sexual Revolution of the 'Roaring Twenties': Practice or Perception," https://soar.suny.edu/bitstream/handle/20.500.12648/2671/hashtaghistory/vol1/iss1/7/fulltext%20%281%29.pdf?sequence=1andisAllowed=y.
5. Dale Cockrell, *Everybody's Doin' It: Sex, Music, and Dance in New York, 1840–1917* (W. W. Norton and Company, 2019).
6. Charyn, *Gangsters and Gold Diggers*, 176.
7. Advertisement in the *New York Times*, October 4, 1920, 14.
8. Michael Goldfarb, "Jews and Blues: Inside Out," *WBUR*, 2001, http://archives.wbur.org/insideout/documentaries/jewsandblues/index2.php.html.
9. Sometimes spelled "Gipsies."
10. Roma dance forms had a similar effect, which can be seen clearly in the striking similarities between traditional Indian dance, Arabic dance (aka belly dance), Flamenco, Passo Doble, and other Spanish dance forms.
11. Remarkably, this demonstrates that the concept of the Broadway musical being the creation of marginalized people starts centuries before the musical is even born. And we see another

Notes

foreshadow of what was to come: the Roma were both outcast by society and at the same time valued as entertainers.

12. Goldfarb, "Jews and Blues."
13. Alan J. Lerner, *The Street Where I Live: A Memoir* (W. W. Norton and Company, 2018), 41.
14. Langston Hughes, *The Big Sea* (DigiCat, 2022).
15. The National Association for the Advancement of Colored People is a national Civil Rights organization established in 1909.
16. Caseen Gaines, *When Broadway Was Black: The Triumphant Story of the All-Black Musical That Changed the World* (Sourcebooks, Inc., 2023).
17. *Shuffle Along*, 1921 script, New York Public Library, https://static.nypl.org/MOTM/ShuffleAlong/ShuffleAlong.html.
18. Caseen Gaines, *Footnotes* (Sourcebooks, 2021), 226.
19. From an interview with Caseen Gaines on the podcast *Broadway Nation*, Episode 37: "100 Years of *Shuffle Along*," September 16, 2021.
20. Gaines, *Footnotes*, 226.
21. *New York Age*, June 10, 1922.
22. Charles Darnton, "Strut Miss Lizzie Full of Life and Color," *Evening World*, June 20, 1922, 24.
23. Written by Ziegfeld regulars: Gene Buck (lyrics) and Louis A. Hirsch and Dave Stamper (music).
24. Gilbert Seldes, *The Seven Lively Arts* (Harper & Brothers, 1924), 141.
25. Lucian H. White, "In The Realm of Music," *New York Age*, December 16, 1922, 6.
26. For a full account of this fascinating story see Gaines, *When Broadway Was Black*.
27. "Broadway Banter," *Atlanta Constitution*, October 11, 1925, 85.
28. Time-Life Books, *The Jazz Age: The 20s* (Time Life Medical, 1998), 35.
29. *Press of Atlantic City*, August 7, 1926, 13.
30. *Pensacola News Journal*, February 11, 1927, 4.
31. *Bridgeport Herald*, March 18, 1926, 1.
32. *Oakland Post Enquirer*, October 21, 1925, 3.
33. *Pensacola News Journal*, February 11, 1927, 4.
34. *Press of Atlantic City*, August 7, 1926, 13.
35. "Who's Who on the Stage," *New York Times*, December 19, 1926.
36. W. M. Cook, "Spirituals and Jazz," *New York Times*, December 26, 1926.
37. Cook, "Spirituals and Jazz."
38. The song and dance "The Varsity Drag" was introduced in the 1927 Desylva, Brown and Henderson musical comedy *Good News*.
39. Gaines, *Footnotes*, 247, 248.
40. Stark Young, "The Play," *New York Times*, September 2, 1924, 22.
41. Ashton Stevens, "White Art Rather Than Black Magic, Says Stevens," *Chicago Herald and Examiner*, March 31, 1924.
42. Gaines, *When Broadway Was Black*.
43. Astaire's father, Friedrich (Fritz) Emanuel Austerlitz, was born in Linz, Austria, on September 8, 1868. He and his family were Jewish, but the family converted to Catholicism, the dominant religion in Austria.

Notes

44. Burns Mantle, "Lady Be Good and the Dancing Astaires," *Daily News*, December 8, 1924, 88.
45. Born Siegmund Rosenberg into a Jewish family in Hungary in 1887, Romberg was a major Broadway composer during the Silver Age, whose biggest hits included *The Student Prince* (1924), *The Desert Song* (1926), and *The New Moon* (1928).
46. Somewhat similar to the off-Broadway hit revue *Forbidden Broadway*.
47. Twenty-eight-year-old Herbert Fields was the choreographer of *The Garrick Gaieties*.
48. Stanley Green, "The World of Musical Comedy," *Philadelphia Inquirer*, May 7, 1961, 85.
49. In a very strange turn of events, as outlined in Barry Kester's *Round in Circles*, it appears that one of the plays that Larry Hart translated for the Shuberts was Molnar's *Lilliam*, and later that translation was used by Rodgers and Hammerstein as the basis for their script for *Carousel*! Whether R&H were aware of this at the time is not clear. Barry Kester, *Round in Circles* (i2i Publishing, 2022).
50. Richard Rodgers, *Musical Stages: An Autobiography* (Random House, 1975), 27.
51. Green, "The World of Musical Comedy," 85.
52. Rodgers, *Musical Stages*, 28.
53. Unattributed, *Daily News*, September 17, 1925, 74.
54. Burns Mantle, "Vagabond King Colorful Show," *Daily News*, September 22, 1925, 122.
55. Unattributed, "Dennis King Shines Amid Friml's Melodies and Reynolds Lovely Scenes and Costumes," *New York Times*, September 22, 1925, 23.
56. Unattributed, "Dennis King Shines," 23
57. Unattributed, "Dennis King Shines," 23.
58. Unattributed, "Dennis King Shines," 23.
59. Dennis King was a major Broadway star who between 1921 and 1969 starred in forty-one Broadway plays and musicals, including Friml's *The Three Musketeers* (1928), the 1932 revival of *Show Boat*, and Rodgers and Hart's *I Married an Angel* in 1938.
60. Unattributed, "Dennis King Shines," 23.
61. Burns Mantle, "Vagabond King Colorful Show," 122.
62. "Broadway Banter," *Atlanta Constitution*, Sunday Magazine, October 11, 1925, 85.
63. Herald Tribune.
64. Arthur Pollock, "The Vagabond King Opens at Casino," *Brooklyn Daily Eagle*, September 22, 1925, 7.
65. Unattributed, "The Story of an Operetta," *New York Times*, January 17, 1926, 167.
66. "Hassard Short Director Dead," *New York Times*, October 10, 1956.
67. Billy J. Harbin, Kim Marra, and Robert A. Schanke, *The Gay and Lesbian Theatrical Legacy: A Biographical Dictionary of Major Figures in American Stage History in the Pre-Stonewall Era* (University of Michigan Press, 2005), 334.
68. In modern stagecraft lingo we would call this a "wagon" or "palette."
69. Harbin, Marra, and Schanke, *The Gay and Lesbian Theatrical Legacy*.
70. John Corbin, "The Play: New Music Box Revue is Dazzling," *New York Times*, October 24, 1922.
71. Harbin, Marra, and Schanke, *The Gay and Lesbian Theatrical Legacy*, 336.
72. "The Palate Mixer," *New York Times*, June 18, 1944.
73. Kevin Winkler, *The Gay and Lesbian Theatrical Legacy* (University of Michigan Press, 2010), 336.

Notes

74. Mary Ellin Barrett, *Irving Berlin: A Daughter's Memoir* (Amadeus Press, 1996), 149.
75. Brooks Atkinson, "First Night at the Theatre," *New York Times*, December 11, 1953, 42.
76. John Murray Anderson and Hugh Abercrombie Anderson, *Out Without My Rubbers: The Memoirs of John Murray Anderson* (Pickle Partners Publishing, 2018).
77. This was an often lucrative line of work for attractive, charming, young men who could dance, but it came with a significant degree of scandal attached to it. Male taxi dancers were often referred to as "gigolos" or "tango pirates" and, perhaps because the masculinity of any man who made a living as a dancer and would acquiesce to being "rented" by a woman, even if just for a dance, was already called into question, many Queer men seem to have been drawn to this profession, including future silent film legend, Rudolph Valentino, and future Broadway and Hollywood star, Clifton Webb.
78. Anderson and Anderson, *Out Without My Rubbers*.
79. Anderson and Anderson, *Out Without My Rubbers*.
80. Anderson and Anderson, *Out Without My Rubbers*.
81. Anderson and Anderson, *Out Without My Rubbers*.
82. Alexander Woollcott, "The Play: John Murray Anderson's Revue," *New York Times*, March 20, 1920, https://www.proquest.com/historical-newspapers/play/docview/97886345/se-2.
83. 1932, 1936, and 1943.
84. Anderson and Anderson, *Out Without My Rubbers*.
85. Raul Pen DuBois (1912–1985) designed the sets and/or costumes for more than fifty Broadway musicals between 1934 and 1980.
86. Anderson and Anderson, *Out Without My Rubbers*.
87. Anderson and Anderson, *Out Without My Rubbers*.
88. *New York Times*, January 10, 1924.
89. Which introduced three songs by Coward, including "Poor Little Rich Girl."
90. Some 697 performances in London, and 159 on Broadway, where it opened just as the stock market crashed.
91. Oliver Soden, *Masquerade: The Lives of Noel Coward* (Weidenfeld and Nicolson, 2024), 207.
92. Manuscript, *Bitter Sweet*, book, music and lyrics by Noel Coward, https://static.nypl.org/MOTM/BitterSweet/BittersweetMusic.html.
93. Soden, *Masquerade*, 207.
94. *Central New Jersey Home News*, January 15, 1930, 9.
95. "Wilkes-Barre Times Leader," *Evening News*, November 19, 1929, 2.
96. *Central New Jersey Home News*, January 15, 1930, 9.
97. "Wilkes-Barre Times Leader," *Evening News*, November 19, 1929, 2.
98. "Masquerade, The Lives Of Noel Coward," Episode 125, *Broadway Nation* https://www.broadway-nation.com/episode-125-masquerade-the-lives-of-noel-coward/.
99. Deborah Grace Winer, *On the Sunny Side of the Street: The Life and Lyrics of Dorothy Fields* (Schirmer Trade Books, 1997).
100. Herbert Fields and Richard Rodgers had attended Columbia University together.
101. Michael Feinstein relates this story in an interview with Terry Gross on the NPR show *Fresh Air*, October 17, 2012.

Notes

102. Armond Fields and L. Marc Fields, *From the Bowery to Broadway: Lew Fields and the Roots of American Popular Theatre* (Oxford University Press, USA, 1993).
103. Frederick Nolan, *Lorenz Hart: A Poet on Broadway* (Oxford University Press, 1994).
104. Stephen Sondheim, *Finishing the Hat: Collected Lyrics (1954–1981) with Attendant Comments, Principles, Heresies, Grudges, Whines and Anecdotes* (Knopf, 2010), 212.
105. Kim Marra and Robert A. Schanke, *Staging Desire: Queer Readings of American Theater History* (University of Michigan Press, 2002), 149.
106. Marra and Schanke, *Staging Desire*, 149.
107. Marra and Schanke, *Staging Desire*, 164.
108. Edited with commentary by Thomas S. Hishchak and Jack Macauly.
109. John C. Wilson, *Noel, Tallulah, Cole, and Me: A Memoir of Broadway's Golden Age* (Rowman and Littlefield, 2015), 23.
110. Soden, *Masquerade*, 169.
111. Soden, *Masquerade*, 169.
112. Soden, *Masquerade*, 170.
113. Wilson, *Noel, Tallulah, Cole, and Me*, 23.
114. Soden, *Masquerade*, 170.
115. Alice Hughes, "New Commedianne Recreates 'Gentlemen Prefer Blondes,'" *Buffalo Currier Express*, December 17, 1949, 15.
116. Brooks Atkinson, "First Night at the Theatre," *New York Times*, December 9, 1949, 35.
117. John Chapman, "'Gentlemen Prefer Blondes' Just Perfect; Carol Channing Supurb," *Daily News*, December 10, 1949, 95.
118. Louis Sheaffer, "Theater," *Brooklyn Daily Eagle*, December 9.
119. John Chapman, "A Blonde From Little Rock," *Daily News*, December 18, 1949, 583.
120. Wilson, *Noel, Tallulah, Cole, and Me*, 98.
121. Wilson, *Noel, Tallulah, Cole, and Me*, 98.
122. Brooks Peters, "King Of Queens," *An Open Book*, May 9, 2020, https://brookspeters.blogspot.com/2020/05/king-of-queens-karyl-norman.html.
123. Darryl W. Bullock, "Panzy Craze," *Guardian*, September 14, 2017.
124. "Pansy Places on Broadway," *Variety*, September 19, 1930.
125. "Bowery Boys, Welcome to the Pansy Club," *The Bowery Boys Blog*, June 2010.
126. *Variety*, December 17, 1930.
127. July 14, 1932.
128. https://www.queermusicheritage.com/MWFM.html.
129. https://www.queermusicheritage.com/MWFM.html.
130. Ford Dabney (March 15, 1883–June 21, 1958). Among his many other credits, for eight years, from 1913 to 1921, Dabney was the music director of *Ziegfeld's Midnight Frolic*, where he led his own "Syncopated Orchestra."
131. Uncredited, "Rang Tang Opens at the Royale Theatre," *New York Times*, July 13, 1927, 20.
132. Uncredited, "Rang Tang Opens at the Royale Theatre."
133. Uncredited, "Rang Tang Opens at the Royale Theatre."

Notes

134. "Keep Shufflin' Given at Break-Neck Pace," *New York Times*, February 28, 1928, 24.
135. "Hot Chocolates Highly praised by Broadway Critics," *New York Age*, June 29, 1929.
136. Winter, "Juba and American Minstrelsy," 39.
137. Elizabeth Blair, "Shirley Temple and Bojangels: Two Stars, One Lifelong Friendship," *All Things Considered*, NPR, February 14, 2014, https://www.npr.org/2014/02/14/276986764/shirley-temple-and-bojangles-two-stars-one-lifelong-friendship.
138. A 1932 version of this routine can be seen in an unfortunately very grainy film clip on YouTube: *Bill "Bojangles" Robinson Stair Dance, 1932*.
139. Stewart F. Lane, *Black Broadway: African Americans on the Great White Way* (Square One Publishers, 2015), 80.
140. "Two To New York," *Montclair Times*, May 12, 1928, 28.
141. Blair, "Shirley Temple and Bojangels."
142. Lane, *Black Broadway*, 80.
143. Weber and Fields are credited with originating (or at least popularizing) the famous comic exchange: Weber: "Who vas dat lady I seen you wid last night?" Fields: "Dat vass no lady, dat vass mine wife."
144. Fields and Fields, *From the Bowery to Broadway*, 470.
145. *New York Age*, October 4, 1930, 6.
146. *Brooklyn Daily Eagle*, October 8, 1930, 21.
147. Ethan Mordden, *When Broadway Went to Hollywood* (Oxford University Press, 2016), 41.
148. Mordden, *When Broadway Went to Hollywood*, 41.
149. Brooks Atkinson, "The Play," *New York Times*, May 20, 1932, 22.

Chapter 6

1. Technically it was the Shubert's corporate entity that went bankrupt.
2. From IBDB.
3. Eventually the U.S. government provided at least some work for tens of thousands of actors, singers, dancers and other theater professionals through its Federal Theatre Project, established in 1935. This WPA "New Deal" program produced nearly 64,000 performances of more than 1,500 plays and musicals in sixty-two cities across America that were attended by more than 30 million people. The dramatic controversy surrounding the FTP's 1937 production of Marc Blitzstein's musical *The Cradle Will Rock* created a theatrical legend.
4. Stanley Green, *Ring Bells! Sing Songs!: Broadway Musicals of the 1930's* (Galahad Books, 1971), 12.
5. "Brother Can You Spare A Dime," VCU Social Welfare History Project, https://socialwelfare.library.vcu.edu/eras/great-depression/brother-can-you-spare-a-dime-1932/.
6. "Brother Can You Spare A Dime," VCU Social Welfare History Project, https://socialwelfare.library.vcu.edu/eras/great-depression/brother-can-you-spare-a-dime-1932/.
7. "E.Y. Harburg," Songwriters Hall of Fame, https://www.songhall.org/profile/EY_Harburg.
8. Billy Rose Theatre Division, New York Public Library. "The 'Brother Can You Spare a Dime?' scene from the stage production Americana," New York Public Library Digital Collections, https://digitalcollections.nypl.org/items/64069640-67fc-0130-2ba0-58d385a7bbd0.

Notes

9. *Standard Union*, October,15, 1930, 11.
10. *Times Union*, October 15, 1930, 7.
11. *Brooklyn Daily Eagle*, October 15, 1930, 21.
12. Willie Howard (1883–1949) was one of the biggest stars of the Silver Age. Between 1912 and 1948 he appeared in more than twenty Broadway musical comedies and revues. In *Girl Crazy* he played a New York cab driver who becomes sheriff of Custerville, Arizona.
13. *Standard Union*, October, 15, 1930, 11.
14. *Standard Union*, October, 15, 1930, 11.
15. Born Harry Reichman, Jr., in Cincinnati, Ohio, in 1895 to Russian Jewish parents, he was a singer, actor, dancer, songwriter, bandleader, and nightclub owner who starred in eight Broadway shows, including two editions of *George White's Music Hall Varieties* and the *Zeigfeld Follies of 1931*.
16. Green, *Ring Bells! Sing Songs!*, 39.
17. Robert Kimball, *The Complete Lyrics of Cole Porter* (Da Capo Press, 1992), 145.
18. Elizabeth Welch Interview, *Wolfgang's Documentaries and Interviews*, YouTube channel, July 6, 1980.
19. Lee Davis, *Bolton and Wodehouse and Kern—the Men Who Made Musical Comedy* (James H. Heinman, Inc., 1993), 334.
20. Geoffrey Block, *Enchanted Evenings: The Broadway Musical from Show Boat to Sondheim and Lloyd Webber* (Oxford University Press, 2009), 42–3.
21. Lee, *Bolton and Wodehouse and Kern—the Men Who Made Musical Comedy*, 330–5.
22. Porter, Cole, Eisen, Cliff, and McHugh, Dominic, *The Letters of Cole Porter* (Yale University Press, 2019), 97.
23. A restaging of the 2011 Broadway production directed and choreographed by Kathleen Marshall.
24. Scott Miller, "Inside Anything Goes," https://www.newlinetheatre.com/anythinggoeschapter.html.
25. Which forty-seven years later would serve as the basis for the 1981 Sondheim/Furth musical of the same name.
26. Steven Bach, *Dazzler—The Life and times of Moss Hart.* (Alfred A. Knoff, 2001).
27. Rowland Field, "The New Play," *Times Union*, October 14, 1935.
28. Burns Mantle, "Citizens, Jubilee is a Hit!," *Daily News*, October 13, 1935, 90.
29. "The Premiere," *Brooklyn Citizen*, October 14, 1935, 16.
23. Rowland Field, "The New Play," *Times Union*, October 30, 1936, 10.
31. Field, "The New Play," *Times Union*, October 30, 1936, 10.
32. This was the last of seven Broadway musicals that Bob Hope appeared in and which included *Roberta* (1933) and *The Zeigfeld Follies of 1936*.
33. Burns Mantle, "'Red Hot and Blue' at the Alvin," *Daily News*, October 29, 1936.
34. Brooks Atkinson, "The Play," *New York Times*, October 30, 1936, 26.
35. Field, "The New Play," *Times Union*, October 30, 1936, 10.
36. Field, "The New Play," *Times Union*, October 30, 1936, 10.
37. Brooks Atkinson, "Of Thee I Sing," *New York Times*, January 3, 1932, 146.

Notes

38. Ruth Faxon Macrea, *Chattanooga Daily Times*, May 22, 1932, 54.
39. *California Eagle*, June 3, 1932, 7.
40. Kaufman worked as a "show doctor" on many additional productions for which he was not credited.
41. Robert Gottlied, "The Hitmaker," *New York Times*, November, 21, 2004.
42. In collaboration with Moss Hart.
43. All written in collaboration with Morris Ryskind.
44. With Abe Burrows and Leueen McGrath.
45. *At Home Abroad* (1935).
46. *As Thousands Cheer* (1933).
47. *Pins and Needles* (1937).
48. *Sing Out The News!* (1938).
49. Born Mechel Salpeter in NYC, Max Gordon (1892–1978) produced more than fifty Broadway plays and musicals.
50. The classic Dietz and Schwartz songs introduced in these revues include "Dancing in the Dark," "By Myself," "Shine on Your Shoes," and "Alone Together."
51. Actor, singer, dancer Clifton Webb was one the era's biggest stars. He headlined *As Thousands Cheer* and twenty-two other Broadway musical comedies, plays, and revues. He was openly Gay, not to the general public, of course, but certainly within the professional worlds of Broadway and Hollywood, where later in midlife he became a major movie star.
52. Waters can be seen on YouTube performing the song thirty years later as a guest on the March 8, 1969 episode of *Hollywood Palace*, hosted by Diana Ross. https://www.youtube.com/watch?v=itrOY1H941s.
53. Green, *Ring Bells! Sing Songs!*.
54. Waters was only the fifth black woman to ever make a recording.
55. Initially Clifton Webb, Marilynn Miller and Helen Broderick were billed over the title, with Waters billed fourth, under the title. However, she would be billed above the title for the subsequent national tour.
56. The Works Progress Administration was one of several "New Deal" programs instituted during the Roosevelt presidency to help counteract severe unemployment caused by the Great Depression.
57. Including her retrospective show *An Evening With Dorothy Fields*, recorded April 9, 1972 at the Kaufman Concert Hall in NYC.
58. Laurence Maslon, "Broadway and Hollywood," *Broadway—The American Musical*, https://www.pbs.org/wnet/broadway/essays/broadway-hollywood/.
59. Scott Miller, *Strike Up the Band: A New History of Musical Theatre* (Heinemann Drama, 2007), 37–8.
60. William McBrien, *Cole Porter* (Vintage Books, 1998).
61. *42nd Street* (1932), *Stage Mother*, (1933), and *Go into Your Dance* (1934).
62. Lillian Schlissel, *Three Plays by Mae West: Sex, The Drag and Pleasure Man* (Routledge, 2013), 24.
63. Richard Rodgers, *Musical Stages* (Da Capo Press, 1995), 115.
64. Chauncey, *Gay New York*, 301.

Notes

65. Julianne Lindberg, *Pal Joey: The History of a Heel* (Oxford University Press, USA, 2020), 141.
66. Brent Phillips, *Charles Walters: The Director Who Made Hollywood Dance* (University Press of Kentucky, 2014).
67. Claude Conyers, "Alton, Robert," *Grove Music Online*, February 23, 2011, https://www.oxfordmusiconline.com/grovemusic/view/10.1093/gmo/9781561592630.001.0001/omo-9781561592630-e-1002092292.
68. Phillips, *Charles Walters*.
69. John Martin, "Robert Alton, Harold Lang and a Masterpiece," *New York Times*, February 17, 1952.
70. Charles Walters danced in five Broadway musicals, and choreographed five. He also had a significant career in Hollywood as a choreographer and director.
71. The brother of musician Ravi Shankar, who was perhaps most famous for collaborating with the Beatles.
72. In 1978, Bob Fosse created his own version of "Sing, Sing, Sing" for his Broadway show *Bob Fosse's Dancin'*, dedicated to Jack Cole.
73. This was the standard practice of almost all classic film musicals—the choreographers would direct the camerawork and all aspects of the major musical sequences, and the official directors of those movies were likely not even on the set during the filming.
74. Claude Conyers, "Cole, Jack," *Grove Music Online*, June 2, 2011.
75. Nolan, *Lorenz Hart*.
76. Geoffrey Block, *The Richard Rodgers Reader* (Oxford University Press, USA, 2006), 79.
77. Marilynn Berger, "George Abbott, Broadway Giant With Hit After Hit, Dead at 107," *New York Times*, February 1, 1995.
78. Three years later, Richard Rodgers (this time with Hammerstein) would write memorable music for another sexy, "boytoy" hustler character who is kept by an older woman, and another anti-hero—Billy Bigalow in *Carousel*.
79. Lorenz Hart, Robert Kimball, and Dorothy Hart, *The Complete Lyrics of Lorenz Hart* (Alfred a Knopf Incorporated, 1986), 272–3.
80. Robert Gottlieb, "Rodger's and Hart's Dysfuntional Partnership," *The Atlantic*, April 2013, https://www.theatlantic.com/magazine/archive/2013/04/words-and-music/309249/.

Chapter 7

1. Laurie Winer, *Oscar Hammerstein II and the Invention of the Musical* (Yale University Press, 2023), 38.
2. Karl Hoschna (1876–1911) was born in Bohemia and educated in Austria. He emigrated to the U.S. in 1896 and eventually joined the Victor Herbert Orchestra as an oboist. He composed music for twelve Broadway shows, including *Madame Sherry*, prior to his premature death in 1911.
3. Mark Eden Horowitz, *The Letters of Oscar Hammerstein II* (Oxford University Press, 2022).
4. Todd S. Purdum, *Something Wonderful: Rodgers and Hammerstein's Broadway Revolution* (Henry Holt, 2018), 24.

Notes

5. Warren Hoffman, *The Great White Way: Race and the Broadway Musical* (Rutgers University Press, 2020).
6. Martin Gottfried, *Sondheim* (Harry N. Abrams, Inc., 1993/2000), 12.
7. Martin Gottfried, *Sondheim* (Harry N. Abrams, Inc., 2000), 12.
8. Gottfried, *Sondheim*, 13.
9. Gottfried, *Sondheim*, 15.
10. Burns Mantle, "'Oklahoma' Links the Ballet with the Prairie Beautifully," *Daily News*, April 1, 1943, 145.
11. Gottfried, *Sondheim*, 15.
12. Craig Zadan, *Sondheim and Co.* (Macmillan, 1974), 52.
13. Zadan, *Sondheim and Co.*, 15.
14. Richard Rodgers, *Musical Stages* (Da Capo Press, 1995), 234.
15. Richard F. Pender, *Stephen Sondheim Encyclopedia* (Rowman & Littlefield, 2000), 222.
16. Sondheim, *Finishing the Hat*, 379.
17. Sondheim, *Finishing the Hat*, 3
18. Meryle Secrest, *Stephen Sondheim: A Life* (Vintage, 2011), 53.
19. Jim Lovensheimer, *South Pacific: Paradise Rewritten* (Oxford University Press, 2010), 85.
20. Horowitz, *The Letters of Oscar Hammerstein II*, 464–6.
21. Horowitz, *The Letters of Oscar Hammerstein II*, 689.
22. Laurence Maslon, *Broadway to Main Street: How Show Tunes Enchanted America* (Oxford University Press, 2018), 89.
23. Richard Eyre, *Talking Theatre: Interviews with Theatre People* (Nick Hern Books, 2009).
24. Lin-Manuel Miranda, "Stephen Sondheim, Theater's Greatest Lyricist," *New York Times Magazine*, October 16, 2017.
25. Hugh Fordin, *Getting to Know Him: A Biography of Oscar Hammerstein II* (Random House, 1977), xxiii.
26. "Stephen Sondheim, Titan of the American Musical is Dead at 91," *New York Times*, November 26, 2021.
27. Julie Bloom, "Lin-Manuel Miranda on Mary Poppins Returns and Movie Musicals," *New York Times*, November 22, 2018.
28. Bloom, "Lin-Manuel Miranda on Mary Poppins Returns and Movie Musicals."
29. Bloom, "Lin-Manuel Miranda on Mary Poppins Returns and Movie Musicals."
30. Patricia Cohen, "Same City, New Story," *New York Times*, March 11, 2009, https://www.nytimes.com/2009/03/15/theater/15cohe.html.
31. After numerous complaints from non-Spanish speaking audience members that the Spanish dialogue and lyrics were difficult to follow, some of the original English was restored to the show.
32. With Tom Kitt and Amanda Green.
33. Miranda, "Stephen Sondheim."
34. https://www.nytimes.com/2015/02/18/theater/review-in-hamilton-lin-manuel-miranda-forges-democracy-through-rap.html.
35. Kat Sherrell, *Experiencing Broadway Music: A Listener's Companion* (Rowman and Littlefield, 2016), 206.

Notes

36. Isaac Butler, "Stephen Sondheim Solved the Puzzle to Being Alive," *Slate*, November 27, 2021.
37. Butler, "Stephen Sondheim Solved the Puzzle to Being Alive."

Chapter 8

1. Sam Zolotow, "Ziegfeld Follies Closing Next Week," *New York Times*, July 14, 1944.
2. Lewis Nichols, "The Ziegfeld Follies . . . Opens Broadway Run at the Wintergarden," *New York Times*, April 2, 1943.
3. Opened June 17, 1943, and played 380 performances.
4. Lewis Nichols, "The Play," *New York Times*, June 18, 1943.
5. Gertrude Lawrence (1898–1952). *The King and I* was the last of fifteen plays and musicals the charismatic British star appeared in on Broadway, including her debut in *Andre Charlot's Revue of 1924*, and *Charlot Revue* (1925); the Gershwins' *Oh, Kay!* (1926) and *Treasure Girl* (1928); *The International Revue* (1930); Noel Coward's *Private Lives* (1931) and *Tonight At 8:30* (1936); and *Lady In The Dark* (1941). Lawrence died during the run of *The King and I* and was buried in the ballgown she wore in the "Shall We Dance" scene.
6. Kurt Weill, *Speak Low (When You Speak Love): The Letters of Kurt Weill and Lotte Lenya* (University of California Press, 1997), 218.
7. Edgar Price, "The Premier," *Brooklyn Citizen*, January 24, 1942, 12.
8. Purdum, *Something Wonderful*, 83–4.
9. Bradley Rogers, *The Song is You: Musical Theatre and the Politics of Bursting into Song and Dance* (University of Iowa Press, 2020), 128.
10. Opened October 7, 1943, and played 567 performances.
11. Lewis Nichols, "The Play," *New York Times*, June 18, 1943.
12. Ward Morehouse, "The New Play," *New York Sun*, October 8, 1943.
13. Morehouse, "The New Play," *New York Sun*, October 8, 1943.
14. Lewis Nichols, "One Touch of Venus . . . Opens at The Imperial," *New York Times*, October 8, 1943.
15. Edgar Price, "The Premiere," *Brooklyn Citizen*, October 8, 1943.
16. Wilella Waldorf, "Two On The Aisle," *New York Post*, October 6, 1943.
17. Rowland Field, *Newark Evening News*, October 8, 1943.
18. Wilella Louise Waldorf (1899–1946) was the only woman drama critic of a New York newspaper and was the Drama Editor of the *New York Post* from 1928 to 1946 and drama critic from 1941 to 1946.
19. Wilella Waldorf, "Two on the Aisle," *New York Post*, October 6, 1943.
20. Lewis Nichols, "One Touch of Venus," *New York Times*, October 17, 1943.
21. Keith Garebian, *The Making of My Fair Lady* (ECW Press, 1993), 48.
22. People/Community Member, University of Washington, Department of Dance website, https://dance.washington.edu/people/helen-tamiris.
23. Pauline Tisch, "Helen Tamiris," *Jewish Women's Archive*, https://jwa.org/encyclopedia/article/tamiris-helen.
24. Tamaris was also presumably in the "corps de ballet" that backed up Fanny Brice in the number, "I Want to be a Ballet Dancer."

Notes

25. Playbill, *Music Box Revue* (1924).
26. "Katherine Dunham Timeline," Library of Congress, https://www.loc.gov/collections/katherine-dunham/articles-and-essays/katherine-dunham-timeline/.
27. Heather Zahra Caldwell, "Imaging Her Selves: Black Women Artists, Resistance, Image and Representation, 1938–1956," Ph.D. dissertation, University of Massachusetts (2015).
28. Caldwell, "Imaging Her Selves," 62.
29. *Tropical Revue*, Playbill, https://playbill.com/production/tropical-revue-martin-beck-theatre-vault-0000008302#carousel-cell211328.
30. Copy from original flyers and posters, https://www.ebay.com/itm/153881461465.
31. https://www.nytimes.com/2006/05/23/arts/dance/23dunham.html?searchResultPosition=5.
32. Susan Stone and Katherine Dunham Honers.
33. Wolfgang Saxon, "Trude Rittmann, an Arranger of Broadway Favorites, Dies at 98," *New York Times*, March 10, 2005, A 25.
34. Saxon, "Trude Rittmann," A 25.
35. Saxon, "Trude Rittmann," A 25.
36. In "Another Opnin' Another Show," from *Kiss Me, Kate*.
37. Kester, *Round in Circles*, 142.
38. Purdum, *Something Wonderful*.
39. Purdum, *Something* Wonderful.
40. Purdum, *Something* Wonderful.
41. Laurence Maslon (ed.), *American Musicals: The Complete Books and Lyrics of Eight Broadway Classics* (Library of America, 2014), 529.
42. *American Musicals*, 529.
43. *American Musicals*, 529.
44. Peter Howard (1927–2008) created the dance and/or vocal arrangements for twenty-two Broadway musicals, including *Carnival, Hello, Dolly!, Chicago, Annie*, and *Crazy For You*.
45. John Chapman, "Carmen Jones Simply Superb Negro Adaption of Carmen," *Daily News*, December 3, 1943, 332.
46. Chapman, "Carmen Jones Simply Superb Negro Adaption of Carmen."
47. Chapman, "Carmen Jones Simply Superb Negro Adaption of Carmen."
48. *The Hot Mikado* starred Bill "Bojangles" Robinson. *The Swing Mikado* was a production of the Federal Theatre Project of the WPA. Both had brief runs in the spring of 1939.
49. Nichols, Lewis, "About Carmen Jones," *New York Times*, December 12, 1943.
50. Jack O'Brian, "Carmen Jones Acclaimed on Broadway," *Buffalo Evening News*, December 4, 1943,18.
51. Chapman, "Carmen Jones Simply Superb Negro Adaption of Carmen," 332.
52. Arthur Pollock, "The Theater," *Brooklyn Daily Eagle*, December 3, 1943,16.
53. Chapman, "Carmen Jones Simply Superb Negro Adaption of Carmen," 332.
54. One result of these casting challenges is that *Carmen Jones* never entered the Broadway canon and has only rarely been revived.
55. Arthur Pollock, "The Theater," *Brooklyn Daily Eagle*, December 3, 1943, 16.

Notes

56. Danton Walker, "Broadway," *Daily News*, December 4, 1943, 13.
57. Arthur Pollock, "The Theater," *Brooklyn Daily Eagle*, December 3, 1943, 16.
58. O'Brian, "Carmen Jones Acclaimed on Broadway," 18.
59. O'Brian, "Carmen Jones Acclaimed on Broadway," 18.
60. O'Brian, "Carmen Jones Acclaimed on Broadway," 18.
61. James Baldwin, "Carmen Jones: The Dark is Light Enough," in *Notes of a Native Son* (Beacon Press, 1955).
62. Lewis Nichols, "The Play," *New York Times*, January 29, 1944.
63. Herbert Fields and Dorothy Fields, manuscript, *Mexican Hayride*, NYPL-LC.
64. Music and lyrics by Dan Shapiro, Milton Pascal, and Phil Charig.
65. Second to *Oklahoma!*
66. In 1955, Wright and Forrest had another hit, adapting the music of Alexander Borodin for the musical *Kismet*, which was retitled *Timbuktu* when it was revived and revised for an all-Black cast in 1978.
67. Harold Meyerson and Ernest Harburg, *Who Put the Rainbow in the Wizard of Oz?: Yip Harburg, Lyricist* (University of Michigan Press, 1995), 184.
68. Meyerson and Harburg, *Who Put the Rainbow in the Wizard of Oz?*, 184.
69. Meyerson and Harburg, *Who Put the Rainbow in the Wizard of Oz?*, 187.
70. Meyerson and Harburg, *Who Put the Rainbow in the Wizard of Oz?*, 197.
71. Arthur Pollock, "American Musical Comedy Blooms With 'Bloomer Girl' and 'Oklahoma!,'" *Brooklyn Daily Eagle*, October 15, 1944, 23.
72. Pollock, "American Musical Comedy Blooms With 'Bloomer Girl' and 'Oklahoma!.'"
73. John Chapman, *Daily News*, December 25, 1944, 180.
74. Claude Conyers, "Loring, Eugene," *Grove Music Online*, February 23 2011.
75. Kidd would add his own spin to the Americana movement with his acclaimed choreography for the 1954 movie musical *Seven Brides For Seven Brothers*.
76. Betty Comden and Adolph Green, *The New York Musicals of Comden and Green* (Applause Theatre and Cinema, 1997), 2.
77. Robert Berkvist, "Betty Comden, Lyricist for Musicals, Dies at 89," *New York Times*, November 23, 2006.
78. Berkvist, "Betty Comden, Lyricist for Musicals, Dies at 89."
79. Richard Severo, "Adolph Green, Playwright and Lyricist Who Teamed With Comden, Dies at 87," *New York Times*, October 25, 2002, A 32.
80. Berkvist, "Betty Comden, Lyricist for Musicals, Dies at 89."
81. Kester, *Round in Circles*, 63.
82. Kester, *Round in Circles*, 94.
83. Josh Logan, "Honoring Richard Rodgers," *New York Times*, March 17, 1985, Section 2, 6.
84. Which is also introduced in the previous number. To a great extent, "the Bench Scene" can be considered to begin with Carrie and Julie's "You're a Queer One."
85. Kester, *Round in Circles*, 129–30.
86. Kester, *Round in Circles*, 113.

Notes

Chapter 9

1. Gene Lees, *The Musical World of Lerner and Loewe* (University of Nebraska Press, 2005), 9–25.
2. Ibid., 26–42.
3. Atkinson, Brooks, The New Play, *New York Times*, March 14, 1947, 28.
4. Tom Shales, "Master of the Musical," *Washington Post*, June 16, 1986.
5. Garebian, *The Making of My Fair Lady*.
6. Dominic Mchugh, *Loverly—The Life and Times of My Fair Lady* (Oxford: Oxford University Press, 2012), 4-6.
7. Garebian, *The Making of My Fair Lady*.
8. Mchugh, *Loverly—The Life and Times of My Fair Lady*.
9. Lees, *The Musical World of Lerner and Loewe*.
10. John Chapman, "*My Fair Lady* a Superb, Stylish Musical Play with a Prefect Cast," *Daily News*, March 16, 1956, 537.
11. Maslon, *Broadway to Mainstreet*, 115–16.
12. Alan Jay Lerner, "Why Can't The English?," in *The Street Where I Live* (Norton and Co., 1978), 322.
13. Gene Lees, *The Musical World of Lerner and Loewe* (Lincoln and London, University of Nebraska Press, 2005).
14. Charlotte Greenspan, *Pick Yourself Up—Dorothy fields and the American Musical* (Oxford University Press, 2010), 150.
15. Bergreen, *As Thousands Cheer*, 450.
16. Deborah Grace Winer, *On the Sunny Side of the Street—The Life and Lyrics of Dorothy Fields*. (Schirmer Books, 1997).
17. Rodgers, *Musical Stages*, 188.
18. Joshua Logan, *Josh, My Up and Down, in and Out Life* (Delacorte Press, 1976), 16.
19. Purdum, *Something Wonderful*, 128.
20. Written by Paul Osborn.
21. Logan, "Honoring Richard Rodgers," Section 2, 6.
22. Rodgers, *Musical Stages*, 190.
23. Rodgers, *Musical Stages*, 190.
24. Rodgers, *Musical Stages*, 190.
25. Lloyd Moss, March 27, 1981 interview with Joshua Logan, WNYC Radio, https://www.wnyc.org/story/joshua-logan/.
26. By Anita Loos as a vehicle for Helen Hayes.
27. By Norman Krasna.
28. There are several versions of this story, but Logan and Rodgers' memoirs agree on this point.
29. By William Inge.
30. By Paul Osborn.
31. On both of these musicals he collaborated with composer and lyricist Harold Rome.

Notes

32. With reportedly some uncredited help from Jerome Robbins.
33. Lovensheimer, *South Pacific: Paradise Rewritten*, 187.
34. Logan, *Josh, My Up and Down, in and Out Life*, 297.
35. The shows were *Let's Face It* (1941), *Something for the Boys* (1943), and *Mexican Hayride* (1944).
36. *Seven Lively Arts* (1944) and *Around The World* (1946).
37. Erik Haagensen, "Rainbow Revivals: Contempoary Reception and Interpretation of Gay themed Classics," Backstage, November 5, 2019. https://www.backstage.com/magazine/article/rainbow-revivals-contemporary-reception-interpretation-gay-41489/.
38. Jennifer Erin Book, "How Do You solve A Problem Like Petruchio: Kiss Me Kate as a Product of its Time and Place," *Americana Magazine*, October 2006. https://americanpopularculture.com/archive/music/kiss_me_kate.htm.
39. Stephen Holden, "Saint Subber, Theater Producer And a Niel Simon Partner, 76," *New York Times*, April 21, 1994, Section B, 8. https://www.nytimes.com/1994/04/21/obituaries/saint-subber-theater-producer-and-a-neil-simon-partner76.html.
40. William Hawkins, *World Telegram*, quoted in Steven Suskin, *Opening Night on Broadway: A Critical Quotebook of the Golden Era of the Musical Theatre, Oklahoma! (1943) to Fiddler on the Roof (1964)* (Schirmer Trade Books, 1990), 370.
41. Hawkins, *World Telegram*, quoted in Suskin, *Opening Night on Broadway*, 370.
42. Brooks Atkinson, *New York Times*, quoted in Suskin, *Opening Night on Broadway*, 369.
43. Atkinson, *New York Times*, quoted in Suskin, *Opening Night on Broadway*, 369.
44. Kinsey's second volume, *Sexual Behavior in the Human Female*, was not published until 1953.
45. Michael Bedwell, "How Alfred Kinsey Armed the Gay Rights Movement With Research," *LGBTQ Nation*, October 29, 2019.
46. Hawkins, *World Telegram*, quoted in Suskin, *Opening Night on Broadway*, 370.
47. "I Love Paris," "C'est Magnifique," and "It's Alright With Me" from *Can-Can*, and "All Of You" from *Silk Stockings*.
48. Sondheim, *Finishing the Hat*, 212.
49. Sondheim, *Finishing the Hat*, 212.
50. Misha Berson, *Something's Coming, Something Good: West Side Story and the American Imagination* (Applause Theatre and Cinema, 2011), 35.
51. Helen Gallagher (1926–) appeared in eighteen Broadway musicals, including the revivals of *Pal Joey* (1953) and *No, No, Nanette* (1971), receiving Tony Awards for both performances.
52. And in fact, in 1989, Gallagher assisted Jerome Robbins in recreating the Keystone Cops sequence from *High Button Shoes* for his retrospective, *Jerome Robbins' Broadway*.
53. "Stephen Sondheim, Jerome Robbins: Something to Dance About," American Masters Digital Archive (WNET), September 24, 2007, https://www.pbs.org/wnet/americanmasters/archive/interview/stephen-sondheim.
54. Liza Gennaro, *Making Broadway Dance* (Oxford University Press, 2021).
55. "Savoy Theatre," Electric Light Demonstration, n.d., https://www.gsarchive.net/carte/savoy/electric.html.
56. Dale Stinchcomb, "Edison Bulb in the Spotlight," *Houghton Library Blog*, https://blogs.harvard.edu/houghton/edison-bulb/.

Notes

57. Victoria Nedweski, "Through the Stage Door, a Spotlight on Backstage Work: Women Designers and Stagehands in Theatrical Production," https://digitalcommons.slc.edu/cgi/viewcontent.cgi?article=1057andcontext=womenshistory_etd.
58. Between 1936 and 1969, Rosenthal designed the lighting for fifty-three dances in the Graham company's repertory.
59. Dinitia Smith, "Peggy Clark, Pioneer Designer of Stage Lighting Dies at 80," *New York Times*, June 22, 1996.
60. "Broadway Lighting Seminar, 1989," https://performingartslegacy.org/billingtonken/broadway-lighting-seminar-1989/.
61. Oliver Smith designed the sets for more than 130 Broadway musicals and plays, including the original productions of *Brigadoon*, *My Fair Lady*, *West Side Story*, *The Sound of Music*, *Hello, Dolly!*, and *Camelot*.
62. Douglas Martin, "Tharon Musser, Stage Lighting Designer, Dies at 84," *New York Times*, April 21, 2009.
63. The National Association for the Advancement of Colored People.
64. "Any Place I Hang my Hat is Home," "(I Had Myself a) True Love," and "Come Rain or Come Shine."
65. Suskin, *Opening Night on Broadway*, 587.
66. In the film of *South Pacific*, Hall's singing voice is dubbed by Muriel Smith, who had starred in *Carmen Jones* and played Bloody Mary in the first London production.
67. William Hawkins, *World-Telegram and Sun*, as quoted in Steven Suskin's *Opening Night on Broadway*, 322.
68. "Eartha Kitt Signs RCA Victor Pact," *New York Age*, November 1, 1952, 31.
69. Brooks Atkinson, *New York Times*, as quoted in Steven Suskin's *Opening Night on Broadway*, 352.
70. Peter B. Flint, "Sammy Davis Dies at 64, Top Showman Broke Barriers," *New York Times*, May 17, 1990, 1, https://www.nytimes.com/1990/05/17/obituaries/sammy-davis-jr-dies-at-64-top-showman-broke-barriers.html.
71. "To Close For Comfort," recorded by Eddie Gorme, and "Mr. Wonderful," recorded by Peggy Lee.
72. http://sammydavisjr.info/biographical/about-sammy/1925-50/.
73. In 1942, singer Lena Horne signed a seven-year movie deal with MGM and became the first African American to sign a contract with a major studio.
74. *Dance With Your Gods* opened at what was then called the Mansfield Theatre and later was named the Brooks Atkinson Theatre. Although Horne and the show played only a total of nine performances there, in 2022 that venue was re-christened The Lena Horne Theatre in her honor.
75. With Fred Saidy.
76. Steve Cohen, "Jamaica's Troubled Past," *The Cultural Critic*, https://theculturalcritic.com/jamaica-returns-after-a-troubled-past/.
77. Robert Coleman in the *Daily Mirror*, as quoted in Steven Suskin's *Opening Night on Broadway*, 344–6.
78. Woll, *Black Musical Theatre*, 245.
79. http://sammydavisjr.info/stage/musical-theatre-broadway/golden-boy-1964-66-broadway/.
80. John McLain in the *Journal-American*, as quoted in Steven Suskin's *Opening Night on Broadway*, 264.

81. *Golden Boy* ran for 568 performances.
82. https://zvbxrpl.blogspot.com/2012/01/obscure-musicals-golden-boy.html.
83. Woll, *Black Musical Theatre*, 247.
84. Following a run of 293 performances.
85. Or "Best Composer And Lyricist" as the category was called that year.
86. Clive Barnes writing for the *New York Times*, as quoted in Steven Suskin's *Opening Night on Broadway*, 419.
87. Sheldon Epps, *My Own Directions: A Black Man's Journey in the American Theatre* (McFarland, 2022), 34–5.
88. Barnes, *New York Times*, as quoted inSteven Suskin's *Opening Night on Broadway*, 418–19.
89. In the 1970s both Pearl Bailey and Sammy Davis, Jr. would return to Broadway: Bailey in a revival of *Hello, Dolly!*, this time with an integrated cast, and Davis in a revival of the Leslie Bricusse/Anthony Newley musical *Stop The World I Want to Get Off* (1978). During the show's original London and Broadway engagements, Davis had released hit recordings of three of the score's songs. Despite being well received in its sold-out Los Angeles and Chicago pre-Broadway engagements, the New York critics were happy to see Davis back on Broadway but found that the show had not aged well and regretted his choice of vehicle.
90. Berson, *Something's Coming*, 21–2.
91. Deborah Jowitt and Jerome Robbins, *Jerome Robbins: His Life, His Theater, His Dance* (Simon and Schuster, 2004), 267.
92. Berson, *Something's Coming*, 35.
93. Richard L. Coe, *Washington Post*.
94. John Chapman, *New York Daily News*.
95. Chapman, *New York Daily News*.
96. Wolcott Gibbs, *The New Yorker*.
97. Brooks Atkinson, *New York Times*.
98. In June of 1959.
99. In April of 1960.
100. This was the National Tour bringing the show back to Broadway.
101. Chita Rivera, *Chita: A Memoir* (HarperCollins, 2023).
102. Willson's mentor, Frank Loessor, accomplished the same remarkable feat in 1956, one year prior to The Music Man.
103. Domonic McHugh, *The Big Parade—Meredith Willson's Musicals from The Music Man to 1491* (Oxford University Press, 2021), 14.
104. *And There I Stood With My Piccolo* (1948).
105. McHugh, *The Big Parade*, 6–7.
106. Scott Miller, *Strike Up the Band: A New History of Musical Theatre* (Heinemann Drama, 2007), 73.
107. Raymond Knapp, *The American Musical and the Formation of National Identity* (Princeton University Press, 2005), 146.
108. Knapp, *The American Musical and the Formation of National Identity*, 146.
109. Jerome Lawrence and Robert E. Lee, *Auntie Mame* (Dramatist Play Service, Inc (Revised Edition), 1999), 87.

Notes

110. Meredith Willson, *The Music Man* (Libretto, MTI, 1962).
111. Knapp, *The American Musical and the Formation of National Identity*, 144.
112. Scott Miller, *Strike Up The Band: A New History of Musical Theatre* (Heinmann, 2007), 73.
113. Suskin, *Opening Night on Broadway*, 460–3.
114. Born Bella Cohen.
115. Mary Rodgers and Jesse Green, *Shy: The Alarmingly Outspoken Memoirs of Mary Rodgers* (Straus and Giroux, 2022), 3.
116. Logan Cullwell-Block, "A Century of the Boy Who Wouldn't Grow Up—A History of Peter Pan on Stage," Playbill, December 2, 2014. https://playbill.com/article/a-century-of-the-boy-who-wouldnt-grow-up-a-history-of-peter-pan-on-stage-com-336472.
117. Stacy Ellen Wolf, *A Problem Like Maria: Gender and Sexuality in the American Musical* (University of Michigan Press, 2002).
118. https://www.tiktok.com/@broadway1011/video/7273997455320993067.
119. "New Musical in Manhattan," *Time*, December 15, 1956.
120. Meryle Secrest, *Stephen Sondheim: A Life* (Vintage, 2011), 134.
121. Secrest, *Stephen Sondheim*, 134.
122. Secrest, *Stephen Sondheim*, 134.
123. Jesse Green, "Review: In a Stripped-Down 'Gypsy,' Audra's Gonna Show It to Ya," *New York Times*, Dec. 20, 2024, Section C, Page 1.
124. *New York Herald Tribune*, May 22, 1959.
125. *New York Times*, September 24, 1974.
126. Green, "Review: In a Stripped-Down 'Gypsy,' Audra's Gonna Show It to Ya," *New York Times*.
127. Rodgers, *Musical Stages*, 299.
128. For more on Layton's work on *The Sound of Music*, see page 181.
129. Peter Lev, *Twentieth Century-Fox: The Zanuck–Skouras Years, 1935–1965* (University of Texas Press, 2013), 266.
130. Michael Quinn, "No Show Too Big," *The Stage*, May 14 2021. https://www.thestage.co.uk/features/no-show-too-big---raymond-gubbay-the-impresario-with-a-flair-for-spectacle.
131. Ethan Mordden, *When Broadway Went to Hollywood* (Oxford University Press, 2016).
132. Knapp, *The American Musical and the Formation of National Identity*, 232–6.
133. The music for *Once Upon a Mattress* was written by Mary Rogers, making this the only time in Broadway history that a father and daughter have competed for a Tony Award—at least so far.

Chapter 10

1. And just four years later, in 2006, *The Fantasticks* reopened at the Theater Center, a small venue in Times Square, where it ran for an additional 4,390 performances.
2. Scott Miller, *Literally Anything Goes: 14 Great Oddball Musicals and What Makes Them Tick* (Createspace Independent Publishing Platform, 2018).
3. Alvin Hanson, "Elvis On the Ed Sullivan Show," Elvis History Blog, November 2011, http://www.elvis-history-blog.com/elvis-sullivan.html.

Notes

4. John Chapman, "Fresh Talent in A New Hit," *Daily News*, April 24, 1960, 564.
5. John Chapman, "'Bye Bye Birdie,' a Funny, Fresh, And Captivating Musical Show," *Daily News*, April 16, 1960, 42. https://www.newspapers.com/article/daily-news-bye-bye-birdie-review-daily/103242964/?locale=en-US.
6. *Do Re Mi.*
7. *The Unsinkable Molly Brown.*
8. Bernard Carragher, "What's So Great Musicals? the Books!," *New York Times*, September 30, 1979, D1. https://www.nytimes.com/1979/09/30/archives/whats-so-great-about-old-musicals-the-books-the-old-musicals.html.
9. Wakefield Poole, *Dirty Poole: A Sensual Memoir* (Lethe Press, 2011).
10. Chapman, "Fresh Talent in A New Hit," 564.
11. *42nd Street* opened at the Wintergarden Theater on August 25, 1980.
12. *Newsday* (Suffolk edition), December 18, 1959, 69.
13. Poole, *Dirty Poole*.
14. Jack Gaver, "Rodgers has Another Hit," *UPI*, April 11, 1962.
15. *Daily News*, May 2, 1980, 8.
16. Rex Reed, *Daily News*, May 2, 1980, 347.
17. Poole, *Dirty Poole*.
18. Suskin, *Opening Night on Broadway*, 299.
19. Howard Taubman, "Theater: 'Hello, Dolly!' Has Premiere: Carol Channing Star of Musical at St James," *New York Times*, January 17, 1964.
20. Walter Kerr of the *Herald Tribune*, as quoted in Jack Gaver, "Hello, Dolly With Carol Channing Wins Acclaim of New York Critics," *Stockton Evening and Sunday Record*, January 18, 1964.
21. Suskin, *Opening Night on Broadway*, 299.
22. Gaver, "Hello, Dolly With Carol Channing Wins Acclaim of New York Critics."
23. John Chapman, "Carol Channing and David Burns Delightful in Hello, Dolly," *Daily News*, January 17, 1964.
24. Gaver, "Hello, Dolly With Carol Channing Wins Acclaim of New York Critics."
25. Suskin, *Opening Night on Broadway*, 299.
26. Associated Press, "Wilder's Matchmaker Becomes Hit Musical," *Arizona Daily Star*, January 18, 1964, 11.
27. Kerr, quoted in "Hello, Dolly With Carol Channing Wins Acclaim of New York Critics."
28. Gaver, "Hello, Dolly With Carol Channing Wins Acclaim of New York Critics." (*Stockton Evening and Sunday Record.* January 18 1964.)
29. John Chapman, Carol Channing and David Burns Delightful in Hello, Dolly,"
30. Associated Press, "Wilder's Matchmaker Becomes Hit Musical."
31. Howard Taubman, "Theater: 'Hello, Dolly!' Has Premiere: Carol Channing Star of Musical at St James," *New York Times*, January 17, 1964.
32. Louis Armstrong's hit single "Hello, Dolly!" reached No. 1 on the U.S. *Billboard*'s Hot 100 and spent nine weeks atop the adult contemporary chart.
33. Jerry Herman and Marilyn Stasio, *Showtune: A Memoir* (Dutton, 1996), 65.

Notes

34. Robert D. McFadden, "Jerry Herman, Composer of 'Hello, Dolly!' and Other Broadway Hits, Dies at 88," *New York Times*, December 27, 2019.
35. John Chapman, "'Funny Girl' Has Opening with Miss Streisand as Miss Brice," *Daily News*, March 27, 1964, 395.
36. Only the 1974 film version of the stage musical starring a miscast Lucile Ball failed to achieve major success.
37. Brook had previously directed the 1954 Truman Capote/Harold Arlen musical *House Of Flowers*, produced by Saint Subber.
38. William Glover, Associated Press Drama Critic, "Broadway Play Preaches Sermon Against War," *The Bee*, October 1, 1964.
39. Until *Grease* broke that record.
40. Alisa Solomon, *Wonder of Wonders: A Cultural History of Fiddler on the Roof* (Macmillan and ORM, 2013), 221, 220.
41. Solomon, *Wonder of Wonders*, 221.
42. Alisa Solomon, "Tradition! The Indestructable" Fiddler On The Roof," *The New Yorker*, October 8, 2015.
43. Howard Taubman, "Theater: Mostel as Tevye in Fiddler On The Roof," *New York Times*, September 23, 1964, 56.

Chapter 11

1. Sheela Lambert, "The Man Behind the 'Hair,'" *Advocate.Com*, August 13, 2008, https://www.advocate.com/arts-entertainment/theater/2008/08/13/man-behind-hair.
2. Lambert, "The Man Behind the 'Hair.'"
3. Lambert, "The Man Behind the 'Hair.'"
4. Lambert, "The Man Behind the 'Hair.'"
5. Lambert, "The Man Behind the 'Hair.'"
6. Lambert, "The Man Behind the 'Hair.'"
7. Lambert, "The Man Behind the 'Hair.'"
8. "Remembering 1968: When 'Hair' Took Root in Pop Culture," *CBS News*, May 27, 2018, https://www.cbsnews.com/news/remembering-1968-when-hair-took-root-in-pop-culture/.
9. Lambert, "The Man Behind the 'Hair.'"
10. Jay Lustig, "Hair, 20 Covers by pop and Rock artists of songs from the musical," NJArts.Net, October 15, 2023, https://www.njarts.net/hair-20-covers-by-pop-and-rock-artists-of-songs-from-the-musical-with-videos/.
11. The third was the play *Lenny*.
12. John-Michael Tebelak was born in Berea, Ohio, in 1949 and died in NYC in 1985.
13. Steve Cohen, "Stephen Schwartz at Mid-Career," *The Cultural Critic*, https://theculturalcritic.com/stephen-schwartz-at-mid-career/.
14. "Stephen Schwartz—On Composing Godspell," masterworksbwayVEVO, https://www.youtube.com/watch?v=7OD-mD5aNPU.
15. "Stephen Schwartz—On Composing Godspell."

Notes

16. Walter Kerr, "Why Make St. Mathew Dance? For the Fun of It," *New York Times*, May 30 1971, D1. https://www.nytimes.com/1971/05/30/archives/why-make-st-matthew-dance-for-the-fun-of-it-kerr-on-godspell.html?searchResultPosition=2.

17. George Gent, "Superstar: The Cheers and Jeers Build," *New York Times*, October 14, 1971, 56.

18. Angel Castillo, "Frampton Suit Puts Focus On Cohabitation Law," *New York Times*, May 12 1981, B1. https://www.nytimes.com/1981/05/12/nyregion/frampton-suit-puts-focus-on-cohabitation-law.html.

19. Peter Schjedahl, "An Up-to-Date and Sexy Verona," *New York Times*, August 8, 1971.

20. Guare co-authored the book with the show's director, Mel Shapiro.

21. Walter Kerr, "Simply Carefree, Simply Wonderful," *New York Times*, December 12, 1971.

22. John S. Wilson, "Broadway—Rock, Calypso and Doo Be Doo," *New York Times*, February 6, 1972, D28.

23. Clive Barnes, "Stage: Two Gentlemen of Verona," *New York Times*, December 2, 1971.

24. Barnes, "Stage: Two Gentlemen of Verona."

25. Clive Barnes, "Purlie is a Victor Again in New Version," *New York Times*, March 16, 1970, 53.

26. Barnes, "Purlie is a Victor Again in New Version," 53.

27. Ben West, *The American Musical: Evolution of an Art Form* (Taylor and Francis, 2024).

28. Clive Barnes, "Theater: Raisin in Musical Form," *New York Times*, October 19, 1973, 59.

29. Walter Kerr, "Raisin is Sweet, Could Be Sweeter," *New York Times*, October 28, 1973, 127.

30. Anita Gates, "Donald McKayle, 87, Broadway and Modern Dance Choreographer, Dies," *New York Times*, April 10, 2018.

31. Barnes, "Theater: Raisin in Musical Form," 59.

32. The score of *The Wiz* included additional songs by George Faison, Timothee Graphenreed, and Luthor Vandross.

33. Stephen Suskin, *More Opening Nights on Broadway* (Schirmer Books, 1997), 972.

34. https://www.facebook.com/Marcelluss/videos/10221961298834236?idorvanity=202792086939939.

35. Douglas Watt, "'Don't Bother Me' is Slick and Spirited," *Daily News*, April 21, 1972, 20.

36. William McGaffen, "All Black Mini Musical Opens at Ford's Theatre," *Los Angeles Times*, September 24, 1971, 75.

37. McGaffen, "All Black Mini Musical Opens at Ford's Theatre," 75.

38. Watt, "'Don't Bother Me' is Slick and Spirited," 20.

39. Robert Wahls, "Footlights—Micki Great Vibes," *Daily News*, May 7, 1972, 208.

40. Woll, *Black Musical Theatre*, 269.

41. Both *Little Mary Sunshine* and *The Boy Friend* became popular long-running hits, with *The Boy Friend* transferring to Broadway in 1954, where it ran for 485 performances.

42. Rachel Kahn, "Cafe Cino and Off-Off Broadway: Finding My Great Grandfather in the Library for the Performing Arts," *New York Public Library Blog*, https://www.nypl.org/blog/2023/12/06/caffe-cino-and-broadway-finding-my-great-grandfather-library-performing-arts.

43. First at the Bouwerie Lane Theatre in December of 1968, and then to the larger Theater de Lys (today's Lucill Lortell Theater) in April of 1969.

Notes

44. George Gent, "Nanette Brings Out the Nostalgia Buffs," *New York Times*, January 21, 1971.
45. *Grease* had first been produced at a small fringe theater in Chicago.
46. Until *A Chorus Line* broke *Grease*'s record.
47. Douglas Watt, *Daily News*, March 13, 1976, 28.
48. Walter Kerr, "A Rousing 'Ain't Missbehavin,'" *New York Times*, May 14, 1978.
49. Now named The Dutch National Ballet.
50. Henry LeTang, Performing Arts Database, Library of Congress, https://memory.loc.gov/diglib/ihas/loc.music.tdabio.128/.
51. Between 1940 and 1947, Felicia Sorel (1906–72) choreographed thirteen Broadway plays and musicals, including *Pins and Needles*.
52. Claude Conyers, "Le Tang, Henry," *Grove Music Online*, February 23, 2011.
53. Nathaniel G Nesmith, "How George Faison Orders His Steps," American Theatre, November 10, 2022. https://www.americantheatre.org/2022/11/10/how-george-faison-ordered-his-steps/.
54. Richard Altman, Mervyn D. Kaufman, *The Making of a Musical: Fiddler on the Roof* (New York: Crown Publishers, 1971), 30.
55. Ibid., Altman and Kaufman, *The Making of a Musical: Fiddler on the Roof*, 30–4.
56. *Broadway Song & Story: Playwrights/lyricists/Composers Discuss Their Hits* (Dodd, Mead, 1985).
57. *Cabaret*'s first revival in 1986 was directed by Harold Prince and choreographed by Ron Field, who largely recreated their original staging, although several significant changes were made in the script and score, including the cutting of two songs, "Meesskite" and "Why Should I Wake Up?," which was replaced with "Don't Go," and an interpolation of one song ("Money") written for the movie version, and a song that had been cut from the original production, "I Don't Care Much." The 1998 revival (which began at London's Donmar Warehouse) was radically reimagined by director by Sam Mendes and co-director and choreographer Rob Marshall, who set the show entirely onstage at the Kit Kat Klub. Further changes in the book were made, two more songs were dropped ("The Telephone Song" and "Sitting Pretty"), and two addtional songs from the film were added ("Mein Heir" and "Maybe This Time"). That same production was revived on Broadway in 2014. The 2024 production (which also began in London), directed by Rebecca Frecknall and choreographed by Julia Cheng, was retitled *Cabaret at the Kit Kat Klub* and is staged in an in-the-round, environmental production.
58. Sondheim, *Finishing the Hat*, 219.
59. Kevin Kelly, *One Singular Sensation: The Michael Bennett Story* (Doubleday, 1990), 3.
60. Kelly, *One Singular Sensation*, 39.
61. Bennett danced in the musicals *Subways are for Sleeping* and *Here's Love* for choreographer Michael Kidd, in *Bajour* for Peter Gennaro, and both danced in and assisted choreographer Ron Field on *Nowhere To Go But Up*.
62. *A Joyful Noise* and *Henry, Sweet Henry*.
63. Stephen Sondheim, Finishing the Hat: Collected Lyrics (1954–1981) with Attendant Comments, Principles, Heresies, Grudges, Whines and Anecdotes.
64. The "Best Musical" Tony was controversially awarded to *Two Gentlemen of Verona*.
65. *Rachael Lily Rosenbloom (And Don't You Ever Forget It)* (1973).
66. Robert Viagas, Baayork Lee, Thommie Walsh, *On the Line: The Creation of A Chorus Line* (Limelight Editions, 2006).

Notes

67. Clive Barnes, "Clive Barnes on the Dance Explosion," *After Dark*, June 1978.
68. Bob Fosse's nine Tony Awards include "Best Director" for *Pippin*, and a final "Best Choreography" Tony for the 1986 flop musical, *Big Deal*.
69. Originally credited only as "Lead-ins and Crossovers" by Stewart, Bramble and Ropes.
70. A year earlier, Bob Fosse had staged his own response to Bennett's *A Chorus Line* opening with the opening sequence of his 1979 film, *All That Jazz*.
71. Scenery by Robin Wagner, costumes by Theoni Aldredge, and lighting by Tharon Musser.
72. *Dear World* (1969), *Mack and Mabel* (1974), *The Grand Tour* (1979).
73. Still the eleventh highest grossing foreign language movie in U.S. history.
74. Lawrence K. Altman, "Rare Cancer Seen in 41 Homosexuals," *New York Times*, July 3, 1981, 20.
75. Jeremy Gerard, "Creative Arts Being Reshaped By The Epidemic," *New York Times*, June 9, 1987, 1.
76. About Broadway Cares/Equity Fights AIDS, https://broadwaycares.org/about-broadway-cares-equity-fights-aids/#:~:text=By%20drawing%20upon%20the%20talents,50%20states%2C%20Puerto%20Rico%20and.

Chapter 12

1. "What Happened in New York Between 1981 and 1983," *New York Times Magazine*, April 22, 2018, 37.
2. Webber and Rice's already strained relationship had come to an end when Rice was asked to create the lyrics for one song in *Cats*, the song that eventually became "Memory," but then had his lyric rejected in favor of one written by the director of *Cats*, Trevor Nunn.
3. Mervyn Rothstein, "The Musical is Money to His Ears: Cameron Mackintosh is a Theatrical Producer Who Knows what He Likes, and what He Likes is what He Puts on Stage. As Mackintosh's Financial and Critical Success Attests, Audiences the World Over Share His Vision. 'I'm a Terrible Interferer,' Mackintosh Says. 'There Isn't an Element of the show that I Don't have a Go at.'" *New York Times*, December 9, 1990, https://www.proquest.com/historical-newspapers/musical-is-money-his-ears/docview/108441968/se-2.
4. Margaret Gray, "For Alain Boublil, The man behind Les Miserables, the revolution isn't over," *Los Angeles Times*, May 23, 2019.
5. Gray, "For Alain Boublil."
6. Gray, "For Alain Boublil."
7. https://us-tour.lesmis.com/about-the-show/.
8. Jacques Le Sourd, "On Broadway," *The Standard-Star*, February 14, 1988, 86.
9. Douglas Watt, "*Phantom*, Close But No Opera," *Daily News*, February 6, 1988, 101
10. Broadway In Cincinnati News, https://broadwayincincinnati.news/2019/02/01/point-of-inspiration-for-miss-saigon/.
11. Edward Behr and Mark Steyn, *The Story of Miss Saigon* (Random House (UK), 1991), 26.
12. Behr and Steyn, *The Story of Miss Saigon*, 28.
13. Stephanie Bunbury, "Jonathan Price on the controversy that almost sunk Miss Saigon," *Sydney Morning Herald*, September 26, 2016.

Notes

14. Bunbury, "Jonathan Price on the controversy that almost sunk Miss Saigon."
15. Nancy Rosati, "Interview with Frank Wildhorn," *The Scarlet Pimpernel*, http://www.thepimpernel.com/cgi/interview.cgi?spot=Frank_Wildhorn.
16. *Jekyll and Hyde* was first produced in 1990 at the Alley Theatre in Houston, Texas, where it broke box office records. Then, in 1995, a new co-production was mounted by Houston's Theatre Under The Stars and Seattle's 5th Avenue Theatre. Based on the success of the runs at both of those theaters, a national tour was launched later that year.
17. Prince and Sondheim had parted ways following the failure of *Merrily We Roll Along* in 1981, and did not work together again until *Bounce* (an early version of *Road Show*) in 2003.
18. However, they were born eighteen years apart, Sondheim in 1930, and Lloyd Webber in 1948.
19. https://www.youtube.com/watch?v=4o4z6bMiuVw.
20. Frank Rich, "On Broadway, the Lights Get Brighter," *New York Times*, May 31, 1992.
21. Kevin Winkler, *Everything is Choreography: The Musical Theater of Tommy Tune* (Oxford University Press, 2021).
22. 1,584 performances.
23. Clive Barnes, "*A Day in Hollywood* is a Night of Magic," *New York Post*, May 2, 1980.
24. Winkler, *Everything is Choreography*.
25. Winkler, *Everything is Choreography*.

Chapter 13

1. John Kenrick, "2001: The Revenge of The Musical Comedy," *Musicals101.com*, https://www.musicals101.com/revenge.htm.
2. Frank Rich, "A Fresh Chorus of Gershwin on Broadway," *New York Times*, February 20, 1992, Section 2, 15.
3. Michael Riedel, *Singular Sensation: The Triumph of Broadway* (Simon and Schuster, 2021), 97.
4. This revival of *Chicago* is still running today and has become the second longest-running show in Broadway history.
5. Mervyn Rothstein, "A Life in the Theatre: Choreographer Patricia Birch," *Playbill*, May 26, 2005, https://playbill.com/article/a-life-in-the-theatre-choreographer-patricia-birch-com-126153.
6. Rothstein, "A Life in the Theatre: Choreographer Patricia Birch."
7. Lawrence Thelen, *The Show Makers: Great Directors of the American Musical Theatre* (Routledge, 2002).
8. Thelen, *The Show Makers*.
9. Previously Daniele and LaChuisa colloboted on *Cronicle of a Death Foretold* (1995), and *Marie Christine* (1999).
10. Nina Lannan, "The Art of the Theater is Togetherness—An Interview with Dame Gillian Lynne," *SDC Journal* (Summer, 2016), https://sdcweb.org/wp-content/uploads/2018/07/The-Art-Of-Theatre-Is-Togetherness-Dame_GillianLynne.pdf.
11. Lannan, "The Art of the Theater is Togetherness."

12. Which today is the Royal Ballet.
13. Lannan, "The Art of the Theater is Togetherness."
14. Lannan, "The Art of the Theater is Togetherness."
15. Originally named the New London Theater.
16. https://www.susanstroman.com/productions/show-boat.
17. https://www.susanstroman.com/productions/show-boat.
18. Victoria Meyers, "An Interview with Kathleen Marshall," *The Interval*, February 18, 2015, https://www.theintervalny.com/interviews/2015/02/an-interview-kathleen-marshall/.
19. Nelson Pressley, "Kathleen Marshall, Broadway's Vintage Girl," *Washington Post*, June 7, 2013, https://www.washingtonpost.com/entertainment/theater_dance/kathleen-marshall-broadways-vintage-girl/2013/06/06/1aee2bcc-cc99-11e2-8573-3baeea6a2647_story.html.
20. Pressley, "Kathleen Marshall, Broadway's Vintage Girl."
21. Lisa Jo Sagolla, "Kathleen Marshall in Converstaion: Reflecting on a Chorography Career," *Backstage*, November 4, 2019, https://www.backstage.com/magazine/article/kathleen-marshall-conversation-reflecting-choreography-career-28089/.
22. Pressley, "Kathleen Marshall, Broadway's Vintage Girl."
23. Michael Kurchwara, Associated Press, "Privates on Full Parade," *Bangor Daily News*, October 28, 2000, 33.
24. Prolific playwright Terrence McNally (1938–2020) created the books for seven Broadway musicals: *The Rink* (1984), *Kiss of The Spider Woman* (1993), *Ragtime* (1998), *The Full Monty* (2000), *Catch Me If You Can* (2011), *The Visit* (2015), and *Anastacia* (2017).
25. Elysa Gardner, "Frank Humor Gives Musical its Fresh A-Peel on Broadway," October 28, 2000.
26. Kurchwara, "Privates on Full Parade," 33.
27. David Hinckly, "Stage Monty Full of Fun," *Daily News*, October 27, 2000, 95.
28. Fintan O'Toole, "Full Monty Bares its Soul," *Daily News*, November 5, 2000, 790.
29. "David Yazbek," *Masterworks Broadway*, https://masterworksbroadway.com/artist/david-yazbek/.
30. Michael Phillips, "Full Monty Something to Behold," *Los Angeles Times*, December 9, 2000, 56.
31. Ben Conner, "The music is completely different but I know it is you," *Brown University Interviews*, December 15, 2020, https://browninterviews.org/the-music-is-completely-different-but-i-know-its-you-brown-interviews-david-yazbek-82/.
32. Vanessa Thorpe, "What Have They Done to Our Monty?," *Guardian*, November 4, 2000.
33. Ben Brantley, "Theater Review: A Scam That'll Knock'em Dead," *New York Times*, April 20, 2001.
34. "Mel Brooks," *American Film Institute*, https://www.afi.com/laa/mel-brooks/.
35. From an interview with Terry Gross on *Fresh Air*, NPR, December 7, 2021, https://www.npr.org/2021/12/07/1061836388/mel-brooks-all-about-me.
36. From an interview with Terry Gross on *Fresh Air*.
37. "Mel Brooks," *American Film Institute*.
38. Working in that writer's room with Brooks were Neil Simon, Carl Reiner, and Larry Gelbart.
39. 1957's *Shinbone Alley* was Brooks' second Broadway musical.
40. With music by Charles Strouse and lyrics by Lee Adams.

Notes

41. Suskin, *Opening Night on Broadway*, 37–8.
42. Five years earlier, filmmaker Blake Edwards' Broadway adaptation of his movie *Victor/Victoria* had failed, even with his wife Julie Andrews as the star, and Paul Simon's 1998 musical, *The Capeman*, had been a disaster.
43. Heather Salerno, "Luck, Pluck Needed for Producers Ticket," *Journal News*, April 20, 2001, 1.
44. Robert Feldberg, "Political Incorrectness with a Wink," *The Record*, April 20, 2001, 25.
45. Brantley, "Theater Review: A Scam That'll Knock'em Dead."
46. Feldberg, "Political Incorrectness with a Wink."
47. Brantley, "Theater Review: A Scam That'll Knock'em Dead."
48. Jacques Le Sourd, "The Producers a Triumph on Broadway," *Journal News*, April 21, 2001.
49. Michael Kuchwara, Associated Press, "Producers on Broadway: Putting the Hit in Hitler," *Chicago Tribune*, April 21, 2001, 33.
50. Le Sourd, "The Producers a triumph on Broadway."
51. Linda Weiner, "Springtime for Brooks," *Newsday*, April 20, 2001, B3.
52. Le Sourd, "The Producers a triumph on Broadway."
53. Salerno, "Luck, Pluck Needed for Producers Ticket," 2A.
54. Brantley, "Theater Review: A Scam That'll Knock'em Dead."
55. "Working in the Theater," American Theatre Wing Seminar, CUNY TV, December 9, 2002. https://tv.cuny.edu/show/atwworkinginthetheatre/PR2002348.
56. Brantly, Ben, "Through Hot Pink Glasses, a World That's Nice," *New York Times*, August 16, 2002, Section E, 1.
57. Only *The Drowsy Chaperone*, *Curtains*, and *A Gentleman's Guide To Love And Murder* do not have (pop)Rock scores.
58. https://www.myp-magazine.com/interview/john-deluca-rob-marshall-true-love-is-deeper-than-appearances/.
59. Choreographed by Sergio Trujillo.
60. Janet Maslin, "Review/Film; Disney's 'Beauty and the Beast' Updated in Form and Content," *New York Times*, November 13, 1991, Section C, 17.
61. Frank Rich, "The Year in The Arts: Theater/1991; Throw Away Those Scripts. Some of the Greatest Moments Were Wordless," *New York Times*, December 29, 1991, Section 2, 5.
62. Jay Root and Michael Paulson, "Broadway Hits Reap Millions in Tax Breaks," *New York Times*, May 18, 2024, 1.
63. That remarkable $10B figure does not include any of the film or video versions of this property, only the Broadway production and its international and touring stage incarnations.
64. Michael Paulson, "How The Lion King Got to Broadway and Ruled for 25 Years (So Far)," *New York Times*, November 16, 2022.
65. Disney, however, does not give up easily, and both *The Little Mermaid* and *Tarzan* have since been reworked and successfully staged around the world.
66. "Guest column: Judy Craymer on the origins of Mamma Mia!," *Denver Center for the Performing Arts*, April 4, 2017, https://www.denvercenter.org/news-center/guest-column-judy-craymer-on-the-origins-of-mamma-mia/.
67. Grace Barnes, *National Identity and the British Musical: From Blood Brothers to Cinderella* (Bloomsbury Publishing, 2022), 204–5.

Notes

68. Michael Gioa, "The Creation of Rent," *Playbill*, Febuary 5, 2016, https://playbill.com/article/the-creation-of-rent-how-jonathan-larson-transformed-an-idea-into-a-groundbreaking-musical.
69. *Hair* had, in fact, a significant impact on Larson, who used it as direct inspiration in creating *Rent*.
70. Patrick Pacheco, "Theater, Will it be a Day at the Beach?," *Los Angeles Times*, March 20, 1994, https://www.latimes.com/archives/la-xpm-1994-03-20-ca-36463-story.html.
71. Jennifer AshleyTepper, "Is Michael Greif Setting a Record by Directing 3 Shows This Season?," *Broadway World*, March 10, 2024, https://www.broadwayworld.com/article/Is-Michael-Greif-Setting-a-Record-by-Directing-3-Shows-This-Season-20240310.
72. Bernardo Sim, "The 'Wicked' box office sales keep soaring & breaking al-time records," Out, December 30, 2024. https://www.out.com/film/wicked-box-office#rebelltitem1.
73. Josh Sharpe, "Wicked Movie Enters Top 50 All-time Box Office Hits in the United States," Broadway World, December 26, 2024. https://www.broadwayworld.com/article/WICKED-Movie-Enters-Top-50-All-Time-Box-Office-Hits-in-the-United-States-20241226.
74. Logan Culwell-Block, Broadway Grosses Analysis: Wicked is 1st Show Ever to Gross $5 Million," Playbill, December 31, 2024. https://playbill.com/article/broadway-grosses-analysis-wicked-is-1st-show-ever-to-gross-5-million.
75. Although *Grand Hotel* was written by Luther Davis (book) and Robert Wright and George Forrest (score), with additional songs by Maury Yeston, director and choreographer Tommy Tune was primarily responsible for shaping and editing the show into its unconventional mosaic-like structure.
76. Catherine Wright, "Six Creators Reveal Which Modern-Day Pop Stars Influenced Each of Henry VIII's Wives in the Musical," *cheatsheet.com*, December 20, 2023, https://www.cheatsheet.com/entertainment/six-the-musical-which-modern-day-pop-stars-are-the-queens-inspired-by.html/
77. Wright, "Six Creators Reveal Which Modern-Day Pop Stars Influenced Each of Henry VIII's Wives in the Musical."
78. https://www.nytimes.com/2021/12/01/theater/company-stephen-sondheim-marianne-elliott.html.
79. The final directing slot went to *Hell's Kitchen*'s director Michael Greif, his fifth nomination in this category.
80. The previous winners are Marianne Elliott, Rachel Chavkin, Diane Paulus, Susan Stroman, and Julie Taymor.
81. Michael Paulson, "What to Know About This Crazily Crowded Broadway Spring Season," *New York Times*, February, 21, 2004, https://www.nytimes.com/2024/02/21/theater/broadway-musicals-plays-spring-season.html.
82. https://www.broadwayleague.com/press/press-releases/broadways-2023-2024-end-of-season-statistics-reveal-123-million-attendances-and-grosses-of-154-billion/.
83. https://www.broadwayleague.com/press/press-releases/broadways-2023-2024-end-of-season-statistics-reveal-123-million-attendances-and-grosses-of-154-billion/.

Chapter 14

1. Stacy Wolf, *Changed for Good: A Feminist History of the Broadway Musical* (Oxford University Press, 2011), 3.

Notes

2. Wolf, *Changed for Good*, 3.
3. "Flappers Are We" from *No, No, Nanette*, lyrics by Irving Caesar and Otto Harbach, music by Vincent Youmans.
4. "I Want to be Bad," music and lyrics by DeSylva, Brown and Henderson from *Follow Thru*.
5. Maslon (ed.), *American Musicals*, 244.
6. The exception is *South Pacific*, in which Bloody Mary's inspirational songs are focused on the young leading man, Lt. Cable.
7. Laurence, Bergreen, *As Thousands Cheer*, 447.
8. In the lyrics to the song "Old Fashioned Wedding," that Berlin added to the show for the 1966 revival.
9. Many modern audience members will have at least some awareness of the "Little Rock Nine" and the events surrounding them that took place there a decade or so after the story of *South Pacific* is set.

Chapter 15

1. For example, according to the IBDB, the show included characters named Minnehaha, Chief Lowdog, and Sambo Simmons.
2. Paul Robeson ended up not being available for the original 1927 Broadway production, but the next year played the role to great acclaim in the original London production, the 1932 Broadway revival, and the 1936 film version of *Show Boat*. Robeson recorded the song with Paul Whiteman and his Concert Orchestra in 1928, and multiple times during the 1930s, and would perform it in concert throughout the rest of his life.
3. James Ferguson, "Old Man River—a powerful indictment of black oppression," *Financial Times*, September 20, 2020, https://ig.ft.com/life-of-a-song/ol-man-river.html.
4. The placement of "Supper Time" in *As Thousands Cheer* has a remarkably similar dynamic to the way the song "I Know Where I've Been" functioned in *Hairspray* nearly seventy years later: one deadly serious, deeply moving song in the midst of an otherwise wildly comic and effervescent show.
5. The original stories were titled *Fo' Dolla'* and *Our Heroine*.
6. In both the original short story and the musical, Liat and her mother, Bloody Mary, are not Polynesian—they are "Tonkinese"—meaning that they are from Tonkin, an area that today is part of northern Vietnam. Tonkin was a French colony at the time, and French planters on the French-colonized South Pacific islands brought people from Tonkin to work on their estates. And as such, they would have been relatively dark-skinned, which feeds into Cable's fears and cowardice.
7. Purdum, *Something Wonderful*, 159.
8. Jim Crow Museum Timeline, part 5 (1944–1972), https://jimcrowmuseum.ferris.edu/timeline/civilrights.htm#:~:text=August%2028%2C%201963,I%20Have%20a%20Dream%20 speech.
9. Charles McNulty, "Review: Black, queer and laceratingly honest, *A Strange Loop* liberates Broadway," *Los Angeles Times*, April 26, 2022, https://www.latimes.com/entertainment-arts/story/2022-04-26/review-a-strange-loop-michael-r-jackson-musical-broadway.

Chapter 16

1. Jeffrey Sweet, *The Dramatist's Toolkit: The Craft of the Working Playwright* (Heinemann, 1993).
2. After viewing these two numbers side by side you might think the writers of *Les Misérables* owed at least some of their immense earnings to the *West Side Story* team. But that's how art works. There is a famous saying, "Bad artists copy and great artists steal"—which has been attributed to everyone from Picasso to T. S. Eliot to John Lennon. Wherever it came from, what it means is that, if you are a truly gifted artist you can co-opt a work of art that someone else has created and then reimagine it, reinvent it, and make something new that is entirely your own.
3. Kimball, *The Complete Lyrics of Cole Porter*, 180.
4. Knapp, *The American Musical and the Formation of National Identity*, 128.
5. Short for "involuntary celibate."
6. Maslon (ed.), *American Musicals*, 281.
7. Maslon (ed.), *American Musicals*, 281.
8. Maslon (ed.), *American Musicals*, 281.
9. Maslon (ed.), *American Musicals*, 290.
10. Alan Jay Lerner, *Brigadoon* (Chappell and Co., 1947), 36.
11. Sondheim, *Finishing the Hat*, 102.
12. Richard Coe, "Chorus Line: A Sensation from the Very First Step," *Washington Post*, September 11, 1977.
13. Book, music, and lyrics by Irene Sankoff and David Hein; directed by Christopher Ashley; musical staging by Kelly Devine; musical supervisor, Ian Eisendrath.

SELECTED BIBLIOGRAPHY

Anbinder, Tyler. *Five Points: The Nineteenth-Century New York City Neighborhood*. Simon and Schuster, 2012.
Anderson, John Murray, and Hugh Abercrombie Anderson. *Out Without My Rubbers: The Memoirs of John Murray Anderson*. Pickle Partners Publishing, 2018.
Artz, Matt. "European Immigration and Defining Whiteness (1910–1920)." Understanding RACE, January 27, 1910. https://understandingrace.org/history/government/european-immigration-and-defining-whiteness-1910-1920/.
Barnes, Grace. *National Identity and the British Musical: From Blood Brothers to Cinderella*. Bloomsbury Publishing, 2022.
Barrett, Mary Ellin. *Irving Berlin: A Daughter's Memoir*. Amadeus Press, 1996.
Behr, Edward, and Mark Steyn. *The Story of Miss Saigon*. Random House (UK), 1991.
Bergreen, Laurence. *As Thousands Cheer: The Life of Irving Berlin*. Da Capo Press, 1996.
Berson, Misha. *Something's Coming, Something Good: West Side Story and the American Imagination*. Applause Theatre and Cinema, 2011.
Block, Geoffrey. *The Richard Rodgers Reader*. Oxford University Press, USA, 2006.
Bloom, Julie. "Lin-Manuel Miranda on 'Mary Poppins Returns' and Movie Musicals." *New York Times*, November 2, 2018. https://www.nytimes.com/2018/11/02/movies/lin-manuel-miranda-mary-poppins-returns.html.
Bloom, Ken, and Frank Vlastnik. *Broadway Musicals: The 101 Greatest Shows of All Time*. Black Dog and Leventhal Publishers, 2010.
Bordman, Gerald. *American Musical Theater: A Chronicle*. Oxford University Press, 2001.
Brockett, Oscar Gross. *History of the Theatre*. Allyn and Bacon, 1974.
Charyn, Jerome. *Gangsters and Gold Diggers: Old New York, the Jazz Age, and the Birth of Broadway*. Thunder's Mouth Press, 2003.
Chauncey, George. *Gay New York: Gender, Urban Culture, and the Making of the Gay Male World, 1890–1940*. Basic Books, 1995.
Chude-Sokei, Louis. *The Last "Darky": Bert Williams, Black-on-Black Minstrelsy, and the African Diaspora*. Duke University Press, 2005.
Cockrell, Dale. *Everybody's Doin' It: Sex, Music, and Dance in New York, 1840–1917*. W. W. Norton and Company, 2019.
Comden, Betty, and Adolph Green. *The New York Musicals of Comden and Green*. Applause Theatre and Cinema, 1997.
Craft, Elizabeth T. *Yankee Doodle Dandy: George M. Cohan and the Broadway Stage*. Oxford University Press, USA, 2024.
Cullen, Frank, Florence Hackman, and Donald McNeilly. *Vaudeville Old and New: An Encyclopedia of Variety Performances in America*. Psychology Press, 2007.
Dickens, Charles. *American Notes for General Circulation*. Chapman and Hall, 1842.
Electric Light Demonstration. "Savoy Theatre." n.d. https://www.gsarchive.net/carte/savoy/electric.html.
Epps, Sheldon. *My Own Directions: A Black Man's Journey in the American Theatre*. McFarland, 2022.
Erdman, Andrew L. *Beautiful: The Story of Julian Eltinge, America's Greatest Female Impersonator*. Oxford University Press, 2024.

Eyre, Richard. *Talking Theatre: Interviews with Theatre People*, Nick Hern Books, 2009.
Fields, Armond, and L. Marc Fields. *From the Bowery to Broadway: Lew Fields and the Roots of American Popular Theatre*. Oxford University Press, USA, 1993.
Forbes, Camille F. *Introducing Bert Williams: Burnt Cork, Broadway, and the Story of America's First Black Star*. Civitas Books, 2008.
Fordin, Hugh. *Getting to Know Him: A Biography of Oscar Hammerstein II*. Random House, 1977.
Furia, Philip. *Irving Berlin: A Life in Song*. Schirmer Trade Books, 1998.
Gaines, Caseen. *When Broadway Was Black: The Triumphant Story of the All-Black Musical That Changed the World*. Sourcebooks, Inc., 2023.
Ganzl, Kurt. *Lydia Thompson: Queen of Burlesque*. Routledge, 2014.
Garebian, Keith. *The Making of My Fair Lady*. ECW Press, 1993.
Gennaro, Liza. *Making Broadway Dance*. Oxford University Press, 2021.
Goldfarb, Michael. "Jews and Blues: Inside Out." WBUR, 2001. http://archives.wbur.org/insideout/documentaries/jewsandblues/index2.php.html.
Gordon, Joanne. *Stephen Sondheim: A Casebook*. Routledge, 2014.
Gottfried, Martin. *Sondheim*. Harry N. Abrams, Inc., 2000.
Green, Stanley. *Ring Bells! Sing Songs!: Broadway Musicals of the 1930's*. Galahad Books, 1971.
Green, Stanley. *The World of Musical Comedy*. Da Capo Press, 1984.
Harbin, Billy J., Kim Marra, and Robert A. Schanke. *The Gay and Lesbian Theatrical Legacy: A Biographical Dictionary of Major Figures in American Stage History in the Pre-Stonewall Era*. University of Michigan Press, 2005.
Hart, Lorenz, Robert Kimball, and Dorothy Hart. *The Complete Lyrics of Lorenz Hart*. Alfred a Knopf Incorporated, 1986.
Hayter-Menzies, Grant. *Charlotte Greenwood: The Life and Career of the Comic Star of Vaudeville, Radio and Film*. McFarland, 2007.
Herman, Jerry, and Marilyn Stasio. *Showtune: A Memoir*. Dutton, 1996.
Hoffman, Warren. *The Great White Way: Race and the Broadway Musical*. Rutgers University Press, 2020.
Horowitz, Mark Eden. *The Letters of Oscar Hammerstein II*. Oxford University Press, 2022.
Hughes, Langston. *The Big Sea: An Autobiography*. Macmillan, 1993.
Hyman, Alan. *The Gaiety Years*. Weidenfeld and Nicolson, 1975.
Jablonski, Edward. *Harold Arlen*. Da Capo Press, Incorporated, 1985.
Jowitt, Deborah, and Jerome Robbins. *Jerome Robbins: His Life, His Theater, His Dance*. Simon and Schuster, 2004.
Kenrick, John. "History of Burlesque Part I." Musicals101.com, 2003. https://www.musicals101.com/burlesque.htm.
Kester, Barry. *Round in Circles: The Story of Rodgers and Hammerstein's Carousel*. i2i Publishing, 2023.
Kimball, Robert. *The Complete Lyrics of Cole Porter*. Da Capo Press, 1992.
Knapp, Raymond. *The American Musical and the Formation of National Identity*. Princeton University Press, 2018.
Lambert, Sheela. "The Man Behind the 'Hair.'" Advocate.Com, August 13, 2008. https://www.advocate.com/arts-entertainment/theater/2008/08/13/man-behind-hair.
Lane, Stewart F. *Black Broadway: African Americans on the Great White Way*. Square One Publishers, 2015.
Lerner, Alan J. *The Street Where I Live: A Memoir*. W. W. Norton and Company, 2018.
Lev, Peter. *Twentieth Century-Fox: The Zanuck–Skouras Years, 1935–1965*. University of Texas Press, 2013.
Levy, Emanuel. *Vincente Minnelli: Hollywood's Dark Dreamer*. St. Martin's Press, 2009.
Lindberg, Julianne. *Pal Joey: The History of a Heel*. Oxford University Press, USA, 2020.
Logan, Joshua. *Josh, My Up and Down, In and Out Life*. Delacorte Press, 1976.

Selected Bibliography

Lovensheimer, Jim. *South Pacific: Paradise Rewritten*. Oxford University Press, 2010.
Magriel, Paul. *Chronicles of the American Dance*. Van Rensselaer Press, 2010.
Marra, Kim. *Strange Duets: Impresarios and Actresses in the American Theatre, 1865–1914*. University of Iowa Press, 2009.
Marra, Kim, and Robert A. Schanke. *Staging Desire: Queer Readings of American Theater History*. University of Michigan Press, 2002.
Maslon, Laurence. *American Musicals: The Complete Books and Lyrics of Eight Broadway Classics*, 2014.
Maslon, Laurence. *American Musicals*. n.p., 2014.
Maslon, Laurence. *Broadway to Main Street: How Show Tunes Enchanted America*. Oxford University Press, 2018.
McBrien, William. *Cole Porter*. Vintage, 2011.
McGilligan, Patrick. *George Cukor: A Double Life*. University of Minnesota Press, 2013.
McHugh, Dominic. *The Big Parade: Meredith Willson's Musicals from The Music Man to 1491*. Oxford University Press, 2021.
McLane, Derek, and Eila Mell. *Designing Broadway: How Derek McLane and Other Acclaimed Set Designers Create the Visual World of Theatre*. Running Press Adult, 2022.
Meyerson, Harold, and Ernest Harburg. *Who Put the Rainbow in the Wizard of Oz? Yip Harburg, Lyricist*. University of Michigan Press, 1995.
Mille, Agnes De. *America Dances*. Macmillan, 1980.
Miller, Scott. *Rebels with Applause: Broadway's Groundbreaking Musicals*. Heinemann Drama, 2001.
Miller, Scott. *Strike Up the Band: A New History of Musical Theatre*. Heinemann Drama, 2007.
Miller, Scott. *Literally Anything Goes: 14 Great Oddball Musicals and What Makes Them Tick*. Createspace Independent Publishing Platform, 2018.
Miranda, Lin-Manuel. "Stephen Sondheim, Theater's Greatest Lyricist." *New York Times*, October 16, 2017. https://www.nytimes.com/2017/10/16/t-magazine/lin-manuel-miranda-stephen-sondheim.html.
Mordden, Ethan. *When Broadway Went to Hollywood*. Oxford University Press, 2016.
Nolan, Frederick. *Lorenz Hart: A Poet on Broadway*. Oxford University Press, 1995.
Okrent, Daniel. *Last Call: The Rise and Fall of Prohibition*. Simon and Schuster, 2010.
Pender, Rick. *The Stephen Sondheim Encyclopedia*. Rowman and Littlefield, 2021.
Pepusch, John Christopher. *Gay's The Beggar's Opera*. Palala Press, 1920/2018.
Phillips, Brent. *Charles Walters: The Director Who Made Hollywood Dance*. University Press of Kentucky, 2014.
Poole, Wakefield. *Dirty Poole: A Sensual Memoir*. Lethe Press, 2011.
Purdum, Todd S. *Something Wonderful: Rodgers and Hammerstein's Broadway Revolution*. Henry Holt, 2018.
Riedel, Michael. *Singular Sensation: The Triumph of Broadway*. Simon and Schuster, 2021.
Rivera, Chita. *Chita: A Memoir*. HarperCollins, 2023.
Rodgers, Richard. *Musical Stages: An Autobiography*. Random House, 1975.
Rogers, Bradley. *The Song is You: Musical Theatre and the Politics of Bursting into Song and Dance*. University of Iowa Press, 2020.
Schlissel, Lillian. *Three Plays by Mae West: Sex, The Drag and Pleasure Man*. Routledge, 2013.
Schultz, William Eben, Oliver Baty Cunningham Memorial Publication Fund, and Elizabethan Club (Yale University). *Gay's Beggar's Opera: Its Content, History and Influence*. Yale University Press, 1923.
Secrest, Meryle. *Stephen Sondheim: A Life*. Vintage, 2011.
Seldes, Gilbert. *The Seven Lively Arts*. Harper & Brothers, 1924.
Sherrell, Kat. *Experiencing Broadway Music: A Listener's Companion*. Rowman and Littlefield, 2016.

Selected Bibliography

Soden, Oliver. *Masquerade: The Lives of Noel Coward*. Weidenfeld and Nicolson, 2024.

Solomon, Alisa. *Wonder of Wonders: A Cultural History of Fiddler on the Roof*. Macmillan and ORM, 2013.

Sondheim, Stephen. *Finishing the Hat: Collected Lyrics (1954–1981) with Attendant Comments, Principles, Heresies, Grudges, Whines and Anecdotes*. Knopf, 2010.

Sondheim, Stephen. *Look, I Made a Hat: Collected Lyrics (1981–2011) with Attendant Comments, Amplifications, Dogmas, Harangues, Digressions, Anecdotes and Miscellany*. Knopf, 2011.

Stalter-Pace, Sunny. *Imitation Artist: Gertrude Hoffmann's Life in Vaudeville and Dance*. Northwestern University Press, 2020.

Stearns, Marshall, and Jean Stearns. *Jazz Dance: The Story of American Vernacular Dance*. Da Capo Press, 1994.

Stempel, Larry. *Showtime: A History of the Broadway Musical Theater*. W. W. Norton, 2010.

Suskin, Steven. *Opening Night on Broadway: A Critical Quotebook of the Golden Era of the Musical Theatre, Oklahoma! (1943) to Fiddler on the Roof (1964)*. Schirmer Reference, 1990.

Thelen, Lawrence. *The Show Makers: Great Directors of the American Musical Theatre*. Routledge, 2002.

Time-Life Books. *The Jazz Age: The 20s*. Time Life Medical, 1998.

Toll, Robert C. *On with the Show: The First Century of Show Business in America*. Oxford University Press, 1976.

Weill, Kurt. *Speak Low (When You Speak Love): The Letters of Kurt Weill and Lotte Lenya*. University of California Press, 1997.

Wilson, John C. *Noel, Tallulah, Cole, and Me: A Memoir of Broadway's Golden Age*. Rowman and Littlefield, 2015.

Winer, Deborah Grace. *On the Sunny Side of the Street: The Life and Lyrics of Dorothy Fields*. Schirmer Trade Books, 1997.

Winkler, Kevin. *Everything is Choreography: The Musical Theater of Tommy Tune*. Oxford University Press, 2021.

Winter, Marian Hannah. "Juba and American Minstrelsy." In *Chronicles of the American Dance*, 39. Da Capo Press, Inc., 1948.

Wolf, Stacy. *A Problem Like Maria: Gender and Sexuality in the American Musical*. University of Michigan Press, 2002.

Wolf, Stacy. *Changed for Good: A Feminist History of the Broadway Musical*. Oxford University Press, 2011.

Woll, Allen L. *Black Musical Theatre: From Coontown to Dreamgirls*. Louisiana State University Press, 1989.

Zadan, Craig. *Sondheim and Co*. Da Capo Press, Incorporated, 1994.

INDEX

(pop)Rock Musical, x, 253, 254–264, 279, 286, 307, 316, 400
& Juliet, 313, 314, 347
1600 Pennsylvania Avenue, 201, 270
1776, 166, 176, 300, 349
25th Annual Putnam County Spelling Bee, 307
42nd Street (film), 92, 264
42nd Street (novel), 92, 382
42nd Street (stage musical), 92, 211, 229, 241, 242–243, 267, 279, 296, 393
5th Avenue Theatre, The, xxi, 306, 312, 398
9/11, 305–306

A Day Well Spent, 244
Abbott, Cary, 98
Abbott, George, 129–130, 190, 200, 203, 204, 205, 237, 247, 271, 272, 383
Abie's Irish Rose, 217
Abyssinia, xii, 49, 52–53, 66, 134, 373
Academy Award, 207, 220, 235, 303
Acis and Galatea, 12
acknowledged (diegetic) songs, 27
Act One, 117
act-one-finale-of-female-self-assertion, 340, 346, 347, 355
Actors' Equity Association, 282, 284, 290
Adams Lee, xvi, 216, 240, 280, 326, 328, 399
Adams, Maude, 58
"Adelaide's Lament," 27
Adele, 318
Adler and Ross, x, 204–205
Adler, Richard, x, 204–205
Advocate, The, 254–256, 394, 405
African diaspora, 209, 404
African Grove Theater, 41
Africana, 122
After Midnight, 310
"After The Ball," 17, 35
"Ah, Sweet Mystery of Life," xii, 31, 62, 63, 133, 286
Ahrens, Lynn, 348, 355
Aida (musical), 347
Aida (opera), 177
AIDS (Auto Immune Deficiency Syndrome) 282–284, 308, 316, 397
Ailey, Alvin, 213, 270
Ain't Got No," 255
Ain't Misbehavin' (musical), xvii, 268, 313, 330

"Ain't Misbehavin'" (song), 103
Ain't Supposed to Die a Natural Death, 262
Ain't Too Proud—The Life and Times of the Temptations, 309
Aladdin, (story), 64
Aladdin, Disney's, xvii, 44, 307, 310–312
Aldredge, Theoni, 209
Alessandrini, Gerard, 45, 289
"Alexander's Ragtime Band," 34–35
Algonquin Round Table, 120
"Alice Blue Gown," 37
All About Eve, 280
All American, 303
"All I Ask of You," 286
All I Care About is Love," 277
All That Glitters, 160
All That Jazz (film), 278, 397
All That Jazz," viii, 71, 82
"All The Things You Are," 156
Allegro, 160, 175
Allen, Debbie, 263
"Almost Like Praying," 165
Alton, Robert, xii, xiv, 69, 94, 117, 125–127, 130–131, **142**, 171, 188, 234, 383
Alvin Ailey Dance Theater, 270
AMC Empire 25 Theater, 60
"America, (I Like To Be In)" 209, 354
America's Got Talent, 17
America's Sweetheart, 98
American Ballet Theater, 205, 208
American Graffiti, 267
American Idiot, 310
American Musical and the Formation of National Identity, The, 361, 391, 392, 403, 405
American Playhouse, 292
American Psychiatric Association, 118
American Society of Composers, Authors, and Publishers (ASCAP), 63
Americana movement in dance, xix, 174, 189, 287
Americana, 110, 127, 380
An American In Paris (film), 113, 315
An American In Paris (stage musical), 310
"An American In Paris" (symphonic work), 113
Anbinder, Tyler, 56, 374, 404
"And I Am Telling You, I'm Not Going," 340, 346
Anderson-Lopez, Kristen, xvii, 332
Anderson, Benny, 314

Index

Anderson, John Murray, 76, 92–94, 101, 125, 201, 204, 214, 378, 404
Anderson, Maxwell, 162, 199
Andre Charlot's Revue of 1924, 94–95, 385
Andrews, Julie, 196, 197, 400
Animal Crackers, 120
Anna and the King of Siam (novel and film), 162
Annie (television adaptation), 308
Annie Get Your Gun, x, xv, 96, 175, 198, 200, 201, 203, 246, 247, 297, 308, 322, 344, 348
Annie, 209, 241, 267, 308, 386
Anti-Irish/Catholic prejudice, 30, 71
Anyone Can Whistle, 163
"Anyplace The Old Flag Flies," xii, 21
Anything Goes, xii, 23, **69**, 89, 115–117, 118, 119, 126, 202, 241, 265, 300, 303, 309, 342, 381, 392, 406
"Anything Goes" (song), 23
"Anything You Can Do, I Can Do Better," viii, 62, 344
Applause, xvi, 190, 211, 241, 280, 283, **328**
Aquacade (*Billy Rose's World's Fair*), 93
Arden, Eve, 245
Arenal, Julie, xv, 251
Arms and the Girl, 209
Armstrong, Louis, 103, 245, 393
Aronson, Will, 357
Around The World In 80 Days, 15
Arsenic and Old Lace, 116
Art Deco, 97, 264–265, 277
Artaud, Antonin, 245
Artists And Models, 112, 374
As Thousands Cheer, xiii, 91, 118, 121, 122, 123, 127, 137, 255, 349, 352, 371, 382, 388, 402, 404
Ashley, Christopher, xvii, 337, 403
Ashman, Howard, 283, 311
Assassins, 164
Astaire, Adele, 85, 91, 113, 115, 228
Astaire, Fred, 32, 61, 85, 91, 104, 113–115, 123, 207, 228, 376, 377
At Home Abroad, 121, 382
Auberjonois, Rene, 280
Auntie Mame (film), 222, 229
Auntie Mame (play), 222, 391
Austin Powers, 13
Avatar, 312
Avenue Q, xvii, 10, 307, 332, 349, 356
Avian, Bob, 292
Away We Go!, ix, 157

Babes In Arms, 129
Babes In Toyland, 31
baby boom generation, 239, 265, 268, 274
Bacall, Lauren, xvi, 280, **328**
Bacharach, Burt, 259
Back to the Future, 307
Bailey, Pearl, xvi, 213, 216, 245, 253, **326**, 391

Baker Street, 293
Baker Word, 238–239
Baker, Josephine, 79, 83, 122
Balanchine, George, 176, 179, 205, 213, 269
Baldwin, James, 184
"Bali Hai," 160
ballad opera, 12
Ballard, Lucinda, 209
Ballet Russe de Monte Carlo, 174
Ballroom dance craze (Ragtime Era), 44, 92
"Band Played On, The", 35
Band Wagon, The (film), 315
Band Wagon, The, xiv, 91, 113, 120, 121, 146, 208
Band's Visit, The, 302, 318, 356
Bandana Land, xii, 49, 50, 52, 134
Bandstand, 309
Bankhead, Tallulah, 100
Barclift, Nelson, 124
Barefoot in the Park, 201
Bareilles, Sarah, 166
Barnes, Clive, 217, 233, 261, 262, 263, 266, 391, 395, 397, 398
Barnes, Grace, 314
Barnum, xvi, 241, 309, 327
Bart, Lionel, 248
Bart, Roger, 305
Baryshnikov, Mikhail, 278
Bathing Beauty (film), 93
Battle, Hinton, 263
Baum, Frank L., 15, 263, 317
Bays, Nora, 63, 93, 230, 340, 374
Beach Boys, The, 259
Beach, Gary, 304
"Beatlemania", 235
Beatles, The, 245, 258, 259, 265, 383
Beatles' Second Album, The, 245
Beatty, Talley, 176
Beautiful Noise — The Neil Diamond Musical, 310, 313
Beautiful, 313
Beauty and the Beast (animated film), 289, 311, 366, 400
Beauty and the Beast (stage musical), 289, 311–312, 366
Beetlejuice, 307
"Before the Parade Passes By," 340
Beggar's Opera, The, 12, 369, 406
"Begin The Beguine," 118
Beguelin, Chad, xvii, **335**
Belafonte, Harry, 94, 214
Belcher, Earnest, 242
Bell, Lou, 103
Bells Are Ringing, 190, 203, 207, 209, 211, 269, 301, 347, 348
"Bench Scene, The" (*Carousel*), xix, 159, 191–193, 261, 284, 387

409

Index

Benjamin, Nell, 348
Benjamin, Rick, 30, 370, 371
Bennett, Tony, 204
Benny, Jack, 76
Berea College, 211
Bergreen, Laurence, 34, 344, 371, 388, 402, 404
Berkley, Busby, 38, 93, 125, 264, 265, 266, 305
Berle, Milton, xvii, 76, 171, 269, **331**
Berlin Stories, The, 273
Berlin, Irving, xii, xiii, xv, 32–34, 39, 59, 60, 63, 75, 78, 79, 91, 92, 93, 96, 99, 113, 117, 121, 122, 123, **133**, 137, 172, 175, 198–199, 201, 203, 221, 228, 231, 247, 254, 255, 271, 295, 322, 344, 350, 352
Berlin, Mrs. Irving (Ellin), 92
Bernstein, Elmer, 226
Bernstein, Felicia Montealegre, 218
Bernstein, Leonard, xv, 102, 163, 179, 188, 189, 190, 205, 217–219, 226, 271, 286, 323, 354
Berson, Misha, xxii, 206, 218, 389, 404
Besoyan, Rick, 265
Best Foot Forward, 265
"Best Is Yet To Come, The," 226
Best Little Whorehouse Goes Public, The, 294
Best Little Whorehouse in Texas, The, 293, 308
"Best Things In Life Are Free, The," 107, 192
"Bewitched, Bothered, and Bewildered," 130–131
Beyoncé, 166, 318
"Bidin' My Time," 111
Big Apple, The (dance), 44, 83
Big Fish, 299
"Big Lady Shows," 247
Big River, 308, 317
"Big Transgressive Lady Shows," x, 247, 280, 346
Big—The Musical, 299
"Big, Blonde, and Beautiful," 347, 355
Billboard Magazine, 161, 196, 232, 245, 257, 259, 393
Billion Dollar Baby, 206
Billy Elliot, 310, 318
Billy Rose Theatre Division, New York Public Library for the Performing Arts, xxii, 69, 323, 380
Billy the Kid, 189, 208
Birch, Patricia (Pat), 267–268, 297, 309, 398
Birdcage, The, 282
"Birth of the Blues," 83
Bissell, Richard, 204–205
Bitter Sweet, 95, 378
Bjornson, Maria, 288
Black Bottom (dance), 44, 82, 83, 107
Black Bottom, The" (song), 83, 107
"Black Boys/White Boys," 255
Black Crook, The, 14–16, 64
Black Musical Theatre, 51, 373, 390, 391, 395, 407
Black musical, vii, ix, x, xiii, 41, 46, 47–54, 71, 77–84, 102–105, 106, 108, 123, 135, 183–184, 212–217, 253, 261–264, 268–270, 279, 326, 329, 350, 373, 376, 380, 387, 390, 391, 395, 402, 405, 407

Black Patti Troubadours, The, 46, 47, 52
Black Sabbath, 219
Blackbirds of 1928 (Lew Leslie's), 104, 105, 106, 108
Blackbirds of 1939, 214
blackface performance, 26, 42–46, 78, 104, 372
Blake, Eubie, xiii, 19, 75, 78–79, 84, 94, 135, 268, 270, 369
Bland, James, 43–44
Blankenbuehler, Andy, 309
Blazing Saddles, 303
Bless You All, 213, 262
Blithe Spirit, 100
Blitzstein, Marc, 179, 211, 238
Bloomer Girl, xv, 100, 175, 185–188, **321**, 343, 349, 352, 387
Bloomer, Amelia, 186
Blossom Time, xiv, 86, 144
"Blow High, Blow Low," 180
"Blow, Gabriel, Blow," xii, **69**
Blue Holiday, 214
"Blue Skies," 34
Blues scale, 74–75
Bock and Harnick, 237, 249–250, 271
Bock, Jerry, 214, 237, 249–250, 271
"Body and Soul," 91
Bolger, Ray, xiv, 142, 204
Bolshoi Ballet, 290
Bolton, Guy, xii, 36–37, 69, 111, 115, 185, 381
Bontemps, Arna, 212
Book of Mormon, The, xvii, 44, 307, 310, 332, 348
BOOP! The Betty Boop Musical, 309
"Born In A Trunk," 305
Boston Globe, The, 38, 210, 272
Boublil and Schönberg, 166, 286–290, 316
Boublil, Alain, 166, 286–290, 316. 377
Boy Friend, The, 265, 395
"Boy Like That/I Have a Dream, A," 165, 220–221
Boy Meets Girl, 225
Boys From Syracuse, The, 129, 156, 265
Bradford, Alex, xvii, 264, 329
Bradley, Clarence "Buddy," 83, 269
Braham, David, 26–27
Bramble, Mark, 279, 397
Brando, Marlon, 177
Brecht, Bertolt, 12, 172, 238, 248, 366
Brennan, Jay, 61
Brice, Fanny, 40, 59, 63, 67, 230, 247, 340, 346, 385, 394
Bricusse, Leslie, 248, 391
Bridge, Andrew, 288
Brigadoon, 175, 178, 195, 211, 297, 309, 343, 363, 366, 390, 403
Brightman, Sarah, 288
Bring in the Noise, Bring in the Funk, 56, 166
Bring It On, 165, 166
British Actors Equity, 278
"British invasion of Broadway," x, 285, 286, 291

410

Index

"British invasion" of Pop music," 235
Brittan, Robert, 262
Broadway Cares/Equity fights AIDS, 384
Broadway Theater District, xii, 4, 5, **6**, 79, 193, 285
Broadway To Mainstreet: How Showtunes Enchanted America, 196, 235
Brook, Peter, 245, 248
Brooklyn Citizen, 185, 385
Brooklyn Daily Eagle, 50, 187, 373, 374, 377, 379, 380, 381, 386, 387
Brooks, Harry, 103
Brooks, Mel, x, 13, 299, 303–306, 399, 400
Brooks, Shelton, 106
"Brother Can You Spare a Dime," ix, 110, 380
Brothers Grimm, 292
Broun, Haywood, 38, 372
Brown Buddies, 106
Brown University, 301
Brown, Jason Robert, 164, 166
Brown, Lew, 83, 106–107, 376, 402
Brown, Russ, 205
Brown, William Alexander, 41
Browne, Bothwell, 60
Browning, Elizabeth Barrett, 123
Bubbling Brown Sugar, xvii, 268, 269, 283, **330**
Buchanan, Jack, 94
Bullets Over Broadway, 299
Bunraku, 312
burlesque, 13–14, 18, 19, 28, 38, 45–46, 64–66, 80, 185, 203, 207, 229, 267, 303, 305, 372, 375, 405
Burns, Robert H., 38
Burton, Richard, 197
Bus Stop (film), 200–201
"Bushell and a Peck, A" 27
Busker's Alley, 294
"But Alive," 280
"But Not for Me," 111
"Button Up Your Overcoat," 107
By George!, 158
By Jupiter, xiv, 142, 199
"By My Side," 259
Bye Bye Birdie, x, 10, 211, 221, 239–242, 301, 347, 393

Cabaret (film), 207, 273
Cabaret (stage musical), 172, 211, 236, 253, 271, 272–273, 277, 283, 308, 318, 346, 349, 354, 396
Cabin in the Sky, xiv, 122, 147, 176–177
Caesar, Sid, 303
Café Cino, 265
Café La MaMa, 259
Cahill, Marie, 52
Cahn, Sammy, 203
cakewalk dance, xii, xiii, xiv, 44, 47, 52, 65, 66, 134, 135, 147, 177, 372
Caldwell, Anne, 62–63, 374, 386
Calhoun, Jeff, 308, 310

Call Me Madam, 116, 182, 205, 220, 228, 271
"Call On Dolly," 246
Callen, Michael, 283
Callow, Simon, 184
Calloway, Cab, 217, 268
Camelot (film), 201
Camelot, 175, 178, 196–197, 201, 240, 347, 390
"Camptown Races," 43
can-can (dance), 65
Can-Can (musical), 182, 202, 208, 220, 389
Candide, 297
cantor (vocalist), 33, 40, 75, 172
Cantor, Eddie, xiii, 40, 53, 59, 61, 63, 101, **133**, 277, 319, 373
Cantu, Maya, xxii, 92
Capers, Virginia, 263
Carlyle, Warren, 310
Carmen (opera), 183
Carmen Jones (film), 184
Carmen Jones, ix, 183–184, 188, 189, 269, 349, 352, 386, 387, 390
Carnegie Hall, 47, 85
Carnegie Mellon University, 259
Carnival, 241, 242, 386
Carousel, ix, 159, 171, 175, 178, 179–180, 191–193,195, 212, 288, 300, 343, 347, 352, 263–264, 377, 383, 405
Carroll, Diahann, xvi, 213, 215, **325**
Carroll, Earl, 76, 121
Carroll, Vinnette, xvi, 264, 319, **329**
"Carry Me Back To Old Virginny," 44
Carter, Nell, 268
Casa Manana, Billy Rose's, 93
Casablanca, 162, 187
Casey, Warren, 267, 283
Cash, Johnny, 315
Casino Girl, The, xii, 134
Castle, Irene, 34
Castle, Vernon, 34, 92
Cats, xvii, 164, 277–278, 285–285, 289, 296, 298, 300, 308, 309, 317, 318, 332, 365, 397
Cavendish, Millie, 14
Ceasar, Irving, 89, 264, 402
Chadman, Christopher, 283, 296
Champion, Gower, xvi, 128, 216, 241–245, 253, 278, 279, 284, 326
Champion, Marge (Belcher), 242
Chanel, Coco, 280
Changed for Good—A Feminist History of the Broadway Musical, 340, 401, 402, 407
Channing, Carol, xvi, 203, 244–245, **326**, 379, 393
Chaplin, 310
Chapman, John, 196, 244, 379, 386, 387, 388, 391, 393, 394
Charles, Ray, 315
Charleston dance, xix, 44, 72, 77, 81–83, 84, 85, 107, 108, 209, 341

411

Index

Charleston Rag, The," 78
Charleston, The" (song), 81, 107, 341
Charley's Aunt, 60, 204
Charlot, Andre, 94–95, 385
Charnin, Martin, 267
Charyn, Jerome, 71, 375, 404
Chattanooga Daily Times, 119, 382
Chauncey, George, 57, 374, 382, 404
Chavkin, Rachel, 318, 401
Cheetah, The, 255–256
Chenoweth, Kristin, 317
Cher, 243, 314
Chernow, Ron, 165
Chess, 283
Chicago (film), 308
Chicago College of Music, 203
Chicago Tribune, 400
Chicago, (musical), 44, 53, 82, 207, 208, 220, 221, 272, 277, 278, 283, 296, 297, 298, 308, 318, 346, 386, 398
Chita Rivera: The Dancer's Life, 221
Choate (Rosemary-Hall) School, 194
Chocolate Dandies, The, xiii, 83–84, 135
Chorus Line, A, xvi, 65, 165, 211, 212, 276–279, 281, 283, 285, 289, 309, 318, 328, 347, 359, 365, 396, 397, 403
Chris Cross, 62
Christiansen, Lew, 189
Christmas Story, A, 307, 310
Churchill, Frank, 112
Cino, Joe, 265
Circus Girl, The, 19
City College, 204, 208
City of Angels, 295, 347
civil rights movement, 187, 212, 249, 255, 261, 255
Civil War Ballet," 187
Civil War, The (musical), 291
Civil War, The, xv, 17, 43, 45, 47, 55, 186, 187, 321, 353
Clark Bobby, 184–185
Clark, Peggy, xv, xx, 209, 211–212, 323, 390
Classic Stage Company, 184
"Climb Every Mountain," 343
Climb High, 162
Clooney, Rosemary, 205
Clorindy, or The Origin of the Cakewalk, xii, 47–48, 52, 134
Club Abbey, 101–102
Club, The, 293
Coco, 280, 297
Coconuts, The, 120
Coe, Peter, 216, 248
Cohan, George M., viii, xii, **21**, 28–31, 33–34, 35, 37, 50, 59, 63, 78, 117, 129, 138, 152, 166, 223, 279, 315, 350, 370, 404
Cohan, Helen "Nellie" Costigan, 29
Cohan, Jerry, 29
Cohan, Josie, 29

Cold War, 222
Cole, Bob, xvii, 46–47, 51–52, 54, 61, 63, **134**, 350
Cole, J.O., 97
Cole, Jack, 127–128, 171, 208, 215, 269, 383
Coleman, Cy, 190, 226–227, 231
Collins, Dorothy, 275
Collins, Judy, 259
Collins, Pat, 212
Color Purple, The, 318, 346
"Colored Actors Declaration of Independence," 51
"Colored Spade," 255
Columbia University, 77, 87, 152, 272, 378
Comden and Green, xvi, xix, 190–191, 203, 216, 229, 240, 254, 271, 280, 295, 328, 387, 404
Comden, Betty, xvi, xix, 190–191, 203, 216, 229, 240, 254, 271, 280, 295, 328, 348, 387, 404
Come From Away, xviii, **337**, 347, 349, 356, 367
"Come Up To My Place," 342
Commedia dell'Arte, 1, 15, 239
Company, 163, 231, 273–274, 275, 276, 283, 319, 347, 365, 401
concept album, 165, 258–259, 261, 287
concept musical, x, xi, 216, 248, 254, 258, 270–278, 279, 285, 291, 294, 298, 307, 318–319, 320, 366
Connecticut Yankee, A, 100, 182
Connelly, Marc, 120
Connie's Inn, 103
Conrad, Con, 103
Consumer Rapport, 263
Contact, xvii, 299, 334
Cook, Barbara, 222
Cook, Will Marion, xii, xiii, 46–47, 49–50, 52, 83–83, **134**, 135
"Cool," 219
Cooper, George W., 104
Copland, Aaron, 179, 189
Corbet, "Gentlemen" Jim, 60
Cort, John, 79
Cotton Club, The (film), 270
Cotton Club, The, 114, 122
Count Me In, 112
Coveney, Michael, 299
Coward, Noel, xiv, 79, 94–96, 98, 100, 122, **141**, 195, 197, 247, 378, 385, 407
Cradle Will Rock, The, 211, 380
Crane, Raymond, 38
Crawford, Cheryl, 174
Crawford, Joan, 121
Crawford, Katherine, 114
Crawford, Michael, 288
Craymer, Judy, xvii, 314–315, **333**, 400
Crazy For You, xvii, 296, 298, 310, 334, 386
Creamer, Henry, 53, 80, 103
Crinoline Girl, The, 60
Crouse, Russell, xii, 69, 115–116, 118, 233–234
Crowley, Bob, xvii, **335**

Index

"Cuddle Up A Little Closer, Lovey Mine," 151
Cullen, Countee, 212
Curious Incident of the Dog in the Night, The, 310
Curtains, 307, 309, 400

D'Oyly Carte, Richard, 118
da Costa, Morton, 222
Dabney, Ford, 102, 379
Daily Mail, 299
Daily News (New York), 37, 89, 188, 240, 241, 264, 271, 377, 379, 381, 384, 386, 387, 388, 391, 393, 394, 395, 396, 387, 399
Dallas Summer Musicals, 293
Daly, Tyne, 233
Dames At Sea, 265–266
Damn Yankees, 205, 207, 208, 271, 274, 307, 308, 343
"Dance at the Gym," 219, 224
"Dance Explosion, The," 278
Dance With Your Gods, 214
Dancin' (Bob Fosse's), 207, 279, 283
"Dancing," 246
Danse Macabre," 219
Dante, Nicholas, 276, 283
Darktown Strutter's Ball," 106
Darling, Peter, 310
Davis, Clifton, 217, 262
Davis, Eddie, 185
Davis, Ossie, 215. 261
"Day by Day," 259
Day in Hollywood/A Night in the Ukraine, A, 293
Days of Wine and Roses, 226, 316, 318
De Carlo, Yvonne, 245, 275
de Lappe, Gemze, 300
de Lavallade, Carmen, 213
De Leon, Michael or Noel, xv, 169
De Mille, Agnes, xiv, xix, 55, 113, 126, 128, 142, 173, 174–175, 178–180, 187, 189–190, 195, 205, 243, 254, 296–300, 309, 368, 373, 406
De Shields, Andre, 268
Dead Outlaw, 302
Dean, James, 177
Dear Evan Hanson, 317, 349
Dearest Enemy, 93
Death Becomes Her, 307, 309, 347
Death of a Salesman, 303
DeCarlo, Yvonne, 245, 275
Deep Blue Sea, The, 100
Delaney, Jere, 38
DeLuca, John, 308
DeMille, Cecil, B., 174
"Den of Iniquity," 129
Denishawn School and Dance Company, 127, 208
Dennis, Patrick, 247
Denver, John, 314, 403
Desert Song, The, 153, 377
Destry Rides Again, 208

DeSylva, Brown, and Henderson, 83, 106–107, 376, 402
DeSylva, Buddy G., 83, 106–107, 376, 402
Devine, Kelly, xvii, 337, 403
Dewhurst, Coleen, 282
"diabolus in musica," 219
Diamond Horseshoe, Billy Rose's, 93
Diamond, John, 55–56
Diamond, Neil, 279, 310, 313
Dickens, Charles, 55, 167, 373, 404
Die Lustige Witwe, (The Merry Widow), 32
diegetic (acknowledged) songs, 27
Dietz and Schwartz, ix, xiv, 87, 91, 113, 120, 121, 146, 182, 195, 315, 382
Diller, Phylis, xvi, 245, 326
Dillinger, John, 117
Dillingham, Charles, viii, xiii, 58–59, 61, 62, 100, 137
Dinner At Eight, 120
director-choreographer, xx, 11, 200, 205, 215, 241–243, 262, 277, 281, 283, 292, 293–294, 296–300, 308–310, 331, 333, 335, 365, 367, 368
Dirty Dancing, 246
Dirty Rotten Scoundrels, 302, 307, 309
Disney (Walt Disney Company, Disney Theatricals), xi, xvii, 10, 40, 44, 112, 162, 166, 196, 232, 283, 289, 308, 310, 311–313, 366, 400
"Disney Renaissance," 282, 311
Dixie Jass Band One Step," 72
DMX, 166
Do Re Mi (musical), 301
"Do, Re, Mi (song)," 181
"Doin' What Comes Naturally," x, 198
Don't Bother Me I Can't Cope, xvi, 263–264, 270, 329
"Don't Fence Me In," 360
"Don't Rain On My Parade," xi, 340, 341
Donahue, Vincent J., 233
Donnelly, Dorothy, xiv, 19, 86, 123, **144**
Douglass, Margaret, xv, **321**
"Down In The Depths on the Ninetieth Floor," 119
Doyle, John, 184
Drake, Alfred, 202
Drama of King Shottaway, The, 41
"Dream a Little Dream of Me," 265
dream ballet, 126, 173, 190, 232, 255
Dreamgirls, 211, 279, 283, 294, 340, 346, 349, 355, 373, 407
"Drink With Me," 286
Drowsy Chaperone, The, 307, 310, 400
Druten, John Van, 273
DuBois, Raul Pen, 94, 378
Dulcy, 119
Dunbar, Paul, xii, 47, 49, 135
Duncan, Isadora, 175
Dunham School of Dance and Theatre, 177, 209
Dunham, Katherine, xiv, **147**, 176–178, 209, 213, 214, 262, 386

413

Index

Durante, Jimmy, 29, 76, 114, 118
"Eagle and Me, The," 187

Earhart, Amelia
Earl Carroll's Vanities, 76, 121
Early to Bed, 171
"Ease On Down the Road," 263
Easter Parade (film), 126, 294
"Easter Parade" (song), 91, 121
Eastman School of Music, 240
"Easy To Be Hard," 257
"Easy To Love," 124
Easy Virtue, 94–95
Ebb, Fred, 53, 272–273, 277, 298, 308, 318
Ed Sullivan Show, The, 197, 239, 392
Eddy, Nelson, 265
"Edelweiss," 234
Edison, Thomas, 210, 389
Edwardian Musical Comedy, vii, 18, 35
Edwards, Blake, 400
Edwards, George, 18, 19
Eisendrath, Ian, xviii, 337, 403
Eisenhour, Peggy, 212
Eisenhower, Mamie, 347
Elf, 307, 310
Ellington, Duke, 13, 48, 211, 268, 270
Elliott, Marianne, 319
Elliott, T. S., 278
Eltinge Theatre, 60
Eltinge, Julian, xiii, 59–60, 67, 101, **138**, 374, 404
"Embraceable You," 111
Eminem, 166
Emmons, Beverly, 212
Encanto, 166
"Epiphany," 159
Epps, Sheldon, xxii, 216, 391, 404
Epstein, Jules J, 162
Epstein, Phillip, 162
Equity Fights AIDS, 384
Erdman, Jean, 260
Estefan, Gloria, 314
Etting, Ruth, 315
Eubie!, xvii, 269, 270, 283, 330
Europe, James Reese, 77
Evangeline, 15
Evans, Albert, xxii, 192, 219, 223
Evans, Wilber, 180
Everglades Club, 101
"Everything's Coming Up Roses," 340
Evita, 261, 309, 346
Eyen, Tom, 265, 279, 283

Face The Music, 91, 113
Fagan, Garth, 312
Fairbanks Jr., Douglas, 121
Fairfax High School, 241

Faison, George, 263–264, 270, 395, 396
Fall River Legend, 189
Falsettoland, 283
Falsettos, 283
Fame, 278
Fancy Free, 188–189, 190, 205
Fanny, 200
Fantasticks, The, x, 238–239, 248, 253, 292, 392
Faria, Arthur, 268
"Farmer and the Cowman, The," 360
"Fascinating Rhythm," 85
Fascinating Widow, The, 60
Faust, 13, 14, 64
Fearnow, Mark, 99
Feder, Abe, 210
Federal Theater Project, 122, 211, 386
Ferber, Edna, 108, 120, 153
Ferguson, James, 351, 402
Ferrer, Jose, 177
Feuer, Cy, 204
Fiddle De Dee, 28
Fiddler on the Roof (film), 246
Fiddler on the Roof, x, 24, 32, 166, 182, 206, 211, 216, 246, 249–250, 253, 257, 267, 271, 345, 349, 354, 359, 389, 394, 396, 407
Field, Ron, xvi, 253, 272, 281, 283, 318, 328, 396
Fielding, Marjory, 126
Fields, Armond, 96, 379, 405
Fields, Dorothy, x, xiv, xv, xix, 28, 79, 93, 96, 105, 112, 123–124, **143**, 184, 189, 201, 226–227, 254, 281, 322, 344, 348, 378, 382, 387, 388, 407
Fields, Herbert (Herbie), x, xiv, xv, 28, 93, 96–98, 105, 114, 124, 125, 143, 182, 184, 198, 201, 322, 344, 377, 378, 387
Fields, Lew, viii, xiii, 25, 27–28, 50, 64, 87, 96, 105, 134, 289, 380, 379, 405
Fields, W. C., 53, 86
Fierstein, Harvey, xvii, 282, 306, 307, 333, 356
Fifty Million Frenchmen, 98
Filling Station, The, 189
Fine And Dandy, 112
Finian's Rainbow, 175, 178, 208, 262, 310, 349
Finn, William, 281, 284
Fiorello!, 209, 236, 237, 271
Fish, Daniel, 362
Fisk University, 77
Fitch, Clyde, 58
Five Points (book), 56, 374, 404
Five Points district, 55–56
flapper, 72, 82, 341, 375, 402
Flapper, The (film), 72
Flappers and Philosophers, 72
"Flappers Are We," 341
Flashdance, 278
Flora the Red Menace, 272, 296
Florodora, 18, 19

Flower Drum Song, 163, 211, 213, 233, 239
Floyd Collins, 226
Flying Colors, xiv, 113, 120, 121, 146
Flying High, 107
Folies Bergère (nightclub), 72
folk opera, 187
Follies, 163, 211, 260, 274, 275–276, 283, 297, 300, 310, 347
Follow the Girls, ix, 184, 185
Follow Thru, 107, 342, 402
Fonda, Henry, 199., 200
Footlight Parade, 264
Footloose (film), 278
Forbidden Broadway, 45, 289, 377
Ford 50th Anniversary Show, The, 228
Ford Motor Company, 228
Forrest, George, 94, 185, 387, 401
Forty Thieves, The, 65, 66
Forty-Five Minutes From Broadway, 151
Fosse (musical), 279, 309
Fosse style, 207
Fosse, Bob, 29, 53, 128, 204, 205, 207, 208, 209, 226, 227, 260, 283, 269, 273, 277, 278, 279, 283, 284, 293, 296, 297, 367, 368, 383, 397
Fosse/Verdon, 166
Foster, Stephen, 43, 44
Foster, Sutton, 116
Four Cohans, The, 29
Fox, George, L., 15
Freaky Friday (book), 226
Frederika, 91
Freedley, Vinton, 115
Freeman Sisters, 47
Freeman, Johnathan, xvii, **335**
Freeman, Morgan, 217
Freidman, Maria, 320
Freud, Sigmund, 32, 172
Friml, Rudolph, 84, 90, 153, 377
Frogs, The, 299
Frohman, Charles, viii, xiii, 58–59, 90, **137**
Frozen, Disney's, xvii, 309, 313, 332
Full Monty, The, x, 296, 301–303, 305–306, 307, 309, 399
Fun Home, 318, 347
Funny Girl, 40, 203, 245, 247, 340, 348, 394
"Funny Honey," 277
Funny Thing Happened on the Way to the Forum, A, 128, 163, 182, 211, 271
Furs and Frills, 152
Furth, George, 273–274, 381

Gaga, Lady, 34
Gaiety Girl, The, 18, 19
Gaiety Theater, 18
Gaines, Caseen, xxii, 78, 80, 83, 84, 376, 405
Galati, Frank, 316

Gallagher, Helen, 206–207, 266, 289
Gandhi, Mahatma, 122
Gangs Of New York, 55
Ganzel, Kurt, 64
Garbo, Greta, 228
Gardens of Anuncia, The, 297
Garland, Judy, 52, 228, 280, 305
Garrick Gaieties, The, 84, 86–87, 377
Gay and Lesbian Theatrical Legacy, The, 91, 372, 377, 405
Gay Divorce, 114–115
Gay Divorcee, The, 115.
Gay Pride parade, 280
Gay rights, 202, 280, 351, 355, 356, 389
Gay, John, 12, 406
Gaynor, Janet, 234
"Gee, Officer Krupke," 219, 354
Geld, Gary, 261
Gentleman's Guide to Love and Murder, A, 307, 400
Gentlemen Prefer Blondes, 100, 128, 175, 203, 211, 243, 245, 343, 379
George M!., 243, 253, 327
George School, The, 158
George Washington, Jr., 30
George White Scandals, The, 76, 82, 106, 113, 121
Gershwin, George, 35, 36, 61, 63, 75, 79, 85, 96, 106, 111–113, 119–120, 123, 161, 172, 230, 264, 267, 315, 350
Gershwin, Ira, xiv, 61, 63, 79, 85, 96, 110–111, 119–120, 123, 146, 172, 230, 267
"Gethsemane," 159
"Getting To Know You," 163
Ghalili, Nava, 357
Ghostly, Alice, 94
Gibbs, Lloyd G., 47
Gibson, William, xvi, 215–216, 326
Gilbert and Sullivan, 13, 18, 19, 104, 110, 119–120, 166, 183, 210, 267
Gingold, Hermione, 94
Girl Crazy, ix, 111–112, 230, 295, 381
Girl From Utah, The, 19, 35, 58
Girl Scouts of the USA, 226
"Give My Regards To Broadway," 29
Gleason, Joanna, 292
Glickman, Will, 214
Glover, Savion, 56
Godspell, xvii, 248, 258–260, 332, 394, 395
Gold Diggers of 1933, 264
Golden Boy, xvi, 215, 216, 262, 263, **326**, 349, 390, 391
Goldfarb, Michael, 73–75, 375, 376, 405
Goldman, James, 260, 275
Goldwyn, Samual, 159
Gonzales, Brian, xvii, 335
Good Morning Dearie, 62
"Good Morning Starshine," 257

415

Index

Good News, 107–108, 192, 342, 376
Goodman, Benny, 111, 128, 279
"Goodnight My Someone," 223
Gorney, Jay, 110–111
gospel music, xvi, 259, 260, 261, 263, 264, 329, 356
Gottfried, Martin, 158, 384, 405
Gould, Morton, 189
Grable, Betty, xvi, 128, 208, 245, 326
Graham, Martha, 127, 210, 262, 297, 273
Grammy Hall of Fame, 245
Grand Guignol, 366
Grand Hotel, 293, 294, 318, 401
Grand Opera House, 86
grand opera, 1, 13, 183
Grande, Ariana, 318
Grant, Micki, xvi, xvii, 264, 329
Grass Harp, The, 201
Gray, Gilda, 80
Grease (film), 268, 297
Grease 2, 297
Grease, 267–268, 277, 283, 297, 300, 308, 346, 394
"Greased Lightnin'," 268
Great American Songbook, 73, 257
Great Comet, The, 318
Great Depression, The, 108, 109, 111, 113, 116, 215, 303, 342, 382
Great Gatsby, The, 318
Great Migration (Black), 48, 71
Great Migration (Puerto Rican), 218
"Great White Way, The", xii, 4, 153, 210, 372, 380, 384, 402, 404, 405
Green Grow The Lilacs, 130, 157, 191
Green, Adolph, xvi, xix, 190–191, 229, 328, 387, 404
Green, Al, 264
Green, Jesse, xxii, 233, 392
Green, Stanley, 109, 186, 371, 377, 380, 405
Greenwich Village Follies 1918, 61
Greenwich Village Follies 1919, 93
Greenwich Village Follies 1920, 61
Greenwich Village Follies 1922, 61
Greenwich Village Follies 1924, 101, 125
Greenwich Village Follies 1925, 91, 93
Greenwich Village Follies, 61, 76, 91, 93, 101, 125
Greenwich Village Theatre, 92
Greenwich, Ellie, 314
Greenwillow, xvi, 327
Greif, Michael, 316–317, 401
Greig, Edvard, 185
Grey Gardens, 308, 317
Grey, Joel, 253
Griffith, Robert (Bobby) E., xv, 271, **323**
Grossinger's Resort, 303
Grotowski, Jerzy, 248
Guare, John, 260, 395
Guettel, Adam, 226, 301
Guinan, Texas, 116

Guys and Dolls, 27, 120, 175, 196, 204, 208, 209, 220, 269, 283, 296, 302, 307, 309, 361, 362
Gynt, Kaj, 102
Gypsy, x, 159, 163, 182, 203, 206, 217, 227, 228, 229–233, 236, 237, 241, 244, 247, 257, 272, 340, 346, 392

H.M.S. Pinafore, 13
Hadestown, 44, 318, 347
Hague, Albert, 226
Haimsohn, George, 266
Hair, x, xv, xvi, 2, 165, 173, 248, 251, 253, 254–262, 264, 268, 271, 274, 280, 301, 316, 328, 349, 355, 364, 394, 401, 405
"Hair" (song), 255
Hairspray (1988 film), 306
Hale, George, 119
"Half of It, Dearie Blues, The," 61, 85
Hall, Adelaide, 79, 105, 106, 215
Hall, Juanita, 161, 213
Hallelujah, Baby!, 216, 262
"Hallelujah," 89
Halliday, Richard, 234
Hamilton, 4, 10, 30, 44, 159, 161, 164–166, 196, 309, 312, 318, 347, 349, 356, 384
Hamlisch, Marvin, 276
Hammerstein, Arthur, 39, 151, 152
Hammerstein, Dorothy, 156, 353
Hammerstein, Oscar, I, viii, 39, 51, 67
Hammerstein, Oscar, II, ix, xiv, xv, xvi, 2, 31, 39, 71, 84, 87, 91, 108, 126, 129, 131, 140, **149**, 151–167, 169, 171–175, 179, 181–188, 191–193, 194–195, 198, 200, 204, 213, 215, 228, 231, 233–236, 238–239, 243, 255, 286, 295, 315, 325, 340, 342, 343, 360–354, 360, 362–364, 375, 377, 383, 384, 405, 406
Hammerstein's Victoria Theatre, 67, 151
Hand's Up!, 98
Handel, George Frideric, 12
Haney, Carol, 205, 207
Happy Birthday, 200
Happy Days, 267
Happy Hunting, 231
Harbach, Otto, ix, xiii, xv, 2, 59, 63, 84, 89, 91, 138, **149**, 151–153, 167, 264, 402
Harburg, E. Y. "Yip", ix, 110–111, 185–187, 195, 214–215, 380, 387, 406
Harburg, Ernest, 187, 387, 406
"Harlem Hellfighters," 77
Harlem Renaissance, The, viii, xiii, 77, 135, 212, 268, 350
Harlem: The Crucible of Modern African American Culture, 77
Harmony, 310
Harnick, Sheldon, 249–250, 271
Harper, Ken, 263

Index

Harrigan and Hart, vii, xii, 25–31, 48, 64, **132**, 199, 370
Harrigan, Edward, vii, xii, 25–31, 48, 64, **132**, 199, 370
Harrigan, Nedda, 199
Harris, Charles, K., 17
Harrison, Rex, 196
Harry Potter and the Cursed Child, 310
Hart, Charles, 288
Hart, Lorenz (Larry), xiii, xiv, xix, 79, 86–88, 93, 96, 98, 111, 120, 125, 126, 129–131, **140**, 142, 156, 182, 199, 203, 217, 267, 315, 344, 377, 379, 383, 405, 496
Hart, Moss, xiii, xiv, xix, 92, 98, 113, 117–118, 120, 121, 137, 146, 172–174, 196–197, 352, 381, 382
Hart, Tony, vii, xii, 25–31, 48, 64, **132**, 199, 370
Harvard Law School, 98
Harvey Girls, The, 126
Hasty Pudding show, 194
Hatch, Heather, 348
Have A Heart, 36
Hay Fever, 94
Haynes, Tiger, 263
Hays Code, The, 115, 123–124
Hayward, Leland, 227–229, 233–244
hazanuth, 75
Hazel Flagg, 126
"Heart Full of Love," 286
"Heat Wave (We're Having A)," xiii, xix, 121, 122, **137**
Hein, David, xviii, 318, 327
Helburn, Teresa, 157, 174
Hell's Kitchen, 313, 314, 317, 347, 349, 401
Hello Daddy, 93
"Hello Twelve, Hello Thirteen, Hello Love," 359
Hello, Dolly!, x, xvi, 10, 211, 216–217, 229, 244–247, 249, 253, 310, 326, 340, 386, 390, 391, 393, 394
Hellzapoppin', 188, 201, 371
Hemsley, Sherman, 262
Henderson, Ray, 83, 106–107, 376, 402
Henry, Sweet, Henry, 396
Hepburn, Katherine, 280
Herbert, Victor, vii, xii, 30–31, 37, 39, 59, 61, 62, 63, 79, 84, 85, 113, **133**, 350, 383
Here We Are, 164
Herman, Jerry, x, xvi, xix, 216, 244–247, 253, 281, 282, 284, 292, **326**, 393, 394, 405
Herman's Hermits, 265
Herzig, Sid, 186
"Hey, There," 205
High Anxiety, 304
High Button Shoes, 203, 205, 206, 211, 243, 389
High Tor, 162
Higher and Higher, 199
Hippodrome Theatre, 93, 113
History of the World, Part 1, 304

HIV/AIDS, 284
Hoffmann, Gertrude, xiv, 66–67, 112, 148, 375, 407
Hoffmann, Max, 67, 375
Hoggett, Stephen, 310
Hoity-Toity, 28
Hokey Pokey, 28
Hold Everything!, 107
Holder, Geoffrey, xv, 213, 263, **324**
Holiday Inn, 34
Holiday, Billie, 122, 315
Holler If Ya Hear Me, 166
Holliday, Judy, 203
Hollywood blacklist, 110, 206
Hollywood Production Code, 115, 123–124
Holm, Celeste, xv, 186–187, 321
Holm, Hanya, xiv, **142**, 175, 178, 182, 196, 202
Holzman, Winnie, 317, 340, 356
Home, James, 152
Honeydew, 91
Hoochie-coochie dance, 60
Hood, Basil, 32
Hooker, Brian, 90
Hope, Bob, 76, 118, 381
Hopkins, George James, 56, 374
Horne, Lena, xv, 106, 212, 214–215, 216, 269, **324**, 390
Hoschna, Karl, 151, 283
Hot Chocolates, 103, 105, 380
Hot Mikado, The, 104, 183, 386
Hould-Ward, Anne, 209
House of Flowers, 201, 213, 394
House Un-American Activities Committee (HUAC), 206
Houston, Whitney, 290
How Now Dow Jones, 226, 293
How the Grinch Stole Christmas!, Dr. Suess', 308
Howard University, 46, 270
Howard, Peter, 181, 386
Howard, Willie, 111, 381
Howells, William Dean, 26
Hudes, Quiara, Alegria, 348
Hudson Theater, 103
Hughes, Allen, 177
Hughes, Langston, 77, 212, 376, 405
Hugo, Victor, 286, 287
Humphrey-Weidman Company, 127
Humphrey, Doris, 127
Humpty Dumpty, xiii, 15, 134
Hunchback of Notre Dame, Disney's The, 289, 366
Hutchinson Prize, 162, 281

I am a Camera, 273
"I Am What I Am," x, 279, 282
"I Can't Give You Anything But Love," 105
I Do! I Do! 242, 253
"I Feel A Song Coming On," 123

417

Index

"I Feel Pretty," 165
"I Got Life," 255
"I Got Love," 262
"I Got Rhythm," 111, 229
"I Know Where I've Been," 356
I Love My Wife, 241
"I Never Has Seen Snow," 213
"I Put My Hand In," 246
"I Want To Be Happy," xviii, 88, 89
I'd Rather Be Right, 120, 127, 129
"I'd Rather Charleston," 85
"I'd Rather Have Nothin' All of the Time Than Something for a Little While," 50
"I'm Falling In Love With Someone," 63
"I'm Gonna Wash That Man Right Out of My Hair," 160
"I'm Henry The Eighth, I Am," 265
"I'm In Love With a Wonderful Guy," 160
"I'm Just a Girl Who Can't Say No," 197
"I'm Just Wild About Harry," 79
"I've Got You Under My Skin," 124
"I've Grown Accustomed To Her Face," 159
"If I Loved You," 193
If I Were King, 89
"If It Wasn't For The Irish and the Jews," 28
Iglehart, James Monroe, xviii, **335**
Illustrators' Show, The, 203
Immigrants/Immigration: Catholic, 24, 29, 30, 40, 59, 71, 86, 217, 376
Immigrants/Immigration: German/German heritage, vii, xii, 17, 23, 24–25, 26, 28, 33, 34, 39, 40, 52, 55, 87, 88, 106, 120, 127, 132, 151, 156, 172, 175, 178, 179, 194, 204, 229, 303
Immigrants/Immigration: Irish/Irish heritage, vii, xii, xix, 21, 24–25, 26, 28, 29, 30, 37, 40, 48, 54–56, 59, 66, 71, 86, 105, 127, 132, 133, 217, 218, 220, 341, 370
Immigrants/Immigration: Jewish /Jewish heritage, vii, viii, xii, xiv, 1, 3, 17, 18, 24–25, 26, 27–28, 32–34, 37, 39, 40, 46, 52, 55, 58, 62, 62, 71, 73–75, 85, 87, 88, 89, 105, 106, 110, 112, 117, 119, 120, 121, 132, 146, 151, 156, 172, 175, 178, 179, 188, 190, 191, 194, 201, 203, 204, 205, 206, 208, 210, 217, 218, 225, 229, 240, 241, 246, 248, 249, 259, 261, 262, 267, 271, 272, 274, 281, 286, 287, 290, 301, 303, 316, 339, 354, 355, 375, 376, 377, 381, 285, 405
Importance of Being Ernest, The, 58
In Dahomey, xii, xiii, 47–49, 52, 66, 134, **135**, 350, 373
"In The Evening By The Moonlight," 43
In The Heights, 10, 159, 164, 166, 309, 318, 347, 348, 349, 356
"In The Still of the Night," 124
In Town, 18
In Trousers, 281

"Indian Love Call," 85, 286
international style musical, 290, 291
Into The Woods (film), 308
Into The Woods, 159, 164, 288, 292, 308, 316, *347*, *383*
Into the Woods, JR, 292
Irene, viii, xv, xviii, 37–39, 77, **148**, 173, 266, 305, 341, 371, 372
Irish (Potato) Famine, 24, 55
Irish Travelers, 55
Irma La Douce, 248, 293
Isherwood, Christopher, 273
"It Don't Mean a Thing if it Ain't Got That Swing," 268
"It Was Good Enough For Grandma," 186–187
"It Was Just One Of Those Things," 99
"It's Getting Dark On Old Broadway," 80
"It's Not Where You Start, It's Where You Finish," 293
"Italian Street Song, The," 31

Jack, Sam T., 46, 47, 372
Jackson, Clayton, and Durante, 114
Jackson, Ernestine, 217, 263
Jackson, Michael R., 319, 356–357, 402
Jackson, Michael, 220, 283
Jacobs, Adam, xvii, 335
Jacobs, Jim, 267
Jacques Brel is Alive and Well and Living in Paris, 313
Jamaica, xv, 214–215, 269, 324, 390
James Reese Europe's Society Orchestra, 77
Jarret, Henry, 14
"Javert's Suicide," 159
Jazz Singer, The, 34
Jefferson Airplane, 259
Jefferson, Margo, 42–43
Jeffersons, The, 262
Jekyll and Hyde, 290, 398
Jerome Robbins, His Life, His Theater, His Dance, 217, 391
Jerome Robbins' Broadway, 309, 389
Jersey Boys, 309, 313, 317
Jesus Christ Superstar, 159, 258–259, 261, 287
"*Jet Song, The*," 219
Jewish shofar call, 219
Jewish Women's Archive, 175
Jews and Blues: Inside Out, 73, 375, 376, 405
Jim Crow era, 42, 71, 153, 261, 402
jitterbug, 44, 83
"Joey Looks Into the Future," 126
John Loves Mary, 200
John Murray Anderson's Almanac, 94, 204, 214
John, Elton, 315
Johnny Johnson, 172
Johnson, Catherine, xvii, 314–315, **333**
Johnson, Chic, 166

Johnson, J. Rosamond, xii, xiii, 51–52, 63, 75, **134**, 350
Johnson, James P., 81, 101
Johnson, James Weldon, xiii, 50, 52, 134
Johnson, Louis, 213, 261, 270
Jolson, Al, 34, 40, 59, 63, 72, 109, 272, 315
Jones and Schmidt, 238–239, 253
Jones, Douglass R., Jr., 263
Jones, Matilda Sissoretta Joyner (Black Patti), 46
Jones, Tom, 238–239, 253
Joplin, Scott, 30, 46
Jordan, Joe, 51, 53
Jowitt, Deborah, 217, 391, 405
Joyful Noise, A, 293, 396
Juba, Master (William Henry Lane), 55–56, 103–104, 374, 380, 407
Jubilee, 98, 113, 118, 381
Juilliard School, The, 111, 194, 221, 259
jukebox musical, xi, xvii, 12, 313–315, 333
Jumbo, 93, 129, 130
"Jump Jim Crow," 41, 83
"Just Imagine," 107
"Just One of Those Things," 118

Kabuki, 1, 239
Kael, Pauline, 235
Kander and Ebb, 53, 272–273, 277, 298, 308, 318
Kander, John, 53, 272–273, 277, 298, 308, 318
Katherine Dunham Dance Company, 176
"Katrina," 194
Katz, Natasha, xvii, 212, **335**
Kaufman, George S., xix, 96, 117, 119, 120, 160, 382
Kaye, Danny, 173, 280
Kaye, Judy, 288
Kearns, Allen, 111
Keeler, Ruby, 264
"Keep It Gay," 305
Keep Shufflin', 103, 380
Kelly, Gene, 29, 104, 113, 131
Kelly, Glen, xvii, 304, **335**
Kelly, Patsy, 266
Kelly, Ray, 124
Kennedy Center Honors, 178
Kennedy, Jacqueline (Jackie), 197
Kennedy, John F., 194, 197
Kenny, Sean, 248
Kenrick, John, 65, 295, 375, 398, 405
Kern, Jerome, viii, xiii, 34–37, 39, 59, 60, 61, 62, 63, 87, 91, 108, 123, 138, 153, 156, 166, 167, 198, 242, 266–267, 315, 350, 351, 381
Kerr, Walter, 233, 244, 260, 393, 395, 396
Kert, Larry, 283
Kester, Barry, xxii, 192–193, 377, 386, 387, 495
Keys, Alicia, 317, 318
Kidd, Michael, 128, 175, 182, 189, 208, 209, 220, 387, 396

Kiley, Richard, xvi, 215, 325
Kiley, Richard, xvii, 215, **325**
Kim, Willa, 209
Kimberly Akimbo, 318, 347
King And I, The, 162, 178, 181, 205–206, 343, 349, 253–254, 385
King Kong, 289
King of Jazz (film), 93
King, Carol, 258
King, Dennis, 90, 377
Kinky Boots, xvii, 307, 309, 333
Kinsey Report, The, 202
Kinsey, Alfred, 202
Kiralfy Brothers (Imre, Bollossy, and Arnold), 15
Kirkwood, James, 276, 283
Kismet, 127, 128, 211, 214, 387
Kiss Me Kate (film), 207
Kiss Me, Kate, x, 100, 175, 182, 201–203, 207, 226, 300, 310, 343, 348, 386, 389
Kiss of the Spider Woman, 221, 308, 399
Kissell, Howard, 263
Kitt, Eartha, 94, 117, 390
Kitt, Tom, 166
Kleban, Edward, 276
Klezmer music, 74
Kline, Kevin, 267
Klotz, Florence, 209
Knapp, Raymond, 222, 236, 361, 391, 392, 401, 405
Knickerbocker Holiday, 172, 199
Knox College, 151
Kochno, Boris, 124
Korean War, 222, 271
Korins, David, 10
Kosarin, Michael, xvii, **335**
Krupa, Gene, 111
Kubie, Dr. Lawrence, 117–118

La Cage aux Folles (2004 Revival), 309
La Cage aux Folles, 281–282, 284, 292, 308
La Révolution Française, 287
LaBelle, Patti, 264, 270
Ladd, William "Billy", 92
"Ladies Who Lunch, The," 302
Lady and the Slipper, The, 62
Lady, Be Good!, 61, 84–85, 228, 377
Lady Do, 101
Lady in the Dark, xiv, xvi, 113, 146, 171–174, 280, 305, 328, 343, 385
LaGuardia, Fiorello, 237
Lahr, Burt, 107
Lamour, Dorothy, 245
Landon, Margaret, 162
Lane, Burton, 182, 188
Lane, Nathan, 296, 304
Lane, William Henry (Master Juba), 55–56, 103–104, 374, 380, 407

419

Index

Langer, Laurence, 157
Lansbury, Angela, 231, 232
Lapine, James, 281, 284, 288, 291–292, 295, 363
Larson, Jonathan, xi, 164, 166, 316, 401
Late Show with David Letterman, The, 301
Latouche, John, 13
Lauder, Harry, 213
Lauper, Cyndi, xvii, 333
Laurence Olivier Awards, xvii, 333
Laurents, Arthur, xv, 102, 163, 164, 216, 217, 231–322, 232, 281, **323**, 354
"Laurey Makes Up Her Mind," 126, 173
Lawrence and Lee, 247–248, 391
Lawrence, Carol, 220, 253
Lawrence, Gertrude, 94, 172–173, 385
Lawrence, Jerome, 247–248, 391
Layton, J. Turner, 53, 80
Layton, Joe, xvi, 181, 215, 234, 243, 253, 283, 293, 309, 325, **327**, 367, 392
Le Tang, Henry, 269–270, 386
Leave It To Jane, 36, 234, 265
Leave It To Me!, 225, 234
Lee Robert E., 247–248, 391
Lee, Gypsy Rose, 229, 232
Lee, Ming Cho, 260
Lee, Sammy, xii, **133**
Legally Blonde, 307, 309. 347, 348
Léhar, Franz, 13, 31, 91
Leigh, Carolyn, 226, 231, 348
Lennart, Isabel, 348
Lennon, John, 314
LeNoire, Rosetta, 268
Lenya, Lotte, 172, 385, 407
Léon, Viktor, 32
Leonowens, Anna, 162
Lerner and Loewe, ix, 194–197, 211, 240, 254, 363, 388
Lerner Shops, 194
Lerner, Alan Jay, ix, 77, 99, 182, 194–197, 211, 240, 254, 280, 363, 376, 388, 403, 405
Les Misérables (aka *Les Miz*), 10, 159, 164, 166, 248, 286–288, 359, 397, 403
Les Romanesques, 238
Leslie, Lew, 105, 106, 108, 112
"Let The Sunshine In," x, 253, 256, 257
Let Them Eat Cake, 119, 120
"Let's Do It," 97, 99
Let's Face It, 124, 389
"Let's Go Out In the Open Air," 112
"Let's Misbehave," 99
Letterman, David, 301
Levine, Avril, 318
Lew Leslie's International Revue, 112
Lewis, Marsha, 277
Lewis, Ted, 277
Liberty Theater, 228

"Lida Rose"/"Will I Ever Tell You," 223
Lif, Vincent, 283
"Life Is Just A Bowl of Cherries," ix, 106
Life Magazine, 29, 175, 266, 275
Life With Father, 116, 185
Life With Father, 116, 185
Light in the Piazza, 226, 318
Lil' Abner, 182, 208, 301
Lillie, Beatrice, 94
Lilliom, 159
Lilo, 208
Limón, José, 127
Lincoln, Abraham, 255
Lindberg, Charles, 107
Lindsay and Crouse, xii, 69, 115–116, 118, 234–235
Lindsay, Howard, xii, 69, 115–116, 118, 234–235
Lindy Hop, 44, 83, 127
Lion King, Disney's The, 289, 311–313, 319, 320, 400
Lion, Margo, 306
"Little Jazz Bird," 85
Little Johnny Jones, 29
Little Mary Sunshine, 265
Little Me, 207, 226, 347, 348
Little Mermaid, The (animated film), 311
Little Mermaid, The (live-action film), 166, 308
Little Mermaid, The (stage musical), 312, 400
Little Millionaire, The, xii, **21**
Little Night Music, A, 160, 163, 211, 274, 297, 347
Little Orphan Annie, 267
Little Red Riding Hood, 63
Little Shop of Horrors, 283, 300, 311, 366
Littlewood, Joan, 245
"Livery Stable Blues," 72
Living Theatre, The, 254
Liza With a Z, 207
Liza, 80
Lloyd, Phyllida, xvii, 314, **333**
Loessor, Frank, x, 203–204, 247, 302
Loewe, Frederick (Fritz), ix, 194–197, 211, 240, 254, 363, 388
Logan, Joshua, xiv, xv, xx, **142**, 180, 198, 199–201, 322, 352, 353, 387, 388, 389, 405
London Palladium, 216
"Lonely Room," 197, 362
Look to the Lillies, 201
Look, I Made A Hat, 166, 407
Lopez, Robert (Bobby), xvii, **323**
Lorelei, 190
Loretta Young Show, The, 230
Loring, Eugene, 184, 189, 387
Los Angeles Times, 38, 286, 316, 356, 371, 395, 397, 399, 401
Lott, Eric, 42
Louise, Mary, 213
"Love For Sale," 114
Ludwig, Ken, 296

Luna, Barbara, xv, **169**
Lunt, Alfred, 100
Lunt, Lynn Fontaine, 100
LuPone, Patti, 233
Lusitania, 59
Lydia Thompson—Queen of Burlesque, 64
Lynde, Paul, 94
Lynn, Loretta, 315
Lynne, Gillian, xvii, 278, 288, 293, 298, **332**, 398
Lyon, Genevieve, 92

MacDermott, Galt, xv, 251, 255, 260
Mack and Johnson, 81
Mack, Cecil, 81
Mackintosh, Cameron, x, 285–290, 297
Macrea, Ruth Faxon, 119–120
Madame Butterfly, 289
Maderia, Marcia, 212
Majestic Theater, xvi, 288, 326
Malin, Jean, 101
Maltby, Richard, 268, 290
Mamas & the Papas, The, 259, 265
Mame, 176, 211, 222, 247, 253
Mamma Mia!, xvii, xx, 313–315, 317, 333, 400
Man of La Mancha, 128, 248–249, 253, 346
Man Who Came To Dinner, The, 98, 112, 120
"Manhattan," 86, 88, 217
Mantle, Burns, 81, 89, 118, 157, 377, 381, 384
"Many A New Day," 343
March of the Falsettos," 281, 283
Marge and Gower Champion Show, The, 242
"Maria," 165, 219
"Marian, The Librarian," 224
"Marie From Sunny Italy," 33
Marlow, Toby, 318
"Marry The Man Today," 27
Marshall, Kathleen
Marshall, Rob
Martin, Ernest H., 204
Martin, John, 126, 383
Martin, Mary, xv, xix, 163, **169**, 174, 180, 203, 226, 227–228, 233, 234, 235, 244, 245
Marx Brothers, The, 120, 293
Mary Poppins Returns, 166, 308, 368, 384, 404
Mary Poppins, 40, 162, 235, 312
"Masculine Women, Feminine Men," 101–102
Maslon, Laurence, 123, 196, 382, 384, 386, 388, 402
Massey, Ilona, 171
Mast, Gerald, 88
"Master of the House," 289
Masteroff, Joe, 273
Mastin, Will, 214
Matchmaker, The, 244
Matilda, 310
Mattox, Matt, 297
Maybe Happy Ending, 318, 357

Maytime, 63
McAnuff, Des, 316
McCarthy and Tierney, 37, 39, 61, 77, 113
McCarthy Era, 110, 206, 222, 362
McCarthy, Joe, 37, 39, 61, 77, 113
McCarthy, Justin Huntley, 89
McCollum, Kevin, 10, 368
McCracken, Joan, xv, 187, **321**
McCrea, Gordon, 253
McDonald, Audra, 233, 392
McDonald, Jeanette, 265
McDowell, Roddy, 197
McGilligan, Partick, 57, 374, 406
McGowan, John, 111
McHugh, Dominic, 221, 381, 388, 406
McHugh, Jimmy, 93, 105, 112
McKayle, Donald, xvi, 213, 216, 262–263, 269, 270, 326, 395
McNally, Terrence, 301, 355, 399
McNally's Row of Flats," 26
McNeil, Lonnie, xvii, **330**
McNulty, Charles, 356, 402
McPherson, Aimee Semple, 116
McQueen, Armelia, 268
McSorleys, The, 26
Me and Juliet, 126
"Me and My Baby," 277
Me Nobody Knows, The, 297
Mean Girls, 307, 310
Meehan, Thomas, 267, 299, 304, 306, 307
Meet Me In St. Louis, 52
Meet the Beatles, 245
mega-musical, 261, 285, 289, 291, 282
Meilziner, Jo, 210
Melvin Van Peebles, 262
Member of the Wedding, The, 122
Memphis, 309, 318, 347, 356
Mendes, Sam, 308, 396
Menken, Alan, xvii, 311, **335**
Menzel, Idina, 317
Mercer, Johnny, 212
Mercer, Mabel, 129
Mercury, Freddie, 315
Merman, Ethel, xii, xv, xvi, **69**, 111, 115–119, 124, 163, 198, 203, 228–229, 230–233, 237, 244–247, 271, 303, **322**, 326, 342
Merrick, David, xvi, 214, 216, 229, 242, 244–247, 248, 279, 298, 326
Merrill, Bob, 203, 247
Merrily We Roll Along (musical), 163, 274, 320, 398
Merrily We Roll Along (play), 117
"Merry Widow Waltz, The," 32, 50
Merry Widow, The, (*Die Lustige Witwe*), xix, 31–32, 50, 194, 371
Metcalf, James, 29
Metropolitan Opera Ballet, 175

421

Index

Metropolitan Opera, 30, 121, 175, 177, 183
Mexican Hayride, ix, 124, 184–185, 397, 389
Meyerson, Harold, 187, 406
MGM (Metro-Goldwyn Mayer), 15, 52, 113, 190, 207, 208, 214, 242, 317, 390
Michiko, 209
Midler, Bette, 243, 245, 269
Midnight Frolic, Ziegfeld's, 232
Mikado, The, 13, 183
Milk and Honey, 182, 246
Miller and Lyles, 77, 78, 81, 102, 103
Miller, Ann, xvii, 267, **391**
Miller, Boots, 103
Miller, Buzz, 128
Miller, Flournoy, 77, 78, 80, 81, 102, 103
Miller, Gladys, xv, **148**
Miller, Glenn, 111
Miller, Irwin C., 80–81
Miller, Marilynn, 91, 121, 382
Miller, Robin, 266
Miller, Scott, 117, 221, 223, 239, 381, 391, 392, 406
Mills, Florence, 79
Mills, Stephanie, 263
Millstein, Gilbert, 130
Minaj, Nicki, 166, 318
Minelli, Liza, 207, 272
minstrel show, viii, 19, 26, 42–45, 48, 51, 56, 65, 255, 405, 407
Minstrelsy, viii, 43, 374, 380, 404, 407
Miranda, Carmen, 242
Miranda, Lin-Manuel, xv, 2, 4, **149**, 151, 164–167, 368, 384, 404, 406
Miss 1917, 36, 61
Miss Information, 98
Miss Jack, 60
Miss Saigon, 286, 289–290, 292, 311, 347, 349, 397, 398, 404
Mister Roberts, 200
Mitchel, Abrea "Abbie", 51
Mitchel, Lofton, 268
Mitchell, Anais, 318
Mitchell, Arthur, 177, 213
Mitchell, Jerry, xvii, 301, 307, 309, 333
Mitchell, Julian, 15, 92, 94
MJ the Musical, 313, 313
Mlle. Modiste, xiv, 31, 113, 146
Moana, 166
Molnar, Ferenc, 191, 192, 377
Moloney, Mick, 30
Monaco, James, 39, 102
Monroe, Marilynn, 128
Montalbán, Riccardo, 214, 215
Montgomery, David,, 15
Montgomery, James, 37
Moore, Constance, xiv, **142**
Moore, Melba, 262

Moore, Tom, 267
Moore, Victor, 115
Mordden, Ethan, 37, 235, 247, 380, 392, 406
Mordkin, Mikhail, 125
"More Than You Know," 89
Morrison, Patricia, 202
Morton, James J., 373
Morton, Joe, 263
Moscow Art Theatre, 199
Moses, Gilbert, 262
Moses, Itamar, 302
Moss, Lucy, 318
Most Happy Fella, The, 204
Mother Courage, 366
Mother Goose, 15, 31
Motley, 209
Motown, 235, 259, 260, 279
Moulin Rouge!, 313, 314
Mourning Becomes Electra, 119
"Mr. Cellophane," vii, 53, 277
Mr. President, 201
Mr. Wix of Wickham, 59
Mr. Wonderful, 214, 220, 390
Mufasa: The Lion King, 166
Mulligan Guard Ball, The, 26, 370
Mulligan Guard Christmas, The, 26
Mulligan Guard Marching Song", The, 26
Mulligan Guard Picnic, The, 26
Murphy, Donna, 292
Music Box Revue, Irving Berlin's, 91, 92, 121, 175, 377, 386
musical comedy, viii, ix, x, 15, 18, 28, 30, 31, 37, 45, 75–76, 84, 86, 106, 107, 111, 112, 117, 118, 119, 120, 135, 157, 174, 182, 184, 185, 187, 188, 190, 192, 195, 197–205, 212, 224, 227, 223, 240, 244, 253, 261, 264, 267, 295–296, 301–307, 311, 236, 340, 362
musical play, xi, xiv, xx, 31, 130, 140, 151, 152, 157, 163, 171, 183, 185, 187, 195, 197, 212, 223, 227, 238, 253, 257, 258, 265, 273, 274, 279, 295, 315–316, 317, 320, 340, 342, 362, 366
Musser, Tharon, xv, xix, 209–212, **323**, 390. 397
My Fair Lady, 159, 164, 175, 178, 195–196, 245, 257, 309, 385, 388, 390, 405
"My Heart Belongs to Daddy," 234
My One and Only, 267, 294, 308
My Three Angels, 226
Mystery of Edwin Drood, 297

NAACP (The National Association for the Advancement of Colored People), 77, 212, 376, 390
NASA (National Aeronautics and Space Administration), 5
Nash, Ogdon, 174
National Tap Dance Day, 104

Naughton, James, 277
Naughty Marietta, xii, 31, 63, 133, 286
Negro spirituals, 73, 74, 376
Nelson, Gene, 275
Nemiroff, Robert, 262
Nestroy, Johann, 244
Neumann, David, 318
Neuwirth, Bebe, 277
New Amsterdam Theatre, 31, 232, 371
New Faces of 1952, Leonard Sillman's, 94, 214, 303
New York Age, 80
New York City Ballet (NYCB), 179, 206, 284
New York City Ballet, 179, 206, 284
New York College of Music, 34
New York Herald Tribune, 38, 244, 272, 377, 392, 393
New York Mail, 49
New York Public Library for the Performing Arts, xxii, 69, 323, 380
New York Shakespeare Festival, 282
New York Stock Exchange, 109
New York Times, The, 5, 31, 49, 82, 84, 93, 102, 103, 119, 126, 130, 142, 165, 166, 174, 177, 178, 182, 185, 191, 185, 201, 217, 218, 233, 234, 241, 244, 249, 258, 259, 260, 261, 262, 266, 268, 282, 283, 285, 286, 291, 296, 302, 307, 311, 316, 319, 368, 370, 371, 372, 373, 375, 376, 377, 378, 379, 380, 381, 382, 383, 384, 385, 386, 387, 388, 389, 390, 391, 392, 393, 394, 395, 396, 397, 398, 399, 400, 401, 404, 406
New York University (NYU), 190, 201, 204, 205, 272
New York World, 225
New York, New York (stage musical), 299
"New York, New York, (Theme From)," 272
New Yorker, The, 249, 391, 394
New Yorkers, The (musical), 98, 114
Newley, Anthony, 248, 391
Newsboys' Home Club, 50
Newsies, Disney's, 33, 308, 309, 312
Next to Normal, 309, 317, 318
Niblo's Garden, 14, 16, 369
Nice Work if You Can Get it, 300
Nicholas Brothers, 212
Nicholas Nickleby, 278
Nicholas, Fayard, 270
Nicholas, Paul, xvi, **328**
Nicholaw, Casey, xvii, 310, **335**
Nichols, "Red," 111
Nichols, Lewis, 182, 385, 386, 387
"Night and Day," 115
Night Boat, The, 62
Night in Paris, A, 112
Night in Spain, A, 112
Nine (film), 308
Nine, xvii, 214, 293, 294, 308, 331
No, No, Nanette, viii, 84, 88–89, 100, 264–266, 267, 275, 341, 389, 396, 402

"No One Is Alone," 363
No Strings, xvi, 215, 243, **325**, 327, 349
"Nobody," 53
Noel, Tallulah, Cole and Me, 99, 379, 407
Noh theater, 1, 239
Nolan, Frederick, 96, 379, 383, 406
Nora Bayes Theater, 93
Norman, Karyl, 101, 379
Norman, Marsha, 348
Northwestern University, 316
Norworth, Jack, 63
"nostalgia craze," x, xvii, 38, 89, 253, 264–268, 278, 279, 295, 330
Notebook, The, 317, 318, 319
Nothing Like A Dame," 160
Notorious BIG, 166
Novello, Ivor, 94
nudity, 16, 200, 256-257
Nunn, Trevor, 248, 278, 299, 397
Nureyev, Rudolf, 278

O' Dea, James, 62
O'Brien, Jack, 301, 307
O'Brien, Margaret, 52
O'Brien, Richard, 257
O'Donnell, Mark, 307
O'Hara, John, 130
O'Horgan, Tom, xv, xvi, 251, 256–259, **328**
O'Neil, Brandon, xvii, **335**
O'Neil, Eugene, 119
Oakland Tribune, 11
Obama, Barack, 165
Obama, Michelle, 165
Oberlin College, 272
Odd Couple, The, 201
Odets, Clifford, 215
Of Thee I Sing, 119, 120, 161, 185, 381
Offenbach, Jacques, 13, 65
Oh, Boy!, 36
Oh, Coward!, 313
"Oh, Dem Golden Slippers," 43–44
Oh, Lady! Lady!, 36
"Oh, What A Beautiful Morning," 156
Oh, What A Lovely War!, 248
"Oh! Susanna," 43
Oklahoma! (2019 revival), 362
Oklahoma!, ix, 2, 71, 126, 128, 131, 157, 158, 159, 160, 172–175, 182–183, 184–193, 195, 196, 197, 199, 212, 243, 299, 300, 310, 342–343, 352, 360–363, 367, 387, 389, 407
Okrent, Mike, 296
"Old Folks At Home," 43
"Old Man River," 351
Old Vic Theatre, 184
Oliver! (film), 176
Oliver! (stage musical), 216, 229, 248, 287, 243

Index

Olsen and Johnson, 188
Olsen, Ole, 188
On Borrowed Time, 199
On Stage!, 208
On The Twentieth Century, 190, 310, 347, 348
On With The Dance, 100
On Your Feet, 309
On Your Toes, 129, 267, 309
Once And Future King, The, 196
Once In A Lifetime, 117, 120
Once On This Island, 297, 311, 347, 348, 349, 355
Once Upon a Mattress, xvi, 226, 236, 243, 327, 347, 392
Once, 310, 318
"One Day More," 359
"One Song Glory, " xi, 316
One Touch of Venus, 174, 175, 178, 179,182, 385
"Only A Rose," 286
"Only Make Believe," 193
Open Theater, The, 254
operetta, vii, viii, x, xii, xiv, 13, 18, 19, 31, 32, 39, 47, 51, 63, 65, 75, 76, 81, 84–86, 89, 90, 95, 97, 104, 119, 133, 144, 151, 152, 166, 185, 194, 210, 211, 256, 284, 286, 289, 341, 352, 362, 375, 377
Oppenheimer, George, 162
Orbach, Jerry, 277
Original Dixieland Jass (Jazz) Band, 72–73
Our Town, 160
"Out of My Dreams," 173
Out of this World, xiv, 142, 201
Out Without My Rubbers, 92, 378, 404
Outsiders, The, 318, 320
Over Here!, 297
"Over the Rainbow," 280
Oxenford, John, 244

Pacific Overtures, 160, 162, 163, 211, 274, 297, 302, 349, 355
Padula, Edward, 240
Page, Ken, 268
Paint Your Wagon (film), 201
Pajama Game, The, 204–205, 207, 209, 271, 274, 300, 302, 362
Pal Joey, ix, 126, 129–131, 342, 383, 389, 405
Palace Theatre, 104
Palais des Sports, 287
Palais Royal (nightclub), 92
Pale of Jewish Settlement, The, 74, 249, 354
Paley, Natalie, 100
Pansy Club, The, 101
"Pansy Craze, The", 101–102, 305, 379
Papp, Joseph, 255, 276, 282
Parade, 355, 356
Paragon Ragtime Orchestra, 30
Paramount Studios, 203
Pardon My Sarong, 177

Paris, 99
"Parisian Pierrot," 94
Park, Hue, 357
Passion, 164, 292
Patience, 210
Patinkin, Mandy, 291
Patricola, Tom, 83
Payton, Lew, 83
PBS (Public Broadcasting Service), 292
Peacock, Michon, 276
Penn, Arthur, 216
Penna, Erik Della, 302
Pennington, Ann, 83, 114
"People Will Say We're In Love," 193
Perlman, S.J., 174
Peter Pan (musical), 178, 190, 203, 206, 211, 226, 234, 392
Peter Pan (play), 58
Peters, Bernadette, 233, 266, 291, 292
Peters, Michael, 279, 283
Phantom of the Opera, The, xvii, 85, 164, 286, 288, 289, 292, 296, 298, 312, 332, 366, 397
Phillios, Michael, 302
Phillips, Brent, 126, 383, 407
Phrygian scale, 74–75
"Pick a Little Talk a Little"/"Goodnight Ladies," 223
Picnic, 200
Picon, Molly, 246
Pinkard, Maceo, 80
Pins and Needles, 176, 382, 396
Pinza, Ezio, xv, **169**
Pippin, xvii, 207, 248, 260, 261, 283, 318, 332, 365, 397
Pirate, The (play), 100
Pirates of Penzance, The, 13, 267, 297
Pitot, Genevieve, 182
Plaza Suite, 201
"Please Hello," 302
Pollack, Murial, 112
Pollock, Arthur, 90, 187, 377, 386, 387
Poole, Wakefield, 241, 243, 393, 406
poperetta, 166, 284, 286, 290, 291, 307
Poppy, 86
Porgy and Bess, 42, 108, 112, 270, 347, 349, 352
Porter, Cole, ix, x, xii, xiv, 23, 69, 79, 89, 96, 97–101, 111, 113–119, 120, 124–126, 129, **142**, 143, 179, 182, 184–185, 189, 195, 198, 201–203, 208, 225, 230–231, 234, 241, 247, 295, 303, 305, 315, 361, 381, 382, 403, 405, 406
Porter, Linda Lee Thomas, 98, 100, 124, 202
Post, William, H., 90
Powell, Eleanor, 107
Premice, Josephine, 215
Preminger, Otto, 184
Present Laughter, 100
Presley, Elvis, 239–240, 315, 392

Preston, Robert, 222
"Pretty Girl Is Like A Melody, A" 39
Pretty Woman, 307, 309
Previn, Andre, 280
Primus, Pearl, 262
Prince of Broadway, 299
Prince, Faith, 296
Prince, Harold (Hal), x, xiv, xv, 200, 253, 260, 270–276, 288, 291, 293, 299, 308, 318, 323, 366, 396, 398
Princeton Triangle Club, 199
Princeton University, 199, 227
Problem Like Maria, A, 230, 392, 407
Producers—The New Mel Brooks Musical, The, x, xvii, 161, 244, 299, 296, 303–306, 307, 310, 334, 440
Producers, The (1968 film), 299, 303, 304
Producers, The, x, xiii, xvii, 161, 244, 296, 299, 303–307, 310, 334
Prohibition, 24, 71, 82, 83, 101, 117, 361, 370, 406
Prom, The, 307, 310
Promises, Promises, 229, 275, 297, 309, 347
Pryce, Jonathan, 290
Public Theatre, 165, 255, 256, 276, 277, 365
Puccini, Giacomo, 202, 285, 316
Puck, Eva, xv, **148**
Pulitzer Prize for Drama, 4, 117, 119–120, 161, 200, 237, 277, 292, 353, 356
Purdam, Todd, 152, 180
Purlie Victorious, 261
Purlie, 261–262, 270, 349, 355, 395
"Put On Your Sunday Clothes," 246
"Puzzlement, A," 353

Quadrille, 100

R&B (rhythm and blues), 261, 280, 290
Rado, James, xv, xvi, 251, 254, 255, 256, 258, 328
Ragni, Gerome, xv, xvi, 251, 254, 255, 256, 258, 328
"Rags to Riches," 204
Ragtime Era, 44, 46
ragtime music, xi, 29, 30, 31, 49, 66, 73, 75, 77, 78, 106
Ragtime, (musical), 24, 32, 297, 316, 317, 347, 348, 355, 399
"Rainbow 'Round My Shoulder," 263
Rainbow Flag, 280
Rainbow, Randy, 45
Rainey, Ma, 48
Raisin in the Sun, A, 262
Raisin, 262, 263, 249, 255, 295
Rang Tang, 102–103, 379
Rasch, Albertina, xiv, 112, 113, 118, **146**, 172
Rattigan, Terrence, 100
Ravel, Maurice, 99
Raye, Matha, xvi, 326

Razaf, Andy, 103
Reagan, Ronald, 282
Reams, Lee Roy, 280, **329**
Red Mill, The, 31
Red Moon, The, xiii, 51–52, 134, 377
Red, Hot and Blue!, 118, 119, 342
"Red, Red Rose," 50
Redhead, 207, 226, 263, 293
Reed, Courtney, xvii, **335**
Reed, Vivian, xvii, **330**
Reinking, Ann, 277
Reisenweber's 400 Club. 72–73
Renault, Francis, 101
Rennagel, Marilyn, 212
Rent, xi, 10, 316–317, 401
revue, viii, ix, xiii, xiv, xvi, xvii, 18, 35, 39, 40, 48, 61, 67, 75, 76, 80, 83, 84, 86, 90, 91, 92–94, 95, 100, 103, 104, 105, 106, 107, 110, 112, 113, 118, 120–123, 127, 137, 139, 145, 146, 171, 175, 176, 177, 184, 188, 190, 201, 204, 213, 214, 240, 241, 242, 246, 255, 258, 262, 263, 267, 268, 269, 270, 273, 274, 276, 278, 279, 286, 289, 291, 293, 294, 298, 300, 303, 313, 315, 318, 329, 330, 352, 364, 370, 371, 374, 375, 377, 378, 381, 382, 385, 386
Revuers, The, 190
Reynolds, Debbie, 38, 164, 266
Reynolds, Herbert, 35
Rhapsody In Blue, 85
rhythm and blues (R&B), 261, 280, 290
Rice, Elmer, 212
Rice, Thomas Dartmouth "Daddy," 41–42
Rice, Tim, 258, 261, 285, 397
Rich, Buddy, 303
Rich, Frank, 233, 288, 296, 311, 398, 400
Richard III, 41
Richman, Harry, 112, 381
Riedel, Michael, 296, 398, 406
Rigby, Harry, 94, 264
Rihanna, 318
Ring Bells, Sing Songs, Broadway Musicals of the 1930s, 109
Ringling Bros. and Barnum and Bailey Circus, 93
Rink, The, 221
Rio Rita, xiv, 146
Rittmann, Trude, 178
Rivera, Chita, xix, 177, 220–221, 240, 269, 277, 298, 308, 391, 406
Road Show, 164
Roan, Juvia ("The Cuban Nightingale"), 47
Roar of the Greasepaint—Smell of the Crowd, 248, 298
Robbins, Jerome, xv, xix, 102, 126, 128, 178, 181, 188, 190, 203, 205–207, 209, 217–218, 220, 223, 228, 231–232, 241, 243, 244, 247, 249, 254, 263, 269, 271–272, 275, 284, 286, 293, 297, 308, **323**, 354, 359, 367, 368, 389, 391, 405

Index

Roberta, 127, 381
Robeson, Paul, 79, 351, 402
Robin Hood, 13, 64
Robinson Caruso, 13, 64
Robinson, Bill "Bojangles," xiii, 104, 105, 106, **136**, 380, 386
rock music, x, 35, 105, 219, 253, 254, 258–261, 264, 265, 279, 286, 287, 290, 301, 307, 316
rock n' roll, 239–240
rock opera, 258, 287, 316
Rockettes, The Radios City Music Hall, 64
Rocky Horror Picture Show, The, 235
Rocky Horror Show, The, 257
Rodeo, 174
Rodgers and Hammerstein, ix, xiv, xv, xvi, 2, 31, 39, 71, 87, 126, 131, 140, 151, 157, 159–164, 166, 169, 171–172, 174–175, 179, 181–182, 185–188, 191–193, 194–195, 198, 200, 204, 213, 215, 228, 233–234, 238–239, 243, 255, 288, 295, 315, 325, 340, 342–343, 352–353, 360, 362–364, 377, 383, 384, 405, 406
Rodgers and Hart, xiii, xiv, xix, 79, 86–88, 93, 96, 98, 111, 117, 120, 125–126, 129–131, **140**, 142, 156, 182, 199, 217, 267, 315, 377, 383
Rodgers, Ginger, xvi, 32, 111, 132, 225, 245, 326
Rodgers, Richard, xiii, xvi, 36, 39, 86, 87–88, **140**, 156–157, 161, 180–182, 191–193, 199, 204, 215, 226, 234, 243, 254, 289, 301, 325, 377, 378, 382, 383, 384, 387, 388, 404, 405, 406
Rogers, Kenny, 290
Rolling Stone Magazine, 285
Roma people (aka Romani, Romany), 74, 375–376
Romburg, Sigmund, 63, 86, 153, 182
Rome, Harold, 182, 388
Romeo and Juliet, 217, 224, 238, 287
Ronell, Ann, 112
Ronstadt, Linda, 267
Rooney, Mickey, 267
Roosevelt, Franklin D., 121, 129, 382
roots movement, 349, 354
Ropes, Bradford, 92, 125, 397
Rosalie, 112
Rosalinda, 211
Rose-Marie, 84–85, 90, 152, 286, 341
Rose, Billy, 93, 183
"Rose's Turn," 159, 232
Rosenthal, Jean, xv, xix, 209–212, 218, 323, 390
Rosie the Riveter, 183
Ross, Adrian, 32
Ross, Diana, 243, 282
Ross, Jerry, x, 204–205
Ross, Ted, 263
Rostand, Edmund, 238
Round In Circles—The Story of Rodgers and Hammerstein's Carousel, 192, 377, 386, 387, 405
Roxy Theatre, 275

Royal Family, The, 120
Runaway Girl, A, 19
Runnin' Wild, 77, 81, 83, 215, 341
Russell, Evelynn, 243
Russell, Jane, 128
Russell, Lillian, 28, 87
Russian Tea Room, The (Albertina Rasch), 113
Ryskind, Morrie, 119, 120, 382

S.S. Morro Castle, 115
Saddler, Donald, 94, 126, 243, 309
Sadler Wells Ballet, 298
"Saga of Jenny, The," 173
Saidy, Fred, 186, 390
Saint-Saëns, Camille, 219
Saint-Subber, Arnold, xiv, 94, 142, 201, 213, 389, 394
Sally In Our Alley, 52
Salomania craze," 67
Salonga, Lea, 290
Sam T. Jack's Creole Show, 46, 47, 372
Sanchez, Alex, 297
Sankoff, Irene, xviii, 318, 337, 403
Saturday Night Fever, 278
Saturday Night Live, 45, 76
Saturday Night, 162
Savoy Theatre, 210, 389, 404
Savoy, Bert, 60–61, 85, 93, 101, 305, 374
Sayonara, 201
Scarlet Pimpernel, The, 291, 398
Scary Movie, 13
Schmidt, Harvey, 238–239, 253
Schola Cantorum, 99
Schönberg, Claude-Michel, 166, 286–290, 316
Schwartz, Stephen, xvii, 166, 259, 260, 261, 291, 317, **332**, 340, 356, 394
Scorsese, Martin, 55
Scottsboro Boys, The, 299
Seattle Men's Chorus, 307
Secret Garden, The, 211, 311, 347, 348
See America First, 98
Seesaw, 227, 281, 293
Seldes, Gilbert, 80, 376, 406
Selena, 315
Sellars, Peter, 294
Set To Music, 100
Seurat, Georges, 291
Seven and a Half Cents, 205
Seven Brides for Seven Brothers (film), 208, 387
Seven Brides for Seven Brothers (stage musical), 308
Seventh Heaven, 209
"Seventy-six Trombones," 223
Sgt. Pepper's Lonely Hearts Club Band, 258
Shaiman, Marc, 166, 307
Shakespeare, William, x, 41, 52, 92, 166, 167, 201, 217, 224, 225, 260, 280
"Shall We Dance?," 353

Index

Shankar, Ravi, 383
Shankar, Uday, 127
Shapiro, Mel, 260
Sharaff, Irene, 209
Shaw, George Bernard, 195–196
Shawn, Ted, 127
She Loves Me, 308, 310
Sherell, Kat, 165, 166
Sherlock Holmes, 58
Sherman, Alan, 45
"Shine On Harvest Moon," 63
Shipp, Jesse A, xiii, 49, 135
Shoo-Fly Regiment, The, xiii, 51, 134
Shoot The Works, 112
Shop Girl, The, 19
Short, Hassard, xiii, 90–94, 113, 118, 121, 137, **139**, 172, 183–185, 210, 377
Show Boat, xvii, 108, 153, 156, 159, 299, 334, 249, 350–352, 377
Show Girl, 113, 264
Show Girl, The, 33
showtune, viii, 18, 19, 44, 72–75, 85, 87, 196, 198, 231, 235, 238, 259, 260, 280, 351, 393, 405
Shubert Theatre, 92, 296
Shubert, Franz, 86
Shubert, Lee, 39, 59
Shucked, 307
Shuffle Along, viii, xiii, 47, 77–81, 83, 86, 105, 123, 135, 215, 262, 269, 270, 341, 350, 376
Shultz, Dutch, 102
Silent Movie, 304
Silk Stockings, 120, 175, 189, 202, 399
Sillman, Leonard, 94, 214
Silverman, Leigh, 320
Silvers, Phil, 203
Simon, Lucy, 348
Simon, Neil, 201, 226, 227, 389, 399
Simpsons, The, 220
"Sing, Sing, Sing," 128
Singing In The Rain (film), 190, 315
Singular Sensation: the Triumph of Broadway, 296, 398, 406
Sissle and Blake, viii, 77–81, 83, 94, 104, **135**, 270
Sissle, Noble, xiii, 77–81, 83, 94, 104, **135**, 270
"Sit Down, John," 166
Sitting Bull, 255
Six, 10, 318–319, 347, 401
"Sleepin' Bee, A," 213
"Small House of Uncle Thomas Ballet," 178, 181, 354
Smalls, Charlie, 263
Smith College, 211, 300
Smith, Alexis, 275
Smith, Bessie, 48, 230
Smith, Oliver, 211
Smokey Joe's Café, 313

Smuin, Michael, 270, 309
Soden, Oliver, xxii, 95, 96, 100, 378, 378, 379, 407
"Soliloquy," 159, 193
"Some Enchanted Evening," 160
Some Like It Hot, 307, 310
"Some Of These Days," 106
Something Bad is Happening," 282
Something for the Boys, xiv, 124, 143, 389
Something Rotten, 307, 310
Something's Coming, Something Good, West Side Story, and the American Imagination, 218
"Something's Coming," ix, 171, 219
Sondheim, 158
Sondheim, Foxy (Janet Fox), 156
Sondheim, Herbert, 156
Sondheim, Stephen, ix, x, xv, 2, 97, 102, **149**, 151, 156, 158–160, 162–167, 191, 202–203, 207, 218, 230–232, 254, 260, 273–276, 281, 287–288, 291–292, 295, 302, 304, 316, 319, **323**, 354, 362, 379, 381, 384, 385, 389, 392, 396, 398, 401, 403, 405, 406, 407
Song Of Norway, The, 184
"Song of the Vagabonds," 90
song plugger, 33
songlets, 192
Sophisticated Ladies, xvii, 269, 270, 330
soul music, 260, 261, 262, 263, 264
Sound of Music, The, x, xvi, 116, 163, 164, 178, 181, 211, 217, 227–228, 233–237, 243, 283, 327, 340, 343, 345, 390, 392
South Before The War, The, 104
South Pacific (film), 201
South Pacific, ix, xi, xv, 160–162, **169**, 178, 180–181, 200–201, 213, 228, 234, 244, 288, 309, 343, 344–345, 349, 352–353, 384, 389, 390, 402, 406
Southern Syncopated, Orchestra, 48
Spamalot, Monty Python's, 28, 307, 310
Spanish-American War, 51
Spears, Britney, 318
Speranzeva, Ludmilla, 176
Spewack, Bella, 202, 225–226, 348
Spewack, Sam, 202, 225–226
Spring Awakening, 318
St. Denis, Ruth, 127
St. Louis Woman, 212, 213
Stage Door, 120
Staging Desire—Queer Readings of American Theater History, 97
Stalter-Pace, Sunny, xxii, 67, 375, 407
Stanislavsky, Konstantin, 199
Star Spangled Rhythm, 177
Star Wars, 312
Starlight Express, 166, 289
Staunton, Imelda, 233, 245
"Steam Heat," 207
Steel Pier, 299

Index

Stein, Joseph, 214, 249, 318
Stein, Leo, 32
Stempel, Larry, 14, 31–32, 369, 371, 407
Stepping Stones, 62
Stevens, Tony, 276
Stewart, James, 199
Stewart, Leslie, 19
Stewart, Michael, xvi, 241, 244, 246, 279, 326, 397
Steyn, Mark, 36, 371, 397, 404
Stilgoe, Richard, 288
stock market crash, 108, 115, 378
Stone, Fred, 15
Stone, Jessica, 320
Stonewall Inn, 279, 281
Stonewall Uprising, The, 279–280, 281
Stop the World—I Want to Get Off, 248, 269, 391
Stormy Weather (film), 177
"Stormy Weather" (song), 122
Stothart, Herbert, 84
Stowe, Harriett Beecher, 354
"Strange Fruit," 122
Strange Loop, A, 319, 349, 356–357, 402
Strauss II, Johan, 13
Stravinsky, Igor, 99
Street Scene, 212
Street Where I Lived, The, 77
"Streets of New York," 31
Streets of Paris, 242
Streisand, Barbra, 203, 243, 247, 394
Strike Up The Band, 119, 120
striptease, 14, 64, 80, 207, 229, 234
Stritch, Elaine, 232
Stroman, Susan, xvii, 296, 298–299, 304, 309, 310, **334**, 399, 401
Strouse, Charles, xvi, 216, 240–241, 267, 280, 326, 328, 399
Strutt Miss Lizzie, 80, 376
Student Prince, The, xiv, 84–86, 144, 286, 341, 377
Styne, Jule, x, 126, 163, 182, 190, 203–204, 214, 216, 229, 232, 240, 247, 254
Subways are for Sleeping, 229, 396
Suffs, 318, 320, 347, 348, 349, 351
Sugar Babies, 267
Sullivan Street Playhouse, 238
Sullivan, Margaret, 199
Summer, Donna, 314
"Summertime," 52
"Sun and Moon," 286
Sunday Afternoon on the Island of La Grande Jatte, A. 291
Sunday In The Park With George, 164, 166, 291–292, 309, 347
"Sunday," 291
sung-through musicals, 166, 261, 284, 291, 316
"Sunny Side of the Street, The" ix, 111, 112, 378, 388, 407

Sunny, 91, 153
Sunset Boulevard, 347
Supremes, The, 259, 279
Swanson, Gloria, 275
Sweeney Todd: The Demon Barber of Fleet Street, 159, 160, 163, 274, 310, 316, 346, 366
Sweet Charity, 128, 207, 208, 227, 243, 248
"Sweet Georgia Brown," xvii, 81, 330
Sweet, Jeffrey, 358, 403
Swift, Kay, 111–112
"Swing Along!," 47, 49
swing dancing, 126, 128, 117
swing era, 44
Swing Time, 123
Swinging on a Star, 300
Sword in the Stone, The, 196

Tale of Two Cities, A, 310
Tales of the South Pacific (book), 160, 200, 352
Talosa, 51
Taming of the Shrew, The, 201, 225
Tamiris, Helen, xv, 175, 182, 198, 262, 322, 385
tap dance, xix, 54–56, 103–104, 106, 126, 136, 178, 207, 209, 266, 269, 270, 279, 293
Tapestry, 258
Tars and Bars, 242
Tarzan, Disney's, 312, 400
Taub, Shaina, 348
Taubman, Howard, 244, 249, 393, 394
Tausch, Boris, 124
taxi dancer, 92, 378
Taylor, James, 259
Taymor, Danya, 320
Taymor, Julie, 312, 320, 401
"Tea For Two," 89, 264
Tebelak, John-Michael, 259, 394
Ted Shawn and his Men Dancers, 127
"Telephone Hour, The," 10
"Tell Me Pretty Maiden," 18
Temple, Shirley, 104, 164, 380
"Ten Crack Commandments," 166
Tepper, Jennifer Ashley, 316
Tesori, Jeanine, 164, 348
Tharp, Twyla, 278
Theatre Comique, 25–26
Theatre Guild, The, 86, 115, 131
Theatre Magazine, 53
"Them There Eyes," 80
thematic revue, 120–123, 255, 276, 278
Theodore, Lee Becker, 293
There's No Business Like Show Business (film), 34
There's No Business Like Show Business, (film), 34, 126–127
"There's No Business Like Show Business," (song), vii, 25, 198
"They Didn't Believe Me," 35–36, 371

Index

"They Say It's Wonderful," 198
They're Playing Our Song, 297
"This Was A Real Nice Clambake," 192
Thompson, Lydia, 14, 64–66, 340, 375, 405
Thompson, Virgil, 179, 189
Thoroughly Modern Millie, 63, 307, 310
Thou Shalt Not, 299
Three Little Pigs, The, 112
Three Twins, 151
Three's A Crowd, xiv, 91, 113, 121, 146
Threepenny Opera, The, 12–13, 172, 238
"Thriller," 283
Tick, Tick. . .Boom!, 164, 166
Tickle Me, 152
Tierney, Harry, 37–39, 61, 62, 77, 113
Till the Clouds Roll By, 242
Timbuktu!, 214, 387
Time Magazine, 117, 238, 266
"Time On My Hands," 89
Times Square, xii, 4, 5, 30, 60, 80, 166, 210, 285, 311
Times, The (London), 18, 210
Tin Pan Alley, vii, 17–18, 19, 29, 31, 33, 34, 61, 75, 202, 204, 257
Tipton, Jennifer, 212
Titanic, 318
"To Life," 359
Tobias, Oliver, xvi, **328**
Todd, Mike, 157
Tommy, The Who's (album), 258
Tonight At 8:30, 100
"Tonight Quintet," 359
Tonight Show, The, 45
Tony Award, xv, xvi, xxii, 4, 56, 94, 126, 161, 163, 164, 175, 200, 202, 205, 206, 207, 208, 213, 214, 215, 216, 217, 220, 221, 223, 225, 226 227, 233, 236, 237, 240, 242, 243, 244, 245, 248, 249, 260, 263, 264, 266, 269, 270, 271, 273, 274, 275, 276, 277, 279, 280, 281, 282, 284, 288, 290, 292, 293, 294, 295, 298, 299, 302, 303, 305, 307, 308, 309, 310, 312, 316, 318, 319, 320, 324, 325, 326, 327, 329, 331, 333, 334, 366, 389, 392, 396, 397
"Too Darn Hot," 202
Tootsie, 302
Topper, 162
Tostee, Lucille, 65
"Tradition," 359
transgressive women, xi, xx, 2, 191, 236, 247–248, 320, 339–348, 356
Trapp Family, The, 233
Travolta, John, 356
Treacher, Arthur, 171
Tree Grows in Brooklyn, A, 226
Tree, Beerbohm, 92
Trent, Jo, 102
Trip To Coontown, A, 47, 373, 407
Tropical Revue, 177

Tropics and Le Jazz Hot: From Harlem to Haiti, 176
Truman, Harry S., 79
Trump, Donald, 288
Tucker, Sophie, 106, 230, 234, 269, 277, 319
Tune, Tommy, x, xvii, 267, 281, 292, 293–294, 296, 308, 309, 310, 318, **331**, 398, 401, 407
Turning Point, The, 278
Tuskegee Institute, 51
Twiggy, 267, 294
"Twin Soliloquies," 180
Twirly-Whirly, 28
Two for the Seesaw, 281
Two Gentlemen of Verona, 260, 395, 396
Tyler, Gene, 241

Udel, Peter, 261
Uggams, Leslie, 203, 216, 269
Ulvaeus, Björn, 314
unacknowledged songs, xix, 27
Uncle Tom's Cabin, 354
"Under The Bamboo Tree," 52
underground railroad, xv, 187, 321
Universal Pictures, 10
University of Chicago, 176
University of Miami, 246
University of Pennsylvania, 271
University of Rochester, 240
Unsinkable Molly Brown, The, 209, 211, 343, 393
"Unspoken Thoughts," 180
Up In Central Park, 175
Urinetown, 365

Vagabond King, The, 81, 84, 89–90, 286, 377
Van Dyke, Dick, 240
"Varsity Drag, The," 83, 107, 376
vaudeville, vii, xii, xiii, 16–17, 18, 19, 25, 28, 29, 33, 39, 45, 48, 52, 60, 61, 63, 66, 67, 77, 78, 80, 85, 92, 101, 104, 105, 109, 113, 122, 132, 135, 136, 151, 178, 185, 208, 214, 229, 230, 234, 248, 258, 265, 269, 277, 319, 374, 375, 404, 405, 407
Verdon, Gwen, 166, 205, 208, 220, 226, 227, 277, 298
Vereen, Ben, 43, 269, 372
Verne, Jules, 15, 369
Very Good Eddie, 36, 63, 267
Very Warm For May, 156
Victor/Victoria, 310, 400
Viet Rock, 254
Vietnam War, 254, 255, 256, 289
Villon, Francois, 90
Visit, The, 297
Vogue Magazine, xiv, 143, 172
von Trapp, Maria Rainer, 233, 234
Vortex, The, 94

Waitress, 318
Walburg, Betty, 182

429

Index

Waldorf, Willella, 174, 385
Walker, Aida Overton, xiii, xiv, 50, 52, 54, 66–67, **135**, 145
Walker, George, vii, viii, xiii, 25, 28, 48–50, 52, 53, 54, 64, 66, **135**, 373
"Walkin' The Dog," 106
Waller, Thomas "Fats", 103, 171, 268
Wallop, Douglas, 205
Walston, Ray, 205
Walt Disney Company (Disney, Disney Theatricals), xi, xvii, 10, 40, 44, 112, 162, 166, 196, 232, 283, 289, 308, 310, 311–313, 366, 400
Walters, Charles, 126, 212, 383, 406
Washington, Booker T., 54
Washington, George, 255
WASP (White Anglo Saxon Protestants), 23–24, 89, 92, 129, 227, 348, 355
Watch Your Step, 34
Water for Elephants, 318, 320
Watergate era, 277
Waters, Ethel, xiii, xix, 106, 121–122, **137**, 352, 382
Waters, John, 306, 356
Watkins, Maurine Dallas, 277
Watson, Bobby, xv, 38, **148**
"Way You Look Tonight, The," 123
"We All Wear A Green Carnation," 95
"We're Getting Away With It," 38
We're No Angels, 226
Webb, Clifton, 121, 378, 382
Webb, Lyda, 81, 341
Webber and Rice, 258, 261, 285, 397
Webber, Andrew Lloyd, 166, 258, 261, 278, 285, 288–289, 291, 316, 381, 387, 398
Weber and Fields, vii, xiii, 25, 27–28, 50, 64, 72, 87, 96, 105, 134, 289, 380
Weber, Joe, vii, xiii, 25, 27–28, 50, 64, 72, 87, 96, 105, 134, 289, 380
"Wedding of a Solid Sender, The," 128
Wedding Singer, The, 309
Weidman, Charles, xiii, 121, 127, 137
Weidman, Jerome, 237
Weil, Kurt, xiv, xix, 12–13, 146, 171–174, 182, 199, 212, 238, 385, 407
Weiss, George David, 214
Welch, Elizabeth, 114, 381
"Welcome to the 60s," 347
Weser transposing piano, 34
Wesleyan University, 164
West Side Story, x, xv, 128, 163–165, 177, 206, 209, 211, 215, 217–225, 231, 241, 244, 269, 271, 272, 275, 281, 283, 286, 297, 302, 323, 349, 353, 354, 356, 359, 362, 365, 367, 368, 375, 382, 389, 390, 403, 405, 407
West, Mae, 61, 125, 382, 406
"What Is This Thing Called Love?," 99
What Makes Sammy Run?, 297

What's In A Name?, 92
Wheatley, William, 14
Wheeldon, Christopher, 310
When Broadway Was Black (aka *Footnotes*) 78, 376, 405
"When I'm Sixty Four," 265
"When Your Good to Mamma," 277
"Where Do I Go," 255
Where In The World is Carmen Sandiego?, 301
Where's Charley?, 204
Whiffenpoofs, Yale, 97
Whirl-i-Gig, 28
White Christmas (film), 34, 126
White Christmas (stage adaptation), 34
White Faun, The, 64
white savior narrative, 355
White, George, 76, 79, 81, 82, 106, 113, 121, 381
White, Onna, 175, 182, 220, 224, 248, 253, 269
Whitman College, 151
Whitman, Scott, 307
"Who's Afraid of the Big Bad Wolf," 112
"Who's That Woman?," 275
Whoop-De-Doo, xiii, 134
Wicked, xvii, 15, 289, 312, 317, 332, 340, 343, 349, 356, 401
Wigman, Mary, 175
Wildcat, 226
Wilde, Oscar, 58, 95
Wilder, Thornton, 160, 116, 244, 293
Wildhorn, Frank, 290
Will Mastin Trio, 214
Will Rogers Follies, The, 190, 294, 295, 308, 309, 311, 373, 385
Williams and Walker, vii, 25, 28, 48–50, 52, 53–54, 64, 66, **135**
Williams College, 160, 162, 281
Williams, Bert, vii, viii, xiii, 25, 28, 48–50, 52, 53–54, 64, 66, **135**, 277, 327, 373, 375, 404, 405
Williams, Esther, 93
Williams, Ethel, 122
Williams, Sammy, xvi, **328**
Williams, Schele, 319, 320
"Willow, Weep for Me," 112
Willson, Meredith, 221–225, 240, 391, 406
Wilson, Billy, xvii, 268, 269, 270, 283, 330
Wilson, Dooley, xv, 187, **321**
Wilson, Doric, 266
Wilson, John C. (Jack), xiv, 98, 99–100, 124, **141**, 182, 202, 379, 395, 407
Wilson, Lanford, 266
Wilson, Sandy, 265
Winer, Laurie, xxii, 151, 383
Winkler, Kevin, xxii, 91, 293, 377, 398, 407
"Winner Takes It All," 314
Winslow Boy, The, 100
Winter, Marion Hannah, 56, 103

Index

Wintergarden Theater, 72
"Wintergreen For President," ix, 119
Winters, Newton, xvii, **330**
Wise, Jim, 266
Wish You Were Here, 200
"Witchcraft," 226
Wiz, The, xv, 211, 263, 270, 285, 319, 324, 347, 369, 395
Wizard Of Oz, The (stage show), 15, 369
Wizard Of Oz, The Wonderful (book), 15, 283, 263, 317
Wizard Of Oz, The, (film), 15, 186, 204, 235, 317, 387, 406
Wodehouse, P.G., xii, 36–37, 59, 63, 69, 115, 116, 381
Woldin, Judd, 262
Wolf, Stacy, xxii, 230, 340, 392, 401, 407
Woll, Allen, 51, 373, 390, 391, 395, 407
Women on the Verge of a Nervous Breakdown, 302
women's liberation movement, 249, 253, 255, 345
Wonderful Town, 190, 211, 243, 271, 300, 347, 348
Woodard, Charlaine, 268
Wooley, Monty, xix, 97, 98, 100, 114, 117
Wooster Academy, 97
World of Suzie Wong, The, 200
World War I, 2, 24, 54, 59, 71, 72, 78, 98, 106, 107, 152, 194, 341
World War II, 160, 174, 183, 189, 194, 199, 204, 207, 209, 242, 265, 272, 303, 342, 363
Wouldn't it be Loverly," 178
WPA (Works Progress Administration), 122, 211, 386
Wright and Forrest, 94, 185, 387, 401
Wright, Orville, 47
Wright, Robert, 94, 185, 387, 401

Yale University, 89, 97, 98, 100, 211, 241
"Yankee Doodle Boy," 28, 29, 35
Yankovic, Weird Al, 45
Yazbek, David, xx, 301–303, 399
Year the Yankees Lost the Pennant, The, 205
Yellen, Sherman, 166
yellowface, 290
Yiddish Theater, vii, 18, 19, 86, 110, 204, 205, 246
Yiddish, 110, 204, 249, 369
"You Can't Get a Man With a Gun," 198
You Can't Take It With You, 117, 120

"You Do Something To Me," 99
"You Naughty, Naughty, Men," 14
"You Walk With Me," 305
"You Won't Succeed on Broadway (If You Don't Have Any Jews," 28
"You'll Never Walk Alone," 343, 364
You're A Good Man Charlie Brown, 297
"You're A Grand Old Flag," 29, 371
"You're A Queer One," 192, 387
You're Arms Too Short Too Box With God, xvii, 264, 320, 329
"You're The Cream In My Coffee," 107
"You've Got That Thing," 99
"You've Got To Be Carefully Taught," 161, 166
Youmans, Vincent, viii, 62, 79, 88–89, 96, 153, 264, 402
Young Frankenstein (film), 13, 63, 303
Young Frankenstein (stage musical), 299
Young, Loretta, 230–231
Young, Rida Johnson, xii, 31, 63, 133
Your Show of Shows, 303
Yuriko, 209

Zaltzberg, Charlotte, 262
zarzuelas, 13
Ziegfeld Follies of 1908, 63
Ziegfeld Follies of 1910, The, xii, 53, 134
Ziegfeld Follies of 1914, 40
Ziegfeld Follies of 1917, 40, 80
Ziegfeld Follies of 1918, 61
Ziegfeld Follies of 1924, 125
Ziegfeld Follies of 1927, The, xii, xiv, 113, **133**, 146
Ziegfeld Follies of 1934, 125
Ziegfeld Follies of 1936, 126
Ziegfeld Follies of 1943, 126, 128, 171, 201
Ziegfeld Follies, The, xii, xiii, xiv, 39, 40, 53, 58, 61, 63, 80, 86, 91, 93, 113, 121, 126, 128, 133, 134, 135, 146, 171, 201, 275, 294, 385
Ziegfeld Girls, xii, 53, 133
Ziegfeld, Florenz, viii, xii, 10, 39, 40, 53, 59, 61, 63, 72, 76, 79, 81, 91, 94, 100, 102, 106, 108, 109, **133**, 171, 229, 233, 264, 294, 375, 376, 379, 385
Zien, Chip, 292
Zipprodt, Patricia, 209
Zorba, 318
Zuber, Katherine, 209